PENGUIN REFERENCE

The Penguin Dictionary of
FIRST NAMES

David Pickering graduated in English from St Peter's College, Oxford.
An experienced reference books compiler, he has contributed to (and
often been sole author and editor of) some 150 reference books, mostly
in the areas of the arts, language, local history and popular interest.
These include a *Dictionary of Theatre* (1988), an *Encyclopedia of Panto-*
mime (1993), *Brewer's Twentieth-Century Music* (1994, 1997), a *Dictionary*
of Superstitions (1995), a *Dictionary of Witchcraft* (1996), a *Dictionary of*
Proverbs (1997), a *Dictionary of Folklore* (1999) and the *Pears Factfinder*
(2002). He lives in Buckingham with his wife and two sons.

Dear Francesca (04/11/14)

Thought this might help us
begin to plan the next exciting
part of our lives.
Will Waite II is however, not
an option.
All my love,
James.
x x p

The Penguin Dictionary of
FIRST NAMES

David Pickering

SECOND EDITION

PENGUIN BOOKS

PENGUIN BOOKS

Published by the Penguin Group
Penguin Books Ltd, 80 Strand, London WC2R 0RL, England
Penguin Group (USA) Inc., 375 Hudson Street, New York, New York 10014, USA
Penguin Books Australia Ltd, 250 Camberwell Road, Camberwell, Victoria 3124, Australia
Penguin Books Canada Ltd, 10 Alcorn Avenue, Toronto, Ontario, Canada M4V 3B2
Penguin Books India (P) Ltd, 11 Community Centre, Panchsheel Park, New Delhi – 110 017, India
Penguin Group (NZ) Ltd, Cnr Airborne and Rosedale Roads, Albany, Auckland 1310, New Zealand
Penguin Books (South Africa) (Pty) Ltd, 24 Sturdee Avenue, Rosebank 2196, South Africa

Penguin Books Ltd, Registered Offices: 80 Strand, London WC2R 0RL, England

www.penguin.com

First published 1999
This revised and updated second edition first published 2004
014

Set in 7.5/10.5pt Adobe Stone
Typeset by Rowland Phototypesetting Ltd, Bury St Edmunds, Suffolk
Printed in England by Clays Ltd, St Ives plc

ISBN-13: 978–0–141–01398–5

www.greenpenguin.co.uk

MIX
Paper from
responsible sources
FSC
www.fsc.org
FSC™ C018179

Penguin Books is committed to a sustainable
future for our business, our readers and our planet.
This book is made from Forest Stewardship
Council™ certified paper.

CONTENTS

INTRODUCTION

First names are more than simply means of identification. They reveal a huge amount of information about a culture's history, religions and artistic heritage and provide evidence of the diverse foreign influences that have operated upon it over the centuries. The origins of some names used in the English-speaking world are now lost to us, while others came about as the result of mistaken renderings of earlier equivalents – as appears to have been the case with Oprah (originally Orpah) and Imogen (which was Innocens prior to Shakespeare's day).

The names used in Anglo-Saxon England belonged to two main groups – Celtic (Welsh, Irish Gaelic and Scots Gaelic) and Old German (these were often based on physical appearance or temperament). Many Anglo-Saxon names disappeared from use after the Norman Conquest, when they were replaced by Norman French equivalents derived from the same Old German sources. Others lay dormant for centuries before enjoying a new lease of life in a popular revival.

During the medieval period saints' names became more frequent, often in the belief that naming an infant after a saint guaranteed the child divine protection. Other first names were derived from surnames, which themselves began as place names, occupational titles or borrowings of older personal names.

Saints' names fell from favour after the Reformation, when Puritans on both sides of the Atlantic turned to the Bible for inspiration and also introduced a variety of 'virtue' names, such as Grace, Prudence, Faith, Hope and Charity. Names with ancient Greek and Roman roots were popular in the 18th century, while Arthurian, medieval, flower and jewel names were among those that came into fashion in the 19th century. The 20th century witnessed the rise of names associated with cinema and television and other branches of the media.

Recent years have seen a richer mix of names to choose from than was the case in any previous era. As well as new coinages, parents today may choose from, among others, revivals of ancient Celtic or Old German names, names dating back to medieval times and names with strong biblical connections (in the year 2000 at least half of the most popular first names in use in the English-speaking world appear in the Bible). Many people select names for their meaning or for their cultural associations (names from Shakespeare have proved very popular), while others follow family tradition or select names purely because they find them attractive.

The Mythology of First Names

Names have always had special magical and ritual significance. In Britain in times gone by it was widely believed that witches spoke the names of their intended victims in their spells in order to guarantee their effectiveness, and it was thus considered important to prevent names being bandied about too freely. In some rural areas people were often addressed by nicknames rather than their real names to stop evil spirits exerting their malevolent influence over them. For much the same reason, new parents were careful not to reveal their choice of name to too many people before the christening, and tales are still told of wives who only learned what name their husbands had selected at the font itself.

Some old names have special significance. It used to be said that no one called George had ever been hanged and that the name was thus a lucky one to have. Couples who bore the names Joseph and Mary were widely thought to have special powers of healing and were often visited by people suffering from whooping cough. More ominously, it was once believed in parts of England (for long-obscure reasons) that women called Agnes were especially prone to insanity.

It was supposed to be unlucky to change one's name after being christened, and if the vicar faltered during the christening service the child itself would suffer from a stutter as it grew up. It was considered a good omen if the number of letters in a name added up to seven or some other propitious total, but unlucky of course if they added up to thirteen. It was also thought to be unwise in some parts to name a child after a dead sibling, an older relative or a family pet, as the fates may get confused and carry off the infant well before its allotted time. By the same token, it was thought to be a good idea to name a child after some great personality, as the infant might then enjoy a share of the other person's good fortune in life. Contrary to modern feeling, it also used to be thought lucky for a person's initials to spell out a word.

Such notions are not as moribund as might be imagined. As recently as the late 1990s the media carried news of an expert who offered to treat various ailments through analysis of the sufferers' names. In one case analysis of a female migraine sufferer's name 'revealed' several references to the head: it was claimed that once she accepted advice to change her name to something less pernicious her condition quickly improved.

Names in the 21st Century

Examination of the lists of newly registered first names published by various government agencies around the English-speaking world each year reveals much about trends and changing tastes in the naming of children. The most cursory study of these records quickly shows how contemporary parents continue to be divided between traditional choices that have been popular for generations and other newer coinages, typically ones that have been promoted in various branches of the media. Thus, lists of the most popular names in the past five years have been dominated not only by such well-established choices as Jack, James, Charlotte and Emma but also by such new or rediscovered names as Callum, Oliver, Chloe and Jessica.

Modern parents seem to be more conservative in naming their sons than they are in naming their daughters. According to the records for the year 2002 some 2,430 different boys' names were registered, considerably fewer than the 3,089 names selected for girls. Many of the choices themselves have, however, been far from conservative. Several long-standing favourites for both sexes, which might have been expected to remain top choices for years to come, have recently gone into substantial decline, notable amongst them such examples as David (ending some fifty years as one of the top ten favourite choices) and Sarah. Also languishing in the lower reaches of the tables are former staples such as Robert, Andrew, John, Susan and Alexandra. Other names that were briefly at a peak a decade ago (among them Jason, Kylie, Chelsea and Imogen) have retreated into the relative obscurity from which they came. Only time will tell if a similar fate awaits Ethan, Tyler, Maisie, Willow and other recently emerged choices that have taken their place.

Parents continue to range widely for inspiration. While names from the Bible (Joshua, Matthew, Rebecca, etc.) continue to play a significant role, many of the other names in the lists appear to reflect the influence of contemporary celebrity-obsessed society, as fuelled by the media, with bursts of interest in names borne by top sports players, film stars, fictional characters and so forth. In the last couple of years television has provided several candidates, including the girl's name Chardonnay, as featured in the drama series *Footballers' Wives*, while the cinema has suggested, among others, Amelie (after the central character in the French film of that name), Angelina (after actress Angelina Jolie), Erin (from the film *Erin Brockovich*) and Maximus (after the name of the hero in *Gladiator*). Children's literature has inspired a renewal of interest in the old favourite Harry (as a result of the success of the *Harry Potter* stories) and in politics the birth of the Prime Minister's son Leo Blair focused the spotlight on another previously neglected name.

Imitation being the sincerest form of flattery, many people have followed the lead of various celebrities in taking up the names the latter have selected for their own children. Highlights in this category have included such names as Brooklyn and Romeo (as bestowed upon David and Victoria Beckham's two sons), Dylan (the name of Catherine Zeta-Jones's first child) and Mia (the name of Kate Winslet's daughter).

A natural conservatism has, however, continued to exert itself with regard to more outlandish choices and parents seem to have been on the whole reluctant to accept the baton proffered by the late Paula Yates, whose daughters by Bob Geldof are named Fifi, Peaches and Pixie. Other recently recorded names that seem destined to remain unique include those of three Brazilian sisters who were called Xerox, Photocopier and Authenticated (reportedly because their birth resulted from a romp on a photocopying machine) and the British baby girl born in the 1990s with the name Room 21A (named apparently for similar reasons).

Lists of the most popular first names from different parts of the English-speaking world reveal the extent to which first names appear to be becoming increasingly universal, perhaps through the influence of the international media. There remain, however, some regional preferences, examples including Cameron, Ryan and Caitlin in Scotland, Brandon and Taylor in the USA and Lachlan and Liam in Australia. If richness of choice is to be preserved through the new century such divergences are only to be welcomed.

Selected lists of popular names around the English-speaking world are given in the appendices.

Practical Matters

The naming of children has always been taken seriously by state and church authorities. French parents were (until relatively recently) limited in their choice by a law of 1803 that gave official sanction only to saints' names and names from ancient history. In the Nordic countries the relevant authorities produce lists of names from which all new parents must choose, the rationale behind this policy being that the interests of children will thereby be protected. Parents must obtain permission if they wish to select a name not on the official list. In the year 1996–7 there were around 500 cases of conflict between adventurous parents and the authorities in these countries. In most cases the parents won, although the Swedish couple who wanted to give their child an unpronounceable name consisting of twenty-seven random letters and numbers were obliged to give up the struggle after two-and-a-half years' wrangling in court and several fines. The Roman Catholic Church has its own lists of approved names. Jewish children are often given a Hebrew name in a formal naming ceremony but have a less formal, secular name for daily use. Such rules protect the legitimacy of traditional names but would result in less variety if it were not for the stubborn intransigence of thousands of parents around the world, who follow their own inclinations.

Parents in English-speaking countries face no such restrictions (although registrars in Scotland have the right to refuse names they consider potentially offensive). In England and Wales births must be registered within forty-two days (twenty-one in Scotland), but it is possible to arrange to wait for a whole year before notifying the authorities of the child's name.

Acknowledgements

I would like to thank Dr Amanda Ellison, Dr Philip Fine and Alistair Alcock for their assistance with name pronunciations, and Jane Birdsell for her editing skills.

A

Aaron (m) Biblical name of obscure origin, possibly Egyptian or else derived from the Hebrew Aharon, variously interpreted as meaning 'bright' or 'high mountain'. It appears in the Bible as the name of the brother of Moses and was consequently taken up by English Puritans in the 17th century. It has remained in use among both Christians and Jews ever since, with a recent peak in popularity in the 1970s and 1980s. Notable bearers of the name have included the villainous Aaron the Moor in William Shakespeare's *Titus Andronicus* (1590–94), English poet Aaron Hill (1685–1750), US Vice-President Aaron Burr (1756–1836), Aaron Winthrop in the George Eliot novel *Silas Marner* (1861) and US composer Aaron Copland (1900–1990). Also encountered as **Aaran** or **Arn**. Other variants include the Arabic **Haroun** or **Harun**.

Abbas (m) Arabic name derived from *abbas* ('austere' or 'stern'). Also an informal name for a lion, it was borne by Muhammad's uncle Abbas ibn Abd-al-Muttalib in the 6th century.

Abbey (f) English first name that was taken up as a diminutive of ABIGAIL. It appeared with increasing regularity during the 19th century but has been a less frequent choice since the early 20th century. Also encountered as **Abbie** or **Abby**.

Abbie/Abby *See* ABBEY.

Abdullah (m) Arabic name meaning 'servant of Allah'. One of the most popular of all Arabic names, it has special significance in the Islamic world as the name of Muhammad's father, although records of the name actually predate the development of Islam itself. Also spelled **Abdalla**.

Abe *See* ABEL; ABNER; ABRAHAM.

Abel (m) Biblical first name of uncertain origin. One theory claims that it comes from the Hebrew Hebel, itself derived from *hevel* ('breath' or 'vapour') and thus interpreted as suggesting vanity or worthlessness, while another suggests it comes from the Assyrian for 'son'. It appears in the Bible as the name of Adam and Eve's younger son, famously murdered by his jealous brother Cain, and was consequently taken up by English Puritans after the Reformation. It continued in irregular use on both sides of the Atlantic over the next two centuries, but is now rare. Notable bearers of the name have included the Dutch explorer Abel Tasman (1603–59), the fictional Abel Drugger in the Ben Jonson play *The Alchemist* (1610) and Abel Magwitch in the Charles Dickens novel *Great Expectations* (1860–61). Sometimes abbreviated to **Abe**.

Abigail (f) Biblical name derived from the Hebrew Abigayil, meaning 'my father rejoices' or 'father's joy'. It appears in the Bible both as the name of the beautiful and intelligent wife of Nabal of Carmel, who went on to marry King David, and as that of King David's sister. As a result of its biblical connections, the name was taken up by English Puritans in the 17th century and remained in fairly common currency into the 19th century. Its appearance as the name of a lady's maid in Beaumont and Fletcher's play *The Scornful Lady* (1616) prompted a literary tradition of using the name for ladies' maids during the later 17th and 18th centuries – a notion that harked back to the biblical Abigail, who described herself as King David's handmaid – and the name soon entered wider use as a slang term for any such servant. Subsequently it suffered a prolonged decline in popularity, partly through association with the controversial Abigail Masham (1680–1734), who wielded considerable influence as lady-in-waiting to Queen Anne. It regained some lost ground as the result of a considerable revival in the 1970s.

Other famous bearers of the name over the centuries have ranged from Barabas' ill-fated daughter in Christopher Marlowe's tragedy *The Jew of Malta* (1633) to one of the young girls at the centre of the witchcraft hysteria in Arthur Miller's play *The Crucible* (1952). Familiar forms of the name include **Abbie**, **Abby**, ABBEY, GAIL, **Gale** and **Gayle**.

Abilene (f) English first name derived ultimately from a Hebrew place name that is thought originally to have meant 'grass'. It appears in the Bible as the name of a region of the Holy Land and was consequently adopted as a place name for various settlements in the USA, including a city in Kansas. It is unclear to what extent the development of Abilene as a first name resulted from its use as a place name; it could also be the result of the influence of ABBEY and relatively commonplace '-lene' feminine endings.

Abla (f) Arabic name meaning 'full-figured'. It predated the rise of Islam but has retained its status as a popular choice into modern times, often through association with a 6th-century beauty who was the subject of celebrated love poems written by her cousin Antarah ibn-Shaddad.

Abner (m) Biblical name derived from the Hebrew for 'father of light'. It appears in the Bible as the name of Saul's cousin, who served as the commander of his army, and was consequently taken up by English Puritans in the 16th century (although it has never been in very widespread use). Since the early 19th century the name has been more common in the USA than it has been elsewhere. Famous bearers of the name have included the fictional detective Uncle Abner, who was created in the mystery

novels of Melville Davisson Post early in the 20th century, Abner Small in the Eugene O'Neill play *Mourning Becomes Electra* (1931); and 'L'il Abner', a cartoon strip character invented by Al Capp in the 1930s and later the subject of the musical *L'il Abner* (1956). Commonly abbreviated to **Ab** or **Abe**. Variants include the Jewish **Avner**.

Abraham (m) Biblical name derived from the Hebrew Avraham, itself from the Hebrew *av hamon* ('father of a multitude' or 'father of many nations'). It appears in the Bible as the name of the father of the Hebrew nation and was consequently among the biblical names adopted by the Puritans in the 17th century. It continued to appear with some regularity into the early 20th century, since when it has become much less common outside Jewish communities. Famous bearers of the name have included English pioneering industrialist Abraham Darby (c.1678–1717), the fictional Revd Abraham Adams in the Henry Fielding novel *Joseph Andrews* (1742) and US President Abraham Lincoln (1809–65). Diminutive forms of the name include **Abe**, **Ham** and **Bram** – as borne by Irish novelist Bram Stoker (1847–1912), who is remembered as the author of the classic horror story *Dracula* (1897). Also encountered occasionally as **Abram**, the original version (meaning 'high father') of the biblical character's name (Abraham being the new name given to him by God), and as the Yiddish **Avrom**.

Abram *See* ABRAHAM.

Absalom (m) Biblical name derived from the Hebrew Abshalom, meaning 'father of peace'. It appears in the Bible as the name of King David's favourite son and was consequently in use among English speakers as early as the 12th century. It continued in irregular use into the 19th century but has since fallen out of favour and is highly unusual today. Notable bearers of the name have included the fictional Absalom in John Dryden's satirical poem *Absalom and Achitophel* (1681), in which the character was understood to represent the Duke of Monmouth. Later occurrences of the name in fiction have included the William Faulkner novel *Absalom, Absalom!* (1936). Variants include the French **Absolon** – in which form it appears as the name of the lecherous student in Geoffrey Chaucer's *The Miller's Tale* (1387). *See also* AXEL.

Absolon *See* ABSALOM.

Acacia (f) English first name ultimately derived from a Greek word meaning 'immortality' or 'resurrection'. It is best known as the name of a flowering shrub, and its adoption as a first name would appear to be a fairly recent development.

Achilles (m) Greek name supposedly derived from the Greek *a-* ('without') and *khelle* ('lips'), and thus interpreted as meaning 'lipless', or else based on the name of the River Akheloos. It was borne in Greek mythology by the hero Achilles, the greatest of the Greek warriors who fought at the siege of Troy and whose name reflected the tradition that he was never suckled. Although the name was also borne by a number of early minor saints, it has made only rare appearances as a first name among English speakers, chiefly in relatively recent times. Variants in other languages include the French **Achille**, the Italian **Achilleo** and the Spanish **Aquiles**.

Acke *See* AXEL.

Ada (f) English first name possibly derived ultimately from the Old German *adal* ('noble') under the influence of the biblical ADAH. It appeared with increasing regularity among English speakers from the late 18th century, when it appears to have been imported from Germany, and remained in fairly common currency until the middle of the 20th century, since when it has virtually disappeared from use. Famous bearers of the name have included Lord Byron's daughter, the mathematician Ada Byron (1815–52). **Ad**, **Addie** and **Adie** are all diminutive forms of the name.

Adah (f) Biblical name derived from the Hebrew for 'decorated' or 'ornamented'. It appears in the Bible as the name of the wives of Lamech and Esau and was consequently taken up by English Puritans after the Reformation. It has made few appearances in succeeding centuries, however, having been eclipsed by the otherwise unrelated ADA, with which it is sometimes confused.

Adair (m) Irish first name meaning 'oak wood' and interpreted as 'dweller by the oak wood' or 'attendant of the oak grove', a reference to the druids who attended sacred oaks in Celtic folklore. It also appears in Scottish tradition as a variant of EDGAR.

Adam (m) Biblical name derived from the Hebrew *adama* ('earth') and usually interpreted as meaning 'human being' or 'man'. It is sometimes traced back to the Hebrew for 'red' (a reference either to the colour of human skin or to the red colour of the clay from which God fashioned the first man). As the name of the biblical Adam, the first man, it has special significance among Christians (although Jews have never considered it suitable for use as a first name). English speakers adopted the name with some enthusiasm during the medieval period and it was among the most popular names in England in the 13th century. It has remained in regular use throughout the English-speaking world ever since (with the exception of a brief lapse towards the end of the 19th century) and has enjoyed a recent peak in popularity since the 1960s.

Notable bearers of the name have included the servant Adam in William Shakespeare's *As You Like It* (1599), Scottish economist and philosopher Adam Smith (1723–90), the central character in the George Eliot novel *Adam Bede* (1859) and British pop singer Adam Faith (Terence Nelhams; 1940–2003). Diminutive forms of the name include the Scottish **Adie**. **Adamina** is a rare feminine equivalent. Variants in other languages include the Italian **Adamo**, the Spanish **Adan** and the Finnish **Aatami**. **Adamnan** is a related Irish name interpreted as meaning 'little Adam' and famous from the 7th-century St Adamnan, Abbot of Iona.

Adamina/Adamnan *See* ADAM.

Adan *See* AIDAN.

Addi *See* ADELINE.

Addie *See* ADA; ADELAIDE; ADRIAN.

Addy *See* ADELINE.

Ade *See* ADRIAN.

Adela (f) English and German first name derived from the Old German *adal* ('noble'). It came to England with the Normans in the 11th century, when it was borne by William the Conqueror's youngest daughter Adela (1062–1137) among others. The name enjoyed a peak in popularity among English speakers towards the end of the 19th century but has been in only irregular use since then. Notable bearers of the name have included the fictional Adela Quested in the E. M. Forster novel *A Passage to India* (1924). Also encountered as **Adella**, **Adele**, **Adelle** or the French **Adèle** (the form generally preferred by English speakers in recent decades). *See also* DELLA.

Adelaide (f) English first name derived from the Old German Adalheit, itself from the Old German *adal* ('noble') and *heit* ('kind', 'state' or 'condition') and thus interpreted as meaning 'woman of noble estate'. English speakers took up the name during the 19th century after it became well known through William IV's popular German-born wife Queen Adelaide (1792–1849), after whom the city of Adelaide in Australia was named. Other famous bearers of the name have included the 10th-century St Adelaide, who married Otto the Great and became Empress of the Holy Roman Empire, and US jazz singer Adelaide Hall (1901–93). Commonly abbreviated to **Addie**. Also encountered in the form **Adelia**. Variants in other languages include the German, Dutch and Scandinavian **Adelheid** and the Hungarian **Alida**. *See also* ALICE; HEIDI.

Adele/Adèle *See* ADELA.

Adelheid *See* ADELAIDE.

Adelice *See* ALICE.

Adelina *See* ADELINE.

Adeline (f) French first name that developed as a variant of ADELA and has been in occasional use among English speakers since the 11th century. It came to England with the Normans, appearing in the 'Domesday Book' of 1086, and enjoyed a modest vogue towards the end of the 19th century, but is very rare today. Notable bearers of the name have included a Lady Adeline in Lord Byron's poem *Don Juan* (1818–23) and the subject of the Harry Armstrong and Richard Husch Gerard hit song 'Sweet Adeline' (1903). **Addi**, **Addy** and **Aline** are diminutive forms of the name. Variants in other languages include the Italian **Adelina** – as borne by the Italian soprano Adelina Patti (1843–1919).

Adelise *See* ALICE.

Adella/Adelle *See* ADELA.

Aden *See* AIDAN.

Adie *See* ADA; ADAM; ADRIAN; AIDAN.

Adlai (m) Biblical name derived via Aramaic from the Hebrew Adaliah, meaning 'God is just' or alternatively 'my ornament'. It appears in the Bible as the name of the father of Shaphat, a herdsman who lived during the reign of King David. It was taken up by English speakers in the 19th century but has never been in very common use. Notable bearers of the name have included the US Vice-President Adlai E. Stevenson (1835–1914) and his grandson the Democratic politician Adlai E. Stevenson (1900–65).

Adnan (m) Arabic name derived from *adana* ('to settle down'). It predated the rise of Islam but also appears in Islamic tradition as the name of a descendant of the patriarch Ibrahim and is consequently in common use throughout the Arab world.

Adolf *See* ADOLPH.

Adolph (m) German first name descended from the Old German Adalwolf, itself from the Old German *adal* ('noble') and *wolf* ('wolf'). It was introduced to England by the Normans in the 11th century, replacing the Old English equivalent Aethulwulf. Having fallen into neglect, it was revived on a limited basis by English speakers in the wake of the Hanoverian Succession in the 18th century but never enjoyed widespread adoption and became a very unpopular choice indeed after the outbreak of war with Nazi Germany in 1939 when it became identified with the dictator Adolf Hitler (1889–1945) – **Adolf** being the usual modern German form of the name. It has yet to regain acceptance in the English-speaking world. Variants of the name in other languages include the French **Adolphe** – as borne by the French-American actor Adolphe Menjou (1890–1963). *See also* ADOLPHUS.

Adolphus (m) Latinized equivalent of the German and English ADOLPH. It made infrequent appearances as a first name among English speakers in the 19th century but has never been in common use. Notable bearers of the name have ranged from Swedish monarch King Gustavus Adolphus II (1594–1632), one of several members of the Swedish royal house to bear the name, to the fictional Adolphus Cusins in the George Bernard Shaw play *Major Barbara* (1905). **Dolly**, **Dolph** and **Dolphus** are all diminutive forms of the name.

Adonis (m) Greek name derived from the Phoenician *adon* ('lord'). It appears in Greek mythology as the name of a beautiful youth who captivated Aphrodite and established itself centuries later as a literary name popular among English poets. As well as appearing as the name of a character in Edmund Spenser's *The Faerie Queene* (1590, 1596), it was also used in a variant form by Percy Bysshe Shelley for the title of his elegy *Adonaïs* (1821), dedicated to John Keats.

Adria *See* ADRIAN.

Adrian (m) English first name derived from the Roman Hadrian, itself from the Latin for 'man of Adria' (a reference to a town in northern Italy). It made relatively few appearances in the English-speaking world between its first appearance around the end of the 12th century and the middle of the 20th century, when it suddenly came into vogue, enjoying a peak in popularity during the 1960s before falling out of favour once more. Famous bearers of the name have included the 4th-century martyr St Adrian, the English Pope Adrian IV (Nicholas Breakspear; *c*.1100–1159), minor characters in William Shakespeare's plays *Coriolanus* (*c*.1608) and *The Tempest* (1611), British conductor Sir Adrian Boult (1889–1983), British poet and painter Adrian Henri (1932–2000) and the fictional teenage narrator of Sue Townsend's *The Secret Diary of Adrian Mole, Aged 13¾* (1982). **Ade**, **Addie** and **Adie** are all recognized diminutives of the name. Variants in other languages include the French **Adrien** and the Italian **Adriano**. **Adria** is a rare feminine equivalent. *See also* ADRIENNE.

Adriana/Adriane/Adrianna/Adrianne *See* ADRIENNE.

Adrienne (f) French first name that developed as a feminine version of ADRIAN. It was adopted by English speakers in the early years of the 20th century. Well-known bearers of the name have included US poet Adrienne Rich (b.1929). Among diminutives are **Drena** and **Drina**. Variants include **Adriane**, **Adrianne**, **Adrianna** and **Adriana** – as borne by the wife of Antipholus of Ephesus in William Shakespeare's *The Comedy of Errors* (*c*.1594).

Aed (m) Scottish and Irish first name meaning 'fiery one'. Pronounced 'aigh', it was common among the early Irish and was borne by several early kings of Ireland.

Aelwyn (m) Welsh first name meaning 'fair-browed'. **Aelwen** is a feminine equivalent.

Aeneas (m) Greek first name of obscure

origin, possibly derived from the Greek *ainein* ('to praise'). It appears in Greek mythology as the name of the Trojan hero whose voyages were recorded in Virgil's *Aeneid* (30–19 BC). The Trojan Aeneas appears in William Shakespeare's *Troilus and Cressida* (1602) and there is a character called Aeneas Manston in Thomas Hardy's *Desperate Remedies* (1871), although the name has never been in common use in the English-speaking world except in Scotland, where it is also regarded as an Anglicization of the Gaelic **Aonghas** or **Aonghus**, and in Ireland, where it is considered an equivalent of the Gaelic **Eighneachan**.

Aeronwy (f) Welsh first name meaning 'berry stream'. The name refers to the River Aeron in Ceredigion. Also encountered in the variant form **Aeronwen**.

Afonso *See* ALPHONSE.

Afra *See* APHRA.

Africa (f) English first name derived from the name of the continent. It has enjoyed modest popularity in relatively recent times as a first name among African-Americans eager to demonstrate their African origins.

Agatha (f) English first name derived ultimately from the Greek Agathe, itself from the Greek *agathos* ('good'). Borne by the 3rd-century virgin martyr St Agatha, it was introduced to England by the Normans in the 11th century, being borne by a daughter of William the Conqueror. It was in widespread use throughout medieval times, when it often appeared in the Latinized form Agacia, but subsequently became much less common. It was revived among English speakers in the 19th century and remained in frequent use into the early 20th century, but has since become rare. Well-known bearers of the name have included British crime novelist Agatha Christie (1890–1976) and the fearsome Aunt Agatha in the Jeeves and Wooster stories of P. G. Wodehouse. Commonly abbreviated to **Aggie**. Variants in other languages include the French and German **Agathe**, the

Italian, Polish and Scandinavian **Agata** and the Spanish **Agueda**.

Aggie *See* AGATHA; AGNES.

Agnes (f) English, German, Dutch and Scandinavian first name descended from the Greek Hagne, itself derived from *hagnos* ('chaste' or 'pure'). Its popularity as a name may also owe something to the influence of the Latin *agnus* ('lamb'), with its Christian connotations. It was in common use in medieval England, becoming one of the top three girls' names by the 16th century, but suffered a decline following the Reformation because of its lack of biblical connections. It was among the many medieval names revived in the 19th century and has remained in irregular use ever since, especially in Scotland, although it has appeared much less frequently since the early 20th century.

Notable bearers of the name have included the 4th-century virgin martyr St Agnes, Charles VII of France's mistress Agnes Sorel (1422–50), the title character in the Anne Brontë novel *Agnes Grey* (1847) and US ballerina and choreographer Agnes de Mille (1905–93). Commonly abbreviated to **Aggie**. Other diminutives include **Nessie** and the Welsh **Nesta** (or **Nest**). Variants in other languages include the French **Agnès**, the German **Agnethe**, the Italian **Agnese**, the Spanish **Inés** (or **Inez**) and the Swedish **Agneta**. *See also* ANNIS.

Agneta *See* AGNES.

Agostino/Agustín *See* AUGUSTINE.

Ahmed (m) Arabic name derived from the Arabic *hamida* ('to praise') and thus usually interpreted as meaning 'more praiseworthy'. Well-known bearers of the name have included Egyptian soldier and nationalist leader Ahmed Arabi (1839–1911). Also encountered as **Ahmad** – as borne by Ahmad Shah Durani (1724–73), the founder and first monarch of Afghanistan – or **Ahmet** – as borne by three 17th- and 18th-century sultans of Turkey.

Aidan (m) English version of the Irish

Aodan, itself a diminutive of Aodh (the name of a Celtic sun god, meaning 'fire'). The Anglicized form of the name succeeded the Irish form in Ireland early in the 20th century and the name subsequently became popular elsewhere in the English-speaking world towards the end of the century. Notable bearers of the name have included the 7th-century St Aidan, remembered for his evangelical work in northern England and for the foundation of the monastery at Lindisfarne, and in more recent times US actor Aidan Quinn (b.1959). **Adie** is a fairly common diminutive form of the name. Occasionally also encountered as **Adan, Aden** or **Edan**. **Ethne** is a feminine form of the name. *See also* HAYDN.

Ailbhe *See* ELVIS.

Aileen *See* EILEEN.

Ailie *See* AILSA.

Ailsa (f) Scottish place name (from the isle of Ailsa Craig in the Firth of Clyde) that has made occasional appearances as a first name over the years, presumably under the influence of ELSA and other similar names. The original place name came from the Old Norse **Alfsigesey** (meaning 'island of Alfsigr'). Pronounced 'eyela', it has yet to win significant acceptance outside Scotland itself. **Ailie** is a diminutive form of the name.

Aimée (f) French first name derived from the ordinary vocabulary word *aimée* ('beloved') that has also made occasional appearances as a first name among English speakers. Records of the name's use among the French go back to the medieval period, but it was not taken up in the English-speaking world until the end of the 19th century, when it was adopted alongside the already established English equivalent AMY. It has remained in irregular use ever since, with and without the accent, with a modest peak in popularity since the 1980s. Well-known bearers of the name have included the Canadian-born US evangelist Aimee McPherson (1890–1944). Also spelled **Aimi**.

Aimi *See* AIMÉE.

Aine (f) Irish first name from the Gaelic meaning 'brightness'. Pronounced 'anyeh', it was borne in legend by a fertility goddess who was subsequently identified as a fairy queen in Irish folklore.

Ainsley (m/f) English place name (common to Nottinghamshire and Warwickshire) derived from the Old English *an* ('one') and *leah* ('clearing' or 'wood') and interpreted as meaning 'lonely clearing' or 'my meadow' that was subsequently taken up as a surname and occasional first name. As a surname it was long associated with a powerful family on the Scottish border. As a first name it enjoyed a boost in the 1990s through British television chef Ainsley Harriott. Occasionally encountered as **Ainslee** or **Ainslie**.

Aisha (f) Arabic name derived from *aisha* ('alive') and pronounced 'eye-eesha'. It was borne by Muhammad's third and favourite wife Aisha bint-Abi-Bakr (*c*.613–78) and consequently has a long history as a favourite choice of name in the Arabic world. Also encountered as **Ayesha** – as spelled in the H. Rider Haggard novel *Ayesha* (1905) – and as **Asia**.

Aisling (f) Irish first name (pronounced 'ashling'), derived from the Gaelic for 'dream' or 'vision', that became popular in Ireland in the 1960s. Also found as **Aislinn**, **Ashling** or **Isleen**.

Aithne *See* EITHNE.

Ajay (m) Indian first name derived from a Sanskrit word meaning 'unconquerable'.

Akash (m) Indian first name derived from a Sanskrit word meaning 'sky'.

Akim *See* JOACHIM.

Al (m/f) English first name in common use as a diminutive of such masculine names as ALAN, ALASTAIR, ALBERT, ALEXANDER, ALFRED and ALVIN and of the feminine

ALICE and ALISON. It entered general usage in the USA in the 19th century and has continued in common currency ever since. Famous bearers of the name have included the US singer and film actor Al Jolson (Asa Yoelson; 1886–1950), US gangster Al Capone (1899–1947), US film actor Al Pacino (b.1939) and US singer-songwriter Al Stewart (b.1945). **Allie** and **Ally** are diminutive forms.

Alain *See* ALAN.

Alan (m) English and Scottish first name of Celtic origin, supposedly derived from the Celtic *alun* ('concord' or 'harmony') or otherwise interpreted as meaning 'shining' or 'rock'. It was introduced to England by the Normans in the 11th century and became a fairly frequent choice during the medieval period. It subsequently experienced a decline in popularity before it became the subject of a significant revival throughout the English-speaking world, along with other medieval names, in the 19th century. It was at its most widespread in the 1950s but has since tailed off considerably. Notable bearers of the name have included Alan-a-Dale (one of Robin Hood's Merry Men), Alan Breck in the Robert Louis Stevenson novel *Kidnapped* (1886), British actor Alan Bates (1934–2003), British playwright Alan Bennett (b.1934) and US film actor Alan Alda (b.1936). Variants include **Allan**, **Allen**, the Welsh **Alun**, the Scottish Gaelic **Ailean** and the French **Alain**. Commonly abbreviated to AL. **Alana** is a feminine form.

Alana *See* ALAN.

Alaric (m) German and English first name derived from the Old German *ala* ('all'), *ali* ('stranger') or *adal* ('noble') and *ric* ('power' or 'ruler') and usually interpreted as meaning 'ruler of all'. Famous as the name of Alaric I, a 5th-century king of the Visigoths, it came to England with the Normans in the 11th century and has made rare appearances as a first name among English speakers since the middle of the 19th cen-

tury. **Alarice** and **Alarica** are rare feminine forms of the name.

Alasdair *See* ALASTAIR.

Alastair (m) English first name derived from the Scottish Gaelic Alasdair, itself a variant of ALEXANDER. Having established itself among the Scots, it began to appear more widely among English speakers during the 19th century and remained fairly popular across the English-speaking world through the 20th century, although it has been in less frequent use since the 1950s. Well-known bearers of the name have included Scottish actor Alastair Sim (1900–1976) and British television newsreader Sir Alastair Burnet (b.1928). Sometimes abbreviated to ALY. Also encountered in the variant form **Alistair** – as borne by Anglo-American radio journalist Alistair Cooke (b.1909) and British novelist Alistair MacLean (1922–87). Less common variants include **Alister**.

Alban (m) English first name possibly derived ultimately from the Roman place name Alba Longa (a district of Rome), itself from the Latin *albus* ('white'), or else from the Celtic *alp* ('rock' or 'crag'), and usually interpreted as meaning 'white hill'. It became well known as the name of the 3rd- or 4th-century Romano-British St Alban, after whom the city of St Albans was named, and was in fairly common use during the medieval period. It subsequently fell into disuse, with the exception of a minor revival in the 19th century. Commonly abbreviated to **Albie** or **Alby**. Also found as **Albany** or **Albin**. **Albina** and **Albinia** are rare feminine forms of the name – the first record of Albinia in use among English speakers going back to 1604.

Albany *See* ALBAN.

Alberic *See* AUBREY.

Albert (m) English and French first name derived from the Old German Adalbert, itself from the Old German *adal* ('noble') and *berht* ('bright' or 'famous') and thus interpreted as meaning 'nobly famous'. Although records of its sporadic use among English speakers go back as far as the Norman Conquest, when the French variant Aubert replaced the Old English ETHELBERT, it did not establish itself as a popular choice among English speakers until the 19th century when it suddenly shot to prominence in its modern form through Queen Victoria's German-born husband Prince Albert of Saxe-Coburg-Gotha (1819–61). It remained in common currency into the 20th century, although it has gradually decreased in frequency since the 1920s and is now rare among the young.

Other notable bearers of the name have included French missionary Albert Schweitzer (1875–1965), German-born US physicist and mathematician Albert Einstein (1879–1955) and British actor Albert Finney (b.1936). Diminutive forms of the name include AL and BERT (or BERTIE). Variants in other languages include the Italian and Spanish **Alberto** and the German **Albrecht**. *See also* ALBERTA.

Alberta (f) English first name that developed as a feminine equivalent of ALBERT. It enjoyed a minor vogue among English speakers during the 19th century but has been in very rare use since the beginning of the 20th century. Famous bearers of the name have included Queen Victoria's and Prince Albert's fourth daughter Princess Louise Caroline Alberta (1848–1939) – after whom the Canadian province of Alberta was named in response to the wish of her husband the Marquess of Lorne, governor-general of Canada (1878–83). Variants include **Albertina** and **Albertine**.

Albertina/Albertine *See* ALBERTA.

Alberto *See* ALBERT.

Albie/Albina/Albinia *See* ALBAN.

Albrecht *See* ALBERT.

Aldo *See* ALDOUS.

Aldous (m) English first name apparently derived from the Old German Aldo, itself from the Old German *ald* ('old'). It was a fairly frequent choice in eastern England during the 13th century but has never been in common general use, despite a minor resurgence in the 19th century. The most famous bearer of the name to date has been the British novelist Aldous Huxley (1894–1963). Variants include **Aldus**.

Alec (m) English first name that developed as a diminutive of ALEXANDER around the middle of the 19th century, proving especially popular in Scotland. It enjoyed a peak in popularity in the first half of the 20th century but has since suffered a marked decline in frequency, in part because of the rise of the rival ALEX. Notable bearers of the name have included Scottish Prime Minister Sir Alec Douglas-Home (Baron Alexander Frederick Douglas-Home; 1903–95) and British actors Sir Alec Guinness (1914–2000) and Alec McCowen (b.1925). Commonly abbreviated to **Lec**. Variants include **Alic**, **Alick** and **Aleck**.

Aled (m) Welsh first name meaning 'offspring'. It enjoyed considerable exposure outside Wales in the 1980s through Welsh soprano boy-singer Aled Jones (b.1971). **Aledwen** is a feminine form of the name.

Aleksandr *See* ALEXANDER.

Alessandra *See* ALEXANDRA.

Alessandro *See* ALEXANDER.

Alethea (f) English first name derived from the Greek *aletheia* ('truth'). It seems to have made its first appearances among English speakers in the 17th century, perhaps in reference to Princess Maria Alatea of Spain, who was briefly considered as a possible bride for Charles I of England, or else as a result of the Puritan enthusiasm for 'virtue' names. The name has remained in occasional use ever since, with a modest vogue among US Blacks in recent decades. Also spelled ALTHEA, although the two names are otherwise unconnected. Famous bearers of the name have included a character called Alethea Pontifex in Samuel Butler's novel *The Way of All Flesh* (1903).

Letty is a diminutive form. Also encountered as **Aleta** or **Aletha**.

Alex (m/f) English first name that developed as a diminutive of the masculine ALEXANDER and also of the feminine ALEXANDRA or ALEXIS but which is now often considered a name in its own right. It appears to have been an early 20th-century introduction that has steadily increased in frequency over the decades. Well-known bearers of this form of the name have included US novelist Alex Haley (1921–92), the protagonist in the Anthony Burgess novel *A Clockwork Orange* (1962) and Northern Irish snooker player Alex Higgins (b.1949). LEX and **Lexie** are diminutive forms of the name. Also encountered as **Alix**. *See also* ALEC.

Alexa *See* ALEXANDRA; ALEXIS.

Alexander (m) Greek name derived from the Greek *alexein* ('to defend') and *aner* ('man') and thus interpreted as meaning 'defender of men' that has been in widespread use among English, German, Dutch and Hebrew speakers since the medieval period. Famous in classical history as the name of Alexander the Great, King of Macedon (356–323 BC), after whom the Egyptian city of Alexandria was named, it was also associated with the Trojan hero Paris and appeared in the New Testament. During the medieval period it became especially popular in Scotland and was borne by several medieval Scottish kings.

Other notable bearers of the name over the centuries have included several early Christian saints, eight popes, three Russian emperors, a servant in William Shakespeare's *Troilus and Cressida* (1602), Scottish-born US inventor Alexander Graham Bell (1847–1922), British bacteriologist Sir Alexander Fleming (1881–1955), US writer and theatre critic Sir Alexander Woollcott (1887–1943), Russian novelist Alexander Solzhenitsyn (b.1918) and US politician Alexander Haig (b.1924). Among the many diminutive forms of the name are ALEC, ALEX, **Sandy** and SASHA. Variants in other languages include the Scottish **Alasdair**, the French **Alexandre**, the Italian **Alessandro** (and its shortened form **Sandro**), the Spanish **Alejandro**, the Polish **Aleksander**, the Hungarian **Sandor** and the Russian **Aleksandr**. *See also* ALEXANDRA.

Alexandra (f) English first name that was taken up as a feminine variant of ALEXANDER. It was in frequent use among English speakers during the medieval period and was among the many medieval names to enjoy a significant revival in the 19th century. It appeared with less frequency from the early 20th century but has been in more common use since the 1970s. Famous bearers of the name have included Edward VII of England's Danish-born wife Queen Alexandra (1844–1925), Empress Alexandra of Russia (1872–1918) and Elizabeth II's cousin Princess Alexandra (b.1936). Among common diminutive forms of the name are ALEX, SANDRA, SASHA and **Zandra**. Less frequent diminutives include **Alexa** and **Alexia**. Variants include **Alexandria** and **Alexandrina** – a version that enjoyed a brief vogue in the 19th century through its fame as Queen Victoria's first name. Versions of the name in other languages include the Italian **Alessandra**, the Spanish **Alejandra** and the Russian **Aleksandra**. *See also* ALEXIS.

Alexandria/Alexandrina *See* ALEXANDRA.

Alexia/Alexie/Alexina *See* ALEXIS.

Alexis (m/f) English and Russian first name descended ultimately from the Greek Alexios, itself like ALEXANDER and ALEXANDRA derived from the Greek *alexein* ('to defend'). It has appeared with decreasing frequency as a masculine name in recent times as it has become more common as a feminine name. Notable bearers of the name have included (among the men) the 5th-century St Alexis, who was noted for his generosity to the poor, and British pop musician Alexis Korner (1928–84) and (among the women) the character Alexis Carrington played by Joan Collins in the popular 1980s television soap opera *Dynasty*. **Alexa**, **Alexia** and **Alexie** are relatively rare variants of the name. **Lexie** and **Lexy** are diminutive forms of the name. Variants include the Scottish **Alexina** and the Italian **Alessia**.

Alf (m) English first name that was widely adopted as a diminutive form of ALFRED towards the end of the 19th century. Famous bearers of the name have included British football manager Sir Alf Ramsey (1920–99) and British television character Alf Garnett, played by Warren Mitchell from the 1960s. Diminutive forms include **Alfie** – as borne by British comedian and actor Alfie Bass (1921–87).

Alfie *See* ALF; ALFRED.

Alfonso *See* ALPHONSE.

Alfred (m) English first name descended from the Old English Aelfraed, itself derived from the Old English *aelf* ('elf') and *raed* ('counsel') and usually interpreted as meaning 'inspired advice'. Another derivation links the name with the Old English Ealdfrith, meaning 'old peace'. It was well established in its Old English form centuries before the Norman Conquest, becoming widely known as the name of Alfred the Great, King of Wessex (849–99). It was in common currency among English speakers during the early medieval period, when it was often written as **Alured**, but later fell into disuse before enjoying a marked revival among other medieval names in the 19th century. It has been in decline, however, since the early years of the 20th century.

Well-known bearers of the name have included Swedish inventor Alfred Nobel (1833–96), the fictional Alfred Jingle in the Charles Dickens novel *Pickwick Papers* (1836–7), British poet Alfred, Lord Tennyson (1809–92) and British film director Alfred Hitchcock (1899–1980). Diminutive forms of the name include AL, ALF, **Alfie** and FRED. Variants in other languages include the Italian and Spanish **Alfredo**. *See also* ALFREDA; AVERY.

Alfreda (f) English first name descended from the Old English ELFREDA, itself interpreted as meaning 'elf strength', but now generally regarded as a feminine equivalent of ALFRED. It enjoyed a modest peak in popularity towards the end of the 19th century but has appeared only irregularly since then. FREDA is a diminutive form of the name.

Alger (m) English first name (pronounced 'aljer') derived ultimately from the Old English Aelfgar, itself from the Old English *aelf* ('elf') and *gar* ('spear'). As **Algar**, it was in fairly common use during the medieval period but subsequently fell from favour, with a minor revival in the 19th century. The name received renewed exposure in the 1930s as a result of the furore surrounding Alger Hiss (1904–96), the US government agent accused of being a Soviet spy.

Algernon (m) English first name derived from the Norman French *als gernons* ('with whiskers'). It was employed originally as a nickname for anyone with a moustache or whiskers. Having come to England as the nickname of two of William the Conqueror's companions (who were unusual among the Norman invaders in not being clean-shaven), it became particularly identified with the powerful Percy family and consequently acquired a reputation as a rather aristocratic name. It was in more widespread use during the 19th century, when it received renewed exposure as the name of Algernon Moncrieff, a character in the classic Oscar Wilde comedy *The Importance of Being Earnest* (1895). Other notable bearers of the name have included British poet Algernon Swinburne (1837–1909) and British writer Algernon Blackwood (1869–1951). Commonly abbreviated to **Algie** or **Algy** – as borne by Algy (properly Captain Algernon Lacy), the hero's best friend in the *Biggles* books of Captain W. E. Johns.

Algie/Algy *See* ALGERNON.

Ali (m) Arabic name derived from *ali* ('elevated' or 'sublime'). As the name of Muhammad's cousin and the first Islamic convert, it is a traditional favourite throughout the Islamic world. *See also* ALICE; ALISON.

Alia *See* ELLA.

Alice (f) English and French first name derived ultimately from the Old German Adalheit, meaning 'noble woman'. It was in common currency among English speakers during the medieval period, when variant forms included **Alse**, **Adelice** and **Adelise,** but subsequently fell from favour in the 17th century. It was revived in the 19th century, when it became well known from Lewis Carroll's stories *Alice's Adventures in Wonderland* (1865) and *Through the Looking-Glass* (1872), but appeared less frequently in the 20th century before enjoying another significant revival in the 1990s.

As well as Lewis Carroll's Alice, famous bearers of the name in literature have included Katherine of France's attendant Alice in William Shakespeare's *Henry V* (1599) and a maidservant in the George Eliot novel *The Mill on the Floss* (1860). Among bearers of the name in real life have been British writer Alice B. Toklas (1877–1967) and Princess Alice, Duchess of Gloucester (b.1901). The name of US rock singer Alice Cooper (Vincent Furnier; b.1948), taken from the name of the band in which he appeared as lead vocalist, is a possibly unique instance of the name being treated as masculine. Commonly abbreviated to AL or **Ali** – as borne by US film actress Ali McGraw (b.1938). Variants include the Welsh **Alys** and the Irish **Alis**, **Ailis** or **Ailish**. *See also* ALICIA; ALISON.

Alicia (f) English first name that was taken up as a Latinized variant of ALICE in the 19th century. It has continued to appear alongside other forms of the name up to the present. Famous bearers of the name have included British ballerina Dame Alicia Markova (Lilian Alice Marks; b.1910). Variants of the name include **Alisa**, **Alissa** and **Alyssa**. **Lyssa** is a diminutive form.

Alick *See* ALEC.

Alida *See* ADELAIDE.

Aline *See* ADELINE.

Alis *See* ALICE.

Alisa *See* ALICIA.

Alison (f) English and French first name that developed as a Norman French diminutive of ALICE. It was taken up during the medieval period, when it also appeared in the form **Alyson** (or **Alysoun**), but seems to have fallen out of favour outside Scotland after the 15th century. It enjoyed a substantial revival throughout the English-speaking world during the 1920s and subsequently reached a peak in frequency in the 1960s, largely superseding Alice and other diminutives of that name. Notable bearers of the name have included the character Alysoun in Geoffrey Chaucer's *The Miller's Tale* (1387), British children's writer Alison Uttley (Alice Jane Uttley; 1884–1976), British actress Alison Steadman (b.1946) and British rock singer Alison Moyet (b.1961). Commonly abbreviated to AL, **Ali**, **Allie** or **Ally**. Also spelled occasionally as **Allison**.

Alissa *See* ALICIA.

Alistair/Alister *See* ALASTAIR.

Alix *See* ALEX.

Allan *See* ALAN.

Allegra (f) English and Italian first name derived from the Italian *allegro* ('happy', 'lively' or 'merry'). It is possible that the name was actually invented by the British poet Lord Byron, who bestowed it upon his illegitimate daughter Allegra Byron (1817–22) and thus established it as an accepted if select first name among English speakers.

Allen *See* ALAN.

Allie *See* AL; ALISON.

Allison *See* ALISON.

Ally *See* AL; ALISON.

Alma (f) English first name of obscure origin, possibly derived from the Latin *alma* ('kind'), but often associated with the Italian *alma* ('soul'). It made rare appearances in earlier times but was only taken up with enthusiasm among English speakers around the middle of the 19th century with reference to the British Army's victory over the Russians at the Battle of Alma (1854) during the Crimean War. It has appeared infrequently since the early years of the 20th century. Well-known bearers of the name have included British singer Alma Cogan (1932–66). There was also a well-known fictional character called Alma in the long-running British television soap opera *Coronation Street*.

Almira (f) English first name probably derived from the Arabic *amiri* ('princess'). It made early appearances as a first name among English speakers in the 19th century, but has been in only sporadic use since then, chiefly confined to the USA.

Alois/Aloisia/Aloisie *See* ALOYSIUS.

Alonso/Alonzo *See* ALPHONSE.

Aloysius (m) English, German, French and Dutch first name representing a fanciful Latinized variant of LOUIS. It was in common currency in medieval Italy and subsequently enjoyed wider fame through the Lombardy-born Jesuit St Aloysius Gonzaga (1568–91). Because of its connections with St Aloysius the name became a favourite choice among Roman Catholics around Europe from the 17th century. Famous bearers of the name in the English-speaking world have included Sebastian Flyte's teddy bear in the Evelyn Waugh novel *Brideshead Revisited* (1945). It is pronounced 'aloishus'. Variants in other languages include the German **Alois**. **Aloisia**, **Aloysia** and **Aloisie** are rare feminine forms of the name.

Alpha (m/f) English first name derived from the first letter of the Greek alphabet and thus suggesting excellence or prime importance. Its use as a first name in the English-speaking world goes back to the 19th century, although it has never been in common use. Variants include **Alfa**. *See also* OMEGA.

Alphonse (m) French first name derived from the Old German *adal* ('noble') and *funs* ('ready' or 'prompt'), or else *ala* ('all') and *hadu* ('struggle') or *hild* ('battle'), that has made occasional appearances among English speakers since the 19th century, chiefly among Black Americans. **Fonsie** and **Fonzie** are among diminutive forms of the name. Variants in other languages include the Latinate **Alphonsus**, the Spanish **Alfonso** (or its variants **Alonso** or **Alonzo**) – as borne by eleven kings of Spain – and the Portuguese **Afonso** – as borne by four kings of Portugal. Feminine variants of the name include **Alphonsine**.

Alphonsine/Alphonsus *See* ALPHONSE.

Althea (f) English first name descended from the Greek Althaia, itself derived from the Greek *althein* ('to heal') and thus interpreted as meaning 'wholesome'. It appeared in Greek mythology as the name of the mother of the hunter Meleager and was consequently taken up as a poetic name by English speakers in the 17th century. It became famous in English literature as the pseudonym by which English poet Richard Lovelace addressed his beloved in his celebrated poem 'To Althea, from Prison' (1642). *See also* ALETHEA.

Alun *See* ALAN.

Alured *See* ALFRED.

Alva (m/f) English first name derived from the Hebrew Alvah, meaning 'height' or 'exalted', but also in use as a feminine equivalent of ALVIN. It appears in the Bible as the name of one of the leaders of Edom and was taken up on a very limited scale by English speakers in the 19th century. Famous bearers of the name have included US scientiest and inventor Thomas Alva Edison (1847–1931).

Alvar (m) English first name descended from the Old English Aelfhere, itself derived from *aelf* ('elf') and *here* ('army' or 'warrior'), but also occasionally encountered in use as an Anglicized form of the Spanish **Alvaro**. Records of its use among English speakers go back as far as the 'Domesday Book' of 1086. Well-known bearers of the name in relatively recent times have included British radio announcer Alvar Liddell (1908–81).

Alvaro See ALVAR.

Alvie See ALVIN.

Alvin (m) English first name descended from the Old English Aelfwine, itself derived from the Old English *aelf* ('elf') and *wine* ('friend'). It made rare appearances among English speakers before the 20th century, when it began to appear with more frequency, chiefly in the USA. Notable bearers of the name have included US ballet dancer and choreographer Alvin Ailey (1931–89) and British pop singer Alvin Stardust (Bernard Jewry; b.1942). Commonly abbreviated to AL or **Alvie**. **Alwyn** and **Aylwin** are variants of the name, and ALVA a feminine equivalent.

Alwyn See ALVIN.

Aly (m) Scottish first name adopted as a diminutive of **Alasdair** (*see* ALASTAIR). Notable bearers of the name in recent times have included the Scottish fiddle player Aly Bain (b.1946).

Alys/Alyson See ALISON.

Alyssa See ALICIA.

Amabel (f) English first name derived from the Latin *amabilis* ('lovable'). It made early appearances among English speakers during the medieval period and was the subject of a minor revival in the 19th century in the wake of its appearance in the Harrison Ainsworth novel *Old St Paul's* (1841). It is very rare today. *See also* ANNABEL; MABEL.

Amal (m/f) Arabic name derived from *amal* ('hope' or 'expectation'). It is in common use as a feminine name, but continues to make appearances as a masculine name in various parts of the Arab world.

Amalia/Amalie *See* AMELIA.

Amanda (f) English first name derived ultimately from the Latin *amanda* ('lovable'), apparently under the influence of MIRANDA. There are suggestions that the name was in occasional use in the English-speaking world during the medieval period, but otherwise its first appearance appears to have been as the name of a character in the Colley Cibber play *Love's Last Shift* (1696). It went on to make appearances in several more notable literary works, including Sir John Vanbrugh's play *The Relapse* (1696), and has remained in currency as a first name ever since, with a recent peak in popularity in the 1960s. Well-known bearers of the name have included a character in the Tobias Smollett novel *Peregrine Pickle* (1751), the fictional Amanda Prynne in the Noël Coward comedy *Private Lives* (1930) and British actresses Amanda Bairstow (b.1960), Amanda Donahoe (b.1962) and Amanda Holden (b.1971). Commonly abbreviated to **Manda** and **Mandy** (or **Mandi**).

Amaryllis (f) Greek name possibly derived from the Greek *amaryssein* ('to sparkle') and thus a reference to sparkling eyes. The name appeared in both Virgil and Ovid and was subsequently taken up by English poets in the 17th century, although it has made only very infrequent appearances as a first name in wider use since then, despite reinforcement in the 19th century as a flower name. Famous bearers of the name in literature have included characters in John Milton's *Lycidas* (1637), in Edmund Spenser's poem *Colin Clouts Come Home Againe* (1595) and in John Fletcher's play *The Faithful Shepherdess* (c.1609).

Amata *See* AMY.

Amber (f) English first name derived from that of the gemstone. It was taken up along with other jewel names towards the end of the 19th century and has continued in limited use ever since, with a recent peak since the 1970s. Well-known bearers of the name have included Amber St Clair, who is described as having amber-coloured eyes, in Kathleen Winsor's popular historical novel *Forever Amber* (1944). **Ambretta** is a rare variant.

Ambrose (m) English first name descended from the Roman Ambrosius, itself derived from the Greek *ambrosios* ('immortal' or 'divine'). Well known as the name of the 4th-century St Ambrosius of Milan and also as that of the semi-legendary 5th-century English leader Ambrosius Aurelianus, a prototype for King Arthur, it has been in regular use among English speakers since at least the 11th century, particularly among Irish Roman Catholics. It enjoyed a resurgence in popularity in the 19th century but has since become relatively uncommon. Famous bearers of the name have included US satirist Ambrose Bierce (1824–c.1914) and British bandleader Ambrose (Albert Ambrose; 1897–1971). Variants in other languages include the French **Ambroise**, the Italian **Ambrogio** and the Spanish and Portuguese **Ambrosio**. **Ambrosina** and **Ambrosine** are rare feminine forms of the name. *See also* EMRYS.

Amelia (f) English first name descended from the Roman Aemilia ('striving/eager') under the influence of the Old German *amal* ('labour'). It became popular among English speakers in the 18th century after it became widely known as the first name of William IV's wife Queen Adelaide (1792–1849) and subsequently as that of Princess Amelia (1783–1810), the youngest daughter of George III. It has continued in use ever since, although it has been rather less frequent since the end of the 19th century. Other notable bearers of the name have included the fictional Amelia Booth in the Henry Fielding novel *Amelia* (1751), Amelia Sedley in the William Makepeace Thackeray novel *Vanity Fair* (1847–8) and US aviator Amelia Earhart (1897–1937). **Millie** and **Milly** are diminutive forms of the name. Variants include the less well-known **Amalia**, the French **Amélie** and the German **Amalie**. *See also* EMILIA.

Amélie *See* AMELIA.

Amethyst (f) English first name derived from that of the semi-precious gemstone.

Amey *See* AMY.

Amias *See* AMYAS.

Amice (f) English first name derived from the Roman Amica, itself from the Latin *amitia* ('friendship'). It was fairly popular in medieval times but was subsequently largely superseded by AMITY. **Amicia** is a variant form.

Amie *See* AMY.

Amin (m) Arabic name meaning 'honest' or 'trustworthy' that ranks among the most common names in the Islamic world. Variants include the feminine **Amina**.

Aminadab (m) Hebrew name meaning 'my people are generous'. It appears in the Bible as the name of the man whose house gave shelter to David and the Ark of the Covenant and the name was consequently taken up by English Puritans in the 17th century, but is virtually unknown today.

Aminta *See* ARAMINTA.

Amita *See* AMITY.

Amity (f) English first name derived from the Latin *amitia* ('friendship'). Variants include **Amita**, a relatively modern version of the name. *See also* AMICE.

Amory (m) English first name of Germanic origin, meaning 'famous ruler'. Also encountered in the variant forms **Amery**, **Emery** and **Emmery**.

Amos (m) Hebrew name possibly meaning 'borne' or 'carried' and usually interpreted as meaning 'borne by God'. Another derivation suggests it comes from the Hebrew for 'strong' or 'courageous'. It appears in the Bible as the name of the Old Testament prophet whose prophecies were collected in the Book of Amos and was taken up by

English Puritans after the Reformation. It remained in fairly regular use until the end of the 19th century, since when it has become much less common – perhaps because it has over the years acquired a reputation as an essentially rustic name. Notable bearers of the name have included the Revd Amos Barton in George Eliot's *Scenes of Clerical Life* (1858).

Amy (f) English first name derived from the Old French *amee* ('beloved'), itself descended from the Latin *amare* ('to love') and possibly ultimately from a pre-Roman source. It was taken up by English speakers in the 18th century and has remained in use ever since, with a recent peak in popularity in the 1980s and 1990s. Well-known bearers of the name have included Amy Robsart (d.1560), the ill-fated wife of the Earl of Leicester, whose death allegedly came about as the result of poison administered by her husband, the fictional Amy Dorrit in the Charles Dickens novel *Little Dorrit* (1857) and Amy March in Louisa M. Alcott's novel *Little Women* (1868–9), US poet Amy Lowell (1874–1925), British aviator Amy Johnson (1903–41), and Amy Carter (b.1969), daughter of US President Jimmy Carter. Variants of the name include **Amey** and **Amie**. Occasionally encountered in the Latinized form **Amata** – as borne by the 13th-century St Amata of Bologna. *See also* AIMÉE.

Amyas (m) English first name (pronounced 'am-ee-ass') derived either from the Roman Amatus, from the Latin for 'loved', or alternatively from a French surname meaning 'person from Amiens'. It has made occasional appearances among English speakers since the 16th century, with a modest peak in frequency in the 19th century. Famous bearers of the name have included a minor character in Edmund Spenser's *The Faerie Queene* (1586) and Captain Sir Amyas Leigh in the Charles Kingsley novel *Westward Ho!* (1855). Also encountered as **Amias**.

Amynta *See* ARAMINTA.

Ana *See* ANNA.

Anaïs (f) French first name derived from the Greek for 'fruitful'. Famous bearers of the name in the English-speaking world have included US writer Anaïs Nin (1903–77).

Anand (m) Indian first name derived from the Sanskrit word for 'joy'. Borne by a Hindu god, it may also be adopted as a name for girls, variously rendered as **Ananda** or **Anandi**.

Anarawd (m) Welsh first name meaning 'most eloquent'. It is pronounced 'anarod'.

Anastasia (f) English and Russian first name descended from the Greek Anastasios, itself derived from the Greek *anastasis* ('resurrection'). Because of its meaning the name was popular among early Christians and was borne by a widely venerated 4th-century saint, although it was not adopted by English speakers until the 19th century. Today the name is most often associated with Princess Anastasia (1901–18), the youngest daughter of Czar Nicholas II, who was executed with the rest of the Russian royal family after the Russian Revolution, but who was for many years rumoured to have survived death at the hands of the Bolsheviks and to have lived under an assumed identity in the West. Diminutive forms of the name include STACEY. *See also* TANSY.

Anatole (m) French first name descended from the Roman Anatolius, itself derived from the Greek *anatole* ('sunrise' or 'east'). It was a popular choice among early Christians but was not taken up by English speakers until the 19th century, and even then only on a very modest scale. Famous bearers of the name have included French writer Anatole France (Jacques-Anatole-François Thibault; 1844–1924) and the fictional valet Anatole in the William Makepeace Thackeray novel *Pendennis* (1848–50). Variants in other languages include the Russian **Anatoli**.

Anders *See* ANDREW.

Andi/Andie *See* ANDREA; ANDREW.

André *See* ANDREW.

Andrea (f) English first name that developed as a variant of the masculine ANDREW, possibly under the influence of the original Greek Andreas. It seems to have made its first appearances as early as the 17th century but it was not until after the Second World War that the name began to appear with any regularity. Famous bearers of the name have included British writer Andrea Newman (b.1938) and US tennis player Andrea Jaeger (b.1965). **Andie**, **Andi** and **Andrée** are among the name's diminutive forms.

Andreas/Andrei/Andrés *See* ANDREW.

Andrew (m) English, Russian and Greek first name derived from the Greek Andreas, itself from the Greek *andreia* ('manliness') and thus interpreted as meaning 'manly' or 'brave'. It appears in the Bible as the name of one of the apostles, subsequently venerated as St Andrew and adopted as the patron saint of Scotland, Greece and Russia – hence the name's particular popularity in those countries. It was established in regular use among English speakers by medieval times and has remained in currency ever since, with a recent peak in popularity in the 1960s and 1970s.

Famous bearers of the name have included Sir Andrew Aguecheek in William Shakespeare's comedy *Twelfth Night* (1601), US Presidents Andrew Jackson (1765–1845) and Andrew Carnegie (1835–1919), Scottish actor Andrew Cruickshank (1907–88) and Queen Elizabeth II's second son Prince Andrew, Duke of York (b.1960). The most common of the name's various diminutive forms is **Andy** – as borne by US pop artist Andy Warhol (1926–87) and US singer Andy Williams (Howard Andrew Williams; b.1928). Among less frequent familiar forms are **Andie**, **Andi** and the Scottish DREW. Variants of the name in other languages include the Scottish **Andra**, the French **André**, the German **Andreas**, the Dutch **Andries**, the Spanish

Andrés, the Italian **Andrea**, the Scandinavian **Anders** and the Russian **Andrei**. **Andrine**, **Andrene**, **Andrena** and **Andreana** are rare feminine forms. *See also* DANDY.

Andries/Andy *See* ANDREW.

Aneka/Aneke *See* ANNEKA.

Aneirin *See* ANEURIN.

Aneurin (m) Welsh first name, originally in the form Neirin, of obscure origin, possibly derived from the Welsh *an* ('all') and *eur* ('gold') and thus interpreted as meaning 'precious one'. Attempts have also been made to trace it back to the Roman Honorius, meaning 'honourable'. Usually pronounced 'an-eye-rin', it was in use in Wales by the medieval period and became well known in the 20th century as the name of Welsh Labour politician Aneurin Bevan (1897–1960). **Nye** is an accepted diminutive form of the name. Also encountered as **Aneirin** – as borne by the 7th-century Welsh poet Aneirin. **Aneira** is a rare feminine form of the name.

Ange *See* ANGEL; ANGELA.

Angel (m/f) English first name derived via Latin from the Greek *angelos* ('messenger') and usually interpreted as meaning 'messenger of God' or simply 'angel'. It seems to have been adopted on a very occasional basis by English speakers as early as the 17th century and has continued to make rare reappearances ever since. Famous bearers of the name have included Angel Clare in the Thomas Hardy novel *Tess of the D'Urbervilles* (1891). **Ange** and **Angie** are diminutive forms of the name. Variants in other languages include the Spanish **Ángel** and the Italian **Angelo**, which has also enjoyed some favour among English speakers since the 19th century. *See also* ANGELA.

Angela (f) English and Italian first name that developed as a feminine equivalent of the masculine ANGEL. It was taken up by English speakers in the 19th century and remained in common currency until the

1960s, since when it has experienced something of a decline. In its early history it was often reserved for children born on 29 September, the feast of St Michael and All Angels. Notable bearers of the name have included St Angela of Brescia (1474–1540), who founded the order of the Ursuline nuns, British actress Angela Lansbury (b.1925) and British television presenter Angela Rippon (b.1944). Commonly abbreviated to **Ange**, **Angie** or **Angy**. *See also* ANGELICA.

Angelica (f) English and Italian first name derived from the Latin *angelicus* ('angelic') but often regarded as a variant of ANGELA. It was imported to England from Italy in the 17th century and enjoyed a modest peak in popularity in the 19th and early 20th centuries, although it has tailed off significantly since the 1950s. Well-known bearers of the name have included Princess Angelica in Ludovico Ariosto's epics *Orlando Innamorato* (1487) and *Orlando Furioso* (1532), Juliet's nurse Angelica in William Shakespeare's tragedy *Romeo and Juliet* (1595), Angelica in William Congreve's play *Love for Love* (1695), Swiss artist Angelica Kauffman (1741–1807) and US actress Angelica Huston (b.1951). Commonly abbreviated to **Ange** or **Angie**. Variants of the name include **Anjelica**, **Angelina**, **Angeline**, **Angelita** and the French **Angélique**.

Angelina/Angeline/Angélique/ Angelita *See* ANGELICA.

Angelo *See* ANGEL.

Angharad (f) Welsh first name derived from the Welsh *an* ('more') and *car* ('love') and usually interpreted as meaning 'much loved'. Its history among Welsh speakers goes back at least to the 12th century and it appears as the name of a character in the medieval *Mabinogion* collection of Welsh folk tales. It has generally been confined to Wales ever since, becoming more popular in the 1940s and for a time enjoying wider exposure in the 1970s through Welsh actress Angharad Rees (b.1949) after she ap-

peared in the British television drama series *Poldark*. Usually pronounced 'anharad'.

Angie *See* ANGEL; ANGELA; ANGELICA.

Angus (m) English version of the Scottish Gaelic **Aonghas** or **Aonghus**, itself derived from the Gaelic *aon* ('one') and *ghus* ('choice') and thus interpreted as meaning 'sole choice'. The name's history in Scotland goes back to at least the 15th century, when it was particularly associated with the clan McDonnell. It retains its distinctive Scottish character but was taken up more widely among English speakers towards the end of the 19th century and has remained in irregular use across the English-speaking world ever since. Notable bearers of the name have included British novelist Sir Angus Wilson (1915–91) and British television presenter Angus Deayton (b.1956). Commonly abbreviated to GUS. **Angusina** is a rare feminine version of the name. *See also* AENEAS; ENOS; INNES.

Angy *See* ANGEL; ANGELA; ANGELICA.

Anil (m) Indian first name derived from the Sanskrit word for 'wind'. The name of a Hindu god, it may also be encountered in the equivalent feminine form **Anila**.

Anita (f) Spanish first name that evolved as a diminutive form of Ana (*see* ANNE). It was taken up by English speakers in the 19th century, initially in the USA but later more widely through the English-speaking world, enjoying a peak in popularity in the 1960s. Notable bearers of the name have included US writer Anita Loos (1888–1981), Swedish actress Anita Ekberg (b.1931), British novelist Anita Brookner (b.1938) and British businesswoman Anita Roddick (b.1942). **Nita** is a diminutive form.

Anjelica *See* ANGELICA.

Anke *See* ANNE.

Ann (f) English first name that developed as a variant of the Hebrew HANNAH and is thus usually interpreted as meaning 'grace' or 'favour'. It became a popular choice of name among English speakers during the medieval period and continued in regular use into the 20th century, although it has been eclipsed in recent decades by the French form of the name, ANNE. Diminutives of the name include ANNIE, **Nan**, **Nana**, NANCY and NINA.

Anna (f) English, French, Dutch, German, Italian, Scandinavian and Russian first name that began life as the Greek or Latin form of HANNAH and is thus interpreted as meaning 'grace' or 'favour'. It appeared as the name of Dido's sister in Virgil's *Aeneid*, written in the 1st century BC, and was subsequently adopted in many European cultures. It was taken up by English speakers in the 19th century, alongside ANN and other variants of the same name, and has remained in fairly regular use ever since, with a recent peak in the 1980s. Notable bearers of the name have included British writer Anna Sewell (1820–78), the central character in Tolstoy's novel *Anna Karenina* (1877), British actress Anna Massey (b.1937) and British television newsreader Anna Ford (b.1943). Variants in other languages include the Spanish **Ana** (Anglicized as **Anya**).

Annabel (f) English first name that came about through the combination of ANN or ANNA with the French *belle* ('beautiful'), possibly under the influence of AMABEL. It made its first appearances in Scotland as early as the 12th century, when it was sometimes spelled Annaple, but was not taken up more widely among English speakers until the 19th century. Commonly abbreviated to **Bel** or **Belle**. Also encountered as **Annabella** or **Annabelle**.

Annabella/Annabelle *See* ANNABEL.

Annalisa *See* ANNELIESE.

Anne (f) French first name that was taken up by English speakers as a variant of ANN during the medieval period. It has remained in regular use ever since and established itself as the most common form of the name around the middle of the 20th century, al-

though it has since tailed off somewhat. Notable bearers of the name over the centuries have included Henry VIII's wives Anne Boleyn (1507–36) and Anne of Cleves (1515–57), William Shakespeare's wife Anne Hathaway (1557–1623), Queen Anne of England (1665–1714), the central character in L. M. Montgomery's *Anne of Green Gables* (1908), US film actress Anne Bancroft (b.1931) and Queen Elizabeth II's daughter Princess Anne (b.1950). Diminutives of the name include ANNIE, **Nan**, **Nana** and NANCY. Variants in other languages include the French ANNETTE, the German **Anke**, the Spanish ANITA and the Swedish ANNEKA. It is also found in combination with various other names, as in **Mary Anne** and the French **Anne-Marie**.

Anneka (f) Swedish variant of ANNE that was adopted by English speakers in the 1950s. Well-known bearers of the name have included British television presenter Anneka Rice (b.1958). Commonly abbreviated to ANNIE. Other forms of the name include **Anneke**, **Annika**, **Aneka** and **Aneke**.

Anneliese (f) German and Scandinavian first name that resulted from the combination of ANNE and Liese (a diminutive of ELIZABETH). It has made occasional appearances as a first name among English speakers in the phonetic form **Annalisa**.

Annette (f) French diminutive of ANNE that has also been in use as a first name among English speakers since the 19th century. It enjoyed a peak in popularity around the middle of the 20th century. Well-known bearers of the name have included Scottish actress Annette Crosbie (b.1934) and US actress Annette Bening (b.1958). Also encountered as **Annetta** or **Annett**. Diminutives include **Netta** and **Nettie**.

Annie (f) Diminutive form of the English first names ANN, ANNE and their many variants. It was taken up by English speakers around the middle of the 19th century, popularized by the Scottish song 'Annie Laurie' (1838), and has remained in regular use ever since, having reached a peak in frequency during the early years of the 20th century. Its popularity in the USA was promoted by the popular Harold Gray comic strip featuring 'Little Orphan Annie', which subsequently provided the basis for the musical *Annie* (1977). Famous bearers of the name have included British social reformer Annie Besant (1847–1933), US sharpshooter Annie Oakley (Phoebe Anne Oakley; 1860–1926) and Scottish pop singer Annie Lennox (b.1954). **Anny** is a rare variant, confined largely to Ireland.

Annis (f) English first name that was taken up during the medieval period as a variant of AGNES. Although rare, it is still in occasional use among English speakers today. Also encountered as **Anis**, **Annys** or **Annice**.

Annora *See* HONOR.

Anona (f) English first name of uncertain origin, derived either from the Latin for 'harvest' or else the result of the combination of ANN and FIONA or similar names. It has made infrequent appearances among English speakers since the early years of the 20th century.

Anouska (f) Russian first name that developed as a variant of ANN. It has made occasional appearances among English speakers since the early 20th century. Famous bearers of the name have included British actress Anouska Hempel (b.1941). Also encountered as the phonetic **Anushka**.

Anselm (m) English first name derived from the Old German Anshelm, itself from the Old German *ans* ('god') and *helm* ('helmet') and thus interpreted as meaning 'protected by God'. It is famous chiefly as the name of St Anselm (1033–1109), Archbishop of Canterbury, and has made occasional appearances among English Roman Catholics in the centuries since then, with a minor revival in the 19th century. **Ansel** and **Ansell** are related forms of the name. Variants in other languages

include the Italian **Anselmo**. **Anselma** is a rare feminine equivalent.

Anselma *See* ANSELM.

Anthea (f) English first name descended from the Greek Antheia, itself derived from the Greek *antheios* ('flowery') and borne in Greek mythology as a title of the goddess Hera. It made early appearances in 17th-century English literature, in the poetry of Robert Herrick among others, but was not taken up as a first name on a significant scale until the 20th century. It enjoyed a peak in popularity in the 1950s but has since become much less common. Well-known bearers of the name in recent times have included British television presenter Anthea Turner (b.1960).

Anthony (m) English first name descended from the Roman Antonius, popularly (although mistakenly) believed to derive ultimately from the Greek *anthos* ('flower') but in fact of obscure (possibly Etruscan) origin. It was borne by several early saints, notably St Anthony of Egypt (251–356) and St Anthony of Padua (1195–1231), and was in regular use among English speakers by the 12th century. It appeared in its modern spelling from the 17th century and subsequently enjoyed a peak in popularity throughout the English-speaking world in the 1950s, since when it has tailed off somewhat.

Notable bearers of the name have included Sir Anthony Absolute in the Richard Brinsley Sheridan comedy *The Rivals* (1775), British Prime Minister Sir Anthony Eden (1897–1977), Mexican-born film actor Anthony Quinn (1915–2001), British novelist Anthony Burgess (1917–93), US actor Anthony Perkins (1932–92) and British actor Sir Anthony Hopkins (b.1937). Commonly abbreviated (since the 17th century) to **Tony** – as borne by such well-known figures as the fictional Tony Lumpkin in the Oliver Goldsmith comedy *She Stoops to Conquer* (1773), US film actor Tony Curtis (Bernard Schwarz; b.1925), US singer Tony Bennett (Antonio Benedetto;

b.1926) and British Prime Minister Tony Blair (Anthony Charles Lynton Blair; b.1953).

Also spelled **Antony** (the usual form of the name before the introduction of the 'h' after the Reformation). It is usually pronounced 'antony' in Britain and 'anthony' in the USA. Variants in other languages include the French **Antoine**, the Spanish and Italian **Antonio** and the German and Russian **Anton** – as borne by Russian playwright Anton Chekhov (1860–1904). *See also* ANTOINETTE; ANTONIA.

Antoine *See* ANTHONY.

Antoinette (f) French first name that developed as a feminine diminutive of **Antoine** (*see* ANTHONY). It is usually associated with the French queen Marie-Antoinette (1755–93) and has been in occasional use among English speakers since the middle of the 19th century. Notable bearers of the name in recent times have included British ballerina Antoinette Sibley (b.1939). Sometimes abbreviated to **Toni** or **Toinette**.

Anton *See* ANTHONY.

Antonia (f) English, German, Dutch, Italian, Spanish, Portuguese and Scandinavian first name descended from the Roman family name Antonius that was adopted as a feminine form of **Antony** (*see* ANTHONY). It was already long established as a first name in continental Europe before English speakers took it up in the early 20th century. Famous bearers of the name have included British novelist and historian Lady Antonia Fraser (b.1932). Commonly abbreviated to **Toni** and less commonly to **Tonia** or **Tonya**. Variants include **Antonina**.

Antonio/Antony *See* ANTHONY.

Anushka *See* ANOUSKA.

Anwar (m) Arabic name derived from *anwar* ('brighter' or 'clearer'). It became well known in the 20th century as the name of Egyptian President Anwar Sadat (1918–81).

Anwen (f) Welsh first name meaning 'very beautiful'.

Anya *See* ANNA.

Aodh *See* AIDAN; EGAN; EUGENE; HUGH; IAGAN; MADOC.

Aonghas/Aonghus *See* AENEAS; ANGUS; ENOS; INNES.

Aphra (f) English first name of obscure origin. It may have evolved from an ancient Irish name or else from the Roman Afra (denoting a woman from Africa), a name that was usually applied to people with dark hair or swarthy colouring. It appears in the Bible as a place name derived from the Hebrew for 'dust' and it might have been a misinterpretation of the phrase 'the house of Aphrah' that led to it being first taken up as a personal name. The name is most familiar in the English-speaking world as that of the English playwright and adventuress Aphra Behn (1640–89), the first professional female writer in English literature. A rare variant is **Affery**, which is how the name appears in the Charles Dickens novel *Little Dorrit* (1855–7).

April (f) English first name derived from the name of the month, presumably inspired by its associations with spring and new growth. It does not appear to have been taken up with much enthusiasm until the 20th century and subsequently enjoyed a modest peak in popularity in the 1960s and 1970s. Variants include the French AVRIL.

Arabella (f) English first name that is thought to have evolved as a variant of Annabella (*see* ANNABEL) or else from the Latin *orabilis* ('entreatable', 'obliging' or 'yielding to prayer'). It was taken up by English speakers during medieval times, becoming particularly well established in Scotland, and became a popular choice of the English aristocracy in the 18th century, promoted by Alexander Pope's *The Rape of the Lock* (1712), which was inspired by an incident involving the real Arabella Fermor. It continued in regular use until the end of the 19th century, but has since appeared much less frequently and is now rare. Other notable bearers of the name in literature have included Arabella Harlowe in the Samuel Richardson novel *Clarissa* (1748), Arabella Briggs in the William Makepeace Thackeray novel *Vanity Fair* (1847–8) and Arabella Donn in Thomas Hardy's *Jude the Obscure* (1894–5). Commonly abbreviated to BELLA and **Belle**. Variants of the name include **Arabel** and **Arabelle**.

Araminta (f) English first name of obscure origin, possibly the result of the combination of ARABELLA and the older **Aminta** or **Amynta**, derived from the Greek for 'protector'. It has enjoyed modest popularity among English speakers since the 17th century. Famous bearers of the name have included the female lead in the William Congreve comedy *The Old Bachelor* (1693) and one of the central characters in Sir John Vanbrugh's play *The Confederacy* (1705). Familiar forms of the name include **Minta** and **Minty**.

Archibald (m) English first name that evolved from the Norman French Archambault itself derived from the Old German *ercan* ('genuine') and *bald* ('bold') and thus interpreted as meaning 'truly brave'. It was taken up by English speakers during the 12th century and subsequently became especially well established in Scotland, where it was considered to be an Anglicized form of GILLESPIE and became particularly associated with the powerful Campbell and Douglas families. It has appeared with less frequency since the early years of the 20th century. Famous bearers of the name have included British military commander Archibald Wavell (1883–1950) and US poet Archibald MacLeish (1892–1982). The most common diminutive form is **Archie** (or **Archy**) – as borne by the fictional Archie Osbaldistone in the Walter Scott novel *Rob Roy* (1817) and Archie Rice in the John Osborne play *The Entertainer* (1957). **Baldie** is a less frequently encountered familiar variant.

Archie/Archy *See* ARCHIBALD.

Ardal (m) Irish first name meaning 'high valour'. Well-known bearers of the name in recent years have included Irish comedian Ardal O'Hanlon (b.1965).

Ardan (m) Irish first name derived from the Irish Gaelic word meaning 'pride'. The name appears in Irish mythology as the brother of Deirdre's lover Naoise.

Aretha (f) English first name descended from the Greek Arete, itself derived from the Greek *arete* ('excellence'). Also associated occasionally with ARETHUSA. It became widely known in the latter half of the 20th century as the name of US soul singer Aretha Franklin (b.1942).

Arethusa (f) Greek name of obscure origin, possibly derived from the Greek *arete* ('excellence'). It appears in Greek mythology as the name of a wood nymph and was revived as a literary name by English writers of the 17th century, appearing in such works as Beaumont and Fletcher's play *Philaster* (*c*.1609). It has made rare appearances as a first name in succeeding centuries.

Ariadne (f) Greek name possibly derived from the Greek *ari* ('more') and *agnos* ('chaste' or 'pure') and thus interpreted as meaning 'very holy'. It appears in Greek mythology as the name of the daughter of King Minos who shows Theseus how to find his way out of the Labyrinth using a trail of thread. The name was borne by the 2nd-century St Ariadne and was consequently taken up by early Christians. It has made irregular appearances among English speakers over the centuries and continues in rare use today. Variants in other languages include the French **Arianne** and the Italian **Arianna**.

Arianna/Arianne *See* ARIADNE.

Arianrhod (f) Welsh first name meaning 'silver disc'. The allusion is to the moon and the name appears in the *Mabinogion* as that of the moon goddess.

Ariel (m/f) Jewish name derived from the

Hebrew for 'lion of God'. It appears in the Bible as the name of Ezra's messenger and was consequently taken up by English Puritans after the Reformation. It is most famous today as the name of the sprite in William Shakespeare's last play, *The Tempest* (1611).

Arlan (m) Cornish first name possibly derived from Allen or Elwin. It was borne by a saint in early Cornish legend.

Arlene (f) English first name that appears to have evolved as a diminutive of such names as CHARLENE and MARLENE. A 20th-century introduction that was taken up initially in the USA, it has also made appearances in such variant forms as **Arline, Arleen** and **Arlena**.

Arlette (f) French first name of obscure origin, possibly a diminutive of CHARLOTTE or otherwise derived from the Old German *arn* ('eagle'). It has been in occasional use among English speakers since the middle of the 19th century. Famous bearers of the name in France have ranged from William the Conqueror's mother to the French actress Arletty (Arlette-Léonie Bathiat; 1898–1992). Variants include **Arletta**.

Arline *See* ARLENE.

Armand *See* HERMAN.

Arn *See* AARON; ARNOLD.

Arnaud/Arndt *See* ARNOLD.

Arnold (m) English and German first name derived from the Old German Arinwalt, itself from the Old German *arn* ('eagle') and *wald* ('ruler') and thus interpreted as meaning 'eagle ruler'. It was brought to England by the Normans in the 11th century but became rare towards the end of the medieval period. It enjoyed a revival alongside many other medieval names in the 19th century and continued in fairly regular use into the early 20th century, since when it has lost ground. Famous bearers of the name have included British novelist Arnold Bennett (1867–1931), British composer

Arnold Bax (1883–1953), US golfer Arnold Palmer (b.1929) and US film actor and politician Arnold Schwarzenegger (b.1947). Commonly abbreviated to **Arn** or **Arnie**. Variants include the French **Arnaud**, the German **Arndt** and the Italian **Arnaldo**.

Art (m) English first name that evolved as a diminutive of ARTHUR. It was taken up towards the end of the 19th century, chiefly in the USA, and has become peculiarly associated with the jazz world, being borne by such luminaries as jazz pianist Art Tatum (1909–56) and jazz saxophonist Art Pepper (1925–82). Other notable bearers of the name have included US pop singer Art Garfunkel (b.1941).

Artair *See* ARTHUR.

Artemus (m) Greek name that is thought to have evolved from the feminine Artemis which appears in Greek mythology as the name of the virgin Greek goddess of the moon and the hunt. Also spelled **Artemas**, in which form it appears in the New Testament, it was taken up by English Puritans in the 17th century but has made few reappearances among English speakers since then. Famous bearers of the name have included the US humorist Artemus Ward (Charles Farrar Browne; 1834–67). Variants include the feminine **Artemisia**, which has made occasional appearances in the English-speaking world since the middle of the 18th century.

Arthur (m) English first name of obscure Celtic origin, possibly derived from the Celtic *artos* ('bear') or the Irish *art* ('stone') or else descended from the Roman clan name Artorius. It is famous in the English-speaking world (and beyond) as the name of the semi-legendary English King Arthur, who is thought to have reigned in the 5th or 6th century, and it was subsequently borne by another three royal princes – Henry II's son Prince Arthur (1187–1203), Henry VII's son Prince Arthur (1486–1502) and Queen Victoria's third son Prince Arthur (1850–1942). It was in fairly regular use throughout the medieval period but became less common after the 14th century. It was revived more widely as a first name in the 18th century and enjoyed a peak in popularity towards the end of the 19th century in response to the contemporary enthusiasm for Arthurian myth embodied in Alfred, Lord Tennyson's *Idylls of the King* (1859–85) and in the historical paintings of the Pre-Raphaelite Brotherhood.

Famous bearers of the name over the years have included Arthur Wellesley, Duke of Wellington (1769–1852), British comedian Arthur Askey (1900–1982), US playwright Arthur Miller (b.1915) and US tennis player Arthur Ashe (1943–93). Commonly abbreviated to ART. Variants in other languages include the Scottish Gaelic **Artair** and the Italian and Spanish **Arturo**. **Arthurine**, **Arthurina** and **Arthuretta** are rare feminine forms.

Asa (m) Jewish name derived from the Hebrew for 'healer' or 'doctor'. It appears in the Bible as the name of a king of Judah and was consequently adopted by English Puritans in the 17th century. It has continued in irregular use ever since. Notable bearers of the name have included British historian Asa Briggs (b.1921).

Ash *See* ASHLEY.

Asha (f) Indian first name derived from the Sanskrit for 'hope' or 'hopeful'.

Asher (m) Jewish name derived from the Hebrew for 'fortunate' or 'happy'. It appears in the Bible as the name of one of Jacob's sons and was consequently taken up on a rather limited scale by English Puritans in the 17th century. **Osher** is a rare variant.

Ashia (f) First name derived from the English ASH or the Arabic AISHA. Notable bearers in recent times have included English athlete Ashia Hansen (b.1971).

Ashley (m/f) English surname, derived from a place name based on the Old English *aesc* ('ash') and *leah* ('clearing' or 'wood'), that was taken up as a first name around the middle of the 19th century. It enjoyed a considerable boost in the middle of the

20th century following the success of the film *Gone with the Wind* (1939), based on the novel by Margaret Mitchell, in which Ashley Wilkes becomes the focus of Scarlett O'Hara's passion. Its use as a feminine name appears to date from the 1940s. Well-known bearers of the name in its early history included the humanitarian Anthony Ashley Cooper, Earl of Shaftesbury (1801–85). Commonly abbreviated to **Ash**. Also encountered (when in use as a name for females) as **Ashleigh**, **Ashlee** or **Ashlea**.

Ashling *See* AISLING.

Asia *See* AISHA.

Aspasia (f) Greek name meaning 'welcome one' that has been in occasional use as a first name in the English-speaking world since the 19th century. It appears in classical history as the name of the lover of the 5th-century Athenian statesman Pericles and was taken up centuries later by English speakers in response to a contemporary interest in classical culture. There is a character called Aspasia Fitzgibbon in the Anthony Trollope novel *Phineas Finn* (1869). Variants include **Aspatia**, in which form it appears in Beaumont and Fletcher's *The Maid's Tragedy* (1610).

Asta *See* ASTRID.

Astra (f) English first name derived ultimately from the Greek *aster* ('star') but often considered to be a variant of ESTHER, STELLA or other names sharing the same source. It has made rare appearances among English speakers since the end of the 19th century.

Astrid (f) English and Scandinavian first name derived from the Old Norse Astrithr, itself from the Norse *ans* ('god') and *frithr* ('fair') and thus interpreted as meaning 'divinely beautiful'. It has been in occasional use among English speakers since the early 20th century. Famous bearers have included the 11th-century Queen Astrid, who was the wife of St Olaf of Norway, Queen Astrid of Belgium (1905–35) and

Princess Astrid of Norway (b.1932). **Asta** and **Sassa** are diminutive forms.

Athairne *See* HERCULES.

Athelstan (m) English first name descended from the Old English Aethelstan, itself derived from the Old English *aethel* ('noble') and *stan* ('stone') and thus interpreted as meaning 'nobly strong'. It was in fairly common use prior to the Norman Conquest, borne by a 10th-century king of Wessex among others, but fell from use during the medieval period. It was among the historical names revived in the 19th century, promoted by its appearance in the Walter Scott novel *Ivanhoe* (1820), and has made rare reappearances since then.

Aub *See* AUBREY.

Auberon (m) English first name of obscure origin, possibly a variant of AUBREY. It has made occasional appearances among English speakers since the 19th century. Famous bearers of the name have included British writer and critic Auberon Waugh (1939–2001). A variant is **Oberon,** as borne by the king of the fairies in Shakespeare's *A Midsummer Night's Dream* (1595–6). Sometimes abbreviated to **Bron**.

Aubrey (m/f) English and French first name derived from the Old German Alberic, itself from the Old German *alb* ('elf') and *richi* ('riches' or 'power') and thus interpreted as meaning 'elf ruler' or 'supernaturally powerful'. It came to England with the Normans in the 11th century and remained in use throughout the medieval period, when it was regarded as a masculine name, but it subsequently fell into neglect before enjoying a marked revival towards the end of the 19th century, when it was also adopted for girls. Notable bearers of the name have included British actor C. Aubrey Smith (1863–1948) and British artist Aubrey Beardsley (1872–98). Sometimes abbreviated to **Aub**. *See also* AUBERON.

Aud/Audra *See* AUDREY.

Audrey (f) English first name descended from the Old English Aethelthryth, itself derived from the Old English *aethel* ('noble') and *thryth* ('strength') and thus interpreted as meaning 'noble strength'. It became well known as the name of the 7th-century St Audrey (originally called St ETHELDREDA), Queen of Northumbria, but fell from favour during the medieval period through its association with the ordinary vocabulary word 'tawdry' (which itself represented a contraction of 'St Audrey' and was first applied to the low quality trinkets sold at medieval fairs held in her name). It was not until the early years of the 20th century that the name became popular in its modern form. It has been encountered with less frequency since the 1920s.

Famous bearers of the name have included a minor character in William Shakespeare's *As You Like It* (1599) and Belgian-born US actress Audrey Hepburn (Edda Hepburn; 1929–93). Also encountered as **Audrie** or **Audry**. Among the name's diminutive forms are **Aud**, **Audi** and **Audie**, which has also made appearances as a name for males, notably US film star Audie Murphy (1924–71). **Audra** and **Audrina** are rare variants.

Augie/August *See* AUGUSTUS.

Augusta (f) English and German first name that evolved originally as a feminine equivalent of the Roman AUGUSTUS. Roman emperors traditionally styled themselves *Augustus* and the feminine form of the title was consequently bestowed upon female members of their families. English speakers took up the name after it became widely known through Frederick, Prince of Wales' wife Princess Augusta of Saxe-Coburg-Gotha (1719–72), who became the mother of the future George III. It enjoyed a peak in popularity towards the end of the 19th century but has since become rare. Other notable bearers of the name have included the Irish playwright Lady Augusta Gregory (1852–1932). Familiar forms include **Gus** and **Gussie**. Among variant forms are **Augustina** and AUGUSTINE.

Auguste *See* AUGUSTUS.

Augustine (m/f) English first name descended from the Roman Augustinus, a diminutive of AUGUSTUS. Famous as the name of St Augustine of Hippo (354–430) and of the 6th-century St Augustine (d.604), the first Archbishop of Canterbury, it was in limited use as a first name among English speakers during the medieval period and subsequently enjoyed a modest revival alongside many other old names in the 19th century. It retains its ecclesiastical associations – there is a character called Father Augustine in the Richard Brinsley Sheridan comedy *The Rivals* (1775). Occasionally encountered as **Augustin**. Commonly abbreviated to GUS or **Gussie**. Variants in other languages include the Italian **Agostino** and the Spanish **Agustín**. *See also* AUSTIN.

Augustus (m) Roman name derived from the Latin *augustus* ('august', 'great' or 'magnificent') that has been in use as a first name among English speakers since the 18th century. It was adopted as a title by the Roman Emperor Octavian in 27 BC and was similarly borne by a number of his successors. As a first name it was introduced to Britain from Germany as a consequence of the Hanoverian Succession and enjoyed a peak in popularity in the English-speaking world in the 19th century, but has since become rare. Notable bearers of the name have included the fictional Augustus Snodgrass in the Charles Dickens novel *Pickwick Papers* (1836–7) and the British painter Augustus John (1878–1961). Diminutive forms of the name include GUS, **Gussie** and **Augie**. Variants in other languages include the French **Auguste**, the Italian, Spanish and Portuguese **Augusto** and the German and Polish **August**. *See also* AUGUSTA; AUGUSTINE; AUSTIN.

Aurelia (f) English first name that developed originally as a feminine equivalent of the Roman Aurelius itself derived from the Latin *aurum* ('gold') and thus sometimes interpreted as meaning 'golden-haired'. Borne by an 11th-century French saint, it was taken up by English speakers in the 17th century and remained in occasional use until the end of the 19th century, since when it has become very rare. Occurrences of the name in fiction have included the Duchess Aurelia in John Marston's play *The Malcontent* (1604) and Aurelia Darnel in the Tobias Smollett novel *Sir Launcelot Greaves* (1762). Variants in other languages include the French **Aurélie**.

Aurélie *See* AURELIA.

Auriol (f) English first name derived ultimately from the Latin *aureus* ('golden'), although also associated with the Roman clan name Aurelius. It was taken up by English speakers in the 19th century. Familiar forms of the name include **Aurie** and **Aury**. Also encountered as **Auriel** or **Auriole**.

Aurora (f) English, German and French first name derived from the Latin *aurora* ('dawn'). It appears in Roman mythology as the name of the goddess of the dawn and was revived throughout Europe during the Renaissance. It was taken up with some enthusiasm by English poets in the 19th century. Famous bearers of the name have included the central characters in Charles Perrault's fairy tale *The Sleeping Beauty* (1697) and Elizabeth Barrett Browning's narrative poem *Aurora Leigh* (1856). Variants in other languages include the French **Aurore**.

Austen *See* AUSTIN.

Austin (m) English first name that developed as a variant of AUGUSTINE. It was taken up by English speakers in the medieval period and has remained in occasional use ever since, also appearing as a surname. Famous bearers of the name have included the fictional Dr Austin Sloper in the Henry James novel *Washington Square* (1880). Also encountered as **Austen**.

Autumn (f) English first name derived from that of the season. Like other season names it appears to be of 19th-century origin and remains relatively rare.

Ava (f) English first name that is thought to

have evolved as a variant of EVE, although it is often assumed to have links with the Latin *avis* ('bird'). It enjoyed early exposure through the 9th-century St Ava of Hainault but appears to have fallen into disuse before the end of the medieval period. It was revived among English speakers around the middle of the 20th century, promoted by the fame of US film actress Ava Gardner (Lucy Johnson; 1922–90).

Avaril *See* AVERIL.

Aveline (f) French first name derived from the Old German Avila, itself a variant of AVIS. It came to England with the Normans in the 11th century and was subsequently among the many historical names revived by English speakers in the 19th century. It remains in limited use.

Averil (f) English first name that evolved either as a variant of AVRIL or else from the Old English Eoforhild (or Everild), itself derived from the Old English *eofor* ('boar') and *hild* ('battle') and thus interpreted as meaning 'boarlike in battle'. It was borne by a 7th-century English saint and has enjoyed a modest revival as a first name since the early years of the 20th century. Variants include **Avaril**, **Averill** and **Averell**.

Avery (m) English surname, derived from ALFRED in medieval times, that has been in occasional use as a first name since the end of the 19th century.

Avice *See* AVIS.

Avila *See* AVELINE.

Avis (f) English first name of obscure origin, possibly related to the German HEDWIG (meaning 'struggle') or else derived from the Latin *avis* ('bird'). Recorded in use among English speakers in medieval times, it made occasional reappearances between the 16th and 18th centuries and was in more frequent use from the early years of the 20th century, although it has never been very common. Variants include **Avice**

– as borne by the fictional Avice Caro in the Thomas Hardy novel *The Well-Beloved* (1897).

Avner *See* ABNER.

Avril (f) English first name derived from the French *avril* ('April'), or otherwise descended from the Old English Eoforhild, itself derived from the Old English *eofor* ('boar') and *hild* ('battle') and thus interpreted as meaning 'boarlike in battle'. It was adopted by English speakers early in the 20th century, often being reserved for girls born in the month of April, but has declined in frequency since reaching a peak in the 1950s. *See also* APRIL; AVERIL.

Avrom *See* ABRAHAM.

Axel (m) Scandinavian variant of ABSALOM that has also been in occasional use among English speakers – chiefly in the USA, where it was introduced by Scandinavian immigrants. Famous bearers of the name have included the Swedish physician and writer Axel Munthe (1857–1949). **Acke** is a familiar form of the name. Also found occasionally as the feminine variant **Axelle**.

Ayesha *See* AISHA.

Aylmer (m) English first name descended from the Old English Aethelmaer, itself derived from the Old English *aethel* ('noble') and *maere* ('famous') and thus interpreted as meaning 'nobly famous'. The Old English form of the name was in common use before the Norman Conquest, after which it continued in such forms as Ailemar, Eilemar and the modern Aylmer. It fell from favour after the medieval period but was the subject of a modest revival in the 19th century. *See also* ELMER.

Aylwin *See* ALVIN.

Azalea (f) English flower name that was taken up as a first name among English speakers towards the end of the 19th century. It has never been in frequent use.

Azaria (m) Biblical name derived from the

Hebrew Azaryah, meaning 'helped by God'. It appears in the Bible as the name of King Solomon's chief prophet and of a king of Judah and it has consequently been in occasional use as a first name among English speakers since the 17th century, when it was taken up by Puritans on both sides of the Atlantic. Also spelled **Azariah**.

Aziz (m) Arabic name meaning 'invincible' or 'beloved'. **Aziza** is a feminine variant.

B

Bab See BARBARA.

Babar (m) Indian name derived from the Turkish *babar* ('lion'). It was borne by a 15th-century Mogul ruler, whose sphere of influence extended from northern India to Bengal, but is today better known throughout the world as that of the fictional Babar the Elephant in the children's stories of Jean de Brunoff (1899–1937) and his son Laurent de Brunoff (b.1925). Sometimes encountered as **Baber**.

Babette (f) French first name that developed as a diminutive form of ELIZABETH. It is also in use among English speakers as a diminutive of BARBARA. The name became more widely familiar through the release of the film *Babette's Feast* (1988), which was based upon a story by Karen Blixen. **Babbetta** is a rare variant.

Babs See BARBARA.

Badr (m/f) Arabic name derived from *badr* ('full moon'). Variants include **Budur**, in which form it is usually reserved for females.

Baha (m) Arabic name derived from *baha* ('splendour' or 'glory'). It is in common use throughout the Arabic world. *See also* BAHIYYA.

Bahiyya (f) Arabic name derived from *bahiyya* ('beautiful') and also representing a feminine form of BAHA. It is well known in Egyptian folklore as the name of a legendary character whose lover was put to death on the orders of a local chief; she is now widely depicted as a personification of Egypt itself.

Bakr (m) Arabic name derived from *bakr* ('young camel'). It features in mythology

as the name of the caliph Abu-Bakr al-Siddiq (573–634), Muhammad's successor.

Bala (m/f) Indian name derived from the Sanskrit *bala* ('young'). It appears in various ancient texts and is sometimes applied to the young Krishna. Variants include **Balu** and **Balan**.

Baldassare See BALTHAZAR.

Baldev (m) Indian name derived from the Sanskrit *bala* ('strength') and *deva* ('god') and thus interpreted as meaning 'god of strength'. As **Baldeva** it is borne in Indian mythology by Krishna's elder brother. It is most frequent today among Sikh communities.

Baldie See ARCHIBALD.

Baldric (m) English first name derived from the Old German Baldarich, itself from the Old German *balda* ('bold') and *ricja* ('rule'). It came to England with the Normans in the 11th century and remained in fairly frequent use through the medieval period, after which it fell from favour. It became familiar to British television audiences in the 1990s in the popular historical comedy series *Blackadder*. Variants include **Baldri**, **Baudri** and **Baudrey**.

Baldwin (m) English surname derived from the Old German Baldawin, itself from the Old German *bald* ('bold' or 'brave') and *wine* ('friend') and thus interpreted as meaning 'brave friend', that has made occasional appearances as a first name since its introduction from Flanders around the 12th century. Having fallen into disuse after the medieval period, it was the subject of a modest revival in the 19th century. Notable bearers of the name over the centuries have included several medieval rulers of Flanders. Variants include the Welsh MALDWYN and the French **Baudouin**.

Balthasar *See* BALTHAZAR.

Balthazar (m) English version of the biblical Belshazzar, which was itself derived from the Babylonian Belsharrausur (meaning 'Baal protect the king'). The name appears in the Bible as that of one of the Three Wise Men who come to praise the infant Jesus in Bethlehem. It also features several times in the plays of William Shakespeare, notably as the assumed identity of Portia when she adopts the disguise of a lawyer in *The Merchant of Venice* (1596–8). Also encountered as **Balthasar**. Variants in other languages include the Italian **Baldassare** and the Spanish **Baltasar**.

Baptist *See* BAPTISTE.

Baptiste (m) French first name derived ultimately from the Greek *batistes* ('baptist'). Because of its biblical associations with John the Baptist the name has a long history in the Christian world. Variants in other languages include the English and German **Baptist**, the Italian **Battista**, the Spanish **Bautista** and the Portuguese **Batista**.

Barbara (f) English, German and Polish first name derived ultimately from the Greek *barbaros* ('strange' or 'foreign') and thus interpreted as meaning 'foreign woman'. It is thought that the Greek word was originally intended to imitate the stammering of foreigners unable to speak Greek with any fluency. English speakers took up the name during the medieval period and it remained in regular use until after the Reformation, when it suffered from its absence in the Bible. It remained in neglect until the early years of the 20th century, when it enjoyed a substantial revival. It enjoyed a peak in popularity in the early 1950s but has since become a much less common choice once more.

Notable bearers of the name have included the 3rd-century martyr St Barbara, British romantic novelist Barbara Cartland

(1900–2000), the central character in the George Bernard Shaw play *Major Barbara* (1905), US actress Barbara Stanwyck (Ruby Stevens; 1907–90), British politician Barbara Castle (1911–2002) and British singer Barbara Dickson (b.1947). Diminutive forms of the name include **Bab**, **Babs**, **Bar**, **Barb**, **Barbie**, BOBBIE and the French BAB-ETTE. A fairly common variant of 20th-century introduction is **Barbra** – as borne by US singer and actress Barbra Streisand (b.1942). Versions of the name in other languages include the Irish **Bairbre**, the Swedish **Barbro** and the Russian **Varvara**.

Barbie/Barbra *See* BARBARA.

Barclay *See* BERKELEY.

Bardolph (m) English first name derived from the Old German Bartholf, itself from the Old German *beraht* ('bright') or *barta* ('axe') and *wolf* ('wolf') and thus interpreted as meaning 'famous wolf'. It was taken up by English speakers during the medieval period but subsequently fell into disuse. Today it is familiar chiefly as the name of one of Falstaff's friends in William Shakespeare's plays *Henry IV* (1597), *Henry V* (1599) and *The Merry Wives of Windsor* (1597).

Barnabas (m) English first name derived ultimately from the Aramaic Barnebhuah, meaning 'son of consolation'. It appears in the Bible as the name of one of St Paul's companions and was taken up by English speakers during the medieval period. It was eventually eclipsed by BARNABY. **Barney** (or **Barny**) is a diminutive form. Variants in other languages include the French **Barnabé** and the Spanish **Bernabé**.

Barnaby (m) English first name that developed as a variant of BARNABAS and established itself as the dominant form of the name in the 19th century. It has been out of favour since the early years of the 20th century (with the exception of a modest revival in the 1960s). Notable bearers of the name have included the title character in the Charles Dickens novel *Barnaby Rudge* (1841). Often encountered today in the diminutive form **Barney**.

Barnard *See* BERNARD.

Barney *See* BARNABAS; BARNABY.

Barrie *See* BARRY.

Barry (m) English first name derived either from the Gaelic *bearach* ('spear') or else from the Irish Barra, a diminutive of Fionnbarr (*see* FINBAR). It entered general usage among English speakers around the middle of the 19th century and was at its most frequent in the 1950s. Notable bearers of the name in recent times have included Australian comedian Barry Humphries (b.1930), US soul singer Barry White (1944–2003) and US pop singer Barry Manilow (b.1946). The variant form **Barrie** did not emerge until the 1920s and enjoyed a peak in popularity between the 1930s and the 1950s. **Bas**, **Baz** or **Bazza** are common diminutive forms of the name.

Bart *See* BARTHOLOMEW.

Bartholomew (m) Biblical name derived from the Aramaic for 'son of Talmai' (Talmai meaning 'abounding in furrows'). It appears in the New Testament as a name borne by one of the apostles (possibly Nathaniel) and has been in occasional use among English speakers since medieval times. Commonly abbreviated to **Bart** or **Barty** and less commonly to **Bat** or **Tolly**. Variants in other languages include the French **Barthélemy**, the Spanish **Bartolomé** and the Italian **Bartolomeo**.

Baruch (m) Jewish name derived from the Hebrew *baruk* ('blessed'). It appears in the Bible as the name of one of the prophet Jeremiah's companions and has made rare appearances as a first name among English speakers.

Bas *See* BARRY; BASIL.

Basant *See* VASANT.

Basil (m) English first name derived from the Greek Basileois, itself from the Greek *basileus* ('king') and thus usually interpreted as meaning 'royal'. It became well known as the name of the 4th-century St Basil, Bishop of Caesarea, and made occasional appearances among English speakers in medieval times, having been imported with returning Crusaders. It was the subject of a significant revival in the 19th century (promoted through its link with the herb basil) and enjoyed a peak in popularity in the 1920s but has been in rather less common use since then. Well-known bearers of the name have included British actor Basil Rathbone (1892–1967), British Roman Catholic prelate Cardinal Basil Hume (George Hume; 1923–99), the British children's television puppet character Basil Brush and the fictional Basil Fawlty in the 1970s British television comedy series *Fawlty Towers*. Commonly shortened to **Bas** (or **Baz**). Variants in other languages include the Russian **Vasili**. Rare feminine forms of the name include **Basilia**, **Basilic** and **Basilla**.

Bastian/Bastien *See* SEBASTIAN.

Basu *See* VASU.

Bat *See* BARTHOLOMEW.

Bathsheba (f) Hebrew name variously interpreted as meaning 'seventh daughter' or 'daughter of the oath'. It appears in the Bible as the name of the beautiful wife of Uriah, who became the lover and subsequently the wife of King David, and was taken up by English Puritans in the 17th century (presumably with the biblical character's beauty in mind, rather than her faithlessness towards her first husband). Notable bearers of the name have included the fictional Bathsheba Everdene in the Thomas Hardy novel *Far From the Madding Crowd* (1874). **Sheba** is a diminutive form.

Battista *See* BAPTISTE.

Baudouin *See* BALDWIN.

Bautista *See* BAPTISTE.

Baz *See* BARRY; BASIL; SEBASTIAN.

Bazza *See* BARRY; SEBASTIAN.

Bea *See* BEATRICE.

Beata (f) Roman first name derived from the Latin *beatus* ('blessed' or 'happy'), and pronounced 'beearta'. It was borne by the early African martyr St Beata and subsequently became popular among Roman Catholics throughout Europe, although it has made few appearances in the English-speaking world since the 18th century. Also in occasional use as a diminutive form of BEATRICE.

Beatrice (f) Italian, French and English first name derived ultimately from the Latin *beatus* ('happy' or 'blessed'). It was in fairly common use in medieval Italy and became lastingly famous as the name of Beatrice Portinari (1266–90), the object of the affections of the celebrated Italian poet Dante and the model for Beatrice in his *Divine Comedy*. Having made only infrequent appearances among English speakers during the medieval period, the name was taken up with more enthusiasm in the 19th century after it became well known as the name of Queen Victoria's youngest daughter Princess Beatrice (1857–1944). Other notable bearers of the name have included a character in William Shakespeare's play *Much Ado About Nothing* (1598–9), British social reformer Beatrice Webb (1858–1943), British singer and entertainer Beatrice Lillie (Constance Sylvia Munston; 1898–1989) and the Duke and Duchess of York's daughter Princess Beatrice (b.1988). Familiar forms of the name include **Bee**, **Bea**, **Beattie** (or **Beatty**), **Tris**, **Triss** and **Trissie**. Versions of the name in other languages include the Welsh **Betrys** or **Bettrys** and the Spanish **Beatriz**. *See also* BEATA; BEATRIX.

Beatrix (f) English, German and Dutch first name derived like BEATRICE from the Latin *beatus* ('happy' or 'blessed'). It was borne by a 4th-century Christian martyr and was consequently fairly common among early Christians. Records of the name's use among English speakers go back as far as the 'Domesday Book' and it was still a fairly frequent choice in the early years of the 20th century, although it has become rare since then. Notable bearers of the name have included Beatrix Esmond in the William Makepeace Thackeray novels *The History of Henry Esmond* (1852) and *The Virginians* (1857–9), British children's author Beatrix Potter (Helen Beatrix Potter; 1866–1943) and Queen Beatrix of the Netherlands (b.1938). Diminutive forms of the name include **Trix** and **Trixie**.

Beattie/Beatty *See* BEATRICE.

Beau (m) English first name derived from the French *beau* ('handsome'). It became well known as the adopted first name of the British dandies Beau Nash (Richard Nash; 1674–1762) and Beau Brummell (George Bryan Brummell; 1778–1840) but did not begin to appear with any regularity among English speakers until after the publication of the P. C. Wren novel *Beau Geste* (1924), which itself inspired several sequels and film versions. It enjoyed another boost as the name of Beau Wilkes, a character in Margaret Mitchell's novel *Gone with the Wind* (1936). Notable bearers of the name in recent times have included US film actor Beau Bridges (b.1941).

Beavis *See* BEVIS.

Becca/Becky *See* REBECCA.

Bee *See* BEATRICE.

Bel *See* ANNABEL; BELINDA.

Belinda (f) English first name derived either from the Italian *bella* ('beautiful') or possibly from the Old German *lint* ('snake') and thus suggestive of a cunning nature. Today it is often assumed to have resulted from the combination of BELLA and LINDA. It was in fairly regular use throughout Europe in medieval times but does not appear to have been taken up by English speakers before the 17th century. It was at its most frequent in the English-speaking world around the 1950s. Notable bearers of the name have included characters in

William Congreve's play *The Old Bachelor* (1693), Sir John Vanbrugh's comedy *The Provok'd Wife* (1697) and Alexander Pope's poem *The Rape of the Lock* (1714) as well as, in more recent times, British television actress Belinda Lang (b.1955) and US pop singer Belinda Carlisle (b.1958). Commonly abbreviated to **Bel** – as borne by British writer Bel Mooney (b.1946). Other diminutives include **Bindy**, LINDA or **Lindy**.

Bella (f) English and Italian first name that developed as a diminutive form of such names as ARABELLA and ISABELLA, apparently promoted through association with the Spanish and Italian *bella* or the French *belle* ('beautiful'). It emerged in general use among English speakers in the 18th century and has remained in currency into modern times. Variants in other languages include the French **Belle**.

Bellamy (m) English first name derived from the Old French for 'handsome friend'. It was in use as a surname before being adopted on an occasional basis as a first name.

Belle *See* BELLA.

Ben (m) English first name that developed as a diminutive form of BENEDICT or BENJAMIN. Although occasional records of this diminutive form go back as far as the medieval period, it was not until the 19th century that it began to appear on a significant scale among English speakers. It has maintained its popular status ever since. Notable bearers of the name have included English playwright Ben Jonson (1572–1637), the fictional Ben Gunn in the Robert Louis Stevenson novel *Treasure Island* (1883), British playwright Ben Travers (1886–1980), Anglo-Indian actor Ben Kingsley (Krishna Banji; b.1944) and British comedian Ben Elton (b.1959).

Benedict (m) English first name derived from the Latin *benedictus* ('blessed'). Borne by the 6th-century St Benedict, who founded the Benedictine order of monks,

and by no less than fifteen popes, it became a popular name among English Roman Catholics and was a common choice during the medieval period, when variant forms included **Benedick** and **Bennett**. It enjoyed a relatively recent resurgence in popularity in the 1980s and 1990s. It has suffered somewhat in the USA through identification with Benedict Arnold (1741–1801), the American Revolutionary soldier who is remembered today for his collusion with the British. Commonly abbreviated to BEN. Variants in other languages include the German **Benedikt**, the Italian **Benedetto** and the Spanish **Benito** – as borne by Italian dictator Benito Mussolini (1883–1945), who was named in honour of the Mexican revolutionary Benito Pablo Juarez (1806–72). **Benedicta** is a rare feminine version of the name. *See also* BENITA.

Benedicta *See* BENEDICT.

Benita (f) Spanish first name that developed as a feminine equivalent of Benito, a Spanish version of BENEDICT. It has made occasional appearances among English speakers since the early years of the 20th century, chiefly in the USA.

Benito *See* BENEDICT.

Benjamin (m) English, French and German name derived from a Hebrew name variously interpreted as meaning 'son of the right hand', 'son of the south' or 'son of my old age', but often interpreted as meaning 'favourite'. It appears in the Bible as the name of the youngest of the sons of Jacob and Rachel, who became the founder of one of the twelve tribes of Israel. It made occasional appearances among English speakers in medieval times, often being reserved for children whose mothers had died in childbirth (as the biblical Benjamin's mother Rachel did). It was taken up with renewed enthusiasm by Puritans in the 17th century and has remained in fairly regular use ever since, having long since shed its rather gloomy medieval implications. It is also a well-established Jewish name. Notable bearers of the name have included

American statesman and scientist Benjamin Franklin (1706–90), British Prime Minister Benjamin Disraeli (1804–81) and British composer Benjamin Britten (1913–76). It enjoyed a relatively recent boost in popularity following the release of *The Graduate* (1967), in which Dustin Hoffman played a character of the same name. Commonly shortened to BEN, BENNY and **Benjie** (or **Benjy**).

Benjie/Benjy *See* BENJAMIN.

Bennett *See* BENEDICT.

Benny (m) English first name that developed as a diminutive of BENJAMIN. It began to appear with increasing frequency from the early years of the 20th century. Famous bearers of the name have included US jazz musician Benny Goodman (1909–86) and British comedian Benny Hill (Alfred Hill; 1925–92). Also encountered as **Bennie**. *See also* BEN.

Bentley (m) English place name (occurring in several counties of England) derived from the Old English *beonet* ('bent grass') and *leah* ('wood' or 'clearing') and thus interpreted as meaning 'place of coarse grass' that was subsequently taken up as a surname and occasional first name. There is a character called Bentley Drummle in the Charles Dickens novel *Great Expectations* (1860–61).

Beppe (m) Italian first name derived ultimately from **Giuseppe** (*see* JOSEPH). It is pronounced 'beppay'.

Berenice *See* BERNICE.

Berkeley (m) English place name (from Gloucestershire) derived from the Old English *beorc* ('birch') and *leah* ('wood') that was subsequently taken up as a surname and occasional first name. It is pronounced 'barklee' in Britain and 'burklee' in the United States. Variants of the name include **Barclay** and **Berkley**.

Bernadetta *See* BERNADETTE.

Bernadette (f) Feminine equivalent of BERNARD, which was taken up by English speakers in the 19th century. Borne by the French St Bernadette of Lourdes (Marie-Bernarde Soubirous; 1844–79), whose visions made Lourdes a celebrated place of pilgrimage, it became particularly popular among Roman Catholics, especially in Ireland. Well-known bearers of the name have included the Northern Ireland political activist Bernadette Devlin (b.1947). Sometimes abbreviated to **Bernie** or **Detta**. Variants include **Bernardette**, **Bernardine** and the Italian **Bernadetta**.

Bernard (m) English and French first name derived either from the Old English Beornheard, from the Old English *beorn* ('man' or 'warrior') and *heard* ('brave'), or else from the Old German Berinhard, itself from the Old German *ber* ('bear') and *hart* ('bold') and thus interpreted as meaning 'brave as a bear'. It came to England at the time of the Norman Conquest, appearing several times in the 'Domesday Book', and has remained in currency ever since, although it became less frequent after the middle of the 20th century. Notable bearers of the name have included three medieval saints, Irish-born British playwright George Bernard Shaw (1856–1950), British actor Sir Bernard Miles (1907–91) and British journalist Bernard Levin (b.1928). Commonly abbreviated to **Bernie** and, less frequently, to **Bunny**. Also encountered in the form **Barnard**. Variants in other languages include the Italian and Spanish **Bernardo**, the German **Bernhard** and the Scandinavian **Bernt**.

Bernardine *See* BERNADETTE.

Bernhard *See* BERNARD.

Bernice (f) English and Italian first name derived ultimately from the Greek Pherenike, meaning 'victory bringer'. It appears in the Bible as the name of a sister of King Herod Agrippa II and became widespread through Europe and Asia through the conquests of the Greeks under Alexander the Great. It was consequently taken up by English speakers after the Reformation and enjoyed a modest peak in popularity in the late 19th and early 20th centuries but has since become infrequent once more. Well-known bearers of the name in recent times have included British novelist Bernice Rubens (b.1928). Diminutive forms of the name include **Bernie**, BERRY, BINNIE and **Bunny**. Also encountered occasionally in the older form **Berenice** – as borne by US photographer Berenice Abbott (1898–1991). Variants in other languages include the Scottish **Bearnas** and the French **Bérénice** – as it appears in the title of the tragedy *Bérénice* (1679) by the celebrated French playwright Jean Racine.

Bernie *See* BERNARD; BERNICE.

Berry (f) English first name derived from the ordinary vocabulary word 'berry' that enjoyed modest popularity among English speakers towards the end of the 19th century. Unlike some of the other flower and fruit names that were taken up around the same time, Berry fell from favour early in the 20th century and is now very rare. *See also* BERNICE; BERYL.

Bert (m) English first name that developed as a diminutive of such names as ALBERT, BERTRAM and HERBERT. It appeared with increasing frequency among English speakers from the 19th century and remained a common choice until the middle of the 20th century, since when it has suffered a gradual decline. Well-known bearers of the name have included US actor Bert Lahr (1895–1967), who played the Cowardly Lion in the film *The Wizard of Oz* (1939). Also encountered as **Burt** – as borne by US film actor Burt Lancaster (1913–94), US composer Burt Bacharach (b.1928) and US film actor Burt Reynolds (b.1936). *See also* BERTIE.

Berta *See* BERTHA; ROBERTA.

Bertha (f) English and German first name derived from the Old German Berahta, itself from the Old German *beraht* ('bright' or 'famous'). Early records of the name's use among English speakers go back as far as the 11th century, although it fell into neglect after the 14th century. It appeared with increasing frequency during the 19th century but became rare from the early 20th century because of its German origin and associations (the large howitzers that pounded Liège, Namur and Paris during the First World War were nicknamed 'Big Bertha' after Frau Bertha Krupp, wife of the head of the German Krupps munitions manufacturing company – although the guns were in fact made by Skoda). Other notable bearers of the name have included the mother of the Holy Roman Emperor Charlemagne and Rochester's mad first wife in Charlotte Brontë's novel *Jane Eyre* (1847). Familiar forms of the name include **Bert** and **Bertie**. Variants of the name include **Berta**, **Bertina** and the French **Berthe**.

Berthold (m) German first name derived from the Old German *berht* ('bright' or 'famous') and *wald* ('ruler') or *hold* ('fair' or 'lovely'). Variants include **Barthold** and **Bertolt** – as borne by the German playwright Bertolt Brecht (1898–1956).

Bertice (f) English first name that is thought to have resulted from the combination of BERTHA and BERNICE. It appears to have made its first appearances among English speakers in the USA in the early years of the 20th century.

Bertie (m) English first name that developed as a diminutive of such names as ALBERT and BERTRAM (*see also* BERT). It was taken up by English speakers towards the end of the 19th century and was in regular use until the 1940s, since when it has largely fallen out of favour. It became particularly well known in the early years of the 20th century as the nickname of King George VI (1895–1952), whose full name was Albert Frederick Arthur George. Other well-known bearers of the name have included the fictional Bertie Wooster in the Jeeves and Wooster stories of P. G. Wodehouse. *See also* BERTHA.

Bertina *See* BERTHA.

Bertram (m) English first name derived via French from the Old German Berahtram, itself from the Old German *beraht* ('bright' or 'famous') and *hramn* ('raven') and thus interpreted as meaning 'famous raven' or more loosely – because ravens were symbols of wisdom in Germanic mythology – 'wise person'. It was fairly common as a first name among English speakers in medieval times and enjoyed a significant revival alongside other medieval names in the 19th century, although it was eclipsed by such diminutive forms as BERT (or **Burt**) and BERTIE from the early 20th century. Notable bearers of the name have included Bertram, Count of Roussillon in William Shakespeare's *All's Well That Ends Well* (1603–4). Variants include **Bartram** and the English and French **Bertrand**, as borne by the British philosopher Bertrand Russell (1872–1970), although this can also be traced back to the Old German for 'bright shield'.

Bertrand *See* BERTRAM.

Beryl (f) English first name derived from the name of the precious gem. It was among the many jewel names that were adopted as first names by English speakers towards the end of the 19th century and enjoyed some popularity until the middle of the 20th century, since when it has suffered a sharp decline. Famous bearers of the name have included British actress Beryl Reid (1920–96), British artist Beryl Cook (b.1926) and British writer Beryl Bainbridge (b.1933). BERRY is a diminutive form.

Bess (f) English first name that developed as a diminutive of ELIZABETH. Queen Elizabeth I was nicknamed 'Good Queen Bess' but the name did not establish itself as a particular favourite until the 17th century. It remained in fairly regular use until the end of the 19th century, but is now very rare. Other notable bearers of the name have included the English noblewoman 'Bess of Hardwick' (Elizabeth Hardwick, Countess of Shrewsbury; 1518–1608), President Harry S. Truman's wife Bess

Truman (1885–1982) and the fictional Bess in the George Gershwin opera *Porgy and Bess* (1935). Also encountered as **Bessie** (or **Bessy**) – as borne by US blues singer Bessie Smith (1894–1937).

Bessie/Bessy *See* BESS.

Bet *See* BETH; BETSY; ELIZABETH.

Beth (f) English first name that developed as a diminutive of ELIZABETH or BETHANY. It appeared with increasing frequency in the 19th century and has continued in fairly regular use ever since, with a recent peak in popularity in the 1990s. Well-known bearers of the name have included Beth March in the Louisa M. Alcott novel *Little Women* (1868–9) and British singer–songwriter Beth Orton (b.1970). Sometimes abbreviated to **Bet**. Also found in combination with various other names, as in **Jobeth** and **Mary Beth**. Variants include the Welsh **Bethan**.

Bethan *See* BETH; ELIZABETH.

Bethany (f) English first name derived from a Hebrew place name meaning 'house of figs'. It appears in the New Testament as the name of the village near Jerusalem that Christ passed through shortly before his Crucifixion and also as the name of Mary of Bethany, sister of Martha and Lazarus, as a result of which it has been a traditional favourite among Roman Catholics. Also rendered in the form **Bethanie**. Sometimes abbreviated to BETH.

Bethia (f) English first name derived from the Hebrew *bith-yah* ('daughter of God'), or alternatively from the Gaelic *beath* ('life'). It appears in the Old Testament in the variant form **Bithiah** and was taken up in its modern form among English speakers in the 17th century, becoming modestly popular in Scotland but falling into disuse by the 20th century. Sometimes abbreviated to BETH.

Betrys *See* BEATRICE.

Betsy (f) English first name that developed as a diminutive of ELIZABETH, apparently through the combination of **Bet** and **Bessie**. It was in fairly widespread use by the middle of the 19th century but has been rare since the early years of the 20th century. Also encountered as **Betsey** – as borne by Betsey Trotwood in the Charles Dickens novel *David Copperfield* (1849–50).

Bette (f) English first name that developed as a diminutive of ELIZABETH (*see also* BETTY). Originally a French variant of the name made famous through the Honoré de Balzac novel *La Cousine Bette* (1847), it is today usually associated with the US film actress Bette (pronounced 'Betty') Davis (Ruth Elizabeth Davis; 1908–89). Other notable bearers of the name have included US actress Bette Midler (b.1944).

Bettina *See* BETTY.

Bettrys *See* BEATRICE.

Betty (f) English first name that developed as a diminutive of ELIZABETH. It appeared with increasing frequency among English speakers from the 18th century, but has become relatively rare since a peak in popularity in the 1920s. Famous bearers of the name have included US film actresses Betty Grable (1918–73) and Betty Hutton (b.1921). Also encountered as **Bettye**. Other variants include the Italian and Spanish **Bettina**, which enjoyed some popularity in the English-speaking world in the 1960s. *See also* BETTE.

Beulah (f) Hebrew name for Israel, meaning 'she who is married', that was taken up as a first name among English speakers in the 17th century, becoming particularly popular within the Black community in the USA. The original Hebrew 'land of Beulah' is also sometimes interpreted as a reference to heaven.

Bev *See* BEVAN; BEVERLEY; BEVERLY.

Bevan (m) Welsh surname derived from the Welsh *ap Evan* ('son of Evan') that was subsequently taken up as an occasional first name. Commonly abbreviated to **Bev**.

Beverley (m) English place name (from Humberside) derived from the Old English *beofor* ('beaver') and *leac* ('stream') that was subsequently adopted as a surname and occasional first name. It became a modestly popular choice of first name in the 19th century but has become rare since enjoying a peak in the 1950s, largely because of increasing competition from the female form of the name, BEVERLY. Famous bearers of the name have included British novelist Beverley Nichols (1898–1983). Commonly abbreviated to **Bev**.

Beverly (f) English first name that developed as a feminine equivalent of BEVERLEY and is now more widespread than the original from which it evolved. It first became popular in the USA in the early years of the 20th century – promoted by the fame of Beverly Hills, the glamorous Los Angeles home district of many US film stars – and has continued in fairly regular use on both sides of the Atlantic ever since, enjoying a peak in popularity in the 1960s. Well-known bearers of the name have included US opera singer Beverly Sills (Belle Miriam Silverman; b.1927). Often abbreviated to **Bev**. Occasionally also encountered as **Beverley**.

Bevis (m) English surname possibly derived from the French *beau fils* ('handsome son'), or else from the French place name Beauvais, that has been in occasional use as a first name since the 11th century. The name came to England with the Normans and enjoyed a revival among English speakers towards the end of the 19th century, promoted by the Richard Jefferies novel *Bevis: The Story of a Boy* (1882). Variants include **Beavis**, a form of the name that became well known in the late 1990s through the adult television cartoon series *Beavis and Butthead*.

Bharat (m) Indian first name derived from the Sanskrit *bharata* ('being maintained'). It appears in Indian mythology as an alternative name of Agni, god of fire, and also as that of a celebrated hero, the son

37

of King Dushyanta. **Bharati** is a feminine form of the name.

Bhaskar (m) Indian first name derived from the Sanskrit *bhas* ('light') and *kara* ('making') and thus interpreted as meaning 'shining'. It appears in Indian mythology as a name borne by Shiva and was also borne by a famous medieval astronomer and mathematician.

Bianca (f) Italian first name derived from the Italian *bianca* ('white' or 'pure'). English speakers adopted the name in the 16th century, when it also appeared as the name of characters in William Shakespeare's plays *The Taming of the Shrew* (*c*.1592) and *Othello* (1602–4), both of which have Italian settings. Notable bearers of the name in more recent times have included British rock star Mick Jagger's former wife, the Nicaraguan model Bianca Jagger (Bianca Pérez Mora Macías; b.1945). *See also* BLANCHE; CANDIDA.

Biddy/Bidelia *See* BRIDGET.

Bijay/Bijoy *See* VIJAY.

Bill/Billie/Billy *See* WILLIAM.

Bina *See* SABINA.

Bindy *See* BELINDA.

Bing (m) English first name of obscure origin. It may have been adopted originally as an abbreviated form of **Bingo**, as borne by a well-known cartoon character, and subsequently enjoyed a boost as the stage-name of US singer and film actor Bing Crosby (Harry Lillis Crosby; 1901–77).

Binnie (f) English first name that developed as a diminutive of BERNICE or any longer name ending '-bina' but may also be encountered as a familiar form of several other names with no apparent connection. It was a fairly common choice around the middle of the 19th century but has become increasingly rare in modern times. Notable bearers of the name have included British actress Binnie Hale (Beatrice Mary Hale-Munro; 1899–1984).

Birgit/Birgitta/Birgitte *See* BRIDGET.

Bjork (f) Icelandic first name. Pronounced 'beeyork', it became familiar outside Iceland through Icelandic pop star Bjork Gudmundsdottir (b.1965).

Björn (m) Swedish first name derived from the Old Norse for 'bear'. Also encountered in the Norwegian forms **Bjørn** – as borne by Swedish tennis player Bjørn Borg (b.1956) – or **Bjarne**.

Blaine (m) Scottish surname of obscure origin that has been in occasional use as a first name among English speakers since the early 20th century. It would appear to be a modern reworking of Blane, a much older name celebrated as that of the 6th-century Scottish bishop St Blane (or Blaan).

Blair (m/f) Scottish place name derived from the Gaelic *blar* ('field' or 'plain') that was subsequently adopted as a surname and occasional first name. It has enjoyed a modest revival since the middle of the 20th century, chiefly in Canada and the USA.

Blaise (m) English and French first name derived from the Roman Blasius, itself from the Latin *blaesus* ('lisping' or 'stammering'). It was borne by the 4th-century St Blaise, the patron saint of wool-workers who was also famed for his work among those suffering from diseases of the throat and became the subject of veneration in medieval times. A long-established favourite in France, the name has made only infrequent appearances among English speakers since the medieval period, when its relative popularity probably owed much to St Blaise's links with the all-important wool trade. Other famous bearers of the name have included the French philosopher and mathematician Blaise Pascal (1623–62). Also encountered as **Blase** or **Blaze**. Among variants in other languages are the Italian **Biaggio**, the Spanish **Blas**, the Portuguese **Bras** and the Russian **Vlas**.

Blake (m) English surname derived either from the Old English *blaec* ('black') or conversely *blac* ('pale' or 'white') that has been in use as a first name since at least the 19th century. The name has sometimes been bestowed in honour of the English admiral Robert Blake (1599–1657) or in tribute to the British poet William Blake (1757–1827). Notable bearers of the name in recent times have included US film director Blake Edwards (William Blake McEdwards; b.1922).

Blanche (f) English and French first name derived from the French *blanc* ('white' or 'pure') and originally normally bestowed upon blondes. It was adopted initially among the French as a translation of the Roman CANDIDA. English speakers used the name on an irregular basis in medieval times and it was among the names to enjoy a brief revival towards the end of the 19th century before becoming infrequent once again. Notable bearers of the name have ranged from Louis VIII of France's queen Blanche of Castile (1188–1252) and Henry I's queen Blanche of Artois (d.1300) to the fictional Blanche Du Bois in the Tennessee Williams play *A Streetcar Named Desire* (1949). Variants in other languages include the Spanish **Blanca** and the Polish **Blanka**. *See also* BIANCA; CANDIDA.

Blane *See* BLAINE.

Blase/Blaze *See* BLAISE.

Blod *See* BLODWEN.

Blodwen (f) Welsh first name derived from the Welsh *blodau* ('flowers') and *gwyn* ('white') and possibly first taken up under the influence of the French Blanchefleur. It was fairly common in medieval times and enjoyed a significant revival in the late 19th century, although still confined chiefly to Wales. Famous bearers of the name have included the fictional Blodwen Evans in the Richard Llewellyn novel *How Green was My Valley* (1939). Commonly abbreviated to **Blod**. Also encountered in the form **Blodwyn**. Related names include **Blodwedd**, meaning 'flower face', and **Blodyn** or **Blodeyn**, meaning 'flower'.

Blondie (f) English first name that evolved

as a nickname for anyone with blonde hair. It appears to have been a relatively recent introduction that probably made its first appearances in the 1920s. It became well known in the 1930s through the Chic Young strip cartoon *Blondie*, featuring the character Blondie Bumstead.

Blossom (f) English first name derived from the ordinary vocabulary word 'blossom'. It was among the various flower names and related terms that were adopted as first names among English speakers towards the end of the 19th century.

Bluebell (f) English first name derived from the name of the bluebell flower. It has made rare appearances among English speakers since the late 19th century.

Blythe (f) English surname probably derived from the ordinary vocabulary word 'blithe' that has made occasional appearances as a first name since the 1940s. Its first appearances coincided with the success of the Noël Coward comedy *Blithe Spirit* (1941).

Boaz (m) Hebrew name of uncertain origin, possibly meaning 'swiftness' or perhaps 'man of strength'. It appears in the Bible as the name of Ruth's husband and was consequently taken up on a rather modest scale by English speakers in the 17th and 18th centuries, generally confined to the Jewish community. Also spelled **Boas**.

Bob (m) English first name that developed as a diminutive of ROBERT. This form of the name was in use among English speakers by at least the early 18th century, appearing with increasing frequency from around the middle of the 19th century. Well-known bearers of the name have included the fictional Bob Acres in the Richard Brinsley Sheridan comedy *The Rivals* (1775), Bob Cratchit in Charles Dickens' *A Christmas Carol* (1843), British film actor Bob Hoskins (b.1942) and West Indian reggae musician Bob Marley (1945–81). *See also* BOBBIE; BOBBY.

Bobbie (f) English first name that developed as a diminutive of ROBERTA. It is sometimes also encountered as a diminutive of BARBARA or as a feminine version of BOBBY. Famous bearers of the name have included US pop singer Bobbie Gentry (Roberta Streeta; b.1944).

Bobby (m) English first name that developed as a diminutive of ROBERT. It seems to have become established as an accepted abbreviation of Robert early in the 18th century and has continued in regular use ever since. Famous bearers of the name in relatively recent times have included US golfer Bobby Jones (1902–71), British footballers Sir Bobby Charlton (b.1937) and Bobby Moore (1941–93) and US soul singer Bobby Womack (b.1944). Sometimes encountered in combination with other names, as in **Bobby Joe**. *See also* BOB; BOBBIE.

Boniface (m) English first name derived ultimately from the Roman Bonifatius, itself from the Latin *bonum* ('good') and *fatum* ('fate') or alternatively *bonum* ('good') and *facere* ('to do') and thus interpreted as meaning either 'good fate' or 'well-doer'. It was borne by several early saints and nine popes and was a fairly frequent choice among English speakers during the medieval period, but has appeared with less regularity since the Reformation. Famous bearers of the name have included a character in the George Farquhar comedy *The Beaux' Stratagem* (1707). Variants include the German **Bonifaz** and the Italian, Spanish and Portuguese **Bonifacio**.

Bonita (f) English first name derived from the Spanish *bonito* ('pretty'). The name does not appear to have originated in Spain itself, having made its first appearances among English speakers in the USA in the 1920s. *See also* BONNIE.

Bonnie (f) English first name derived from the Scottish 'bonny' (meaning 'pretty' or 'fine'), itself ultimately from the Latin *bonus* ('good'). It is also in occasional use as a diminutive of BONITA. It was taken up by English speakers on both sides of the Atlantic early in the 20th century and became increasingly common around the middle of the century after appearing as the name of Scarlett O'Hara's baby in Margaret Mitchell's novel *Gone with the Wind* (1936). Other notable bearers of the name have included US bank robber Bonnie Parker (1911–34), whose violent end was depicted in the film *Bonnie and Clyde* (1967), US blues singer Bonnie Raitt (b.1949) and British actress, singer and dancer Bonnie Langford (Bonita Langford; b.1964). Also encountered as **Bonny**.

Booth (m) English first name derived from the Old Norse for 'hut' or 'shed'. It was in use as a surname before being adopted on an occasional basis as a first name.

Boris (m) Russian first name derived either from the Old Slavonic *bor* ('fight' or 'struggle') or more likely from the Tartar nickname Bogoris, meaning 'small'. It was taken up by English speakers in the 19th century and has continued in irregular use into modern times. Notable bearers of the name have included a 10th-century Russian saint, Russian tsar Boris Godunov (1552–1605), US horror film actor Boris Karloff (William Pratt; 1887–1969), Russian poet Boris Pasternak (1890–1960), Russian President Boris Yeltsin (b.1931) and German tennis player Boris Becker (b.1967). Among familiar forms of the name are **Boba** and **Borya**.

Boyce (m) English surname derived from the French *bois* ('wood') that has made occasional appearances as a first name since the early 20th century.

Boyd (m) Scottish surname derived from the Gaelic *buidhe* ('yellow') that has made occasional appearances as a first name among English speakers since the early 20th century. Its history as a first name among the Scots goes back several hundred years, having been reserved initially for people with blonde hair (although another derivation suggests it evolved as a reference to people from the island of Bute). There is a character called Boyd Tarleton in Margaret Mitchell's novel *Gone with the Wind* (1936).

Brad *See* BRADFORD; BRADLEY.

Bradford (m) English place name (from various locations in northern England) derived from the Old English *brad* ('broad') and *ford* ('ford') that was subsequently taken up as a surname and occasional first name. **Brad** is the usual diminutive form of the name.

Bradley (m) English place name derived from the Old English *brad* ('broad') and *leah* ('wood' or 'clearing') that was subsequently taken up as a surname and occasional first name since the 19th century, chiefly in the USA. Well-known bearers of the name have included the ill-fated Bradley Headstone in the Charles Dickens novel *Our Mutual Friend* (1864–5). Commonly abbreviated to **Brad** – as borne by US film actor Brad Pitt (b.1965).

Brady (m) Irish surname possibly derived ultimately from the Gaelic *bragha* ('chest' or 'throat'), and thus interpreted as meaning 'large-chested', that has also been in occasional use as a first name among English speakers.

Bram *See* ABRAHAM.

Bramwell (m) English place name (from Derbyshire) meaning 'place of brambles' that was subsequently taken up as a surname and occasional first name. Famous bearers of the name have included British religious campaigner William Bramwell Booth (1829–1912), leader of the Salvation Army. Variants include **Branwell** – as borne by Patrick Branwell Brontë (1817–48), the artist brother of the celebrated Brontë sisters.

Brandon (m) English place name derived from the Old English *brom* ('broom' or 'gorse') and *dun* ('hill') that was subsequently taken up as a surname and, from the 19th century, as an occasional first name, apparently under the influence of the Irish BRENDAN. More common in the

USA than elsewhere, with a recent peak in popularity in the 1980s. Sometimes abbreviated to **Brandy**. Variants include **Branton**.

Brandy *See* BRANDON.

Branwell *See* BRAMWELL.

Branwen (f) Welsh first name derived from the Welsh *bran* ('raven') and *gwyn* ('white' or 'blessed'), but also in existence as a variant of BRONWEN. It appears in the *Mabinogion* as the name of the beautiful sister of King Bran and is still in occasional use in Wales.

Bras *See* BLAISE.

Bren *See* BRENDA.

Brenda (f) English first name derived from the Old Norse *brandr* ('sword' or 'torch'), but also sometimes regarded as a feminine equivalent of the Irish BRENDAN. It was taken up initially as a first name in the Shetland Isles but subsequently became more widespread during the course of the 19th century, although it has become much less frequent since enjoying a peak in popularity in the middle of the 20th century. Notable bearers of the name have included US pop singer Brenda Lee (b.1944) and Irish actress Brenda Fricker (b.1944). Commonly shortened to **Bren**.

Brendan (m) Irish first name derived from the Gaelic Breanainn, meaning 'prince' – although alternative derivations suggest it means 'stinking hair' or 'dweller by the beacon'. It appeared with increasing frequency among English speakers from the early 20th century and had become one of the top fifty names in Australia by the 1970s. Well-known bearers of the name over the centuries have ranged from the 6th-century Irish St Brendan the Voyager, who is supposed to have discovered America, to Irish playwright Brendan Behan (1923–64) and British athlete Brendan Foster (b.1948). Variants include **Brandan,** BRANDON and the Irish Gaelic **Breandan**.

Brent (m) English place name (from Devon and Somerset), apparently derived from the Old English word for 'hill', that was subsequently adopted as a surname and, from the 1930s, as an occasional first name, chiefly in Canada and the USA. It enjoyed a peak in popularity on both sides of the Atlantic in the 1970s and 1980s. Famous bearers of the name have included Brent Tarleton in Margaret Mitchell's novel *Gone with the Wind* (1936).

Brett (m) English surname originally bestowed upon Breton settlers in medieval England that has been in increasing use as a first name since the middle of the 20th century, chiefly in the USA. Also encountered as **Bret** – as borne by the US writer Bret Harte (Francis Brett Harte; 1836–1902).

Brian (m) English and Irish first name derived ultimately from the Irish Gaelic *brigh* ('strength' or 'power'). It appears in Irish mythology as the name of the 10th-century king Brian Boru but came to England with the Bretons who arrived with William the Conqueror. It was in fairly regular use during the medieval period but subsequently became much less common until its eventual revival as an import from Ireland in the 18th century. It enjoyed relatively recent peaks in popularity in the UK in the 1950s and in the USA in the 1970s but has since experienced a gradual decline. Famous bearers of the name in relatively recent times have included British cricketer Brian Close (b.1931) and British actor Brian Blessed (b.1937). Also encountered as **Brien** or **Bryan** – as borne by British novelist and film director Bryan Forbes (b.1926) and British pop singer Bryan Ferry (b.1945). Sometimes abbreviated to **Bri**. **Brianna** is a rare feminine version of the name. *See* also BRYONY.

Brice *See* BRYCE.

Bride *See* BRIDGET.

Bridget (f) English first name derived from the Gaelic Brighid, itself from the Celtic *brigh* ('strength' or 'power'). In its original

Gaelic form the name of a Celtic fire goddess, it consequently became especially popular in Ireland and Scotland, although it has appeared with increasing regularity elsewhere in the English-speaking world since the 18th century. It enjoyed a peak in popularity in the 1950s, since when it has become rather less common.

Famous bearers of the name have included the 6th-century St Bridget of Kildare (also known as St Bride), the fictional Bridget Allworthy in the Henry Fielding novel *Tom Jones* (1749), British artist Bridget Riley (b.1931) and US film actress Bridget Fonda (b.1964). Also encountered as **Brigit** or **Brigid** – as borne by British novelist Brigid Brophy (1929–95). Diminutive forms of the name include GITA, **Bride**, **Bridie** and **Biddy** – as borne by the fictional Biddy Gargery in the Charles Dickens novel *Great Expectations* (1860–61). **Bidelia** is a rather fanciful elaboration of the name. Variants in other languages include the French **Brigitte**, as borne by the French film actress Brigitte Bardot (b.1933), the Italian **Brigida**, the Swedish **Britt**, as borne by Swedish film actress Britt Ekland (b.1942), the German **Birgit** and the Scandinavian **Birgitta**, **Birgitte** and **Brigitta**.

Bridie *See* BRIDGET.

Brien *See* BRIAN.

Brigham (m) English place name (from Cumbria and North Yorkshire) derived from the Old English *brycg* ('bridge') and *ham* ('homestead') that was subsequently taken up as a surname and occasional first name. In the USA the name is usually associated with the US Mormon leader Brigham Young (1801–77).

Brigid/Brigit/Brigitta/Brigitte *See* BRIDGET.

Brin *See* BRYN.

Briony *See* BRYONY.

Britney (f) English first name that may have evolved from BRITTANY. It became widely familiar from the late 1990s through the international success enjoyed by US pop singer Britney Spears (b.1981).

Britt *See* BRIDGET.

Brittany (f) English first name derived from the name of the province of Bretagne (Anglicized as Brittany). It has enjoyed modest popularity as a first name among English speakers since the middle of the 20th century.

Broderick (m) English surname meaning 'son of Roderick' that has made occasional appearances as a first name in relatively recent times, apparently under the influence of RODERICK. Famous bearers of the name have included US actor Broderick Crawford (b.1910).

Brodie (m) Scottish first name derived from the Scots Gaelic for 'ditch'. Also encountered as **Brody**, it was in use as a surname before being adopted as an occasional first name.

Bron *See* AUBERON; BRONWEN.

Bronwen (f) Welsh first name derived from the Welsh *bron* ('breast') and *gwen* ('white') and thus interpreted as meaning 'fair-bosomed'. It has long been a favourite in Wales but has also made occasional appearances among English speakers elsewhere since the end of the 19th century. Notable bearers of the name have included Bronwen Morgan in the Richard Llewellyn novel *How Green was My Valley* (1939). Also encountered as **Bronwyn** and sometimes confused with the otherwise unrelated BRANWEN. Commonly abbreviated to **Bron**.

Brook (m) English surname derived from the ordinary vocabulary word 'brook' and thus originally meaning 'dweller by a stream' that was taken up as a first name towards the end of the 19th century. It was adopted initially by Black Americans but has since made sporadic appearances throughout the English speaking world. The feminine form is BROOKE.

Brooke (f) Feminine equivalent of BROOK that has been in occasional use since around the middle of the 20th century. Well-known bearers of the name have included US film actress Brooke Shields (b.1965).

Brooklyn (m/f) English first name derived from the Brooklyn district of New York City. Also found as **Brooklynn** and **Brooklynne**, it enjoyed a significant boost in 1999 when English footballer David Beckham and pop singer Victoria Beckham selected it as the name for their newborn son (New York being where the couple discovered they were expecting a baby).

Bruce (m) Scottish surname that was widely adopted as a first name throughout the English-speaking world from the late 19th century. It was originally imported into Scotland as the Norman French baronial name de Brus, itself taken from an unidentified place name in northern France. The name has largely lost its uniquely Scottish character, although it is still often associated with the Scottish king Robert the Bruce (1274–1329). It has proved particularly popular in recent years in Australia, to the extent that it is also used as a generic name for any adult male (*see also* SHEILA). Notable bearers of the name in recent times have included British television presenter Bruce Forsyth (b.1927), US rock musician Bruce Springsteen (b.1949) and US film actor Bruce Willis (b.1955). **Brucie** is a fairly common diminutive form of the name.

Brunella *See* BRUNO.

Brunhilde (f) German first name derived from the Old German *brun* ('armour' or 'protection') and *hild* ('battle'). It is well known as the name of the legendary warrior queen who was a central character in the *Nibelungenlied* and subsequently in Richard Wagner's opera cycle *The Ring of the Nibelung*. Variants include **Brunhild** and **Brynhild**.

Bruno (m) English and German first name derived ultimately from the Old German *brun* ('brown') and originally usually reserved for people with brown hair, brown eyes or a swarthy complexion. It was in use among English speakers in medieval times and was subsequently revived towards the end of the 19th century, possibly under the influence of Lewis Carroll's *Sylvie and Bruno* (1889) but also as a result of the arrival of German immigrants in the USA. Famous bearers of the name have ranged from three 10th-century German saints to the German-born US conductor Bruno Walter (1876–1962). **Brunella** and **Brunette** are rare feminine versions of the name.

Bryan *See* BRIAN.

Bryce (m) English surname of obscure Celtic origin that has also been in occasional use as a first name over the centuries. Also encountered as **Brice**.

Bryn (m) Welsh first name derived from the Welsh *bryn* ('hill') but also in use as a diminutive form of BRYNMOR. It appears to have been an early 20th-century introduction. Also encountered as **Brin**.

Brynmor (m) Welsh place name (from Gwynedd) derived from the Welsh *bryn* ('hill') and *mawr* ('large') that was adopted as an occasional first name in the 20th century. Sometimes abbreviated to BRYN.

Bryony (f) English first name derived from that of the wild hedgerow plant, although also in occasional use as a feminine equivalent of BRIAN. It appears to have been taken up by English speakers towards the middle of the 20th century, in the wake of many other flower names adopted around the end of the 19th century. Also encountered as **Briony**.

Buck (m) English first name derived from the ordinary vocabulary word 'buck' (denoting a male deer or goat) and thus suggesting a lively, spirited young man. It emerged as a modestly popular choice of name in the USA in the early years of the 20th century and was subsequently promoted by the space adventures of the cartoon strip character Buck Rogers, first published in the 1920s. Other notable bearers of the name have included US jazz musician Buck Clayton (Wilbur Dorsey Clayton; b.1911).

Bud *See* BUDDY.

Buddy (m) English first name that developed as a nickname meaning 'friend' or 'pal', possibly originally as a variant of 'brother'. It has been in fairly regular use in the USA since the early 20th century. Notable bearers of the name have included US bandleader Buddy Rich (Bernard Rich; 1917–87) and US rock and roll singer Buddy Holly (Charles Hardin Holley; 1936–59). **Bud** is a diminutive form of the name – as borne by the US comedian Bud Abbot (William Abbott; 1895–1974).

Budur *See* BADR.

Bunny *See* BERNARD; BERNICE.

Buntie *See* BUNTY.

Bunty (f) English first name of uncertain origin, possibly with its roots in a nickname derived from a dialect term for a lamb. It became fairly common in the UK in the wake of the popular play *Bunty Pulls the Strings* (1911) and subsequently became familiar as the title of the popular British girls' comic *Bunty*. Also encountered as **Buntie**.

Burl (m) English first name derived from the Germanic for 'cup bearer'. Confined chiefly to the USA, it is most familiar as the first name of US singer and actor Burl Ives (1909–95).

Burt *See* BERT.

Buster (m) English first name that developed as a nickname presumably derived from the verb 'bust' and thus suggesting a person given to breaking or smashing things. It was taken up by English speakers in the USA towards the end of the 19th century. Famous bearers of the name have included US silent film comedian Buster

Keaton (Joseph Francis Keaton; 1895–1966).

Byron (m) English surname derived from the Old English *aet thaem byrum* ('at the byres') that has made rare appearances as a first name in relatively recent times. The name is usually associated with the celebrated British poet Lord Byron (George Gordon, 6th Baron Byron; 1784–1824).

C

Caddy *See* CANDICE; CAROLINE.

Cade (m) English first name derived ulti-mately from a traditional nickname meaning 'round'. It enjoyed some popularity among English speakers after appearing as the name of a character in the Margaret Mitchell novel *Gone with the Wind* (1936).

Cadell (m) Welsh first name derived from the Old Welsh *cad* ('battle'). Also encountered as **Cadel**.

Cadfael (m) Welsh first name meaning 'battle metal', and pronounced 'cadful'. It was popularized in the late 20th century through the medieval mystery novels of Ellis Peters featuring the detective monk Brother Cadfael.

Cadogan (m) Welsh first name derived from the Welsh word *cad* (meaning 'battle'). Rendered **Cadwgan** among Welsh speakers, it has particular connections with Glamorgan, which was ruled by a chieftain of that name in the 10th century.

Cadwalader (m) Welsh first name derived from the Welsh *cad* ('battle') and *gwalad* ('disposer') and thus interpreted as meaning 'general' or 'commander'. Borne by a 7th-century saint who died fighting the Saxons and by several other Welsh kings and princes, it remains a uniquely Welsh name that has yet to win acceptance elsewhere in the English-speaking world. Also encountered as **Cadwallader** or **Cadwaladr**.

Caerwyn (m) Welsh name derived from *caer* ('fort') and *wyn* ('white'), pronounced 'curwin'. Also spelled CARWYN.

Caesar (m) Roman name possibly derived from the Latin *caesaries* ('head of hair') or otherwise from *caedere* ('to cut') that has made occasional appearances as a first name among English speakers since the 18th century, usually in tribute to the celebrated Roman emperor Gaius Julius Caesar (100–44 BC). Variants include **Cesar** – as borne by US actor Cesar Romero (1907–94) – and the Italian **Cesare** – as borne by Cesare Borgia (1476–1507), one of the notorious Borgia family who dominated Renaissance Italy in the late 15th century.

Caetano *See* GAETANO.

Cahal *See* CAROL.

Cai *See* CAIUS.

Caitlin *See* CATHERINE; KATHLEEN.

Caius (m) Roman first name (pronounced 'kyus') derived from the Latin for 'rejoice' that has continued in irregular use among English speakers into modern times. Sometimes abbreviated to **Cai** or **Kai**, although this form of the name can also be traced as a Welsh name. Also encountered as **Gaius**.

Cal *See* CALUM; CALVIN; CATHAL.

Caleb (m) Biblical name derived from the Hebrew **Kaleb**, variously interpreted as meaning 'intrepid', 'bold' or 'dog' (presumably intended to suggest a doglike devotion to God). It appears in the Bible as the name of one of Moses' companions on the journey to the Promised Land and was consequently taken up with some enthusiasm by Puritans after the Reformation, becoming especially popular in the USA. Famous bearers of the name have included the central character in the William Godwin novel *Caleb Williams* (1794).

Calista *See* CALLISTA.

Calliope (f) Greek name meaning 'beautiful face', and pronounced 'kallee-opee'. Borne by the ancient Greek muse of epic poetry, it has made occasional reappearances among English speakers over the centuries, although it has never been in common use. Sometimes abbreviated to **Cally**.

Callista (f) Feminine equivalent of the Italian Callisto, itself descended from the Roman Callistus, which came from the Greek *kalos* ('fair' or 'good'). It became widely known among English speakers in the altered form **Calista** in the late 1990s through the US actress Calista Flockhart (b.1964), star of the US television series *Ally McBeal*, who was named after her grandmother.

Callisto *See* CALLISTA.

Callum *See* CALUM.

Calum (m) Scottish first name derived from the Roman Columba, meaning 'dove'. Although it has a fairly long history as a Scottish name, initially in tribute to the 6th-century St Columba, it has enjoyed increasing acceptance among English speakers since the middle of the 20th century, with a recent peak in the 1990s. Also spelled **Callum**. Commonly shortened to **Cal**, **Cally** or **Caley**. **Calumina** is a rare feminine version of the name.

Calvin (m) French surname derived via the Old French *chauve* from the Latin *calvus* ('bald'), and thus meaning 'little bald one', that was taken up as a first name among English speakers in the 16th century in tribute to the French Protestant theologian Jean Calvin (1509–64). Famous bearers of the name have included US President Calvin Coolidge (John Calvin Coolidge; 1872–1933) and US fashion designer Calvin Klein (b.1942). Commonly shortened to **Cal**.

Calypso (f) Greek first name meaning 'concealer'. In Greek myth, Calypso was a sea nymph who kept Odysseus prisoner for seven years.

Cameron (m/f) Scottish surname derived from the Gaelic *cam shron* ('crooked nose') that has been in occasional use as a first name among English speakers since the beginning of the 20th century. It has retained its strong Scottish connections, being well known as a famous clan name, but has appeared with increasing regularity elsewhere in the English-speaking world from the 1990s. Notable bearers of the name have included British theatrical producer Cameron Mackintosh (b.1946). In recent times it has become equally familiar as a name for females through US film actress Cameron Diaz (b.1972).

Camilla (f) Feminine version of the Roman Camillus, thought to mean 'attendant at a sacrifice', that has been in use as a first name among English speakers since the 13th century. It appears as the name of a warrior queen in Virgil's *Aeneid* (30–19 BC) and was regarded initially as a literary name when adopted in the English-speaking world. Notable bearers of the name have included the central character in the Fanny Burney novel *Camilla* (1796), which did much to make the name a popular choice, as well as the heroine in the Alexandre Dumas novel *La Dame aux camélias* (1848) and, in more recent times, the British aristocrat Lady Camilla Parker Bowles (b.1946). Also encountered as **Camellia**. The usual French version of the name is **Camille**. Among diminutive forms of the name are **Cam**, **Cammie**, **Millie** and **Milly**. The modern masculine equivalent of the name, **Camillo**, is popular among Italians but has not won acceptance in the English-speaking world to the extent that the feminine version has.

Camille/Camillo *See* CAMILLA.

Campbell (m) Scottish surname derived from the Gaelic *cam beul* ('crooked mouth') that has been in occasional use as a first name over the centuries, chiefly in Scotland. It is best known as the surname of one of the most famous of the Scottish clans, historically the sworn enemies of the Mac-Donalds.

Candace *See* CANDICE.

Candi *See* CANDIDA; CANDY.

Candice (f) English first name of uncertain origin. It represents a modern variant of **Candace** (pronounced 'candiss'), in which form the name appears in the Bible as that of a queen of Ethiopia. Early records of Candace being used as a first name by English speakers go back to the 17th century. As Candice it was taken up by English speakers early in the 20th century, becoming particularly popular in the USA. Candace Compson is the central character in the William Faulkner novel *The Sound and the Fury* (1929). Other famous bearers of the name have included the US actress Candice Bergen (b.1946). Commonly abbreviated to **Caddy** or CANDY. Variants include **Candis**.

Candida (f) Roman name derived from the Latin *candidus* ('white') that has been in use among English speakers since the medieval period. Having been borne by several saints and become popular among early Christians, it has remained in irregular use among English speakers into modern times, enjoying a minor peak in popularity in the early years of the 20th century, promoted by the George Bernard Shaw play *Candida* (1894). Familiar forms of the name include **Candi**, **Candia**, **Candie** or CANDY. Variants in other languages include the French **Candide** – as borne by the male central character in Voltaire's *Candide* (1759).

Candie *See* CANDIDA.

Candis *See* CANDICE.

Candy (f) English first name that evolved as a diminutive form of CANDICE and CANDIDA, possibly under the influence of the ordinary vocabulary word 'candy' (a word of Indian origin). Also encountered as **Candi**.

Caprice (f) English first name apparently derived from the ordinary vocabulary word meaning 'whim'. It has become widely familiar through US glamour model Caprice Bourret (b.1971).

Cara (f) English first name derived from the Latin or Italian *cara* ('dear'). It is also possible to trace the name back to the Irish *cara* ('friend' or 'dear one'). It was taken up by English speakers around the beginning of the 20th century and enjoyed something of a revival in the 1970s. Notable bearers of the name have included a character in the Evelyn Waugh novel *Brideshead Revisited* (1945). Variants include **Kara** and **Carita**. *See also* CARINA.

Caradoc (m) Welsh name derived from the Welsh *car* ('love') and thus interpreted as meaning 'amiable'. As **Caradog** or **Caractacus**, it was borne by a famous 1st-century British chieftain who led the resistance against the Romans. It has been in irregular use among the Welsh since the medieval period.

Cardew (m) English first name derived from the Welsh meaning 'black fort'. It was in use as a surname before being adopted on an occasional basis as a first name.

Careen (f) English first name of uncertain origin. It appears to have been one of the names that were created by the US novelist Margaret Mitchell in her novel *Gone with the Wind* (1936), perhaps under the influence of CARA or CARINA.

Carey (m/f) English first name that developed as a variant of CARY in the 19th century. In Irish use it may have evolved from the Gaelic O Ciardha ('descendant of the dark one'). The Welsh may trace it back to the place name **Carew**. It was used initially as a boys' name but since the 1950s has been reserved almost exclusively for girls.

Cari *See* CERI.

Carina (f) Scandinavian, German and English first name derived from both CARA and KAREN. It appears to have made its debut towards the end of the 19th century.

Variants include **Karina** and **Karine**.

Carissa (f) English first name derived from the Latin for 'dear one'.

Carita See CARA.

Carl (m) English first name derived from the Old English *ceorl* ('free man'), or otherwise encountered as a diminutive of CARLTON. It was taken up by English speakers around the middle of the 19th century and has continued in modest use on both sides of the Atlantic ever since, with a recent peak in popularity in the 1970s and 1980s. Notable bearers of the name have included US astronomer Carl Sagan (1934–96), US composer Carl Davis (b.1936) and US athlete Carl Lewis (b.1961). Sometimes also encountered in the German form **Karl**. A Swedish variant is **Kalle**. See also CARLA; CARLENE; CHARLES.

Carla (f) English, German and Italian first name that evolved as a feminine form of CARL. It was taken up by English speakers on both sides of the Atlantic in the 1940s and enjoyed a peak in popularity in the 1980s. Notable bearers of the name have included British television screenwriter Carla Lane (b.1935). Familiar forms of the name include **Carly** – as borne by US pop singer Carly Simon (b.1945) – and **Karly**.

Carlene (f) English first name that developed as a variant form of CARL under the influence of such names as CHARLENE and DARLENE. Famous bearers of the name have included the US singer-songwriter Carlene Carter (b.1955). Also spelled CARLEEN.

Carleton See CARLTON.

Carley/Carlie See CARLA.

Carlo/Carlos See CHARLES.

Carlotta See CHARLOTTE.

Carlton (m) English place name derived from the Old English *ceorl* ('man') and *tun* ('settlement') that was subsequently adopted as a surname and from the end of the 19th century as an occasional first name. Commonly shortened to CARL. Also en-

countered as **Carleton**. See also CHARLTON.

Carly See CARLA.

Carlyn See CAROLINE.

Carmel (f) Hebrew place name meaning 'vineyard' or 'garden' that has made occasional appearances as a first name among English speakers since the end of the 19th century. It appears in the Bible as the name of the sacred Mount Carmel in Israel. Well known from the Carmelite order of nuns founded on Mount Carmel, it was taken up as a first name by English-speaking Roman Catholics towards the end of the 19th century. Variants of the name include **Carmela**, **Carmelina**, **Carmelita** and **Carmencita**. See also CARMEN.

Carmela See CARMEL.

Carmen (f) Spanish equivalent of CARMEL that is often associated with the Latin *carmen* ('song'). The huge success of Bizet's opera *Carmen* (1873–4), based on Prosper Mérimée's short story *Carmen* (1845), made the name popular among English speakers in the 19th century. The musical *Carmen Jones* (1943), based on Bizet's opera, gave the name another boost in the middle of the 20th century, although it remains relatively rare today. Notable bearers of the name have included Portuguese singer and actress Carmen Miranda (Maria do Carmo Miranda da Cunha; 1909–55) and US jazz singer Carmen McCrae (1922–94).

Caro See CAROLINE.

Carol (m/f) English first name that developed as a diminutive of CAROLINE, although it is also closely associated with the ordinary vocabulary word 'carol' and has thus often been reserved for children born during the Christmas season. It appeared with increasing frequency towards the end of the 19th century and enjoyed a peak in popularity in the 1950s, but has since become much less common. As a masculine name, it is usually encountered as an Anglicized form of the Roman **Carolus** and was fairly widespread in the 19th century but has since become very rare under pressure from the feminine form of the name. Notable bearers of the name have included (among the men) British film director Sir Carol Reed (1906–76) and (among the women) US actress Carol Channing (b.1921). Variants of the feminine version of the name include **Carola**, CAROLE and CARYL. **Caroll** is a variant in use for both sexes. Equivalents of the masculine form of the name in other languages include the Irish **Cahal** or CATHAL (meaning 'battle-mighty'), the Polish **Karol** – as borne by Polish-born Pope John Paul II (Karol Wojtyla; b.1920) – and the Czech **Karel** – as borne by Czech-born British film director Karel Reisz (1926–2002).

Carola See CAROL.

Carole (f) English and French first name that evolved as a variant of CAROL. English speakers adopted the name from the French around the middle of the 20th century and it enjoyed a peak in popularity in the 1960s, since when it has become much less common. Well-known bearers of the name have included the US actress Carole Lombard (Jane Peters; 1908–42) and US singer-songwriter Carole King (b.1942).

Carolina See CAROLINE.

Caroline (f) English first name derived from the Italian Carolina, itself a feminine equivalent of Carlo (see CHARLES). It came to England with George II's wife Queen Caroline of Ansbach (1683–1737) and has remained in common currency ever since, with a recent peak in popularity in the 1960s and 1970s. Its popularity in the USA reflects its use as the name of the states of North and South Carolina, which were named originally in honour of Charles I. Notable bearers of the name have included Lord Byron's notorious lover Lady Caroline Lamb (1785–1828) and, in more recent times, Princess Caroline of Monaco (b.1957). Among the name's various diminutive forms are **Caddy**, **Carlyn**, **Caro** and LINA. Also encountered (since the early 20th century) as **Carolyn** or, more rarely,

Carolyne. Variants in other languages include the German **Karoline** and the Scandinavian **Karolina**. See also CARRIE.

Carolus See CHARLES.

Carolyn/Carolyne See CAROLINE.

Caron (f) Welsh first name derived from the Welsh *caru* ('to love') but also in use as a variant of KAREN, perhaps under the influence of CAROL. It was taken up by English speakers in the 1950s and has remained in occasional use ever since. Well-known bearers of the name have included British television presenter Caron Keating (b.1962).

Carrie (f) English first name that emerged as a diminutive form of CAROLINE in the 19th century. Interest in the name reached a peak in the USA during the 1970s, possibly under the influence of the Stephen King horror novel *Carrie* (1974). Also found as **Carri** or **Carry** – as borne by the celebrated US temperance campaigner Carry Nation (1846–1911). Sometimes found in combination with other names, as in **Carrie-Ann**.

Carroll See CAROL; CEARBHALL.

Carry See CARRIE.

Carson (m/f) English surname that has been in occasional use as a first name since the 19th century. Records of its use as a surname go back as far as the 13th century, when it may have been based on an unidentified place name. As a first name, it is associated primarily with people with Irish or Scottish connections, sometimes bestowed in honour of the celebrated Irish Protestant leader Edward Carson (1854–1935). In the USA it is popularly linked with the famed frontiersman Kit Carson (1809–68). Famous bearers of the name have included the US novelist Carson McCullers (Lula Carson McCullers; 1917–67).

Carsten See CHRISTIAN.

Carter (m) English surname, denoting a

person who transports goods by cart, that has made occasional appearances as a first name over the years. In Scotland it is sometimes treated as an Anglicization of the Gaelic Mac Artair, meaning 'son of Artair'.

Carver (m) English first name derived from the Cornish Gaelic for 'great rock'. It is most familiar as the name of the villainous Carver Doone in R. D. Blackmore's classic romance *Lorna Doone* (1869).

Carwyn (m) Welsh first name derived from the Welsh *car* ('love') and *gwyn* ('white' or 'blessed'). *See also* CAERWYN.

Cary (m/f) English place name (the River Cary in Somerset and the River Carey in Devon) that was subsequently adopted as a surname and has been in occasional use as a first name since the 19th century. It enjoyed a peak in popularity in the 1940s and 1950s when it became well known as the name of the British-born US film star Cary Grant (Alexander Archibald Leach; 1904–86). *See also* CAREY.

Caryl (f) English first name that developed as a variant of CAROL, possibly under the influence of BERYL and other similar names. It was taken up by English speakers in the 19th century. Notable bearers of the name have included British playwright Caryl Churchill (b.1938).

Caryn *See* KAREN.

Carys (f) Welsh first name derived from the Welsh *car* ('love') that developed under the influence of such names as GLADYS. Variants include **Cerys**.

Casey (m/f) English first name that can be variously traced back to an Irish surname meaning 'vigilant in war' or else to the US folk hero and engine-driver Casey Jones (John Luther Jones; 1863–1900), who lost his life saving his passengers on the 'Cannonball Express'; he was named after his birthplace, Cayce, Kentucky. Also spelled **Kasey**.

Casimir (m) English version of the Polish Kazimierz, itself from *kazic* ('to destroy') and *meri* ('great') but often interpreted to mean something like 'proclamation of peace'. It was famous as the name of several Polish kings in medieval times. Variants include **Kasimir** and the feminine **Casimira** or **Kasimira**.

Caspar (m) Dutch version of the English JASPER that was adopted as a first name by English speakers in the 19th century. Traditionally associated with one of the biblical Three Wise Men (who are not actually named in the Bible), it is also found in the variant forms **Casper**, **Kaspar** and **Kasper**. Other variants include the French GASPARD and the Italian **Gasparo** and **Gaspare**. Well-known bearers of the name have included German painter Caspar David Friedrich (1774–1840) and US statesman Caspar Weinberger (b.1917).

Cass *See* CASSANDRA.

Cassandra (f) Greek name meaning 'ensnaring men' that has been in occasional use among English speakers since the medieval period. It appears in Greek mythology as the name of a celebrated prophetess, the daughter of Priam and Hecuba, whose prophecies were fated never to be believed. As a result of its mythological origins it has entered the language as a name for any purveyor of gloomy predictions about the future. Famous bearers of the name have included a prophetess in William Shakespeare's *Troilus and Cressida* (1602) and Jane Austen's sister, Cassandra Austen (1775–1817). During the middle years of the 20th century the name became well known in the UK as the pseudonym under which Sir William Connor wrote a long-running column in the *Daily Mirror*. Diminutives of the name include **Cass**, **Cassie** and occasionally SANDRA.

Cassia *See* KEZIA.

Cassidy (m/f) English first name derived from the Irish surname O Caiside. A relatively recent introduction, it is mostly confined to the USA.

Cassie *See* CASSANDRA.

Cassius (m) Roman name of uncertain meaning, possibly derived from the Latin *cassus* ('empty'), that has made occasional appearances as a first name among English speakers since the 19th century. It is most famous in history as the name of a Roman general who was one of the organizers of the plot to assassinate Julius Caesar. Well-known bearers of the name in modern times have included the US boxer Cassius Clay, later Muhammad Ali (b.1942). Commonly abbreviated to **Cass** or **Cassie**.

Cat (m/f) English first name that evolved initially as a nickname for anyone with a tempestuous character. It has appeared in generally informal use among English speakers since the early 20th century, enjoying particular popularity among jazz musicians. Notable bearers of the name have included the British pop musician Cat Stevens (Steven Georgiou; b.1947) and the central character played by Jane Fonda in the comedy western *Cat Ballou* (1965). It is commonly encountered in use as an abbreviated form of CATHERINE, as borne by British television presenter Cat Deeley (b.1976).

Catalina/Catarina/Caterina/Cath/ Catha *See* CATHERINE.

Cathal (m) Irish first name derived from the Gaelic *cath* ('battle') and *val* ('rule'), and pronounced 'carhal'. Notable bearers of the name have included a 7th-century Irish saint. Occasionally abbreviated to **Cal**. Also found as **Cahal**, **Kathel**, **Catheld** or **Cathaldus**.

Cathán *See* KANE.

Catharine *See* CATHERINE.

Catherine (f) English first name derived ultimately from the Greek Aikaterina, which is itself of unknown meaning. The link with the 4th-century St Catherine of Alexandria, who was tortured on a spiked wheel before being beheaded, has led to the name being popularly associated with the Greek *aikia* ('torture'), although it has also been linked with the Greek *katharos* ('pure'),

hence the alternative spellings **Katherine**, **Katharine** and **Catharine**. English speakers took up the name during the medieval period in response to the cult of St Catherine, which was brought back from the Middle East by returning Crusaders. Notable early bearers of the name included three of Henry VIII's wives. It has remained in common use throughout the English-speaking world ever since.

Famous bearers of the name in its various forms since medieval times have included Catherine Earnshaw in the Emily Brontë novel *Wuthering Heights* (1847), British romantic novelist Catherine Cookson (1906–98), US actress Katharine Hepburn (1909–2003) and British actress Catherine Zeta Jones (b.1969). Among the name's many diminutives are CAT, **Cath** (or **Kath**), **Catha**, KATE, **Katie** (or **Katy**), **Cathy** (or **Kathy**), KAY, **Kat**, **Kit** and KITTY. Other variants include **Kathryn** (or **Cathryn**), **Katarine** (or **Catarine**), the Welsh **Catrin**, the Irish **Caitlin** (from which KATHLEEN and **Cathleen** evolved), the Spanish **Catalina**, the Portuguese **Catarina**, the Italian **Caterina**, the Swedish **Katarina**, the Russian **Katerina** and **Katya** and the German **Käthe**. *See also* CATRIONA; KAREN.

Cathleen *See* CATHERINE; KATHLEEN.

Cathryn/Cathy/Catrin *See* CATHERINE.

Catrina *See* CATHERINE; CATRIONA.

Catriona (f) Scottish and Irish first name that developed as a variant of CATHERINE. Usually pronounced 'catreena', it was adopted more widely throughout the English-speaking world in the 19th century and has remained in fairly regular use into modern times. Notable bearers of the name have included the fictional Catriona Drummond in Robert Louis Stevenson's novel *Catriona* (1893). Sometimes abbreviated to **Trina** or, chiefly among the Irish, to **Riona**. Also encountered as **Katrina**, **Catrina** or **Catrine**.

Cayetano *See* GAETANO.

Ceallagh *See* KELLY.

Cearbhall (m) Irish first name of uncertain meaning, possibly from the Gaelic *cearbh* ('hacking'), and pronounced 'keerval' or 'curval'. It was fairly frequent in Ireland during the medieval period and in the 20th century became more widely known as that of the Irish President Cearbhall O Dalaigh (1911–78). Sometimes Anglicized as **Carroll** or CHARLES.

Cecil (m) English first name derived either from the Roman Caecilius, itself from the Latin *caecus* ('blind'), or else from the Welsh Seissylt, ultimately from the Latin *sextus* ('sixth'). It became well known in England as the surname of the Cecil family, who wielded considerable power in Elizabethan England, but was not adopted as a first name until around the middle of the 19th century. It was at its most frequent at the beginning of the 20th century but has since become very rare, having acquired something of a reputation as an aristocratic name. Notable bearers of the name have included British statesman Cecil Rhodes (1853–1902), after whom Rhodesia (now Zimbabwe) was named, US film director and producer Cecil B. DeMille (1881–1959) and Irish-born British poet Cecil Day-Lewis (1904–72). *See also* CECILIA.

Cécile *See* CECILIA.

Cecilia (f) English first name derived from the Roman Caecilia, itself from the Latin *caecus* ('blind'). English speakers took up the name during the medieval period and it was subsequently the subject of a strong revival towards the end of the 19th century, since when it has become much less frequent. Notable bearers of the name have included the 2nd-century St Cecilia (the patron saint of music), a daughter of William the Conqueror and the fictional Cecilia Beverley in the Fanny Burney novel *Cecilia* (1782). **Cecil**, **Ciss** (or **Sis**), CISSIE (or **Cissy**) and **Sissie** (or **Sissy**) are diminutive forms of the name. Variants that are now in more common use than the source name include **Cicely** – as borne by British actress Cicely Courtneidge (1893–1980) –

and **Cecily** (or **Cecilie**) – as borne by the fictional Cecily Cardew in the Oscar Wilde comedy *The Importance of Being Earnest* (1895). Other less well-known variants include **Sisley**. Variants in other languages include the French **Cécile** (which is borne in France by both sexes). *See also* CELIA.

Cecilie/Cecily *See* CECILIA.

Cedric (m) English first name derived from the Old English Cerdic, itself of uncertain meaning, or alternatively from the Welsh Cedrych, derived from *ced* ('bounty') and *drych* ('pattern') and interpreted as meaning 'pattern of generosity'. As Cerdic it was borne by the first king of Wessex in the 6th century. Although Scottish novelist Sir Walter Scott may have had the Welsh form of the name in mind, it is traditionally believed that the modern form of the name resulted from an inaccurate rendering of the Old English name in his historical novel *Ivanhoe* (1819). Other notable bearers of the name have included the fictional Lord Cedric Errol Fauntleroy in the Frances Hodgson Burnett novel *Little Lord Fauntleroy* (1886) – an association that did much to destroy the name's attractiveness for many people in the 20th century – and British actor Sir Cedric Hardwicke (1893–1964).

Cedrych *See* CEDRIC.

Cees *See* CORNELIUS.

Ceinwen (f) Welsh first name (pronounced 'Kane-wen') derived from *cain* ('fair') and *gwen* ('white' or 'blessed') and sometimes interpreted as meaning 'beautiful gems'. Well-known bearers of the name have included a 5th-century Welsh saint.

Celeste (f) English first name derived via the masculine French name Céleste from the Roman Caelistis, itself from the Latin *caelestis* ('heavenly'). It was taken up by English speakers in the 20th century, though only as a name for girls. Variants include **Celestina** and **Celestine** (in which form it was borne by five popes).

Celestina/Celestine *See* CELESTE.

Celia (f) English and Italian first name derived from the Roman Caelia, itself probably from the Latin *caelum* ('heaven'), but often also treated as a diminutive of CECILIA. Although records of the name go back to the 16th century, it only became popular among English speakers in the 19th century and has continued in modest use ever since, with a minor peak in popularity in the 1950s. Notable bearers of the name have included characters in William Shakespeare's comedy *As You Like It* (1599) and Ben Jonson's *Volpone* (1605–6) and British actresses Dame Celia Johnson (1908–82) and Celia Imre (b.1952). Variants include the French **Célie** and the German **Silke**. *See also* CÉLINE; SHEILA.

Célina *See* CÉLINE; SELINA.

Céline (f) French first name derived from the Roman Caelina, itself probably from the Latin *caelum* ('heaven'). Often treated as an elaboration of CELIA or as a diminutive of **Marcelline**. Variants include **Célina**. *See also* SELINA.

Celso (m) Italian and Spanish first name (pronounced 'kelso') derived from the Roman Celsus, itself from the Latin *celsus* ('tall'). It was borne by a number of early saints. It is also in use in Ireland where it is often regarded as an equivalent of the Gaelic **Ceallagh**.

Cenydd *See* KENNETH.

Cera (f) Irish first name of obscure meaning. Pronounced 'keera', it was borne by a queen of ancient Irish legend as well as by three Irish saints. Also encountered in the variant form **Ceara**.

Cerdic *See* CEDRIC.

Ceri (f) Welsh first name derived from the Welsh *caru* ('to love'), and thus interpreted as meaning 'loved one', but also often encountered as a diminutive form of CERIDWEN or as a variant of KERRY. It is a relatively recent introduction that does not appear to have been in use before the 1940s.

Still largely confined to the Welsh community.

Ceridwen (f) Welsh first name derived from the Welsh *cerdd* ('poetry') and *gwen* ('white' or 'blessed') and thus interpreted as meaning 'poetically fair'. It was borne by the Celtic goddess of poetical inspiration and mother of the legendary poet Taliesin and is still in occasional use today, although rare outside Wales itself. Sometimes abbreviated to CERI.

Cerys *See* CARYS.

Cesar/Cesare *See* CAESAR.

Chad (m) English first name derived from the Old English Ceadda, possibly based on the Celtic *cad* ('battle' or 'warrior'). Borne by the 7th-century St Chad, Archbishop of York, it became widely known in the 1940s through graffiti drawings featuring a character called Chad and subsequently enjoyed a modest peak in popularity as a first name during the 1970s, chiefly in the USA. Notable bearers of the name have included the Revd Chad Varah (b.1911), British founder of the Samaritans organization.

Chae *See* CHARLES.

Chaim (m) Jewish first name (pronounced 'hyim') derived from the Hebrew Hyam, itself from the Hebrew *hayyim* ('life'). It is in fairly common use within Jewish communities around the world, especially in the USA. Israeli President Chaim Herzog (1918–97) ranks among the more famous bearers of the name. Variants include the feminine equivalent **Chaya**.

Chance (m) English first name derived from the ordinary vocabulary word denoting fortune or luck.

Chandan (m) Indian first name derived from the Sanskrit *candana* ('sandalwood'). Extracts of sandalwood have special significance among Hindus, who use the perfume in religious ceremonies.

Chander *See* CHANDRA.

Chandler (m) English surname, denoting

a maker of candles, that has made occasional appearances as a first name in recent times. It enjoyed a boost in the late 1990s as the name of one of the flatmates in the popular US television series *Friends*. Other notable bearers of the name have included the US author Joel Chandler Harris (1848–1908), creator of the *Uncle Remus* tales.

Chandra (m/f) Indian first name derived from the Sanskrit *candra* ('moon') and thus often interpreted as meaning 'shining'. Variants include **Candra** and **Chander**.

Chandrakant (m) Indian first name derived from the Sanskrit *candra* ('moon') and *kanta* ('beloved') and thus interpreted as meaning 'beloved of the moon'. Variants include the feminine **Chandrakanta**.

Chanel (f) French first name derived from the surname of French couturier and perfumier Coco Chanel (1883–1971). Also encountered in the variant forms **Shanel** and **Shanelle**.

Chantal (f) French first name derived from the Old Provençal *cantal* ('stone' or 'boulder') but popularly associated with the French *chant* ('song'). English speakers took up the name in the 20th century and it may be encountered today within English-speaking communities all over the world. It has enjoyed particular popularity among French-speaking Canadians. In France the name is well known as the surname of the French saint Jeanne-Françoise de Chantal (1572–1641), co-founder of an order of nuns. Variants include **Chantale**, **Chantalle**, **Chantelle**, **Shantel** and **Shantelle**.

Chantale/Chantalle/Chantelle
See CHANTAL.

Chapman (m) English surname denoting a merchant or pedlar that has been in occasional use as a first name over the years. Notable bearers of the name have included British journalist and novelist Chapman Pincher (Henry Chapman Pincher; b.1914).

Chardonnay (f) English first name alluding to the celebrated Chardonnay wine. The name enjoyed a boost in Britain in 2001 with the screening of the popular television series *Footballers' Wives*, which featured a character of that name. Also found as **Chardonay**.

Charis (f) English first name derived from the Greek *kharis* ('grace') and pronounced 'kariss'. Borne in classical mythology by one of the three Graces, it was taken up by English speakers in the 17th century alongside numerous other 'virtue' names that became popular among Puritans on both sides of the Atlantic. In the variant form **Charissa** (possibly influenced by CLARISSA) it made an early appearance in Edmund Spenser's epic *The Faerie Queen* (1590). It has continued to make irregular appearances into modern times, although it has never been in common use.

Charissa *See* CHARIS.

Charity (f) English first name derived from the ordinary vocabulary word 'charity'. It was among the many 'virtue' names that were taken up with some enthusiasm by English Puritans after the Reformation and was often bestowed alongside FAITH and HOPE (although it is now much less common than these). Notable bearers of the name have included the fictional Charity Pecksniff in the Charles Dickens novel *Martin Chuzzlewit* (1843–4). CHERRY and **Chattie** are diminutive forms of the name. Variants in other languages include the Spanish **Caridad**, the Portuguese **Caridade** and the Scandinavian **Karita**.

Charlene (f) English first name (pronounced 'sharleen') that developed as a feminine variant of CHARLES. It is a relatively recent coinage, dating only to the middle of the 20th century. It enjoyed a peak in popularity in the 1980s when it became widely known as the name of the character played by Kylie Minogue in the popular Australian soap opera *Neighbours*. Commonly abbreviated to **Charlie**,

Charley or **Charly**. Variants include **Charleen**, **Charline** and **Sharlene**.

Charles (m) English and French first name derived ultimately from the Old German *karl* ('free man'). Also encountered in Ireland as an Anglicization of CEARBHALL. It was in occasional use among English speakers during the medieval period but did not become generally popular until the 16th century when Mary, Queen of Scots imported the name from France, giving it to her son Charles James Stuart who became King James VI of Scotland and I of England. It reached a peak in frequency between the middle of the 19th century and the early 20th century. It has remained in general use throughout the English-speaking world to the present day, with a recent peak from the 1980s. It is well known as a royal name, having been borne by the Holy Roman Emperor Charlemagne (otherwise known as Charles the Great or Carolus Magnus; *c.*742–814) as well as two kings of England, ten kings of France, the Scottish pretender Bonnie Prince Charlie (Charles Edward Stuart; 1720–88), and in more recent times the current heir to the British throne Prince Charles (b.1948).

Other notable bearers of the name over the centuries have included such luminaries as Dr Charles Primrose in the Oliver Goldsmith novel *The Vicar of Wakefield* (1766), British novelist Charles Dickens (1812–70), French poet Charles Baudelaire (1821–67), British-born US film comedian Charlie Chaplin (Charles Spencer Chaplin; 1889–1977) and French President Charles de Gaulle (1890–1970). Among familiar forms of the name are **Charlie**, **Chas**, **Chaz**, CHUCK and CHICK. Variants in other languages include the Scottish **Chae** or **Chay**, as borne by British lone yachtsman Chay Blyth (Charles Blyth; b.1940), the German CARL and **Karl**, the Italian **Carlo**, the Spanish and Portuguese **Carlos**, the Polish **Karol**, the Dutch **Karel**, the Hungarian **Karoly** and the Finnish **Kaarle**. *See also* CAROL.

Charley *See* CHARLENE; CHARLOTTE.

Charlie *See* CHARLENE; CHARLES; CHARLOTTE.

Charline *See* CHARLENE.

Charlotte (f) English and French first name (pronounced 'sharlot') derived from the Italian Carlotta, itself a feminine variant of Carol (*see* CHARLES). English speakers took up the name as early as the 17th century and it became a particularly frequent choice in the 18th and 19th centuries. It has continued in general use at a rather reduced level ever since, with a relatively recent peak in popularity in the 1970s. Notable bearers of the name have included Charlotte Sophia of Mecklenburg-Strelitz (1744–1818), who was the wife of George III, British novelists Charlotte Brontë (1816–55) and Charlotte M. Yonge (1823–1901) and British actress Charlotte Rampling (b.1946). Diminutive forms of the name include **Charley**, **Charlie**, **Charly**, **Chattie**, **Lotta**, **Lottie**, **Lotty**, **Tottie** and **Totty**. Among variants are **Charlotta**, the German **Karlotte** and the rare **Sharlott**.

Charlton (m) English place name derived from the Old English *ceorl* ('free man') and *tun* ('settlement'), and thus interpreted as meaning 'settlement of free men', that was subsequently taken up as a surname and, from the 19th century, as an occasional first name. The most famous bearer of the name to date has been the US film actor Charlton Heston (John Charlton Carter; b.1924), who inherited it as his mother's maiden name. *See also* CARLTON.

Charly *See* CHARLENE; CHARLOTTE.

Charmaine (f) English first name (pronounced 'sharmain') that is thought to have evolved either as a variant of CHARMIAN or else from the ordinary vocabulary word 'charm'. It became fairly popular among English speakers around the middle of the 20th century, promoted by the popular song 'Charmaine' (1926). Variants include **Charmain**, **Sharmain**, **Sharmaine** and **Sharmane**.

Charmian (f) English first name derived from the Greek Kharmion, itself from the Greek *kharma* ('joy' or 'delight'). It was in use among English speakers by the 16th century, when it became more widely known as the name of Cleopatra's lady-in-waiting in William Shakespeare's *Antony and Cleopatra* (1606–7). *See also* CHARMAINE.

Charo *See* ROSARIO.

Chas *See* CHARLES.

Chase (m) English surname that has made occasional appearances as a first name, chiefly in the USA. It came originally from the ordinary vocabulary word 'chase' and was in use in medieval times as a nickname for a hunter.

Chastity (f) English first name that was among the 'virtue' names that were adopted by Puritans on both sides of the Atlantic in the 17th century. Like PRUDENCE and TEMPERANCE it has continued to make occasional appearances in modern times.

Chattie *See* CHARITY; CHARLOTTE.

Chauncey (m) English surname of uncertain Norman French origin that has been in occasional use as a first name among English speakers since the 13th century. Today it is found chiefly in the USA, where it has made rare appearances over the years in tribute to a number of famous early Americans to bear it as a surname, including Harvard College President Charles Chauncy (1592–1672). Also found as **Chauncy**.

Chay *See* CHARLES.

Chaya *See* CHAIM.

Chaz *See* CHARLES.

Chelle *See* MICHELLE.

Chelo *See* CONSUELO.

Chelsea (f) English place name (from central London) meaning 'landing-place for limestone' that was taken up as a first name among English speakers from the 1950s, initially in Australia and the USA but later more widely throughout the English-speaking world. The popularity of the name in the 1960s reflected Chelsea's (and London's) fame as a fashion centre and the birthplace of the 'swinging sixties'. It enjoyed renewed exposure in the 1990s through Chelsea Clinton (b.1980), daughter of US President Bill Clinton. Also encountered as **Chelsie**, presumably under the influence of such names as ELSIE.

Cher (f) French first name (pronounced 'share') derived from the French *chère* ('dear'), but sometimes also employed as a diminutive form of such names as CHERRY and CHERYL. It has made occasional appearances among English speakers since the 1940s and enjoyed a boost in the 1960s through the US pop singer and film actress Cher (Cherilyn Sarkasian LaPierre; b.1946).

Cheralyn/Cherelle *See* CHERYL.

Cherida (f) English first name that appears to have resulted from the combination of CHERYL and PHYLLIDA. It is a relatively recent coinage, possibly influenced by the Spanish *querida* ('dear').

Cherie (f) French first name (pronounced 'sheree') derived from the French *chérie* ('dear one' or 'darling'). It was taken up by English speakers in the 1950s. Well-known bearers of the name have included the British actress Cherie Lunghi (b.1954) and British Prime Minister Tony Blair's wife Cherie Booth (b.1954). Also spelled **Sheree**, **Sheri**, **Sherie** or **Sherry**. *See also* CHER; CHERRY; CHERYL.

Cherill/Cherilyn *See* CHERYL.

Cherish (f) English first name derived from the ordinary vocabulary word 'cherish'. A relatively recent introduction that has yet to win wide acceptance.

Cherry (f) English first name that developed as a diminutive form of such names as CHARITY, CHERIE and CHERYL but is now sometimes treated as a name in its own right and associated with the fruit of the same name. It appeared with increasing regularity among English speakers from the middle of the 19th century but is now rare. Instances of the name in literature have included characters in the George Farquhar play *The Beaux' Stratagem* (1707) and the Charlotte M. Yonge novel *The Daisy Chain* (1856). In the Charles Dickens novel *Martin Chuzzlewit* (1844), the two Pecksniff girls Charity and Mercy are sometimes referred to informally as Cherry and Merry. Variants include **Cherrie** and the fairly uncommon **Cherelle**.

Cheryl (f) English first name (pronounced 'sherril') that is thought to have resulted from the combination of CHERRY and BERYL (or other similar names) perhaps under the influence of CHERIE. It seems to have made early appearances among English speakers in the early years of the 20th century but did not become a frequent choice of name until the 1940s and 1950s, since when it has become much less common. Famous bearers of the name have included US actress Cheryl Ladd (b.1951) and British pop singer and television presenter Cheryl Baker (Rita Crudgington; b.1954). Variants include **Cheryll**, **Cherill**, **Sherill** and **Sheryl**. Among the name's diminutives are various combinations with LYNN, including **Cheralyn**, **Cherilyn** and **Sherilyn**.

Chesney (m) English surname that has been in occasional use as a first name since the beginning of the 20th century. Notable bearers of the name have included British comedian Chesney Allen (1894–1982). Commonly abbreviated to **Ches** or **Chet** – as borne by US jazz musician Chet Baker (Chesney Baker; 1929–88).

Chester (m) English place name (from the city of Chester in Cheshire), derived from the Latin *castra* ('camp' or 'fort'), that has made occasional appearances as a first name since the end of the 19th century. Notable bearers of the name have included US President Chester A. Arthur (1830–86). Sometimes abbreviated to **Chet** – as borne by US

country-and-western musician Chet Atkins (Chester Burton Atkins; 1924–2001).

Chet *See* CHESNEY; CHESTER.

Chevonne *See* SIOBHAN.

Chiara *See* CLAIRE.

Chick (m) English first name that is sometimes regarded as a diminutive form of CHARLES or otherwise as a nickname for a youth or person of small build. It appeared with increasing frequency among English speakers from the 19th century, mainly in the USA. Well-known bearers of the name have included US jazz musicians Chick Webb (William Henry Webb; 1909–39) and Chick Corea (Armando Anthony Corea; b.1941).

Chip *See* CHRISTOPHER.

Chiquita (f) Spanish first name meaning 'little one'. It is pronounced 'chickeeta'.

Chita *See* CONCEPCIÓN.

Chloe (f) English first name derived from the Greek Khloe, meaning 'young green shoot', that was first adopted by English speakers in the 17th century. It appeared in Greek mythology as an alternative name for the Greek goddess of agriculture Demeter and featured in the legend of *Daphnis and Chloe* (later turned into a ballet by Maurice Ravel), but owed its adoption in post-Reformation England to its appearance in the Bible as the name of a convert of St Paul. The name did not appear with much frequency in the English-speaking world until the 20th century, although it was not uncommon among Black slaves in the USA in the 19th century – as shown by its appearance in the Harriet Beecher Stowe novel *Uncle Tom's Cabin* (1852), in which it is the name of Uncle Tom's wife. It enjoyed a recent peak in popularity in the 1990s. Notable instances of the name in literature have included a shepherdess bearing the name in the prose romance *Arcadia* (1590) by Sir Philip Sidney. Sometimes abbreviated to **Clo**. Also spelled **Chlöe**.

Chloris (f) Greek name derived from *khloros* ('green' or 'fresh'). Representing fertility, it appears in the poetry of the Roman poet Horace and was consequently taken up by English poets in the 17th and 18th centuries. Also encountered as **Cloris**.

Chris (m/f) English first name that developed as a diminutive form of various longer names, including the masculine CHRISTOPHER and CHRISTIAN and the feminine CHRISTINE, CHRISTABEL and CRYSTAL. This shortened version of the name appeared with increasing regularity from the end of the 19th century and enjoyed a peak in popularity in the 1950s and 1960s. Well-known bearers of the name have included British mountaineer Chris Bonington (b.1934), Irish pop singer Chris De Burgh (b.1948), US tennis player Chris Lloyd (Christine Evert; b.1954) and British television presenter Chris Tarrant (b.1946). Variants of the masculine form of the name include **Kris** – as borne by the US pop singer and film actor Kris Kristofferson (b.1936). Variants of the feminine form of the name include **Chrissie** and **Chrissy** – as borne by US-born British rock singer Chrissie Hynde (b.1951)

Chrissie/Chrissy See CHRIS.

Christa See CHRISTINA; CHRISTINE.

Christabel (f) English first name derived from the Latin *Christus* ('Christ') and *bella* ('beautiful') and thus interpreted as meaning 'beautiful Christian'. It made its first appearance among English speakers as early as the 16th century and became popular following the publication of Samuel Taylor Coleridge's poem *Christabel* (1797), although it is relatively rare today. Notable bearers of the name have included British suffragette Christabel Pankhurst (1880–1958). Commonly abbreviated to CHRIS, **Chrissie**, **Chrissy**, **Christie**, **Christy**, BELLA or **Belle**. Variants include **Christobel**, **Christabelle** and **Christabella**.

Christelle See CRYSTAL.

Christen See CHRISTINE.

Christian (m) English first name derived from the Roman Christianus, itself from the Latin for 'Christian'. It was taken up by English speakers in the 17th century, since when it has continued in irregular use. Its adoption in the English-speaking world was promoted through Christian, the allegorical central character in John Bunyan's *The Pilgrim's Progress* (1678, 1684). Famous bearers of the name have included the Danish writer Hans Christian Andersen (1805–75), French couturier Christian Lacroix (b.1951) and US actor Christian Slater (b.1967). Sometimes abbreviated to CHRIS. Variants in other languages include the German **Carsten** or **Karsten** and the Scandinavian **Kristen** or **Kristian** – as borne by ten kings of Denmark, Sweden and Norway. See also CHRISTIANA.

Christiana (f) Feminine variant of CHRISTIAN. It seems to have made its first appearances among English speakers in the 17th century, at much the same time that the masculine version of the name was adopted. It remained in fairly common currency until the end of the 19th century but has since become very rare, under pressure from CHRISTINE. Commonly abbreviated to CHRIS or **Christie** (or **Christy**). Variants include **Christiania** and **Christianna**. See also CHRISTINA.

Christie See CHRISTABEL; CHRISTIANA; CHRISTINE.

Christina (f) English first name that developed as a variant of CHRISTIANA. It was taken up alongside the older form of the name as early as the 18th century and is still in occasional use today, although it has been eclipsed to a large extent since the beginning of the 20th century by CHRISTINE. Famous bearers of the name have included the British poet Christina Rossetti (1830–94) and Greek-born US businesswoman Christina Onassis (1950–88). Diminutive forms of the name include CHRIS, **Christa**, KIRSTY and TINA. Variants in other languages include **Kristina**, the

Italian, Spanish and Portuguese **Cristina** and the Polish **Krystyna**.

Christine (f) English and French first name derived via CHRISTINA from CHRISTIANA. This modern variant of the name established itself among English speakers towards the end of the 19th century. It reached a peak in frequency in the 1950s and has since experienced a gradual decline in popularity. Notable bearers of the name have included British tennis player Christine Truman (b.1941). Commonly abbreviated to CHRIS, **Chrissie**, **Chrissy**, **Christa**, **Christie**, **Christy** or KIRSTY. Variants include **Christen**, **Kristen**, **Kristin**, **Kristine** the Scandinavian KIRSTEN (now in common use among English speakers) and the Welsh **Crystin**.

Christmas (m) English surname based on the name of the festival that has made rare appearances as a first name since the 13th century, usually reserved for children born on Christmas Day itself. There is a character called Christmas Evans in the Richard Llewellyn novel *How Green was My Valley* (1939). *See also* CAROL; NATALIE; NOEL.

Christobel *See* CHRISTABEL.

Christopher (m) English first name derived from the Greek Khristophoros, itself from the Greek *Khristos* ('Christ') and *pherein* ('to bear') and thus interpreted as meaning 'bearing Christ' – a reference to the legend of St Christopher, who carried the boy Jesus over a stream and thus became the patron saint of travellers. Popular among early Christians, the name was taken up by English speakers around the 13th century and has continued in regular use ever since, becoming relatively infrequent in the 19th century but reviving to enjoy a peak in popularity around the middle of the 20th century.

Famous bearers of the name have included Genoese-born explorer Christopher Columbus (1451–1506), English playwright Christopher Marlowe (1564–93), English architect Sir Christopher Wren (1632–1723), British-born US novelist Christopher Isherwood (1904–86), British playwright Christopher Fry (b.1907), the fictional Christopher Robin in the *Winnie-the-Pooh* stories of A. A. Milne and Canadian actor Christopher Plummer (b.1927). Familiar forms of the name include CHRIS, **Christy**, **Kit** and **Chip**. Variants in other languages include the French **Christophe**, the German **Christoph**, the Italian **Cristoforo**, the Spanish **Cristóbal**, the Scandinavian **Kristoffer**, the Czech **Krystof** and the Polish **Krzysztof**. *See also* KESTER.

Christy *See* CHRISTINE; CHRISTOPHER.

Chrystal/Chrystalla *See* CRYSTAL.

Chucho *See* JESUS.

Chuck (m) English first name that developed as a diminutive form of CHARLES but which is also used informally as a term of endearment. It can be traced back to the Old English *chukken* (to cluck). It has been in common use among English speakers in the USA since the 19th century. Famous bearers of the name have included US pop singer Chuck Berry (Charles Edward Berry; b.1926). Variants include **Chuckie**.

Chus *See* JESUS.

Ciabhan (m) Irish first name derived from the Irish Gaelic for 'full-haired'. Pronounced 'keevan', it is sometimes Anglicized as **Keevan**.

Cian (m) Irish name (pronounced 'kain' or 'keern') derived from the Gaelic for 'ancient'. It appears in Irish mythology as the name of the son-in-law of Brian Boru. Also encountered as KEAN or **Keane**. **Ciannait** is a feminine form of the name.

Ciannait *See* CIAN.

Ciara/Ciaran *See* KIERAN.

Cibor *See* CZCIBOR.

Cicely *See* CECILIA.

Cilla (f) English first name that developed as a diminutive of PRISCILLA and of the less frequent DRUSILLA. It seems to have made its first appearances among English speakers around the middle of the 20th century. It has become particularly well known in the UK through the British pop singer and television presenter Cilla Black (Priscilla White; b.1943).

Cillian *See* KILLIAN.

Cimmie *See* CYNTHIA.

Cinderella (f) English version of the French Cendrillon, meaning 'little cinders'. Best known from the classic fairy tale *Cinderella*, it has made occasional appearances as a first name, usually reserved for children with rather dull surnames. CINDY is a diminutive form of the name.

Cindy (f) English first name that developed as a diminutive form of such names as CYNTHIA, LUCINDA and even CINDERELLA but which is now often encountered as a name in its own right. It began to appear with increasing frequency among English speakers in the 1950s and is now fairly common. Well known bearers of the name have included US model Cindy Crawford (b.1966). Variants include **Cindie**, **Cindi**, **Cyndi** – as borne by US pop singer Cyndi Lauper (b.1953) – and **Sindy** (best known as the brand name for a popular make of children's dolls).

Cinzia *See* CYNTHIA.

Cipriano (m) Italian name (pronounced 'chipreearno') derived from the Roman Cyprianus, itself from the Latin for 'person from Cyprus'. It was borne by a number of early Christian saints and has continued in use among Italians ever since, although it has never won acceptance among English speakers.

Ciriaco (m) Italian and Spanish name (pronounced 'chireeako') derived via the Roman Cyriacus from the Greek Kyriakos from *kyrios* ('lord'). It became a popular choice of early Christians and was borne by several minor saints.

Cis/Ciss *See* CISSIE.

Cissie (f) English first name that developed as a diminutive form of FRANCES and CECILIA and its variants. English speakers began to use the name in the 19th century and it remained common until the 1930s, since when it has become much more rare, partly because the ordinary vocabulary word 'sissy' has come to mean 'effeminate' or 'weak'. Commonly abbreviated to **Cis** or **Ciss**. Also found as **Cissy**, **Sissie** or **Sissy** – as borne by US film actress Sissy Spacek (Mary Elizabeth Spacek; b.1949).

Cissy *See* CECILIA; CISSIE.

Claire (f) English and French first name derived from the Roman **Clara**, itself from the Latin *clarus* ('clear' or 'pure'). It came to England with the Normans in the 11th century but remained infrequent among English speakers until the 19th century, during which time it usually appeared as **Clare** – as borne by the 13th-century St Clare of Assisi, founder of the Franciscan order of the 'Poor Clares'. In the French form Claire, the name was at its most common in the 1970s, since when it appears to have lost ground. Well-known bearers of the name in its various forms have included US writer and politician Clare Boothe Luce (1903–87), US actress Claire Luce (1904–89), British actress Claire Bloom (b.1931), British 'agony aunt' Claire Rayner (b.1931) and British politician Clare Short (b.1946). Also found as **Clair** or, more rarely, **Clarette** or **Claretta**. Variants in other languages include the Italian **Chiara**. *See also* CLARA.

Clancy (m) English and Irish first name that developed variously from the Irish surname Mac Fhlannchaidh ('son of Flannchadh') or else as a diminutive of CLARENCE. It was taken up by English speakers in the 19th century, chiefly in the USA. Also spelled **Clancey**.

Clara (f) English, German and Italian first name derived ultimately from the Latin *clarus* ('clear' or 'pure') that was taken up in the English-speaking world as a Latinized version of the already accepted CLARE (*see* CLAIRE). In Scotland it is sometimes considered to be an Anglicized form of SORCHA. It became popular among English speakers in the 19th century but has declined somewhat since the beginning of the 20th century. Notable bearers of the name have included the fictional Clara Peggotty in the Charles Dickens novel *David Copperfield* (1849–50), British singer Dame Clara Butt (1872–1936) and US film actress Clara Bow (1905–65). **Clarrie** is a diminutive form of the name. Variants in other languages include the German **Klara**. *See also* CLARIBEL; CLARICE; CLARINDA.

Clare *See* CLAIRE.

Clarence (m) English name meaning 'of Clare' that was adopted in the 14th century as a ducal title, appearing subsequently as a surname and, from the 19th century, winning acceptance as an occasional first name. The original ducal title was created by Edward III in 1362 when his third son, Lionel, married the heiress of Clare in Suffolk. Its use among English speakers towards the end of the 19th century owed much to the desire to pay tribute to Edward VII's son Albert Victor, Duke of Clarence (1864–92), whose premature death attracted public sympathy. It has, however, generally proved more popular in the USA than it has in the UK over the years. Other notable bearers of the name have included US lawyer Clarence Darrow (1857–1938) and US blues musician Clarence Brown (b.1924). Commonly abbreviated to **Clarrie** and less frequently to CLANCY.

Clarette *See* CLAIRE.

Claribel (f) English first name that resulted from the combination of CLARA and such names as ANNABEL and ISABEL. It was adopted as a literary name in the 16th century, when notable instances of its use included a character in Edmund Spenser's epic poem *The Faerie Queene* (1590, 1596) and the Queen of Tunis in William Shakespeare's play *The Tempest* (1611), but is rare today.

Clarice (f) English and French name derived from the Roman Claritia, itself from the Latin *clara* ('clear' or 'pure') or else from the Latin *clarus* ('famous' or 'renowned'). It was taken up by English speakers in medieval times and revived towards the end of the 19th century but has since become very rare. Famous bearers of the name have included a character in the legends of Roland and Charlemagne and the British ceramic designer Clarice Cliff (1899–1972). *See also* CLARISSA.

Clarinda (f) English first name that appears to have resulted from the combination of CLARA and BELINDA, LUCINDA or other similar names. It was taken up by English speakers in the late 16th century, appearing possibly for the first time as the name of a character in Edmund Spenser's epic poem *The Faerie Queene* (1590, 1596). Spenser's choice of name may have been influenced by the already extant **Clorinda**, which appears in Torquato Tasso's *Gerusalemme Liberata* (1580). Thus established as a literary name, it reappeared in many other notable works of literature over the following 200 years. It enjoyed a peak in popularity in the 18th century, when it was further popularized by Robert Burns' love poems published as *To Clarinda* (1787) – the name the poet used for his close friend Agnes McLehose. The name has appeared only rarely since the early 19th century and is virtually unknown today.

Clarissa (f) English first name derived from CLARICE. The name was recorded in use in medieval times and became very well known in the 18th century through the Samuel Richardson novel *Clarissa* (1748). It has remained in occasional use ever since. Notable bearers of the name since the 18th century have included a character in the Charles Dickens novel *David Copperfield* (1849–50) and Clarissa Dalloway in the Virginia Woolf novel *Mrs Dalloway* (1925). Sometimes abbreviated to **Clarrie**, **Clarry** or **Claris**. Variants in other languages include the Spanish **Clarisa**.

Clark (m) English surname denoting a clerk or secretary that has been in occasional use as a first name since the end of the 19th century, chiefly in the USA. Well-known bearers of the name have included US film actor Clark Gable (William Clark Gable; 1901–60) and the fictional Clark Kent, the assumed identity of the US comic-strip superhero Superman. Also encountered as **Clarke**.

Clarrie See CLARA; CLARENCE; CLARISSA.

Clarry See CLARISSA.

Claud See CLAUDE.

Claude (m) English and French first name descended from the Roman Claudius, itself derived from the Latin *claudus* ('lame'). It was borne early in its history by several saints, the most notable of whom was the 7th-century St Claude of Besançon, whose fame brought the name lasting popularity in France (where it has been used for both sexes). It was taken up by English speakers during the 16th century and was at its most frequent towards the end of the 19th century but fell from favour around the middle of the 20th century. Notable bearers of the name have included French artists Claude Lorraine (1600–1682) and Claude Monet (1840–1926), French composer Claude Debussy (1862–1918) and British actor Claude Rains (1889–1967). Occasionally encountered as **Claud**. Variants in other languages include the Italian, Spanish and Portuguese **Claudio**.

Claudette See CLAUDIA.

Claudia (f) English, French and German first name descended ultimately from the Roman Claudius, itself derived from the Latin *claudus* ('lame'). It appears in the Bible as the name of a Roman woman mentioned in one of Paul's letters and seems to have made its first appearances among English speakers during the 16th century. It has remained in irregular use ever since, with a recent peak in popularity since the 1980s. In Wales it is sometimes treated as an equivalent of GLADYS. Notable bearers of the name have included Italian actress Claudia Cardinale (b.1939) and German model Claudia Schiffer (b.1971). Variants in other languages include the French **Claudette** (also in use among English speakers since the early 20th century) – as borne by the French-born US actress Claudette Colbert (1905–96) – and **Claudine** – as borne by the heroine of a series of novels written by the French writer Colette (1873–1954) in the years 1900–1903. *See also* CLODAGH.

Claudine See CLAUDIA.

Claudio See CLAUDE.

Claudius See CLAUDE; CLAUDIA.

Claus (m) German first name (pronounced 'klaowce') that evolved from Niclaus or Niklaus (*see* NICHOLAS). English speakers know the name best as that of Father Christmas, or Santa Claus ('Saint Claus'). Also encountered as **Klaus**, the Dutch **Klaas** and the Finnish **Launo**.

Clay See CLAYTON.

Clayton (m) English place name (shared by several places in north and central England) that was subsequently adopted as a surname and has been in use since the early 19th century as an occasional first name. The original place name came from the Old English *claeg* ('clay') and *tun* ('settlement'). **Clay** is a diminutive form.

Cledwyn (m) Welsh name derived from the Welsh *caled* ('hard' or 'rough') and *gwyn* ('white' or 'blessed').

Clelia (f) English and Italian name descended from the Roman Cloelia. It appears in Roman mythology as the name of a legendary heroine who escaped capture by the Etruscans.

Clem See CLEMENT; CLEMENTINA.

Clement (m) English first name derived from the Latin *clemens* ('merciful'). Borne by several early saints and by no less than fourteen popes, it was in common currency among English speakers during the medieval period and is still in use, although it has become very rare. Notable bearers of the name have included the fictional Sir Clement Willoughby in the Fanny Burney novel *Evelina* (1778), British Prime Minister Clement Attlee (1883–1967) and British politician, food writer and media personality Clement Freud (b.1924). Commonly abbreviated to **Clem**. Variants include **Clemence**, the French **Clément**, the German **Klemens**, the Hungarian **Kelemen**, the Russian and Czech **Kliment** and the Italian, Spanish and Portuguese **Clemente**. *See also* CLEMENTINA.

Clementina (f) English first name that developed as a feminine version of CLEMENT. It seems to have made its first appearances among English speakers in the 17th century but has been rarely encountered since the early part of the 20th century. Famous bearers of the name have included a character in the George Eliot novel *Daniel Deronda* (1876). The French variant **Clementine** has also made occasional appearances among English speakers and is best known as the name of Lady Clementine Spencer-Churchill (1885–1977), wife of British Prime Minister Winston Churchill. Diminutive forms of the name include **Clem**, **Clemmie**, **Clemmy** and **Cleo** – as borne by British jazz singer Cleo Laine (Clementine Dinah Campbell; b.1927). Variants in other languages include the Polish **Klementyna**.

Clementine/Clemmie/Clemmy
See CLEMENTINA.

Cleo *See* CLEMENTINA; CLEOPATRA.

Cleopatra (f) English version of the Greek Kleopatra, derived from the Greek *kleos* ('glory') and *pater* ('father') and thus interpreted as meaning 'father's glory', which has made occasional appearances among English speakers over the centuries. Universally associated with the historical queen of Egypt famed for her liaisons with Julius Caesar and Mark Antony, it has proved fairly popular within the Black community in the USA. Commonly abbreviated to **Cleo**.

Clidna See CLIONA.

Cliff (m) English first name that developed as a diminutive of CLIFFORD, although it is also sometimes encountered in use as an abbreviated form of CLIFTON. It was taken up by English speakers early in the 20th century and enjoyed a peak in popularity in the late 1950s and 1960s, largely in response to the popularity of British pop singer Cliff Richard (Harold Webb; b.1940). Other well-known bearers of the name have included British broadcaster Cliff Michelmore (b.1919) and Canadian snooker player Cliff Thorburn (b.1948).

Clifford (m) English place name (common to the counties of Gloucestershire, Herefordshire and Yorkshire) that was subsequently taken up as a surname and adopted as a first name in the 19th century. The original place name came from the Old English *clif* ('cliff' or 'riverbank') and *ford* ('ford') and can thus be interpreted as meaning 'ford by a slope'. It enjoyed a peak in popularity in the first half of the 20th century, especially in the USA, but has become much less common since then. Notable bearers of the name have included US playwright Clifford Odets (1906–63) and British pianist Sir Clifford Curzen (1907–82). Commonly abbreviated to CLIFF.

Clifton (m) English place name (common to several English counties) that was subsequently taken up as a surname and from the 19th century as a first name, chiefly in the USA. The original place name came from the Old English *clif* ('cliff' or 'riverbank') and *tun* ('settlement') and can thus be interpreted as meaning 'town on a cliff'. Sometimes abbreviated to CLIFF.

Clint (m) English first name derived from the surname Clinton (also in occasional use as a first name) that has enjoyed modest popularity among English speakers on both sides of the Atlantic since the early 20th century. The original surname may have come from the same source as CLIFTON, thus meaning 'town on a cliff', although another suggestion is that it began as a place name meaning 'headland farm'. It was adopted initially by English speakers in the USA in tribute to the notable Clinton family, which produced two early governors of New York, but is today usually identified with the US film actor and director Clint Eastwood (b.1930), whose popularity in the 'spaghetti westerns' of the 1960s and 1970s brought the name new exposure. Other bearers of the name in recent times include US country musician Clint Black (b.1962).

Clinton *See* CLINT.

Clio (f) English first name descended from the Greek Kleio, itself derived from the Greek *kleos* ('glory' or 'praise'). Borne in classical mythology by one of the Muses, it is sometimes encountered today as a variant of **Cleo** and thus regarded as a diminutive form of CLEOPATRA.

Cliona (f) Irish first name derived from the Gaelic Cliodhna (or Clidna). Borne in Irish legend by a beautiful fairy princess, it was taken up with some enthusiasm as a first name in the 20th century, although chiefly confined to the Irish community.

Clitus (m) English first name descended from the Greek Kleitos, which may itself have come from the Greek *kleos* ('glory'). Borne by one of Alexander the Great's generals, it has made occasional appearances as a first name in modern times, chiefly in the USA.

Clive (m) English place name (common to several English counties) that was subsequently taken up as a surname and seems to have been adopted as a first name around the middle of the 19th century. The original place name was based on the Old English *clif* ('cliff' or 'riverbank') and as a surname meant 'dweller by the cliff'. Perhaps the earliest bearer of the name was the fictional Clive Newcombe in the William Makepeace Thackeray novel *The Newcomes* (1853–5),

who was apparently named after the British soldier and colonial administrator Robert Clive (1725–74), better known as 'Clive of India'. The name continued in fairly regular use into the 20th century, enjoying a peak in popularity in the 1950s before going out of fashion. Notable bearers of the name since then have included Australian-born British broadcaster and writer Clive James (b.1939) and British television presenter Clive Anderson (b.1953).

Clo *See* CHLOE; CLODAGH.

Clodagh (f) Irish first name (pronounced 'cloda') derived from that of a river in County Tipperary, Ireland. A relatively recent introduction that appears to have begun with the bestowal of the name upon the daughter of the Marquis of Waterford early in the 20th century, it is sometimes treated as an Irish equivalent of CLAUDIA. It has made occasional appearances elsewhere in the English-speaking world but has retained its essentially Irish associations. It received a boost in the early 1970s as the name of Northern Ireland pop singer Clodagh Rogers (b.1947). Sometimes abbreviated to **Clo**.

Clorinda *See* CLARINDA.

Clothilde *See* CLOTILDA.

Clotilda (f) English version of the French Clothilde, which was itself derived from the Old German *hlod* ('famous' or 'loud') and *hild* ('battle'). It became widely known as the name of a 5th-century Burgundian princess who became the wife of King Clovis and persuaded him to convert to Christianity. It enjoyed a modest peak in popularity among English speakers in the 19th century but has never been in very common use. Variants include **Clotilde**.

Clover (f) English first name derived from the name of the wild flower. A relatively rare choice of first name (perhaps because it is also a traditional name for a cow), it enjoyed some exposure in the 19th century as the name of a character in the *Katy* books of US children's writer Susan Coolidge, published between 1870 and 1890, including *Clover* (1888). Variants include **Clova**.

Clovis (m) English first name that was taken up in the 19th century as part of the fashion for all things medieval. In its origins it was closely related to LUDWIG and therefore to the later LOUIS. Never a common choice of name, it was borne by the 6th-century Clovis, king of the Franks, and enjoyed renewed exposure early in the 20th century through the collection of short stories entitled *The Chronicles of Clovis* (1911), written by the British author Saki.

Clyde (m) Scottish surname derived from that of the River Clyde in southwest Scotland that was taken up as a first name in Scotland and elsewhere in the 19th century. The name of the river can be interpreted as meaning 'the washer' and is of ancient origin, predating the Roman occupation and possibly having its roots in the name of a local goddess. It established itself fairly early on in its history as a first name as a popular choice among Black Americans (perhaps because many US plantation owners were of Scottish descent) and continued in fairly regular use among both Blacks and Whites through the 20th century. Notable bearers of the name have included US bank robber Clyde Barrow (1900–1934), whose violent career in crime was the subject of the highly successful 1967 film *Bonnie and Clyde*, and the fictional Clyde Griffiths in the Theodore Dreiser novel *An American Tragedy* (1925).

Cody (m/f) English first name that is thought to have evolved from an Irish surname meaning 'descendant of a helpful person'. Although rare in the UK, it has enjoyed some popularity in the USA and elsewhere in the English-speaking world, perhaps through association with the celebrated Wild West hero Buffalo Bill Cody (William Frederick Cody; 1846–1917). Also encountered as **Codey** or **Kody**.

Coinneach (m) Scottish first name (pronounced 'kooinock') derived from the

Gaelic for 'handsome' or 'fair'. It continues in occasional use in Scotland itself but elsewhere has given way to KENNETH.

Cokkie *See* CORNELIA.

Colan *See* COLIN.

Colbert (m) English first name derived from the Old German *col* (of uncertain meaning) and *berht* ('bright' or 'famous'). It was in common use during the medieval period and has made occasional reappearances into modern times.

Cole (m) English surname of uncertain origin that has made occasional appearances as a first name over the years. It may have evolved originally from the Old English *cola* ('swarthy') or else be a variant of NICHOLAS or an abbreviated form of **Coleman** (*see* COLMAN). Old King Cole in the nursery rhyme was originally Coel, a 3rd-century king of Colchester in Essex. The name is best known today as the name of the celebrated US songwriter Cole Porter (1891–1964).

Coleen/Colene *See* COLLEEN.

Coleman *See* COLMAN.

Colette (f) French first name derived from the French Nicolette (*see* NICOLA) that also has a long history as a first name in the English-speaking world, recorded as early as the 13th century. Borne by a 15th-century French saint, it was taken up with increasing regularity among English speakers in the early years of the 20th century, partly in response to the popularity of the French novelist Colette (Sidonie Gabrielle Colette; 1873–1954). Also encountered as **Collette**.

Colin (m) English first name that developed via the medieval diminutive Col from NICHOLAS but is now widely regarded as an independent name. In Scotland it is sometimes considered to be an Anglicization of the Gaelic Cailean, meaning 'puppy' or 'whelp'. It was established among the English by at least the 12th century and remained in common use until the 16th century, by which time it was being thought of as a predominantly rural name – as shown by Edmund Spenser's choice of the name for the shepherd Colin Clout in his pastoral poems *The Shephearde's Calendar* (1579) and *Colin Clouts Come Home Againe* (1595). It fell into disuse in subsequent centuries but enjoyed a revival in the first half of the 20th century and was at its most frequent in the 1950s and 1960s. In Scotland the name is particularly associated with the Campbell clan. Well-known bearers of the name have included British conductor Sir Colin Davis (b.1927), British actor Colin Blakely (1930–87), British cricketer Sir Colin Cowdrey (1932–2000) and British actors Colin Welland (b.1934) and Colin Firth (b.1960). Variants include **Collin**, **Colyn**, the Welsh **Collwyn** and the Irish **Colan**. **Colina**, **Colene**, **Coletta** and **Colinette** are rare feminine versions of the name.

Colina/Colinette *See* COLIN.

Coll (m) Scottish first name derived from the Gaelic Colla, itself from the Old Celtic for 'high'. Sometimes encountered in use as a diminutive of COLIN.

Colleen (f) Irish first name derived from the Gaelic *cailin* ('girl'). Sometimes considered to be a feminine form of COLIN, it was adopted by English speakers in the 19th century, becoming particularly popular in Australia, Canada and the USA from the 1940s. Despite its strong Irish connections it is not very common in Ireland itself. Notable bearers of the name have included British actress Colleen Dewhurst (1926–91) and Australian novelist Colleen McCullough (b.1937). Variants include **Coleen** and **Colene**.

Collette *See* COLETTE.

Colley (m) Irish surname meaning 'swarthy' that has been in occasional use as a first name over the centuries. Famous bearers of the name have included the celebrated 18th-century English actor and playwright Colley Cibber (1671–1757), who inherited it as his mother's maiden name.

Collin/Collwyn *See* COLIN.

Colm *See* COLUM.

Colman (m) Irish first name that developed like COLUM out of the Roman Columba, itself from the Latin for 'dove'. It was borne by several early Irish saints. Also spelled Coleman. Equivalents in other languages include the French **Colombain**, the Italian **Columbano** and the Czech **Kolman**.

Colombe (f) French first name derived from the Roman Columba, from the Latin for 'dove'. Famous bearers of the name have included the 3rd-century French St Colombe of Sens.

Colum (m) Irish first name derived from the Roman Columba, itself from the Latin for 'dove'. Its popularity in Ireland can be traced back to St Columba (521–97), who brought Christianity to the country. Variants include **Colm** and **Colom**.

Columba *See* COLOMBE; COLUM; COLUMBINE.

Columbine (f) English version of the Italian Columbina, itself descended from the Roman Columba, from the Latin for 'dove'. It became well known in France and England as the name of Harlequin's lover in traditional harlequinade entertainments. The name enjoyed some popularity among English speakers in the 19th century, when its association with the flower columbine led to its inclusion among the many flower names that were taken up as first names during that era. (The flower itself was named columbine through a fancied similarity between its petals and a cluster of five doves.)

Comfort (m/f) English first name that enjoyed some popularity among English speakers after the Reformation. It continued to make rare appearances among both sexes into the 19th century but now appears to be defunct.

Con *See* CONNOR; CONRAD; CONSTANCE; CONSTANTINE.

Conal (m) Irish first name derived from the Irish Gaelic for 'wolf' and 'strong' or otherwise meaning 'high mighty'. Notable bearers of the name have included several famous Irish warriors and chieftains. Also spelled **Conall** or, in Scotland, as **Comhnall**.

Conan (m) Irish first name derived from the Irish Gaelic *cu* ('hound' or 'wolf', or otherwise 'high') that was in fairly common use among English speakers between the 12th and 15th centuries and has remained in currency throughout the English-speaking world since a revival in the 19th century. In the USA the name is usually pronounced with a long 'o', whereas the Irish generally prefer a short 'o' ('Connan'). Notable bearers of the name have included several early Celtic saints, the British writer Sir Arthur Conan Doyle (1859–1930), creator of the detective Sherlock Holmes, and the comic-strip hero and film character Conan the Barbarian.

Concepción (f) Spanish first name (pronounced 'konhepthion') derived from a Spanish title for the Virgin Mary (translated as 'Mary of the Immaculate Conception'). The name was popular during the medieval period and is in widespread use today among people of Spanish descent. English speakers have never taken up the name, although it is familiar among Spanish immigrant communities in the English-speaking world. Familiar forms of the name include **Concha** and **Conchita** (and its pet form **Chita**). *See also* IMMACULATA.

Concepta *See* CONCETTA.

Concetta (f) Italian first name (pronounced 'konchetta') derived from *Maria Concetta* ('Mary of the Immaculate Conception'), a title of the Virgin Mary. Variants include the Latinate **Concepta**, a version of the name that became popular among Irish Catholics. Sometimes abbreviated to CONNIE.

Concha/Conchita *See* CONCEPCIÓN.

Conchobar/Conchobhar/Conn
See CONNOR.

Connee *See* CONNIE.

Connie (f) English first name that evolved as a diminutive of CONSTANCE. It is also in occasional use as a familiar form of the Italian CONCETTA. It seems to have made its first appearance among English speakers towards the end of the 19th century. Well-known bearers of the name have included US singer Connie Francis (Concetta Francis; b.1938) and British actress Connie Booth (b.1941). Commonly abbreviated to **Con**. Also spelled **Connee**.

Connor (m) Irish first name derived from the Gaelic Conchobar or Conchobhar, itself thought to mean 'hound lover' or 'wolf lover' and thus usually bestowed originally upon hunters. It appears in mythology as the name of a legendary Irish king. Commonly abbreviated to **Con** or **Conn** (which is, however, sometimes traced back to a different origin and interpreted as meaning 'wisdom'). **Conor** is a modern variant of the name – as borne by Irish writer Conor Cruise O'Brien (b.1917).

Conor *See* CONNOR.

Conrad (m) English version of the German Konrad, itself derived from the Old German *kuon* ('bold') and *rad* ('counsel') and thus interpreted as meaning 'bold counsel'. It was taken up by English speakers during the medieval period and has continued in modest use ever since, with a marked revival in the 19th century. Well-known bearers of the name have included four medieval German kings, the fictional Conrad in the Horace Walpole novel *The Castle of Otranto* (1765), US writer Conrad Aiken (1889–1973) and German-born actor Conrad Veight (1893–1943). Commonly abbreviated to **Con**. Variants include the German **Curt** or KURT.

Conroy (m) English first name derived from the Gaelic for 'wise'.

Consolata *See* CONSUELO.

Constance (f) English and French first name derived from the Roman Constantia, meaning 'constancy' or 'perseverance'. Borne by a daughter of William the Conqueror, it was fairly common among English speakers in the medieval period and enjoyed renewed popularity in the 17th century when the Puritans included it among the numerous 'virtue' names that they selected for their children. The name has remained in currency ever since, although it has become less common since the early 20th century. The Roman form of the name was revived among English speakers in the 19th century but subsequently went out of fashion. Famous bearers of the name have included the fictional Constance Neville in the Oliver Goldsmith comedy *She Stoops to Conquer* (1773), US actress Constance Bennett (1904–65) and US-born British actress Constance Cummings (b.1910). Commonly abbreviated to **Con** or CONNIE. Variants include **Constancy** and **Constantina**.

Constancy *See* CONSTANCE.

Constant (m) English and French first name descended from the Roman Constans, itself from the Latin *constantis* ('constant' or 'steadfast'). Recorded in use during medieval times, it was among the 'virtue' names taken up by Puritans after the Reformation, but had become very rare by the 19th century and is now in infrequent use. Famous bearers of the name have included British composer and conductor Constant Lambert (1905–51). Sometimes shortened to **Con** or CONNIE.

Constantia *See* CONSTANCE.

Constantine (m) English and French version of the Roman Constantinus, itself from the Latin *constantis* ('constant' or 'steadfast'). It was taken up by English speakers in the 19th century in response to renewed interest in classical history but has never been in common use. Notable bearers of the name over the centuries have included the 4th century Roman emperor Constantine the Great, who sanctioned the toler-

ation of Christianity in the Roman Empire, three Scottish kings and two kings of modern Greece. Variants in other languages include the German, Scandinavian and Russian **Konstantin**, the Russian **Kostya** and the Polish **Konstantyn**.

Consuelo (m) Spanish first name derived from a Spanish title for the Virgin Mary, *Nuestra Señora del Consuelo* ('Our Lady of Consolation'). The name enjoyed renewed exposure in France through the George Sand novel *Consuelo* (1842–4). Familiar forms of the name include **Chelo** and **Suelo**. An Italian equivalent is **Consolata**.

Cooper (m) English first name meaning 'barrel maker'. It was in use as a surname before being adopted as a first name. Sometimes abbreviated to **Coop**.

Cor *See* CORNELIUS.

Cora (f) English first name derived from the Greek *kore* ('girl'). In the Greek form Kore, it appeared in classical mythology as an alternative name for Persephone, goddess of the underworld. It became fairly popular in its modern form in the 19th century but has been increasingly uncommon since the early 20th century, with the exception of a modest vogue among Black Americans in the 1930s. Famous bearers of the name have included Cora Munro in the James Fenimore Cooper novel *The Last of the Mohicans* (1826), possibly the very first instance of the name. Variants include **Coretta** – as borne by US civil rights leader Martin Luther King's widow. *See also* CORALIE; CORINNE.

Coral (f) English first name that appears to have been adopted as a result of the fashion for coral jewellery in the late 19th century. It is sometimes suggested, however, that the name can be considered a variant of CORA. It has continued to appear on an irregular basis into modern times. **Cory** is a diminutive form of the name. *See also* CORALIE.

Coralie (f) French first name of uncertain meaning that has also made occasional appearances as a first name among English speakers. It was one of a range of new names that enjoyed some popularity in France in the years immediately following the Revolution of 1789. It is still in fairly selective use, sometimes regarded as a variant of CORA or CORAL (both of which it apparently predates).

Corbin (m) English first name derived from the Old French for 'black-haired' or 'raucous'. Notable bearers of the name include US television actor Corbin Bernsen (b.1954).

Cordelia (f) English first name of obscure origin, possibly a variant of the Celtic Cordula, itself derived from the Latin *cor* ('heart'). Rarely encountered in modern times except in reference to Cordelia, the loving daughter of the king in William Shakespeare's tragedy *King Lear* (1605). Shakespeare himself adapted the name from **Cordeilla**, in which form it appears in Raphael Holinshed's *Chronicles* (1577). Diminutive forms of the name include **Cordy** and DELIA.

Coretta *See* CORA.

Corey (m) English surname of uncertain origin that has made occasional appearances as a first name since the 1960s, chiefly within the Black community in the USA. Also found as **Cory**.

Corin (m) French first name descended from the Roman Quirinus, which may have evolved ultimately from the Sabine *quiris* ('spear'). It was borne by a number of early Christian martyrs and has made irregular appearances as a first name among English speakers in relatively recent times. Notable bearers of the name have included British actor Corin Redgrave (b.1939).

Corinna *See* CORINNE.

Corinne (f) English and French first name derived ultimately from the Greek Korinna, itself probably from the Greek *kore* ('girl'). Promoted by Madame de Staël's novel *Corinne* (1766–1817), it was adopted by

English speakers in the late 19th century, when it was often considered a variant of CORA. The variant **Corinna** – the name of a celebrated 5th-century BC Greek poetess and of the woman to whom the Roman poet Ovid addressed many of his love poems – became well known from Robert Herrick's poem 'Corinna's going a-Maying' (1648) and is still in occasional use.

Cormac (m) Irish first name derived from the Gaelic *corb* ('defilement') and *mac* ('son') or otherwise interpreted as meaning 'charioteer'. It was borne by many notable figures in early Irish history, including a 3rd-century king, and has remained in common currency to the present day, being borne by (among others) Cormac Murphy-O'Connor (b.1932), head of the Roman Catholic Church in Britain. Variants include **Cormick** and the Scottish **Cormag**.

Cormag/Cormick *See* CORMAC.

Cornel *See* CORNELL.

Cornelia (f) English, German and Dutch first name that developed originally as a feminine version of the Roman CORNELIUS. It was adopted by English speakers in the 19th century and has remained in limited currency ever since. Notable bearers of the name have ranged from the 2nd-century BC Roman matron Cornelia, who was the mother of the admired but ill-fated Roman statesmen Caius and Tiberius Gracchus, to the celebrated US actress Cornelia Otis Skinner (1901–79). Diminutive forms of the name include **Cornie**, **Corrie**, **Nellie** and the Dutch **Cokkie**.

Cornelis *See* CORNELIUS.

Cornelius (m) Biblical name of uncertain origin, possibly derived originally from the Latin *cornu* ('horn'). It appears in the Bible as the name of a Roman centurion converted to Christianity by St Peter. It was imported to the English-speaking world from the Netherlands around the 15th century and was at its most frequent in the 19th century, when it became particularly popular among Black Americans. Notable bearers of the name have included a 3rd-century pope, minor characters in William Shakespeare's plays *Hamlet* (1599–1601) and *Cymbeline* (1609–10), US financier Cornelius Vanderbilt (1794–1877) and one of the main characters in the *Babar* stories of Jean de Brunoff (1899–1937). Familiar forms of the name include **Cornie**, **Corney** and **Corny**. Variants in other languages include the Polish and Czech **Kornel**, the French **Corneille** and the Dutch **Cornelis** (sometimes abbreviated to **Cor**, **Cees** or **Kees**). *See also* CORNELIA.

Cornell (m) English surname that has been in occasional use as a first name since the 19th century, chiefly in the USA. It is thought that it may have begun originally as a medieval diminutive of CORNELIUS. **Cornel** is a variant form – as borne by US actor Cornel Wilde (1915–89).

Corney/Cornie/Corny *See* CORNELIUS.

Corrie *See* CORNELIA.

Cory *See* CORAL; COREY.

Cosima/Cosimo *See* COSMO.

Cosmo (m) English, German and Italian first name derived from the Greek Kosmas, itself from the Greek *kosmos* ('order', 'harmony' or 'beauty'). It was introduced to the English-speaking world by the Scottish dukes of Gordon in the 18th century, who encountered it in Tuscany in the Italian form **Cosimo**. Famous bearers of the Italian form of the name over the centuries have included two members of the Florentine Medici family – the financier and statesman Cosimo Medici (1389–1464) and the soldier and patron of the arts Cosimo de' Medici (1519–74). Notable bearers of the name in the English-speaking world, where it has never been in frequent use, have included the Scottish-born Archbishop of Canterbury Cosmo Gordon Lang (1864–1945). **Cosima** – as borne by Franz Liszt's daughter Cosima Wagner (1837–1930) – is a feminine form of the name in use among the English, the Germans and the Italians.

Courtney (m/f) English surname that has been in occasional use as a masculine first name since the middle of the 19th century, chiefly in the USA. The original surname came from the Norman French place name Courtenay (meaning 'domain of Curtius'), although it was also in use as a nickname based on the French *court nez* ('short nose'). As a name for girls it appears to have been first adopted around the middle of the 20th century. It enjoyed a resurgence in popularity as a name for both sexes in the 1990s. Well-known bearers of the name have included (among the men) West Indian cricketer Courtney Walsh (b.1962) and British jazz musician Courtney Pine (b.1964) and (among the women) US rock musician Courtney Love (b.1963). Variants include **Courtenay** and **Courteney**.

Coy (m) English first name of uncertain origin, possibly taken from an identical surname or else from the ordinary vocabulary word 'coy'. Mostly confined to the USA.

Craig (m) Scottish place name derived from the Gaelic *creag* ('crag') that was subsequently adopted as a surname and from the middle of the 19th century as a first name. It has largely lost its uniquely Scottish character and is now in fairly widespread use throughout the English-speaking world. It enjoyed a peak in popularity in the 1970s. Famous bearers of the name have included Australian actor Craig McLachlan (b.1965).

Crawford (m) Scottish place name meaning 'ford where the crows gather' that was subsequently taken up as a surname and occasional first name.

Creighton (m) Scottish place name derived from the Gaelic *crioch* ('border' or 'boundary') and the Old English *tun* ('settlement') that was subsequently taken up as a surname and occasional first name.

Cressida (f) English version of the Greek Khryseis, derived from the Greek *khrysos* ('gold'). It is well known in the English-speaking world from the legend of *Troilus* *and Cressida*, as related by Geoffrey Chaucer and William Shakespeare – although this appears to be a largely medieval invention based on a brief mention in Homer's *Iliad*. Chaucer's immediate source was the Italian writer Boccaccio, who gave the name as **Criseida** through an apparent misreading of **Briseida** (meaning 'daughter of Brisis'). In Chaucer's version of the legend the name appeared as **Criseyde**. In its modern form the name was taken up on a very selective basis among English speakers in the 20th century. Sometimes abbreviated to **Cressy**.

Crispian *See* CRISPIN.

Crispin (m) English version of the Roman Crispinus, itself derived from the nickname Crispus (meaning 'curly-haired'). It was taken up by English speakers in the 17th century and remained in fairly common currency well into the 20th century before suffering a marked decline. Famous bearers of the name over the centuries have included a 3rd-century saint, usually associated with the rousing 'St Crispin's day' speech from William Shakespeare's play *Henry V* (1599). **Crispian** is an equally rare variant of the name.

Cristina *See* CHRISTINA.

Cristóbal/Cristoforo *See* CHRISTOPHER.

Crystal (f) English first name derived from the ordinary vocabulary word 'crystal'. It was taken up as a first name by English speakers on both sides of the Atlantic towards the end of the 19th century, when many similar names connected with gemstones and jewellery were adopted as first names. In the 20th century it enjoyed particular popularity among Black Americans. Well-known bearers of the name have included US country singer Crystal Gayle (Brenda Gail Webb; b.1951). Commonly abbreviated to CHRIS or **Chrissie**. Also encountered as **Chrystal**, **Christel**, **Cristal**, **Crystle**, **Krystle** or **Krystal** (in which form it appeared in the popular 1980s US television soap opera *Dynasty*) and, more rarely, as **Christelle** or **Chrystalla**.

Crystin *See* CHRISTINE.

Cuddie/Cuddy *See* CUTHBERT.

Cullan (m) Scottish and Irish first name derived from the Gaelic for 'at the back of the river'. Also found as **Cullen**.

Curt *See* CONRAD; CURTIS; KURT.

Curtis (m) English surname derived from the Old French *curteis* ('courteous') that has been in use as an occasional first name among English speakers ever since the 11th century, when it was borne by the eldest son of William the Conqueror. Early in its history it acquired a new derivation, from the Middle English *curt* ('short') and *hose* ('leggings'). It has proved particularly popular in modern times among Black Americans, notable bearers including soul musician Curtis Mayfield (1942–99). Sometimes abbreviated to **Curt**.

Cuthbert (m) English first name derived from the Old English Cuthbeorht, itself from *cuth* ('known') and *beorht* ('bright' or 'famous') and thus interpreted as meaning 'well known'. It became famous as the name of the 7th-century English St Cuthbert, Bishop of Lindisfarne, and continued in fairly common currency right up until the 1930s, since when it has fallen into disuse. Diminutives include BERT and the Scottish **Cuddie** or **Cuddy**.

Cy *See* CYRUS.

Cybill *See* SYBIL.

Cyndi *See* CINDY.

Cynthia (f) English version of the Greek Kynthia, a name borne in mythology by the goddess Artemis whose birthplace was supposed to have been Mount Kynthos (a name of obscure origin) on the island of Delos. The 1st-century BC Roman poet Propertius addressed some of his love poetry to one Cynthia (otherwise identified as Hostia) and the name was subsequently taken up by English speakers in the 16th century, being adopted by Edmund Spenser, Ben Jonson and other notable writers as a poetical name for Elizabeth I. The name has remained in currency ever since, although it has appeared with decreasing frequency since the middle of the 20th century and is now rare among the young. Diminutives include **Cimmie** and CINDY (a version of the name that is now rather more common than the source name). Variants in other languages include the Italian **Cinzia**.

Cyprian (m) English first name derived from the Roman Cyprianus, itself from the Latin for 'man of Cyprus'. Borne by a 3rd-century saint from Carthage, it was taken up by English speakers during the medieval period but has since made only very occasional appearances in the English-speaking world, possibly because it came to be used as a slang term for 'prostitute'.

Cyra *See* CYRUS.

Cyril (m) English first name derived from the Greek Kyrillos, itself from the Greek *kurios* ('lord'). It was borne by several early saints, including the 9th-century St Cyril who invented the Cyrillic alphabet, and became popular among English speakers towards the end of the 19th century. It has been in decline since the 1920s, however, and is now very rare among the young. Notable bearers of the name have included Cyril Beardsall in the D. H. Lawrence novel *The White Peacock* (1911), British politician Sir Cyril Smith (b.1928) and British foot-baller Cyril Knowles (1944–91), whose prowess on the football pitch inspired the 1970s pop song 'Nice one, Cyril'. Variants in other languages include the French **Cyrille** and the Russian **Kirill**. **Cyrilla** is a rare feminine form of the name.

Cyrilla/Cyrille *See* CYRIL.

Cyrus (m) Biblical name derived from the Greek Kyros, which may have evolved originally from the Greek *kurios* ('lord'), although this derivation is disputed and it may equally have come from Persian words meaning 'sun' or 'throne'. It was borne by several kings of ancient Persia and made irregular appearances among English speakers from the 17th century. It enjoyed a modest peak in popularity in the USA in the 19th century. Notable bearers of the name in recent times have included the US statesman Cyrus Vance (b.1917). The diminutive form **Cy** has been in use, chiefly in the USA, since the early 20th century, being borne by such luminaries as US baseball player Cy Young (Denton True Young; 1867–1955) and US pop musician Cy Coleman (Seymour Kaufman; b.1929). Variants in other languages include the Italian **Ciro**. **Cyra** and **Kyra** are rare feminine versions of the name.

Czcibor (m) Polish first name (pronounced 'cheebor') derived from the Old Slavonic *chest* ('honour') and *borit* ('to fight'). Variants include **Cibor**.

D

Dacre (m) English place name (from Cumbria), meaning 'trickling stream', that was subsequently taken up as a surname and has made occasional appearances as a first name (pronounced 'dayker'). A strongly aristocratic name, it has become very rare since the beginning of the 20th century.

Daff See DAFFODIL; DAPHNE.

Daffodil (f) English first name derived from the name of the flower. Like other flower names it made its first appearances towards the end of the 19th century, but has never been common. **Daff** and **Dilly** are diminutive forms of the name.

Daffy See DAPHNE.

Dafydd See DAVID.

Dag (m) Scandinavian first name derived from the Old Norse *dagr* ('day'). Famous bearers of the name have included the Swedish statesman Dag Hammarskjöld (1905–61).

Dagmar (f) Scandinavian first name of uncertain meaning. It may have evolved from the Old Scandinavian *dag* ('day') and *mar* ('maid') or else from the Slavonic *dorog* ('dear') and *meri* ('great' or 'famous'). It has made occasional appearances as a first name among English speakers, chiefly among Scandinavian immigrants.

Dahlia (f) English first name (pronounced 'dayleea') that was among the many flower names that were taken up by English speakers towards the end of the 19th century. The flower itself was named in honour of the celebrated Swedish botanist Anders Dahl (1751–89). Bertie Wooster has an Aunt Dahlia in the comic 'Jeeves' novels of P. G. Wodehouse. Also spelled **Dalia** or **Dalya**.

Dai (m) Welsh first name derived originally from the Old Celtic *dei* ('to shine') but often considered to be a diminutive form of DAVID. Since the 19th century it has become established as one of the most characteristic of all Welsh names, but is virtually unknown as a first name outside Welsh-speaking communities. Usually pronounced as 'die'.

Daibhidh See DAVID.

Daisy (f) English first name derived from the name of the flower, itself from the Old English *daegeseage* ('day's eye') – so called because it opens its petals at daybreak. Through association with the French *marguerite*, the French name for the daisy, it came to be regarded as a familiar form of MARGARET. It was taken up by English speakers in the 19th century and remained popular into the early years of the 20th century, since when it has gone into a gradual decline until it is now quite rare. Notable bearers of the name have included the central character in the Henry James story *Daisy Miller* (1879), British children's writer Daisy Ashford (1881–1972) and Daisy Buchanan in the F. Scott Fitzgerald novel *The Great Gatsby* (1925).

Dalal (f) Arabic name derived from *dalal* ('coquettishness').

Dale (m/f) English surname, originally borne by people living in a dale or valley, that was taken up as a first name among English speakers in the 19th century, primarily in the USA. It was employed initially as a boys' name, in which role it enjoyed a peak in popularity in the 1960s. As a name for girls it appears to have made early appearances in the first decade of the 20th century and became fairly well known in the 1930s. Notable bearers of the name have included the US writer Dale Carnegie (1888–1955) and the fictional Dale Evans, the girlfriend of the US comic-strip hero Flash Gordon in the 1930s.

Daley (m) Irish surname derived from the Gaelic for 'descendant of Dalach', a surname that came from *dal*, meaning 'assembly' or 'gathering', that has also made occasional appearances as a first name. Sometimes encountered as **Daly**.

Dalia *See* DAHLIA.

Dallas (m) English place name derived from the Old English for 'dweller in the dale' that has made occasional appearances as a surname and first name. Its use in the USA has been promoted through the name of the city of Dallas, Texas.

Daly *See* DALEY.

Dalya *See* DAHLIA.

Damaris (f) Biblical name thought to have evolved from the Greek *damar* ('wife') or alternatively from *damalis* ('calf' or 'heifer') and thus interpreted as signifying 'gentleness'. It appears in the Bible as the name of an Athenian convert of St Paul and was consequently taken up by English Puritans in the 17th century. It has become much less common since then but has continued to make occasional appearances into modern times.

Damayanti (f) Indian name derived from the Sanskrit *damayanti* ('subduing'). It features in Indian legend as the name of a beautiful princess.

Damhnait *See* DYMPHNA.

Damian (m) English first name derived from the Greek Damianos itself from the Greek *daman* ('to subdue' or 'to rule') and thus interpreted as meaning 'tamer'. It was borne by a 4th century Christian martyr, the patron saint of doctors, and made

appearances among English speakers as early as the 13th century. It did not appear with any regularity, however, until the 20th century. It enjoyed a peak in popularity in the late 1970s, when the variant **Damien** (the usual French version of the name) became internationally famous through the *Omen* series of horror films, in which Damien is the name borne by the Antichrist central character. Variants in other languages include the Italian **Damiano** and the Russian **Demyan**. *See also* DAMON.

Damodar (m) Indian name derived from the Sanskrit *dama* ('rope') and *udara* ('belly') and usually interpreted as meaning 'having a rope round his belly'. The name has its origins in the story of Krishna, who as a child was tied up with rope after causing mayhem in the home of his foster-mother. **Damodari** is a feminine version of the name.

Damon (m) English variant of DAMIAN that emerged as an alternative form of the name around the middle of the 19th century. It features in Greek mythology in the legend of the two devoted friends Damon and Pythias. Notable bearers of the name since then have included Damon Wildeve in the Thomas Hardy novel *The Return of the Native* (1878), US writer Damon Runyon (1884–1946) and British motor-racing driver Damon Hill (b.1962).

Dan (m) English first name derived from the Hebrew Dan, meaning 'judge' but more often in use today as a diminutive of DANIEL or other similar names. It appears in the Bible as the name of a son of Jacob, the founder of one of the twelve tribes of Israel. Famous bearers of the name have included the fictional 1950s space hero Dan Dare, US politician Dan Quayle (James Danforth Quayle; b.1947) and Canadian comedian Dan Aykroyd (b.1950). *See also* DANNY.

Dana (m/f) English first name that evolved as a diminutive form of DANIEL in the 19th century, although it can also be traced back to the identical surname – promoted by the popularity of the US poet and novelist

Richard Dana (1787–1879), who was admired for his work on behalf of runaway slaves in the USA. Today it is unusual to find it in use as a masculine name and is more often bestowed upon girls, in which case it developed as a variant of such names as DANIELLE and DONNA. Famous bearers of the name (among the men) have included the US actor Dana Andrews (Carver Daniel Andrews; 1909–92) and (among the women) the Irish pop singer and politician Dana (Rosemary Brown; b.1952). Variants in other languages include the Polish **Danuta**.

Dandy (m/f) English first name derived from the ordinary vocabulary word 'dandy', but also in use as a familiar form of such names as DANIELLE and ANDREW. It has made occasional appearances among English speakers since the early years of the 20th century. Well-known bearers of the name have included the British actress Dandy Nichols (1907–86).

Dane (m) English surname and first name that is thought to have developed as a variant of DEAN. It has appeared with increasing frequency since the early 20th century, but is now rare outside the USA.

Danette *See* DANIEL.

Daniel (m) English, French and German first name derived from the Hebrew Daniel, meaning 'God is my judge' or 'God has judged'. In Ireland, where it has long been especially popular, it is also regarded as an Anglicized form of the Irish Domhnall. In Wales it may be treated as an Anglicization of Deiniol, meaning 'attractive' or 'charming'. It appears in the Bible as the name of the Old Testament prophet Daniel, famous for his escape from the lions' den. It made early appearances among English speakers before the Norman Conquest, although initially it was confined to members of the clergy. It became more widely popular during the medieval period and has remained in currency ever since, with a temporary fall from favour in the second half of the 19th century and first half of the

20th century. Having revived around the middle of the 20th century, it has enjoyed recent peaks in popularity in the 1970s and 1990s.

Notable bearers of the name have included English novelist Daniel Defoe (1660–1731), US frontiersman Daniel Boone (1723–1820), the central character in the George Eliot novel *Daniel Deronda* (1876), British actor Daniel Day-Lewis (b.1957) and the central character in Roald Dahl's children's story *Danny the Champion of the World* (1975). Commonly shortened to DAN or DANNY (or **Dannie**). Variants in other languages include the Welsh **Deiniol**, the Italian **Daniele** and the Russian **Daniil**. Among feminine equivalents of the name are DANIELLE, **Daniella**, **Danette**, **Danita** and **Danuta**. *See also* DANA.

Daniela/Danièle/Daniella
See DANIELLE.

Danielle (f) French feminine equivalent of DANIEL that has become popular as a first name among English speakers since the 1940s. It enjoyed a peak in popularity in the 1980s. Well-known bearers of the name have included the US writer Danielle Steel (b.1947). Diminutive forms of the name are **Dan**, **Danny**, **Dannie** and **Dani** – as borne by British television presenter Dani Behr (b.1974). Variants include **Daniella**, **Daniela** and **Danniella**. A French version of the name is **Danièle**.

Danika (f) Slavonic name derived from the name for the morning star. It has made occasional appearances as a first name among English speakers.

Danita *See* DANIEL.

Dannie *See* DANIEL; DANNY.

Danny (m) English first name that was taken up as a diminutive form of DANIEL early in the 20th century. Like Daniel, it has strong Irish associations, as celebrated in the popular song 'Danny Boy' (1913). Well-known bearers of the name have included US actor Danny Kaye (David Daniel

Kaminsky; 1913–87), Irish-born entertainer Danny La Rue (Daniel Patrick Carroll; b.1927) and US actor Danny de Vito (b.1944). Commonly abbreviated to DAN. Also encountered as **Dannie**.

Dante (m) Italian name derived ultimately from the Latin *durare* ('to endure') and thus interpreted as meaning 'enduring' or 'steadfast'. It is famous as the name of the celebrated Italian poet Dante Alighieri (1265–1321). Other notable bearers of the name have included the British poet and painter Dante Gabriel Rossetti (1828–82).

Danuta *See* DANA.

Daph *See* DAPHNE.

Daphne (f) Greek name derived from the Greek *daphne* ('laurel tree'). Borne in Greek mythology by a nymph who was transformed by her father into a laurel tree when pursued by Apollo, it was taken up as a first name among English speakers in the 18th century. It was at its most popular between the late 19th century and the 1930s, when it was among the many flower names taken up in the English-speaking world, but has become much less frequent since the 1950s. Famous bearers of the name have included the British novelist Daphne du Maurier (1907–89). Sometimes shortened to **Daff**, **Daffy** or **Daph**.

Dara (m/f) Irish first name derived from the Gaelic Mac Dara. Sometimes Anglicized as DUDLEY. The name is also familiar as a girls' name among the world's Jewish communities, in which context it is traced back to the Hebrew for 'pearl of wisdom' (although when it appears in the Old Testament it is given as a boys' name). Also encountered as **Darach**.

Darby (m) English surname derived from the place name Derby that has been in occasional use as a first name since the medieval period. The original place name came from the Old Norse *diur* ('deer') and *byr* ('settlement') and thus interpreted as meaning 'deer park'. Sometimes used in Ireland as an Anglicization of DERMOT. Many

English speakers know the name from 'Darby and Joan', who were formerly familiar as the archetypal loving and virtuous elderly couple and made their first appearance in a ballad by Henry Woodfall, published in the *Gentleman's Magazine* in 1735. Also encountered as **Derby**.

Darcey (f) English first name that developed as a feminine equivalent of the masculine DARCY. It has made irregular appearances as a first name among English speakers since the early 20th century, primarily in the USA. Famous bearers of the name have included the British ballerina Darcey Bussell (b.1969).

Darcy (m) English first name, derived from the Norman surname d'Arcy (referring to the town of Arcy in France), that has been in occasional use among English speakers since the 19th century. The popularity of the name was promoted by the stern but handsome aristocrat Fitzwilliam Darcy in the Jane Austen novel *Pride and Prejudice* (1813). Also spelled **D'Arcy**.

Darel/Darell *See* DARRYL.

Daria (f) English, Italian and Polish name that evolved originally as a feminine equivalent of the Roman masculine name Darius. It was borne by a 3rd-century Greek martyr and has made irregular appearances as a first name among English speakers into modern times. Variants in other languages include the Russian **Darya** (and its familiar form **Dasha**). *See also* DARIO.

Darina (f) Irish first name derived from the Irish Gaelic *daireann* (meaning 'fruitful'). Also encountered as **Daireann**, **Doirend** or **Doirenn**.

Dario (m) Italian first name derived from the Roman Darius, itself from the Persian *daraya* ('to hold' or 'to possess') and *vahu* ('good' or 'well') and thus variously interpreted as meaning 'protector' or 'wealthy'. Borne by several Persian kings and by an early Christian martyr, it has made occasional appearances as a first name among

English speakers into modern times, sometimes in its original form **Darius**, as borne by English pop singer Darius Danesh (b.1980). Famous bearers of the name have included the Italian playwright and actor Dario Fo (b.1926). *See also* DARIA.

Darius *See* DARIO.

Darlene (f) English first name that is thought to have evolved from the ordinary vocabulary word 'darling' under the influence of such similar coinages as CHARLENE and RAELENE. It became fairly popular in the USA in the 1950s and has remained in occasional use ever since, enjoying particular popularity in Australia in the 1980s. Also found as **Darleen** or **Darline**.

Darran *See* DARREN.

Darrell *See* DARRYL.

Darren (m) English first name that is thought to have developed as a variant of DARRYL. It seems to have made its first appearance among English speakers in the USA in the 1920s and enjoyed a peak in popularity in the 1960s and 1970s before falling out of favour. Well-known bearers of the name have included the British footballer Darren Anderton (b.1972). Also found as **Darran** or **Darrin** – as borne by one of the leading characters in the popular 1960s US television comedy series *Bewitched*. Another variant is **Darin**, a version of the name made famous by the US pop singer Bobby Darin (Walden Robert Cassotto; 1936–73), who admitted to selecting the name from a telephone directory. **Darrene** is a rare feminine form of the name.

Darrin *See* DARREN.

Darryl (m/f) English first name derived ultimately from the Norman baronial surname d'Airelle (referring to Airelle in Calvados) that has made appearances throughout the English-speaking world since the beginning of the 20th century. An alternative derivation traces the name back to the Old English *deorling* ('darling'). In such variant forms as **Darel**, **Darell** or

Darrell it made early appearances among English speakers towards the end of the 19th century. Also spelled **Daryl**. Famous bearers of the name have included US film producer Darryl F. Zanuck (1902–79) and US pop singer Daryl Hall (b.1948). Daryl is the usual form when the name is bestowed upon females – examples including the US film actress Daryl Hannah (b.1961).

Daryl *See* DARRYL.

Dassah *See* HADASSAH.

Daud *See* DAWUD.

Dave/Davey *See* DAVID.

David (m) English first name derived ultimately from the Hebrew Dawid, which is thought to have meant 'favourite', 'beloved' or 'darling'. It appears in the Bible as the name of the boy who killed the Philistine giant Goliath with just a sling and subsequently became the greatest of the kings of the Israelites. The name was taken up by English speakers during the medieval period and it has remained one of the most popular of all boys' names ever since. It became especially well established in Wales, where it acquired further significance as the name of the 7th-century St David, the patron saint of Wales, and also in Scotland, where it was famous as the name of two kings. It maintained its status as one of the five most popular boys' names among English speakers from the 1950s to the 1990s.

Notable bearers of the name have included the central character in the Charles Dickens novel *David Copperfield* (1849–50), Welsh statesman David Lloyd-George (1863–1945), David Balfour in the Robert Louis Stevenson novel *Kidnapped* (1886), British actor David Niven (1910–83), British broadcaster Sir David Attenborough (b.1926), British novelist David Lodge (b.1935), British artist David Hockney (b.1937) and British pop singer David Bowie (b.1947). **Dave**, **Davie**, **Davey** and **Davy** are well-known diminutive forms of the name – as borne by such luminaries as US frontiersman Davy Crockett (1786–1836), US jazz musician Dave Brubeck (b.1920) and Irish comedian Dave Allen (b.1936). Feminine equivalents include DAVINA, **Davida** and **Davinia**. Among variants in other languages are the Gaelic **Daibhidh**, the Welsh **Dafydd** or DEWI and the Finnish **Taavi**. *See also* DAI; TAFFY.

Davida/Davie *See* DAVID.

Davina (f) Scottish feminine variant of DAVID. It appears to be a fairly recent introduction of early 20th-century coinage. It has acquired a reputation as a strongly aristocratic name. Famous bearers of the name in recent times have included Lady Davina Windsor (b.1977), daughter of the Duke of Gloucester, and British television presenter Davina McCall (b.1967). Sometimes abbreviated to **Vina**. Variants include **Davida**, **Davena** and **Davinia**. *See also* DIVINA.

Davinia *See* DAVINA; DIVINA.

Davis (m) English first name meaning 'David's son'. It is more commonly encountered in use as a surname.

Davy *See* DAVID.

Dawn (f) English first name derived from the ordinary vocabulary word 'dawn'. It seems to have made its first appearances among English speakers in the 1920s and was at its most frequent in the 1960s, but has since become much less common. Well-known bearers of the name have included the British comedienne Dawn French (b.1957). *See also* AURORA.

Dawud (m) Arabic version of DAVID. Another Arabic variant is **Daud**.

Dayaram (m) Indian name derived from the Sanskrit *daya* ('compassion') and Ram (a variant of the name of the god Rama).

Dean (m) English surname that has been in use as a first name among English speakers since the end of the 19th century. The surname can be traced back either to the Old English *denu* ('valley') or to the ecclesiastical

rank 'dean'. It seems to have made its first appearances as a first name in the USA but has since been taken up throughout the English-speaking world, enjoying a peak in popularity in the 1980s, promoted by association with the cult US film actor James Dean (1931–55). Notable bearers of the name have included US statesmen Dean Acheson (1893–1971) and Dean Rusk (1909–94) and US film actor Dean Martin (Dino Crocetti; 1917–95). Variant forms are **Deane** and **Dene**. *See also* DEANNA.

Deanna (f) English first name that evolved as a variant of DIANA in the early 20th century but is also occasionally encountered as a feminine equivalent of DEAN. It has never been in regular use. Famous bearers of the name have included Canadian-born US film actress and singer Deanna Durbin (Edna Mae Durbin; b.1921).

Deanne *See* DIANE.

Dearbhail *See* DERVLA.

Deb *See* DEBORAH; DEV.

Debbie (f) English first name that developed as a diminutive form of DEBORAH and is today sometimes treated as a name in its own right. It became widely heard in the 1950s and enjoyed a peak in popularity in the 1960s and 1970s, since when it has become rather less frequent. Famous bearers of the name have included US film actress Debbie Reynolds (Mary Frances Reynolds; b.1932). Also found as **Debby**.

Debby *See* DEBBIE.

Debdan *See* DEVDAN.

Deborah (f) English first name derived from the Hebrew Deborah, meaning 'bee' and thus suggestive of a diligent, industrious nature. It appears in the Bible as the name of Rebecca's nurse, the wife of Lapidoth and the mother of Ananiel, and was consequently taken up with some enthusiasm by Puritans on both sides of the Atlantic in the 17th century. It enjoyed a peak in popularity in the 1960s but has since become relatively uncommon.

Notable bearers of the name have included the British actress Deborah Kerr (b.1921), US pop singer Deborah Harry (b.1945) and British novelist Deborah Moggach (b.1948). Commonly shortened to **Deb**, **Debs** or DEBBIE (or **Debby**). **Debra** is a variant form of the name – as borne by US actress Debra Winger (b.1955).

Debra/Debs See DEBORAH.

Decima See DECIMUS.

Decimus (m) Roman name derived from the Latin *decimus* ('tenth') that made irregular appearances as a first name among English speakers until the end of the 19th century. It was usually reserved for tenth-born children, hence its rarity in modern times. Notable bearers of the name have included the British architect Decimus Burton (1800–1881). **Decima** is a rare feminine form of the name.

Declan (m) English version of the Irish Deaglan, of uncertain meaning. Borne by a 5th-century Irish saint, it became popular as a first name among the Irish in the 1940s and was subsequently taken up more widely in the English-speaking world from the 1980s. Famous bearers of the name have included the Irish theatre director Declan Donnellan (b.1953).

Dee (f) English first name that evolved as a diminutive form of various names beginning with the letter 'D', including DEIRDRE and DOROTHY. Variants include **DeeDee** (or **Didi**).

Deepak See DIPAK.

Deforest (m) English surname that has made occasional appearances as a first name, chiefly in the USA. In many cases the name has been bestowed in tribute to the US novelist John DeForest (1826–1906). Notable bearers of the name have included US television actor DeForest Kelley (1920–99), best known as Dr Leonard 'Bones' McKoy in the cult 1960s science-fiction television series *Star Trek*. Also encountered as **Deforrest** or **DeForrest**.

Deidre See DEIRDRE.

Deiniol See DANIEL.

Deirbhile See DERVLA.

Deirdre (f) Irish first name derived from the Irish *deardan* ('storm') and thus interpreted as meaning 'raging' or 'tempestuous'. It was adopted more widely in the English-speaking world in the 1930s but it suffered a gradual decline in popularity after the 1950s and is now very rare among the young. The name has featured prominently in Irish literature through retellings of the tragic legend of the beautiful Irish folk heroine Deirdre of the Sorrows, notably in the poetic works of W. B. Yeats and in the J. M. Synge play *Deirdre of the Sorrows* (1910), and she is sometimes considered to be a metaphor for the sufferings of Ireland under English rule. Also encountered as **Deidre**, **Diedre** or **Deidra**.

Del See DELBERT; DELROY; DEREK.

Delbert (m) English first name that is thought to have evolved in parallel with DELMAR and DELROY and other similar names. It appears to have been a relatively recent introduction that made its first appearances among English speakers in the early part of the 20th century and has since been found mainly within Black communities on both sides of the Atlantic. In the UK it became well known in the 1980s as the name of a comic character created by the British television comedian Lenny Henry.

Delfina See DELPHINE.

Delia (f) English first name derived ultimately from the name of the Greek island of Delos, which in Greek mythology was identified as the home of Artemis and Apollo. It is also occasionally encountered as a diminutive form of such names as CORDELIA. It was taken up by English speakers towards the end of the 16th century, when it became established as a favourite literary name – as in Samuel Daniel's sonnet sequence entitled *Delia* (1592). It remained popular with English writers through the 17th and 18th centuries but has since made only irregular appearances as a first name. Famous bearers of the name in modern times have included the British cookery writer and broadcaster Delia Smith (b.1941). Sometimes abbreviated to DEE. DELLA is a variant form.

Delice *See* DELICIA.

Delicia (f) English first name derived from the Roman Delicius, derived from the Latin *deliciae* ('delight'). Variants include **Delys**.

Delight (f) English first name derived from the ordinary vocabulary word meaning 'joy' or 'satisfaction'.

Delilah (f) Hebrew name meaning 'delight', possibly from the Arabic *dalla* ('to flirt' or 'to tease'). It appears in the Bible as the name of Samson's deceitful lover and the cause of his downfall, but despite this connection it was taken up with some enthusiasm by English Puritans in the 17th century, perhaps because the biblical Delilah was also very clever and very beautiful. It is not found as a first name very often today, although it remains familiar not only from the biblical story but also from the Saint-Saëns opera *Samson and Delilah* (1877) and the popular song 'Delilah' (1917 and 1968 – two different songs with the same name). **Delila** is a variant form.

Dell *See* DELLA.

Della (f) English first name that developed as a diminutive form of ADELA and DELIA among other names. It made its first appearances towards the end of the 19th century and became relatively popular in the 20th century. Commonly abbreviated to **Dell**.

Delma *See* FIDELMA.

Delmar (m) English first name of uncertain origin, possibly a variant of ELMER. It has enjoyed some popularity within the Black community in the USA since the middle of the 20th century.

Delores *See* DOLORES.

Delphine (f) French first name derived from the Roman Delphina, meaning 'woman of Delphi'. Madame de Staël's use of the name in her epistolatory novel *Delphine* (1802) undoubtedly promoted awareness of the name and English speakers were using the name on a limited scale by the end of the 19th century, perhaps attracted to it because it brought to mind the flower delphinium. Today it is found primarily among US Blacks. Famous bearers of the name have included the French actress Delphine Seyrig (1932–90). Also encountered in the variant forms **Delfina** (the usual form of the name in Italy and Spain), **Delphina** and **Delvene**.

Delroy (m) English first name that is thought to have evolved as a variant of LEROY. It has enjoyed some popularity in the UK since the middle of the 20th century.

Delwyn (f) Welsh name derived from the Welsh *del* ('pretty' or 'neat') and *wyn* ('white' or 'blessed'). It made its first appearances among the Welsh early in the 20th century. Also encountered as **Delwen**.

Delys *See* DELICIA.

Delyth (f) Welsh name (pronounced 'dellith') derived from the Welsh *del* ('pretty' or 'neat'). It remains confined largely to Wales itself.

Demelza (f) English first name that enjoyed some popularity among English speakers from the 1950s. Although it purported to be a traditional Cornish name, it was in fact the name of a Cornish village, meaning 'hill-fort of Maeldaf', that was selected by the British novelist Winston Graham for the name of one of the leading characters in his *Poldark* series of novels set in historical Cornwall that began with *Demelza* (1946). The televisation of Graham's stories in the 1970s made the name widely familiar.

Demetrio/Demetrius *See* DMITRI.

Demi (f) English first name that evolved as

a diminutive of the lesser known **Demetra**, itself a variant of the Roman **Demetrius**. In Greek mythology **Demeter** was the name of the goddess of the harvest. Notable bearers of the name in recent years have included US actress Demi Moore (b.1962).

Dempsey (m) English first name derived from the Gaelic for 'proud descendant'. It was in use as a surname before being adopted as a first name.

Demyan *See* DAMIAN.

Den *See* DENNIS.

Dene *See* DEAN.

Deneice *See* DENISE.

Denholm (m) English place name derived from the Old English *denu* ('valley') and *holm* ('island') that was subsequently taken up as a surname and occasional first name. Famous bearers of the name have included the British actor Denholm Elliott (1922–92). Variants include **Denham,** meaning 'home in a valley'.

Denice/Deniece *See* DENISE.

Denis *See* DENNIS.

Denise (f) French first name that developed as a feminine version of Denis (*see* DENNIS). It was taken up by English speakers in the 1920s and enjoyed a peak in popularity in the 1950s and 1960s. **Dennie** is a familiar form of the name. Variants include **Deneice**, **Denice** and **Deniece** – as borne by US pop singer Deniece Williams (b.1951).

Dennie *See* DENISE.

Dennis (m) English first name derived via the Roman Dionysius ultimately from the Greek Dionysios, denoting a devotee of the Greek god of wine Dionysos. Borne by a number of early Christian saints, it came to England with the Normans in the 11th century but seems to have fallen from favour in the 17th century. It was revived in the early 20th century and quickly became very popular, although it has been much

less frequent since the 1970s. Notable bearers of the name have included British novelist Dennis Wheatley (1897–1977), British television playwright Dennis Potter (1935–94) and British comic strip character Dennis the Menace. Also spelled **Denys**. A French variant of the name that has enjoyed some popularity among English speakers since the early years of the 20th century is **Denis** – as borne by British politician Denis, Lord Healey (b.1917), British cricketer Sir Denis Compton (1918–97) and British actor Denis Quilley (1927–2003). Commonly abbreviated to **Den** or, more rarely, **Denny**. *See also* DENISE.

Dennison (m) English first name meaning 'son of Dennis'. Also encountered in such variant forms as **Denison**, **Tennyson** and **Tennison**.

Denny *See* DENNIS.

Denton (m) English place name derived from the Old English *denu* ('valley') and *tun* ('settlement') that was subsequently adopted as a surname and has made occasional appearances as a first name.

Denys *See* DENNIS.

Denzel *See* DENZIL.

Denzil (m) English first name derived from a Cornish surname, itself based on the Cornish place name Denzell, alternatively interpreted as meaning 'fort' or 'fertile upland'. Early records of its use as a first name go back to the 16th century, when it became famous as a traditional choice of the celebrated Holles family, whose most notable members included the English statesman Denzil Holles (1599–1680). It has remained in occasional use into modern times. Also encountered as **Denzel** – as borne by US film actor Denzel Washington (b.1954) – or **Denzyl**.

Deo *See* DEV.

Deodan *See* DEVDAN.

Derby *See* DARBY.

Derek (m) English first name derived from

the Old German THEODORIC, meaning 'ruler of the people'. It is thought to have come to England with Flemish immigrants in the 15th century but remained rare until the end of the 19th century and has never been common in the USA. It was at its most frequent between the 1930s and the 1960s, since when it has become much less common. Well-known bearers of the name have included British comedian Derek Nimmo (1932–99), British actor Sir Derek Jacobi (b.1938) and British film director Derek Jarman (1942–94). **Del** and **Derry** are common diminutive forms of the name. Also spelled **Deryck** (or **Deryk**) – as borne by British comedian Deryck Guyler (1914–99) and **Derrick** – as borne in the 17th century by the Tyburn hangman, resulting in the word 'derrick' being used for the gallows themselves and today for a type of crane. Variants in other languages include the German DIETRICH and the Dutch **Dirk** – as borne by the British actor Dirk Bogarde (Derek Gentron Gaspart Ulric van den Bogaerde; 1921–99).

Dermot (m) English version of the Irish Diarmaid or Diarmuid, possibly derived from the Gaelic *dl* ('without') and *airmait* ('envy'). As Diarmaid it was the name of a legendary king of Tara, the lover of Finn MacCool's wife Grainne. As Dermot, it made its first appearances in Ireland in the 19th century and has since been encountered elsewhere in the English-speaking world, although usually among people with strong Irish connections. Variants include **Diarmid**, **Dermid** and the Scottish **Diarmad**. *See also* DARBY; KERMIT.

Derrick *See* DEREK.

Derry *See* DEREK.

Dervla (f) Irish name possibly derived from the Irish *dear* ('daughter') and *file* ('poet') or *Fal* ('Ireland') and often interpreted as meaning 'daughter of Ireland' but sometimes alternatively as meaning 'true desire'. Famous bearers of the name have included Irish television actress Dervla Kirwan (b.1971). It does not appear to have

won acceptance outside Ireland itself. Variants include **Dearbhail**, **Deirbhile** and **Dervila**.

Derwent (m) English first name meaning 'river that flows through oak woods'. It was in use as a place name and surname before being adopted as a first name.

Deryck/Deryk *See* DEREK.

Deryn (f) Welsh first name possibly derived from *aderyn* ('bird'). It seems to have made its first appearance in Wales around the middle of the 20th century but is today rare elsewhere in the English-speaking world.

Des *See* DESMOND.

Desdemona (f) English first name apparently derived from the Greek *dusaimon* ('ill-fated'). It is famous as the name of the doomed wife of the central character in William Shakespeare's tragedy *Othello* (1602–4). Probably because of the sad fate of Shakespeare's character, the name has appeared only very rarely as a first name among English speakers.

Desi *See* DESMOND.

Désirée (f) French first name derived from the French *désirée* ('desired'). It can be traced back ultimately to the Roman Desiderata, meaning 'desired' in Latin. Borne in the early 19th century by Bernardine Eugénie Désirée Clary, one of Napoleon Bonaparte's mistresses, it was subsequently taken up by English speakers and became fairly well known in the 1950s, chiefly in the USA. Often written in English usage without the accents. *See also* DIDIER.

Desmond (m) English first name derived from the Gaelic surname Deas-Mhumhan, meaning 'someone from south Munster'. It appears to have come to England from Ireland towards the end of the 19th century, assuming its present form under the influence of ESMOND, and remained fairly frequent until the middle of the 20th century, since when it has become relatively uncommon. Well-known bearers of the name have included the British novelist Desmond Bagley (1923–83), British zoologist and anthropologist Desmond Morris (b.1928) and British television presenter Desmond Lynam (b.1942). Commonly abbreviated to **Des** – as borne by British singer and entertainer Des O'Connor (b.1932) – or **Desi** (also spelled **Desy** or **Dezi**).

Desy See DESMOND.

Detta See BERNADETTE.

Dev (m) Indian name derived from the Sanskrit *deva* ('god'). Variants include **Deb** and **Deo**. **Devi** is a feminine form of the name.

Devdan (m) Indian name derived from the Sanskrit *deva* ('god') and *dana* ('gift') and thus interpreted as meaning 'gift of the gods'. Variants include **Debdan** and **Deodan**.

Devdas (m) Indian name derived from the Sanskrit *deva* ('god') and *dasa* ('servant') and thus interpreted as meaning 'servant of the gods'.

Deverell (m) Celtic first name meaning 'fertile river bank'. Also found as **Deverill**, it was in use as a surname before being adopted as an occasional first name.

Devereux (m) English surname (pronounced 'deveroh' in Britain and 'deveruh' in the United States) that has made occasional appearances as a first name, chiefly in the USA. The surname was of Norman French origin, evolving originally from the French *de Evreux* ('of Evreux'). It became famous as the surname of the earls of Essex in the 16th century.

Devi See DEV.

Devika (f) Indian name derived from the Sanskrit *devi* ('goddess') and *ka* ('little' or 'like').

Devlin (m) Irish first name derived from the Irish Gaelic for 'fiercely brave'.

Devon (m) English first name derived from the name of the county of Devon. It has

made rare appearances, chiefly within the Black community in the USA, during the second half of the 20th century. Well-known bearers of the name have included the Jamaican-born British cricketer Devon Malcolm (b.1963).

Dewey See DEWI.

Dewi (m) Welsh variant of DAVID. Of ancient origins, it enjoyed a revival in Wales in the 20th century. **Dewey** is a variant of the name in occasional use in the USA.

Dex See DEXTER.

Dexter (m) English surname derived from the Old English *deag* ('dye') and thus meaning 'dyer' that has been in occasional use as a first name among English speakers on both sides of the Atlantic since the 1930s. It is sometimes chosen as a name through association with the Latin *dexter*, meaning 'right-handed' or 'auspicious'. Commonly shortened to **Dex**.

Dezi See DESMOND.

Di See DIANA; DIANE; DINAH.

Diamond (f) English first name derived from that of the gemstone. It was among the various jewel names that enjoyed some popularity in the 19th century but has since become very rare.

Diana (f) English first name derived from the name of the Roman goddess of the moon and of the hunt. Despite its pagan associations, it was taken up by English speakers after the Reformation and subsequently enjoyed a peak in popularity around the middle of the 20th century. Notable bearers of the name have included the central character in the George Meredith novel *Diana of the Crossways* (1885), British actresses Diana Dors (1931–84) and Dame Diana Rigg (b.1938), US pop singer Diana Ross (Diane Earle; b.1944) and Diana, Princess of Wales (1961–97). Commonly shortened to **Di**. *See also* DEANNA; DIANE; DINAH.

Diane (f) French version of the English DIANA that was taken up alongside the existing form of the name by English speakers in the 1930s. It remained popular until the 1970s, when it began to decline in frequency. Famous bearers of the name have included Diane de Poitiers (1499–1566), mistress of Henri II of France, and US actresses Diane Ladd (b.1932) and Diane Keen (b.1946). Commonly abbreviated to **Di**. Variants include **Dian**, **Dianne**, **Deanne**, **Diahann** and **Dyan** (or **Dyanne**) – as borne by the US actress Dyan Cannon (b.1938).

Dianne *See* DIANE.

Diarmaid/Diarmuid *See* DERMOT.

Dick (m) English first name that developed as a diminutive form of RICHARD. It has been suggested that the name evolved via **Rick** as a result of the difficulty English speakers experienced in pronouncing the initial 'R' in the rolled Norman French manner. It was in widespread use among English speakers by the 17th century and remained in common currency until well into the 20th century. Notable bearers of the name have included the English highwayman Dick Turpin (Richard Turpin; 1706–39), the fictional Dick Swiveller in the Charles Dickens novel *The Old Curiosity Shop* (1840–41), British comedian Dick Emery (1917–83), British crime novelist Dick Francis (b.1920) and US comedian Dick van Dyke (b.1925). **Dickie** and **Dicky** are diminutive forms of the name of 19th-century origin – as borne by British pop singer Dickie Valentine (1929–71) and British television presenter Dickie Davies (b.1933).

Dickie *See* DICK.

Dickon *See* RICHARD.

Dicky *See* DICK.

Didi *See* DIDIER.

Didier (m) French first name derived from the Roman Desiderius itself from the Latin *desiderium* ('longing'). It was borne by several early Christian saints. **Didi** is a diminutive form of the name. Variants in other languages include the Italian, Spanish and Portuguese **Desiderio**.

Diederik *See* DIETRICH.

Diedre *See* DEIRDRE.

Diego (m) Spanish first name of uncertain origin, possibly descended from the Greek *didakhe* ('teaching'). It is often treated as a variant of SANTIAGO. Famous bearers of the name in recent times have included Argentinian footballer Diego Maradona (b.1960). Variants include the Portuguese **Diogo**.

Dieter (m) German first name (pronounced 'deeter') derived from the Old German *theuth* ('people' or 'race') and *hari* ('army' or 'warrior'). Notable bearers of the name have included a 6th-century French saint.

Dietmar (m) German first name (pronounced 'deetmar') derived from the Old German *theuth* ('people' or 'race') and *mari* ('famous'). It was borne by two 12th-century German saints.

Dietrich (m) German equivalent of the English DEREK, pronounced 'deetrik'. Notable bearers of the name have included the German baritone Dietrich Fischer-Dieskau (b.1925). Variants in other languages include the Dutch **Diederik**.

Dieudonnée *See* DONATA.

Digby (m) English place name (from Digby in Lincolnshire) derived from the Old Norse *diki* ('ditch') and *byr* ('settlement'), and thus interpreted as meaning 'farm by a ditch', that was subsequently taken up as a surname and, from the 19th century, as an occasional first name. Well-known bearers of the name have included the best friend of the fictional Dan Dare in the famous long-running British cartoon strip that began in the *Eagle* comic in the 1950s.

Diggory (m) English first name of uncertain origin, but possibly derived from the French *l'esgaré* ('the lost one' or 'astray'). The name may have been popularized by the 14th-century romance *Sir Degaré* but it was not until the 16th century that the name began to appear with any regularity among English speakers, most frequently in Cornwall. The name appears to be of largely historical interest today, having fallen out of use some time during the 19th century. Notable instances of the name in literature have included appearances in such works as Oliver Goldsmith's comedy *She Stoops to Conquer* (1773) and Thomas Hardy's novel *The Return of the Native* (1878). Also encountered as **Digory**.

Dil *See* DILYS.

Dilip (m) Indian name possibly derived from the Sanskrit *dili* ('Delhi') and *pa* ('protecting'). In Indian mythology it is borne by several legendary kings. Also spelled **Duleep**.

Dill *See* DILYS.

Dillon *See* DYLAN.

Dilly *See* DILWEN; DILYS.

Dilwen (f) Welsh name that is thought to have resulted from the combination of DILYS and *gwyn* ('white') and is usually interpreted as meaning 'fair' or 'holy'. It appears to be a relatively recent introduction of 20th-century origin. **Dilly** is a diminutive form of the name. Also encountered as **Dilwyn**.

Dilwyn *See* DILWEN.

Dilys (f) Welsh name derived from *dilys* ('genuine', 'steadfast' or 'sincere'). It appears to have been a 19th-century introduction that soon found favour beyond Welsh borders, but has appeared with decreasing frequency since the middle of the 20th century. Well-known bearers of the name have included the British film critic Dilys Powell (1901–95). **Dylis** and **Dyllis** are variant forms of the name. Diminutives include **Dil**, **Dill** and **Dilly**.

Dima (f) Arabic name derived from *dima* ('downpour'). Its attractiveness as a first name among Arabs reflects the fact that rain is generally welcomed in the dry lands of the Middle East.

Dimitri *See* DMITRI.

Dina *See* DINAH.

Dinah (f) Hebrew name derived from the Hebrew *din* ('judgement' or 'lawsuit') and interpreted as meaning 'vindicated'. It often appears as a variant of DIANA, despite the fact that the two names have distinct origins. It appears in the Bible as the name of the daughter of Jacob and Leah, whose rape by Shechem led to her brothers taking bloody revenge. It was taken up by English Puritans after the Reformation and enjoyed a peak in popularity among English speakers on both sides of the Atlantic in the 19th century. Notable bearers of the name have included a character in Laurence Sterne's novel *Tristram Shandy* (1759–67), Dinah Morris in the George Eliot novel *Adam Bede* (1859) and British actress Dinah Sheridan (b.1920). Commonly shortened to **Di**. **Dina** is a variant form of the name.

Dinesh (m) Indian name derived from the Sanskrit *dina* ('day') and *isa* ('lord') and thus interpreted as meaning 'lord of the day' or simply 'sun'.

Dino (m) Italian name representing a diminutive form of Leonardino and other names with similar endings.

Dinsdale (m) English place name meaning 'settlement by a moat' that was subsequently adopted as a surname and occasional first name. Famous bearers of the name have included British actor Dinsdale Landen (b.1932).

Diogo *See* DIEGO.

Dion (m) English first name derived via the Roman Dionysius from the Greek Dionysios (a devotee of the Greek god of wine) or some other similar Greek source. It was taken up by English speakers in the 16th century and has remained in irregular use ever since. Today it is popular within the Black community in the USA. Famous bearers of the name have included the Irish playwright Dion Boucicault (Dionysius Lardner Boursiquot; 1820–90). **Dionne**, **Dione** and **Dionna** are feminine variants in chiefly US use since the 1930s – as borne by US pop singer Dionne Warwick (b.1941).

Dione/Dionna/Dionne See DION.

Dionysios/Dionysius See DENNIS; DION.

Dipak (m) Indian name derived from the Sanskrit *dipa* ('light' or 'lamp') and *ka* ('little' or 'like'). It is sometimes associated with Kama, the god of love in Indian mythology. Also encountered as **Deepak**.

Dirk See DEREK.

Divina (f) English first name that developed as a variant of DAVINA, possibly under the influence of the ordinary vocabulary word 'divine'. It has appeared irregularly as a first name among English speakers since the early part of the 20th century. Variants include **Davinia**, which may reflect the influence of LAVINIA.

Dixie (f) English first name derived from the French *dix* ('ten'). It is popular chiefly in the USA, where it is best known as the nickname of the southern states of the USA. Also found as **Dixee**.

Diya (m) Arabic name derived from *diya* ('brightness' or 'glow').

Djamila See JAMAL.

Dmitri (m) Russian first name derived via the Roman Demetrius from the Greek Demetrios, a derivative of the name of the Greek goddess Demeter, itself from the Greek *de* ('earth') and *meter* ('mother'). Notable bearers of the name have included the 4th-century martyr St Demetrius. **Mitya** is a familiar form. Variants include **Dimitri** and the Italian and Spanish **Demetrio**.

Dod/Dodie/Dodo See DOROTHY.

Doireann See DOREAN.

Dolly (f) English first name that evolved as a diminutive of DOROTHY or DOLORES and is sometimes presumed (inaccurately) to have been inspired by the ordinary vocabulary word 'doll' (which is, however, a later coinage dating from the 17th century). It appears to have been taken up by English speakers in the 16th century and had become relatively common by the 18th century, since when it has become much less frequent. Notable bearers of the name have included Dolly Varden in the Charles Dickens novel *Barnaby Rudge* (1841), US country-and-western singer Dolly Parton (b.1946) and Dolly Levi in Thornton Wilder's play *The Matchmaker* (1955), which subsequently provided the basis for the musical *Hello, Dolly!* (1964). Commonly abbreviated to **Doll** – as borne by Falstaff's mistress Doll Tearsheet in William Shakespeare's *Henry IV, Part 2* (1597). Occasionally encountered as **Dolley**, chiefly in the USA. *See also* ADOLPHUS.

Dolores (f) Spanish first name derived from the Spanish *dolores* ('sorrows') and thus referring to the title *Maria de los Dolores* ('Mary of the Sorrows') borne by the Virgin Mary. It became very popular in the 20th century, when it spread with Spanish emigrants to many parts of the English-speaking world, especially the USA. Famous bearers of the name have included the US actress Dolores Del Rio (1905–83). LOLA, LOLITA and DOLLY are diminutive forms of the name. Variants include **Delores**.

Dolph See ADOLPHUS.

Dom/Domenico/Domingo See DOMINIC.

Dominic (m) English first name descended ultimately from the Roman Dominicus, itself derived from the Latin *dominus* ('lord'). Borne in the 13th century by St Dominic, founder of the Dominican order of monks, it was popular among English speakers in medieval times and remained a favourite choice of Roman Catholics in succeeding centuries, often reserved for children born on Sundays. In Ireland it is sometimes treated as an Anglicization of **Domhnall**. Commonly abbreviated to **Dom**. Also encountered occasionally in the archaic form **Dominick**. Variants in other languages include the French DOMINIQUE, the Italian **Domenico** and the Spanish **Domingo**. **Dominica** is a relatively rare feminine version of the name.

Dominica/Dominick *See* DOMINIC.

Dominique (m/f) French equivalent of the male DOMINIC. The French apply the name to both sexes, more often to boys than to girls in recent times, but it has always been employed as a girls' name among English speakers, who first took up the name in this French incarnation in the 1960s.

Don (m) English first name that developed as a diminutive form of DONALD and DONOVAN. It began to win acceptance as a name in its own right from the 19th century and remained a fairly popular choice among English speakers until the middle of the 20th century, since when it has become less frequent. Notable bearers of the name have included the US writer Don Marquis (1878–1937), US actor Don Ameche (Dominic Felix Amici; 1908–93), Australian cricketer Sir Don Bradman (1908–2001) and US pop singer Don McLean (b.1945). **Donny** is a diminutive form of the name.

Donal *See* DONALD.

Donald (m) English version of the Gaelic Domhnall, itself derived from the Celtic *dubno* ('world') and *val* ('rule' or 'mighty') and thus interpreted as meaning 'world mighty' or 'world ruler'. The final 'd' came either through attempts by English speakers to pronounce the Gaelic name in an authentic manner or else through the influence of such Germanic names as RONALD. It has strong Scottish associations, notably through several early Scottish kings of the name and through the clan MacDonald, one of the most famous of all Scottish clans. English speakers elsewhere took up the name in the 1920s and it has remained in occasional use ever since, often among people with no Scottish connections, al-

though much more rarely by the end of the 20th century.

Famous bearers of the name have included British actor Donald Pleasence (1919–95), British car and speedboat racer Donald Campbell (1921–67), British actor Donald Sinden (b.1923), US actor Donald O'Connor (1925–2003) and Canadian actor Donald Sutherland (b.1935) as well as the cartoon character Donald Duck created by Walt Disney in the 1930s. Commonly abbreviated to DON and less frequently to **Donny** – as borne by US pop singer Donny Osmond (Donald Osmond; b.1957). An Irish form of the name is **Donal**. Feminine equivalents include **Donalda**, **Donaldina** and **Donella**.

Donalda/Donaldina *See* DONALD.

Donat *See* DONATA.

Donata (f) Italian, Spanish and Portuguese name derived from the Roman Donatus, itself from the Latin *donare* ('to give') and thus interpreted as meaning 'given by God'. The masculine form of the name was a frequent choice of early Christians and a common saints' name and is still in use in modern Italy as **Donato** or **Donatello**, although the feminine form of the name is now more common. Variants in other languages include the masculine French forms **Donat** and **Donatien** and the feminine Old French **Dieudonnée**.

Donatello/Donatien/Donato *See* DONATA.

Donella *See* DONALD.

Donna (f) English first name derived from the Italian *donna* ('lady'). It was taken up by English speakers in the 1920s, initially in the USA but later becoming widespread throughout the English-speaking world. It was at its most frequent in the 1960s and again in the 1980s. Notable bearers of the name have included US actress Donna Reed (1921–86) and US soul singer Donna Summer (LaDonna Adrian Gaines; b.1948). *See also* MADONNA.

Donny *See* DONALD; DONOVAN.

Donovan (m) Irish surname derived from the Gaelic *donn* ('brown') and *dubh* ('black' or 'dark'), and thus interpreted as meaning 'dark brown' (referring to the colour of a person's hair, eyes or complexion), that was subsequently taken up as an occasional first name. It was taken up by English speakers early in the 20th century and is borne today by many people with no immediate Irish connections. Well-known bearers of the name have included the Scottish-born British pop singer Donovan (Donovan Leitch; b.1946). Commonly shortened to DON or **Donny**.

Dora (f) English first name that developed as a diminutive of such names as DOROTHY, ISADORA and THEODORA, which all share common origins in the Greek word *doron* ('gift'). It was adopted by English speakers in the 19th century and became fairly common, although it has been in decline since the early 20th century and is now rare. Famous bearers of the name have included the fictional Dora Spenlow in the Charles Dickens novel *David Copperfield* (1849–50), British artist Dora Carrington (1893–1932) and British actress Dora Bryan (b.1924). Familiar forms of the name include **Dorry** and **Dory**. The diminutive forms **Doria**, **Doretta**, **Dorette** and **Dorita** are very rare variants.

Doran (m) English first name derived from an Irish Gaelic surname meaning 'descendant of Deoradhan' (which itself means 'exile' or 'wanderer').

Dorcas (f) English first name derived from the Greek *dorkas* ('doe' or 'gazelle'). It appears in the Bible not as a name in its own right but as a translation of the Aramaic TABITHA. English Puritans adopted it as a first name after the Reformation and it has continued in irregular use into modern times. In Scotland it is sometimes employed as an Anglicization of **Deoiridh**. Notable bearers of the name have included one of the main characters in the anonymous comedy *The Merry Devil of Edmonton* (1608)

and a shepherdess in William Shakespeare's *The Winter's Tale* (1610–11).

Dorean (f) Irish name that developed as an Anglicization of the Gaelic Doireann, itself resulting from the combination of the Gaelic *der* ('daughter') and the name of the legendary Irish hero Finn. It emerged as a popular choice of name among Irish speakers in the 20th century, perhaps in response to the popularity of the English DOREEN.

Doreen (f) English first name that resulted from the combination of such names as DORA, KATHLEEN and MAUREEN. English speakers took up the name towards the end of the 19th century and it was at its most frequent in the 1930s, since when it has become much less common. Variants include **Dorene** and **Dorine**; **Reenie** is a diminutive. *See also* DOREAN.

Doretta/Dorette/Doria *See* DORA.

Dorian (m) English first name derived via the Roman Dorianus from the Greek Dorieus, meaning 'person from Doris' (Doris being the name of a region in ancient Greece). It is well known in the English-speaking world from the Oscar Wilde novel *The Picture of Dorian Gray* (1891), in which it may have made its first appearance, and has since continued in irregular use. Other notable bearers of the name have included the British showjumping commentator Dorian Williams (1914–85). **Dorien** and **Dorrien** are rare variants of the name. The feminine equivalents **Dorianne** and **Doriana** have also made occasional appearances.

Dorinda (f) English first name that resulted from the combination of DORA and the suffix '-inda', as found in such names as BELINDA and CLARINDA. It made appearances as a literary name in the 17th century and has since made infrequent appearances as a first name among English speakers. Notable bearers of the name have included one of the main characters in the

George Farquhar comedy *The Beaux' Stratagem* (1707).

Doris (f) English first name derived from the Greek for 'bountiful' or else 'person from Doris' (Doris being the name of a region in ancient Greece), but also treated as a combination of DOROTHY and PHYLLIS. It appears in mythology as the name of a minor goddess who was the mother of the Nereids and it was adopted by English speakers towards the end of the 19th century. It has become much less common since the middle of the 20th century. Famous bearers of the name have included South African novelist Doris Lessing (b.1919), US film actress Doris Day (b.1924) and the fictional Doris Archer in the long-running British radio soap opera *The Archers*. Diminutive forms of the name include **Dorrie**.

Dorita *See* DORA.

Dorothea *See* DOROTHY.

Dorothy (f) English first name derived via Dorothea ultimately from the Greek *doron* ('gift') and *theos* ('god') and thus interpreted as meaning 'gift of God'. As Dorothea, it was taken up by English speakers in the 16th century and became fairly common in the 19th century before falling from favour. As Dorothy, it made its first appearance as early as the 16th century and, after a period out of favour in the 18th century, gradually eclipsed Dorothea from the late 19th century. It enjoyed a peak in popularity in the 1920s but has since become much less common, perhaps because the name 'Dorothy' has become a slang term for a homosexual (a reference to Dorothy in the 1939 film musical *The Wizard of Oz*, which now enjoys cult status among homosexuals).

Notable bearers of the name in its various forms have included the 4th-century Christian martyr St Dorothea, English actress and royal mistress Dorothea Jordan (1761–1816), the fictional Dorothea Casaubon in the George Eliot novel *Middlemarch* (1872), British crime novelist Dorothy L. Sayers (1893–1957), US humorist Dorothy Parker (1893–1967), US actress Dorothy Lamour (1914–96) and British actress Dorothy Tutin (1930–2001). Diminutive forms of the name include **Thea**, DEE, **Dot**, **Dottie** (or **Dotty**), **Dod**, **Dodo**, **Dodie** – as borne by the British playwright Dodie Smith (1896–1990) – DOLLY and DORA. Variants in other languages include the Russian **Dorofei**.

Dorrie *See* DORA; DORIS.

Dorrien *See* DORIAN.

Dory *See* DORA.

Dosia *See* THEODOSIA.

Dot/Dottie/Dotty *See* DOROTHY.

Doug *See* DOUGAL; DOUGLAS.

Dougal (m) English version of the Gaelic Dubhgall or Dughall, derived from the Gaelic *dubh* ('black') and *gall* ('stranger'). It was applied originally to the dark-haired Danes who settled in Ireland early in that country's history. The Scottish took up the name in subsequent centuries and it began to appear more widely in the English-speaking world after the early 20th century, although it has retained its Gaelic associations. Well-known bearers of the name have included Dougal the long-haired dog in the British 1960s children's television programme *The Magic Roundabout*. Commonly abbreviated to **Doug** (or **Dug**) and **Dougie** (or **Duggy**). Variants include **Dugald** and **Doyle**.

Dougie *See* DOUGAL; DOUGLAS.

Douglas (m) Scottish place name derived from the Gaelic *dubh* ('black') and *glas* ('stream') that was subsequently taken up as a surname and, from the 19th century, as a first name among English speakers. Well known in Scotland from the earls of Douglas, it was applied initially to children of either sex, although it has been reserved exclusively for boys since the 17th century. It remained a popular choice until the middle of the 20th century, since when it has become much less common. Famous bearers of the name have included the US army commander General Douglas MacArthur (1880–1964), US actors Douglas Fairbanks (1883–1939) and Douglas Fairbanks Jnr (1909–2000) and British war hero Sir Douglas Bader (1920–82). Commonly shortened to **Doug** (or **Dug**) and **Dougie** (or **Duggie**).

Doyle *See* DOUGAL.

Drake (m) English first name meaning 'dragon'. It was in use as a surname before being adopted as an occasional first name.

Dreda *See* ETHELDREDA.

Drena *See* ADRIENNE.

Drew (m/f) English first name that evolved as a diminutive of ANDREW or otherwise as a derivation of the Old German DROGO. It established itself in Scotland before winning acceptance elsewhere in the English-speaking world from the 1940s, usually as a name for boys. Famous bearers of the name in modern times have included US film actress Drew Barrymore (b.1975), although in her case she inherited it from the surname of the celebrated theatrical Drew family into which the Barrymores had married.

Drina *See* ADRIENNE.

Driscoll (m) English first name, originally a surname, derived from the Irish Gaelic for 'interpreter'. Also encountered as **Driscol**.

Drogo (m) English name of uncertain meaning, possibly derived from the Old Saxon *drog* ('ghost') or Old German *tragan* ('to bear' or 'to carry') or, more likely, from the Slavonic *dorogo* ('dear'). It was brought to England by the Normans in the 11th century and remained in currency until the late 17th century. It enjoyed a revival among English speakers in the 19th century after it was taken up by the aristocratic Montagu family but is very rare today. DREW is occasionally used as a diminutive form of the name.

Drummond (m) Scottish place name that was subsequently adopted as a surname and is occasionally encountered in use as a first name. Still largely confined to Scotland.

Drusilla (f) English first name derived ultimately from the Roman Drusus, itself supposedly from the Greek *drosos* ('dew') and often interpreted as meaning 'fruitful' or 'dewy-eyed'. It appears in the Bible as the name of the lover of Felix, the Roman procurator of Judaea. It was taken up by English speakers in the 17th century, although it has never been in frequent use. It is still encountered occasionally today, chiefly in the USA. Notable bearers of the name have included the emperor Caligula's sister Livia Drusilla and the fictional Drusilla Fawley in the Thomas Hardy novel *Jude the Obscure* (1894–5). Also found as **Drucilla** or **Druscilla**. *See also* CILLA.

Drystan *See* TRISTRAM.

Dua (f) Arabic name derived from *dua* ('prayer').

Duane (m) English version of the Gaelic Dubhan, itself derived from *dubh* ('black') and interpreted as meaning 'little dark one'. It became popular among English speakers in the 1940s and reached a peak in frequency in the 1970s. It is often associated with the rock 'n' roll era of the 1950s, when famous bearers of the name included the US guitarist Duane Eddy (b.1938). Also found occasionally as **Dwayne** or **Dwane**.

Duarte *See* EDWARD.

Dubhghall *See* DOUGAL.

Dud *See* DUDLEY.

Dudley (m) English place name derived from the Old English for 'wood or clearing of Dudda' that was subsequently adopted as a surname and, from the middle of the 19th century, as an occasional first name. It is also encountered in Ireland as an Anglicization of **Dubhdara** or DARA. It became well known as the surname of Elizabeth I's favourite Robert Dudley, Earl of Leicester (*c*.1532–88). Other notable bearers of the name have included British comedian and actor Dudley Moore (1935–2002) and the fictional Dudley Dursley in the *Harry Potter* books by J. K. Rowling. Commonly shortened to **Dud**.

Duff (m) Scottish first name derived from the Gaelic *dubh* ('dark' or 'black') and originally bestowed upon people with dark hair or complexions. Famous bearers of the name have included the British politician Sir Alfred Duff Cooper, 1st Viscount Norwich (1890–1954).

Dug *See* DOUGAL; DOUGLAS.

Dugald *See* DOUGAL.

Duggie *See* DOUGAL; DOUGLAS.

Duha (f) Arabic name derived from *duha* ('morning').

Duke (m) English first name derived either from the rank or title 'duke' or else as a diminutive of MARMADUKE. It was taken up by English speakers early in the 20th century, chiefly in the USA, where it was further popularized as the nickname of the popular US film actor John Wayne (1907–79). Notable bearers of the name have included the US jazz musician Duke Ellington (Edward Kennedy Ellington; 1899–1974).

Dulce/Dulcibella *See* DULCIE.

Dulcie (f) English first name derived ultimately from the Roman Dulcia, from the Latin *dulcis* ('sweet'). Recorded in use among English speakers in medieval times in such forms as Duce or Dowse, it was revived in its modern form towards the end of the 19th century and enjoyed a peak in popularity in the 1920s and 1930s. It had become uncommon by the end of the 20th century. Famous bearers of the name have included the British actress Dulcie Gray (b.1920). **Dulce** is a diminutive form. Variants include the largely historical **Dulcibella** or **Dowsabel**, the 19th-century **Dulcia** and the Spanish **Dulcinea**.

Dulcinea *See* DULCIE.

Duleep *See* DILIP.

Duncan (m) English version of the Gaelic Donnchadh, derived from the Old Celtic *donn* ('dark') and *cath* ('battle') and thus interpreted as meaning 'dark warrior'. It has a long history as a Scottish name, having been borne by a 7th-century Scottish saint and three 11th-century Scottish kings. It was taken up on a wider basis throughout the English-speaking world in the 20th century and today is often borne by people with no immediate Scottish connections. It enjoyed a peak in popularity in the 1960s but had become rather less common by the end of the century. Notable bearers of the name have included Scottish painter Duncan Grant (1885–1978) and British swimmer Duncan Goodhew (b.1957). Commonly abbreviated to **Dunk**, **Dunkie** or **Dunky**.

Dunlop (m) Scottish first name meaning 'muddy hill'. It was in use as a surname before being adopted as a first name on an occasional basis.

Dunstan (m) English place name derived from the Old English *dun* ('dark') and *stan* ('stone') and interpreted as meaning 'stony hill' that was subsequently taken up as a surname and from the medieval period as an occasional first name, chiefly among Roman Catholics. It is best known as the name of the 10th-century English St Dunstan, Archbishop of Canterbury. Other bearers of the name have included the fictional Dunstan Cass in the George Eliot novel *Silas Marner* (1861).

Durand (m) French and English first name derived from the Latin *durans* ('enduring'). It came to England with the Normans in the 11th century and remained in fairly common currency until the end of the medieval period. It has made rare reappearances in succeeding centuries. *See also* DANTE.

Durga (f) Indian name derived from the Sanskrit *durga* ('unattainable'). It appears in

Indian mythology as the name of Shiva's fierce twelve-armed wife.

Dustin (m) English surname of uncertain origin that has made occasional appearances as a first name among English speakers since the early 20th century. It has been suggested that the name evolved as a Norman version of the Old Norse THUR-STAN, meaning 'Thor's stone', or else from the Old German for 'brave fighter'. The most famous bearer of the name to date has been US actor Dustin Hoffman (b.1937), who is supposed to have been named in honour of the earlier US film actor Dustin Farman (1874–1929). *See also* DUSTY.

Dusty (m/f) English first name that emerged either as a feminine equivalent of the masculine DUSTIN or else as a borrowing of the ordinary vocabulary word 'dusty' (referring to the colour of a person's hair or complexion). It has made occasional appearances as a first name since the 1950s. The most famous bearer of the name to date has been the British pop singer Dusty Springfield (Mary O'Brien; 1939–99).

Dwane/Dwayne *See* DUANE.

Dwight (m) English surname possibly derived from the medieval French Diot that has made irregular appearances as a first name since the end of the 19th century, chiefly in the USA. It has been suggested that the medieval form of the name can be traced back ultimately to the Roman Diony-sius (*see* DENNIS). Its popularity in the USA reflects the fame of US President Dwight D. Eisenhower (1890–1969), who was himself named after the noted clergyman and educationist Timothy Dwight (1752–1817), an early President of Yale University.

Dyan/Dyanne *See* DIANE.

Dylan (m) Welsh first name that may have evolved via the Welsh *dylif* ('flood') from the Celtic word for 'sea'. Attempts to interpret the name more exactly have included 'son of the wave' and 'influence'. Long established in Wales, where it was borne by a legendary Welsh hero who appears in the *Mabinogi*, it was taken up by English speakers in the 1950s and received a boost from the 1960s as the surname of the US singer-songwriter Bob Dylan (Robert Allen Zimmerman; b.1941), who claimed that he got the name from his uncle **Dillon** – a fairly common variant spelling. The most famous bearer of the name to date has been the Welsh poet Dylan Thomas (1914–53).

Dylis/Dyllis *See* DILYS.

Dymphna (f) Irish first name that is thought to have evolved from the Gaelic Damhnait, itself from *damh* ('fawn' or 'stag', or alternatively 'poet'). Sometimes interpreted as meaning 'eligible'. It is little known outside Ireland itself. Notable bearers of the name have included the obscure Irish St Dymphna, patron saint of lunatics. **Dympna** is a variant form.

E

Eachann (m) Scottish name (pronounced 'ackan') derived from the Gaelic *each* ('horse') and *donn* ('brown'). Sometimes considered to be a Gaelic equivalent of HECTOR.

Eadan (f) Irish name derived from the Old Irish Etain, possibly based on the Old Irish *et* ('jealousy'). Usually pronounced 'aidan' or 'adan', it features in Irish legend as the name of a sun goddess and became popular among English speakers following the success of the opera *The Immortal Hour* (1914), which retold the mythological story of Princess Etain of the Fair Hair. Also encountered as **Etan**.

Eamon (m) Irish equivalent of the English EDMUND, pronounced 'aimon'. Notable bearers have included the celebrated Irish President Eamon de Valera (1882–1975). Also encountered as **Eamonn** – as borne by Irish-born British television presenter Eamonn Andrews (1922–87).

Earl (m) English surname and first name derived from the aristocratic rank, itself from the Old English *eorl* ('nobleman' or 'chieftain'). As a surname it was often bestowed upon those who worked as servants and retainers in the households of English earls. Records of the name in use among English speakers go back as far as the 12th century. It became more common in the 17th century and has remained popular ever since, particularly among Black Americans in the 20th century. Notable bearers of the name have included US jurist Earl Warren (1891–1974) and US jazz musician Earl 'Fatha' Hines (1903–81). It acquired some notoriety in 1968 through James Earl Ray (1929–98), the assassin who in that year shot dead the US Black civil rights leader Martin Luther King. Also encountered as **Earle** or **Erle** – as borne by the US crime fiction novelist Erle Stanley Gardner (1889–1970). *See also* DUKE; EARLENE; ERROL; KING; PRINCE.

Earlena *See* EARLENE.

Earlene (f) English first name that developed as a feminine equivalent of EARL. Variants include **Earlena**, **Erlean**, **Erleen** and **Erlinda**.

Earnest *See* ERNEST.

Eartha (f) English first name derived from the ordinary vocabulary word 'earth'. Often associated with the notion of 'Mother Earth', it has made irregular appearances among English speakers through the 20th century. Famous bearers of the name have included US jazz singer and actress Eartha Kitt (b.1928). Variants include **Ertha** and **Erthel**.

Easter (m/f) English first name derived from the name of the Christian festival of Easter, which itself got its name from that of the Germanic spring goddess Eostre. Sometimes also treated as a variant of ESTHER, it was often reserved for children born during the Easter season but seems to have disappeared from use since the end of the 19th century.

Ebba (f) English first name derived from the Old English Eadburga, itself from *ead* ('riches') and *burg* ('fortress'). It was among the traditional English names that were revived during the 19th century but unlike some of the others appears to have fallen into disuse since then. The name is also in use among German speakers, who trace it back to the Old German *eber* ('wild boar').

Ebbe *See* EBERHARD.

Eben *See* EBENEZER.

Ebenezer (m) English first name derived from the Hebrew *ebenhaezer* ('stone of help'). It appears in the Bible as the name of the stone erected by Samuel to commemorate his triumph over the Philistines and was consequently taken up as a first name by Puritans on both sides of the Atlantic in the 17th century. Well-known bearers of the name have included the fictional miser Ebenezer Scrooge in *A Christmas Carol* (1843) by Charles Dickens as well as Ebenezer Balfour in the Robert Louis Stevenson novel *Kidnapped* (1886). Sometimes shortened to **Eb** or **Eben**.

Eberhard (m) German first name derived from the Old German *eber* ('wild boar') and *hardu* ('brave' or 'hardy'). Commonly abbreviated to **Ebbe**. Variant forms include **Evert**.

Ebo *See* EBONY.

Ebony (f) English first name derived from the name of the black wood ebony. It was taken up as a first name chiefly among Black Americans in the 1970s and by the 1980s ranked among the top three most popular names among female members of the Black community in the USA. Commonly abbreviated to **Ebo**.

Ebrahim *See* IBRAHIM.

Echo (f) English first name derived from the ordinary vocabulary word 'echo'. In Greek legend, Echo was a nymph whose unceasing chatter irritated the goddess Hera, who robbed her of the power of independent speech and allowed her only to repeat the last fragment of what others said. When Echo's love for the beautiful youth Narcissus was not returned she wasted away until all that was left was her voice.

Eckhard (m) German first name derived from the Old German *ek* ('edge') and *hardu* ('brave' or 'hardy'). Also found as **Eckhardt** or **Eckehard**.

Ed (m) English first name that developed as a diminutive of various longer names such as EDGAR, EDMUND, EDWARD and EDWIN but is now frequently treated as a name in its own right. It became more frequent among English speakers around the beginning of the 20th century. Well-known bearers of the name have included US crime novelist Ed McBain (Salvatore A. Lombino; b.1926) and US actor Ed Begley (b.1949). **Eddie** and **Eddy** are diminutive forms that emerged at much the same time – as borne by US actors Eddie Cantor (Edward Israel Itskowitz; 1892–1964) and Eddie Murphy (b.1961).

Eda *See* ADA.

Edan *See* AIDAN.

Edda *See* HEDDA.

Eddie/Eddy *See* ED.

Ede *See* EDITH.

Eden (m/f) English first name derived from the Old English Edun or Edon, which came in turn from the Old English *ead* ('riches') and *hun* ('bearcub'). As the name of the biblical Paradise, itself from the Hebrew *eden* ('delight' or 'paradise'), Eden was taken up as a first name by Puritans in the 17th century, although it has never been very common. Famous bearers of the name have included the British novelist Eden Phillpotts (1862–1960).

Edgar (m) English first name derived from the Old English Eadgar, itself based on the Old English *ead* ('riches') and *gar* ('spear') and thus interpreted as meaning 'rich in spears' or 'owner of many spears'. The modern form of the name was in common use among English speakers during the medieval period and it was among the many neglected historical names to be revived towards the end of the 19th century, particularly after it appeared as the name of a central character in the Walter Scott novel *The Bride of Lammermoor* (1819). It has been in decline since the early 20th century and is now relatively rare.

Famous bearers of the name have included the 10th-century English king Edgar the Peaceful (d.975), the 11th-century English prince Edgar the Aetheling (c.1060–c.1125), the Duke of Gloucester's son in William Shakespeare's tragedy *King Lear* (1604–5), US writer Edgar Allan Poe (1809–49), the fictional Edgar Linton in the Emily Brontë novel *Wuthering Heights* (1847) and US novelist Edgar Rice Burroughs (1875–1950). Commonly abbreviated to ED or **Eddie**. Variants include **Adair**.

Edie *See* EDITH.

Edina *See* EDNA; EDWINA.

Edith (f) English, French, German and Scandinavian first name derived from the Old English Eadgyth, itself based on the Old English *ead* ('riches') and *gyth* ('strife') and thus interpreted as meaning 'rich in war'. It was popular among English speakers in medieval times and was among the traditional first names revived towards the end of the 19th century. It suffered a gradual decline over the course of the 20th century and is now rare. Notable bearers of the name have included William the Conqueror's wife Edith (d.1075), British children's writer Edith Nesbit (1858–1924), US novelist Edith Wharton (1862–1937), British nurse Edith Cavell (1865–1915), British poet Dame Edith Sitwell (1887–1964), British actress Dame Edith Evans (1888–1976) and the French singer Edith Piaf (1915–63). Sometimes shortened to **Edie** or **Eda**. Variants include **Edyth** and the rare **Edythe**, **Edytha** or **Editha**.

Edmé *See* ESMÉ.

Edmond *See* EDMUND.

Edmund (m) English first name derived from the Old English Eadmund, itself based on the Old English *ead* ('riches') and *mund* ('protector') and thus interpreted as meaning 'protector of wealth' or 'happy protection'. The modern form of the name was in regular use among English speakers during the medieval period and it has remained in use ever since, although it has become much less common since the early years of the 20th century. Notable bearers of the name have included the 9th-century English king and saint after whom Bury St Edmunds was named, English poet Edmund Spenser (1552–99), a character in William Shakespeare's tragedy *King Lear* (1604–5), English actor Edmund Kean (c.1787–1833), British poet Edmund Blunden (1896–1974) and New Zealand mountaineer Sir Edmund Hillary (b.1919). Diminutive forms of the name include ED, **Eddie** (or **Eddy**), **Ned**, **Neddie** (or **Neddy**), **Ted** and **Teddie** (or **Teddy**). Variants in other languages include the French **Edmond**, the Italian **Edmondo** and the Spanish and Portuguese **Edmundo**. *See also* EAMON.

Edna (f) English first name possibly derived from the Hebrew *ednah* ('rejuvenation' or 'pleasure') or alternatively and more likely from the Irish EITHNE, itself from the Irish Gaelic for 'kernel'. It appears in the Apocrypha as the name of Sarah's mother. Sometimes considered a feminine equivalent of EDEN, it was taken up by English speakers in the 18th century and was at its most common from the late 19th century to the 1920s. It has since suffered a decline in popularity and is now very rare among the young. Well-known bearers of the name have included US writer Edna Ferber (1887–1968), US actress Edna Purviance (1894–1958) and Irish novelist Edna O'Brien (b.1932). Variants include **Edina**.

Edoardo *See* EDWARD.

Edom (m) Biblical name derived from the Hebrew for 'red'. It is supposed to have been an alternative name borne by the biblical Esau and was taken up in Scotland during the medieval period as a variant of ADAM.

Édouard *See* EDWARD.

Edric (m) English first name derived from the Old English *ead* ('riches') and *ric* ('power') and thus interpreted to mean 'rich and powerful'. Common in Anglo-Saxon times, it has appeared only very infrequently in modern times.

Edsel (m) German first name that is thought to have developed as a variant of ETZEL. The most famous bearer of the name in the English-speaking world to date has been Edsel Ford (1893–1943), son of the US industrialist Henry Ford.

Eduard/Eduardo/Edvard *See* EDWARD.

Edvige *See* HEDWIG.

Edward (m) English first name derived from the Old English Eadweard, itself from the Old English *ead* ('riches') and *weard* ('guard') and thus variously interpreted to mean 'guardian of riches', 'fortunate guardian' or 'wealth guardian'. The name's long history among the English goes back to at least the 9th century and it is still in common use today. It appeared regularly among English speakers during the medieval period, by which time it was already established as a royal name, and it was among the many historical names subsequently revived in the 19th century. It enjoyed a peak in popularity in the 1920s and has remained in currency throughout the English-speaking world (and beyond) ever since.

Famous bearers of the name have included three Anglo-Saxon kings and another eight kings of England, British humorist and artist Edward Lear (1812–88), the British composer Sir Edward Elgar (1857–1934), US film actor Edward G. Robinson (Emanuel Goldenberg; 1893–1973), British Prime Minister Edward Heath (b.1916) and Queen Elizabeth II's youngest son Prince Edward (b.1964). Commonly abbreviated to ED, **Eddie**, **Eddy**, **Ned**, **Neddie**, **Neddy**, **Ted**, **Teddie** or **Teddy**. Variants in other languages include the French **Édouard**, the German **Eduard**, the Italian **Edoardo**, the Spanish **Eduardo**, the Portuguese **Duarte** and the Russian and Scandinavian **Edvard**.

Edweena/Edwena *See* EDWINA.

Edwige *See* HEDWIG.

Edwin (m) English first name derived from the Old English Eadwine, itself based on the Old English *ead* ('riches') and *wine* ('friend') and thus interpreted to mean 'friend of riches' or 'rich friend'. Celebrated as the name of the 7th-century King Edwin of Northumbria, who was venerated as a saint after his death in battle, it was in fairly regular use among English speakers during the medieval period and was subsequently among the historical names revived in the 19th century. It is now very rare. Well-known bearers of the name have included British artist Sir Edwin Landseer (1802–73), the fictional central character in the unfinished Charles Dickens novel *Edwin Drood* (1870), Scottish poet Edwin Muir (1887–1959) and the central character in Arnold Bennett's *Clayhanger* (1910). ED and **Eddie** are common diminutives of the name. Sometimes spelled **Edwyn** or **Edwy**. *See also* EDWINA.

Edwina (f) English first name that evolved as a feminine form of EDWIN. It does not seem to have been in use in medieval times and probably made its first appearances in the 19th century when Edwin was revived. Today it is more common in Scotland than it is elsewhere. Notable bearers of the name have included Lord Mountbatten's wife Lady Edwina Mountbatten (1901–60), who was named in honour of Edward VII, and British politician, writer and broadcaster Edwina Currie (b.1946). Variants include **Edweena**, **Edwena** and **Edwyna**.

Edwy/Edwyn *See* EDWIN.

Edwyna *See* EDWINA.

Edyth/Edytha/Edythe *See* EDITH.

Effie *See* EPHRAIM; EUPHEMIA.

Efisio (m) Italian first name derived ultimately from the Roman Ephesius, a name applied to anyone from the Greek city of Ephesus. It was borne by a 4th-century Christian martyr from Sardinia.

Efrain *See* EPHRAIM.

Egan (m) Irish first name derived from

the Gaelic Aogan, itself a variant of Aodh, meaning 'fire'.

Egbert (m) English first name derived from the Old English Ecgbeorht from the Old English *ecg* ('edge') and *beorht* ('bright' or 'famous') and thus interpreted to mean 'bright sword' or 'famed swordsman'. It was in common use in Anglo-Saxon England prior to the Norman Conquest, being borne by two 8th-century saints and a 9th-century king of Wessex, among others. It appears to have fallen into disuse following the medieval period and, after a brief revival in the 19th century, is virtually unknown today.

Egidio *See* GILES.

Eglantine (f) English flower name based on that of the plant usually identified as sweetbrier (which has the French name *aiglent*), but often confused with honeysuckle. The name was in use among English speakers during the medieval period, as shown by its appearance as the name of the central character in 'The Prioress's Tale' in Geoffrey Chaucer's *The Canterbury Tales* (1387). It was revived on a modest scale in the 19th century but has since failed to make more than very occasional appearances. Variants include **Eglantina**, **Eglantyne** and **Eglentyne**.

Egon (m) German first name derived from the Old German *ek* ('edge') and thus usually interpreted to mean 'swordpoint'. Notable bearers of the name have included the Hungarian-born British food writer Egon Ronay.

Eibhlin *See* EILEEN.

Eileen (f) English first name derived from the Irish Eibhlin, an Irish equivalent of AVELINE (from AVIS, meaning 'struggle' or 'bird'), but also often treated as an Irish form of HELEN. It was taken up by English speakers towards the end of the 19th century (when it was exported widely throughout the English-speaking world by Irish emigrants) and enjoyed a peak in popularity in the 1920s, since when it has suffered a prolonged decline. **Eily** is a

familiar form of the name. Variants include **Aileen** (a Scottish variant), **Eilean**, **Eilene**, **Ilean**, **Ileene**, **Ilene** and **Ileen**.

Eilert (m) Scandinavian first name derived from the Old German *eg* ('edge') and *hardu* ('brave' or 'hardy'). It was exported to Scandinavia from Germany in the 17th century.

Eiluned *See* ELUNED.

Eilwen (f) Welsh name meaning 'fair brow'.

Eily *See* EILEEN.

Einar (m) Scandinavian first name (pronounced 'eyenar') derived from the Old Norse *einn* ('one') and *herr* ('warrior') and thus interpreted as meaning 'warrior chief'. It has made rare appearances as a first name among English speakers over the years.

Eira (f) Welsh first name (pronounced 'eera' or 'eye-ra') meaning 'snow'. It is a relatively recent introduction that has yet to win acceptance outside Wales.

Eirian (f) Welsh first name (pronounced 'evan' or 'eye-ree-an') meaning 'bright', 'beautiful' or 'silver'. Apparently a recent coinage dating back to around the middle of the 20th century, it seems to have remained confined to Wales. Variants include **Eireen**, **Arian** and **Ariane**.

Eirlys (f) Welsh first name (pronounced 'airlees' or 'eyer-liss') meaning 'snowdrop'. It made its first appearances towards the end of the 19th century but still appears to be in exclusively Welsh use.

Eithne (f) Irish first name probably derived from the Gaelic *eithne* ('kernel'), although often treated as a feminine version of AIDAN. Borne by an Irish goddess, several Irish queens and nine saints, the name remains rare outside Ireland itself. English speakers usually pronounce the name as 'ethnee', whereas the Irish know it as 'eenya' – hence the Irish variant **Enya,** as borne by the Irish pop singer Enya (Eithne ni Bhraonain; b.1962). Other variants include **Ethne, Ethna, Etna** and **Aithne**. *See also* ENA.

Eladio (m) Spanish first name derived via the Roman Helladius from the Greek Hellas ('Greece').

Elain (f) Welsh first name meaning 'fawn' or 'hind'. Sometimes confused with the otherwise unrelated ELAINE.

Elaine (f) English first name derived via Old French from HELEN. It appeared with increasing frequency among English speakers from the late 19th century, following its appearance in Alfred, Lord Tennyson's *Idylls of the King* (1859), reaching a peak in the 1960s and then falling off markedly in popularity. Famous bearers of the name have included the mother of Sir Galahad and the lover of Sir Lancelot in Arthurian legend, US actress Elaine Stritch (b.1926) and British singer and actress Elaine Paige (b.1952). Variants include **Elayne**. *See also* ELAIN.

Eldon (m) English place name (from County Durham) derived from the personal name Ella and the Old English *dun* ('hill'), thus interpreted as meaning 'Ella's hill', that was subsequently taken up as a surname and, from the 19th century, as an occasional first name. **Elden** is a variant form.

Eldred (m) English first name derived from the Old English Ealdred, itself from the Old English *eald* ('old') and *raed* ('counsel') and thus interpreted to mean 'long-established counsel'. Common among English speakers in medieval times and earlier, it has made only very occasional appearances in modern times. Variants include the rare feminine form **Eldreda** (sometimes shortened to **Dreda**).

Eldreda *See* ELDRED.

Eleanor (f) English first name of disputed origin. It is generally accepted that as a first name in use among English speakers it evolved either as a French version of HELEN, or else from an Old German name derived from *al* ('all'). The name came to England with Henry II's wife Eleanor of Aquitaine (1122–1204) and has remained in use ever since, with recent peaks in popularity in the 1960s and 1990s, although it has lost ground to Helen since 1400. Other notable bearers of the name have included Edward I's wife Eleanor of Castile (1246–90), in whose memory the 'Eleanor crosses' were erected in eastern England, British children's writer Eleanor Farjeon (1881–1965), US President Franklin D. Roosevelt's wife Eleanor Roosevelt (1884–1962) and British actress Eleanor Bron (b.1934). **Ellie,** NELL, **Nellie, Nelly,** NORA and **Norah** are diminutive forms. Alternative versions of the name include **Elenora, Lenore** and **Elinor** – as borne by Elinor Dashwood in Jane Austen's *Sense and Sensibility* (1811) and British novelist Elinor Glyn (1864–1943). Variants in other languages include the German **Eleonore** and the Italian **Eleonora**.

Eleanora *See* ELEANOR.

Eleazar *See* LAZARUS.

Electra (f) English version of the Italian Elettra, itself derived from the Greek *elektor* ('brilliant'). It is usually associated with the legend of Orestes and Electra, the children of Agamemnon who avenged their father's murder.

Elen (f) Welsh equivalent of HELEN. It is sometimes suggested that the name developed not directly from Helen but perhaps from the Welsh *elen* ('nymph'). The name was borne by a shadowy figure in Welsh myth, sometimes identified as the mother of Constantine the Great. Variants include **Elin**.

Elena *See* HELEN.

Elenora/Eleonora/Eleonore *See* ELEANOR.

Eleri (f) Welsh first name of uncertain meaning. It appears in Welsh mythology as the name of the daughter of the legendary chieftain Brychan.

Elettra *See* ELECTRA.

Elfleda (f) English first name derived from the Old English Aethelflaed, from the Old English *aethel* ('noble') and *flaed* ('beauty'). It enjoyed a short-lived revival among English speakers in the 19th century.

Elfreda (f) English first name derived from the Old English Aelfthryth, from the Old English *aelf* ('elf') and *thryth* ('strength'). It was common in Anglo-Saxon England, when notable bearers of the name included the mother of Ethelred the Unready. It vanished after the Norman Conquest but resurfaced among English speakers in the 19th century. It has since disappeared from general use once more. Also found as **Elfrida** or ALFREDA. Variants in other languages include the German **Elfriede**, commonly shortened to FREDA or **Friede**.

Elfrida *See* ELFREDA.

Eli (m) Hebrew name meaning 'high', 'elevated' or 'exalted'. It appears in the Bible as the name of a priest and judge who brought up the prophet Samuel and it was consequently adopted as a first name by English speakers in the 17th century. It enjoyed a peak in popularity in the 19th century but has been rare since the middle of the 20th century. Famous bearers of the name have included the US actor Eli Wallach (b.1915). **Ely** is a variant form.

Éliane (f) French first name derived via the Roman Aeliana from the Greek *helios* ('sun'). In English, Italian and other languages it often appears in the form **Eliana**.

Elias (m) Greek version of the biblical ELIJAH. It was taken up by English Puritans in the 17th century but became infrequent after the 19th century. Notable bearers of the name have included Elias Ashmole (1617–92), the founder of Oxford's Ashmolean Museum. Variants include ELLIS, which has been in rare use since the 15th century, and the Russian **Ilya**. *See also* ILIE.

Eliezer *See* LAZARUS.

Eligio *See* ELOY.

Elihu (m) Hebrew name meaning 'God is he' or 'the Lord is Yah'. It appears in the Old Testament and was consequently taken up by English Puritans after the Reformation, but is now uncommon.

Elijah (m) Biblical name derived from the Hebrew Eliyahu, meaning 'God is Yah' (Yah being another name for Jehovah). It appears in the Bible as the name of a celebrated prophet of the Israelites and also as an alternative name borne by John the Baptist. It was among the many biblical names adopted by Puritans on both sides of the Atlantic in the 17th century, although it was not until the 19th century that it began to appear with any regularity. It is now rare, confined largely to Black Muslims in the USA. Variants include the Yiddish **Elye**. *See also* ELIAS.

Elinor *See* ELEANOR.

Eliot/Eliott *See* ELLIOTT.

Eliphalet (m) Biblical name derived from the Hebrew Eliphelet, meaning 'God is release'. It appears in the Bible as the name of a son of King David and was subsequently taken up by English Puritans in the 17th century. Notable bearers of the name have included the US inventor and small-arms manufacturer Eliphalet Remington (1793–1861).

Elisa/Elisabet/Elisabeth/Elisabetta/Elise *See* ELIZABETH.

Eliseo *See* ELISHA.

Elisha (m) Hebrew name derived from *el* ('God') and *sha* ('to help' or 'to save') and thus interpreted as meaning 'God is salvation'. It appears in the Bible as the name of a revered Old Testament prophet, a disciple of Elijah, and was consequently taken up by English Puritans in the 17th century. It has appeared only infrequently since then. Variants include the Italian and Spanish **Eliseo** and the Russian **Yelisei**.

Elissa *See* ELIZABETH.

Elita (f) English first name derived from the French *élite* ('chosen').

Eliyahu *See* ELIJAH.

Eliza (f) English first name that evolved as a diminutive form of ELIZABETH. It was taken up by English speakers in the 16th century and enjoyed a peak in popularity in the 18th century. It continued in common currency until the end of the 19th century, since when it has become much less frequent under pressure from other variants of Elizabeth. Notable bearers of the name have included the fictional Eliza Doolittle in George Bernard Shaw's play *Pygmalion* (1913), which was later made into the musical *My Fair Lady* (1956). *See also* LISA.

Elizabeth (f) English first name derived via the Roman Elisabetha and the Greek Elisabet from the Hebrew Elisheba, meaning 'oath of God' or 'God has sworn'. It appears in the Bible as the name of John the Baptist's mother and consequently became popular among English speakers during the medieval period. During the late 16th century it was often bestowed in tribute to Elizabeth I of England (1533–1603): in 1600 around one in every five female infants born in England were being given the name. It has remained a frequent choice of name ever since, often found in one of numerous variant forms.

Notable bearers of the name have included the 13th-century St Elizabeth of Hungary (1207–31), British poet Elizabeth Barrett Browning (1806–61), Elizabeth the Queen Mother (Elizabeth Bowes-Lyon; 1900–2002), British-born US actress Elizabeth Taylor (b.1932) and Elizabeth II of Great Britain and Northern Ireland (b.1926). Also encountered as **Elisabeth,** especially in continental Europe. Diminutive forms of the name include BESS, **Bessie**, **Bessy**, **Bet**, BETH, BETSY, BETTY, ELIZA, **Else**, ELSIE, **Ilsa**, **Ilse**, **Libby**, **Lillah**, LISA, **Lisbeth**, **Liz**, **Liza**, **Lizzie**, **Lizzy** and **Tetty**. Variants in other languages include the Welsh **Bethan,** the French and German **Elisabeth** (often shortened to

Elli Lili or **Lilli**), the French **Elise**, **Lise** and **Lisette**, the German **Liese** and **Liesl**, the Italian **Elisabetta** and the Scandinavian **Elisabet**. *See also* BABETTE; ELSA; ELSPETH; ISABEL.

Elkanah (m) Hebrew name meaning 'God has created' or 'the Lord is possessing'. It appears in the Bible as the name of the father of the prophet Samuel and was consequently taken up by English speakers in the 17th century. Famous bearers of the name have included the English playwright Elkanah Settle (1648–1724).

Elke (f) Jewish first name derived from the Hebrew *elkahan* ('possessed by God'), although it is also regarded as a Yiddish version of ELAINE, a Dutch diminutive (*see* ADELAIDE) or as a German equivalent of ALICE. Famous bearers of the name have included the German film actress Elke Sommer (Elke Schletz; b.1940). Also found as **Elkie** – as borne by British singer Elkie Brooks (b.1945).

Ella (f) English first name derived via French from the Old German Alia, itself from the German *al* ('all'). It is often considered to be a diminutive form of such names as ELEANOR and ELLEN. It came to England with the Normans in the 11th century but it was not until the 19th century that it began to appear with significant regularity on both sides of the Atlantic. It has suffered a marked decline since the early years of the 20th century. Well-known bearers of the name have included US poet Ella Wheeler Wilcox (1850–1919) and US jazz singer Ella Fitzgerald (1918–96). **Ellie** is a common diminutive form.

Ellar (m) Scottish first name that developed as an Anglicization of the Gaelic Eallair, itself from the Latin *cella* ('cellar'). The name was originally borne by butlers or stewards in monasteries.

Ellen (f) English first name that was taken up by English speakers as a variant form of HELEN in the 16th century. Popular towards the end of the 19th century, it went into decline in the first half of the 20th century, but subsequently picked up in popularity later in the century. Famous bearers of the name have included British actress Dame Ellen Terry (1848–1928). Variants include **Ellie**, NELL, **Nellie** and **Nelly**.

Ellery (m) English surname that has made occasional appearances as a first name among English speakers since the early 20th century. Well-known bearers of the name have included detective Ellery Queen, actually the pseudonym of Frederick Dannay (1905–82) and Manfred B. Lee (1905–71). Occasionally spelled **Ellerie,** in which form it is also sometimes bestowed upon females.

Elli See ELIZABETH.

Ellie See ELEANOR; ELLA; ELLEN; ELSA; HELEN.

Elliott (m) English surname that made early appearances among English speakers in the 16th century and has remained in fairly common use ever since. The surname itself came originally from a Norman French variant of ELIAS. Also encountered as **Eliot,** it has enjoyed a recent peak in popularity in the 1990s. Famous bearers of the name have included US actor Elliott Gould (Elliot Goldstein; b.1938). Other variants include **Eliott** and **Elliot**.

Ellis (f) English first name that evolved either from the identical surname, derived from ELIAS, or as a variant of ISABEL or ALICE, or as an Anglicization of the Irish Eilis or the Welsh Elisud, itself from *elus* ('kind'). Famous bearers of the name have included the British novelist Ellis Peters (Edith Pargeter; 1913–95).

Elly See ELEANOR; ELLA; ELLEN; HELEN.

Elma (f) English first name that is thought to have evolved through the combination of ELIZABETH and MARY. Largely confined to the USA, it is also found as a diminutive form of various names ending '-elma' and occasionally as a feminine equivalent of ELMER. *See also* WILHELMINA.

Elmer (m) English surname derived from the Old English *aethel* ('noble') and *maer* ('famous') that was taken up as a first name in the 19th century, chiefly in the USA. Old English versions of the name included Ethelmer and Ethelward. The name's popularity in the USA may be traced back to admiration for the brothers Ebenezer and Jonathan Elmer, who were prominent figures during the American War of Independence. Other notable bearers of the name have included US writer Elmer Rice (1892–1967) and the central character in the Sinclair Lewis novel *Elmer Gantry* (1927). **Elm** and **Elmy** are diminutive forms of the name. *See also* AYLMER.

Elmo (m) Italian first name derived ultimately from the Old German *helm* ('helmet' or 'protection') that has made irregular appearances as a first name among English speakers since the 19th century. Also encountered as a familiar form of ERASMUS.

Elmore (m) English first name, originally a surname, meaning 'river bank with elms'. Famous bearers of the name include US novelist Elmore Leonard (b.1925).

Elodia (f) Spanish first name derived from the Germanic *ali* ('other' or 'foreign') and *od* ('riches'). Notable bearers of the name have included a 9th-century martyr. Variants in other languages include the French **Élodie**.

Élodie See ELODIA.

Elof (m) Swedish first name derived from the Old Norse *ei* ('ever' or 'always') or *einn* ('one') and *lafr* ('heir'). Also encountered as **Elov**. Variants in other languages include the Danish **Eluf**.

Eloi See ELOY.

Eloisa See ÉLOISE.

Éloise (f) French first name of uncertain Germanic origin that has made irregular appearances (usually without the accent) among English speakers over the centuries. Attempts have been made to trace the name back to the Old German for 'hale' or 'wide'.

It came to England with the Normans in the 11th century, possibly as a feminine equivalent of LOUIS, but has never been widely used. Famous bearers of the name have included the beautiful Eloise whose ill-fated 12th-century romance with the French philosopher Abelard became the subject of legend. Also encountered as **Eloisa** or **Héloïse**.

Elov *See* ELOF.

Eloy (m) Spanish first name derived ultimately from the Roman Eligius, itself from the Latin *eligere* ('to choose'). Variants include the French and Portuguese **Eloi** and the Italian **Eligio**.

Elroy (m) English first name that developed as a variant of LEROY. It has proved particularly popular among Black Americans since the 19th century. Famous bearers of the name have included the British poet James Elroy Flecker (1884–1915).

Elsa (f) English, German and Swedish first name derived from ELIZABETH. It became popular among English speakers in the 19th century, promoted by the appearance of the name as that of Lohengrin's bride in the Wagner opera *Lohengrin* (1846–8). **Ellie** is a familiar form of the name. Well-known bearers of the name have included British-born US actress Elsa Lanchester (Elizabeth Sullivan; 1902–86) and the lioness whose story was told in Joy Adamson's book *Born Free* (1960), subsequently filmed (1965). *See also* AILSA.

Elsdon (m) English place name (from Northumbria) that was adopted as a surname during the medieval period and has subsequently made occasional appearances as a first name, chiefly in the USA. The original place name appears to have been based on the Old English for 'Elli's valley'.

Else *See* ELSIE.

Elsie (f) English first name that developed via Elspie as a diminutive form of ELSPETH, although it is also sometimes encountered as an abbreviated form of ELIZABETH, de-

spite the fact that this is an otherwise unrelated name. It was popular among English speakers in the 18th and 19th centuries, particularly in Scotland, but has been less common since the 1920s. Well-known bearers of the name have included the central character in the Oliver Wendell Holmes novel *Elsie Venner* (1861) and the fictional Elsie Tanner in the long-running British television soap opera *Coronation Street*. Sometimes abbreviated to **Else**.

Elspeth (f) English and Scottish first name that developed as a diminutive form of ELIZABETH in the 19th century. Famous bearers of the name have included the Kenyan-born British writer Elspeth Huxley (1907–97). **Elspie** is a familiar form of the name. *See also* ELSIE.

Elspie *See* ELSPETH.

Elton (m) English place name derived from the Old English for 'Ella's settlement' that was subsequently adopted as a surname and made occasional appearances as a first name among English speakers during the 20th century. The name is most familiar as that of the British pop singer Elton John (Reg Dwight; b.1947), who was inspired to adopt the name by saxophonist Elton Dean (of the rock band Soft Machine).

Eluf *See* ELOF.

Eluned (f) Welsh first name that is thought to have evolved out of the earlier Luned or Lunet, names which may have evolved out of the Welsh *eilun* ('image'). Rarely found outside Wales. Also encountered in the forms **Elluned** or **Elinod**. *See also* LYNETTE.

Elvie/Elvin/Elvina *See* ALVIN.

Elvira (f) Spanish name of uncertain origin, possibly derived from the Old German Alwara, itself from the Old German *al* ('all') and *wer* ('true') and thus interpreted as meaning 'true to all'. It was not taken up by English speakers until the 19th century and has never been a very frequent choice of name. Notable bearers of the name have included characters in several classic operas, including Don Juan's wife in Mozart's *Don Giovanni* (1787), as well as central characters in the Noël Coward play *Blithe Spirit* (1941) and the Swedish film *Elvira Madigan* (1967).

Elvis (m) English first name that is thought to have evolved from the surname Elwes, which had its origins in ÉLOISE, or alternatively from the Irish Ailbhe. Today it is universally associated with the US rock and roll singer Elvis Presley (1935–77), who inherited the name from his father Vernon Elvis Presley. Other famous bearers of the name have included the British pop singer Elvis Costello (Declan Patrick McManus; b.1955).

Elwin *See* ELWYN.

Elwyn (m) Welsh first name that is thought to have evolved from the Welsh for 'fair brow' or 'elf friend'. It has also been suggested that it may have come about as a variant of ALVIN. Other versions of the name include **Elwin**.

Ely *See* ELI.

Elye *See* ELIJAH.

Elysia (f) English first name derived from the Greek for 'blissful'. It evolved as a feminine version of Elysium, the name of heaven in Greek mythology.

Em *See* EMILY; EMMA; EMMELINE.

Emanuel (m) Biblical name derived from the Hebrew Immanuel, meaning 'God with us'. It appears in the Bible as a name for the expected Messiah and was consequently taken up by English speakers in the 17th century. It has appeared with less regularity in succeeding centuries. Notable bearers of the name have included the British politician Emanuel Shinwell (1884–1986). Often spelled **Emmanuel** and, in the USA, in the Spanish variant **Manuel**. Familiar forms of the name include **Man** and **Manny**. **Emanuelle** and **Manuela** are feminine equivalents of the name. Further variants of the name in other languages include the Italian **Emanuele**.

Emanuela/Emanuele/Emanuelle *See* EMANUEL.

Emblem/Emblin/Emblyn/Emeline/Emelyn *See* EMMELINE.

Emer (f) Irish name of uncertain origin, pronounced 'eemer'. It is famous in Irish mythology as the name of the hero Cuchulain's beloved, who was depicted as the personification of all female qualities. **Emir** is a rare variant form.

Emerald (f) English first name derived from the name of the gem. Like other jewel names, it enjoyed some popularity among English speakers towards the end of the 19th century, but has reappeared only rarely since then. Occasionally encountered as a familiar form of ESMERALDA.

Emerson (m) English surname meaning 'son of Emery' that has made occasional appearances as a first name in relatively recent times. Famous bearers of the name have included Brazilian motor-racing driver Emerson Fittipaldi (b.1946). **Emmerson** is a rare variant.

Emery (m) English first name derived from the Old German Emmerich or Amalric, itself from the Old German *amal* ('labour') and *ric* ('ruler') and usually interpreted as meaning 'powerful noble'. It came to England with the Normans in the 11th century and until the 18th century was borne by both sexes but is now reserved exclusively for males. Occasionally encountered as **Emory**.

Emil *See* EMILE.

Emile (m) French first name descended, possibly via French Huguenots, from the Roman Aemilius, itself from the Latin for 'striving' or 'eager'. Usually spelled Émile in France, it made irregular appearances among English speakers around the middle of the 19th century and has remained in sporadic use ever since. Notable bearers of the name have included the celebrated

French writer Émile Zola (1840–1902) and England footballer Emile Heskey (b.1978). Variants in other languages include the German **Emil** and the Italian, Spanish and Portuguese **Emilio**.

Emilia (f) English first name derived from AMELIA. It emerged as a variant among English speakers during medieval times and is still in use today, although it has never been very common. Well-known bearers of the name have included three characters in the plays of William Shakespeare, notably Iago's wife Emilia in *Othello* (1602–4) and Hermione's maid Emilia in *The Winter's Tale* (1610–11).

Émilie *See* EMILY.

Emily (f) English first name derived from the Roman Aemilia, itself from the Latin for 'striving' or 'eager'. It was adopted by English speakers in the 18th century and enjoyed a peak in popularity during the 19th century, but suffered a lapse in frequency in the 20th century. It has enjoyed a marked revival since the 1970s. Notable bearers of the name have included British novelist Emily Brontë (1818–48), US poet Emily Dickinson (1830–86), the fictional Emily Peggoty in the Charles Dickens novel *David Copperfield* (1849–50) and British actress Emily Lloyd (b.1971). **Em**, **Emmie**, **Emmy** and **Milly** (or **Millie**) are diminutive forms of the name. Variants in other languages include the French **Émilie**. *See also* AMELIA.

Emir *See* EMER.

Emlyn (m) Welsh first name sometimes traced back to the Roman Aemilius, itself from the Latin for 'striving' or 'eager', or else from unknown Celtic roots. It has retained its strong Welsh associations and is today rarely found outside Wales itself. Well-known bearers of the name have included the Welsh actor and playwright Emlyn Williams (1905–87).

Emma (f) English first name derived from the Old German *ermen* ('entire' or 'uni-versal'). It was in use among English speakers during medieval times and was at its most frequent in the 19th century. It has remained in regular use ever since, with a recent peak in popularity in the 1980s. Famous bearers of the name have included Emma of Normandy, the wife of the 11th-century English kings Ethelred the Unready and Canute, Nelson's mistress Lady Emma Hamilton (1765–1815), the fictional Emma Woodhouse in the Jane Austen novel *Emma* (1816), the central character in Gustave Flaubert's *Madame Bovary* (1857) and British actress Emma Thompson (b.1959). **Em**, **Emmie** and **Emmy** are diminutive forms of the name. *See also* EMMET.

Emmanuel *See* EMANUEL.

Emmeline (f) English first name that developed as a variant of EMMA but can also be traced back via the Old French Ameline to the Old German *amal* ('labour'). It was taken up by English speakers in medieval times but subsequently fell into disuse before a revival in the 18th century, since when it has continued to make rare appearances, often being treated rather inaccurately as a variant of EMILIA or EMILY. Famous bearers of the name have included a character in the Harriet Beecher Stowe novel *Uncle Tom's Cabin* (1852) and the British suffragette leader Emmeline Pankhurst (1858–1928). Diminutive forms of the name include **Emeline** and **Emelyn** as well as the rarer **Emblem**, **Emblin** and **Emblyn**.

Emmerson *See* EMERSON.

Emmet (m) English surname derived from EMMA that was subsequently taken up as an occasional first name. The surname appears to have made its first appearances in medieval times. As a first name it is sometimes bestowed in Ireland in honour of the Irish rebel Robert Emmet (1778–1803).

Emmie/Emmy *See* EMILY; EMMA; EMMELINE.

Emory *See* EMERY.

Emrys (m) Welsh first name that developed as a variant of AMBROSE. Apparently a 20th-century introduction, it is still largely confined to Welsh speakers.

Ena (f) English version of the Irish EITHNE that is also encountered as a diminutive of EUGENIA, HELENA and various other names with similar endings. It became popular among English speakers towards the end of the 19th century after it was bestowed upon Queen Victoria's granddaughter Princess Ena (Victoria Eugénie Julia Ena; 1887–1969), although popular rumour insisted that she only got the name through a misreading of 'Eva' at her baptism. Well-known bearers of the name since then have included the fictional Ena Sharples in the long-running popular British television soap opera *Coronation Street*. Sometimes encountered as INA.

Engelbert (m) German first name derived from the Old German *Angil* ('Angle') and *berht* ('famous' or 'bright'). Also found as **Englebert** – as borne by British singer Englebert Humperdinck (Arnold George Dorsey; b.1936).

Enid (f) English first name that may have developed out of the Welsh *enaid* ('soul' or 'life') or possibly from *enit* ('woodlark'). It became popular among English speakers towards the end of the 19th century in response to Alfred, Lord Tennyson's 'Geraint and Enid' (1886), which retold the Arthurian legend in which Enid successfully proves her innocence when tested by her husband after he doubts her fidelity to him. The name was at its most frequent in the 1920s, but has since suffered a marked decline in popularity. Notable bearers of the name have included British novelist Enid Bagnold (1889–1981) and British children's writer Enid Blyton (1897–1968).

Enoch (m) English first name derived from the Hebrew Hanok, thought to mean 'dedicated', 'trained' or 'experienced'. It appears in the Bible as the name of the son of Cain and father of Methuselah and was consequently taken up by English Puritans in the 17th century. Well-known bearers of the name have included the central character in Alfred, Lord Tennyson's narrative poem *Enoch Arden* (1864) and British politician Enoch Powell (John Enoch Powell; 1912–98).

Enola (f) English first name of uncertain meaning. A late 19th-century introduction, it acquired some notoriety through the 'Enola Gay', the nickname of the US Superfortress bomber used to drop the first atomic bomb on Hiroshima on 6 August 1945. The aircraft was named after the mother of its pilot, Colonel Paul W. Tibbets. Other notable instances of the name have included a character called Enola Gay in the Martin Amis novel *London Fields* (1989).

Enos (m) Biblical name derived from the Hebrew for 'mankind'. It appears in the Bible as the name of one of Adam and Eve's grandsons and as that of a son of Seth. It is sometimes encountered in Ireland as an Anglicization of the Gaelic **Aonghas** or **Aonghus** (*see* ANGUS). It was taken up by English speakers in the 19th century.

Enrico/Enrique *See* HENRY.

Enya *See* EITHNE.

Enzo (m) Italian first name possibly derived from the Old German *ent* ('giant'). Sometimes also encountered as a diminutive form of LORENZO and various other names ending '-enzo'. Famous bearers of the name have included the Italian racing-car designer Enzo Ferrari (1898–1988).

Eoan *See* EUGENE.

Eoghan (m) Irish and Scottish first name of uncertain origin, pronounced 'yewan'. It may have evolved from the Gaelic words for 'yew' and 'born' and may be interpreted to mean 'born of the yew'. It is sometimes encountered in Ireland as a translation of EUGENE or OWEN and in Scotland of EWAN, EVAN or HUGH.

Eoin *See* JOHN.

Ephraim (m) Biblical name derived from the Hebrew Ephrayim, meaning 'fruitful'. It appears in the Bible as the name of Joseph's second son but unlike many other biblical names was not especially popular among English Puritans and it was not until the 18th century that it appeared with any frequency among English speakers. It has become very rare since the early 20th century, except among Jews. There are characters with the name in Oliver Goldsmith's novel *The Vicar of Wakefield* (1766) and Charles Dickens' novel *Little Dorrit* (1855–7). **Effie** and **Eph** are familiar forms of the name. Variants in other languages include the Spanish **Efrain** (as used throughout Latin America), the Russian **Yefrem** and the Jewish **Evron**.

Eppie *See* EUPHEMIA; HEPHZIBAH.

Erasmus (m) English first name derived via Latin from the Greek Erasmos, itself from *eran* ('to love') and thus interpreted to mean 'beloved', 'desired' or 'longed for'. It became famous as the name of the Dutch humanist Desiderius Erasmus (Gerald Gerards; *c.*1466–1536), who adopted the name in response to his birth as an illegitimate love child. It was taken up by English speakers in the 17th century and remained current until the end of the 19th century before falling into disuse. Other notable bearers of the name have included a 4th-century Italian martyr (the patron saint of sailors), and Charles Darwin's grandfather, the English physician and poet Erasmus Darwin (1731–1802). *See also* ELMO.

Erastus (m) English first name derived from the Greek Erastos, meaning 'beloved' or 'dear one'. It was borne in the 16th century by the Swiss theologian Thomas Erastus (1524–83) and was taken up on a limited basis by English speakers in the 18th century. Today it is equally familiar in its diminutive form **Rastus**.

Ercole *See* HERCULES.

Erdmann *See* HARTMANN.

Erhard (m) German first name derived

from the Old German *era* ('honour' or 'respect') and *hardu* ('brave' or 'hardy').

Eric (m) English first name derived from the Old Norse Eyrekr, itself from *ei* ('ever' or 'always') or *einn* ('one') and *rikr* ('ruler') and thus interpreted as meaning 'ever-ruling' or possibly 'island ruler'. Early bearers of the name included the 10th-century Viking discoverer of Greenland Eric the Red, and it would appear that the name first came to England with Danish settlers before the Norman Conquest. It was not, however, until the middle of the 19th century that the name began to be taken up on a regular basis by English speakers, largely in response to the publication of F. W. Farrar's popular school story *Eric, or, Little by Little* (1858). Very popular in the first half of the 20th century, it has become much less common since the 1960s.

Well-known bearers of the name have included British comedians Eric Sykes (b.1923) and Eric Morecambe (1926–84) and British rock musician Eric Clapton (b.1945). Variants of the name include **Erik** (originally a Swedish version), **Rick** and **Ricky** (or **Rikki**) as well as the German **Erich** and the Finnish **Eero** and **Erkki**. *See also* ERICA.

Erica (f) English first name that developed as a feminine equivalent of ERIC. It has also been suggested that the name may have been influenced by *Erica*, the Latin name for the plant heather. In Scotland it is sometimes treated as an Anglicization of the Gaelic **Oighrig**. It made early appearances as a first name among English speakers towards the end of the 18th century and enjoyed a peak in popularity in the 1960s. Well-known bearers of the name have included US novelist Erica Jong (b.1942). **Rica**, **Ricki**, **Rika** and **Rikki** are diminutive forms of the name. Variants in other languages include the German and Scandinavian **Erika**.

Erik *See* ERIC.

Erika *See* ERICA.

Erin (f) Irish first name derived from *Eire*, the traditional Gaelic name for Ireland itself. It has made occasional appearances as a first name since the end of the 19th century, not only in Ireland but also in Australia, the USA and elsewhere, increasingly among people with no Irish connections. **Errin** and **Eryn** are variant forms.

Erkki *See* ERIC.

Erland (m) Scandinavian first name derived from the Old Norse *örlendr* ('foreigner' or 'stranger'). Also spelled **Erlend**.

Erle *See* EARL.

Erlean/Erleen/Erlinda *See* EARLENE.

Erma *See* IRMA.

Ermanno *See* HERMAN.

Ermenegilde/Ermenegildo *See* HERMENEGILDO.

Ermentraud *See* ERMINTRUDE.

Ermete (m) Italian first name derived from the Greek Hermes, the name of the Greek messenger of the gods (otherwise of unknown meaning). It was in fairly frequent use among early Christians and was borne by many minor early saints.

Ermintrude (f) English, French and German first name derived from the Old German *ermen* ('entire' or 'universal') and *traut* ('beloved') and thus interpreted as meaning 'wholly beloved'. It came to England with the Normans in the 11th century but has never been very common and is today effectively defunct. Notable bearers of the name have included a 9th-century empress of France. Commonly shortened to **Trudie, Trudi** or TRUDY. Variants in other languages include the German **Ermentraud, Ermentrud, Irmtraud** and **Irmtrud**.

Ern *See* ERNEST.

Erna (f) English first name that developed as a diminutive form of Ernesta and Ernestine (*see* ERNEST). It was taken up by English speakers in the 19th century.

Ernest (m) English first name derived from the Old German Ernust, from *eornost* ('earnestness' or 'seriousness'). It made its first appearances among English speakers at the time of accession of the Hanoverian George I during the 18th century and remained popular until the early years of the 20th century, since when it has gradually declined to the point where it is now rare.

Famous bearers of the name have included the fictional Ernest (or Jack) Worthing in the Oscar Wilde comedy *The Importance of Being Earnest* (1895), British politician Ernest Bevin (1881–1951), US novelist Ernest Hemingway (1898–1961) and US film actor Ernest Borgnine (Ermes Effron Borgnino; b.1918). Commonly shortened to **Ern** or **Ernie** – as borne by US actor Ernie Kovacs (1919–62) and British comedian Ernie Wise (Ernest Wiseman; 1925–99). Occasionally found as **Earnest** through confusion with the ordinary vocabulary word. **Ernesta, Ernestina** and **Ernestine** are feminine versions of the name. Variants in other languages include the modern German **Ernst**, the Italian, Spanish and Portuguese **Ernesto** and the Hungarian **Erno**. *See also* ERNA.

Ernesta/Ernestina/Ernestine/ Ernesto/Ernie/Erno/Ernst *See* ERNEST.

Errin *See* ERIN.

Errol (m) Scottish place name and surname that began to appear as a first name among English speakers from the late 19th century. Sometimes associated with EARL, from which it may have evolved, or HAROLD, it proved especially popular among Black Americans in the 20th century. Famous bearers of the name have included Australian-born US film actor Errol Flynn (1909–59) and US jazz musician Errol Garner (1921–77).

Erskine (m) Scottish place name (from Erskine, near Glasgow) that was subsequently taken up as a surname and occasional first name among English speakers from the 19th century. Notable bearers of the name have included the Irish novelist

Erskine Childers (1870–1922) and US novelist Erskine Caldwell (1903–87).

Erwin (m) German first name derived from the Old German *era* ('honour' or 'respect') and *win* ('friend'). It was in fairly regular use among German speakers during the medieval period. Notable bearers of the name in more recent times have included German field marshal Erwin Rommel (1891–1944). Sometimes treated as a variant of IRVING or IRWIN.

Eryn *See* ERIN.

Esau (m) Biblical name derived from the Hebrew Esaw, meaning 'hairy'. It appears in the Bible as the name of one of Isaac and Rebecca's twin sons, who was born covered with red hair, and enjoyed some popularity among English speakers after the Reformation and to a limited extent once more during the 19th century.

Esmaralda *See* ESMERALDA.

Esmé (m/f) French first name derived from the Old French *esme* ('loved' or 'esteemed'). It seems to have been imported to England from France as early as the 16th century, when famous bearers included James VI of Scotland's cousin Esmé Stuart (1542–83). It has continued to make occasional reappearances ever since, borne in its early history by both sexes. As a name for girls, also spelled **Esmée,** it was taken up by English speakers in the 18th century and now appears to be in exclusively feminine use. Sometimes treated as an abbreviated form of the otherwise unconnected ESMERALDA. Variants include the Scottish **Edmé**. *See also* AIMÉE.

Esmée *See* ESMÉ.

Esmeralda (f) English first name derived from the Spanish *esmeralda* ('emerald'). Borne by the gypsy girl loved by Quasimodo in Victor Hugo's *The Hunchback of Notre Dame* (1831), it was taken up by English speakers in the 19th century but has never been common. Sometimes shortened to ESMÉ. Also spelled **Esmerelda** or **Esmaralda**. *See also* EMERALD.

Esmond (m) English first name derived from the Old German Estmund, itself from *est* ('favour' or 'grace') and *mund* ('protection') and thus interpreted as meaning 'favoured protector'. It made early appearances in medieval times but disappeared from use after the 14th century. It was revived among English speakers in the 19th century and has since continued in occasional use, although it is now very rare. Notable instances of the name in literature have included the William Makepeace Thackeray novel *The History of Henry Esmond* (1852). Occasionally spelled **Esmund**.

Esmund *See* ESMOND.

Esperanza (f) Spanish first name derived from the Roman Sperantia, itself from the Latin *sperans* ('hope').

Essa *See* ESTHER.

Essie *See* ESTELLE; ESTHER.

Esta *See* ESTHER; HESTER.

Estéban *See* STEPHEN.

Estella *See* ESTELLE.

Estelle (f) French first name derived from STELLA and thus meaning 'star'. It was taken up by English speakers in the 19th century and enjoyed a recent peak in popularity in the 1970s. Before Estelle became the dominant form of the name in the 20th century it was usually encountered as **Estella** – as borne by one of the central characters in Charles Dickens' novel *Great Expectations* (1860–61). Diminutive forms of the name include **Essie**.

Ester *See* ESTHER.

Esther (f) Biblical name that may have had its roots in the Persian *stara* ('star') but is otherwise associated with the Hebrew HADASSAH, meaning 'myrtle' or 'bride'. Another theory suggests it is a Hebrew version of Ishtar the name of the Persian goddess of love. It appears in the Bible as the name of the Jewish concubine who became the wife of Ahasuerus, king of the Persians.

It was taken up by English speakers in the 17th century, as was the quickly discarded Hadassah, and enjoyed a peak in popularity during the 19th century, since when it has become rather less frequent. Famous bearers of the name have included the fictional Esther Summerson in the Charles Dickens novel *Bleak House* (1852–3), US swimmer and film actress Esther Williams (b.1923) and British television presenter Esther Rantzen (b.1940). **Ess**, **Essa**, **Esta**, **Ettie**, **Etty**, HESTER and **Hetty** are all diminutive forms of the name. Variants in other languages include the Scandinavian **Ester** and the Hungarian **Eszter**.

Esyllt *See* ISOLDE.

Eszter *See* ESTHER.

Etain *See* EADAN.

Eth *See* ETHEL.

Ethan (m) Biblical name derived from the Hebrew Eythan, meaning 'constant', 'firm', 'strong', or alternatively 'long-lived'. It appears in the Bible as the name of four minor characters, the most significant being the wise man Ethan the Ezrahite, whose wisdom is surpassed only by Solomon. It was taken up on a fairly restricted basis by Puritans on both sides of the Atlantic from the 17th century and increased a little in frequency during the 19th century, proving most popular in the USA. Famous bearers of the name have included the American War of Independence hero Ethan Allen (1738–89), the central character in the Edith Wharton novel *Ethan Frome* (1911) and US film director Ethan Coen (b.1958). **Etan** is a Jewish variant.

Ethel (f) English first name derived ultimately from the Old German *ethel* ('noble'). It is thought to represent a shortened version of a range of Anglo-Saxon names all beginning the same way, among them Ethelburga, Ethelthryth, ETHELINDA and Ethelgive. Because of its ancient associations it was taken up by English speakers in the 19th century, when it was further popularized as the name of central charac-

ters in William Makepeace Thackeray's novel *The Newcomes* (1855) and C. M. Yonge's *The Daisy Chain* (1856). It became relatively common in the early years of the 20th century but faltered in popularity later in the century and is now virtually defunct. Notable bearers of the name have included the British composer Dame Ethel Smyth (1858–1944), US actress Ethel Barrymore (1879–1959) and US singer and actress Ethel Merman (1909–84). Commonly shortened to **Eth** and, more rarely, to **Thel**.

Ethelbert (m) English name derived from the Old English Aethelbeorht, itself based on *aethele* ('noble') and *beorht* ('bright'). Borne by a 7th-century king of Kent and subsequently by a 9th-century king of England, brother of Alfred the Great, it continued in very irregular use after the Norman Conquest but enjoyed a brief resurgence in popularity in the 19th century, since when it has effectively disappeared from use. There is a character called Ethelbert Stanhope in the Anthony Trollope novel *Barchester Towers* (1857). An equally rare feminine equivalent of the name is **Ethelberta** – as borne by the central character in the Thomas Hardy novel *The Hand of Ethelberta* (1876). *See also* ALBERT.

Etheldreda (f) English first name derived from the Old English Aethelthryth, itself from the Old English *aethel* ('noble') and *thryth* ('strength'). It was borne by a 7th-century English saint and remained in occasional use through medieval times before giving way to the related AUDREY around the 16th century. It has continued to make very rare reappearances, however, into modern times. **Dreda** is an accepted derivative of the name. *See also* ETHEL.

Ethelinda (f) English first name derived from the Old English Aethelind, itself from the Old German *athal* ('noble') and *lindi* ('snake'). It appears to have vanished from use after the Norman Conquest but enjoyed a modest revival among English speakers in the 19th century. *See also* ETHEL.

Ethelred (m) English name derived from

the Old English Aethelread, itself from *aethele* ('noble') and *raed* ('counsel') and thus interpreted as meaning 'noble counsel'. It was common in England before the Norman Conquest, being borne by two English kings – the 9th-century king of Wessex Ethelred I and the 11th-century king of England Ethelred II, also known as 'Ethelred the Unready' because of his ill-advised policies. It appeared only rarely during the medieval period and is now virtually unknown.

Ethna/Ethne *See* EITHNE.

Étienne (m) French first name that evolved as a variant of STEPHEN. **Étiennette** is a relatively rare feminine form of the name.

Etna *See* EITHNE.

Etta/Ettie *See* HENRIETTA.

Ettore *See* HECTOR.

Etty *See* ESTHER; HENRIETTA.

Etzel (m) German first name derived from the Old German *adal* ('noble') or possibly from the nickname *Atta* ('father'). A medieval introduction, it is also found today in the form EDSEL.

Euan *See* EWAN.

Eudora (f) Greek name derived from *eu* ('good') and *doron* ('gift') and thus interpreted as meaning 'good gift'. It enjoyed some popularity as a first name among English speakers towards the end of the 19th century but has made very few appearances since then. Notable bearers of the name have included the US writer Eudora Welty (1909–2001). Commonly shortened to DORA.

Eufemia *See* EUPHEMIA.

Eugene (m) English first name derived via French from the Greek Eugenios, from the Greek *eugenes* ('noble' or 'well-born'). It was borne by several early Christian saints and popes and subsequently surfaced in several European languages, including Russian. In Ireland it became accepted as an Anglicization of Aodh, EOGHAN or Eoan. English speakers took up the name in the 19th century and it has remained in irregular use ever since, especially in the USA. Famous bearers of the name have included the celebrated military commander Prince Eugene of Savoy (1663–1736), the fictional Eugene Marchbanks in the George Bernard Shaw play *Candida* (1894), US playwright Eugene O'Neill (1888–1953) and the Hungarian-born US conductor Eugene Ormandy (Jeno Ormandy Blau; 1899–1985). Commonly shortened to GENE. Variants in other languages include the French **Eugène**, the Italian and Spanish **Eugenio**, the German **Eugen** and the Russian **Yevgeni**. *See also* OWEN.

Eugenia *See* EUGENIE.

Eugenie (f) French first name (Eugénie) that developed as a feminine equivalent of EUGENE. Famous as the name of Napoleon III's wife the Empress Eugénie (1826–1920), who spent much of her life in England, it was taken up on an occasional basis as a first name among English speakers in the 19th century and has continued to make rare appearances ever since. Notable bearers of the name in more recent times have included Princess Eugenie (b.1990), the daughter of Prince Andrew and Sarah, Duchess of York. Commonly abbreviated to GENE or **Genie**. The variant **Eugenia**, familiar to the English, Italian and Spanish, is now very rare. *See also* ENA.

Eugenio *See* EUGENE.

Eulalia (f) English, Italian and Spanish first name derived from the Greek *eu* ('good') and *lalein* ('chatter' or 'talk') and thus interpreted as meaning 'sweetly speaking'. Borne by a 4th century Spanish saint, it was a popular choice of name in medieval times but is now uncommon. **Lalla**, **Lallie** and **Lally** are diminutive forms. Variants in other languages include the French **Eulalie** and the Spanish **Olalla**.

Eulalie *See* EULALIA.

Eunice (f) Biblical name derived from the Greek *eu* ('good') and *nike* ('victory') and thus interpreted to mean 'good victory'. It appears in the Bible as the name of the mother of Timothy and was consequently taken up by English Puritans in the 17th century (when it was usually pronounced as a three-syllable word – 'you-ni-cee' – compared to the two-syllable pronunciation of modern times). It enjoyed a peak in popularity in the 1920s but has since suffered a sharp decline. Also spelled **Unice**.

Euphemia (f) Greek name derived from *eu* ('well') and *phenai* ('to speak') and thus interpreted as meaning 'well spoken of', 'well regarded' or 'of good repute'. Borne by a number of early saints, it seems to have made its first appearances among English speakers in the 12th century. It enjoyed a modest peak in popularity in the 19th century, particularly in Scotland (where it was used as an Anglicized form of the Gaelic **Oighrig**), and continued in occasional use through the 20th century. The diminutive form **Effie** was particularly common in the 19th century, when notable bearers of the name included the fictional Effie Dean in Walter Scott's novel *The Heart of Midlothian* (1818). Other diminutives of the name are **Eppie**, **Phemie** and FANNY. Variants of the name in other languages include the French **Euphémie** and the Italian, Spanish and Portuguese **Eufemia**.

Eurydice (f) Greek name pronounced 'youridicee' derived from *eurus* ('wide') and *dike* ('right' or 'justice') and thus interpreted as meaning 'wide justice' or 'queen'. It is usually associated with the Eurydice of Greek mythology, whose rescue from Hades after she died was thwarted when her husband Orpheus disobeyed an order not to look back to see if she was following him back to the land of the living. Retellings of the Greek legend in Gluck's opera *Orpheus and Eurydice* (1762) and other works made the name widely familiar in the 18th and 19th centuries, but it has never been a very frequent choice of first name among English speakers.

Eusebio (m) Spanish, Portuguese and Italian first name derived from the Greek Eusebios, from the Greek *eu* ('good') and *sebein* ('to worship'). It was borne by several early saints and has consequently remained in use ever since.

Eustace (m) English first name derived via French from the Greek Eustakhios, from the Greek *eu* ('good') and *stakhus* ('ear of corn' or 'grapes') and thus interpreted as meaning 'rich in corn' or 'good harvest' and hence 'fruitful'. It was borne by the 2nd-century Christian martyr St Eustachius and was subsequently brought to England by the Normans in the 11th century. It appeared less frequently as a first name among English speakers after the medieval period but picked up again in the 19th century, when it enjoyed a significant revival. It has remained in occasional use ever since, although it has lost much ground since the early 20th century. Notable bearers of the name have included one of the two central characters in L. P. Hartley's novel *The Shrimp and the Anemone* (1944) and its two sequels *The Sixth Heaven* (1946) and *Eustace and Hilda* (1947). STACY is an established diminutive form of the name. Variants in other languages include the French **Eustache**, the Italian **Eustachio** and the Spanish **Eustaquio**. *See also* EUSTACIA.

Eustacia (f) English first name that developed as a feminine equivalent of EUSTACE. Never a common choice of name, it is best known from Eustacia Vye, the central character in the Thomas Hardy novel *The Return of the Native* (1878). Sometimes shortened to STACEY or STACY.

Eva (f) Roman name derived from the Hebrew Havvah, meaning 'living'. The usual form of the English EVE in many non-English speaking cultures, it was taken up by English speakers as an alternative form of the name around the middle of the 19th century and enjoyed a peak in popularity early in the 20th century. Famous bearers of the name have included Little Eva in the Harriet Beecher Stowe novel *Uncle Tom's Cabin* (1852), US actress Eva Le Gallienne (1899–1991), Adolf Hitler's mistress Eva Braun (1910–45), Eva Perón (1919–52), the wife of the Argentine President Juan Perón popularly known as **Evita,** and Hungarian-born actress Eva Gabor (1921–95). Variants in other languages include the Polish **Ewa**. *See also* AVA; EVANGELINE.

Evadne (f) Greek name derived from *eu* ('well') in combination with another unknown root. It appears in Greek mythology as the name of the wife of Capaneus, who threw herself onto her husband's funeral pyre, and subsequently made occasional appearances among English speakers from the 17th century – as borne, for instance, by the heroine of the Beaumont and Fletcher play *The Maid's Tragedy* (1619). It enjoyed a modest peak in popularity in the 19th century but is now very rare.

Evaline/Evalyn *See* EVELYN.

Evan (m) Welsh first name derived from Iefan or Ieuan, a Welsh variant of the English JOHN. It seems to have made its first appearance among the Welsh around 1500 and became a popular choice of first name throughout Wales in the 19th century. It began to appear more widely throughout the English-speaking world in the 20th century, although it is still usually thought of as a predominantly Welsh name. A Welsh variant is **Ifan**.

Evander (m) Roman name derived from the Greek Euandros, from the Greek *eu* ('good') and *aner* ('man'). It appears in Roman legend as the name of a hero who founded a city on the site of modern Rome. It was subsequently taken up by English speakers, enjoying special popularity among the Scottish, who sometimes treated it as an Anglicization of the Gaelic Iomhair. Notable bearers of the name in recent times have included the boxer Evander Holyfield (b.1962).

Evangelina *See* EVANGELINE.

Evangeline (f) English first name derived ultimately from the Latin *evangelium* ('gospel'). It appears to have been popularized as the name of Evangeline Bellefontaine in Henry Wadsworth Longfellow's narrative poem *Evangeline* (1847), and subsequently became especially popular among Black Americans. Well-known bearers of the name have included British-born US Salvation Army leader Evangeline Booth (1865–1950). Diminutive forms of the name include EVA and **Evie**.

Evaristo (m) Italian, Spanish and Portuguese first name derived from the Greek Euarestos, from the Greek *eu* ('good') and *areskein* ('to please'). Notable bearers of the name have included a 2nd-century pope and martyr. Variants in other languages include the French **Évariste**.

Eve (f) English and French name derived via Latin from the Hebrew Havvah, based on the Hebrew *hayya* ('living'). As the name of the female companion of the biblical Adam, the name has always had special religious significance among Christians. It was in use among English speakers by the medieval period and has remained modestly popular ever since, with a slight rise in frequency from the 1960s. **Evie** is a familiar form of the name. *See also* EVA; EVELYN.

Eveleen/Evelina/Eveline *See* EVELYN.

Evelyn (m/f) English surname that was subsequently taken up as a first name bestowed upon both sexes. As a masculine name it appears to have made its first appearance early in the 20th century. As a name for girls, possibly influenced by the French AVELINE, it was in use among English speakers by the late 19th century and may have resulted from the combination of EVE and LYNN. It enjoyed a peak in popularity in the 1920s but has since suffered a marked decline in frequency. Famous bearers of the name have included (among the men) British novelist Evelyn Waugh (1903–66) and (among the women) British actress Evelyn Laye (Elsie Evelyn Lay; 1900–1996) and Scottish percussionist Evelyn

Glennie (b.1965). Commonly abbreviated to **Evie** or EVE. Variants include **Evaline**, **Evalyn**, **Evelyne**, **Eveline**, **Eveleen** and **Eibhlin**. Also found as **Evalina** – as borne by the central character in the Fanny Burney novel *Evelina* (1778).

Everard (m) English surname and first name derived from the Old German Everart from *eber* ('boar') and *hart* ('brave' or 'strong') and thus interpreted as meaning 'fierce as a boar'. The name is recorded in use among English speakers in medieval times and was revived in the 19th century, having appeared as the name of a character in the Walter Scott novel *Waverley* (1814). It became much less common after the early part of the 20th century. Variants in other languages include the French **Evrard**.

Everett (m) English surname that was taken up on an occasional basis as a first name among English speakers towards the end of the 19th century. As a surname it is thought to have evolved as a variant of EVERARD. There is a character called Everett Hills in the Eugene O'Neill play *Mourning Becomes Electra* (1931). Also encountered as **Everitt**.

Everild *See* AVERIL.

Evert *See* EBERHARD.

Evette *See* YVONNE.

Evie *See* EVA; EVANGELINE; EVE; EVELYN.

Evita *See* EVA.

Evonne *See* YVONNE.

Evrard *See* EVERARD.

Evron *See* EPHRAIM.

Ewa *See* EVA.

Ewan (m) English version of the Gaelic EOGHAN (also the source of OWEN; pronounced 'yewan'). Although it is now in modest use throughout the English-speaking world, it has retained its strong Scottish associations. Well-known bearers of the name have included Scottish folk musician Ewan McColl (James Millar; 1915–89). Also spelled **Ewen**.

Ewart (m) English surname derived from EDWARD, or else from a place name in Northumbria, that was subsequently taken up as an occasional first name in the 19th century. The name enjoyed modest popularity among English speakers in tribute to Prime Minister William Ewart Gladstone (1809–98).

Ewen *See* EWAN.

Ezekiel (m) Biblical name derived from the Hebrew Yehezqel, meaning 'God will strengthen'. It appears in the Bible as the name of the prophet Ezekiel and was consequently taken up by English Puritans in the 17th century. It remained in fairly regular use until the end of the 19th century, since when it has become much less frequent and is now like many other biblical names confined largely to traditional religious communities. **Zeke** is a common diminutive of the name.

Ezra (m) Hebrew name meaning 'help'. It appears in the Bible as the name of a prophet and was consequently taken up by Puritans on both sides of the Atlantic in the 17th century. It has been rare since the early years of the 20th century. Notable bearers of the name have included the US poet Ezra Pound (1885–1972).

F

Faas (m) Dutch first name derived from the Old Germanic Fastred, itself from the Old German *fast* ('firm') and *red* ('counsel').

Fabia (f) Roman name derived via the masculine Fabianus from the Latin *faba* ('bean'). It was taken up by English speakers in the 19th century but has never been in very frequent use. Notable bearers of the name have included the British actress Fabia Drake (1904–90).

Fabian (m) English first name descended from the Roman Fabianus, itself derived from the Latin *faba* ('bean') and thus signifying a grower of beans. It is thought to have been introduced to England by the Normans, although there is scant evidence of the name's use among the English before the 16th century. Notable bearers of the name have included a 3rd-century pope who was subsequently beatified, Olivia's servant in William Shakespeare's *Twelfth Night* (1601) and the US pop singer and film actor Fabian (Fabian Forte Bonaparte; b.1943). Variants in other languages include the French **Fabien** and the Italian **Fabiano**. **Fabiana** and the French **Fabienne** are feminine variants.

Fabiana/Fabiano/Fabien/Fabienne *See* FABIAN.

Fabio (m) Italian, Spanish and Portuguese name descended from the Roman Fabius, itself derived from *faba* ('bean'). As Fabius the name was borne by the Roman general Quintus Fabius Maximus (d.203 BC). Bearers of the name in more recent times have included the Spanish aristocrat Fabiola de Mora y Aragon, widow of King Baudouin I of Belgium (1930–93). **Fabiola** was a feminine version of the Roman name.

Fabiola *See* FABIO.

Fabrice (m) French name descended from the Roman Fabricius, itself derived from the Latin *faber* ('craftsman'). Variants in other languages include the Italian **Fabrizio** and the Spanish **Fabricio**.

Fachtna (m) Irish name (pronounced 'fokna') of uncertain origin, though possibly derived from the Gaelic for 'malicious' or 'hostile'.

Faddei *See* THADDEUS.

Fadi (m) Arabic name derived from *fadi* ('redeemer' or 'saviour'). **Fadia** is a feminine variant of the name.

Fadil (m) Arabic name derived from *fadil* ('generous' or 'virtuous'). Also found in the form **Fadl**. **Fadila** is a feminine variant of the name.

Fae *See* FAY.

Fahd (m) Arabic name derived from *fahd* ('panther' or 'leopard'). Famous bearers of the name have included King Fahd of Saudi Arabia (b.1923).

Fahim (m) Indian name derived from the Arabic *fahim* ('scholar' or 'learned man'). **Fahmida** is a feminine form of the name.

Fahmida *See* FAHIM.

Faisal (m) Arabic first name derived from *faysal* ('judge'). Famous bearers of the name have included King Faisal I of Iraq (1885–1933) and Faisal of Saudi Arabia. Also found as **Faysal** or **Feisal**.

Faith (f) English virtue name that was taken up by English Puritans in the 17th century, initially as a name for either sex. Unlike some of the other virtue names that became popular around the same time, Faith has remained in use into modern times, although it is now reserved exclusively for females. It was formerly quite common for triplets of girls to be named Faith, Hope and Charity. Well-known bearers of the name have included two legendary saints and British comedienne Faith Brown (b.1944). Familiar forms of the name include FAY and **Faithie**.

Faivish (m) Jewish name (pronounced 'feye-vish') probably derived from the Greek Phoibos or Phoebus (as borne by the sun god Apollo). It has been speculated that the first Jews to acquire the name were slaves captured by the Greeks, who often gave their captives the names of the gods. Familiar forms of the name include **Fayvel** and **Feivel**.

Fakhr-al-Din (m) Arabic name derived from *fakhr* ('pride' or 'glory'), *al* ('the') and *din* ('religion'), thus meaning 'glory of religion'. Also found in the forms **Fakhrid-Din** and **Fakhruddin**.

Fakhri (m) Arabic name derived from *fakhri* ('meritorious' or 'honorary'). **Fakhriyya** is a feminine version of the name.

Falk (m) Jewish name derived from the Yiddish *falk* ('falcon'). Occasionally treated as a translation of the Hebrew Yehoshua (*see* JOSHUA), a reference perhaps to Joshua's hawklike descent upon the Land of Canaan.

Fan *See* FANNY.

Fancy (f) English first name that may have arisen as a variant of FANNY, or possibly under the influence of the ordinary vocabulary word 'fiancée'. It appears to have made its first appearances in the 19th century and is virtually unknown today.

Fannie *See* FANNY.

Fanny (f) English first name that developed as a diminutive form of such names as EUPHEMIA, FRANCES and MYFANWY. It appeared with considerable frequency

among English speakers from the late 17th century but became rare after the 19th century, probably because as an ordinary slang word 'fanny' came to mean 'backside' or 'bottom'. Its popularity as a first name in the UK was also dented by association with the tragic Fanny Adams, a little girl who was the victim of a notorious murder in the 1860s, and whose name became enshrined in the slang euphemism 'sweet Fanny Adams' (meaning 'nothing at all'). Famous bearers of the name have included the fictional heroine Fanny Hill in John Cleland's scandalous *Memoirs of a Woman of Pleasure* (1748–9), British novelist Fanny Burney (1752–1840), British actress Fanny Kemble (1809–93), Fanny Price in Jane Austen's novel *Mansfield Park* (1814), US actress Fanny Brice (Fannie Borach; 1891–1951) and the central character in George Bernard Shaw's play *Fanny's First Play* (1905). Commonly shortened to **Fan**. Also found as **Fannie.**

Faraj (m) Arabic name derived from *faraj* ('remedy' or 'improvement'). Also found in the form **Farag**.

Faramond (m) German name derived from the Old German *fara* ('journey') and *mund* ('protection'). It was borne by the legendary first king of France and came to England with the Normans in the 11th century. Spelt **Pharamond**, the name made a fleeting appearance in William Shakespeare's *Henry V* (1599), but seems to have lain dormant since.

Fardoos (f) Arabic name derived from *firdaws* ('paradise').

Fareed *See* FARID.

Farid (m) Arabic name derived from *farid* ('unique' or 'unrivalled'). A variant is the Indian **Fareed** – as borne by a famous 13th-century Persian poet and Sufi mystic. **Farida** and **Fareeda** (or **Faridah**) are feminine versions of the name – as borne by Princess Farida (b.1921), the first wife of King Farouk I of Egypt.

Farley (m) English surname derived from

the Old English for 'fair meadow' that has made occasional appearances as a first name over the centuries.

Faron *See* FARRAN.

Farouk *See* FARUQ.

Farquhar (m) Scottish first name that developed as an Anglicized form of the Scottish Gaelic Fearchar, derived from the Gaelic for 'man' and 'dear' and thus meaning 'dear one'. Borne by an early Scottish king, it is now better known as a surname than as a first name.

Farrah (f) English first name ultimately derived from the Latin for 'iron'. The name became widely known in the 1970s as that of US actress Farrah Fawcett-Majors (b.1947). **Farrer** is a masculine variant.

Farran (m/f) English surname possibly derived from the Old French for 'pilferer' or 'ferret' or else a medieval variant of FERDINAND. Other forms of the name include **Farren** and **Faron**.

Faruq (m) Arabic name meaning 'person who can tell right from wrong'. Also found in the form **Farouk** – as borne by King Farouk (1920–65), the last king of Egypt.

Fathi (m) Arabic name derived from *faith* ('conqueror'). **Fathiyya** is a feminine form of the name.

Fatima (f) Arabic name derived from *fatima* ('weaning' or 'abstaining'), often interpreted to mean 'chaste' or 'motherly'. Borne in the 7th century by the favourite daughter of Muhammad, it has long been a popular choice among Muslims because it implies chastity and other forms of abstention desirable among Muslim women. It has also made occasional appearances among English speakers in the 20th century, sometimes in tribute to Our Lady of Fatima, who is supposed to have made miraculous appearances to three children at the village of Fatima in Portugal in 1917. Famous bearers of the name in recent times have included British athlete Fatima Whit-

bread (b.1961). Also encountered in the variant form **Fatma**.

Fatin (f) Arabic name derived from **fatin** ('charming' or 'seductive'). A relatively recent introduction, it is best known as the name of the Egyptian actress Fatin Hamama (b.1932), the former wife of film star Omar Sharif.

Faustina *See* FAUSTINE.

Faustine (f) French first name descended from the Roman names Fausta and Faustus, themselves derived from the Latin *faustus* ('fortunate'), that has made occasional appearances over the centuries. **Faustina** is a rare English variant of the name. Both versions of the name are closely associated with the Faust legend as recounted in Christopher Marlowe's play *Doctor Faustus* (*c*.1592) and other celebrated works, but Faust or Faustus themselves do not appear to have survived as first names beyond the end of the Roman era.

Fawn (f) English first name derived either from the ordinary vocabulary word for a young deer or else from the combination of FAY and DAWN or similar names. It made its debut as a first name among English speakers in the 19th century and has continued to appear on an irregular basis ever since.

Fawzi (m) Arabic name derived from *fawz* ('triumph' or 'victory'). **Fawziyya** is a feminine form of the name.

Fay (f) English name derived from the traditional name for a fairy. It is also encountered fairly regularly as a diminutive form of FAITH. It appeared at a relatively early date as a component of the name of Morgan le Fay, the treacherous sister of King Arthur in Arthurian legend, but it does not seem to have been taken up as a first name until the 19th century, since when it has continued to make infrequent appearances. Well-known bearers of the name have included British actress Fay Compton (1894–1978), US film actress Fay Wray (b.1907) and New Zealand-born British novelist Fay

Weldon (Franklin Weldon; b.1931). **Faye** and **Fae** are variant forms of the name – as borne by US film actress Faye Dunaway (b.1941).

Faye *See* FAY.

Fayiz (m) Arabic name derived from *faiz* ('victor'). **Fayza** is a feminine form of the name.

Fayruz (f) Arabic name derived from *fayruz* ('turquoise'). It is thought to have been originally of Persian origin and was initially given to boys, although today it is reserved exclusively for girls.

Faysal *See* FAISAL.

Fayvel *See* FAIVISH.

Fearghal *See* FERGAL.

Fearghas/Feargus *See* FERGUS.

Fedele *See* FIDEL.

Fedelma *See* FIDELMA.

Federico *See* FREDERICK.

Fedora *See* THEODORA.

Fedot (m) Russian first name derived from the Greek Theodotus, itself from the Greek *theos* ('god') and *dotos* ('given'). It was popular among early Christians and was borne by several early saints.

Fedya *See* THEODORE.

Feichin (m) Irish name (pronounced 'feckin') derived from the Irish Gaelic *fiach* ('raven'). Occasionally found as FESTUS.

Feidhelm *See* FIDELMA.

Feige (f) Jewish name derived from the Yiddish Feygl, meaning 'bird'. **Fayge** is a variant form.

Feivel *See* FAIVISH.

Felice *See* FELIX.

Felicia *See* FELICITY.

Feliciano *See* FELIX.

Felicity (f) English first name derived from the ordinary vocabulary word meaning 'good luck' or 'good fortune', ultimately descended from the Latin *felicitas* ('fertility' or 'fortune') and often treated as a feminine equivalent of the masculine FELIX. As **Felicitas**, it was a fairly common Roman name best known as the name of a 3rd-century saint. As Felicity, it was among the group of so-called virtue names that were adopted by English Puritans in the 17th century and it has remained in currency ever since, with a peak in popularity in the 1980s and 1990s. Famous bearers of the name have included British actress Felicity Kendal (b.1946). Familiar forms of the name include **Flick**, **Lis**, **Liss**, **Lissa**, **Lissie**, **Phil** and LUCKY. **Felicia** is a rare variant of the name of 18th-century origin – as borne by English poet Felicia Hemans (1793–1835). Other variants include the Italian **Felicita**, the Spanish **Felicidad** and the Portuguese **Felicidade**.

Felipe *See* PHILIP.

Felix (m) Roman name derived from the Latin *felix* ('happy' or 'lucky') that entered use as a first name among English speakers in medieval times and has been in regular use since the 19th century. It appears in the Bible as the name of a Roman procurator of Judea and was subsequently borne by a number of saints and by four popes. Having declined in use after the middle of the 20th century, it enjoyed a marked resurgence in popularity in the 1990s. Famous bearers of the name have included the central character in the George Eliot novel *Felix Holt* (1866), British actor Sir Felix Aylmer (1889–1979) and Felix the Cat in US cartoon films of the 1920s. Variants in other languages include the Irish **Phelim**, the French **Félix**, the Italian **Felice** and the Italian, Spanish and Portuguese **Feliciano**.

Femie *See* EUPHEMIA.

Fenella (f) Irish first name derived via Fionnuala or Fionnghuala from the Gaelic *fionn* ('fair' or 'white') and *guala* ('shoulder') and thus meaning 'fair-shouldered'. In Irish legend Fionnuala is turned into a swan by her wicked stepmother and is only released from the spell when Ireland adopts Christianity. English speakers took up the name in the 19th century after it was promoted by a character of the name in the Walter Scott novel *Peveril of the Peak* (1823). Well-known bearers of the name have included British actress Fenella Fielding (b.1934). Commonly shortened to **Nella**, **Nola** or **Nuala**. Variant forms include **Finella**, **Finola** and **Fionola**. *See also* PENELOPE.

Fenton (m) English place name (found in several northern counties of England) that was subsequently taken up as a surname and occasional first name. The original place name came from the Old English *fenn* ('marsh' or 'fen') and *tun* ('settlement').

Feodora *See* THEODORA.

Ferapont (m) Russian first name derived from the Greek Therapon, meaning 'servant' or 'attendant' and thus interpreted by early Christians to signify 'follower' or 'worshipper'.

Ferdie *See* FERDINAND.

Ferdinand (m) German, French and English first name derived from the Old German Fridenand, itself from *fridu* ('peace') and *nand* ('bravery') and thus meaning 'peace through bravery'. Another derivation suggests the name developed out of the Old German *farth* ('journey') and *nand* ('prepared'). It came to England with the Normans in the 11th century, sometimes appearing in the Old French form **Ferrand** (or **Ferrant**), but never became as widespread as it was elsewhere in Europe. It enjoyed a brief period in favour among English speakers during the 1550s, when the marriage of Mary I and Philip II of Spain created a short-lived fashion for Spanish names.

Notable bearers of the name have included three Holy Roman emperors as well as Ferdinand I (d.1065), king of Castile and León, and several of his descendants, notably Ferdinand V (1452–1516), who drove the Moors out of Spain and funded the voyages of Christopher Columbus, and (through marriage between the two royal houses) several members of the Austro-Hungarian royal family. Bearers of the name in fiction have included characters in William Shakespeare's plays *Love's Labour's Lost* (*c*.1595) and *The Tempest* (1611). Sometimes shortened to **Ferd**, **Ferdie**, **Ferdy** and **Nandy**. Variants of the name in other languages include the French **Fernand**, the Spanish **Fernando** or **Hernando**, the Italian **Ferdinando** and the Romanian **Nandru**.

Ferdy *See* FERDINAND.

Ferenc *See* FRANCIS.

Fergal (m) Anglicized form of the Irish Fearghal, itself derived from the Gaelic *fear* ('man') and *gal* ('valour'), thus meaning 'man of valour'. Well-known bearers of the name in modern times include British journalist Fergal Keane (b.1961).

Fergie *See* FERGUS.

Fergus (m) English version of the Gaelic Fearghas, derived from *fear* ('man') and *gus* ('force' or 'strength') and thus meaning 'man of force'. Borne by a legendary Irish hero of Ulster credited with being the grandfather of St Columba, the name has retained its strong Scottish and Irish associations but is now found fairly widely across the English-speaking world. Commonly shortened to **Fergie** or **Fergy**. Variant forms of the name include **Feargus** – as borne by the Irish Chartist leader Feargus O'Connor (1796–1855).

Fermin *See* FIRMIN.

Fern (f) English first name derived from the name of the plant, itself from the Old English *fearn*. It is thought to have made its first appearance among English speakers along with other flower and plant names in the 19th century but has never been very common.

Fernand/Fernando *See* FERDINAND.

Fernley (m) Cornish first name of unknown meaning.

Ferrer (m) Spanish name derived from a Catalan surname meaning 'blacksmith'. It became popular among Spanish Catholics in honour of St Vicente Ferrer (d.1418).

Ferruccio (m) Italian name that developed as a diminutive form of the medieval Ferro, meaning 'iron'. It was often given to people with a strong physique or else with grey hair.

Fester (m) German diminutive of SYL-VESTER. The name became familiar to English speakers through a character of the name in the popular 1960s US television series (later filmed) *The Addams Family*. Also encountered as **Vester**.

Festus (m) Roman name meaning either 'festive' or else 'steadfast'. It appears in the Bible as the name of a Roman procurator of Judea who refused to condemn St Paul to death and was subsequently borne by several early saints. As a first name among English speakers it was taken up on an occasional basis in the medieval period and enjoyed a minor resurgence in popularity in the 19th century – there is, for instance, a character called Festus Derriman in the Thomas Hardy novel *The Trumpet Major* (1880).

Ffion (f) Welsh first name meaning 'rose' or 'foxglove finger'. Pronounced 'feeon', it is best known through Ffion Hague, wife of English politician William Hague.

Fi *See* FIONA.

Fiachna *See* FIACHRA.

Fiachra (m) Irish name (pronounced 'fearcra') derived from the Gaelic *fiach* ('raven'). It was borne by a 7th-century French saint who originated in Ireland, the patron saint of gardeners. Also found in the form **Fiachna**, a variant revived in the 20th century.

Fiammetta (f) Italian name derived from the Italian *fiamma* ('fire' or 'flame').

Fidda (f) Arabic name derived from *fidda* ('silver'). Also found as **Fizza**.

Fidel (m) Spanish first name derived from the Roman Fidelis itself from the Latin *fidelis* ('faithful'). It is best known as the name of the Cuban President Fidel Castro (b.1927). **Fedele** is an Italian variant. *See also* FIDELIA.

Fidelia (f) English first name derived from the Latin *fidelis* ('faithful'). It was included among the virtue names that were taken up by English Puritans in the 17th century and remained in occasional use for 100 years or more, with very rare revivals since the 18th century. There are characters of the name in the works of English poet Edmund Spenser and also in William Wycherly's play *The Plain-Dealer* (1676) and Edward Moore's *The Foundling* (1748). A rare masculine version of the name is **Fidelis** – as borne by a 6th-century saint.

Fidelis *See* FIDEL; FIDELIA.

Fidelma (f) Irish name derived from the Gaelic Feidhelm or Fedelm, itself of uncertain meaning, although it has been speculated that it was originally understood to mean 'beauty'. It was borne by an early Irish saint who was converted to Christianity by St Patrick. Sometimes shortened to **Delma**. **Fedelma** is a variant form of the name.

Fife (m) Scottish place name derived from the name of the legendary Pictish hero Fib that was subsequently taken up as a surname and first name. Largely confined to people with strong Scottish associations, it also appears in the variant form **Fyfe** – as borne by Scottish television reporter Fyfe Robertson (1902–87).

Fifi (f) French first name that developed as a diminutive of JOSEPHINE and various other names incorporating 'fi' or 'if' sounds, such as FIONA and YVONNE. The common use of the name for poodles over the decades would appear to have made the name less attractive as a choice for girls.

Fihr (m) Arabic name of uncertain derivation, though possibly from *fihr* ('stone pestle').

Fikri (m) Arabic name derived from *fikri* ('intellectual'). A feminine form of the name is **Fikriyya**.

Filat (m) Russian name derived from the Greek Theophylaktos, from the Greek *theos* ('god') and *phylassein* ('to guard'). It was borne by a 9th-century Greek saint usually identified today as St THEOPHILUS.

Filbert *See* FULBERT.

Filiberto (m) Italian first name derived from the Old German *fil* ('much') and *berht* ('bright' or 'famous'). It made several appearances among members of the royal house of Savoy and remains popular in Italy today.

Filippo *See* PHILIP.

Fina *See* FIONA; SERAPHINA.

Finbar (m) Anglicized form of the Irish Fionnbarr or Fionbharr, itself from the Gaelic *fionn* ('fair' or 'white') and *barr* ('head'). It was borne by several early Irish saints, including a 6th-century bishop of Cork. Also found as **Finnbar**.

Findlay *See* FINLAY.

Finella *See* FENELLA.

Fingal (m) Anglicized form of the Scottish Fionnghall, derived from the Gaelic *fionn* ('fair' or 'white') and *gall* ('stranger'), thus meaning 'pale stranger'. Initially it was borne chiefly by Norse immigrants in Scotland but it subsequently became more widespread. It became well known in the 18th century as the name of the legendary warrior-hero of the Ossianic poems of James Macpherson (1736–96). Also found as **Fingall**.

Finian *See* FINNIAN.

Finlay (m) Scottish name descended from the Gaelic Fionnlagh, itself from the Gaelic *fionn* ('fair' or 'white') and *laogh* ('warrior') and thus interpreted to mean 'fair hero'. It was borne by the father of Macbeth, King

of Scotland. Also found as **Findlay** and **Finley**.

Finn (m) Irish name derived from the Gaelic *fionn* ('fair' or 'white'). Also found in the form **Fionn**, it was borne by the celebrated legendary hero Finn MacCool.

Finnian (m) Irish name derived from the Gaelic *fionn* ('fair' or 'white'). Notable bearers of the name have included two 6th-century Irish bishops. Also found as **Finian**.

Finola *See* FENELLA.

Fiona (f) English first name derived from the Scottish Gaelic *fionn* ('fair' or 'white'). It became well known among English speakers through its appearance in the Ossianic poems of James Macpherson (1736–96), who seems to have been the first person to use the name, and through the pseudonym Fiona Macleod used by Scottish writer William Sharp (1855–1905). Sometimes thought of as an aristocratic name, it enjoyed a peak in popularity in the 1960s. Well-known bearers of the name have included British actress Fiona Fullerton (b.1956), Irish actress Fiona Shaw (b.1958) and British ballerina Fiona Chadwick (b.1960). Commonly shortened to **Fi**. Variants of the name include **Fina** and the rare **Tiona**.

Fionn *See* FINN.

Fionnuala/Fionola *See* FENELLA.

Fiorella (f) Italian name derived from the Italian *fiore* ('flower').

Fiorenzo *See* FLORENCE.

Firdos (m) Arabic name derived from *firdaws* ('paradise'). Notable bearers of the name have included the Persian poet and historian Firdausi (*c*.940–1020). Variant forms include **Firdose**, **Firdoze** and **Firdaus**.

Firmin (m) French name derived from the Roman Firminus, itself from the Latin *firmus* ('firm' or 'steadfast'). It was popular among early Christians and was borne by several saints. Variants in other languages include the Italian **Firmino** and the Spanish **Fermin**.

Firoz (m) Arabic name derived from *firoz* ('victorious' or 'successful'). Variant forms include **Firuz**, **Feroz** and **Feroze**. Famous bearers of the name have included Firuz Shah Tughluq (*c*.1307–88), the builder of many celebrated buildings in Delhi.

Fishl (m) Jewish name derived from the Jewish word *fish* ('fish'), based on a biblical reference to the effect that the descendants of Ephraim and Manasseh would multiply like fish in the sea. Also found as **Fishke**.

Fitz *See* FITZROY.

Fitzgerald (m) English first name meaning 'son of Gerald'. Ultimately of Old French origins, it is more familiar as a surname. Sometimes abbreviated to **Fitz**.

Fitzroy (m) English surname meaning 'son of the king' that has made irregular appearances as a first name since the middle of the 19th century. It was used initially as a nickname for illegitimate sons of English monarchs. Commonly shortened to **Fitz**.

Flann (m) Irish name that developed as a diminutive form of Flannan, itself derived from the Gaelic *flann* ('red' or 'ruddy'). Famous bearers of the name have included the Irish novelist Flann O'Brien (Brian O'Nolan; 1911–66).

Flannan *See* FLANN.

Flavia (f) Roman name derived from *flavus* ('yellow' or 'golden'), probably as a reference to blond hair. Records of its use among English speakers go back to the 16th century. Notable bearers of the name have included a princess in the Anthony Hope novel *The Prisoner of Zenda* (1894). Sometimes shortened to **Flave** or **Flavie** (also a French variant of the name). *See also* FULVIA.

Fletcher (m) English surname, denoting a maker of arrows, that has been in occasional use as a first name since the 19th century.

The original surname developed out of the Old French *fleche* ('arrow'). It is perhaps best known as the name of Fletcher Christian (*c*.1764–94), the English naval officer who was the leader of the infamous 1789 *Bounty* mutiny.

Fleur (f) French first name, meaning 'flower', that was taken up by English speakers in the early years of the 20th century. Recorded in use in France in medieval times, its adoption in the English-speaking world resulted from the popularity of a character bearing the name in John Galsworthy's *Forsyte Saga* novels (1906–22). Well-known bearers of the name since then have included the New Zealand-born British poet Fleur Adcock (b.1934). Related names include FLORA, **Flower** and BLOSSOM. A diminutive form of the name is **Fleurette**.

Flick *See* FELICITY.

Flint (m) English first name meaning 'stream'.

Flip *See* PHILIP.

Flo *See* FLOELLA; FLORA; FLORENCE.

Floella (f) English first name that is thought to have resulted from the combination of FLORA and FLORENCE with ELLA or similar names. It appears to have made its first appearances among English speakers in the 1950s. Well-known bearers of the name have included Trinidad-born British television presenter Floella Benjamin (b.1955). Commonly shortened to **Flo**.

Flora (f) Roman name derived from the Latin *flos* ('flower'). The name of the Roman goddess of the spring, it was taken up by English speakers in the 18th century, although until then it had been considered suitable only as a name for spaniels. It became particularly popular in Scotland in tribute to Flora Macdonald (Fionnaghal Macdonald; 1722–90), the woman who in 1746 assisted Bonnie Prince Charlie in his escape from Scotland following defeat in the Jacobite Rebellion. Other famous bearers of the name have included the British writer Flora Thompson (1876–1947) and British actress Dame Flora Robson (1902–84). Variants include **Floretta**, **Florette** and **Florinda**. Abbreviated forms of the name include **Flo**, **Florrie**, **Floss** and **Flossie**.

Florence (f) English first name derived from the Roman Florentia, itself from the Latin *florens* ('blossoming' or 'flourishing'). It was first taken up by English speakers in the medieval period (when it was also used as a name for boys) and enjoyed a peak in popularity in the 19th century, since when it has largely fallen from favour. Notable bearers of the name have included English nursing reformer Florence Nightingale (1820–1910), who was born in the city of Florence (with which the name is often associated). Shortened forms of the name include **Flo**, **Florrie**, **Floss**, **Flossie** and **Floy**. When borne by males the name was formerly commonly abbreviated to **Flurry**. Masculine variants in other languages include the Italian **Fiorenzo**, the Spanish and Portuguese **Florencio**, the German **Florenz**, the Dutch **Floris** and the Russian **Florenti**.

Florentina (f) Roman name derived from the Latin *florens* ('blossoming' or 'flourishing'). It was borne by a 7th-century Spanish saint.

Floretta/Florette *See* FLORA.

Florian (m) English and German first name derived from the Roman Florianus, itself from *flos* ('flower'). Borne by a 3rd-century Roman saint, it has made irregular appearances among English speakers since medieval times but has become increasingly rare since the end of the 19th century.

Florinda/Floris *See* FLORENCE.

Florrie/Floss/Flossie
See FLORA; FLORENCE.

Flower *See* FLEUR.

Floy *See* FLORENCE.

Floyd (m) English surname derived from the Welsh LLOYD that has made occasional appearances as a first name since the 19th century, chiefly in the USA. Famous bearers of the name have included US heavyweight boxer Floyd Patterson (b.1925).

Fluellen *See* LLEWELLYN.

Flurry *See* FLORENCE.

Flynn (m) Scottish first name derived from the Scots Gaelic for 'son of the red-haired one'. Also encountered as **Flinn**.

Foka (m) Russian name derived from the Greek Phokas derived from *phoke* ('seal'). It was borne by several early saints.

Folke (m) Scandinavian name derived from the Old Norse *folk* ('people'). Variants include the English FULK (or **Fulke**).

Foma *See* THOMAS.

Fonsie *See* ALPHONSO.

Forbes (m) Scottish surname derived from the Gaelic *forba* ('field' or 'district') that has made occasional appearances as a first name, chiefly in Scotland.

Ford (m) English surname denoting a person living close to a river crossing that has made irregular appearances as a first name.

Forrest (m) English surname derived from the ordinary vocabulary word 'forest' that has made occasional appearances as a first name since the 19th century. Its popularity in the USA can be traced back to the fame of Confederate commander Nathan Bedford Forrest (1821–77). Also found as **Forest**.

Forrester (m) English first name meaning 'forester'. Ultimately of Old French origins, it is sometimes rendered in the form **Forster**.

Fortunato (m) Italian, Spanish and Portuguese name derived from the Roman Fortunatus, from the Latin *fortuna* ('fortune' or 'fate'). It was popular among early Christians and was borne by several early saints. **Fortunata** is a feminine form of the name.

Fortune (f) English first name derived from the Latin *fortuna* ('fortune' or 'fate'). It was taken up by English Puritans in the 17th century but is rare today.

Foster (m) English surname of obscure origin that has made irregular appearances as a first name. The original surname may have had one of several meanings, signifying 'foster-parent', 'forester', 'shearer' or 'saddle-tree maker'. Famous bearers of the name have included US statesman John Foster Dulles (1888–1959), whose maternal grandfather bore Foster as a surname.

Fran *See* FRANCES; FRANCESCA.

Franca *See* FRANCESCO.

France (m) English first name derived either from the name of the country or else a diminutive form of FRANCIS. Encountered occasionally in the USA but rare elsewhere.

Frances (f) English first name that developed as a feminine form of FRANCIS. It should be noted that the spelling Frances was formerly used interchangeably for the masculine form of the name. As a name for girls, it was taken up by English speakers in the 17th century and went on to enjoy a peak in popularity in the 19th century, before going into decline in the 20th century. Well-known bearers of the name have included Anglo-US novelist Frances Hodgson Burnett (1849–1924) and British actress Frances de la Tour (b.1944). Commonly shortened to **Fran**, **Frannie** (or **Franny**), **Francie**, **Frankie** or FANNY. Variants of the name include **Francine** (or **Francene**), the French **Françoise** and the Italian FRANCESCA.

Francesca (f) Italian name that developed as a feminine form of FRANCESCO and has made increasingly frequent appearances as a first name among English speakers since the middle of the 20th century. Notable bearers of the name have included the legendary Francesca di Rimini, the subject of a famous romantic tragedy told in Dante's *Inferno* and elsewhere. Commonly shortened to **Fran** or **Franny**. Variants in other languages include the Spanish **Francisca** and the German **Franziska**.

Francesco (m) Italian first name that represents an Italian equivalent of the English FRANCIS, both derived ultimately from the Roman Franciscus. It has been popular among Italians ever since the 13th century, often bestowed in honour of St Francis of Assisi (1182–1226). **Franco** is a common diminutive form of the name. Feminine versions include **Franca** and FRANCESCA. *See also* FRANTISEK; FRANZ.

Francie/Francine *See* FRANCES.

Francis (m) English first name descended from the Roman Franciscus, itself from the Latin for 'Frenchman'. The name is supposed to have had its origin in St Francis of Assisi (1182–1226), who was initially baptized GIOVANNI but was renamed by his father following his return from France. It was after St Francis of Assisi that the Franciscan order of friars took its title. The name Francis was taken up by English speakers in the 16th century and it remained in fairly common currency until the 20th century, when it went into decline. Notable bearers of the name have included the English sailor Sir Francis Drake (d.1596), English philosopher and writer Francis Bacon (1561–1626), British yachtsman Sir Francis Chichester (1901–72) and Irish painter Francis Bacon (1909–92). Commonly shortened to FRANK or **Frankie**. Variants in other languages include the French FRANÇOIS, the Italian FRANCESCO, the Spanish **Francisco** (and its diminutives **Paco** and **Pancho**), and the Hungarian **Ferenc**. *See also* FRANCES.

Francisca *See* FRANCES.

Francisco *See* FRANCIS.

Franco *See* FRANCESCO.

François (m) French version (pronounced 'fronswa') of the English FRANCIS, both descended ultimately from the Roman Franciscus. Notable bearers of this lastingly popular name have included two 16th-century kings of France and, in more recent times, French President François Mitterrand (1916–96). **Françoise** is an equally popular feminine version of the name – as borne by French novelist Françoise Sagan (b.1935).

Françoise *See* FRANÇOIS.

Frank (m) English first name that developed as a diminutive form of FRANCIS or FRANKLIN (and also of the feminine FRANCES and FRANCESCA) but is now frequently considered to be a name in its own right. It is also possible to trace the name all the way back to the Germanic peoples called the Franks, who may have got their name from the distinctive spears they carried. The name became increasingly common among English speakers from the middle of the 19th century but has been in decline since the middle of the 20th century. Well-known bearers of the name have included US architect Frank Lloyd Wright (1869–1959), US film director Frank Capra (1897–1991) and US popular singer and film actor Frank Sinatra (Francis Albert Sinatra; 1915–98). Also found in the diminutive form **Frankie** – as borne by British comedian Frankie Howerd (1921–92) and British popular singer Frankie Vaughan (1928–99).

Frankie *See* FRANCES; FRANCIS; FRANKLIN.

Franklin (m) English surname derived from the Middle English *frankeleyn* ('freeman') that was taken up as a first name in the 19th century. In medieval times the word was used to describe a person who owned land but who was not of noble rank. The name has proved particularly popular in the USA, in part through association with the US statesman and scientist Benjamin Franklin (1706–60) and Presidents Franklin Pierce (1804–69) and Franklin D. Roosevelt (1882–1945). Commonly shortened to FRANK or **Frankie**. Also encountered in the variant form **Franklyn**.

Franklyn *See* FRANKLIN.

Frannie/Franny
See FRANCES; FRANCESCA.

Frantisek (m) Czech variant of the Italian FRANCESCO. **Frantiska** is a feminine form of the name.

Franz (m) German variant of the Italian FRANCESCO. The name was taken up by the Habsburg royal family in the 18th century and was subsequently borne by the Archduke Franz Ferdinand, whose assassination in 1914 precipitated the outbreak of the First World War. A feminine form of the name is **Franziska**.

Fraser (m) Scottish surname that has been in occasional use as a first name among English speakers since the 1930s. Ultimately derived from a Norman place name of uncertain meaning, it has retained its strong Scottish links. Also found as **Frazer**, **Frazier** and **Frasier** – as borne by the central character Frasier Crane in the popular US television series *Frasier*.

Frauke (f) German name (pronounced 'frowker') derived from *frau* ('lady'), but sometimes used as a familiar form of **Veronika** (*see* VERONICA). It became increasingly popular as a first name among German speakers in the 1960s.

Frazer/Frazier *See* FRASER.

Frea *See* FREYA.

Fred (m) English first name that developed as a diminutive form of FREDERICK and which is occasionally considered a name in its own right. Notable bearers of the name have included US dancer and actor Fred Astaire (Frederick Austerlitz; 1899–1987), Austrian-born US film director Fred Zinnemann (1907–2002) and British astronomer Sir Fred Hoyle (1915–2001). Variants include **Freddie** and **Freddy** – as borne by British-born US actor Freddie Bartholomew (1924–92) and Zanzibar-born British rock singer Freddie Mercury (Frederick Bulsara; 1946–91). *See also* ALFRED; FREDA; FREDERICA.

Freda (f) English first name that developed

as a diminutive form of such names as ALFREDA, ELFREDA, FREDERICA and WINIFRED, although it is often treated as a feminine equivalent of FRED or FREDERICK. It was taken up by English speakers in the 19th century and enjoyed a peak in popularity in the 1920s, but has since become rare. Well-known bearers of the name have included US jazz singer Freda Payne (b.1945). Variants of the name include **Frida** and the German **Friede** or **Frieda** – as borne by British novelist D. H. Lawrence's wife Frieda.

Freddie/Freddy *See* FRED.

Frédéric *See* FREDERICK.

Frederica (f) English first name that evolved as a feminine form of FREDERICK. It made its first appearance among English speakers in the 19th century but has never been very common. Often shortened to **Fred**, FREDA, **Freddie**, **Rickie**, **Ricky Rika** or **Rica**. Variants of the name in other languages include **Frédérique** (a French version), **Friederike** (a German form sometimes shortened to **Fritzi**), **Frederika** and **Frederike**.

Frederick (m) English first name derived from the Old German *fridu* ('peace') and *ric* ('ruler' or 'power') and usually interpreted to mean 'peaceful ruler'. It came to England with the Normans in the 11th century but it was not until the 18th century that the name became widespread. It enjoyed a peak in popularity in the English-speaking world in the early 20th century, when it ranked among the most popular of all boys' names. It has since gone into decline.

Notable bearers of the name have included a character in William Shakespeare's play *As You Like It* (1599), the Prussian ruler Frederick the Great (1712–86) and Frederick, Prince of Wales (1707–51), the eldest son of George II. Also encountered as **Frederic** – as borne by British novelist Frederic Raphael (b.1931) – and **Fredric**. Commonly shortened to FRED, **Freddie** or **Freddy**. Variants of the name in other languages include the French **Frédéric**, the

Italian and Spanish **Federico**, the Scandinavian **Frederik** and **Fredrik** and the German **Friedrich** and **Fritz** – as borne by Austrian-born US violinist Fritz Kreisler (1875–1962) and German-born US film director Fritz Lang (1890–1976).

Frederik/Fredric/Fredrik
See FREDERICK.

Freeman (m) English first name meaning 'free man'. It was in use as a surname before being adopted on an occasional basis as a first name.

Freja *See* FREYA.

Freya (f) Scandinavian first name (pronounced 'frayer') derived from that of the Norse goddess of love (after whom Friday was named). It is thought to have come originally from the German *frau* ('woman'). It has made infrequent appearances among English speakers since the late 19th century, chiefly in Scotland and the Shetland Islands. Notable bearers of the name have included British archaeologist and travel writer Dame Freya Stark (1893–1993). Variants include the relatively rare **Frea** and the Swedish **Freja**.

Freyde (f) Jewish name meaning 'joy'.

Frida *See* FREDA.

Frideswide (f) English name derived from the Old English *frith* ('peace') and *swith* ('strong'). It was borne by an 8th-century English saint and has since made occasional appearances as a first name among English Roman Catholics.

Fridtjof *See* FRITJOF.

Frieda/Friede *See* ELFREDA; FREDA.

Friedemann (m) German first name derived from the Old German *frid* ('peace') and *man* ('man'). It is popular among Jews, who treat it as a translation of Shlomo (*see* SOLOMAN). Famous bearers of the name have included the German composer Wilhelm Friedemann Bach (1710–84), eldest son of Johann Sebastian Bach.

Friederike *See* FREDERICA.

Friedrich *See* FREDERICK.

Fritjof (m) Scandinavian name derived from the Old Norse *frithr* ('peace') and *thjofr* ('thief'). Variants include **Fritjov** and **Fridtjof** – as borne by Norwegian explorer Fridtjof Nansen (1861–1930).

Fritz *See* FREDERICK.

Fritzi *See* FREDERICA.

Frode (m) Scandinavian name derived from the Old Norse *frothr* ('learned'). It enjoyed a revival around the middle of the 20th century.

Fuad (m) Arabic name derived from *fuad* ('heart').

Fulbert (m) English name derived from the Old German Filibert, from the Old German *fil* ('much') and *berht* ('bright' or 'famous'). It was borne by a 7th-century saint and subsequently came to England with the Normans, who also occasionally spelled it **Filbert**. The name remained in currency among English speakers for several hundred years but is now very rare. *See also* FILIBERTO.

Fulgencio (m) Spanish name derived from the Roman Fulgentius, itself from the Latin *fulgens* ('shining'). Notable bearers of the name have included a 7th century Spanish saint. Variants in other languages include the Italian **Fulgenzio**.

Fulgenzio *See* FULGENCIO.

Fulk (m) English name meaning 'people' or 'tribe' in Old German. It came to England with the Normans in the 11th century but virtually disappeared from use among English speakers after Tudor times. Also found in the form **Fulke** as borne by the English statesman Sir Fulke Greville (1554–1628).

Fulke *See* FULK.

Fulton (m) Scottish surname, possibly derived from a Scottish place name, that has been in occasional use as a first name since the end of the 19th century. Well-known bearers of the name have included Scottish actor Fulton Mackay (1922–87).

Fulvia (f) Italian and English first name that developed originally as the feminine form of the Roman Fulvius, itself derived from the Latin *fulvus* ('dusky' or 'tawny'). Famous bearers of the name in classical times included the wife of Mark Antony.

Fyfe *See* FIFE.

Fyodor *See* THEODORE.

G

Gab/Gabby/Gabi *See* GABRIEL; GAB-RIELLE.

Gabino *See* GAVINO.

Gabor *See* GABRIEL.

Gabriel (m) Biblical name derived from the Hebrew Gabhriel, meaning 'my strength is God' or 'man of God'. It appears in the Bible as the name of the Archangel Gabriel, who informs Mary of the forthcoming birth of Jesus, and was consequently taken up by English speakers during the medieval period, when it also appeared as **Gabel** or **Gabell**. It remained in fairly frequent use through the 18th and 19th centuries but became less common in the early part of the 20th century before enjoying a temporary revival in the 1940s. Famous bearers of the name have included the fictional Gabriel Varden in the Charles Dickens novel *Barnaby Rudge* (1841) and Gabriel Oak in Thomas Hardy's novel *Far From the Madding Crowd* (1874). **Gabe**, **Gab** and **Gabby** are common diminutive forms of the name. Variants in other languages include the Italian **Gabriele** and the Hungarian **Gabor**. *See also* GABRIELLE.

Gabriella *See* GABRIELLE.

Gabrielle (f) French first name that developed as a feminine equivalent of GAB-RIEL. English speakers adopted the name towards the end of the 19th century. Commonly shortened to **Gab**, **Gabby**, **Gabi** or **Gaby**. Variants include **Gabriela** and **Gabriella** – as borne by Lady Gabriella Windsor (b.1981), daughter of Prince Michael of Kent.

Gaby *See* GABRIELLE.

Gae *See* GAY.

Gaea *See* GAIA.

Gaenor *See* GAYNOR.

Gaetano (m) Italian name (pronounced 'gaytarno') descended from the Roman Caietanus, meaning in Latin 'person from Caieta' (the old name of modern Gaeta). Caieta in turn got its name from the nurse of the legendary Aeneas, who is popularly supposed to have died in that vicinity. Notable bearers of the name have included the 16th-century St Gaetano of Naples. Variants in other languages include the French **Gaétan**, the German **Kayetan**, the Spanish **Cayetano**, the Portuguese **Caetano** and the Polish **Kajetan**.

Gaia (f) Greek name derived from the Greek *ge* ('earth'). In classical mythology it was borne by the goddess of the earth who gave birth to the Titans. In more recent times the name has been taken up to describe the 'Gaia theory' that argues that the earth and all life on it should be considered a single living entity. Also encountered as **Gaea**.

Gail (f) English first name that evolved as a diminutive form of ABIGAIL and is now considered an independent name in its own right. It began to appear among English speakers during the 1930s and enjoyed a peak in popularity in the 1960s, since when it has become rather less frequent. Also found in the forms **Gale** – as borne by US actress Gale Sondergard (Edith Sondergard; 1899–1985) – and **Gayle** – as borne by the US actress Gayle Hunnicutt (b.1942).

Gaius *See* CAIUS.

Gala *See* GALINA.

Galahad (m) English name of uncertain

origin that has made occasional appearances as a first name over the centuries. It would seem to have been invented by early compilers of Arthurian legend as the name of the most virtuous of King Arthur's knights, destined to find the Holy Grail. Attempts have been made to link the name with the Hebrew Gilead. The name increased in frequency among English speakers in the 19th century in the wake of the publication of Alfred, Lord Tennyson's *Idylls of the King* (1859–85).

Gale *See* GAIL.

Galla (f) Jewish name derived from the Hebrew for 'wave'.

Galina (f) Russian name of uncertain meaning, though possibly derived from the Greek *galene* ('calm'). Familiar forms of the name include **Gala** – as borne by Spanish painter Salvador Dali's wife Gala (Yelena Diakonov; 1904–84).

Gamaliel (m) Biblical name derived from the Hebrew Gamliel, meaning 'my reward is God' or 'recompense of God'. It appears in the Bible as the name of a teacher of St Paul and was consequently taken up by English Puritans in the 17th century, although it never entered frequent use. The name features in the Tobias Smollett novel *Peregrine Pickle* (1751) and was the middle name of US President Warren G. Harding (1865–1923).

Ganesh (m) Indian name derived from the Sanskrit *gana* ('host' or 'horde') and *isa* ('lord') and thus meaning 'lord of hosts'. It is found in the *Mahabharata* as one of the many names borne by the god Shiva and also by his elder son. As the god of wisdom, Ganesh is usually depicted with an elephant's head and is widely worshipped throughout India.

Gardenia (f) English flower name that has made irregular appearances as a first name since the 19th century. The flower itself was named after an 18th-century naturalist called Dr Alexander Garden.

Gareth (m) Welsh first name that developed as a variant of GERAINT, although it has also been linked with such names as GARTH, GARY and GERARD and is often interpreted as meaning 'gentle'. Having established itself in Wales, it made its first appearance in England as early as the 16th century. It began to appear elsewhere in the English-speaking world with increasing frequency from the 1930s and by the 1980s had become widely popular among English speakers, although it has since suffered a marked decline and is once more being thought of as a predominantly Welsh coinage. Famous bearers of the name have included King Arthur's nephew Gareth in Malory's *Morte d'Arthur* (1485), British actor Gareth Hunt (b.1943), Welsh rugby player Gareth Edwards (b.1947) and British pop singer Gareth Gates (b.1984). Commonly shortened to GARY or **Gaz**.

Garey *See* GARY.

Garfield (m) English surname derived from the Old English *gar* ('spear') and *feld* ('open country'), and thus interpreted to mean 'person living near a triangular field', that has been in occasional use as a first name, chiefly in the USA, since the end of the 19th century. The name appears to have been adopted initially by English speakers in the USA in tribute to the assassinated US President James A. Garfield (1831–81). Notable bearers of the name since the 19th century have included the West Indian cricketer Sir Gary Sobers (Garfield Sobers; b.1936). It has enjoyed renewed exposure since 1978 as the name of the cartoon cat created by the US artist Jim Davis. Diminutive forms of the name include **Garry** and GARY.

Garnet (m/f) English surname of uncertain meaning that was taken up as an occasional first name in the 19th century, at a time when many other jewel names came into fashion. Notable bearers of the name have included the British Field Marshal Lord Garnet Joseph Wolseley (1833–1913).

Garret (m) Irish and English surname that

was subsequently adopted as an occasional first name from the 17th century, becoming particular popular in Ireland. The surname itself seems to have been derived from GERALD or GERARD. Well-known bearers of the name have included former Irish Prime Minister Garret FitzGerald (b.1926). Also found as **Garrett**. **Garry** and GARY are diminutive forms of the name. *See also* GARRISON.

Garrick (m) English surname derived from the Old English *gar* ('spear') and *ric* ('ruler') that has made rare appearances as a first name among English speakers over the years. Its initial popularity may have been promoted by the fame of the cele-brated 18th-century British actor David Garrick (1717–79).

Garrison (m) English place name (from Garriston in North Yorkshire) that was sub-sequently taken up as a surname and oc-casional first name. Another possibility is that the name evolved simply as 'Garrett's son'. The name was boosted in the USA through admiration for William Lloyd Garrison (1805–79), who was a noted campaigner against slavery. Well-known bearers of the name in more recent times have included the US writer Garrison Keillor (b.1942).

Garry *See* GARFIELD; GARRET; GARY.

Garth (m) English surname derived from the Old Norse *garthr* ('enclosure') that was taken up as a first name around the begin-ning of the 20th century. Sometimes treated as a variant of GARETH, it enjoyed a peak in popularity in the 1940s. Notable bearers of the name have included Garth, the fictional superhero in a British 1940s newspaper comic strip, and US country singer Garth Brooks (b.1962).

Gary (m) English surname that emerged as a popular choice of first name from the 1930s. The surname was probably of Norman French origin, derived in turn from the Germanic *gar* ('spear'). Often linked to the Welsh GARETH, it was at its most popular between the 1930s and the 1960s, since when it has become rather less fre-quent. The name became widely known through the US film actor Gary Cooper (Frank James Cooper; 1901–61), who based his pseudonym on the name of Gary, Indiana, where his agent lived (the town was named in its turn after an industrialist named Elbert Gary). Other notable bearers of the name have included South African golfer Gary Player (b.1935), British pop singer Gary Glitter (Paul Francis Gadd; b.1940) and British footballer Gary Lineker (b.1960). Also found as **Garry** – as borne by Russian chess player Garry Kasparov (b.1963) – and **Garey**. Sometimes abbrevi-ated to **Gaz**. *See also* GARFIELD; GARRET.

Gaspar *See* CASPAR.

Gaspard (m) French variant of CASPAR. The final '-d' is thought to have been added through association with the Germanic *hardu* ('brave' or 'hardy').

Gaston (m) French name of uncertain origin. It seems to have made its first appear-ances in southern France in medieval times and may have come originally from the German *gast* ('guest' or 'stranger'). Alterna-tively, it may have been adopted as a version of the French *Gascon* (signifying anyone from Gascony). It remains common in France and has made occasional appear-ances as a first name in the English-speaking world over the years.

Gauri (f) Indian name derived from the Sanskrit *gauri* ('white'). It was borne in Indian mythology by the wife of Shiva, who acquired a pure white complexion through meditation in the Himalayas after Shiva had criticized her dusky colouring. Also en-countered as **Gowri**.

Gautam (m) Indian name derived from the Sanskrit *gautama* ('descendant of Go-tama'). It was borne by the Buddha and thus became a frequent name among Buddhists. It is also popular among Jains. *See also* GOTAM.

Gavin (m) Scottish first name derived from

GAWAIN that has been taken up throughout the English-speaking world since the early 20th century. It enjoyed a peak in popularity in the 1970s and 1980s. Notable bearers of the name have included British novelist Gavin Maxwell (1914–69).

Gavino (m) Italian name that is thought to have developed as a modern equivalent of the Roman Gabinus, a name borne by natives of the city of Gabium in Latium. Notable bearers of the name have included a 2nd-century saint martyred in Sardinia. Variants in other languages include the Spanish **Gabino**.

Gawain (m) Welsh name possibly derived from the Welsh *gwalch* ('hawk'). It became relatively well known among English speakers during the medieval period, when it was also found as **Gauvain** or **Gawayne**. The name is usually associated with Sir Gawain, one of the knights of the Round Table in Arthurian legend and the central character in the 14th-century tale of *Sir Gawain and the Green Knight*. It seems to have virtually disappeared from use by the 16th century, but subsequently returned to favour in the modernized variant form GAVIN.

Gawel (m) Polish name (pronounced 'garwul') derived ultimately from the Roman Gallus, meaning 'cock' but usually interpreted to mean 'Gaul'. Early bearers of the name included a 7th-century Irish saint who did missionary work in central Europe, although in his case the name probably came from the Irish *gall* ('stranger'). Variants in other languages include the Czech **Havel**.

Gay (f) English first name derived from the French *gai* ('joyful' or 'cheerful'). It became popular among English speakers in the 1930s, initially in the USA, and in its early history was occasionally borne by men as well as women. It continued in fairly regular use until the 1960s, when it went into a sudden and rapid decline after the word 'gay' became widely understood to mean 'homosexual'. Variants include **Gaye** and the rarer **Gae**.

Gaye *See* GAY.

Gayle *See* GAIL.

Gaylord (m) English surname derived from the French *gaillard* ('dandy') that was taken up as a first name among English speakers from the 19th century. Often assumed to mean literally 'gay lord', it disappeared from use during the latter half of the 20th century when the word 'gay' acquired its modern meaning of 'homosexual'. **Gayelord** is a variant form.

Gaynor (f) English first name that evolved in medieval times as a variant of GUINEVERE. It enjoyed a shortlived revival in the 1960s. **Gaenor** is a Welsh variant.

Gaz *See* GARETH; GARY.

Gebhard (m) German name derived from the Old German *geb* ('gift') and *hardu* ('brave' or 'hardy'). The name was borne by a 10th-century saint who served as bishop of Constance. Also encountered as **Gebbert**.

Geena *See* GINA.

Gem *See* GEMMA.

Gemma (f) English, Irish and Italian first name derived from the Italian for 'gem' or 'jewel'. A long-established favourite in Italy, it has become relatively common in the English-speaking world, perhaps under the influence of EMMA, enjoying a peak in popularity from the 1960s to the 1980s. Well-known bearers of the name have included the Italian St Gemma Galgani (1878–1903) and Irish-born British actress Gemma Craven (b.1950). Sometimes abbreviated to **Gem**. Also found as **Jemma**.

Gena *See* GINA.

Gene (m/f) English first name that developed as a diminutive form of EUGENE and EUGENIA, and as a variant of JEAN. It was particularly popular in the USA in the first half of the 20th century. Notable bearers of the name have included (among the men) US boxer Gene Tunney (James Joseph Tunney; 1898–1978), US film actors Gene Autry (1907–98), Gene Kelly (1912–96), Gene Hackman (b.1930) and Gene Wilder (Jerry Silberman; b.1934) and US pop singer Gene Pitney (b.1941) and (among the women) US actress Gene Tierney (1920–91).

Genette *See* JEANETTE.

Geneva (f) English first name of uncertain origin. It may have been inspired by the name of the city in Switzerland, although it has also been suggested that it developed as a variant of GENEVIÈVE or JENNIFER.

Geneviève (f) French first name possibly derived from the Old German *geno* ('people' or 'race') and *wefa* ('woman') and thus interpreted to mean 'lady of the people' or more simply 'female'. Having already established itself in France, it was adopted by English speakers (usually without the accent) in the 19th century and enjoyed a resurgence in popularity following the release of the popular British film *Genevieve* (1953), in which the name was borne by a vintage car. Other notable bearers of the name have included the 5th-century St Geneviève, the patron saint of Paris, and, in more recent times, French-Canadian actress Geneviève Bujold (b.1942). Sometimes shortened to **Ginny**, GINA, **Ginette** or **Veva**. Variants in other languages include the Italian **Genoveffa** and GINEVRA.

Genevra *See* GINEVRA.

Genie *See* EUGENIE.

Genista (f) English first name derived from *genista*, the Latin name of the plant otherwise known as broom. The name was introduced to English speakers through the Plantagenet royal family, whose name came from the Latin *planta genesta* – a reference to the fact that the founder of the dynasty, Geoffrey Plantagenet (d.1151), wore a sprig of broom when going into battle.

Gennadi (m) Russian name derived from the Greek Gennadios, itself of disputed origin. The Greek name may possibly have developed as a diminutive form of various other names, such as Diogenes. Celebrated bearers of the name have included two early saints and, in more recent times, Russian politician Gennadi Gerasimov.

Gennaro (m) Italian name that developed as a modern equivalent of the Roman Januarius, itself from the Latin *Januarius* ('January'). In its historical form Januarius, the name was borne by several early saints. Variants in other languages include the Spanish **Jenaro**.

Genoveffa *See* GENEVIÈVE.

Geoff *See* GEOFFREY.

Geoffrey (m) English first name derived from the German Gaufrid, itself from the Old German *gavja* ('territory') and *fridu* ('peace') and thus interpreted as meaning 'peaceful ruler'. Another derivation suggests that it may have evolved as a variant of GODFREY. Whatever its origins, it came to England with the Normans in the 11th century and was in relatively frequent use among the English until the beginning of the 15th century, after which it became much less common. It enjoyed a resurgence in popularity in the 19th century when many medieval names were revived but has become increasingly rare since the 1950s.

Notable bearers of the name have included the English poet Geoffrey Chaucer (*c*.1343–1400), British novelist Geoffrey Household (1900–1988), British politician Sir Geoffrey Howe (b.1926) and British cricketer Geoffrey Boycott (b.1940). Commonly shortened to **Geoff**. Variants include **Jeffrey** (or **Jeffery**) and its abbreviated form **Jeff** as well as the French **Geoffroi**, the Italian **Goffredo** and the Spanish and Portuguese **Godofredo**.

Geordie *See* GEORGE.

George (m) English first name derived via the Latin Georgius from the Greek Georgios, itself from the Greek *georgos* ('farmer'). Already famous as the name of several early saints, including St George, the patron saint of England since the 14th century, it made irregular appearances among English speakers in medieval times but only became a popular choice after the accession to the throne of the Hanoverian George I in 1714. Over succeeding centuries its status as a traditional royal name was strengthened through another five English monarchs of the name. It remained in common currency into the early 20th century, then experienced a temporary decline before returning to favour in the 1960s and once again in the 1990s.

Notable bearers of the name have included US President George Washington (1732–99), British novelist George Eliot (Mary Ann Evans; 1819–80), US Presidents George Bush (b.1924) and George W. Bush (b. 1946), British pop musician George Harrison (1943–2001), Northern Ireland-born footballer George Best (b.1946) and British pop singer George Michael (Yorgos Panayiotou; b.1963). Diminutive forms of the name include **Georgie**, **Georgy** and **Geordie** (a variant commonest in northern England and Scotland). Variants in other languages include the French **Georges**, the Italian **Giorgio**, the Spanish and Portuguese **Jorge**, the German **Georg** and **Jürgen**, the Dutch **Joris**, the Swedish **Göran**, the Hungarian **György**, the Russian **Georgi** and YURI, the Polish **Jerzy** and the Czech **Jiri**. *See also* GEORGETTE; GEORGIA; GEORGIANA; GEORGINA; JODY.

Georgene *See* GEORGINA.

Georgette (f) French variant of the masculine GEORGE that was taken up by English speakers in the early years of the 20th century. Well-known bearers of the name have included British historical novelist Georgette Heyer (1902–74). Sometimes shortened to **Georgie** or **George**.

Georgia (f) English first name that developed as a feminine version of GEORGE, promoted in the USA through association with the state of Georgia. It was taken up

by English speakers towards the end of the 19th century and enjoyed a peak in popularity in the 1990s. Well-known bearers of the name have included a 5th-century French saint, US artist Georgia O'Keeffe (1887–1986) and British actress and singer Georgia Brown (Lilian Klot; 1933–92). Diminutive forms include **Georgie** and **George**.

Georgiana (f) English first name that developed from GEORGIA or GEORGINA as a feminine version of GEORGE, perhaps under the influence of JULIANA. This Latinate form of the name enjoyed considerable popularity among English speakers in the 18th century and remained fairly frequent until the end of the 19th century, since when it has become much rarer under pressure from Georgina. Aristocratic bearers of the name have included Georgiana, 5th Duchess of Devonshire (1757–1806). Sometimes shortened to **Georgie** or **Georgy**. Occasionally encountered in the form **Georgeana**.

Georgie *See* GEORGE; GEORGETTE; GEORGIA; GEORGIANA; GEORGINA.

Georgina (f) English first name that developed as a feminine version of GEORGE. It was taken up by English speakers in the 18th century, becoming especially popular in Scotland but subsequently winning acceptance throughout the English-speaking world and beyond, although GEORGIA is generally preferred in the USA. It largely replaced GEORGIANA as the usual form of the name in the 19th century. Commonly shortened to **Georgie**, **George** or GINA. The English **Georgene** and the French **Georgine** are among variant forms of the name.

Georgine *See* GEORGINA.

Georgy *See* GEORGE; GEORGIANA.

Ger *See* GERALD; GERARD.

Geraint (m) Welsh name (pronounced 'ger eye nt') of uncertain meaning, possibly derived via the Roman Gerontius from the

Greek *gerontos* ('old man'). Early records of the name include its appearance as **Gerente** in the *Anglo-Saxon Chronicle* of 705. It also features in Arthurian legend as the name of one of the knights of the Round Table and as such it reappeared in Alfred, Lord Tennyson's *Idylls of the King* (1859–86). Famous bearers of the name have included the Welsh opera singer Sir Geraint Evans (1922–92).

Gerald (m) English and Irish first name derived from the Old German Gerwald, itself from the German *ger* ('spear') and *wald* ('rule') and thus interpreted to mean 'spear rule'. The name came to England with the Normans in the 11th century and continued in use until the late 13th century, when it seems to have fallen out of favour everywhere except Ireland, where it was first introduced in the 12th century and became closely associated with the Fitzgerald family, who enjoyed great influence as the Earls of Kildare. It was revived among English speakers in the 19th century, acquiring a reputation as an aristocratic name, but has become infrequent since the middle of the 20th century.

Well-known bearers of the name have included Welsh writer Gerald of Wales (Giraldus Cambrensis; *c.*1146–*c.*1223), British actor-manager Gerald du Maurier (1873–1934), the fictional Gerald Arbuthnot in the Oscar Wilde play *A Woman of No Importance* (1893) and British zoologist and writer Gerald Durrell (1925–95). Commonly shortened to **Ger**, GERRY or JERRY. **Jerrold** is a variant of largely historical interest. Variants in other languages include the Welsh **Gerallt**, the Irish Gaelic **Gearóid**, the German **Gerhold**, the Dutch **Gerolt**, the French **Gérald** and **Géraud** and the Italian **Giraldo**. *See also* GARRET; GERALDINE.

Geraldine (f) English first name that was taken up as a feminine version of GERALD. Records of its use go back as far as the 16th century, when it made several appearances in literature, notably as a pseudonym of Lady Elizabeth Fitzgerald, the object of the love poetry of Henry Howard, Earl of Surrey (1514–47). It entered general usage as a first name in the English-speaking world in the 19th century, partly in response to its appearance in Samuel Taylor Coleridge's poem *Christabel* (1816), and subsequently enjoyed a peak in popularity in the 1950s. Famous bearers of the name have included US opera singer and actress Geraldine Farrar (1882–1967), US actress Geraldine Page (1924–87) and British actress Geraldine James (b.1950). Diminutive forms of the name include **Gerrie**, GERRY, **Jerrie** and JERRY.

Gerallt *See* GERALD.

Gerard (m) English, Irish and Dutch first name descended from the Old German **Gerart** or **Gairhard** itself from *ger* ('spear') and *hardu* ('brave' or 'hardy') and thus interpreted to mean 'brave with the spear'. Having been brought to England by the Normans in the 11th century, it remained fairly frequent among English speakers during the medieval period but became less common from the 17th century. It revived around the middle of the 19th century and remained in currency until the 1950s, since when it has suffered another sharp decline, being thought of as a strongly aristocratic name unsuitable for more general use, although it has lingered on among Roman Catholics. Well-known bearers of the name have included the British poet Gerard Manley Hopkins (1844–89) and German-born British musician and cartoonist Gerard Hoffnung (1925–59). Commonly shortened to **Ger**, GERRY or JERRY. Variants in other languages include **Gerrard** and **Jerrard** as well as the French **Gérard**, the Italian **Gerardo**, the German **Gerhard** or **Gerhart** and the Hungarian **Gellért**. *See also* GARETH; GARRET.

Gerasim (m) Russian name derived from the Greek Gerasimos, itself from *geras* ('old age' or alternatively 'honour'). Notable bearers of the name have included a 5th-century saint. **Garsha** is a familiar form of the name.

Gerda (f) Scandinavian, German, Dutch and English name derived from the Old Norse *garthr* ('enclosure') or else treated as a feminine equivalent of GERARD or a diminutive of GERTRUDE. Borne by a Norse goddess of peace and fertility, it was taken up by English speakers in the 19th century. Notable bearers of the name have included the young heroine Gerda in Hans Christian Andersen's fairytale *The Snow Queen* (1846). Variants of the name include the German **Gerde**.

Gereon (m) German name derived from the Greek *geron* ('old'). Notable early bearers of the name included a 4th-century Christian martyr.

Gergely *See* GREGORY.

Gerhard *See* GERARD.

Gerlach (m) German and Dutch name derived from the Old German *ger* ('spear') and *laic* ('play'). It was borne by a 12th-century hermit who was subsequently venerated as a saint.

Gerlinde (f) German first name derived from the Old German *ger* ('spear') and *lind* ('weak' or 'soft'). Notable early bearers of the name included an 8th-century saint from Alsace.

Germain *See* GERMAINE.

Germaine (f) English and French first name derived from the masculine French name Germain and thus descended from the Roman Germanus, meaning 'brother'. English speakers began to use the name in the early years of the 20th century. Notable bearers of the name have included a 16th-century French saint and the Australian feminist writer and broadcaster Germaine Greer (b.1939). Also found in the form **Jermaine** – as borne by US pop singer Jermaine Jackson (b.1954).

Gernot (m) German name derived from the Old German *ger* ('spear') and *not* ('need').

Geronimo *See* JEROME.

Gerontius *See* GERAINT.

Gerrard *See* GERARD.

Gerrie *See* GERALDINE.

Gerry (m/f) English first name that evolved as a diminutive form of such names as the masculine GERALD and GERARD and the feminine GERALDINE and now often considered to be a name in its own right. Notable bearers of the name have included British pop musician Gerry Marsden (b.1942) and British footballer Gerry Francis (b.1951). Also found as **Gerrie** or JERRY.

Gershom (m) Hebrew name meaning 'exile' or 'stranger'. It appears in the Bible as the name of a son of Moses and Zipporah, who was born in exile. The name was taken up by Puritans on both sides of the Atlantic in the 17th century but is now defunct in the UK, although it has continued to be recorded in the USA into modern times.

Gert/Gertie *See* GERTRUDE.

Gertrude (f) English, French, German and Dutch name derived from the Old German *ger* ('spear') and *traut* ('strength') and thus meaning 'strong with the spear' or 'ruler of the spear'. It was taken up by English speakers towards the end of the medieval period, perhaps as an import from the Netherlands, but enthusiasm for the name waned in post-medieval times and it was not until the middle of the 19th century that it appeared with any regularity once again. It has suffered another decline among English speakers since the early years of the 20th century. Notable bearers of the name have included two saints, Hamlet's mother in Shakespeare's tragedy *Hamlet* (1599–1601), British garden designer Gertrude Jekyll (1843–1932), US writer Gertrude Stein (1874–1946) and British actress Gertrude Lawrence (Gertrud Alexandra Dagmar Lawrence Klasen; 1898–1952). Diminutive forms of the name include **Gert**, **Gertie** and TRUDY or **Trudl** (or **Trudie**). Variants in other languages include the German **Gertrud**, the Spanish **Gertrudis** and the Portuguese **Gertrudes**.

Gervase (m) English name derived ultimately from the Roman Gervasius, itself from the Greek *geras* ('old age'), or else from the Old German *ger* ('spear') and *vas* ('servant') and thus interpreted to mean 'spear servant'. It was borne by a 1st-century saint whose bones were reportedly discovered by St Ambrose in the 4th century and was consequently taken up by English Roman Catholics in the 16th century. Notable bearers of the name in its early history included the 12th-century English scholars Gervase of Canterbury (*c*.1141–*c*.1210) and Gervase of Tilbury (*c*.1150–*c*.1220). Also encountered as **Gervaise** or JARVIS. A French variant is **Gervais**.

Gerwyn (m) Welsh first name meaning 'fair love'. Also spelled **Gerwen**.

Gethin (m) Welsh first name meaning 'dark-skinned'.

Ghada (f) Arabic name derived from *ghada* ('graceful lady').

Ghadir (f) Arabic name derived from *ghadir* ('brook' or 'stream').

Ghalib (m) Arabic name derived from *ghalib* ('conqueror').

Ghassan (m) Arabic name derived from *ghassan* ('youth'). The name of an ancient Arabian tribe, it is today a very popular Arabic name.

Ghayth (m) Arabic name derived from *ghayth* ('rain'). Also found as **Ghaith**.

Ghislaine (f) French name that developed as a variant of GISELLE. Usually pronounced 'jislane' or 'jilane', it has made occasional appearances as a first name among English speakers since the 1920s. Sometimes shortened to GIGI. Variants include **Ghislane** and **Ghislain**.

Ghufran (f) Arabic name derived from *ghufran* ('forgiveness').

Gianni *See* JOHN.

Gib *See* GILBERT.

Gid *See* GIDEON.

Gideon (m) Biblical name derived from the Hebrew Gidon, meaning 'hewer', 'one who cuts down' or alternatively 'having a stump for a hand', but often interpreted as meaning 'great warrior'. It appears in the Bible as the name of a judge who put the Midianites to flight after being instructed by God to protect the Hebrew people and was consequently taken up by English speakers on both sides of the Atlantic in the 17th century. Today it is more commonly encountered in the USA than it is elsewhere. Sometimes shortened to **Gid**.

Giffard (m) English name derived from the Old German Gebahard, itself from *gib* ('give') and *hardu* ('brave' or 'hardy'). Although now redundant as a first name, it was common among English speakers during the medieval period.

Gigi (f) French first name (pronounced 'jeejee') that developed as a diminutive form of GHISLAINE and other names. In Colette's novel *Gigi* (1958) it is treated as a familiar form of Gilberte (*see* GILBERT).

Gil *See* GILBERT; GILCHRIST.

Gilbert (m) English first name derived via French from the Old German Gisilbert, from *gisil* ('pledge' or 'hostage') and *berht* ('bright' or 'famous') and usually interpreted to mean 'bright pledge'. In Scotland it is sometimes encountered as an Anglicized form of the Gaelic Gilbride, meaning 'servant of St Bridget'. It came to England with the Normans in the 11th century and made irregular appearances until the 17th century, when it began to appear with greater frequency. It has been less common since the early years of the 20th century. Notable bearers of the name have included the 12th-century St Gilbert of Sempringham (d.1189), founder of the Gilbertine order of monks, the British naturalist Gilbert White (1720–93), the

British novelist G. K. Chesterton (Gilbert Keith Chesterton; 1874–1936), the character Gilbert Osmond in the Henry James novel *The Portrait of a Lady* (1881) and British broadcaster Gilbert Harding (1907–60). Commonly shortened to **Gib**, **Gibbie**, **Gil**, **Gilly**, BERT or BERTIE. Feminine equivalents of the name include **Gilberta**, **Gilbertine** and the French **Gilberte**.

Gilberta *See* GILBERT.

Gilberte *See* GIGI; GILBERT.

Gilbertine *See* GILBERT.

Gilchrist (m) English first name derived from the Gaelic for 'servant of Christ'. It has a fairly long history but seems to have disappeared from use since the 19th century and is now found only as a surname.

Gilda (f) Italian name that may have developed as a diminutive form of an Old German name derived from *hild* or *gild* ('sacrifice') or else from the Gaelic for 'servant of God' or the Old English for 'golden'. The name was known in Anglo-Saxon England as Eormenhild and continued to make irregular appearances in its modern form until the end of the 19th century, since when it has become very rare among English speakers. Notable bearers of the name have included the fictional Gilda in the Verdi opera *Rigoletto* (1851) and the central character played by Rita Hayworth in the film *Gilda* (1946).

Giles (m) English first name derived via French and the Roman Aegidius from the Greek Aigidios, itself from the Greek *aigidion* ('kid' or 'young goat') and often interpreted to refer to kid leather as used in the making of shields. The name was moderately common among English speakers of both sexes in medieval times, especially in Scotland, but never became a great favourite, perhaps because of its association with an 8th-century French saint who was venerated as the patron saint of beggars and cripples and whose name thus evoked notions of poverty. The saint himself was

popularly supposed to have fled to France from Athens and got the name from the goatskin he habitually wore.

Giles has remained in currency ever since, though with a significant reduction in popularity between the early years of the 20th century and the 1990s, when it enjoyed something of a revival. The name has strong rustic associations and the title 'Farmer Giles' is often applied to English farmers as a result of English poet Robert Bloomfield's poem 'The Farmer's Boy' (1800).

Notable bearers of the name have included the English poet Giles Fletcher (1588–1623) and the British cartoonist Giles (Carl Ronald Giles; 1916–95). **Gyles** is a variant form of the name borne by, among others, British writer and television presenter Gyles Brandreth (b.1948). Equivalents in other languages include the French **Gilles**, the Spanish and Portuguese **Gil**, the Danish and Dutch **Gillis** and the Italian **Egidio**.

Gill *See* GILLIAN.

Gilles *See* GILES.

Gillespie (m) Scottish name that developed as an Anglicized form of the Gaelic Gilleasbaig, meaning 'servant of the bishop'. Its use as a first name is now very rare and it is more commonly encountered as a surname. *See also* ARCHIBALD.

Gillian (f) English first name that developed either as an elaboration of JILL or as a feminine version of JULIAN. Another theory suggests it evolved from the Scottish Gaelic for 'servant of St John'. It was a popular girls' name during the medieval period but fell from fashion after the 17th century. It was taken up by English speakers once more around the middle of the 20th century and remained in popular use until the 1960s, since when it has lost much ground. Well-known bearers of the name have included British opera singer Gillian Knight (b.1934) and British politician Gillian Shepard (b.1940). Commonly shortened to **Gill**, **Gillie** or **Gilly**. Also found as **Jillian,** a relatively modern form of the name.

Gillie/Gillis/Gilly *See* GILLIAN.

Gilroy (m) Irish and Scottish surname derived from the Gaelic for 'son of the red-haired lad' that has made occasional appearances as a first name since the beginning of the 20th century.

Gina (f) Italian and English first name that developed as a diminutive form of GEORGINA and REGINA. It was taken up by English speakers in the 1920s and has remained fairly common, sometimes being considered a name in its own right. Famous bearers of the name have included Italian film actress Gina Lollabrigida (Luigina Lollabrigida; b.1927). Also found as **Gena** or **Geena** – as borne by US actress Geena Davis (b.1957). *See also* GENEVIÈVE.

Ginette *See* GENEVIÈVE.

Ginevra (f) Italian equivalent of the English GENEVIÈVE or GUINEVERE. This Italian variant has been adopted by English speakers on an occasional basis since the 19th century. There is a character called Ginevra Fanshawe in the Charlotte Brontë novel *Villette* (1853). Sometimes shortened to **Ginnie** or **Ginny**. Related variants include **Genevra**.

Ginger (m/f) English first name that developed as a nickname for anyone with red hair or a tempestuous character. As a girls' name it is sometimes used as a familiar form of VIRGINIA. It appears to be a 20th-century introduction that was at its most popular between the two world wars. Famous bearers of the name have included (among the men) the hero's best friend in the *Biggles* books of Captain W. E. Johns, one of William's gang in the *Just William* stories of Richmal Crompton and British rock drummer Ginger Baker (Peter Baker; b.1939) and (among the women) US film actress and dancer Ginger Rogers (Virginia McMath; 1911–95).

Gini/Ginnie/Ginny *See* GENEVIÈVE; GINEVRA; VIRGINIA.

Gino (m) Italian first name that developed as a diminutive form of numerous longer names ending '-gino'.

Gioacchino/Gioachino *See* JOACHIM.

Gioconda (f) Italian first name (pronounced 'jee-oh-konda') derived from the Latin *jucunda* ('happy'). Borne by a 5th-century Italian saint, it is usually associated with Leonardo da Vinci's masterpiece *Mona Lisa*, his portrait of the wife of Francesco del Giocondo otherwise known as *La Gioconda*.

Giorgio *See* GEORGE.

Giovanni *See* JOHN.

Girolamo *See* JEROME.

Gisela *See* GISELLE.

Giselle (f) French and English name (pronounced 'jeeselle') derived from the Old German *gisil* ('pledge'). Like other names derived from the same source it may have come about through the medieval practice of handing over children to foreign courts as pledges or guarantees of alliances. Because the name was borne by the wife of Duke Rollo of Normandy in the 10th century, who was herself possibly entrusted to Rollo as a hostage, the name enjoyed early popularity among the French but it was not until around the middle of the 19th century that English speakers took up the name, largely in response to the huge success of Adolphe Adam's ballet *Giselle* (1841). It has continued to make rare appearances ever since. Variants in other languages include the French **Gisèle** and the German and Dutch **Gisela**. *See also* GHISLAINE.

Gita (f) Indian name derived from the Sanskrit *gita* ('song'). Also found as **Geeta**. *See also* BRIDGET.

Githa *See* GYTHA.

Giulia *See* JULIA.

Giulietta *See* JULIET.

Giulio *See* JULIUS.

Giuseppe *See* JOSEPH.

Giuseppina *See* JOSEPHINE.

Gjord (m) Swedish name derived either from the Old Norse *guth* ('god') and *frithr* ('peace'), perhaps via the German form, Gottfried. A Norwegian variant is **Gjurd**. *See also* GODFREY.

Glad *See* GLADYS.

Gladstone (m) Scottish place name derived from the Old English *glaed* ('kite') and *stan* ('rock') that was subsequently taken up as a surname and occasional first name. It has made irregular appearances as a first name since the late 19th century, initially in tribute to the British Prime Minister William Gladstone (1809–98).

Gladwin (m) English surname derived from the Old English *glaed* ('bright') and *wine* ('friend') that has also made occasional appearances as a first name since the medieval period.

Gladys (f) English first name derived from the Welsh Gwladys, itself possibly from the Welsh *gwledig* ('ruler over territory' or 'princess'). It is also encountered as a variant of CLAUDIA. Known in Wales in various forms since before the Norman Conquest, it was taken up by English speakers elsewhere towards the end of the 19th century and remained popular into the 20th century before falling into disfavour and virtually disappearing from use by the Second World War. Well-known bearers of the name have included British actress Dame Gladys Cooper (1888–1971) and US soul singer Gladys Knight (b.1944). Commonly shortened to **Glad** and **Gladdie** (or **Gladdy**).

Glanville (m) English surname derived either from a Norman French place name or else from the Old English for 'clean field'. Variants include **Glenvil** and **Glenville**.

Gleb (m) Russian name derived from the Old Norse *guth* ('god') and *leifi* ('life'). It was borne by an 11th-century ruler of Kiev who was made a saint after being murdered.

Glen *See* GLENDA; GLENN.

Glenda (f) Welsh first name derived from the Welsh *glan* ('clean' or 'holy') and *da* ('good'). English speakers elsewhere took up the name around the 1930s but it has never been very common. The most famous bearer of the name to date has been the British actress and politician Glenda Jackson (b.1936). Sometimes abbreviated to **Glen** or GLENN.

Glendower *See* GLYNDWR.

Glenice/Glenis *See* GLENYS.

Glenn (m/f) Scottish and English surname derived from the Gaelic *gleann* ('valley') that was taken up as a first name for boys towards the end of the 19th century and for girls from the 1940s. When applied to girls it is sometimes treated as a diminutive form of GLENDA or GLENYS. It enjoyed a peak in popularity on both sides of the Atlantic in the 1950s and 1960s. Famous bearers of the name have included (among the men) US bandleader Glenn Miller (1904–44), Canadian-born US film actor Glenn Ford (Gwyllyn Ford; b.1916), Canadian pianist Glenn Gould (1932–82) and British footballer Glenn Hoddle (b.1957) and (among the women) US film actress Glenn Close (b.1945). Also spelled **Glen**, as borne by US country singer Glen Campbell (b.1936). **Glenna** is a rare feminine variant. *See also* GLYN.

Glenna *See* GLENN.

Glenys (f) Welsh first name that is thought to have evolved relatively recently as a variant of GLYNIS. Other theories suggest that it may have come about through the combination of such names as GLADYS and GLENDA. It was taken up by English speakers in the 1940s. Notable bearers of the name have included Welsh politician Glenys Kinnock (b.1944), wife of the former Labour Party leader Neil Kinnock. Sometimes shortened to **Glen** or GLENN. Also found as **Glenice** or **Glenis**.

Glinys *See* GLYNIS.

Gloria (f) English first name derived from the Latin *gloria* ('glory'). It seems to have made its first appearance as the name of a character in the George Bernard Shaw play *You Never Can Tell* (1889) and was subsequently taken up by English speakers around the beginning of the 20th century. It was at its most frequent in the 1930s, but has since become much more rare. Notable bearers of the name have included US actress Gloria Swanson (Josephine Swenson; 1899–1983), Irish television presenter Gloria Hunniford (b.1940), US pop singer Gloria Gaynor (b.1949) and Cuban-born US pop singer Gloria Estefan (b.1957). A variant is **Glory**.

Glory *See* GLORIA.

Glyn (m) Welsh first name derived from the Welsh *glyn* ('valley'). Its early development during the early years of the 20th century may have been influenced by the similar GLENN and GWYN. Having established itself as a fairly popular choice of name in Wales it began to make appearances elsewhere in the English-speaking world, reaching a peak in popularity during the 1950s and 1960s. Also found as **Glynn**. *See also* GLENN; GLYNIS.

Glyndwr (m) Welsh place name (pronounced 'glindoor') derived from the Welsh *glyn* ('valley') and *dwr* ('water') that was subsequently taken up as a surname and, from the 20th century, as an occasional first name. Its adoption as a first name in relatively recent times was inspired by admiration for the Welsh hero Owen Glendower (Owain Glyndwr, *c*.1359–1416), who led the Welsh resistance to the English for many years.

Glynis (f) Welsh first name that is thought to have developed from the Welsh *glyn* ('valley') under the influence of GLADYS. It was taken up by English speakers around the beginning of the 20th century and continued to appear fairly regularly until the 1950s, since when it has become less fre-

quent. Well-known bearers of the name have included the Welsh actress Glynis Johns (b.1923). Commonly shortened to GLYN. Sometimes spelled **Glinys** or **Glynnis**.

Glynn *See* GLYN.

Glynnis *See* GLYNIS.

Gobind *See* GOVIND.

Gobnait (f) Irish name of uncertain meaning, but possibly derived from the Gaelic *goba* ('smith'). It is sometimes treated as a Gaelic equivalent of ABIGAIL. Also found as **Gobnet**.

Goddard (m) English surname derived from the Old English *god* ('god') and *heard* ('brave' or 'hardy') that has made occasional appearances as a first name since medieval times, although very rarely since the 17th century. Variants in other languages include the German **Gotthard**.

Godelieve *See* GOTTLIEB.

Godfrey (m) English first name derived from the Old German Godafrid, itself from the Germanic *god* ('god') and *fridu* ('peace') and thus meaning 'God's peace'. It came to England with the Normans in the 11th century and was a popular choice of name through medieval times and beyond, although it has suffered a marked decline since the early 20th century and is now very rare. Well-known bearers of the name have included an 11th-century Norman saint, the fictional Godfrey Cass in the George Eliot novel *Silas Marner* (1861) and British actor Sir Godfrey Tearle (1884–1953). Variants in other languages include the Scottish Gaelic **Goraidh**, the German **Gottfried** and the Dutch **Godfried**.

Godiva (f) English name derived from the Old English *god* ('god') and *gyfu* ('gift') and thus interpreted to mean 'God's gift'. It is uniquely associated with Godiva, the wife of the Mercian Earl Leofric, who became notorious for riding naked through the streets of Coventry in order to persuade her husband not to levy exacting taxes upon the people of the city and has consequently made only very few appearances as a first name in succeeding centuries.

Godric (m) English name derived from the Old English *god* ('god') and *ric* ('powerful'). It ranked among the most common names used by English speakers prior to the Norman Conquest and was so well known that the Normans often used it as a generic name for an Englishman. It does not appear to have been used after the 14th century.

Godwin (m) English first name derived from the Old English Godwine, itself from the Old English *god* ('god') and *wine* ('friend') and thus interpreted to mean 'friend of God'. Borne in the 11th century by Godwin, Earl of Wessex, the father of Harold II, it was in fairly regular use during the medieval period but became much less common subsequently and is virtually unknown today. There is a character called Godwin in the George Eliot novel *Middlemarch* (1871–2). Also found as **Goodwin**.

Golda (f) Jewish first name derived from a Yiddish nickname meaning 'gold'. Notable bearers of the name have included the Israeli Prime Minister Golda Meir (Golda Meyerson; 1898–1978). Also found as **Golde** or **GOLDIE**.

Goldie (f) English first name of uncertain origin, though usually assumed to be from the ordinary vocabulary word 'gold'. It may have been derived from an identical surname or else have been taken up as a name for anyone with blond hair. First recorded in use as a first name during the 19th century. Famous bearers of the name have included US film actress Goldie Hawn (b.1945). *See also* GOLDA.

Goldwin (m) English surname derived from the Old English Goldwine, from *gold* ('gold') and *wine* ('friend'), that was subsequently taken up as a first name. It was relatively common in medieval times but seems to have gone out of use except as a surname after about 1730. **Goldwyn** is a variant form.

Gomer (m) Hebrew name meaning 'complete'. It appears in the Bible as the name of Noah's grandson and was consequently taken up by Puritans on both sides of the Atlantic in the 17th century. It has continued to make rare appearances in the USA into modern times.

Gonzalo (m) Spanish name derived from the Old German *gund* ('strife') and *salv*, possibly from the Latin *salvus* ('whole' or 'safe'). Variants include **Gonzalez**.

Goodwin *See* GODWIN.

Gopal (m) Indian name derived from the Sanskrit *go* ('cow') and *pala* ('protector') and thus interpreted to mean 'cowherd' or, sometimes, 'king'. In the *Mahabharata* the name is borne by Krishna and consequently it became very popular among Hindus.

Goraidh *See* GODFREY.

Goran *See* GEORGE.

Gordon (m) Scottish place name possibly derived from the Scots Gaelic for 'spacious fort' that was subsequently taken up as a surname and first name now commonly encountered throughout the English-speaking world. The name retains its strong Scottish associations, being a famous clan name, but this did not prevent it becoming very popular with English speakers elsewhere from the late 19th century, when many English babies were given the name in tribute to General Charles George Gordon (1833–85) after his death at Khartoum. It enjoyed a peak in popularity in the years between the two world wars. It has since become rather less frequent. Famous bearers of the name have included British jockey Sir Gordon Richards (1904–86), Scottish actor Gordon Jackson (1923–90) and British footballer Gordon Banks (b.1937). Occasionally spelled **Gorden**.

Goretti (f) English, Irish and Italian name that became popular early in the 20th century in tribute to the young Italian St Maria Goretti (d.1902), who became famous for forgiving her own murderer on her deathbed.

Gormlaith (f) Irish and Scottish name derived from the Gaelic *gorm* ('illustrious') and *flaith* ('lady'). Also found as **Gormla** or **Gormelia**.

Goronwy (m) Welsh name of uncertain meaning. It appears in the *Mabinogi* and as a consequence has been taken up on an occasional basis as a first name over succeeding centuries. Notable bearers of the name have included Welsh poet Goronwy Evans (1723–69).

Gosta *See* GUSTAV.

Gotam (m) Indian name derived from the Sanskrit *go* ('cow' or 'ox') and *tama* ('best'). Since ancient times cattle have represented wealth and productivity in Indian culture, hence the reference to cows in this and many other Indian names. Also found as GAUTAM.

Gottfried *See* GODFREY.

Gotthard *See* GODDARD.

Gotthold (m) German name derived from the German *Gott* ('God') and *hold* ('lovely'). Famous bearers of the name have included the German playwright Gotthold Lessing (1729–81).

Gottlieb (m) German name derived from the German *Gott* ('God') and *lieb* ('love'). It appears to have been of 17th-century invention and has remained in regular use among German speakers ever since. Variants include **Godelieve**.

Gottschalk (m) German name derived from the German *Gott* ('God') and *scalc* ('servant'). It was borne by an 11th-century German saint and subsequently became fairly common among German Jews.

Govind (m) Indian name derived from the Sanskrit *go* ('cow') and *vinda* ('finding') and thus interpreted to mean 'one who finds cows'. It appears as one of the names borne by Krishna in the *Mahabharata*. **Gobind** is a variant form of the name.

Gowri *See* GAURI.

Grace (f) English virtue name based on the ordinary vocabulary word 'grace'. It was among the many virtue names adopted by Puritans in the 17th century and, after a dip in the 18th century, it continued in fairly regular use on both sides of the Atlantic into the 19th century and beyond, enjoying a recent peak in popularity in the 1990s. Its 19th-century revival owed much to the fame of British heroine Grace Darling (1815–42), the lighthouse-keeper's daughter on the Farne Islands who in 1838 became nationally known for helping her father rescue nine shipwrecked sailors during a storm. Other notable bearers of the name have included US film actress Grace Kelly (1928–82) and West Indian soul singer Grace Jones (b.1952). Variant forms of the name include **Gracie** – as borne by British singer and comedienne Gracie Fields (Grace Stansfield; 1898–1979). Versions in other languages include the Italian **Grazia**, the Spanish **Gracia** and the German and Dutch **Gratia**. In Ireland the name sometimes appears as an Anglicization of the Gaelic GRAINNE.

Graciano *See* GRATIEN.

Gracie *See* GRACE.

Gracilia (f) English name derived from the Latin *gracilis* ('slender').

Grady (m) Irish surname meaning 'noble' that has also made irregular appearances as a first name.

Graeme *See* GRAHAM.

Graham (m) Scottish surname of 12th-century origin that was subsequently taken up as a first name both in Scotland and elsewhere in the English-speaking world. The original surname seems to have come from an English place name, Grantham in Lincolnshire, which itself came from the Old English *grand* ('gravel') and *ham* ('homestead'), thus meaning 'gravelly place' or alternatively 'Granta's homestead'. It enjoyed a peak in popularity in the 1950s. Notable bearers of the name have included the Earls of Montrose (leaders of the Scottish Graham clan who first took the name to Scotland) as well as British artist Graham Sutherland (1903–80), British novelist Graham Greene (1904–91), British motor-racing driver Graham Hill (1929–75) and Irish television presenter Graham Norton (Graham Walker; b.1963). A variant form of the name that has enjoyed some popularity since the early 20th century, especially in Scotland, is **Graeme** – as borne by Scottish-born comedian Graeme Garden (b.1943) and Scottish footballer Graeme Souness (b.1953). Also encountered as **Grahame**.

Grainne (f) Irish name derived from the Gaelic *gran* ('grain') or *grain* ('disgust'), or otherwise from *graidhne* ('love'). The name appears in Irish legend as that of the daughter of King Cormac, who killed herself after her lover Dermot died following a long pursuit by the jealous Finn MacCool. It is sometimes Anglicized as GRACE. Variants include **Grania** and **Granya**.

Granger (m) English first name meaning 'farmer' or 'bailiff'. It is more commonly used as a surname.

Grania *See* GRAINNE.

Grant (m) Scottish surname probably derived from the Norman French *grand* ('large' or 'tall') that was taken up as a first name throughout the English-speaking world in the 19th century. As a first name it has enjoyed particular popularity in Canada and the USA, where its frequency was promoted by admiration for the US President Ulysses S. Grant (1822–85). It enjoyed a peak in popularity towards the end of the 20th century, promoted perhaps in the UK by the fictional Grant Mitchell in the popular *Eastenders* television soap series.

Granville (m) English surname derived from a Norman baronial name that was subsequently adopted as a first name in the 19th century. The original Norman surname came from a place name based on

grand ('large') and *ville* ('settlement'). It has never been very common as a first name. Also found as **Grenville**.

Granya *See* GRAINNE.

Gratien (m) French first name derived from the Roman Gratianus, itself from the Latin *gratus* ('pleasing'). The name was borne by a 4th-century French saint. Variants in other languages include the Italian **Graziano** and the Spanish and Portuguese **Graciano**.

Graziano *See* GRATIEN.

Greer (f) Scottish surname derived from Gregor (*see* GREGORY) that has made occasional appearances as a first name since medieval times. The most famous bearer of the name to date has been the Anglo-Irish actress Greer Garson (1908–96), whose mother bore it as her maiden name. Occasionally encountered as **Grier**.

Greg/Greger/Gregers/Gregg/ Grégoire/Gregor *See* GREGORY.

Gregory (m) English first name derived via the Latin Gregorius from the Greek Gregorios itself from *gregorein* ('to watch' or 'be vigilant'). Because St Peter had bid his followers to 'be vigilant' the name was taken up with some enthusiasm by early Christians and was borne by no less than sixteen popes, including Gregory the Great in the 6th century. It has remained in fairly common currency among English speakers ever since the Norman Conquest, with a temporary period out of favour because of its Papist associations following the Reformation. It has enjoyed a recent peak in popularity since the middle of the 20th century. Famous bearers of the name have included US film actor Gregory Peck (1916–2003). Common diminutive forms of the name include **Greg**, **Gregg** and **Greig**. Variants in other languages include the Scottish **Gregor**, the Welsh **Grigor**, the French **Grégoire**, the Dutch **Joris**, the Swedish **Greger**, the Danish and Norwegian **Gregers**, the Russian **Grigori**

(sometimes shortened to **Grisha**) and the Hungarian **Gergely**.

Greig *See* GREGORY.

Grenville *See* GRANVILLE.

Gresham (m) English place name derived from the Old English for 'grazing' and 'hamlet' that was subsequently taken up as a surname and occasional first name.

Greta (f) Scandinavian and German first name that developed as a diminutive form of Margareta (*see* MARGARET). It has made infrequent appearances among English speakers since the 1920s. The name was made internationally famous through the Swedish film actress Greta Garbo (Greta Lovisa Gustafsson; 1905–90). Another bearer of the name in more recent times has been the Italian-born British actress Greta Scacchi (b.1960). Sometimes found as **Gretta**.

Gretchen (f) German first name that developed as a diminutive form of Margarete (*see* MARGARET). It was taken up by English speakers in the 19th century and has continued to make rare appearances ever since. It owed its initial popularity to a character of the name in Goethe's *Faust* (1808).

Gretel (f) German first name derived via Grete from Margarete (*see* MARGARET). Both Grete and Gretel have made very occasional appearances as first names among English speakers – often inspired by the character in the 'Hansel and Gretel' fairy tale by the Brothers Grimm.

Gretta *See* GRETA.

Greville (m) English surname that has been in occasional use as a first name since the 17th century. The surname came in its turn from a Norman French surname, which itself began life as Gréville, a place name in La Manche. The name has strong aristocratic associations, having been borne as a surname by the Earls of Warwick, notably Fulke Greville (1554–1628).

Griff *See* GRIFFITH.

Griffin (m) Welsh first name derived from the Roman Griffinus. It appears to have developed as a variant of GRIFFITH.

Griffith (m) English version of the Welsh Gruffudd or Gruffydd, derived from the Welsh for 'lord' or 'prince'. Records of its use in Wales go back to at least the 16th century but it has only rarely been adopted outside the principality in succeeding centuries. The name appears as that of a minor character in the play *Henry VIII* (1613), thought to have been written by William Shakespeare and John Fletcher. In its original Welsh incarnation the name is usually associated with the great Welsh leader Gruffydd ap Llewellyn (d.1063). Sometimes shortened to **Griff** – as borne by Welsh comedian Griff Rhys Jones (b.1953). *See also* GRIFFIN.

Grigor/Grigori *See* GREGORY.

Griselda (f) German and English first name derived from the Old German *gris* ('grey') and *hild* ('battle') and thus interpreted to mean 'grey warrior'. It was reasonably familiar among English speakers in medieval times but has since become very rare. Famous bearers of the name have included characters in Geoffrey Chaucer's *The Canterbury Tales* (1387) and Anthony Trollope's *The Warden* (1855). **Grizzie** and ZELDA are diminutive forms of the name. **Grizel** (or **Grizzel**) is a Scottish variant.

Grisha *See* GREGORY.

Grizel/Grizzel/Grizzie *See* GRISELDA.

Gro (f) Scandinavian name possibly derived from the Old Norse *groa* ('to grow').

Grover (m) English place name derived from the Old English *graf* ('grove') that was subsequently taken up as a surname and occasional first name. As a first name it is confined largely to the USA, partly in tribute to the US President Stephen Grover Cleveland (1837–1908).

Gruffud/Gruffydd *See* GRIFFITH.

Guadalupe (m) Spanish first name derived from a Spanish place name based on the Arabic *wadi al-lubb* ('river of the wolf'). It was taken up by Spanish speakers in honour of the Virgin Mary, sometimes known as 'Our Lady of Guadalupe' because that was how she described herself when she appeared in a vision to a Mexican peasant in 1531. **Lupita** is a diminutive form.

Gudrun (f) German and Scandinavian name derived from *guth* ('battle' or 'god') and *run* ('secret') and thus sometimes interpreted to mean 'wily in battle'. It has made occasional appearances among English speakers since the late 19th century, notably as the name of the principal character in D. H. Lawrence's novels *The Rainbow* (1915) and *Women in Love* (1921).

Guendolen *See* GWENDOLEN.

Guenevere *See* GUINEVERE.

Guglielmo *See* WILLIAM.

Guido *See* GUY.

Guillaume/Guillem/Guillermo *See* WILLIAM.

Guinevere (f) French and English equivalent of the Welsh Gwenhwyfar, itself from the Welsh *gwen* ('white' or 'fair') and *hwyfar* ('smooth' or 'soft'). The name is usually associated with King Arthur's faithless wife, who bore the name, and has otherwise only made occasional appearances as a first name, being superseded long ago by the related JENNIFER. Sometimes shortened to **Gwinny**. **Guenevere** is a variant form. *See also* GAYNOR.

Guiscard (m) French first name (pronounced 'jeescar') derived from the Norman French place name Hauteville-la-Guichard, which was itself in part from the Old German *hardu* ('bold' or 'hardy'). It became a popular name among English speakers following the Norman Conquest. Also spelled **Giscard**.

Gull (f) Scandinavian name derived from the Old Norse *guth* ('god') or alternatively from *gull* ('gold').

Gulzar (m) Indian name derived from the Persian *gulzar* ('blooming').

Gunnar *See* GÜNTHER.

Gunne (m) Scandinavian first name derived from the Old Norse Gunni, itself a diminutive of Gunnar, from the Old Norse *gunnr* ('strife'). Occasionally also encountered as a feminine name.

Gunnhild (f) Scandinavian name derived from the Old Norse *gunnr* ('strife') and *hildr* ('battle'). It has remained in currency among Scandinavians since Viking times but has only made rare appearances among English speakers. Also found as **Gunhild** or **Gunhilda**.

Gunter *See* GÜNTHER.

Günther (m) German first name derived from the Old German *gund* ('strife') and *heri* ('army'). The name appears in German mythology as that of the hero Siegfried's brother-in-law and it enjoyed a revival among German speakers following Wagner's reworking of German legend in his opera *Götterdämmerung* (1876). Long popular among Germans, it was taken up by English speakers in medieval times but seems to have fallen into disuse after the end of the 15th century. Notable bearers of the name in modern times have included German novelist Günter Grass (b.1927). Also found as **Gunter** or **Gunnar**.

Gus (m) English first name that evolved as a diminutive form of such masculine names as ANGUS, AUGUSTUS and GUSTAV and also the feminine AUGUSTA. It was taken up by English speakers in the 19th century. **Gussie** is a familiar form.

Gussie *See* GUS.

Gusta *See* AUGUSTA.

Gustaf *See* GUSTAV.

Gustav (m) Swedish first name derived from Gotstaf, itself possibly from *got* ('god') and *stafr* ('staff') and thus interpreted to mean 'staff of the gods'. Records of its use among English speakers go back to at least the 17th century. Notable bearers of the name have included British composer Gustav Holst (1874–1934), whose parents were Swedish, and King Gustav VI (1882–1973), one of several Swedish monarchs to share it. Commonly abbreviated to GUS. Variants include the Swedish **Gustaf** and **Gosta** and the French **Gustave**.

Guy (m) English first name derived via French from the Old German Wido, from *wit* ('wide') or *witu* ('wood'). It came to England with the Normans in the 11th century and subsequently became popular through the medieval romance *Guy of Warwick*. It was among the medieval names that enjoyed a considerable revival among English speakers in the 19th century. Notable bearers of the name over the years have included the wicked Guy of Gisborne in the Robin Hood legends, the English Catholic conspirator Guy Fawkes (1570–1606), the central character in the Walter Scott novel *Guy Mannering* (1815) and French writer Guy de Maupassant (1850–93). Rarely encountered in the form **Gye**. Variants in other languages include the Italian **Guido**.

Gwen (f) Welsh first name derived from the Welsh *gwyn* ('white', 'fair' or 'blessed') or else as a diminutive form of GWENDOLEN or GWYNETH. Although it still has strong Welsh connections, the name was taken up throughout the English-speaking world during the 20th century, although it has become less frequent since the 1960s. Notable bearers of the name have included a 5th-century Welsh saint, Welsh painter Gwen John (1876–1939) and British actress Gwen Ffrangcon-Davies (1891–1992).

Gwenda (f) Welsh first name derived from the Welsh *gwen* ('white', 'fair' or 'blessed') and *da* ('good') that was taken up on an occasional basis by English speakers early in the 20th century. Occasionally used as a diminutive form of GWENDOLEN. Often abbreviated to GWEN.

Gwendolen (f) Welsh first name derived from the Welsh *gwen* ('white', 'fair' or 'blessed') and *dolen* ('ring' or 'bow') that has become popular throughout the English-speaking world since the middle of the 19th century. Sometimes interpreted as meaning 'white circle' and thus a reference to the moon. Borne by the wife of the legendary Welsh King Locrine and by the wife of the legendary Arthurian sorcerer Merlin, it enjoyed a peak in popularity among English speakers in the 1920s. Notable bearers of the name have included the fictional Gwendolen Fairfax in the Oscar Wilde play *The Importance of Being Earnest* (1895). Variant forms include **Gwendolin**, **Gwendoline**, **Gwendolyn** and the largely historical **Guendolen**.

Gweneth *See* GWYNETH.

Gwenllian (f) Welsh first name (pronounced 'gwent-clee-an') derived from the Welsh *gwen* ('white', 'fair' or 'blessed') and *lliant* ('flood' or 'flow'). Sometimes interpreted to mean 'foamy white' and thus a reference to a pale complexion. Confined largely to Wales itself.

Gwenyth *See* GWYNETH.

Gwilim/Gwill/Gwilym *See* WILLIAM.

Gwinny *See* GUINEVERE.

Gwladys *See* GLADYS.

Gwyllim *See* WILLIAM.

Gwyn (m) Welsh name derived from the Welsh *gwyn* ('white', 'fair' or 'blessed'). It has retained its strong Welsh associations although it has made occasional appearances elsewhere in the English-speaking world since the early years of the 20th century. Famous bearers of the name have included the Welsh writer Gwyn Thomas (b.1936). Also found as **Gwynn**. *See also* WYNN.

Gwynedd *See* GWYNETH.

Gwyneth (f) Welsh first name derived from the Welsh *gwynaeth* ('luck' or 'happiness'). It was imported from Wales during the 19th century and has remained in use throughout the UK (though rarely elsewhere in the English-speaking world) ever since. Famous bearers of the name have included the Welsh poet Gwyneth Vaughan (Annie Harriet Hughes; 1852–1910) and US film actress Gwyneth Paltrow (b.1972). Commonly abbreviated to GWEN. Variants include **Gwynedd**, **Gwynneth**, **Gwenyth**, **Gweneth** and **Gwenneth**. *See also* VENETIA.

Gwynfor (m) Welsh first name derived from the Welsh *gwyn* ('white', 'fair' or 'blessed') and *mawr* ('great' or 'large') and interpreted to mean 'fair lord' or 'fair place'. Apparently an early 20th-century introduction. **Wynfor** is a variant.

Gwynn *See* GWYN.

Gwynneth *See* GWYNETH.

Gye *See* GUY.

Gyles *See* GILES.

György *See* GEORGE.

Gypsy (f) English first name derived from the ordinary vocabulary word 'gypsy'. It was taken up by English speakers during the 19th century, borne both by actual gypsies and also by non-gypsies attracted by the romantic associations of such a name. Notable bearers of the name have included the US actress Gypsy Rose Lee (Rose Louise Hovick; 1913–70). Also found as **Gipsy**.

Gytha (f) English first name derived from the Old English *gyth* ('strife') or the Old Norse *guthr* ('war'). Recorded in use in England before the Norman Conquest, it was revived during the 19th century and has made rare reappearances as a first name among English speakers since then.

Gyula *See* JULIUS.

H

Haakon *See* HAKAN.

Habakkuk (m) Hebrew name meaning 'embrace' that was taken up by English speakers in the 17th century. It appears in the Bible as the name of a minor prophet and was consequently adopted by English Puritans but never enjoyed widespread popularity, apparently disappearing from use after the 19th century. There is a character with the name in the Walter Scott novel *Old Mortality* (1816). Variant forms include **Habacuc**.

Habib (m) Arabic name derived from *habib* ('beloved' or 'dear'). Famous bearers of the name in recent times have included Tunisian President Habib Bourguiba (1903–2000). **Habiba** is a feminine version of the name.

Hadassah (f) Hebrew name that appears in the Bible as an alternative form of ESTHER. It is still sometimes encountered in this ancient Hebrew form among modern Jews. **Dassah** is an abbreviated version of the name.

Hadi (m) Arabic name derived from *hadi* ('leader' or 'guide', or alternatively 'calm' or 'quiet'). **Hadya** is a feminine variant.

Hadil (f) Arabic name derived from *hadil* ('cooing'). It can be traced back to the name of a bird that is supposed to have become extinct in the time of Noah when it was attacked and killed by a hawk.

Hadley (m) English first name meaning 'heathery hill'. It is generally more familiar as a surname.

Hadrian *See* ADRIAN.

Hadyn *See* HAYDN.

Hafiz (m) Arabic name derived from *hafiz* ('guardian'). The name was formerly reserved for devotees who could recite the Koran from memory. Variants include the Indian **Hafeez**.

Hafsa (f) Arabic name of uncertain origin that is usually interpreted to mean 'motherliness'. The name has a long history and was famous as that of one of Muhammad's wives. Variants include **Hafza**.

Hagar (f) Hebrew name meaning 'forsaken' that was taken up by English speakers in the 19th century. It appears in the Bible as the name of Sarah's Egyptian maid, who is sent away ('forsaken') by Sarah after she bears Ishmael by Abraham (despite the fact that Sarah initially sanctioned the birth). It seems to have fallen into disuse as a first name in the English-speaking world after the 1920s. *See also* HAJAR.

Hagen *See* HAKAN.

Haidar (m) Indian name derived from the Arabic *haidar* ('lion'). It was among the names borne by Muhammad's son-in-law Ali. Famous bearers of the name in later centuries have included Haidar Ali (1722–82), Sultan of Mysore, who fought the British in the 18th century. Variant forms include **Haider, Hayder** and **Hyder**.

Haidee (f) English first name (pronounced 'haydee') derived from the Greek *aidoios* ('modest') or else treated as a variant form of HEIDI. It made irregular appearances as a first name among English speakers from the 19th century, popularized as the name of a character in Lord Byron's poem *Don Juan* (1819–24), but is now very rare.

Hailey *See* HAYLEY.

Hajar (f) Arabic name derived from *hajara* ('to emigrate'). It is traditionally considered to be an Arabic equivalent for the biblical HAGAR. It is often given as the name of the mother of Abraham's son Ishmael, and thus that of the mother of all Arabs.

Hakan (m) Swedish name derived from the Old Norse Hakon, itself derived from *ha* ('horse' or 'high') and *konr* ('son' or 'descendant'). Variants elsewhere in Scandinavia include the Danish **Hagen** and the Norwegian **Hakon** or **Haakon** – as borne by seven kings of Norway.

Hakim (m) Arabic name derived from *hakim* ('wise').

Hal *See* HARRY; HENRY.

Hala (f) Arabic name derived from *halo* ('halo'). It was one of the alternative names borne by Muhammad's first wife, Khadija, who became identified after death with the halo round the Moon.

Halcyon (f) Greek name that had its roots in the myth of the daughter of Aeolus, who was transformed into a kingfisher after she threw herself into the water. Sometimes interpreted to mean 'calm'. It has been in occasional use among English speakers but has never been common. **Halcyone** is a variant form.

Haldor (m) Scandinavian name derived from the Old Norse *hallr* ('rock') and Thor (the name of the Norse god of thunder). Also found as **Halldor**.

Hale (m) English place name meaning 'nook' or 'recess' that was subsequently adopted as a surname and has made occasional appearances as a first name.

Haley *See* HAYLEY.

Halina (f) Polish name of uncertain origin, although it may have resulted from a combination of the names HELEN and GALINA.

Hall (m) English surname derived from the ordinary vocabulary word 'hall' that has made occasional appearances as a first name over the centuries. The name was given originally to servants in the halls of great manor houses.

Hallam (m) English place name meaning 'nook' or 'stone' that was subsequently taken up as a surname and occasional first name. British poet laureate Alfred, Lord Tennyson named his son Hallam Tennyson in tribute to his close friend Arthur Hallam, who had died prematurely in 1833.

Halle (f) English first name, pronounced 'halley'. The popularity of Oscar-winning US model and film actress Halle Berry (b.1968) brought the name a degree of prominence from the late 1990s. She herself is reported to have been named after the US department store Halle Brothers. The name may also be encountered as a diminutive of the Scandinavian names HALSTEN and HALVARD.

Halsten (m) Swedish name derived from the Old Norse *hallr* ('rock') and *steinn* ('stone'). Commonly shortened to **Halle**. Variants include **Hallsten** and the Norwegian **Hallstein**.

Halvard (m) Scandinavian name derived from the Old Norse *hallr* ('rock') and *varth* ('guardian'). Commonly shortened to **Halle**. Variants include **Hallvard**, **Halvor**, **Hallvor** and **Halvar**.

Halvdan (m) Scandinavian name derived from the Old Norse *halfr* ('half') and *Danr* ('Dane') and thus applied to people of mixed Danish origin. It was in frequent use in Viking times.

Ham *See* ABRAHAM.

Hamdi *See* HAMID.

Hamid (m) Arabic name derived from *hamid* ('thankful' or 'praising'). Variants include **Hamdi**.

Hamilton (m) English place name that was subsequently taken up as a surname and occasional first name, chiefly in Scotland and the USA. The original place name referred to the (lost) village of Hamilton or Hameldune in Leicestershire, which itself took its name from the Old English *hamel* ('flat-topped') and *dun* ('hill'). Having been imported to Scotland by the 13th century, the name became famous as the title of the Dukes of Hamilton (after whom the Scottish town of Hamilton was named). It seems to have made its debut as a first name among English speakers early in the 19th century, chiefly in the USA, where its popularity may have been boosted by the fame of George Washington's Secretary of the Treasury Alexander Hamilton (d.1804).

Hamish (m) Scottish name derived from the Gaelic Sheumais, itself a version of Seumas (a variant of JAMES). Taken up by English speakers around the middle of the 19th century, it has retained its strong Scottish links, but is today encountered widely across the English-speaking world (usually where the population has Scottish connections). *See also* SEAMUS.

Hamlet (m) English form via French of the Old German Heimo, itself derived from *heim* ('house' or 'home'). As **Hamo** or **Hamon,** the name came to England with the Normans and was in fairly common use during the medieval period. The name is today universally associated with the doomed prince of William Shakespeare's great tragedy *Hamlet* (*c*.1600) and he himself gave the variant **Hamnet** to his own son. In earlier versions of the tale the name appears in such forms as **Amleth** or **Amlothi**. Because of the link with Shakespearean tragedy it has made few appearances as a first name since the end of the 18th century. Variants include **Hamlyn**. *See also* HAMMOND.

Hamlyn *See* HAMLET.

Hammond (m) Scottish surname derived from the Old German *heim* ('house' or 'home') that has been in occasional use as a first name among English speakers since the 19th century. Notable bearers of the name have included British novelist Hammond Innes (Ralph Hammond Innes; 1913–98), Hammond having been the sur-

name of his father and Innes his mother's maiden name.

Hamnet/Hamo/Hamon *See* HAMLET.

Hamza (m) Arabic name derived from *hamuza* ('strong' or 'steadfast'). Of pre-Islamic origin, it was subsequently identified as the name of Muhammad's uncle.

Hana (f) Arabic name derived from *hana* ('happiness').

Hanan (f) Arabic name derived from *hanan* ('tenderness'). Variants include **Hani** and **Haniyya**.

Hanford (m) English first name meaning 'rocky ford'. It remains a relatively rare choice and is generally more familiar as a surname.

Hani *See* HANAN.

Hank (m) English first name that developed as a diminutive form of JOHN. It arose through **Hankin**, a medieval form of John that has long since fallen into disuse. Today (particularly in the USA) the name is also often treated as a diminutive form of HENRY. It established itself during the 19th century, chiefly in the USA. Notable bearers of the name have included US country singer Hank Williams (Hiram King Williams; 1923–53) and British pop guitarist Hank Marvin (Brian Rankin; b.1941).

Hanke *See* JOHN.

Hannah (f) Hebrew name meaning 'favour' or 'grace' and sometimes interpreted to mean 'God has favoured me'. It appears in the Bible as the name of three women, including the mother of Samuel, and was consequently taken up with some enthusiasm by English Puritans during the 17th century. It remained in frequent use until the end of the 19th century but has since become rather less common, although it has enjoyed a strong revival in popularity since the 1970s. Notable bearers of the name have included British playwright Hannah Cowley (1743–1809), a maid in Samuel Richardson's novel *Clarissa* (1748) and Scottish actress Hannah Gordon (b.1941). Also encountered as **Hanna**. Diminutive forms of the name include **Han**, **Hannie** (or **Hanny**) and NANCY. *See also* ANNA.

Hannibal (m) Roman name derived from the Phoenician *hann* ('grace') and Baal (the name of a god), thus meaning 'grace of Baal', that has made occasional appearances as a first name among English speakers since the 16th century. It is famous as the name of the 3rd-century BC Carthaginian general who led his army over the Alps to launch a surprise attack on Rome. Hannibal's reliance upon elephants to cross the Alps is recalled today in the long-standing tradition of giving the name to circus and zoo elephants. Well-known bearers of the name in recent times have included the fictional Hannibal Lector, a serial killer in the Thomas Harris novel (1988) and film (1990) *The Silence of the Lambs*.

Hannie/Hanny *See* HANNAH.

Hans *See* JOHN.

Happy (f) English first name derived from the ordinary vocabulary word 'happy'. It does not appear to have been in use prior to the 20th century.

Harald *See* HAROLD.

Harcourt (m) English first name derived from the Old French for 'from a fortified court' and the Old English for 'falconer's cottage'.

Harding (m) English surname derived from the Old English *heard* ('brave' or 'strong') that has been in occasional use as a first name.

Hardy (m) English surname of uncertain meaning that has been in occasional use as a first name since the early 20th century. It is possible that the name was based originally on the ordinary vocabulary word 'hardy'. Well-known bearers of the name have included the British fashion designer Hardy Amies (Edward Hardy Amies; 1909–2003)

and German actor Hardy Kruger (b.1928).

Hari (m) Indian name derived from the Sanskrit *hari* ('brownish' or 'greenish'). The name has a variety of other meanings in classical mythology and appears as one of the names borne by the gods Indra and Vishnu or Krishna. Variants include **Harinder,** a combination of *hari* and INDRA that is popular among Sikhs.

Harinder *See* HARI.

Harish (m) Indian name derived from the Sanskrit *hari* ('brownish' or 'greenish') and *isa* ('lord'). It became popular during the medieval period as a name borne by Vishnu. Also spelled **Haresh**.

Harith (m) Arabic name derived from *haratha* ('to provide').

Harlan (m) English place name derived from the Old English *hara* ('hare') and *land* ('land') that was subsequently adopted as a surname and occasional first name in the 19th century. It is confined largely to the USA, where its initial popularity was promoted by US judge John Marshall Harlan (1833–1911), a staunch defender of civil rights. **Harland** is a variant form of the name.

Harley (m/f) English surname that was taken up as a first name for boys in the 19th century but which has since also been applied to females.

Harmony (f) English first name derived via Latin from the Greek for 'concord' or 'unity'. A relatively rare choice of first name of 20th-century origin, it is occasionally found in the variant forms **Harmonie** or **Harmonia**.

Harold (m) English first name derived under the influence of the Scandinavian Haraldr or Harald from the Old English Hereweald, itself from *here* ('army') and *wealdan* ('to rule') and thus meaning 'general'. It was borne by the Saxon King Harold II, whose death at the Battle of Hastings in 1066 signalled the beginning of the Norman Conquest. Because of this link with the old royal house of England the name fell out of use during the Norman period and only reappeared in the 19th century, when it enjoyed a significant resurgence in popularity in the wake of Lord Byron's epic poem *Childe Harold's Pilgrimage* (1812) and ranked among the most popular boys' names in the English-speaking world. It went into decline once more from the early years of the 20th century and is now rare.

Famous bearers of the name have included US film comedian Harold Lloyd (1893–1971), British Prime Ministers Harold Macmillan (1894–1986) and Harold Wilson (1916–95) and British playwright Harold Pinter (b.1930). Commonly shortened to HARRY. *See also* ERROL.

Haroun *See* AARON.

Harper (m/f) English surname, denoting someone who plays the harp, that has made infrequent appearances as a first name, chiefly in the USA. Notable bearers of the name have included US novelist Harper Lee (Nelle Harper Lee; b.1926).

Harriet (f) English first name that developed as a feminine equivalent of HARRY. It was taken up among English speakers in the 17th century and remained fairly popular until the early 20th century, when it went into a sharp decline. It revived, however, once more in the 1990s. Famous bearers of the name have included British writer Harriet Martineau (1802–76), US novelist Harriet Beecher Stowe (1811–96), the fictional Harriet Smith in Jane Austen's novel *Emma* (1816) and British actress Harriet Walter (b.1950). Commonly shortened to **Harrie**, **Harry**, **Hatty** or **Hattie** – as borne by British actress Hattie Jacques (1924-80). Variant forms include **Harriett**, **Harriette** and **Harrietta**. *See also* HENRIETTA.

Harrison (m) English surname meaning 'son of Harry' that has been in irregular use as a first name since the 19th century. Its relative popularity in the USA may have been influenced by the names of Presidents William H. Harrison (1773–1841) and Benjamin Harrison (1833–1901). Other notable bearers of the name have included British composer Sir Harrison Birtwistle (b.1934) and US film actor Harrison Ford (b.1942). Commonly shortened to HARRY.

Harry (m) English first name that developed as a diminutive form of HENRY and HAROLD but is now frequently treated as a name in its own right. It was established among English speakers by medieval times, when it was widely encountered as the usual vernacular form of Henry, and subsequently enjoyed another peak in popularity in the 19th century, but later fell out of fashion prior to a revival in the 1990s. The name subsequently enjoyed a further boost in popularity with the publication of the *Harry Potter* series of books by J. K. Rowling. Well-known bearers of the name have included Scottish music-hall singer Sir Harry Lauder (1870–1950), US President Harry S. Truman (1884–1972) and the British Prince Harry (Henry Charles Albert David; b.1984). **Hal** is a diminutive form. *See also* HARRIET; HARRISON.

Harsha (f) Indian first name derived from the Sanskrit word meaning 'happiness'.

Hart (m) English first name meaning 'hart deer'. It is generally more familiar as a surname.

Hartley (m) English place name (found in several counties of England) usually derived from the Old English *heorot* ('hart') and *leah* ('clearing') that was subsequently taken up as a surname and occasional first name. Another derivation suggests it means 'stony meadow'. Notable bearers of the name have included British poet Samuel Taylor Coleridge's son Hartley Coleridge (1796–1849), who was named in tribute to the British philosopher David Hartley (1705–57), and British lawyer Sir Hartley Shawcross (1902–2003).

Hartmann (m) German name derived from the Old German *hard* ('brave' or 'strong') and *man* ('man'). Variants include **Erdmann**.

Hartmut (m) German name derived from the Old German *hard* ('brave' or 'strong') and *muot* ('spirit').

Hartwig (m) German name derived from the Old German *hard* ('brave' or 'strong') and *wig* ('battle').

Hartwin (m) German name derived from the Old German *hard* ('brave' or 'strong') and *wine* ('friend'). Variants in other languages include the Italian **Arduino**.

Harun *See* AARON.

Harvey (m) English surname that was taken up as a first name among English speakers in the 19th century. The surname was of Breton origin, from *haer* ('battle') and *vy* ('worthy'), and came to England with the Normans. It made several appearances in the 'Domesday Book' but seems to have disappeared from use after the 14th century. It was revived in the 19th century and has continued in irregular use ever since. Notable bearers of the name have included a 6th-century Breton saint, US film actor Harvey Keitel (b.1939) and US playwright and actor Harvey Fierstein (b.1954). Commonly shortened to **Harv** or **Harve**. Occasionally spelled **Hervey**. Variants in other languages include the French **Hervé**.

Hasan (m) Arabic name derived from *hasan* ('good' or 'beautiful'). Borne by a celebrated grandson of Muhammad, poisoned by one of his wives, it remains today one of the most common names used in Islamic countries.

Hashim (m) Arabic name derived from *hashim* ('crushing'), but generally understood to refer to a person who breaks up bread to eat. The name was borne by a great-grandfather of Muhammad who took up the responsibility of providing food for pilgrims visiting the holy shrine of Kaba.

Hasim (m) Arabic name derived from *hasim* ('decisive').

Hatim (m) Arabic name derived from *hatim* ('determined' or 'decisive'). The most famous bearer of the name was the 7th-century Hatim ibn-Abd-Allah, who was renowned for his generosity.

Hattie/Hatty *See* HARRIET.

Havel *See* GAWEL.

Havelock (m) English surname (pronounced 'haverlok') that made infrequent appearances as a first name in the 19th century. Notable bearers of the name have included British psychologist Havelock Ellis (Henry Havelock Ellis; 1859–1939). *See also* OLIVER.

Haydn (m/f) Welsh first name (pronounced 'haydun') of uncertain origin, though possibly a development of the English surname Haddon, meaning 'hill with heather'. It may also have evolved as a Welsh version of the Celtic AIDAN. Its popularity among the Welsh owes something to the admiration of many Welsh people for the music of the Austrian composer Josef Haydn (1732–1809). As a Germanic surname it had its roots in the medieval *heiden* ('heathen'). It was treated initially as an exclusively masculine name, but is today also bestowed upon girls, possibly under the influence of HEIDI. Also spelled **Hadyn**, **Hayden** or **Haydon**.

Hayfa (f) Arabic name derived from *hayfa* ('slender' or 'delicate').

Hayley (f) English place name (from Hailey in Oxfordshire) that was subsequently taken up as a surname and as a first name from the 1960s. The original place name came from the Old English *heg* ('hay') and *leah* ('clearing') and was thus understood to mean 'hay field'. It enjoyed a peak in popularity towards the end of the 1980s. Famous bearers of the name have included British actress Hayley Mills (b.1946), whose mother also bore it as her second name. Also found as **Haley**, **Hailey** and **Haylie**.

Haytham (m) Arabic name derived from *haytham* ('young eagle').

Hazel (f) English first name derived from the name of the tree but more often assumed to refer to the nut-brown colour of some people's eyes. It was one of many flower and plant names taken up by English speakers towards the end of the 19th century. It enjoyed a peak in popularity in the 1930s but has since become rather less frequent. Commonly shortened to **Haze**.

Headley *See* HEDLEY.

Heath (m) English first name derived from the ordinary vocabulary word 'heath' that has been in occasional use among English speakers since the 19th century. The most famous bearer of the name to date has been the British cartoonist William Heath Robinson (1872–1944).

Heathcliff (m) English first name meaning 'dweller by the heather cliff'. Also found as **Heathcliffe**, it is indelibly linked with the character of that name in the classic romance *Wuthering Heights* (1847) by Emily Brontë.

Heather (f) English first name derived from the name of the moorland plant. It was taken up by English speakers towards the end of the 19th century, enjoying particular popularity in Scotland where the plant grows most plentifully, and was at its most frequent around the middle of the 20th century but has since lost ground.

Hebe (f) Greek name (pronounced 'heebee'), derived from the Greek *hebos* ('young'), that made its first appearances among English speakers towards the end of the 19th century. The name is borne in Greek mythology by a daughter of Zeus who was revered as a goddess of youth and as cupbearer to the gods.

Heber (m) Hebrew name meaning 'enclave' or 'fellowship' that has made occasional appearances among English speakers, chiefly in Ireland, where it also represents a variant of the Gaelic Eibhear. It appears in the Bible as the name of several minor figures and was consequently taken up by Puritans after the Reformation. It seems to have disappeared from use around the start of the 20th century.

Heck/Heckie *See* HECTOR.

Hector (m) Greek name derived from *ekhein* ('to hold' or 'to resist') and usually interpreted to mean 'holding fast'. It was famous in Greek mythology as the name of the Trojan warrior who met his death at the hands of Achilles. Shakespeare depicted Hector in *Troilus and Cressida* (1602), but the name has never been very widespread among English speakers, although it has made irregular appearances among the Scottish since medieval times. It enjoyed a minor resurgence in popularity towards the end of the 19th century. Notable bearers of the name have included the British writer Hector Munro (1870–1916), better known as 'Saki'. **Heck** and **Heckie** are abbreviated forms of the name in Scotland, where Hector is sometimes encountered as an equivalent of the otherwise unconnected Gaelic EACHANN. Variants of the name in other languages include the Italian **Ettore** and the Portuguese **Heitor**.

Hedda (f) Scandinavian name derived via the Scandinavian Hedvig from the German HEDWIG, itself based on the Old German words *hadu* ('contention' or 'struggle') and *wig* ('war'). Universally identified with the Henrik Ibsen play *Hedda Gabler* (1890), the name has made occasional appearances as a first name among English speakers since the 19th century. Well-known bearers of the name have included US actress Hedda Hopper (Elda Furry; 1890–1966). Variants in other languages include the Italian **Edda**.

Heddwyn (m) Welsh name (pronounced 'hedwin') derived from *hedd* ('peace') and *wyn* ('white' or 'blessed'). The name enjoyed some popularity among Welsh speakers in tribute to the poet Ellis Humphrey Evans (1887–1918), who wrote under the name Hedd Wyn until his death in the First World War.

Hedley (m) English place name (from several locations in northern England) derived from the Old English *haeth* ('heather') and *leah* ('clearing') that was subsequently taken up as a surname and since the 19th century as an occasional first name. Also found in the variant form **Headley**.

Hedvig *See* HEDWIG.

Hedwig (f) German name (pronounced 'hedvig') derived from the Old German *hadu* ('contention' or 'struggle') and *wig* ('war'). It became more familiar in the English-speaking world through the *Harry Potter* books by J. K. Rowling, in which it appears as the name of Harry's owl. Variants in other languages include the French **Edwige**, the Italian **Edvige** and the Scandinavian **Hedvig** – as borne by the central character in the Henrik Ibsen play *The Wild Duck* (1886). *See also* HEDDA; HEDY.

Hedy (f) Diminutive form (pronounced 'hedee') of the German HEDWIG that has made occasional appearances as a first name among English speakers. Notable bearers of the name have included the Austrian actress Hedy Lamarr (Hedwig Kiesler; 1913–2000).

Heidi (f) Swiss first name derived from Adalheit (*see* ADELAIDE). It was taken up with some enthusiasm by English speakers in the 1960s in response to the popularity of the televisation of the Swiss novelist Johanna Spyri's children's story *Heidi* (1881). *See also* HAIDEE.

Heilyn (m) Welsh name derived from *heilio* ('to prepare'). The name, which appears twice in the *Mabinogi*, was originally reserved for servants who worked as stewards or wine-pourers in big houses.

Heino (m) German name derived from the Old German *heim* ('home'), usually encountered as a diminutive of longer names such as Heinrich or **Heinrad**.

Heinrich *See* HENRY.

Heinz (m) German name that developed during the medieval period as a diminutive form of Heinrich (*see* HENRY). It has enjoyed a peak in popularity since the early years of the 20th century. Well-known bearers of the name in recent times have included the British scientist and television presenter Heinz Wolff (b.1928).

Heitor *See* HECTOR.

Heledd (f) Welsh name of uncertain origin. It was borne by a legendary 7th-century Welsh princess. Also found as **Hyledd**.

Helen (f) English first name derived from the Greek Helene itself possibly from *helios* ('sun') and thus meaning 'shining one' or 'bright one'. The name is usually linked with Helen of Troy, the beautiful daughter of Zeus over whom the 10-year Trojan War was fought. The name was in use among English speakers as early as the 16th century and it appears in William Shakespeare's plays *Troilus and Cressida* (1602) and *Cymbeline* (1609). Notable bearers of the name in more recent times have included US actress Helen Hayes (1900–1993), British pop singer Helen Shapiro (b.1946) and British actress Helen Mirren (b.1946). Variants of the name include EILEEN, ELAINE, ELEANOR, ELEN, **Elena**, **Elinor**, ELLA, ELLEN, HELENA, NELL and **Ilona**. Equivalents of the name in other languages include the French **Hélène** and the Irish Gaelic **Léan**.

Helena (f) English first name that developed as a Latinized form of HELEN. The name was borne by a 3rd-century saint identified as the mother of Constantine the Great and as the finder of the True Cross, and the probably erroneous belief that this saint was born in Britain made the name especially popular among English speakers from the medieval period. The name features in William Shakespeare's plays *A Midsummer Night's Dream* (1596) and *All's Well That Ends Well* (1604) and has been in fairly regular use among English speakers ever since. Notable bearers of the name have included Polish-born beautician Helena Rubinstein (1871–1965) and British actress Helena Bonham Carter (b.1966). Variants include LENA, the Italian, Spanish and Portuguese **Elena** and the Russian **Yelena**.

Hélène *See* HELEN.

Helga (f) German and Scandinavian name derived ultimately from the Old Norse *heill* ('hale' or 'hearty'), but later interpreted to mean 'blessed' or 'holy'. The name was recorded in use among English speakers at the time of the Norman Conquest but it seems to have been dropped shortly afterwards and did not reappear until the 20th century, when it enjoyed a limited revival. A variant form is **Hella**. **Helge** is a masculine form of the name. *See also* OLGA.

Helge/Hella *See* HELGA.

Helmfried (m) German name derived from the Old German *helm* ('helmet') and *frid* ('peace'). Also encountered in the variant forms **Helmfrid** and **Helfried**.

Helmut (m) German name derived from the Old German *helm* ('helmet') and *muot* ('spirit'). The name seems to have been a medieval coinage and has remained in currency ever since. Famous bearers of the name have included German statesman Helmut Kohl (b.1930). Also found as **Helmuth**.

Héloïse *See* ÉLOISE.

Hemming (m) Scandinavian name of uncertain origin. It may have had its roots in the Old Norse *hamr* ('shape') but could be interpreted to mean 'werewolf'.

Hendrik *See* HENRY.

Hennie/Henny *See* HENRIETTA.

Henri *See* HENRY.

Henrietta (f) English equivalent of the French Henriette, itself a feminine version of Henri (*see* HENRY). English speakers took up the name in the 17th century after it was introduced to the country with Charles I's French wife Queen Henrietta Maria (Henriette-Marie; 1609–69). Subsequently it was eclipsed by the related HARRIET but went on to enjoy a resurgence in popularity towards the end of the 19th century. It went into decline once more after the early part of the 20th century. It is sometimes used as an Anglicized form of the Scots Gaelic **Oighria**. Among the various diminutive forms of the name are **Etta, Ettie** (or **Etty**),

Hennie (or **Henny**), **Hattie, Hettie** and **Nettie** (or **Netty**).

Henriette *See* HENRIETTA.

Henrik *See* HENRY.

Henrike (f) German name that represents a feminine form of **Heinrich** (*see* HENRY).

Henry (m) English first name derived from the German **Heinrich**, itself from the Old German Haimirich – from *heim* ('house' or 'home') and *ric* ('ruler' or 'owner') and thus meaning 'house owner' or 'lord of the manor'. It was taken up by English speakers in the medieval period and became firmly established as a royal name, being borne by eight English monarchs – although HARRY was the more common form of the name in vernacular use before the 17th century. It was also a frequent choice of royal families elsewhere in Europe and as **Henri** was borne by six kings of France. It became less frequent among English speakers in the 20th century, but enjoyed a revival in the 1990s partly in response to the name's reappearance in the royal family, as borne by Prince Henry (b.1984) – although it was announced at the time of his birth that he was to be known as Harry.

Other notable bearers of the name have included US poet Henry Wadsworth Longfellow (1807–82), British actor Sir Henry Irving (1838–1905), US-born British novelist Henry James (1843–1916), US actor Henry Fonda (1905–82) and US statesman Henry Kissinger (b.1923). As well as Harry, other diminutive forms of the name include HANK and **Hal** – as borne by the young Henry V in William Shakespeare's play *Henry IV* (1597) and later by US film producer Hal Roach (1892–1992) and US theatre director Hal Prince (Harold Smith; b.1928). Variants in other languages include the German **Heinrich**, the Italian **Enrico**, the Spanish **Enrique**, the Portuguese **Henrique**, the Dutch and Scandinavian **Hendrik**, the German and Scandinavian **Henrik** and the Polish **Henryk**. *See also* HEINZ; HENRIETTA; HENRIKE; IMRE.

Hephzibah (f) Hebrew name meaning 'in her is my delight'. It appears in the Bible as the name of the wife of Hezekiah, king of Judah, and also as an alternative name for Israel itself. The name was consequently taken up by Puritans in the 17th century. Today it has virtually disappeared from use among English speakers, with rare exceptions among Jews. Famous bearers of the name have included a young girl in the George Eliot novel *Silas Marner* (1861) and US-born pianist Hephzibah Menuhin (1920–81). Shortened forms of the name include **Eppie**, **Hepsie**, **Hepsey** and **Hepsy**. A variant form is **Hepzibah**.

Hepsey/Hepsie/Hepsy/Hepzibah *See* HEPHZIBAH.

Herb *See* HERBERT.

Herbert (m) English, German and French name derived from the Old German *heri* or *hari* ('army') and *berht* ('bright') and often interpreted to mean 'famous army'. An English version of the name was Herebeorht, but this was replaced by the modern form of the name after the Norman Conquest. The name was relatively common among English speakers during the medieval period but went out of fashion after the 13th century except as a surname borne by the earls of Pembroke, among others. It was revived to enjoy a new peak in popularity in the 19th and early 20th centuries. It has since become much less common. Famous bearers of the name have included British actor Sir Herbert Beerbohm Tree (1853–1917) and US President Herbert C. Hoover (1874–1964). Diminutive forms of the name include **Herb** – as borne by US musician Herb Alpert (b.1935) – and **Herbie** – as borne by US jazz musician Herbie Hancock (b.1940). Variants include the German **Heribert**. *See also* BERT.

Herbie *See* HERBERT.

Hercules (m) Roman equivalent of the Greek Heracles or Herakles that has made occasional appearances as a first name among English speakers since the 16th century. The name resulted from a combination of the name of the Greek goddess Hera and *kleos* ('glory'), thus meaning 'glory of Hera' – although Hercules was not in fact the son of Zeus' wife Hera but the offspring of an encounter between Zeus and the mortal Alcmene. It is sometimes found in Scotland as an Anglicization of the Gaelic **Athairne** and in the Shetlands as an equivalent of the Norse **Hacon**. **Herk** and **Herkie** are shortened forms of the name. Variants in other languages include the French **Hercule** and the Italian **Ercole**.

Hereward (m) English name derived from the Old English *here* ('army') and *weard* ('protection'). It became famous as the name of the Anglo-Saxon leader Hereward the Wake, who rebelled against Norman rule in the 11th century. It remains very rare as a first name.

Heribert *See* HERBERT.

Herk/Herkie *See* HERCULES.

Herleif (m) Scandinavian name (pronounced 'hair-leef') derived from the Old Norse *herr* ('army') and *leifr* ('heir'). Also found as **Härlief**, **Herlof** and **Herluf**.

Herlindis (f) Dutch name derived from the Old German *heri* or *hari* ('army') and *lind* ('weak' or 'soft'). Variants include the German **Herlinde** and the Spanish **Herlinda**.

Herman (m) English first name derived from the Old German Hariman, itself from *hari* ('army') and *man* ('man') and thus interpreted to mean 'soldier' or 'warrior'. It was taken up by English speakers around the middle of the 19th century, chiefly among German immigrants in the USA, but became less frequent after the early 20th century. Notable bearers of the name have included US novelists Herman Melville (1819–91) and Herman Wouk (b.1915). A feminine version of the name is **Hermine**. Variants in other languages include the German **Hermann** – as borne by German Nazi leader Hermann Goering (1893–1946)

– the French **Armand** and the Italian **Ermanno**.

Hermenegildo (m) Spanish and Portuguese name derived from the Old German *ermen* or *irmen* ('whole' or 'entire') and *gild* ('sacrifice'). It was borne by a 6th-century king of the Visigoths who was subsequently made a saint. Variants include the French **Ermenegilde** and the Italian **Ermenegildo**.

Hermia (f) English name that developed as a variant of HERMIONE. It was taken up by English speakers in medieval times but is rare today. Notable bearers of the name have included a character in William Shakespeare's play *A Midsummer Night's Dream* (1595).

Hermine See HERMAN.

Hermione (f) Greek name (pronounced 'herm-eye-oh-nee') that was adopted as a feminine equivalent of Hermes, the name of the Greek messenger of the gods. It may originally have been derived from the Greek for 'stone'. The name appears in Greek mythology as that of the daughter of Menelaus and Helen and was subsequently taken up by English speakers during the medieval period. William Shakespeare gave the name to the queen of Leontes in his play *The Winter's Tale* (1611) and another Hermione features in the Walter Scott novel *The Fortunes of Nigel* (1822). Notable bearers of the name in relatively recent times have included the British actresses Hermione Gingold (1897–1987) and Hermione Baddeley (1906–86).

Hernán/Hernando See FERDINAND.

Hero (f) Greek name of uncertain meaning. It is most familiar in ancient mythology as the name of the lover of Leander. The appearance of the name in William Shakespeare's *Much Ado About Nothing* (*c*.1598) helped to popularize the name among English speakers, although it has never been common.

Hershel See HIRSH.

Hertha (f) German name meaning 'strong' or 'bold'. As Nertha the name was borne by a German goddess of fertility, and it appears to have been subsequently changed to Hertha through a misreading of the initial letter. As Hertha it has made occasional appearances as a first name in the English-speaking world since the 19th century. **Herta** is a variant form.

Hervé/Hervey See HARVEY.

Hesba (f) Greek name derived from *hespera* ('western'). It has made infrequent appearances among English speakers since the 19th century.

Heshel See HIRSH.

Hesketh (m) English place name (shared by several places in northern England) that was subsequently taken up as a surname and first name. The original place name came from the Old Norse *hestr* ('horse') and *skeithr* ('racecourse') and was probably inspired by the long-established tradition of horse-racing in Scandinavia.

Hester (f) English first name that was adopted as a variant form of ESTHER in the 17th century. Notable bearers of the name have included the British writer and friend of Samuel Johnson Hester Thrale (1709–90), British traveller Lady Hester Stanhope (1776–1839) and the fictional Hester Prynne in the Nathaniel Hawthorne novel *The Scarlet Letter* (1850). Shortened forms of the name include **Esta**, **Ester**, **Hettie** and **Hetty**.

Hettie/Hetty See ESTHER; HENRIETTA; HESTER.

Heulwen (f) Welsh name meaning 'sunshine'.

Hew/Hewie See HUGH.

Hezekiah (m) Biblical name derived from the Hebrew Hizqiyah, meaning 'my strength is Yah' or 'Yah is strength' (Yah being an alternative name of Jehovah or God). It appears in the Bible as the name of a king of Judah and was subsequently taken up by English speakers in the 17th century, although it has never been in frequent use. There is a character of the name in the Thomas Hardy novel *Two on a Tower* (1882).

Hiba (f) Arabic name derived from *hiba* ('gift' or 'grant').

Hieronymus *See* JEROME.

Hikmat (m/f) Arabic name derived from *hikma* ('wisdom').

Hilary (m/f) English first name descended ultimately from the Roman Hilarius, itself derived from the Latin *hilaris* ('cheerful'). Borne by the 5th-century St Hilarius of Poitiers, it was taken up by English speakers during the medieval period as a name chiefly for boys. The name fell into disuse after medieval times but was revived during the 19th century as a name for both sexes and has continued in occasional use ever since. Commonly shortened to **Hil** or **Hilly**. **Hillary** – as borne by Hillary Clinton (b.1947), wife of US President Bill Clinton – is a variant spelling used for both boys and girls. Variants of the name in other languages include the Welsh **Ilar**, the French **Hilaire**, the Italian **Ilario**, the Spanish and Portuguese **Hilario** and the Russian **Ilari**.

Hilda (f) German, Dutch, Scandinavian and English name derived from the Old German *hild* ('battle'). The name appears to have developed initially as an abbreviated form of HILDEGARD and other similar names. It was borne by the leader of the Valkyries in Scandinavian legend and by St Hilda, the famous 6th-century abbess of Whitby. The name was taken up more widely by English speakers during the medieval period but became less frequent in Tudor times. It enjoyed a later peak in popularity in the early years of the 20th century, but has since become very rare. Well-known bearers of the name in relatively recent times have included the US writer Hilda Doolittle (1886–1961) and the fictional Hilda Lessways in the *Clayhanger* series (1910–18) written by Arnold Bennett. A

variant form of the name is **Hylda** – as borne by British actress and comedienne Hylda Baker (1909–86). **Hilde** is a German variant.

Hildebrand (m) German name derived from the Old German *hild* ('battle') and *brand* ('sword'). It was borne by the 11th-century Pope Gregory VII but fell out of use among English speakers around the end of the medieval period. It enjoyed a minor revival in the 19th century alongside many other medieval names.

Hildegard (f) German, Scandinavian and English name derived from the Old German *hild* ('battle') and *gard* ('enclosure') and interpreted to mean 'comrade in arms'. The name is largely confined to the German-speaking world but has nonetheless made occasional appearances as a first name among English speakers of German descent, chiefly in the USA. Sometimes shortened to HILDA. Also found as **Hildegarde**.

Hillary *See* HILARY.

Hillel (m) Jewish name derived from the Hebrew for 'praise'. It appears in the Bible as the name of the father of one of the Judges of Israel. Its popularity among Jews can be traced back to a celebrated 1st-century rabbi of the name.

Hillevi (f) Danish first name derived from the German Heilwig, itself from the Old German *heil* ('whole') and *wig* ('war').

Hilly *See* HILARY.

Hilton (m) English first name meaning 'from the hill farm'. More familiar as a surname, it is also found in the form **Hylton**.

Hiltraud (f) German name derived from the Old German *hild* ('battle') and *trud* ('strength'). Also found as **Hiltrud**.

Hind (f) Arabic name of uncertain origin. It was borne by one of Muhammad's wives, noted for her beauty.

Hippolyta *See* HIPPOLYTE.

Hippolyte (m) French name (pronounced

'hipoleet') derived via the Roman Hippolytus from the Greek Hippolytos, from the Greek *hippos* ('horse') and *lyein* ('to free'). It was borne in classical mythology by a youth who died in a chariot accident and was subsequently borne by a number of early saints. The name's popularity in France was inspired by Jean Racine's retelling of the classical legend in his tragedy *Phèdre* (1677). Variants of the name in other languages include the Italian **Ippolito** and the Spanish and Portuguese **Hipolito**. A feminine equivalent of the name is **Hippolyta** – as borne by a legendary queen of the Amazons and later by a character in William Shakespeare's *A Midsummer Night's Dream* (c.1594).

Hippolytus *See* HIPPOLYTE.

Hiram (m) Hebrew name possibly descended from Ahiram, meaning 'my brother is exalted', or else of unknown Phoenician origin. It appears in the Bible as the name of a king of Tyre and was subsequently taken up by Puritans in the 17th century. It remained in occasional use among English speakers until the 19th century, but is now rare outside the USA. Also found in the form **Hyram**.

Hirsh (m) Jewish name derived from the Yiddish for 'hart' or 'deer'. Variants include **Hirsch**, **Hershel**, **Heshel** and **Heshi**.

Hisham (m) Arabic name derived from *hisham* ('generous'). The name was borne by a famous 8th-century caliph whose armies invaded France.

Hjalmar (m) Scandinavian name derived from the Old Norse *hjalmr* ('helmet') and *herr* ('army' or 'warrior'). It fell into disuse at a relatively early date but was revived towards the end of the 18th century. Also found in the form **Hjälmar**.

Hjördis (f) Scandinavian name derived from the Old Norse *hjorr* ('sword') and *dis* ('goddess').

Hob *See* ROBERT.

Hobart *See* HUBERT.

Hodge *See* ROGER.

Hoel *See* HOWELL.

Holden (m) English place name that was subsequently adopted as a surname and occasional first name. The original place name meant 'hollow valley' and as a surname it was usually applied to people living in such a location. As a first name its history goes back as far as the 19th century, but is today most famous as the name of Holden Caulfield, the central character in J. D. Salinger's celebrated novel *The Catcher in the Rye* (1951).

Holger (m) Scandinavian name derived from the Old Norse *holmr* ('island') and *geirr* ('spear'). It was the name of one of the Emperor Charlemagne's generals, supposedly of Danish origin.

Hollie *See* HOLLY.

Hollis (m/f) English surname meaning 'dweller in the holly grove' that was subsequently adopted as an occasional first name among English speakers.

Holly (f) English first name that may have developed out of the ordinary vocabulary word 'holy' or else may have come from the name of the evergreen tree commonly used for Christmas decorations. The name was in use among English speakers on both sides of the Atlantic by the late 19th century and enjoyed a peak in popularity towards the end of the 20th century, often bestowed upon girls born in the Christmas season. Well-known bearers of the name have included a character in John Galsworthy's *Forsyte Saga* series of novels published in the early years of the 20th century, the fictional Holly Golightly in the Truman Capote novel (1958) and film (1961) *Breakfast at Tiffany's*, in which it appears as an abbreviated form of **Holiday**, and the US actress Holly Hunter (b.1959). The name has also made very rare appearances as a masculine name – as in Graham Greene's screenplay for the film *The Third Man* (1949), in which the hero is named Holly Martins. Also found in the form **Hollie**.

Homer (m) Greek and English name possibly derived from the Greek *homeros* ('hostage') or alternatively from an Old English surname meaning 'helmet maker' or 'pool in a hollow'. The name is universally associated with the celebrated 8th-century BC Greek poet, author of the *Odyssey*. It was taken up as a first name among English speakers in the 19th century, chiefly in the USA. Well-known bearers of the name have included the fictional Homer Simpson in the popular 1990s US television cartoon series *The Simpsons*.

Honey (f) English first name derived from the ordinary vocabulary word 'honey', which has been in use as a term of endearment since medieval times. It may also have developed as a diminutive of Honoria (*see* HONOR). Its use in modern times was promoted through a character of the name in the Margaret Mitchell novel (1936) and film (1939) *Gone with the Wind*.

Honor (f) English first name derived either from the Roman Honoria or else from the ordinary vocabulary word 'honour'. Recorded in various forms among English speakers as early as the Norman Conquest, it was among the numerous virtue names taken up by the Puritans in the 17th century and has remained in use ever since. In its early history it was applied to boys as well as girls. Famous bearers of the name in recent times have included the British actress Honor Blackman (b.1926). Sometimes shortened to NORA. As well as the Roman Honoria, which is still occasionally encountered, other variants are **Annora**, **Honora**, **Honorine** and the French **Honore**. **Honoré** is a masculine version of the name in use among French speakers. *See also* ANEURIN; HONEY.

**Honora/Honoré/Honoria/
Honorine/Honour** *See* HONOR.

Hope (f) English virtue name that was taken up by English Puritans after the Reformation. It was sometimes given to sets of triplets alongside FAITH and CHARITY, occasionally as a name for boys as well as

girls. It has remained in use on both sides of the Atlantic ever since, sometimes as an adoption of the surname Hope, derived from the Old English *hope* ('enclosed valley'). It is now reserved exclusively for girls and is more popular in the USA than elsewhere.

Hopkin (m) English and Welsh surname derived in medieval times via Hob from ROBERT that was subsequently taken up as a first name among English speakers. **Hopcyn** is a Welsh variant.

Horace (m) English and French first name derived from the Roman Horatius, itself possibly from the Latin *hora* ('hour' or 'time'). Celebrated as the name of the Roman poet Horace (Quintus Horatius Flaccus; 65–8 BC), it was adopted by English speakers in the 18th century and continued in fairly frequent use until the end of the 19th century but is now very rare. Celebrated bearers of the name have included the British writer Sir Horace Walpole (Horatio Walpole; 1717–97) and US journalist Horace Greeley (1811–72). Occasionally shortened to **Horry**. An Italian variant is **Orazio**. *See also* HORATIO

Horatia *See* HORATIO.

Horatio (m) English first name that developed as a variant of HORACE under the influence of the Roman Horatius. It was in occasional use among English speakers by the 16th century, when it was also borne by the fictional Horatio in William Shakespeare's tragedy *Hamlet* (1599–1601). Other notable bearers of the name have included British admiral Horatio Nelson (1758–1805), British military commander Horatio Herbert Kitchener (1850–1916), disgraced British politician Horatio Bottomley (1860–1933) and the fictional Horatio Hornblower, hero of the *Hornblower* novels of C. S. Forester (1899–1966). Sometimes shortened to **Horry**. **Horatia** is a feminine equivalent – as borne by Nelson's daughter Horatia.

Horatius *See* HORACE; HORATIO.

Horry *See* HORACE; HORATIO.

Horst (m) German name derived either from the German *horst* ('wood') or alternatively from *horsa* ('horse'). Records of this fairly popular name among German speakers go back to the 15th century.

Hortense (f) French first name derived from the Roman Hortensia, itself possibly from the Latin *hortus* ('garden'). English speakers took up the name in the 19th century but it never became very common and is now rare. Notable bearers of the name have included characters in Charlotte Brontë's *Shirley* (1849) and Charles Dickens' *Bleak House* (1852–3). The old Roman form of the name, Hortensia, is still occasionally encountered.

Hortensia *See* HORTENSE.

Hosanna (m/f) English first name derived from the Hebrew *hosanna* ('save now' or 'save pray'). Because of its biblical associations it was taken up as a first name by English speakers early in the 13th century and was used initially for both sexes, although after the 17th century it appears to have been reserved chiefly for girls. Also found in the forms **Hosannah** and among the French as **Osanne** or **Ozanne**.

Hosni (m) Arabic name derived from *husn* ('beauty' or 'excellence'). Notable bearers of the name in recent times have included Egyptian President Hosni Mubarak (b.1928). Also found as **Husni**.

Howard (m) English surname that was taken up as a first name among English speakers early in the 19th century. The surname of the dukes of Norfolk since the 13th century, it may have had its origins in a similar Scandinavian name derived from *ha* ('high') and *ward* ('guardian'). Other suggestions link the name with the Old German Huguard, from *hugu* ('heart') and *vardu* ('protection'), or with the Old French Houard, meaning 'worker with a hoe', or the Old English for 'hog-warden'. As a first name its history goes back to the 19th century. It enjoyed a peak in popularity in the 1960s. Notable bearers of the name have included US film director Howard Hawks (1896–1977), US industrialist and millionaire Howard Hughes (1905–76) and US singer and actor Howard Keel (Harold Keel; b.1917). **Howie** is a common diminutive form of the name.

Howell (m) English first name that was derived either from an English surname or else from the Welsh HYWEL. It made its first appearances among English speakers around the middle of the 19th century. Also found as **Howel** and, in medieval Brittany, as **Hoel**.

Howie *See* HOWARD.

Hrothgar *See* ROGER.

Hubert (m) English, French and German first name derived from the Old German Hugibert, itself from *hug* ('heart' or 'mind') and *berht* ('bright') and thus interpreted to mean 'bright spirit' or 'inspiration'. It came to England with the Normans in the 11th century and was a popular choice in medieval times, perhaps in tribute to St Hubert of Liège, the patron saint of hunters. It fell from fashion between the 16th and 18th centuries but has continued to make irregular appearances into modern times, although it has become much less frequent since the early years of the 20th century. Notable bearers of the name have included a judge in William Shakespeare's *King John* (*c*.1596) and US Vice-President Hubert Humphrey (1911–78). Commonly shortened to BERT. Variants include **Hobart**, the German **Huppert** and **Hupprecht** and the Dutch **Hubrecht**.

Huda (f) Arabic name derived from *huda* ('right guidance').

Hudson (m) English surname meaning 'son of Hudd' or 'son of Hugh' that was subsequently taken up as a first name. Its popularity in Canada and the USA is a reflection of the early exploration of the area by the English adventurer Henry Hudson (d.1611), after whom the Hudson Bay was named.

Huey See HUGH.

Hugh (m) English and Welsh first name derived ultimately from the Old German *hug* ('heart' or 'mind'). It came to England with the Normans in the 11th century and has remained in use ever since, although it was relatively rare between the 17th and 19th centuries, when it enjoyed a resurgence in popularity. It is also found as an Anglicization of various Gaelic names, including the Irish Aodh and the Scottish Uisdean.

Notable bearers of the name have included the 12th-century St Hugh of Lincoln, the nine-year-old martyr St Hugh (1255–64), British novelist Sir Hugh Walpole (1884–1941), British architect Sir Hugh Casson (1910–99) and British film actor Hugh Grant (b.1961). Diminutive forms of the name include **Hughie** – as borne by Canadian-born British television presenter Hughie Green (1920–97) – and **Hewie** (or **Huey**). In Scotland the name sometimes appears in the familiar forms **Shug** or **Shuggie**. A Welsh variant of the name is **Huw** – as borne by Welsh television presenter Sir Huw Wheldon (1916–86). A rare feminine version of the name is **Hughina**. *See also* HUGO; KEGAN.

Hughie See HUGH.

Hugo (m) English first name that developed as a diminutive form of HUGH. It emerged as an alternative Latinized form of Hugh around the middle of the 19th century and the two forms of the name now exist side by side. Variants include the Italian **Ugo**.

Hulda (f) Hebrew name meaning 'weasel'. As Huldah, it appears in the Bible as the name of an Old Testament prophetess and has consequently made occasional appearances as a first name among English speakers. It also exists as a Scandinavian name derived from *huld* ('sweet' or 'lovable' or alternatively 'muffled' or 'covered').

Humbert (m) English, French and German first name derived from the Old German *hun* ('bear-cub' or 'Hun') and *berht* ('bright' or 'famous') and thus interpreted to mean 'famous Hun'. It came to England with the Normans in the 11th century and has resurfaced from time to time ever since, notably as the name of the fictional Humbert Humbert in the Vladimir Nabokov novel *Lolita* (1955). Sometimes abbreviated to **Hum**. An Italian variant is **Umberto**.

Humph See HUMPHREY.

Humphrey (m) English first name derived from the Old German Hunfred, itself from *hun* ('bear-cub' or 'Hun') and *fridu* ('peace') and thus interpreted to mean 'peaceful Hun'. It came to England with the Normans in the 11th century, replacing the earlier equivalent Hunfrith, and was relatively frequent through the medieval period and beyond, although it has become steadily less common since the 19th century and is now rare. It used to be considered a relatively aristocratic name but gradually became acceptable to all classes. Originally spelt **Humfrey,** it may have been altered to its modern spelling through association with the little-known Egyptian saint Onuphrios in an attempt to give the name a suitable Christian context. Famous bearers of the name have included the 15th-century Humphrey, Duke of Gloucester (1391–1447), who appears in William Shakespeare's history play *Henry IV* (1597), US film actor Humphrey Bogart (1899–1957) and British jazz musician and radio presenter Humphrey Lyttelton (b.1921). Commonly shortened to **Humph** or **Huffie**. Also spelled **Humphry** – as borne by the central character in the Tobias Smollett novel *Humphry Clinker* (1771).

Hunter (m) English and Scottish surname derived from the ordinary vocabulary word 'hunter' that has been in occasional use as a first name. Well-known bearers of the name have included the Scottish writer and broadcaster Hunter Davies (Edward Hunter Davies; b.1936).

Husain See HUSSEIN.

Husam (m) Arabic name derived from *husam* ('sword').

Husayn *See* HUSSEIN.

Husni *See* HOSNI.

Hussain *See* HUSSEIN.

Hussein (m) Arabic name derived from *hasan* ('good' or 'beautiful'). It was borne by a grandson of Muhammad who was massacred with his followers in 680, an event that led to the foundation of the Shiite sect. Because of its strong religious associations the name is popular throughout the Arab world. Notable bearers of the name in recent times have included King Hussein of Jordan (1935–99). Also found as **Husain, Hussain, Husayn** or **Hisein**.

Huw *See* HUGH.

Hy *See* HYACINTH; HYMAN.

Hyacinth (f) English flower name that was among the many flower names taken up by English speakers towards the end of the 19th century. It was borne in Roman legend by a youth accidentally killed by Apollo and subsequently by several early saints. It was formerly thought of as a masculine name and it was not until the late 19th century that it began to be regarded as exclusively feminine. It is relatively rare today, although it enjoyed renewed exposure in the 1990s as the name of the central character Hyacinth Bucket in the British television comedy *Keeping Up Appearances*. Sometimes shortened to **Hy** and, in Ireland, to **Sinty**. Variants include **Hya-**cintha and **Jacinth**. Equivalents in other languages include the Spanish and Portuguese **Jacinto**.

Hyacintha *See* HYACINTH.

Hyam *See* HYMAN.

Hylda *See* HILDA.

Hylton *See* HILTON.

Hyman (m) Jewish name derived via **Hyam** from the Hebrew *hayyim* ('life'). Sometimes shortened to **Hy**. **Hymie** and CHAIM are familiar forms of the name.

Hymie *See* HYMAN.

Hypatia (f) Greek name derived from the Greek *hupatos* ('highest') that has made rare appearances as a first name among English speakers since the end of the 19th century. Notable bearers of the name have included a 5th-century philosopher and mathematician whose story was recounted in Charles Kingsley's novel *Hypatia* (1853) and Hypatia Tarleton in George Bernard Shaw's play *Misalliance* (1910). Sometimes abbreviated to **Patsy**.

Hyram *See* HIRAM.

Hywel (m) Welsh first name (pronounced 'huwel' or 'howel') meaning 'eminent' or 'conspicuous'. Borne by several early rulers of Wales, including the 10th-century Hywel Dda (Hywel the Good), it remains rare outside Wales itself despite a resurgence in popularity in the 20th century. Well-known bearers of the name in recent times have included the British actor Hywel Bennett (b.1944). *See also* HOWELL.

I

Iagan (m) Scottish first name representing a Gaelic version of Aodhagan, itself derived from Aodh, meaning 'fire'.

Iago (m) Spanish and Welsh variant of JACOB and also an old Spanish form of JAMES (*see* SANTIAGO). The identification of the name with the villainous Iago of William Shakespeare's tragedy *Othello* (1604) has militated against the name ever being taken up on a significant scale among English speakers.

Iain *See* IAN.

Ian (m) Scottish first name that developed as a variant of the English JOHN. It emerged as a distinct name in Scotland in the 19th century and quickly made the transition to other parts of the English-speaking world (although it has never been particularly popular in the USA). It enjoyed a peak in popularity in the 1950s and 1960s. Notable bearers of the name have included British novelist Ian Fleming (1906–64), who was the creator of secret agent James Bond, British actors Ian Carmichael (b.1920) and Sir Ian McKellen (b.1935), and British novelist Ian McEwan (b.1948). A variant largely confined to Scotland is the Gaelic **Iain**, which similarly made its first appearances in the 19th century and went on to enjoy a peak in popularity in the 1970s and 1980s. Well-known bearers of this Scottish variant have included Scottish actor Iain Cuthbertson (b.1930) and Scottish novelist Iain Banks (b.1954).

Ianthe (f) Greek name (pronounced 'eye-an-thee') derived from *ion* ('violet') and *anthos* ('flower'). It was borne in Greek legend by a sea nymph, daughter of the sea god Oceanus. The name enjoyed some popularity as a literary name in the 19th

century, appearing, for instance, in Lord Byron's *Childe Harold's Pilgrimage* (1812), Percy Bysshe Shelley's *Queen Mab* (1813) and Walter Savage Landor's *Ianthe*, addressed to his love Sophia Jane Swift. Shelley also gave the name to his daughter but it has otherwise remained a very rare choice as a first name. Rare variants include **Iantha**, **Ianthina**, **Janthina** and **Janthine**. *See also* IOLANTHE.

Iarlaith (m) Irish name (pronounced 'eerla') derived from the Gaelic *ior* (of unknown meaning) and *flaith* ('leader' or 'prince'). The name is rarely found outside Galway, where it was borne by a local saint. Sometimes encountered in the Anglicized form **Jarlath**.

Ib (m) Danish first name that is thought to have developed as a diminutive of JACOB. Records of this fairly common name go back as far as medieval times. *See also* ISABEL.

Ibbie/Ibby *See* ISABEL.

Ibrahim (m) Arabic version of ABRAHAM. A revered name in Islamic tradition, it was borne by the father of Ismail, who was also the builder of the temple of Kaba in Mecca and from whom all Muslims claim descent. Also encountered as **Ebrahim** or **Ibraheem**, it remains one of the most popular masculine names in the Arab world today.

Ibtisam (f) Arabic name derived from *ibtisam* ('smiling').

Ichabod (m) Biblical name (pronounced 'ikabod') derived from the Hebrew Ikhabhodh, meaning 'no glory' or 'where is the glory?' It is borne in the Bible by a grandson of Eli, who acquired the name through the fact that he came into the world on the very day that the Ark of the Covenant was captured by the Philistines. Because of its biblical associations, the name was taken up by Puritans in the 17th century, although it never became very frequent. The most famous bearer of the name to date has been the fictional Ichabod Crane who is the central character of Washington Irving's classic short story 'The Legend of Sleepy Hollow' (1820).

Ida (f) English first name derived via Norman French from the Old German *id* ('labour' or 'work') or possibly *itis* ('woman'), or else from the name of the Norse goddess Iduna. Some authorities link the name with Mount Ida in Crete, home of the infant Zeus. In Ireland it is sometimes traced back to the Gaelic Ide or Ita, derived from *ita* ('thirsty'). The name came to England with the Normans but became rare after the 14th century. It was revived among English speakers during the 19th century, when its appearances in fiction included Princess Ida in Alfred, Lord Tennyson's poem *The Princess* (1847) and the central character in Gilbert and Sullivan's opera *Princess Ida* (1884). It fell from favour once more after the 1920s. Bearers of the name in real life have included the British-born US actress and film director Ida Lupino (1918–95).

Ide *See* IDA.

Idonea (f) English first name derived from the Old Norse *idh* ('work' or 'labour'), as borne by the Norse goddess Iduna, or else possibly from the Latin *idoneus* ('suitable'). Also found in the form Idony, it was recorded in fairly common use among English speakers as early as the 12th century and has made rare reappearances in succeeding centuries.

Idoya (f) Spanish first name bestowed in tribute to the Virgin of Idoia (Idoia being a Basque place name meaning 'pool' or 'pond').

Idris (m) Welsh name derived from *iud* ('lord') and *ris* ('ardent', 'fiery' or 'impulsive') and thus meaning 'ardent ruler' or

'fiery lord'. The name appears in Welsh mythology as that of the sorcerer Idris after whom Cader Idris, the second highest mountain in Wales, was named. It was recorded in common use among Welsh speakers by medieval times and has remained in occasional use ever since, with a resurgence in popularity towards the end of the 19th century.

The name is also in use among Indian Muslims, having appeared twice in the Koran and being also borne by the 8th-century founder of the first Shiite dynasty.

Idwal (m) Welsh name derived from *iud* ('lord' or 'master') and *wal* ('wall').

Iefan *See* EVAN.

Iestyn *See* JUSTIN.

Ieuan/Ifan *See* EVAN.

Ifor (m) Welsh name (pronounced 'eye-vor') of uncertain origin, possibly derived from *iôr* ('lord'). The name was borne by several important figures in Welsh legend and history but as a first name was rare before the early 20th century. It is often confused with IVOR, although the names do not come from the same source.

Ignatius (m) Spanish, Russian and English name derived from the Roman family name Egnatius, the origins of which are obscure (possibly Etruscan) – although it later came to be associated with the Latin *ignis* ('fire'). From the 16th century it became popular among Roman Catholics in many countries in tribute to various early saints of the name and particularly to St Ignatius Loyola (1491–1556), the Spanish founder of the Jesuits. Variants in other languages include the French **Ignace**, the Italian **Ignazio**, the Spanish **Ignacio** (commonly shortened to **Nacio** or **Nacho**), the German **Ignatz**, the Dutch **Ignaas** and the Polish **Ignacy**. *See also* INIGO.

Igor (m) Russian name derived either from IVOR or else from the Scandinavian INGVAR, which resulted from the combination of Ing (the name of the Norse god of peace and fertility) and *varr* ('careful') or *arr* ('warrior'), thus meaning 'cared for by Ing' or 'Ing's warrior'. It came to Russia with Scandinavian settlers around Kiev in the 9th century. It made irregular appearances as a name among English speakers in the 19th century but has never enjoyed widespread popularity in the English-speaking world – in part through its identification in popular fiction and cinema with the moronic assistant of Doctor Frankenstein. Other bearers of the name have included the central character in the Borodin opera *Prince Igor* (1890) and Russian-born US composer Igor Stravinsky (1882–1971).

Ihab (m/f) Arabic name derived from *ihab* ('donation' or 'gift').

Ihsan (m/f) Arabic name derived from *ihsan* ('charity').

Ike *See* ISAAC.

Ila *See* ISLA.

Ilana (f) Jewish name derived from the Hebrew for 'tree'. A variant form applied to males is **Ilan**.

Ilar/Ilari/Ilario *See* HILARY.

Ilbert (m) English name derived from the Old German Hildeberht, itself from *hildi* ('strife') and *berht* ('bright'). It was in use before the Norman Conquest in the Old English form Hildebeorht but was adopted by English speakers in its later form in the 11th century, this French version of the name having been brought to England by the Normans. It seems to have disappeared from use during the 13th century.

Ilean *See* EILEEN.

Ileen/Ileene/Ilene *See* EILEEN.

Ilie (m) Romanian variant (pronounced 'Illy') of ELIAS. It became well known in the 1970s as the name of the Romanian tennis player Ilie Nastasie (b.1946). A feminine version of the name is **Ilinca**.

Illona *See* HELEN.

Illtyd (m) Welsh name derived from *il*

('multitude') and *tud* ('land'), thus meaning 'land of the people'. It was borne by a 6th-century Welsh saint but did not make many appearances as a first name among the Welsh until the 19th century. Also found in the variant form **Illtud**.

Ilma *See* WILHELMINA.

Ilona *See* HELEN.

Ilsa/Ilse *See* ELIZABETH.

Ilya *See* ELIAS.

Imam (m) Arabic name derived from *imam* ('leader'). The word is best known as the title conferred on devout Muslims who lead the prayers in Sunni mosques.

Iman (f) Arabic and Indian name derived from the Arabic *iman* ('belief' or 'faith').

Imbert (m) English name derived from the Old German Isenbard, itself from *isan* ('iron') and the name Bard. It came to England with the Normans in the form Imbert or **Isembert**. Records of its use among English speakers cease during the 14th century. Variants include **Isambard**, as borne by the famous British engineer Isambard Kingdom Brunel (1806–59), whose father, Sir Marc Isambard Brunel, was French.

Imelda (f) Spanish and Italian first name derived from the Old German Irmhilde, itself from *irmin* or *ermin* ('whole' or 'entire') and *hild* ('battle'), thus meaning 'all-conquering'. It became popular among Roman Catholics in tribute to the 14th-century St Imelda Lambertini, Virgin of Bologna, and has made occasional appearances as a first name among English speakers during the 20th century, chiefly in Ireland. Famous bearers of the name have included the Filipino politician Imelda Marcos (b.1930) and British actress Imelda Staunton (b.1957).

Imke (f) German first name that evolved as a diminutive form of Imma, itself a variant of IRMA.

Immaculata (f) Irish name derived via the Italian Immacolata from a title borne by the Virgin Mary, *Maria Immacolata* (a reference to the Immaculate Conception). It has made irregular appearances among Roman Catholics over the centuries. *See also* CONCEPCIÓN.

Immanuel *See* EMANUEL.

Immy *See* IMOGEN.

Imogen (f) English name that appears to have evolved through a mistaken reading of the Celtic Innogen, itself derived either from the Latin *innocens* ('innocent') or the Irish Gaelic *inghean* ('daughter', 'maiden' or 'girl'). The mistake seems to have been made when William Shakespeare's play *Cymbeline* (1609) was printed for the first time, the 'nn' becoming 'm'. In earlier versions of the legend on which the play was based (including Holinshed's *Chronicles*) the name is always given as Innogen. As Imogen, the name came into favour among English speakers towards the end of the 19th century and enjoyed a peak in popularity late in the 20th century. As well as the Shakespearean character, well-known bearers of the name have included British composer Imogen Holst (1907–84) and British actress Imogen Stubbs (b.1961). Sometimes shortened to **Immy**.

Imran (m) Arabic first name meaning 'family of Imran'. Notable bearers of the name in recent times have included Pakistani cricketer and politician Imran Khan (b.1952).

Imre (m) Hungarian variant of the German Emeric or Emmerich, either an equivalent of the English HENRY or else derived from the Old German *amal* ('work') and *ric* ('rule'). The name was borne by an 11th-century Hungarian saint.

Ina (f) English and Scottish name (pronounced 'eena') that evolved as a variant of ENA and also as a diminutive of various longer names ending '-ina', including CHRISTINA, EDWINA and GEORGINA. It was taken up by English speakers in the 19th century but has since become very rare.

Inam (f) Arabic name derived from *inam* ('benefaction' or 'bestowal'). Also in use among Indians, who also have the variant **Enam**.

Inderjit (m/f) Indian name derived from INDRA and the Sanskrit *jit* ('to conquer'), thus meaning 'conqueror of Indra'. As **Indrajit**, the name was borne by a demon in the *Ramayana*. Today it is frequently encountered among Sikhs, who apply it to both sexes.

Inderpal (m) Indian name derived from INDRA and the Sanskrit *pala* ('protector'), thus meaning 'Indra's protector'. It is fairly popular among modern Sikhs.

India (f) English first name derived from the name of the country, itself based on the name of the River Indus. The name began to be taken up among English speakers towards the end of the 19th century, when India was the 'jewel of the British Empire'. It was made familiar to a wider audience as the name of a character in the Margaret Mitchell novel (and film) *Gone with the Wind* (1936).

Indiana (m/f) English name of relatively recent invention that developed either as a variant of INDIA or else from the name of the US state Indiana. When it made its first appearance in the early 20th century it was reserved exclusively for girls – there is a young woman with the name in the Edith Wharton novel *The Custom of the Country* (1913). The appearance of the name as that of the hero of the highly popular *Indiana Jones* movies of the 1980s, however, made it an acceptable name for males. Commonly shortened to **Indy**.

Indira (f) Indian name derived from the Sanskrit *indira* ('beauty' or 'splendour'). The name is borne in Indian mythology by Lakshmi, the wife of Vishnu, although it is also often linked with the name of the supreme god INDRA. Famous bearers of the name in modern times have included the Indian Prime Minister Indira Gandhi (1917–84).

Indra (m) Indian name derived from the Sanskrit *ind* ('to drop') and *ra* ('possessing'), thus meaning 'possessing drops' (of rain). The name is borne in Indian mythology by Indra, the supreme god of the atmosphere and the sky, hence also the lord of the rain. It is only rarely encountered in use as a first name today, although it is sometimes found in combination with other names, such as INDERJIT and INDERPAL.

Indy *See* INDIANA.

Inés/Inês/Inez *See* AGNES.

Inga/Inge *See* INGEBORG; INGRID.

Ingeborg (f) Scandinavian and German name derived from an Old Norse name based on that of the fertility god Ing and *borg* ('fortification'), thus meaning 'Ing's fort'. Sometimes shortened to **Inga** or **Inge**.

Ingegerd (f) Scandinavian name derived from an Old Norse name based on that of the fertility god Ing and *garthr* ('stronghold'). Variants include the Swedish **Ingegärd** or **Inger**.

Inger *See* INGEGERD; INGRID.

Inglebert *See* ENGELBERT.

Ingmar (m) Scandinavian name that was taken up as a diminutive form of Ingemar, itself derived from the name of the Norse fertility god Ing and *maerr* ('famous'). This diminutive form of the name became widely known through Swedish film director Ingmar Bergman (b.1918).

Ingram (m) English surname that was subsequently taken up as a first name. The surname is thought to have developed from the Norman Ingelram or Engelram, itself derived from the Germanic name Ingilrammus, from Engel and *hramn* ('raven'). It was in fairly common use among English speakers from medieval times until the 17th century and enjoyed a revival in the 19th century.

Ingrid (f) Scandinavian and German name derived from Ing (the name of a Norse fertility god) and *frithr* ('fair' or 'beautiful') or *rida* ('to ride') and often interpreted to mean 'Ing's ride'. It made a few appearances among English speakers in the 13th century but was not taken up on a significant scale in the English-speaking world until around the middle of the 19th century. It has remained in irregular use ever since. Sometimes shortened to **Inga** or **Inge** (or **Inger**). Well-known bearers of the name have included Swedish-born US actress Ingrid Bergman (1915–82) and Polish-born British actress Ingrid Pitt (b.1944).

Ingvar (m) Scandinavian name derived from Ing (the name of the Norse fertility god) and the Old Norse *varr* ('careful') or *arr* ('warrior'), thus meaning 'cared for by Ing' or 'Ing's warrior'. **Ingvarr** and **Yngvar** are variant forms. *See also* IGOR.

Inigo (m) Spanish variant of IGNATIUS, which was subsequently taken up by English speakers. Records of the name in use in England go back to at least the 16th century, when it was borne by the celebrated English architect Inigo Jones (1573–1652). Jones inherited the name from his father, who acquired the name at about the time when Mary I became the wife of Philip of Spain and there was consequently a short-lived fashion for Spanish names. It continued to be used by Roman Catholic English speakers for some time but it gradually fell out of use, enjoying a brief minor resurgence in popularity in the 19th century.

Innes (m/f) Scottish name that developed as an Anglicization of the Gaelic **Aonghas** or **Aonghus** (*see* ANGUS).

Innokenti (m) Russian name derived from the Roman Innocentius, itself from *innocens* ('innocent'). It was borne by a number of early saints revered in the Eastern Church. Variants in other languages include the Italian **Innocenzo** and the Spanish **Inocencio**.

Iola (f) Greek name meaning 'dawn cloud'. In the variant form **Iole,** the name appears in Greek mythology as that of a princess with whom Hercules falls in love.

Iolanthe (f) English name (pronounced 'eye-oh-lanthee') derived from the Greek *iole* ('violet') and *anthos* ('flower'). This appears to have been a relatively recent invention influenced by other flower names popular around the end of the 19th century. It was made more widely known through the Gilbert and Sullivan opera *Iolanthe* (1882). *See also* YOLANDA.

Iole *See* IOLA.

Iolo (m) Welsh name that developed as a diminutive form of IORWERTH, although it is often considered to be a variant of JULIUS. Welsh speakers had taken up the name by the 18th century. Famous bearers of the name have included the Welsh poet and scholar Iolo Morgannwg (1747–1826). A variant form is **Iolyn**.

Iolyn *See* IOLO.

Iomhar *See* IVOR.

Ion *See* JOHN.

Iona (f) English name derived from that of the Scottish island of Iona (originally Ioua, meaning 'yew-tree island', but supposedly altered to Iona by a misreading) or else possibly descended from the Greek *ion* ('violet'). Iona occupies a special place in the religious history of the British Isles as the location of a famous monastery founded by St Columba in the 6th century. As a first name Iona has been in irregular use since the 19th century, chiefly among Scots. Famous bearers of the name have included British folklorist Iona Opie (b.1923).

Ione (f) Greek name meaning 'violet'. It made irregular appearances as a name among English speakers in the 19th century, apparently in the belief that it was an authentic ancient Greek name, although no records exist of it in use in classical times.

Iorwerth (m) Welsh name derived from the Welsh *iôr* ('lord') and *berth* ('beautiful' or 'handsome'), thus meaning 'handsome lord'. The name is borne by Madawg's brother, a son of Maredudd, in the *Mabinogi*. Largely confined to Wales, where it is sometimes considered a variant of the English EDWARD, it appears to have been taken up as a first name in the 19th century. **Yorath** is a variant form of the name. *See also* IOLO.

Iosif *See* JOSEPH.

Ipati (m) Russian name derived from the Greek Hypatios, itself from the Greek *hypatos* ('highest' or 'best'). It was a fairly common name among early Christians and was borne by several saints. **Patya** is a familiar form.

Ippolito *See* HIPPOLYTE.

Ira (m) Hebrew name meaning 'watchful'. It appears in the Bible as the name of one of King David's generals and in the 17th century was taken up by English Puritans, who introduced it to America, where it has always been more popular than anywhere else. Famous bearers of the name have included US lyricist Ira Gershwin (1896–1983) and US writer Ira Levin (b.1929).

Irena *See* IRENE.

Irene (f) English first name derived from the Greek *eirene* ('peace'). The name of a minor Greek goddess and also of an early Christian martyr, it was taken up by English speakers towards the end of the 19th century and enjoyed a peak in popularity in the 1920s, promoted by the fictional Irene Forsyth in John Galsworthy's popular *Forsyte Saga* novels (1906–22), but has since become infrequent. The name was formerly usually pronounced in the Greek manner as 'eyereenee' but is now more commonly rendered as 'eyereen'. Well-known bearers of the name have included US dancer Irene Castle (1893–1969) and British actress Irene Handl (1901–87). Commonly shortened to **Rene** (pronounced 'reenee') or **Renie**. Variants include **Irena**, a version used in several European countries, the French **Irène** and the Russian **Irina**.

Iréné (m) French first name derived from the Greek *eirenaios* ('peacable'). Closely related to IRENE, it was popular among early Christians and was borne by a 2nd-century French saint. Variants include the Dutch **Ireneus**, the Polish **Ireneusz** and the Russian **Irinei**.

Irial (m) Irish first name of unknown Gaelic origin. It was revived in the 20th century.

Irina See IRENE.

Irinei See IRÉNÉ.

Iris (f) English, German and Dutch first name derived from that of the flower, although it may also have been inspired in part by the identical name of the Greek goddess of the rainbow. It was taken up by English speakers along with other flower names towards the end of the 19th century but became relatively rare after the 1930s. Famous bearers of the name have included British novelist Iris Murdoch (1919–99).

Irma (f) German first name derived from the Old German *ermen*, meaning 'whole', that was taken up to a limited extent by English speakers towards the end of the 19th century. It appeared initially in use among German speakers as a diminutive form of various names beginning 'Irm-', such as IRMGARD. Its popularity in the USA was promoted by the films *My Friend Irma* (1949) and *Irma la Douce* (1963), starring Shirley Maclaine, but generally it became much less common throughout the English-speaking world over the course of the 20th century. Also found as **Erma**. Diminutive forms of the name include **Imma** and **Imke**. See also EMMA.

Irmgard (f) German first name derived from *irmin* or *ermin* ('whole' or 'entire') and *gard* ('enclosure').

Irmtraud/Irmtrud See ERMINTRUDE.

Irvin/Irvine See IRVING.

Irving (m) Scottish surname that has made rare appearances as a first name among English speakers since the 19th century. The surname came originally from a place name in Dumfriesshire. Notable bearers of the name have included Russian-born US songwriter Irving Berlin (Israel Baline; 1888–1989). Variants include **Irvin** and **Irvine**.

Irwin (m) English surname derived from the Old English *eofor* ('boar') and *wine* ('friend'), thus meaning 'boar friend', that has made rare appearances among English speakers since the middle of the 19th century. It has become less frequent since the middle of the 20th century. Famous bearers of the name have included US novelist Irwin Shaw (1913–84). See also ERWIN.

Isa (f) German first name derived from the Old German *isan* ('iron'). Also encountered among English speakers as an abbreviated form of ISABEL.

Isaac (m) Biblical name derived from the Hebrew Yitschaq, possibly meaning 'he laughs' or 'laughter'. It appears in the Bible as the name of the son of Abraham and Sarah, whose birth brought delight to his elderly parents. According to tradition, Sarah laughed in disbelief when informed that at her advanced age (ninety-nine!) she was about to give birth. Having made occasional appearances among English speakers before the Reformation, it was among the biblical names taken up by the Puritans in the 17th century and remained fairly frequent among English speakers until the early 20th century, particularly among Jews.

Famous bearers of the name, also found spelt Izaak (a 17th-century variant), have included English angler and writer Izaak Walton (1593–1683), English scientist Sir Isaac Newton (1642–1727), Polish-born US writer Isaac Bashevis Singer (1904–91), Russian-born US science-fiction writer Isaac Asimov (1920–92) and Russian-born US violinist Isaac Stern (1920–2001). Common abbreviated forms of the name are **Ike** – famous as the nickname of US President Dwight D. Eisenhower (1890–1969), derived from his surname – and **Zak**. Other variants include the German **Izaak**, the Swedish **Isak**, the Hebrew YITZHAK and **Itzhak** – as borne by Israeli violinist Itzhak Perlman (b.1945).

Isabel (f) Spanish equivalent of ELIZA-BETH. The Spanish version of the name evolved out of the French Isabeau, which in turn came from the French Ilsabeth. English speakers started to take up the Spanish version of the name, while still retaining the popular Elizabeth, as early as the medieval period and it ranked among the most popular of all first names during the 13th and 14th centuries. It enjoyed a significant revival in the 19th century but fell from favour during the course of the 20th century before experiencing another resurgence in popularity in the 1990s. Famous bearers of the name have included Isabel Burton (1831–96), the wife of British explorer and writer Sir Richard Burton. Variant forms include ISABELLA, **Ysabel** and the Scottish **Ishbel**, **Isbel** or **Isobel** – as borne by Scottish-born opera singer Isobel Baillie (1895–1983) and British television personality Lady Isobel Barnett (1918–80). Diminutive forms include BELLA, ELLA, **Ib**, **Ibbie** (or **Ibby**), ISA, **Izzie**, **Izzy**, **Nib**, **Sib** and **Tibby**.

Isabella (f) Italian version of ELIZABETH. Having made occasional appearances among English speakers since the 12th century, it began to appear more frequently in the English-speaking world towards the end of the 19th century and continued in irregular use during the 20th century, enjoying particular popularity in Scotland. Notable bearers of the name have included King John's wife Isabella of Angoulême (d.1246), Edward II's wife Isabella of France (1296–1358), Richard II's wife Isabella of France (1389–1409), the Spanish Queen Isabella I (1451–1504), who funded the explorations of Christopher Columbus, the heroine of William Shakespeare's *Measure for Measure* (1604), the subject of the narrative poem *Isabella; or, The Pot of Basil* (1818) by John Keats, and the Italian-born US actress Isabella Rossellini (b.1952). Variant

forms include the French **Isabelle**. *See also* ISABEL; ISLA; SABELLA.

Isabelle *See* ISABELLA.

Isadora (f) English first name that developed as a feminine version of ISIDORE. It made its first appearances among English speakers in the 19th century. The most celebrated bearer of the name to date has been the US dancer Isadora Duncan (1878–1927). Also found as **Isidora**. Familiar forms of the name include **Issy**, **Izzy** and DORA.

Isaiah (m) Biblical name derived from the Hebrew Yeshayah, meaning 'salvation of Yah' (Yah being another name for Jehovah, or God). It features in the Bible as the name of an Old Testament prophet living in the 8th century BC and was consequently taken up by Puritans on both sides of the Atlantic in the 17th century and became enduringly popular among Jews. It has become increasingly rare since the early years of the 20th century. Famous bearers of the name have included Russian-born British philosopher Sir Isaiah Berlin (1909–97). Variants in other languages include the Italian **Isaia**.

Isam (m) Arabic name derived from *isam* ('strap' or 'pledge'). It is usually considered to be an abbreviated version of Isam al-Din ('protector of religion').

Isambard *See* IMBERT.

Isaura (f) Spanish first name descended from the Roman Isaura, which originally denoted a woman from Isauria in Asia Minor.

Isbel *See* ISABEL.

Iser (m) Jewish name derived ultimately from ISRAEL. **Issur** is a variant form of the name.

Iseult *See* ISOLDE.

Ishbel *See* ISABEL.

Ishmael (m) Biblical name derived from the Hebrew Yishmael, meaning 'God will hearken'. It appears in the Bible as the name of Abraham's son by his wife's maidservant Hagar and was consequently taken up by English speakers in the 19th century. Famous bearers of the name have included the narrator in Herman Melville's novel *Moby-Dick* (1851). **Ismail** is a popular Arabic form of the name. An Indian variant is **Esmail**.

Isidora *See* ISADORA.

Isidore (m) English name derived from the Greek Isidoros, itself from the Egyptian Isis (the name of an Egyptian goddess) and the Greek *doron* ('gift'), thus meaning 'gift of Isis'. In ancient times it was sometimes treated as a Christian equivalent of the Jewish ISAIAH. It was taken up by English speakers in the 19th century. Famous bearers of the name have included the 6th-century St Isidore of Seville. Commonly shortened to **Izzy**. Variants in other languages include the German **Isidor**.

Isla (f) Scottish first name of relatively recent invention, apparently unknown before the 1930s. Pronounced 'eyela', it was based on a Scottish place name, that of the Scottish island of Islay, although it is sometimes considered to be a diminutive form of ISABELLA. Well-known bearers of the name have included the Scottish folksinger and television presenter Isla St Clair (b.1952). Also found as **Ila** or **Islay**.

Isleen *See* AISLING.

Islwyn (m) Welsh first name derived from that of a mountain in Gwent, itself from the Welsh *is* ('below') and *llwyn* ('grove').

Ismail *See* ISHMAEL.

Ismat (m/f) Arabic name derived from *isma* ('safeguarding' or 'infallibility').

Ismay (f) English first name of uncertain origin. Recorded in use as early as the 13th century, it is sometimes linked with ESME.

Ismene (f) Greek name of unknown meaning. It is usually associated with the tragic myth of Oedipus, in which the name appears as that of a daughter of Oedipus

and Jocasta. Despite this melancholy association, the name has made occasional appearances among English speakers since the 19th century.

Isobel *See* ISABEL.

Isolda *See* ISOLDE.

Isolde (f) English and French first name derived from the Old French Iseult or Yseult, itself from the Celtic for 'fair' or 'beautiful', or from the Old German Isvald, from the words for 'ice' and 'rule'. The name figures prominently in Arthurian legend as that of the Irish princess in the tragic tale of Tristram and Isolde – as told in Wagner's opera *Tristan and Isolde* (1865) and other famous works. It was fairly common in medieval times but is very rare today. Variant forms include **Isolda** and the traditional Welsh **Esyllt** (meaning 'of fair aspect').

Isra (f) Arabic name derived from *isra* ('night journey'). It developed as a reference to a night journey to Jerusalem supposedly taken by Muhammad to meet Jesus and Moses.

Israel (m) Biblical name derived from the Hebrew Yisrael from *sarah* ('to struggle') and *el* ('God'), thus meaning 'he who struggles with God' or alternatively 'may God prevail'. It features in the Bible as the collective name borne by Jacob's descendants, the source of the name of the modern state of Israel. Jacob acquired the name after he wrestled with the angel of God. Because of its biblical connotations the name was taken up by English Puritans in the 17th century, but it has since remained confined largely to the world's Jewish communities. Notable bearers of the name have included British writer Israel Zangwill (1864–1926) and the fictional pirate Israel Hands in Robert Louis Stevenson's adventure novel *Treasure Island* (1883). Commonly shortened to **Issy** or **Izzy**. Variants include the Yiddish **Iser**, **Issur** and **Sroel**.

Issachar (m) Biblical name derived from the Hebrew for 'hireling'. It was borne in the Bible by one of the sons of Jacob and has remained popular among Jews.

Issur *See* ISRAEL.

Issy *See* ISADORA; ISRAEL.

István (m) Hungarian variant of STEPHEN. It was borne by St Stephen of Hungary (975–1038), the patron saint of Hungary.

Ita *See* IDA.

Italo (m) Italian first name derived from the Roman Italus. According to legend, Italus was the name borne by the father of Romulus and Remus, the founders of Rome, and it was from him that Italy itself took its name (although it is now generally believed that the name of the country came first). **Itala** is a feminine form of the name.

Itamar (m) Jewish name derived from the Hebrew for 'palm island'. It appears in the Bible as the name of one of Aaron's sons.

Ithel (m) Welsh name meaning 'generous lord'.

Itidal (f) Arabic name derived from *itidal* ('temperance' or 'moderation').

Ivah (f) Biblical name derived from an Old Testament place name.

Ivan (m) Russian equivalent of the English JOHN that has been in occasional use among English speakers since the end of the 19th century. It fell into disfavour from the 1930s, largely in response to changes in international relations between Russia and the English-speaking world. Notable bearers of the name have included the Russian emperor Ivan the Terrible (1530–84) and Russian novelist Ivan Turgenev (1818–

83). Commonly shortened to VAN or **Vanya**. Feminine versions of the name include the Ukrainian **Ivanna** and the Czech **Ivana**.

Ivana *See* IVAN.

Ives/Ivo *See* YVES.

Ivor (m) English version of the Scandinavian Ivarr, derived from *ur* ('yew' or 'bow') and *arr* ('warrior') and thus meaning 'bowman'. It appeared with increasing frequency among English speakers during the 19th century, but has become less common since the 1930s. Today it is commonly associated with IFOR, although the two names do not share the same history. Well-known bearers of the name have included an Irish saint, Welsh composer Ivor Novello (David Ivor Davies; 1893–1951) and the 1970s British television cartoon character Ivor the Engine. A Scottish Gaelic variant is **Iomhar**.

Ivy (f) English plant name that was taken up as a first name alongside other plant and flower names towards the end of the 19th century. It enjoyed a peak in popularity in the 1920s but has since fallen out of favour. Famous bearers of the name have included British novelist Ivy Compton-Burnett (1884–1969).

Izaak *See* ISAAC.

Izz-al-Din (m) Arabic name derived from *izz* ('power' or 'glory') and *al* ('the') and *din* ('religion'), thus meaning 'power of religion'. It was borne by a famous 13th-century Egyptian sultan. Also found as **Izz-ed-Din**.

Izzie/Izzy *See* ISABEL; ISADORA; ISIDORE; ISRAEL.

J

Jaakko/Jaap *See* JACOB.

Jabbar *See* JABIR.

Jabez (m) Biblical name derived from the Hebrew Yabets, meaning 'he causes sorrow'. It features in the Bible as the name of a descendant of Judah and was subsequently taken up on occasion by English Puritans in the 17th century. It has largely disappeared from use among English speakers since the end of the 19th century.

Jabir (m) Arabic name derived from *jabir* ('comforter'). Also encountered as **Gabir** and, among Indians, as **Jabbar**.

Jabr (m) Arabic name derived from *jabr* ('consolation'). Also spelled **Gabr**.

Jacaline/Jacalyn *See* JACQUELINE.

Jacek (m) Polish first name (pronounced 'yachek') derived from Jacenty, the Polish equivalent of the English HYACINTH. The longer form of the name, as borne by a 13th-century Polish saint, is now of chiefly historical interest only. Sometimes shortened to **Jach**.

Jacenty/Jach *See* JACEK.

Jacinta/Jacinth/Jacintha/Jacinthe/ Jacinto *See* HYACINTH.

Jack (m) English first name that evolved as a diminutive of JOHN (not, incidentally, as a derivative of the French JACQUES, as is often assumed). It evolved gradually from Johannes via Jehan, JAN and the Middle English form Jankin (an elaboration of JAN) to emerge as Jankin before arriving at its modern form, becoming increasingly popular from around the middle of the 19th century. It enjoyed peaks in popularity in the 1920s and again in the 1990s. As well

as appearing in many nursery rhymes and fairy tales as the name of the archetypal folk hero, as in *Jack and the Beanstalk*, it has also been used on many occasions to refer to actual or mythical characters whose names are otherwise unknown (such as the 19th-century murderer Jack the Ripper or the supernatural demon of Victorian penny-dreadfuls called Spring-heeled Jack).

Notable bearers of the name in real life have included US novelist Jack London (1876–1916), British cricketer Jack Hobbs (1882–1963), US comedian Jack Benny (Benjamin Kubelsky; 1894–1974), US boxer Jack Dempsey (William Harrison Dempsey; 1895–1983), British actor Jack Hawkins (1910–73), US novelist Jack Kerouac (1922–69), US actors Jack Lemmon (1925–2001) and Jack Nicholson (b.1937) and US golfer Jack Nicklaus (b.1940). *See also* JACKIE; JACKSON; JAKE; JOCK.

Jackalyn *See* JACQUELINE.

Jackey/Jacki *See* JACKIE.

Jackie (m/f) English diminutive of the boys' name JACK, itself a derivative of JOHN, and also of the girls' name JACQUELINE. As a name for boys, also found as **Jacky**, it became increasingly common from the end of the 19th century. As a name for girls, also found as **Jackey**, **Jacky** or **Jacqui**, it was taken up by English speakers in the 1930s and remained popular into the 1980s. Well-known bearers of the name have included (among the men) US actor Jackie Coogan (1914–84), US comedian Jackie Gleason (1916–87) and Scottish motor-racing driver Jackie Stewart (John Young Stewart; b.1939) and (among the women) Jackie Kennedy Onassis (1929–94), the wife of US President John F. Kennedy, US novelist

175

Jackie Collins (b.1937) and US athlete Jackie Griffith-Joyner (Jackie Joyner-Kersee; 1962–98).

Jackson (m) English surname meaning 'son of Jack' that was taken up as a first name on an occasional basis in the 19th century. Its popularity in the USA was promoted by admirers of President Andrew Jackson (1767–1845) and Confederate general Thomas 'Stonewall' Jackson (1824–63). Notable bearers of the name in more recent times have included US artist Jackson Pollock (1912–56) and US singer-songwriter Jackson Browne (b.1948). Sometimes shortened to JACK or **Jacky**.

Jacky *See* JACKIE; JACKSON.

Jaclyn *See* JACQUELINE.

Jacob (m) Biblical name derived via the Latin Jacobus from the Hebrew Yaakov or Yakubel, meaning 'May God protect'. It is often popularly supposed that it is descended from the Hebrew *aqeb* ('heel') or *aqab* ('to usurp') and thus interpreted to mean 'supplanter' – evoking the idea of a person who dogs another's footsteps in order to usurp him. This notion reflects the context in which it appears in the Bible, as the name of one of the twin sons of Isaac and Rebecca who with God's approval tricks his less worthy elder brother Esau out of his inheritance and becomes the father of twelve sons (destined to be identified as the founders of the twelve tribes of Israel). It was in occasional use as a clerical name among English speakers before the Norman Conquest, but was relatively rare during medieval times except among Jews, with whom it has always been popular. The name was taken up with new enthusiasm by the Puritans in the 17th century, perhaps because it accorded with their own ideas about usurping others less worthy than themselves, but became much less frequent during the course of the 20th century before enjoying something of a revival in the 1990s.

Famous bearers of the name have included the US-born British sculptor Sir

Jacob Epstein (1880–1959) and the central character Jacob Flanders in Virginia Woolf's novel *Jacob's Room* (1922). JAKE is sometimes treated as a diminutive form. Variants in other languages include the French JACQUES, the German **Jakob**, the Italian **Giacobbe**, the Russian **Yakov**, the Polish **Jakub**, the Finnish **Jaakko** and the Dutch **Jaap**. **Jacoba**, **Jacobine** and **Jacobina** are rare feminine forms of the name that were especially popular in the 18th century among English and Scottish 'Jacobites' (supporters of the deposed Stuart monarchy). *See also* IAGO; IB; JAMES.

Jacoba/Jacobina/Jacobine *See* JACOB.

Jacqueline (f) French diminutive of JACQUES, the French equivalent of the English JAMES. The name was exported to England at a relatively early date, being recorded in use in the 13th century, but it was not until the middle of the 20th century that it became widely popular. Notable bearers of the name have included British actress Jacqueline Bisset (b.1944) and British cellist Jacqueline du Pré (1945–87). Commonly shortened to JACKIE. Variants include **Jacalyn**, **Jacaline**, **Jaclyn**, **Jacklyn**, **Jackalyn**, **Jaqueline** and **Jacquelyn**. *See also* JACQUETTA.

Jacques (m) French first name that represents a French equivalent of the English names JACOB and JAMES. One of the most common of all French first names, it is often used to denote the average Frenchman.

Jacquetta (f) French diminutive (pronouced 'jaketa') of JACQUES, itself an equivalent of the English JAMES. Early records of the name in use among English speakers date from medieval times. It enjoyed a peak in popularity in the 20th century. An historical variant was **Jaquenetta**, as used in the plays of William Shakespeare and others to denote a country wench. Variants in other languages include the Italian **Giachetta**, from which the French form of the name probably evolved. *See also* JACQUELINE.

Jacqui *See* JACKIE.

Jade (f) English first name derived from that of the semi-precious stone. The name of the stone came originally from the Spanish *piedra de ijada* ('stone of the bowels'), which referred to the stone's supposed magical influence upon intestinal disorders. It was taken up by English speakers towards the end of the 19th century and enjoyed a surge in popularity from the 1970s, partly in response to British rock star Mick Jagger giving the name to his own daughter.

Jael *See* YAEL.

Jafar (m) Arabic name derived from *jafar* ('stream'). It was borne by a celebrated 7th-century military commander who died fighting the Byzantines and by an 8th-century Shiite leader. Also found as **Gafar** and, in India, as **Jaffer** or **Jaffar**.

Jaffe (f) Jewish first name (pronounced 'yaffer') derived from the Hebrew *yafe* ('beautiful' or 'lovely'). Variants include **Yaffa**.

Jagannath (m) Indian name derived from the Sanskrit *jagat* ('world') and *natha* ('lord') and thus meaning 'lord of the world'. The name is borne in Indian mythology by Vishnu or Krishna and is the focus of an important religious cult based at Puri in Orissa.

Jagdish (m) Indian name derived from the Sanskrit *jagat* ('world') and *isa* ('ruler') and thus meaning 'ruler of the world'. It was borne by several gods in Indian mythology.

Jagjit (m) Indian name derived from the Sanskrit *jagajjit*, meaning 'conqueror of the world'. Popular chiefly among Sikhs, it appears to have been a medieval invention.

Jago (m) English first name that evolved as a Cornish version of JAMES. It enjoyed a minor revival in popularity in the 20th century.

Jahangir (m) Indian name derived from the Persian *jahan* ('world') and *gir* ('holder').

It was borne by the celebrated Mogul emperor Nur ud-Din Muhammad (1569–1627). Well-known bearers of the name in more recent times have included Pakistani squash player Jahangir Khan (b.1963). Also encountered as **Jehangir**.

Jai *See* JAY.

Jaikie *See* JAMES.

Jaime *See* JAMES.

Jake (m) English first name that developed as a variant of JACK and as a diminutive form of JACOB but which is now often regarded as a name in its own right. It appeared with increasing frequency from the beginning of the 20th century, enjoying a peak in popularity in the 1980s and 1990s.

Jakki *See* JACKIE.

Jakob/Jakub *See* JACOB.

Jalal (m) Arabic name derived from *jalal* ('greatness' or 'glory'). **Galal** is a variant form.

Jalila (f) Arabic name derived from *jalila* ('important' or 'exalted'). Also encountered as **Galila**.

Jamal (m/f) Arabic and Indian name derived from the Arabic *jamal* ('beauty'). Although not one of the older traditional names of the Islamic world, it is nevertheless popular in many countries of the Middle East. In Egypt and several other countries it appears only as a masculine name, whereas in Syria and elsewhere it is generally thought of as a feminine name. Well-known bearers of the name have included Egyptian President Jamal Nasser (1918–70). Also found as **Gamal**, **Gamil** or **Jamil** and in India as **Jameel**. **Jamila** and the Indian **Jameela** are feminine forms of the name that have become increasingly popular among English speakers in recent years. A French variant of Jamila is **Djamila**.

Jameel/Jameela *See* JAMAL.

James (m) Biblical name derived from the

Latin Iacomus or Jacomus, itself a derivative of Iacobus or Jacobus and thus sharing the same roots as JACOB. It appears in the Bible as the name of two of Jesus' disciples and was subsequently taken up by English speakers in the 12th century, when thousands of pilgrims travelled to Spain to visit the shrine of St James at Compostela. Because of its connection with the Catholic Stuart royal family in Scotland, it was thought of as a predominantly Catholic name in 16th-century England, until the thrones of England and Scotland were finally united in 1603 under James I. At that time the name was sometimes spelled **Jeames**, reflecting its usual pronunciation before modern times. The name was popular among Puritans in the 16th and 17th centuries and has since maintained its position as one of the most enduring of all English first names – despite a temporary lapse in popularity in the 1950s and 1960s.

Notable bearers of the name have included six kings of Scotland and two kings of England, English explorer Captain James Cook (1728–79), Irish novelist James Joyce (1882–1941), US film actors James Stewart (1908–97) and James Dean (1931–55), novelist Ian Fleming's fictional secret agent James Bond and British motor-racing driver James Hunt (1947–93). Commonly shortened to JIM, **Jimmy** or **Jimmie** and more rarely to JEM or **Jemmy** (from Jeames). **Jamie** is another diminutive form (originally Scottish), which like **Jami** and **Jaime** has also appeared occasionally as a name for girls – as borne, for instance, by US actress Jamie Lee Curtis (b.1958). Variants in other languages include the Scottish **Jaikie**, the French JACQUES, the Italian **Giacomo**, the Spanish **Jaime** and the Irish SEAMUS. A rare feminine version of the name is **Jamesina** (sometimes shortened to INA). *See also* HAMISH; JAGO; JEMIMA.

Jamesina/Jami/Jamie *See* JAMES.

Jamil/Jamila *See* JAMAL.

Jamshed (m) Indian name of uncertain meaning. Borne by a legendary king of ancient Persia, it subsequently became a favourite name among Parsees and Muslims. The city of Jamshedpur was named after the Indian industrialist Jamshed Tata (1839–1904). Also spelled **Jamshad**.

Jan (m/f) English first name that developed as a diminutive of various masculine and feminine names, including JOHN, JANET, JANICE and JANINE. Alternatively it may also be considered a variant of JANE, JEAN or JOAN or else a borrowing of the Dutch and Scandinavian masculine name Jan (usually pronounced 'yan'). As a Middle English version of John it was in use among English speakers in medieval times. It was taken up once more by English speakers in the early years of the 20th century, but is now much more common as a name for girls and relatively rare as a masculine name. Famous bearers of the name have included British television presenter Jan Leeming (b.1942) and British actress Jan Francis (b.1951). Variants include **Janna** and the Scandinavian **Janne**. In other countries the name may also be encountered as an abbreviated form of such names as the Polish **Janusz** and the Czech **Janacek**.

Janaki (f) Indian name derived from the Sanskrit *janaka* ('descendant of Janaka'). It is found in classical texts as a name borne by Sita, the daughter of King Janaka.

Jancis (f) English first name (pronounced 'jan-siss' or occasionally 'yan-siss') that appears to have resulted from the combination of JANE with FRANCES or Cicely (*see* CECILIA). It made its first appearances in the 1920s, possibly invented by novelist Mary Webb for a character in her book *Precious Bane* (1924). Well-known bearers of the name in recent times have included British wine expert Jancis Robinson (b.1950).

Jane (f) English first name derived via the French JEANNE or Jehane from the Latin Johanna, a feminine variant of Johannes (*see* JOHN). It was taken up by English speakers in the 16th century and gradually eclipsed the related names JEAN and JOAN. During the 19th century it was popularly associated with domestic servants and appeared frequently as the name of housemaids in fiction. It returned to mainstream use in the early 20th century, enjoying peaks in popularity in the 1920s and again in the 1960s.

Notable bearers of the name have included Henry VIII's wife Jane Seymour (1509–37), Lady Jane Grey (1537–54), remembered as the ill-fated 'nine-day queen', English novelist Jane Austen (1775–1817), the heroine of Charlotte Brontë's novel *Jane Eyre* (1847), US frontierswoman 'Calamity Jane' (Martha Jane Cannary; 1852–1903) and British actress Jane Asher (b.1946). Sometimes spelled **Jayne** – as borne by US film actress Jayne Mansfield (Vera Jayne Palmer; 1932–67) and British ice dancer Jayne Torvill (b.1957) – or used in combination with other names, as in **Sarah-Jane**. Familiar forms of the name include **Janie**, **Janey** and **Jaynie**. Variants in other languages include the Spanish **Juana**, the Italian **Giovanna** or **Gianna**, the German **Johanna** and **Hanne**, the Scandinavian **Jensine** and the Polish **Jana**. *See also* JANELLE; JANET; JANICE; JENNY; SHEENA; SIAN; SIOBHAN.

Janelle (f) English first name that developed as an elaboration of JANE. Variants include **Janella**.

Janene *See* JANINE.

Janet (f) English first name that evolved as a diminutive of JANE. It was in use among English speakers in medieval times but subsequently fell into disuse except in Scotland for some 400 years until its revival in the 19th century. Historical variants included Jannet, Jennet, Jonet and Janeta. The name became increasingly widespread in the English-speaking world in the 1950s and 1960s, since when it has been in decline.

Well-known bearers of the name have included US actress Janet Leigh (Jeanette Morrison; b.1927), British opera singer Dame Janet Baker (b.1933), South African actress Janet Suzman (b.1939) and US pop singer Janet Jackson (b.1966). A famous Janet in fiction was the housekeeper in A. J. Cronin's novel *Beyond This Place* (1953), which became hugely popular as the basis for the 1960s British television series *Dr Finlay's Casebook*. Commonly shortened to JAN. Familiar forms of the name include **Jennie**, JENNY, **Jinty** and **Netta** and (in Scotland) **Jess** and JESSIE. Variants in other languages include the French **Janette**. *See also* SINEAD.

Janetta/Janette *See* JANET; JEANNETTE.

Janey *See* JANE.

Janice (f) English first name that evolved as a diminutive form of JANE. It may have made its first appearance with the publication of Paul Leicester Ford's novel *Janice Meredith* (1899) and was subsequently taken up by English speakers with some enthusiasm early in the 20th century. The name enjoyed a peak in popularity in the 1950s, but has since suffered a sharp decline and is now rarely encountered among the young. Commonly shortened to JAN. Also spelled **Janis** – as borne by US rock singers Janis Joplin (1943–70) and Janis Ian (b.1951).

Janie *See* JANE.

Janina *See* JANINE.

Janine (f) English version of the French Jeannine, itself an elaboration of the masculine name Jean. It enjoyed some popularity among English speakers in the 1930s and again in the late 1960s. Commonly shortened to JAN. Also found as **Jannine**, **Janene** and (rarely) **Janina**.

Janis *See* JANICE.

Janne *See* JAN.

Jannine *See* JANINE.

János *See* JOHN.

Janthina/Janthine *See* IANTHE.

Janusz *See* JAN.

Japheth (m) Biblical name derived from the Hebrew Yepheth, meaning 'enlargement' or 'expansion'. It appears in the Bible as the name of Noah's eldest son and was consequently among the biblical names taken up by the Puritans in the 17th century.

Jaqueline *See* JACQUELINE.

Jaquenetta *See* JACQUETTA.

Jared (m) Biblical name derived from the Hebrew *yeredh* ('descended' or 'descent', or possibly 'rose'). It features in the Bible as the name of one of Adam's descendants, who fathered Enoch at the age of 162, and was consequently taken up by Puritans in the 17th century, although it never became very common. It experienced a marked revival in Australia and the USA in the 1960s. Also encountered as **Jarred**, **Jarod** and **Jarrod**. A Hebrew variant is **Yered**.

Jarek (m) Polish and Czech first name (pronounced 'yarek') found as a diminutive of JAROSLAW and other names beginning 'Jaro-'. A feminine variant is **Jarka**.

Jarka *See* JAREK.

Jarlath *See* IARLAITH.

Jarmila *See* JAROMIL.

Jaromierz (m) Polish name (pronounced 'yaromeersh') derived from *jaro* ('spring') and *meri* ('great' or 'famous'). Equivalents in other languages include the Czech **Jaromir**. *See also* JAREK.

Jaromil (m) Polish name (pronounced 'yaromil') derived from *jaro* ('spring') and *milo* ('grace' or 'favour'). A feminine form of the name is **Jarmila**. *See also* JAREK.

Jaropelk (m) Polish name (pronounced 'yaropelk') derived from *jaro* ('spring') and *polk* ('people'). Variants in other languages include the Czech **Jaropluk** and the Russian **Yaropolk**. *See also* JAREK.

Jaroslaw (m) Polish name (pronounced 'yaroslav') derived from *jaro* ('spring') and *slav* ('glory'). Variants in other languages include the Czech **Jaroslav** and the Russian **Yaroslav**. A feminine version of the name is **Jaroslawa**. *See also* JAREK.

Jarvis (m) English surname derived from GERVASE that has made irregular appearances as a first name since the 19th century. There is a character of the name in Charles Dickens' novel *A Tale of Two Cities* (1859). Also encountered as **Jervis**.

Jasmine (f) English first name derived from that of the flower jasmin (ultimately from the Persian *yasmin*). It was adopted by English speakers along with other flower names towards the end of the 19th century but has appeared only infrequently since then. Also found as **Jasmin**, **Yasmin**, **Yasmine** and **Yasmina** and more rarely as **Jessamine**, **Jessamyn** and **Jessamy**.

Jason (m) English first name derived from the Greek Iason, itself probably from the Greek *iasthai* ('to heal'). Familiar in Greek legend from the story of Jason and the Argonauts, it also appears in the Bible as that of a man who plays host to St Paul and in this instance may represent a variant of JOSHUA. It is also supposed to have been the name of the author of the Book of Ecclesiasticus and as such was taken up by English speakers in the 17th century although it was not until the 1970s that it suddenly established itself as a leading favourite. It has since fallen off markedly in popularity. Notable bearers of the name have included US actor Jason Robards (1893–1963) and his identically named son (1920–2000), British actor Jason Connery (b.1963) and Australian television actor and pop singer Jason Donovan (b.1968).

Jasper (m) English first name that may have its origins in the Persian for 'treasurer', although it is usually assumed that it relates to the gemstone jasper. Although it does not appear in the Bible, it (or CASPAR) is traditionally supposed to have been the name of one of the three wise men who came to see the infant Christ at Bethlehem and so was fairly popular among English speakers in the 17th century (although there are records of its use among English speakers as early as the 14th century). It remained in occasional use into the 20th century, when it enjoyed a minor resurgence in popularity. In Victorian times it was a favourite name for the stereotypical villain of popular melodrama and pantomime, usually the local squire. Notable bearers of the name have included US artist Jasper Johns (b.1930), British comedian Jasper Carrott (Robert Davies; b.1945) and US dress designer Jasper Conran (b.1959). Variants in other languages include the Danish **Jesper**.

Jaswinder (f) Indian name derived from the Sanskrit *jasu* ('thunderbolt') and INDRA (a god's name) and thus meaning 'Indra of the thunderbolt'. It is mostly confined to Sikhs.

Jathibiyya (f) Arabic name derived from *jathibiyya* ('attractiveness' or 'charm'). Also found as **Gathbiyya** or **Gazbiyya**.

Javed (m) Indian name derived from the Persian *jawid* ('eternal'). **Javaid** is a variant form.

Javier *See* XAVIER.

Jawahir (f) Arabic name derived from *jawahir* ('jewels').

Jawdat (m) Arabic name derived from *jawda* ('goodness' or 'excellence'). Variants include **Gawdat**.

Jay (m/f) English first name that evolved as a diminutive of various names beginning with 'J', including JAMES and JANE, although it is often assumed that it relates to the bird of the same name or that it is distantly descended from the Roman Gaius (*see* CAIUS). As a name for boys it was taken up by English speakers in the 19th century – although it has been suggested that, inspired by the noisy antics of the birds of the same name, it was employed in medieval times as a nickname for chatterers. It appears to have been applied to girls for the first time in the early years of the 20th century. It is encountered more frequently in

Canada and the USA than it is in the UK. Notable bearers of the name have included US novelist Jay McInerney (b.1955). Sometimes found in the form **Jaye**. The name is also used in India, where it evolved out of the Sanskrit *jaya* ('victory') and is sometimes found as **Jai**.

Jaya (f) Indian name that developed as a feminine equivalent of the Indian name JAY or Jai. Also found in combination with other names, as in **Jayashree**.

Jayakrishna (m) Indian name derived from the Sanskrit *jaya* ('victory') and KRISHNA and thus meaning 'victorious Krishna'.

Jayant (m) Indian name derived from the Sanskrit *jayanta* ('victorious'). **Jayanti** is a feminine variant of the name.

Jayanti *See* JAYANT.

Jayashankar (m) Indian name derived from the Sanskrit *jaya* ('victory') and SHANKAR and thus meaning 'victorious SHIVA'.

Jayashree *See* JAYA.

Jaye *See* JAY.

Jayne *See* JANE.

Jaywant (m) Indian name derived from the Sanskrit *jayavant* ('possessing victory'). Largely confined to the Sikh community.

Jean (f) English first name derived – like JANE and JOAN – from the Old French Jehane, itself a feminine version of the masculine Jean, commonly used in France over centuries as a name for boys. All the various forms of the name are descended ultimately via Johanna from the Latin Johannes (*see* JOHN). It became an established favourite in Scotland in medieval times but was only taken up on a wider basis throughout the English-speaking world towards the end of the 19th century. It enjoyed a peak in popularity in the 1930s but has since been eclipsed by JAN and Jane. Well-known bearers of the name have included British novelists Jean Rhys (Ella Gwendolen Rees

Williams; 1894–1979) and Jean Plaidy (Eleanor Hibbert; 1910–93), British actress Jean Simmons (b.1929), US-born actress Jean Seberg (1938–79) and the fictional Jean Brodie in Muriel Spark's novel *The Prime of Miss Jean Brodie* (1961). **Jeanie** and **Jeannie** are familiar forms of the name with strong Scottish associations. Diminutive forms include **Jeane** or **Jeana** (variants rare outside the USA) and JEANETTE. *See also* GENE; SHEENA.

Jeana/Jeane *See* JEAN.

Jeanette (f) English first name that developed as a diminutive of the French JEANNE. It was taken up in Scotland at a relatively early date but did not enter regular usage elsewhere in the English-speaking world until the 20th century. It enjoyed a peak in popularity in the 1960s. Famous bearers of the name have included US actress Jeanette MacDonald (1901–65) and British novelist Jeanette Winterson (b.1959). Also encountered as **Jeannette** and, more rarely, as **Jennet** or **Genette**. A familiar form of the name in Scotland is **Jinty**; other diminutives include **Netta** and **Nettie**.

Jeanie *See* JEAN.

Jeanne (f) French first name that developed as a feminine equivalent for the masculine Jean (*see* JOHN) and also of JANE and JOAN. The link with Joan is illustrated by the French name of the heroine Joan of Arc – Jeanne d'Arc. Diminutive forms include **Jeannine**.

Jeannette *See* JEANETTE.

Jeannie *See* JEAN.

Jeannine *See* JEANNE.

Jed *See* JEDIDIAH.

Jedidiah (m) Biblical name derived from the Hebrew Jedidyah, meaning 'beloved of God' or 'friend of Yah' ('Yah' being another name for Jehovah, or God). It features in the Bible as an alternative name for King Solomon and was consequently among the

biblical names taken up by English Puritans in the 17th century. It has since become very rare and is today more likely to be encountered in its abbreviated form **Jed**.

Jeetendra *See* JITENDRA.

Jeff *See* GEOFFREY.

Jefferson (m) English surname meaning 'son of Jeffrey' that was adopted as a first name, chiefly in the USA, from the 19th century. The name was adopted by many people in the USA in tribute to US President Thomas Jefferson (1743–1826) and also to Confederate President Jefferson Davis (1808–89). Sometimes shortened to **Jeff**.

Jeffery/Jeffrey *See* GEOFFREY.

Jehane *See* JANE; JEAN.

Jem (m) English first name that evolved as a diminutive form of JAMES, although it is now often associated with JEREMY. It was taken up by English speakers in the 19th century, but has since fallen out of fashion. **Jemmy** is a diminutive form. *See also* JEMIMA; JEREMIAH; JEREMY.

Jemima (f) Biblical name derived from the Hebrew Yemimah, meaning 'wild dove' or possibly 'bright as day'. It appears in the Bible as the name of Job's eldest daughter and was taken up by English Puritans in the 17th century. In the same century Charles II gave the name Charlotte Jemima to one of his illegitimate children. It has remained a relatively popular choice of name in succeeding centuries, being considered by many people a feminine equivalent of the masculine JAMES. Well-known bearers of the name in fiction have included Jemima Pinkerton in William Makepeace Thackeray's novel *Vanity Fair* (1847–8) and Jemima Puddle-Duck in Beatrix Potter's children's story *The Tale of Jemima Puddle-Duck* (1908). JEM, **Jemmy** and **Mima** are familiar forms of the name.

Jemma *See* GEMMA.

Jemmy *See* JEM; JEMIMA.

Jen *See* JENNIFER; JENNY.

Jenaro *See* GENNARO.

Jeni *See* JENNY.

Jenifer *See* JENNIFER.

Jenkin (m) English and Welsh surname that has also made occasional appearances as a first name. It is thought to have evolved originally from the medieval first name Jankin (*see* JACK). It has a strong Welsh flavour, largely because the surname Jenkins is particularly common among the Welsh. **Siencyn** is an historical Welsh variant of the name.

Jenna (f) English first name that developed as a variant of JENNY. It is a relatively recent adoption, making early appearances in the 1970s, when it was promoted through a character of the same name in the US television soap opera *Dallas*.

Jennet *See* JEANETTE.

Jenni/Jennie *See* JENNY.

Jennifer (f) English first name that developed initially as a Cornish variant of GUINEVERE – the name borne by King Arthur's unfaithful wife in Arthurian legend. It became established among English speakers in the 18th century but remained relatively uncommon until the early years of the 20th century, by which time it had eclipsed the older form of the name. It became hugely popular in the 1950s and has since maintained a fairly high position among popular girls' names. Well-known bearers of the name have included a character in George Bernard Shaw's play *The Doctor's Dilemma* (1905), British comedienne Jennifer Saunders (b.1958), US television actress Jennifer Anniston (b.1969) and US tennis player Jennifer Capriati (b.1976). Also encountered as **Jenifer**. Commonly shortened to **Jen**, **Jennie** or JENNY. *See also* GAYNOR.

Jenny (f) English first name that is generally thought of as a diminutive form of JANE, JANET and JENNIFER. It seems to have made early appearances during medieval times as a variant of JEAN but had become connected with several other girls' names by the 18th century, being taken up with particular enthusiasm in Scotland. Commonly shortened to **Jen**. Also found as **Jeni**, **Jenni**, **Jennie** or the Latinate JENNA. Well-known bearers of the name in its various forms have included Swedish soprano Jenny Lind (Johanna Lind; 1820–87), Winston Churchill's mother Jennie Jerome (d.1921), British politician Jennie Lee (1904–88) and British actress Jenny Agutter (b.1952).

Jens *See* JOHN.

Jep *See* JEPSON.

Jephthah (m) Biblical name derived from the Hebrew Yiphtah, meaning 'God opens'. It appears in the Bible as the name of a leader of the Israelites who was commanded to sacrifice his daughter to God in exchange for victory over the Ammonites, and was revived by English speakers in the 19th century. Also found as **Jephtha** and **Jeptha**.

Jepson (m) English surname that has made occasional appearances as a first name. The surname evolved originally out of a medieval variant of GEOFFREY. Sometimes shortened to **Jep**.

Jeremiah (m) Biblical name derived from the Hebrew Yirmeyah, meaning 'appointed by God' or 'exalted by Yah' (Yah being an alternative for Jehovah, or God). It appears in the Bible as the name of the 7th-century BC prophet to whom the Book of Jeremiah and the Book of Lamentations were attributed and was consequently among the biblical names taken up by Puritans in the 17th century. It is now rare, although it continues to make occasional appearances in Ireland, which the Old Testament prophet is traditionally supposed to have visited, and may also be encountered as a variant of the Irish Diarmaid (*see* DERMOT). Famous bearers of the name have included the

English composer Jeremiah Clarke (1659–1707). Commonly shortened to JERRY or JEM. *See also* JEREMY.

Jeremias *See* JEREMY.

Jeremy (m) English first name that evolved out of the biblical JEREMIAH. Also found as Jeremias, it is recorded in use among English speakers during the medieval period and remained in currency even after the Puritans revived the biblical Jeremiah in the 17th century, appearing, for example, as the name of a servant in the William Congreve comedy *Love for Love* (1695). It enjoyed a peak in popularity in the first half of the 20th century, in part through *Jeremy* (1919) and other popular books by British novelist Hugh Walpole, and in the 1970s appeared in the top 50 most popular names being given to babies born in Canada and the USA. Well-known bearers of the name have included British philosopher Jeremy Bentham (1748–1832), a frog called Jeremy Fisher in a children's story by Beatrix Potter, British Liberal politician Jeremy Thorpe (b.1929) and British actor Jeremy Irons (b.1948). Commonly shortened to JERRY or **Jerrie** and, less commonly, to JEM. *See also* JEROME.

Jermaine *See* GERMAINE.

Jerome (m) English first name descended via the Latin Hieronymus from the Greek Hieronymos, itself derived from *hieros* ('holy') and *onoma* ('name') and thus meaning 'one who bears a holy name'. Often confused with the otherwise unconnected JEREMY, it made irregular appearances among English speakers as early as the 12th century, when it often appeared as Geronimus. Other versions of the name were subsequently replaced by the French form **Jérôme**, which went on to enjoy a peak in popularity in the 19th century. Notable bearers of the name have included the 4th-century St Jerome, a monk who translated the Bible into Latin, the British writer Jerome K. Jerome (1859–1927), US songwriter Jerome Kern (1885–1945) and US ballet dancer and choreographer Jerome

Robbins (1918–98). Commonly shortened to JERRY. Variants of the name in other languages have included the Spanish **Jerónimo**, the Dutch **Jeroen** and the Italian **Girolamo** and **Geronimo** – as borne by the celebrated Apache chief (1829–1909).

Jerrard *See* GERARD.

Jerrie *See* GERALDINE; JEREMY; JERRY.

Jerrold *See* GERALD.

Jerry (m) English first name that exists as a diminutive of several other names, including JEREMIAH, JEREMY and JEROME. As a variant of GERRY, it may also be found as an abbreviation of GERALD or GERARD. It appears to have made its debut among English speakers in the 18th century and has remained in wide circulation ever since. Famous bearers of the name have included Jerry Cruncher in the Charles Dickens novel *A Tale of Two Cities* (1859), US actor Jerry Lewis (b.1926), Jerry the Mouse in the long-running US cartoon film series *Tom and Jerry*, US country musician Jerry Lee Lewis (b.1935) and US television comedian Jerry Seinfeld (b.1954). *See also* GERALDINE.

Jervis *See* JARVIS.

Jerzy *See* GEORGE.

Jesper *See* JASPER.

Jess *See* JANET; JESSE; JESSICA.

Jessamine/Jessamy/Jessamyn *See* JASMINE.

Jesse (m) English first name derived from the Hebrew Yishay, meaning 'Jehovah exists' or 'gift of Jehovah'. It features in the Bible as the name of King David's father and thus an ancestor of Jesus Christ. It was taken up by English speakers in the 18th century, becoming particularly popular in the USA. Usually pronounced 'jessee' and accordingly sometimes spelled JESSIE. Notable bearers of the name have included the notorious US outlaw Jesse James (1847–82), US athlete Jesse Owens (James Cleveland Owens; 1913–80) and US politician

Jesse Jackson (b.1941). Sometimes shortened to **Jess**.

Jessica (f) English first name that appears to have been invented by William Shakespeare as the name of Shylock's daughter in his play *The Merchant of Venice* (1596) – hence the name's long-established association with Jews. It seems Shakespeare modelled the name on the Hebrew Iscah or Jesca, meaning 'God beholds', as featured in the Bible. It remained in irregular use from the 16th to the 19th century and subsequently enjoyed a considerable vogue from the 1990s. Notable bearers of the name have included British actress Jessica Tandy (1909–94), British writer Jessica Mitford (1917–96) and US film actress Jessica Lange (b.1949). Commonly shortened to **Jess** or JESSIE.

Jessie (f) English first name that evolved as a diminutive form of JEAN, JANET and JESSICA. It was taken up by English speakers, especially in Scotland, in the 19th century and was fairly common until the 1920s, since when it has become relatively rare. Its popularity in the 19th century is illustrated by its appearance in several celebrated works of fiction, including Charlotte Brontë's *Shirley* (1849) and Mrs Gaskell's *Cranford* (1853). Notable bearers of the name in real life have included British dancer, singer and actress Jessie Matthews (1907–81). Sometimes shortened to **Jess**. Also spelled **Jessi** and **Jessye** – as borne by US concert singer Jessye Norman (b.1945). A Gaelic form of the name is **Teasag**. *See also* JESSE.

Jessye *See* JESSIE.

Jesus (m) Spanish and Portuguese name (pronounced 'haysus') bestowed in honour of Jesus Christ. The name is an Aramaic variant of JOSHUA, meaning 'saviour' or 'Jehovah saves'. The name is relatively common in Spanish and Portuguese-speaking countries, often given to children born on the feast of the Sacred Name of Jesus, but is rare elsewhere, being considered too sacred for secular use. **Chus** and

Chucho are familiar versions of the name. A rare feminine variant is **Jesusa**.

Jethro (m) English name derived from the Hebrew Yitro or Ithra, meaning 'abundance' or 'excellence'. It appears in the Bible as the name of the father-in-law of Moses and was consequently taken up by English Puritans in the 16th century. It remained fairly common until the end of the 19th century, by which time it had acquired strong rural associations, in part through Jethro Tull (1674–1741), the English agricultural reformer who invented the seed drill. Well-known bearers of the name in more recent times have included the 1970s British rock group Jethro Tull and, in the 1980s, the fictional Jethro Larkin in the popular British radio soap opera *The Archers*.

Jetta (f) English first name based on the name of the mineral jet. The name of the mineral came ultimately, via the Old French *Jalet*, from the Latin *gagates* ('stone from Gagai' – a town in Lycia, Asia Minor).

Jewel (f) English first name derived from the ordinary vocabulary word 'jewel'. It was among the many words connected with gemstones that were taken up by English speakers as first names in the 19th century. The word is thought to have come originally via the Old French *jouel* from the Latin *iocus* ('delight').

Jill (f) English first name that evolved as a diminutive form of GILLIAN. Jill began to appear as a replacement for Gill as the usual shortened form of Gillian from the 17th century and enjoyed peaks in popularity in the 1930s and again since the 1970s (although Gill is still in irregular use). Notable bearers of the name have included the nursery rhyme character in 'Jack and Jill' (of 15th-century origin, when the name was treated as a generic name for any young girl). **Jilly** and **Jillie** are diminutive forms of the name – as borne by British writer Jilly Cooper (b.1937).

Jillian *See* GILLIAN.

Jillie/Jilly *See* GILLIAN; JILL; JULIANA.

Jim (m) English first name that evolved as a diminutive of JAMES and is now often considered to be a name in its own right. Medieval in origin, it was taken up on a significant scale by English speakers by the middle of the 19th century and was greatly promoted throughout the English-speaking world by Robert Louis Stevenson's Jim Hawkins, the hero of his adventure novel *Treasure Island* (1883). Well-known bearers of the name since then have included Scottish motor-racing driver Jim Clark (1936–68) and British comedian Jim Davidson (b.1953). In recent years Jim has been substantially eclipsed by its diminutive form **Jimmy** – as borne by US comedian Jimmy Durante (1893–1980), British radio presenter Jimmy Young (Leslie Ronald Young; b.1923), US President Jimmy Carter (b.1924) and the fictional Jimmy Porter in the John Osborne play *Look Back in Anger* (1957). Other variants are **Jimmie** and **Jimi** – famous as the name of US rock guitarist Jimi Hendrix (James Hendrix; 1942–70).

Jimmie/Jimmy *See* JIM.

Jinan (m/f) Arabic name derived from *jinan* ('garden' or 'paradise'). Commonly found throughout countries of the Middle East.

Jinny *See* VIRGINIA.

Jinty *See* JEANETTE.

Jiri *See* GEORGE.

Jitender *See* JITENDRA.

Jitendra (m) Indian name derived from the Sanskrit *jita* ('conquered') and INDRA and usually interpreted to mean 'having conquered Indra' (Indra being the name of a powerful god). Variants include **Jeetendra** and the masculine **Jitender** or **Jitinder**.

Jitinder *See* JITENDRA.

Jo (m/f) English first name that developed as a diminutive form of various longer names, including the masculine JOHN, JONATHAN and JOSEPH and the feminine JOAN, JOANNA, JOANNE and JOSEPHINE. It is also found as a variant of JOE. It emerged during the 19th century and is today more often encountered in use as a name for females, enjoying a peak in popularity between 1940 and 1970. Well-known bearers of the name have included (among men) British Liberal politician Jo Grimond (Joseph Grimond; 1913–93) and (among women) the fictional Jo March in the Louisa M. Alcott novel *Little Women* (1868) and British tennis player Jo Durie (Joanna Durie; b.1960). It is sometimes used in combination with other names, as in **Jobeth**. A rare Scottish variant is **Joina**. JODY is a diminutive form.

Joab (m) Biblical name derived from the Hebrew Yoabh, meaning 'Jehovah is father'. It appears in the Bible as the name of one of King David's generals and was consequently among the biblical names taken up by English Puritans in the 17th century.

Joachim (m) Biblical name (pronounced 'yoakim') derived from the Hebrew Yehoyaqim or Johoiachin, meaning 'Jehovah will establish' or 'established by God'. It features in the Bible as the name of a king of Judah and is traditionally supposed to have been the name of the Virgin Mary's father, hence its popularity among European Christians. It was subsequently taken up by English speakers by the 13th century, but had more or less fallen out of use by the 20th century. Variants in other languages have included the Italian **Gioacchino** or **Gioachino**, the Spanish **Joaquin**, the Portuguese **Joaquim**, the German **Jochim**, **Jochem** and **Jochen**, the Scandinavian **Joakim**, **Jokum** or **Jockum** and the Russian **Yakim** or **Akim**.

Joan (f) English first name derived from the Latin Johanna, itself a feminine version of Johannes (*see* JOHN). Records of the name's use among English speakers go back to the medieval period, when the name was imported from France in the form Jhone or Johan. The modern spelling of the name seems to have been established by the 14th century. Having become one of the top three feminine names among English speakers in the 16th century, it came to be considered a rather vulgar name and went into a sudden and rapid decline, being little used between the 16th and 19th centuries, during which time it was eclipsed by such alternatives as JANE. It subsequently enjoyed a significant revival in the 1920s and 1930s, possibly in response to the canonization in 1920 of the medieval French heroine Joan of Arc (in French, Jeanne d'Arc; 1412–31). It has since suffered another decline and is now rare among the young.

Notable bearers of the name in relatively recent times have included US film actress Joan Crawford (Lucille le Sueur; 1904–77), British actress Joan Hickson (1906–98), New Zealand opera singer Dame Joan Hammond (1912–96), Australian opera singer Dame Joan Sutherland (b.1926), British actress Joan Collins (b.1933) and US folk-rock singer-songwriter Joan Baez (b.1941). *See also* JOANNA; JOANNE; JONI; SIOBHAN.

Joanna (f) English variant of JOAN derived via Hebrew and Latin from the Greek Ionna and in origin one of several feminine versions of JOHN. It appears in the Bible as the name of the wife of King Herod's steward, who was also one of Jesus' followers. In medieval times the name was usually spelled **Johanna** and it was not until the 18th century that the modern spelling became widely accepted, replacing Joan as the dominant form of the name from the 1930s. Notable bearers of the name have included British novelist Joanna Trollope (b.1943) and British actress Joanna Lumley (b.1946). Commonly shortened to JO. *See also* JOANNE.

Joanne (f) English first name borrowed from Old French and, like JOAN, in origin a feminine equivalent of JOHN. It is often equated with JOANNA, although the latter evolved through Greek and Latin. It enjoyed a peak in popularity among English speakers in the 1970s but has since lost

ground. Notable bearers of the name have included the US actress Joanne Woodward (b.1930) and British actress Joanne Whalley-Kilmer (b.1964). Commonly shortened to JO. Also found as **Jo-Anne** and **Jo Anne**.

Joao *See* JOHN.

Joaquim/Joaquin *See* JOACHIM.

Job (m) Biblical name derived from the Hebrew Iyyobh, meaning 'persecuted' or 'hated'. The biblical Job demonstrated his faithfulness to God through a series of trials and misfortunes, as told in the Book of Job, and the name was consequently taken up by English Puritans in the 17th century. It remained in use until the end of the 19th century, since when it has virtually disappeared. The name features in several classic works of English literature, including Charles Dickens' *Pickwick Papers* (1836–7) and Robert Louis Stevenson's *Treasure Island* (1883). **Joby**, **Jobie** and **Joby** are all familiar forms of the name.

Jobeth *See* JO.

Jocasta (f) Greek name of uncertain meaning. According to some authorities, the name comes from the mythical Io (whose name was understood to refer to the moon) combined with *kaustikos* ('burning') and thus meaning 'shining moon'. It is most famous from the various plays and other literary works based on the myth of Queen Jocasta of Thebes, who committed suicide after unknowingly marrying her own son, Oedipus. Despite its association with classical tragedy, it has made rare appearances as a first name among English speakers from time to time, chiefly in the late 19th century. JO is a diminutive form of the name.

Jocelyn (m/f) English surname derived from the Old Norman Joscelin that was itself subsequently taken up as a first name by English speakers. The Old Norman name, which was brought to England with the Normans, may have come originally from the name of a Germanic tribe called the

Gauts or *Gautelen* (sometimes interpreted to mean 'little Goths'). Other suggestions are that it comes from the Old German Josse (meaning 'champion') or else from the old Breton name Jodoc (of obscure meaning). The name was in regular use in England through the medieval period, when it had several variant spellings, but became less common after the 14th century. It enjoyed a substantial revival in the 19th century, when it provided the title for the novel *Jocelyn* (1898) by John Galsworthy, for instance, and continued in regular use into the 20th century but is now very rare (especially as a name for boys). When bestowed upon girls, it is often considered to be a combination of JOYCE and LYNN. Commonly shortened to **Jos** or **Joss**. Variants include **Jocelin**, **Joseline**, **Joscelin**, **Josceline**, **Joselyn** and **Josslyn** (all feminine versions of the name).

Jochem/Jochen/Jochim *See* JOACHIM.

Jock (m) Scottish variant of JACK, itself a diminutive of JOHN. It is strongly associated with Scotland and is in fact a nickname for anyone of Scottish ancestry, although it is not in fact much used as a name in Scotland itself. Famous bearers of the name have included Scottish football manager Jock Stein (1922–85). **Jocky** (or **Jockey**) is a familiar form of the name. A Gaelic variant is **Seoc**.

Jockum *See* JOACHIM.

Jocosa *See* JOYCE.

Jodene/Jodi/Jodie *See* JODY.

Jodoc *See* JOCELYN.

Jody (m/f) English first name that evolved as a diminutive form of the masculine GEORGE, JUDE and JOE and of the feminine JO, JOSEPHINE, Josie and JUDITH. As a boys' name, it was heard with increasing frequency among English speakers during the 19th century. As a girls' name it seems to date from the 1950s, enjoying its greatest popularity in Canada and the USA. Also found in the variant spellings **Jodi** and **Jodie** – as borne by US film actress Jodie

Foster (Alicia Christian Foster; b.1962). Another variant of relatively recent coinage is **Jodene**.

Joe (m) English first name that evolved as a diminutive form of such names as JOSEPH, JOHN and JOSHUA. It became very common among English speakers in the 19th century and in the USA became a generic term for any ordinary member of the public, as in 'he's just an ordinary Joe' or 'Joe Soap' (in the UK, 'Joe Bloggs'). Well-known bearers of the name have included British bandleader Joe Loss (Joshua Loss; 1909–90), US boxer Joe Louis (Joseph Louis; 1914–81), British pop singer Joe Cocker (Joseph Cocker; b.1944) and the fictional Joe Lampton in the John Braine novel *Room at the Top* (1957). Also encountered as JO or **Joey**. *See also* JODY.

Joel (m) Biblical name derived from the Hebrew Yeol, meaning 'Yah is god' (Yah being another name for Jehovah, or God). It appears around a dozen times in the Bible, notably as the name of a minor 8th-century BC prophet, and was in use in medieval England, although in this instance it was usually derived from the Breton Judicael or Juhel, as borne by an early Breton saint. The biblical history of the name led to it being taken up by English Puritans in the 17th century. It is also popular among Jews. Since the 19th century it has been confined largely to the USA, with a minor revival in the UK in the 1970s. Famous bearers of the name have included US children's writer Joel Chandler Harris (1848–1908), US actor Joel McCrea (1905–90) and US film director Joel Coen (b.1955). A French variant is **Joël**. A feminine version of the name is **Joelle**, also found in French as **Joëlle**.

Joelle *See* JOEL.

Joey *See* JOE; JOSEPH.

Johan/Johann *See* JOHN.

Johanna *See* JOANNA.

Johannes *See* JOHN.

John (m) English first name derived via the

Latin Johannes originally from the Hebrew Yohanan or Johanan, meaning 'Yah is gracious' or 'Yah is merciful' (Yah being another name for Jehovah, or God). It features in the Bible as the name of several major characters including John the Baptist, one of the twelve disciples and John the Evangelist, author of the fourth gospel. Because of its strong religious associations, the name was borne by several saints and popes and was also popular among Europe's royal families – although it has not been much favoured by British royalty since the 13th century, when King John brought the name a dubious reputation. It is often identified as the most popular of all Christian names in European history. It came to England with the Normans in the 11th century, initially in the forms Johan or Jon, and has been in regular use among English speakers since the 16th century, reaching a peak in the second half of the 17th century when nearly 30 per cent of all children born in England were given the name. It has fallen off somewhat in popularity since its most recent peak in the 1950s.

Notable bearers of the name have included Sir John Falstaff in Shakespeare's plays *Henry IV* (1597) and *The Merry Wives of Windsor* (1597), British poet and novelist John Masefield (1878–1967), British actor Sir John Gielgud (1904–2000), British poet Sir John Betjeman (1906–84), US President John F. Kennedy (1917–63), British playwright John Osborne (1929–94), British singer-songwriter John Lennon (1940–80) and British Prime Minister John Major (b.1943). A famous mythical John is John Bull, the archetypal Englishman created by the Scottish writer John Arbuthnot (1667–1735) in the early 18th century.

The variant form **Jon** has been revived in relatively recent times – as borne by British actor Jon Pertwee (1919–96), US actor Jon Voight (b.1938) and British television presenter Jon Snow (b.1947). Diminutives of John and Jon include JACK, HANK and **Johnny** (also found as **Johnnie** or **Jonny**) – as borne by such luminaries as US film actor and athlete Johnny Weissmuller

(1904–84), US comedian and chat show host Johnny Carson (b.1925), US pop singer Johnnie Ray (1927–90) and US country musician Johnny Cash (1932–2003). Variants in other languages include the Irish SEAN or **Eoin**, the Scottish IAN or **Iain**, the Welsh EVAN or **Ieuan**, French **Jean**, the Italian **Giovanni** or **Gianni**, the Spanish JUAN or **Juanito**, the Portuguese **Joao**, the Scandinavian **Johan**, **Jens** and JAN, the German **Johan**, **Johann**, **Hanke** or **Hans**, the Dutch JAN or **Joop**, the Romanian **Ion**, the Russian IVAN and the Hungarian **János**.

Johnathan/Johnathon *See* JONATHAN.

Johnnie/Johnny *See* JOHN.

Joisse *See* JOYCE.

Jokum *See* JOACHIM.

Jolana/Jolanda/Jolantha *See* YOLANDA.

Joleen *See* JOLENE.

Jolene (f) English first name that probably resulted from the combination of JO and MARLENE or another name with a '-lene' ending. It appears to be a name of relatively recent coinage, becoming popular in the USA in the 1940s. Many people know it from Dolly Parton's 1974 hit single 'Jolene'. Also found in the form **Joleen**.

Jolie (f) English first name that evolved as a variant of JULIA, JULIE or JULIANA. It appears to be a relatively recent introduction of late 20th-century invention.

Jolyon *See* JULIAN.

Jon *See* JOHN; JONATHAN.

Jonah (m) Biblical name derived from the Hebrew Yonah meaning 'dove'. It appears in the Bible as the name of a prophet who is swallowed by a whale – a story that was very popular in medieval times. It was consequently among the biblical names taken up with new enthusiasm by the Puritans in the 17th century, although later generations tended to avoid the name because to many it signified bad luck. Well-known bearers of the name in relatively recent times have included British squash player Jonah Barrington (b.1940). *See also* JONAS.

Jonas (m) English first name derived from the Greek Ionas, an equivalent of JONAH. It has been in use among English speakers since the 19th century or earlier and, because it does not carry the same association with misfortune, gradually came to eclipse Jonah across the English-speaking world. **Joney** is a familiar form of the name.

Jonathan (m) English first name derived from the Hebrew Yahonathan, meaning 'Yah has given' or 'Yah's gift' (Yah being another name for Jehovah, or God). It appears in the Bible as the name of the son of King Saul, a close friend of David. It was taken up by English speakers as early as the 13th century and has been in regular use since the 17th century, sometimes confused with JOHN. Notable bearers of the name have included Irish clergyman and writer Jonathan Swift (1667–1745), the central character of the Henry Fielding novel *Jonathan Wild* (1743), British theatre director and television presenter Jonathan Miller (b.1934), British broadcaster Jonathan Dimbleby (b.1944) and British actor Jonathan Pryce (b.1947). The title 'Brother Jonathan' is sometimes bestowed upon the average American, or upon the USA itself (thought to be a reference to Jonathan Trumbull, an 18th-century governor of Connecticut). Also encountered as **Jonathon** and occasionally as **Johnathan** or **Johnathon**. Commonly shortened to **Jon**. Diminutive forms of the name include the relatively rare **Jonty**.

Joni (f) English first name that developed via Joani as a variant of JOAN. It was taken up by English speakers in the 1950s, becoming popular chiefly in Canada and the USA. Well-known bearers of the name have included Canadian singer-songwriter Joni Mitchell (Roberta Joan Anderson; b.1943). Sometimes shortened to JO.

Jonny *See* JOHN.

Jonquil (f) A less popular example of the flower names that were taken up by English speakers towards the end of the 19th century and early 20th century; it reached its peak in the 1940s and 1950s.

Jonty *See* JONATHAN.

Jools *See* JULES.

Joop *See* JOHN.

Joost (m) Dutch first name derived ultimately from the Latin JUSTUS, meaning 'fair' or 'just'.

Jordan (m/f) English and German name derived from that of the sacred River Jordan in the Holy Land, in which Jesus Christ was baptized by John the Baptist. The original river name came from the Hebrew *hayarden* ('flowing down'). The name was brought back to England by the Crusaders and was often bestowed upon children (initially boys only) baptized in water from the river itself. The name enjoyed a revival among English speakers in the 19th century, since when it has continued to make occasional appearances as a name borne by both sexes. It was among the thirty most popular names for boys chosen in England and Wales in 2001 and enjoyed a boost as a name for girls through British model Jordan (Katie Price; b.1978). Also found as **Jordyn**. **Judd** is occasionally encountered in use as a diminutive form of the name. Variants in other languages include the French **Jourdain**, the Italian **Giordano** and the Dutch **Jordaan** or **Joord**.

Jorge *See* GEORGE.

Jos *See* JOCELYN; JOSEPH; JOSIAH.

Joscelin/Josceline *See* JOCELYN.

José (m) Spanish equivalent (pronounced 'hosay') of JOSEPH that is also occasionally encountered among English speakers, chiefly in the USA; **Pepe** is a diminutive. It is sometimes used as a name for girls in combination with other names, as in

Maria José. Other feminine variants include **Josée** and **Josiane**.

Josef/Josefa *See* JOSEPH.

Joselyn *See* JOCELYN.

Joseph (m) English and French first name derived from the Hebrew Yoseph, meaning 'Yah may add' or 'Yah added' (in other words, 'God gave this son'). The name appears in the Bible three times, as the name of a son of Jacob who was sold into slavery, as that of the Virgin Mary's husband, and that of Joseph of Arimathea, who retrieved Christ's body and put it in the garden tomb. It made irregular appearances among English speakers in medieval times, becoming increasingly popular after the Reformation and again in the early years of the 20th century. It fell off in subsequent decades before reviving once more in the 1990s.

Well-known bearers of the name have included the central character in the Henry Fielding novel *Joseph Andrews* (1742), Joseph Surface in Richard Brinsley Sheridan's comedy *The School for Scandal* (1777), Polish-born British novelist Joseph Conrad (Josef Konrad Korzeniowski; 1857–1924) and US film actor Joseph Cotten (1905–94). JO, JOE, **Joey** and **Jos** are diminutive forms of the name, as is the German **Sepp**. Variants in other languages include **Josef** in Dutch, German and the Scandinavian languages, the Irish Gaelic **Seosamh**, the Italian **Giuseppe**, the Spanish JOSÉ, the Polish **Jozef**, the Russian **Iosif** or **Osip** and the Arabic **Yusuf**. The Spanish, Portuguese and Scandinavian **Josefa** and the French **Josèphe** are feminine versions of the name. *See also* JOSEPHINE.

Josepha/Josephina *See* JOSEPHINE.

Josephine (f) English first name derived from the French Josèphe or Joséphine, both feminine versions of the masculine JOSEPH. It appears to have made its debut among English speakers around the middle of the 19th century. Notable bearers of the name have included Napoleon's wife the Empress Joséphine (Marie-Josèphe-Rose Beauhar-

nais; 1763–1814), British socialist reformer Josephine Butler (1828–1906) and US-born French dancer and singer Josephine Baker (1906–75). Commonly shortened to JO. Diminutive forms include **Josie**, **Josette**, FIFI and **Pheeny**. Variants include **Josepha** and **Josephina**. Among versions in other languages is the Italian **Giuseppina**. *See also* JODY; PEPITA.

Josette *See* JOSEPHINE.

Josh *See* JOSHUA; JOSIAH.

Joshua (m) Biblical name derived from the Hebrew Yehoshua or Hosea, meaning 'Yah saves' or 'Yah is salvation' (Yah being another name for Jehovah, or God). It appears in the Bible as the name of the man who succeeded Moses as the leader of the Israelites on their journey to the Promised Land. It was taken up by English speakers in the 18th century and became particularly popular among Jews. It became less frequent from the middle of the 19th century but enjoyed a revival in the USA in the 1950s and in the UK in the 1990s. Famous bearers of the name have included the British portrait painter Sir Joshua Reynolds (1723–92) and Zimbabwean politician Joshua Nkomo (1917–99). JOE and **Josh** are common diminutives. Variants in other languages include the Dutch **Jozua**. *See also* JESUS.

Josiah (m) Biblical name derived from the Hebrew Yoshiyah, meaning 'Yah supports' or 'Yah heals' (Yah being another name for Jehovah, or God). It appears in the Bible as the name of a king of Judah. It was taken up by English speakers in the 17th century but has been in decline in recent decades. Notable bearers of the name have included the celebrated British potters Josiah Wedgwood (1730–95) and Josiah Spode (1754–1827) and the fictional Josiah Crawley in Anthony Trollope's novel *Framley Parsonage* (1861). Common diminutives are **Jos** and **Josh**. A rare variant is **Josias**.

Josiane *See* JOSE.

Josias *See* JOSIAH.

Josie *See* JOSEPHINE.

Joss *See* JOCELYN.

Josse *See* JOYCE.

Josslyn *See* JOCELYN.

Jotham (m) Biblical name derived from the Hebrew Yotham, meaning 'Yah is perfect' (Yah being another name for Jehovah, or God). It appears in the Bible as the name of one of Gideon's sons and was subsequently taken up by English speakers in the 17th century.

Jourdain *See* JORDAN.

Joy (f) English first name derived from the ordinary vocabulary word 'joy', itself from the Old French *joie*. Also encountered as a diminutive form of JOYCE. It was in use in England as early as the 12th century and was subsequently taken up by English Puritans in the 17th century, who interpreted it as expressive of the 'joy' of religious faith. It has remained in irregular use ever since, with a small increase in popularity around the middle of the 20th century. It is now relatively rare. Well-known bearers of the name have included Austrian-born wildlife expert Joy Adamson (1910–80). Variants include **Joye**, **Joi** and **Joya**.

Joyce (m/f) English surname that was subsequently adopted as a first name or else an Anglicization of the Norman French name Josce, a Celtic name descended from the Breton Jodoc or Judoc, meaning 'lord' – as borne by a 7th-century hermit saint. Today it is commonly associated with the ordinary vocabulary words 'joy' or 'rejoice'. The name, historically sometimes spelled Joisse or Josse, came to England with followers of William the Conqueror in the 11th century, although in those days it was treated as a masculine name. Having vanished from use by the 14th century, it reappeared (chiefly as a name for girls) around the 17th century and became increasingly common among English speakers from the 19th century. It enjoyed a peak in popularity in the 1920s, since when it has gradually declined.

Well-known bearers of the name have included British comedian Joyce Grenfell (1910–79) and US novelist Joyce Carol Oates (b.1938). Commonly shortened to JOY. **Jocosa** was another historical form of the name, possibly influenced by the Latin *jocosus* ('merry').

Jozafat (m) Polish first name derived from the Hebrew Josaphat or Jehoshaphat, meaning 'God has judged'. Borne by a biblical king of Judah, it became popular in Poland through a 16th-century Polish saint.

Jozef *See* JOSEPH.

Juan (m) Spanish version (pronounced 'hwarn') of the English JOHN now commonly encountered among Hispanic communities throughout the English-speaking world, particularly in the USA. Famous bearers of the name have included Don Juan, the legendary Spanish seducer of women who features in the Mozart opera *Don Juan* (1787) and Lord Byron's poem *Don Juan* (1819–24) among other classic works. A familiar version of the name is **Juanito**. **Juana**, **Janita**, **Junita** and **Juanita** (sometimes abbreviated to **Nita**) are feminine equivalents.

Juana/Juanita/Juanito *See* JUAN.

Jubal (m) Biblical name derived from the Hebrew Jobel, meaning 'horn' or 'trumpet'. It appears in the Bible as the name of a son of Lamech famed for his musical prowess and was consequently among the biblical names taken up by English speakers in the 17th century.

Juda (m) Arabic name meaning 'goodness' or 'excellence'. Also found in the form **Guda**.

Judah (m) Biblical name derived from the Hebrew Yehudhah or Yehuda, meaning 'praised' or 'he who is praised'. It is borne in the Bible by a son of Jacob and Leah, the founder of one of the twelve tribes of Israel, and was consequently among the biblical names taken up by English speakers in the

17th century. **Yehudi** is a variant form. *See also* JUDAS; JUDE.

Judas (m) Biblical name representing a Greek version of JUDAH. Because of its notoriety as the name of Judas Iscariot, Christ's betrayer, the name has only rarely been taken up as a first name among English speakers – although it was also borne by another apostle called Judas and by Judas Maccabaeus, who drove the Syrians out of Judea. *See also* JUDE.

Judd *See* JORDAN.

Jude (m) English variant of the biblical JUDAS. The name is sometimes applied to the apostle Judas Thaddaeus (the patron saint of lost causes) to distinguish him from Judas Iscariot. It was taken up by English speakers in the 17th century. The best-known bearer of the name is the fictional Jude Fawley in the Thomas Hardy novel *Jude the Obscure* (1895). In more recent times the Beatles' song 'Hey Jude' (1968) brought the name into the limelight once again, while another contemporary to bear the name is British actor Jude Law (b.1972). *See also* JODY; JUDITH.

Judi *See* JUDITH.

Judith (f) Biblical name derived from the Hebrew Yehudhith, meaning 'Jewess' or 'woman of Judea'. It appears in the Bible as the name of one of Esau's wives and in the Apocryphal Book of Judith, about a beautiful young widow who saves her town by killing the Persian leader Holofernes. Records of the name's use among English speakers go back beyond the Norman Conquest. It was borne by the stepmother of King Alfred the Great in the 9th century and William the Conqueror had a niece with the name in the 11th century. It was not, however, until the 17th century that the name began to appear with any frequency in the English-speaking world, although it has always been popular among Jews. William Shakespeare was among those who selected the name for his own family, giving it to his second daughter. It

enjoyed a peak in popularity among English speakers in the 1950s and 1960s but has since fallen off somewhat.

Famous bearers of the name in relatively recent times have included the Australian actress Dame Judith Anderson (1898–1992), US novelist Judith Krantz (b.1928) and British television presenter Judith Chalmers (b.1935). Commonly shortened to JUDE, **Judi** (or **Judie**) – as borne by British actresses Dame Judi Dench (b.1934) and Judi Bowker (b.1954) – and **Judy** – as borne by Punch's wife in traditional English 'Punch and Judy' puppet shows as well as by US actress and singer Judy Garland (Frances Gumm; 1922–69) and US folksinger Judy Collins (Judith Collins; b.1939).

The full version of the name is sometimes also encountered in use as an Anglicization of the Gaelic SIOBHAN. Variants in other languages include the Polish **Judyta** and the Czech **Judita**. In Germany the name is sometimes abbreviated to **Jutta** or **Jutte**. *See also* JODY.

Judoc *See* JOYCE.

Judy *See* JUDITH.

Jules (m) French name derived either from JULIAN or JULIUS. It was taken up by English speakers on a limited basis towards the end of the 19th century. Well-known bearers of the name have included French novelist Jules Verne (1828–1905). A variant form of relatively recent invention is **Jools** – as borne by British keyboard player and television presenter Jools Holland (Julian Holland, b.1958). *See also* JULIE; JULIET.

Julia (f) Roman name that evolved as a feminine equivalent of JULIUS and was subsequently taken up by English speakers in the 16th century. It enjoyed a resurgence in popularity in the second half of the 20th century, reaching a peak in the 1960s. Since 1900, however, it has lost much ground to the French form of the name, JULIE. William Shakespeare gave the name to a character in his play *Two Gentlemen of Verona* (1592–3) and Richard Brinsley

Sheridan's comedy *The Rivals* (1775) included a character called Julia Melville. Bearers of the name in more recent times have included British photographer Julia Cameron (1815–79), US author Julia Ward Howe (1819–1910) and US film actress Julia Roberts (Julie Roberts; b.1967). Variants of the name in other languages include **Julitta** and the Italian **Giulia**. *See also* JOLIE; JULIE.

Julian (m) English first name derived from the Roman Julianus, a variant of JULIUS. Borne by the mythical St Julian the Hospitaller (the patron saint of travellers) and by a 4th-century Roman emperor, it made occasional appearances in medieval times, when it was also in use as a variant of the feminine GILLIAN – as borne by the 14th-century English mystic Julian of Norwich. It was not taken up by English speakers on a significant scale, however, until the 18th century. It enjoyed a peak in popularity in the 1960s but has since experienced a marked decline. Well-known bearers of the name have included British scientist Sir Julian Huxley (1887–1975), British guitarist Julian Bream (b.1933), British novelist Julian Barnes (b.1944) and British cellist Julian Lloyd Webber (b.1951). **Jolyon** is a variant of the name formerly in use among English speakers in the north of England – a version that was made more widely familiar through the character Jolyon Forsyth in John Galsworthy's *Forsyte Saga* novel sequence (1906–22), the basis of a highly successful 1960s British television series. A rare variant is **Julyan**. Sometimes shortened to **Jolly** or JULES. Variants in other languages include the French **Julien**. *See also* JULIANA.

Juliana (f) Feminine version of the Roman Julianus. Borne by an early Christian martyr, it was taken up by English speakers as early as the 12th century. It enjoyed a resurgence in popularity in the 18th century and remained in fairly regular use until the end of the 19th century, but has since become rare. Notable bearers of the name have included Queen Juliana of the Nether-

lands (b.1909), where the name has long been an established favourite in tribute to St Juliana. Occasionally abbreviated to **Jilly** or, more rarely, to LIANA. Variant forms include **Julianna**, **Julianne**, **Julie Ann** and the German **Juliane**. *See also* JOLIE.

Juliane/Julianne *See* JULIANA.

Julie (f) French version of the Roman JULIA that was taken up on a wide basis among English speakers around the end of the 19th century. It gradually replaced Julia as the more common version of the name and has remained in regular use to the present day. Well-known bearers of the name have included British actress and singer Julie Andrews (Julia Elizabeth Wells; b.1934), British actress Julie Christie (b.1941) and British comedienne and actress Julie Walters (b.1950). Commonly shortened to **Jules**. *See also* JOLIE.

Julien *See* JULIAN.

Juliet (f) English first name derived from the Italian Giulietta, itself an elaboration of the Italian Giulia (*see* JULIA). Its use among English speakers was much promoted by William Shakespeare's tragedy *Romeo and Juliet* (1595) and he also used the name for a character in *Measure for Measure* (1604). The name has been in regular use ever since, with its most recent peak in the 1960s. Notable bearers of the name in relatively recent times have included British actresses Juliet Mills (b.1941) and Juliet Stevenson (b.1956). Sometimes shortened to JULIE or JULES. Variants in other languages include the French **Juliette**.

Juliette *See* JULIET.

Julio *See* JULIUS.

Julius (m) Roman family name of uncertain origin that was subsequently taken up by English speakers during the 19th century. According to legend, the very first bearer of the name was Iulus, the son of Aeneas. Some authorities suggest that the name comes originally from the Greek meaning 'downy' or 'hairy' – a reference to the first growth of beard in young men. From a relatively early date it became established as a popular choice among both Christians and Jews, common to many European languages. It is most often associated historically with the Roman emperor Gaius Julius Caesar (*c*.102–44 BC). Other notable bearers of the name have included three popes and Tanzanian statesman Julius Nyerere (1922–99). Occasionally shortened to JULES. Variants in other languages include the Italian **Giulio**, the Spanish **Julio**, the Portuguese **Juliusz** and the Hungarian **Gyula**.

Julyan *See* JULIAN.

June (f) English first name derived from the name of the month. Like other first names based on the names of months of the year, it appears to have been taken up by English speakers early in the 20th century, often bestowed upon girls born in June, but became less frequent after the 1930s. Well-known bearers of the name have included British actress June Whitfield (b.1925). *See also* APRIL; MAY.

Junior (m) English first name that developed initially as a common nickname for any young person, derived from the Latin for 'younger'. Long used to distinguish a son from his father, it does not appear to have won acceptance as a formal first name until the early 20th century and is still rare outside the USA. Notable bearers of the name have included US blues musician Junior Wells (Amos Blackmore; 1934–98).

Juniper (f) English first name derived from the name of the plant, itself from the Latin *juniperus* (of unknown meaning). It appears in the Bible as a translation of the Hebrew *rothem* (the name of a desert shrub). It has never been very common as a first name.

Junita *See* JUAN.

Juno (f) Roman name derived from that of the goddess Juno, wife of Jupiter. It was subsequently taken up by the Irish as a variant of UNA. Examples of its use in relatively modern times have included the Sean O'Casey play *Juno and the Paycock* (1924).

Jürgen *See* GEORGE.

Justie *See* JUSTIN; JUSTINE.

Justin (m) English first name descended from the Roman Justinus, itself a derivative of JUSTUS. Borne by several early saints and by two Byzantine emperors, it began to appear with increasing frequency among English speakers in the 1970s. **Justie** and **Justy** are familiar forms of the name. Variants include **Justyn** and the Welsh **Iestyn**. *See also* JUSTINE.

Justina *See* JUSTINE.

Justine (f) French feminine equivalent of the masculine JUSTIN. Its oldest form was Justina (or Justiana), as borne by a 4th-century Christian martyr of Padua, it was taken up by English speakers in the 19th century and enjoyed a minor peak in popularity in the 1970s. Well-known bearers of the name have included the central character in Lawrence Durrell's novel *Justine* (1957). Sometimes shortened to **Justie** or **Justy**.

Justus (m) Roman name derived from the Latin for 'fair' or 'just'. Borne by several early saints, it made irregular appearances as a first name among English speakers towards the end of the 19th century and is also known in Germany, the Netherlands and other countries. *See also* JOOST.

Justy *See* JUSTIN; JUSTINE.

Jutte *See* JUDITH.

Jyoti (f) Indian first name derived from the Sanskrit *jyotis* ('light'). A relatively recent adoption as a first name, it is sometimes also encountered as a name for boys.

K

Kaarle *See* CHARLES.

Kady (f) Irish first name possibly derived from the Irish Gaelic *ceadach* (meaning 'first'). Alternatively, it may have evolved as a variant of KATIE.

Kaety *See* KATE.

Kai (m) Scandinavian first name (pronounced 'kay') of uncertain meaning. It has been suggested that it may have come from the Old Norse *katha* ('chicken'), but others have tried to link it with the Roman CAIUS. It is most commonly heard today in Denmark. Variants include **Kaj**. Also encountered as a Welsh version of CAIUS.

Kailash (m/f) Indian name derived from the Sanskrit *kailasa* (of uncertain meaning). In Indian mythology the name is borne by Shiva's paradise.

Kajetan *See* GAETANO.

Kaleigh/Kaley *See* KAYLEIGH.

Kalidas (m) Indian name derived from the Sanskrit *kali* ('black one') and *dasa* ('servant'), and thus meaning 'servant of Kali' – Kali being the name of the fearsome dark-skinned goddess who was Shiva's wife. Notable bearers of the name have included a celebrated 2nd- or 3rd-century Indian poet and playwright whose works were translated into English in the 18th century.

Kalle *See* CARL.

Kalpana (f) Indian name derived from the Sanskrit *kalpana* ('making' or 'fantasy'), also understood to mean 'ornament'. It appears in classical Indian religious texts and was taken up as a first name in medieval times in deference to feminine beauty.

Kalyan (m) Indian name derived from the Sanskrit *kalyana* ('beautiful' or 'auspicious'). A feminine form is **Kalyani**, as borne as an alternative name by Shiva's wife Durga.

Kamal (m) Arabic and Indian name derived from the Arabic *kamal* ('perfection'). When used by Indians it is usually traced back to the Sanskrit *kamala* ('pale-red'). Variants include **Kamil**. A feminine version of the name in use among Indians is **Kamala**, one of the alternate names borne by the goddess Lakshmi.

Kamala *See* KAMAL.

Kamil *See* KAMAL.

Kane (m) English first name derived from the Gaelic Cathán, itself derived from the Irish *cath* ('battle' or 'fighter'). Another derivation suggests it can also be traced to a Welsh word meaning 'beautiful'. It was first taken up by English speakers in the 1950s and is today more common in Australia and the USA than it is in the UK.

Kanta (f) Indian name derived from the Sanskrit *kanta* ('desired' or 'beautiful'). In classical Indian writings the name is often applied to wives or mistresses.

Kanti (f) Indian name derived from the Sanskrit *kanti* ('beauty'). In Indian mythology it is among the names borne by the goddesses Lakshmi and Durga among others.

Kapil (m) Indian name probably derived from the Sanskrit *kapi* ('monkey') and usually interpreted to mean 'monkey-coloured' or 'red-brown'. Well-known bearers of the name in ancient times included a celebrated sage, occasionally identified as Vishnu.

More recent examples include Indian cricketer Kapil Dev (b.1959).

Kar *See* KAREN.

Kara *See* CARA.

Karam *See* KARIM.

Karan (m) Indian name derived from the Sanskrit *karna* ('ear'). According to the *Mahabharata*, as Karna it was borne by a famous warrior-king of Anga who was eventually killed by his own half-brothers, who did not know who he really was. Today the name is popular chiefly in northern India, especially among Sikhs. *See also* KAREN.

Karel *See* CAROL; CHARLES.

Karen (f) English first name derived from a Danish diminutive of the English CATHERINE. An established favourite among Scandinavians for many years, it was adopted by English speakers in the USA in the 1920s, after it was imported with Scandinavian settlers. Subsequently it became a favourite choice on both sides of the Atlantic, reaching a peak in frequency in the 1960s, and is still popular, although less frequent today than it was. Notable bearers of the name have included the Danish author Karen Blixen (1885–1962), whose experiences in Africa provided the basis for the book *Out of Africa* (1937), and US pop singer Karen Carpenter (1950–83). Occasionally shortened to **Kar** or **Kaz**. Variant forms include **Karin** (originally Swedish), **Karyn**, **Carin**, **Caryn**, CARON, **Caronne**, CARINA, **Karena**, **Karina**, **Karyna** and **Keren**. *See also* CARA.

Karenza *See* KERENSA.

Karim (m) Arabic name derived from *karim* ('noble' or 'generous'). **Karam** is a variant used for both sexes. Another feminine version of the name is **Karima**.

Karin *See* KAREN.

Karina *See* CARINA; CATHERINE; KAREN.

Karita *See* CHARITY.

Karl *See* CARL.

Karla *See* CARLA.

Karlotte *See* CHARLOTTE.

Karol *See* CHARLES.

Karolina/Karoline *See* CAROLINE.

Karoly *See* CHARLES.

Karp (m) Russian first name derived from the Greek Karpos, itself from *karpos* ('fruit'). The original Greek name was a shortening of Karpophoros, meaning 'fruit-bearing'. The name appears in the Bible as that of a companion of St Paul.

Karsten *See* CHRISTIAN.

Karyn/Karyna *See* KAREN.

Kasey *See* CASEY.

Kasi (m) Indian name (pronounced 'carsee') derived from the Sanskrit *kasi* ('shining'). Closely linked with the worship of Shiva, it was the ancient name of Varanasi or Benares, a city well known as a place of pilgrimage, and was inevitably taken up as a name by people hailing from there.

Kasia *See* KEZIA.

Kasimir/Kasimira *See* CASIMIR.

Kaspar/Kasper *See* CASPAR.

Kat *See* CATHERINE; KATE; KATRINA.

Katarina *See* CATHERINE.

Kate (f) English first name that developed as a diminutive of CATHERINE and its many derivatives, such as KATHLEEN. It was first used by English speakers during the medieval period. It features twice in the plays of William Shakespeare, as the name of the central character of the comedy *The Taming of the Shrew* (c.1592), which was later turned into the popular Broadway musical *Kiss Me Kate*, and as the familiar name of the king's wife Katharine in *Henry V* (1599). It became increasingly popular throughout the English-speaking world towards the end of the 19th century, but suffered something of a decline in the middle of the 20th century before reviving once more from the 1970s.

Other notable bearers of the name have included the fictional Kate Hardcastle in Oliver Goldsmith's play *She Stoops to Conquer* (1773), British illustrator Kate Greenaway (1846–1901), British television reporter Kate Adie (Kathryn Adie; b.1945), British pop singer Kate Bush (Catherine Bush; b.1947), British model Kate Moss (b.1974) and British film actress Kate Winslet (b.1975). Also found as **Katie**, **Kati**, **Katy** and **Kaety**. **Kat** is a diminutive form.

Katerina/Kath/Katharine/Käthe/ Katherine *See* CATHERINE.

Kathleen (f) English version of the Irish Caitlin, itself derived from the English CATHERINE. The name was familiar on both sides of the Atlantic by the 19th century, when it was further promoted in the USA by the 1870s song 'I'll take you home again Kathleen'. It enjoyed peaks in popularity within the UK in the 1920s and again in the 1950s, but has since fallen out of favour. Well-known bearers of the name have included British contralto Kathleen Ferrier (1912–53) and US actress Kathleen Turner (b.1954). Variant forms include **Cathleen** and **Kathlyn**. Commonly shortened to **Kath**, **Kathy**, **Kati**, **Katie** or **Katy**.

Kathryn *See* CATHERINE.

Kathy *See* CATHERINE; KATHLEEN.

Kati *See* KATE.

Katie *See* KATE.

Katina/Katinka/Katrien *See* CATHERINE.

Katrina (f) Scottish variant of CATHERINE, probably descended via CATRIONA from the Italian Caterina. Since the middle of the 20th century the name has been encountered with increasing frequency elsewhere in the English-speaking world. Variants include **Katrine** and **Katriona**. **Kat** is a diminutive form.

Katrine/Katriona *See* KATRINA.

Katy *See* KATE.

Katya *See* CATHERINE.

Kausalya (f) Indian name derived from the Sanskrit *kausalya* ('of the Kosala people'). The name is borne by three queens in Indian mythology, one of whom became the mother of the hero Rama.

Kay (m/f) English first name that as a name for boys probably developed ultimately out of the Roman CAIUS, meaning 'rejoice'. It features in Arthurian legend as the name of Sir Kay, King Arthur's steward, and it may have been the unpleasant character of this knight of the Round Table that prevented the name being taken up on a significant scale among English speakers in succeeding centuries. Another character of the same name features in the Hans Christian Andersen story 'The Snow Queen'.

As a name for girls, it probably emerged initially as a simple abbreviation for any longer name beginning with C or K, including CATHERINE and its many derivatives. Also found as **Kaye,** it made its first appearances among English speakers towards the end of the 19th century and reached a peak in popularity during the 1960s before going out of favour.

Well-known bearers of the name have included US bandleader Kay Kyser (James King Kern Kyser; 1906–85) and British actress Kay Kendall (Justine McCarthy; 1927–59).

Kaye *See* KAY.

Kayla *See* KAYLEIGH.

Kayleigh (f) English and Irish first name (pronounced 'kaylee') that is thought to owe its modern popularity to the combination of KELLY or KYLIE and Leigh or LEE. The ultimate source of the name was the Irish O Caollaidhe (meaning 'descendant of Caoladhe'), itself derived from *caol* ('slender'). It enjoyed some popularity among English speakers in the 1970s and 1980s. Also found as **Kayley**, **Kaleigh**, **Kaylee**, **Kayly**, **Kayla** and KEELEY.

Kayley/Kayly *See* KAYLEIGH.

Kaylin (f) Irish first name meaning 'slender fair one'. An Anglicization of the original Irish Caoilfhinn or Caoilfhionn, it is also rendered in the forms **Kayline** and **Keelan**.

Kaz *See* KAREN.

Kazimierz *See* CASIMIR.

Kean (m) Irish first name that developed as an Anglicization of the Gaelic CIAN, meaning 'ancient', or of the Gaelic *cean* ('head'). It was once common in Ireland, where it was particularly associated with the O'Hara family. Also spelled **Keane** or KANE.

Keefe (m) Irish first name meaning 'noble'.

Keeley (f) English and Irish first name that may have evolved as a variant of the Irish names KEELIN and KAYLEIGH. Well-known bearers of the name in recent times have included the British actress Keeley Hawes (b.1976). Also found as **Keely**, **Keeleigh** and KEIGHLEY.

Keelin (f) Irish first name that evolved as an Anglicization of the Gaelic Caoilfhionn, itself derived from *caol* ('slender') and *fionn* ('white'). *See also* KEELEY.

Keenan (m) Irish first name derived from the Irish Gaelic for 'little ancient one'.

Kees *See* CORNELIUS.

Kegan (m) Irish first name meaning 'son of Egan' or alternatively 'little fiery one'. Sometimes considered an Irish equivalent of HUGH.

Keighley (f) English place name (from the town of Keighley in Yorkshire) that was subsequently adopted as a surname and occasional first name, possibly an altered form of KEELEY. Pronounced 'keethly'.

Keir (m) Scottish surname of uncertain origin that was taken up as a first name in the 19th century. One suggestion is that the name came originally from the Gaelic for 'swarthy'. Largely confined to Scotland, it became widely known through British trade unionist and politician Keir Hardie (James Keir Hardie; 1856–1915), the Labour Party leader whose mother had borne it as her maiden name.

Keiran *See* KIERAN.

Keith (m) Scottish surname that was subsequently taken up as a first name throughout the English-speaking world. The original surname had its roots in a Scottish place name (the town of Keith near Elgin in East Lothian), itself possibly derived from the Celtic word for 'wood' or 'windy place'. As a first name, it made its debut in the 19th century and enjoyed a peak in popularity among English speakers in the late 1950s. Well-known bearers of the name have included New Zealand Prime Minister Sir Keith Holyoake (1904–83), British journalist, novelist and playwright Keith Waterhouse (b.1929), British rock musician Keith Richards (b.1943) and British television chef Keith Floyd (b.1956). A rare feminine form of the name is **Keitha**.

Kelan (m) Irish first name representing an Anglicization of the Gaelic Caolan, itself derived from *caol* ('slender').

Kelcey *See* KELSEY.

Keld *See* KETTIL.

Kelda (f) Scandinavian first name meaning 'spring' or 'fountain'. It has made rare appearances in the English-speaking world in recent times.

Kelemen *See* CLEMENT.

Kelley/Kellie *See* KELLY.

Kelly (m/f) Irish surname that was taken up by English speakers as a first name for both sexes from the late 1950s. The usual Irish Gaelic form of the name is **Ceallagh**, meaning 'strife', 'war' or 'warlike'. Its emergence among English speakers may have been influenced initially by the popularity of US film actress Grace Kelly (1928–82), as a result of which it is today usually reserved for girls. Although it has fallen out of favour since the 1980s, it is still fairly popular in Australia. Well-known bearers of the name have included US film actress Kelly McGillis (b.1958). Also spelled **Kelley** or **Kellie**.

Kelsey (m/f) English surname derived from the Old English Ceolsige, itself from the Old English *ceol* ('ship') and *sige* ('victory'), that has appeared on an occasional basis as a first name for both sexes, chiefly since the 1870s. Famous bearers of the name in recent times have included US television actor Kelsey Grammer (b.1955), star of *Frasier*. Also found as **Kelsie** or **Kelcey**.

Kelvin (m) English first name that made its debut in the 1920s, possibly under the influence of such names as CALVIN and MELVIN. It may have had its roots ultimately in the Old English words for 'ship' and 'friend'. The Irish-born Scottish scientist Lord Kelvin of Largs (William Thomson; 1824–1907) acquired his title from the name of the River Kelvin in Scotland, originally thought to mean 'narrow water' in Gaelic. The name is more common in Canada than elsewhere in the English-speaking world.

Kemp (m) English surname in occasional use as a first name. The surname was originally a medieval tradename derived from the Middle English *kempe* ('athlete' or 'wrestler'), itself descended from the Old English *kempa* ('warrior' or 'champion').

Ken *See* KENDALL; KENNETH; KENYON.

Kena *See* KENINA.

Kendall (m) English place name (from Kendal in Cumbria) meaning 'valley of the River Kent' that was subsequently taken up as a surname and occasional first name from the middle of the 19th century. It is also possible that in some circumstances the name evolved from the place name Kendale (in Humberside), itself derived from the Old Norse *keld* ('spring'), or else from the Old Welsh name Cynnddelw, of obscure meaning. Commonly shortened to **Ken**. Also spelled **Kendal**.

Kendra *See* KENDRICK.

Kendrick (m) Welsh and Scottish surname that was taken up as a first name among English speakers around the middle of the 19th century. The original Welsh source was probably the Old Welsh Cynwrig, possibly derived from the Old Celtic for 'high summit'. As used among English speakers it probably evolved from the Old English Ceneric or Cyneric, itself derived from *cene* ('keen' or 'bold') and *ric* ('power'). **Kenrick** is a variant form of chiefly historical interest, recorded throughout medieval times and as late as the 17th century. **Kendra** is a rare feminine version.

Kenelm (m) English first name descended from the Old English Cenelm, itself derived from the Old English *cene* ('bold' or 'keen') and *helm* ('helmet' or 'protection') and thus meaning 'bold defender'. It was fairly common in England during the medieval period but has been only very rarely encountered in modern times. Notable bearers of the name have included the 9th-century St Kenelm of Mercia and the English writer, adventurer and diplomat Sir Kenelm Digby (1603–65).

Kenia *See* KENINA.

Kenina (f) English first name that developed as a feminine version of KENNETH. It was once fairly common in Scotland, but is rarely encountered today. Also found as **Kena**, **Kenna** or **Kenia**.

Kennard (m) English first name that evolved from an Old English name derived from *cene* ('keen' or 'bold') or *cyne* ('royal') and *weard* ('guard') or *heard* ('brave' or 'hardy'). It became rare during medieval times except as a surname but made occasional reappearances as a first name in the 19th and 20th centuries. An historical variant is **Kenward**.

Kennedy (m/f) Irish, Scottish and English surname that was taken up as a first name throughout the English-speaking world from the middle of the 20th century. It evolved as an Anglicization of the Irish

Gaelic Cinneidigh, derived from *ceann* ('head') and *eidigh* ('ugly') and thus meaning 'ugly head', and also as an Anglicized version of the Scottish Gaelic Uarraig. It is occasionally applied to females. It was chosen as a first name by many Americans in the 1960s in tribute to the assassinated President John F. Kennedy (1917–63).

Kenneth (m) Scottish and English first name that is thought to have evolved out of the Gaelic names Cinead (meaning 'born of fire') and Cainneach (meaning 'handsome one') and thus interpreted to mean 'fair and fiery'. It was taken up more widely by English speakers around the middle of the 19th century and enjoyed a peak in popularity in the UK in the 1920s and in the USA in the 1950s. Notable bearers of the name have included two early Scottish kings, Scottish children's writer Kenneth Grahame (1859–1932), British actor Kenneth More (1914–82), Zambian President Kenneth Kaunda (b.1924), British comedian Kenneth Williams (1926–88) and Northern Ireland-born actor Kenneth Branagh (b.1960). The name is commonly shortened to **Ken** or **Kenny** – as borne by British film director Ken Russell (b.1927), British comedian Ken Dodd (b.1931), US writer Ken Kesey (b.1935) and US country singer Kenny Rogers (b.1938). Variants include **Kennith**, **Kenith** and the Welsh **Cenydd**. *See also* KENINA.

Kenny *See* KENNETH.

Kenrick *See* KENDRICK.

Kent (m) English surname that was subsequently taken up as an occasional first name. It may have had its origins in the name of the English county of Kent, itself originally meaning 'border'. It appears to have made its first appearance in the middle of the 20th century and has remained confined largely to Canada and the USA. It is also sometimes employed as a shortened form of the Scandinavian **Kennet** (a variant of KENNETH).

Kentigern (m) English name derived from a Celtic name meaning 'chief lord'. The name is best known from the 7th-century St Kentigern, who served as bishop of Glasgow. As a result of this connection, the name was popular in the Glasgow area until well into the 18th century. *See also* MUNGO.

Kenton (m) English place name derived from the river name Kenn or else from the Old English *cena* ('keen') or *cyne* ('royal') and the Old English *tun* ('settlement') that was subsequently taken up as a surname and occasional first name. Sometimes interpreted to mean 'royal manor'. Rare today, it has received a boost in modern times as the name of a character in the long-running popular British radio soap opera *The Archers*.

Kenward *See* KENNARD.

Kenyon (m) English place name (from Lancashire) derived from the Old English for 'Ennion's mound' that has subsequently been adopted as a surname and occasional first name. Sometimes shortened to **Ken**.

Keren *See* KAREN; KERENHAPPUCH.

Kerena *See* KERENHAPPUCH.

Kerenhappuch (f) Biblical name derived from the Hebrew for 'horn of kohl' (kohl being a type of cosmetic) that was taken up by English Puritans in the 17th century. It features in the Bible as the name of the youngest of Job's beautiful daughters. It has made rare appearances among English speakers in succeeding centuries, often shortened to **Keren** or **Kerena**.

Kerensa (f) English first name of Cornish origin, meaning 'love' or 'affection'. Variants include **Kerenza** and **Karenza**.

Keri *See* KERRY.

Kermit (m) English version of the Gaelic surname **Mac Dhiarmaid** meaning 'son of Diarmad' (*see* DERMOT). It was taken up by English speakers in the USA in the 19th century. A notable bearer of the name was the US soldier and entrepreneur Kermit Roosevelt (1889–1943), son of President Theodore Roosevelt. In modern times the name has become indelibly associated with Kermit the Frog, a puppet character in the 1970s US children's television series *The Muppet Show*.

Kerr (m) English place name derived from the Old Norse *kjarr* ('rough ground with brushwood') that was subsequently taken up as a surname and occasional first name.

Kerri/Kerrie *See* KERRY.

Kerry (m/f) English surname probably derived from the name of the Irish county of Kerry (meaning 'descendants of Ciar') that was subsequently taken up as a first name throughout the English-speaking world in the early 20th century. Having established itself as a favourite boys' name in Australia, it enjoyed a peak in popularity among English speakers elsewhere between the 1960s and the 1980s, chiefly as a name for girls (although it continued to make occasional appearances as a boys' name). Also found as **Kerrie**, **Kerri**, **Keri** or CERI. Well-known bearers of the name have included Australian businessman Kerry Packer (b.1937) and New Zealand novelist Keri Hulme (b.1947).

Kerstin *See* KIRSTEN.

Keshia *See* KEZIA.

Kester (m) Scottish version of CHRISTOPHER. Fairly common in medieval times, it enjoyed a substantial revival in the 20th century.

Kestrel (f) English first name derived from the Old French *cressele* ('rattle'). Popularly associated with the name of the bird of prey, it enjoyed a minor revival in the 20th century.

Kettil (m) Swedish name derived from the Old Norse *ketill* ('cauldron'). It is often used in combination with other names, as in **Thorketill**. It also appears in the form **Kjell**. Other variants include the Norwegian **Kjetil** and the Danish **Kjeld** or **Keld**.

Keturah (f) Biblical name meaning 'incense' or 'fragrance' in Hebrew. It features in the Bible as the name of Abraham's second wife and has consequently made occasional appearances among English speakers since the Reformation.

Kev/Kevan *See* KEVIN.

Kevin (m) English and Irish first name derived from the Gaelic Caoimhin, itself from the Irish Gaelic Caoimhinn ('handsome at birth'), itself based on *caomh* ('comely' or 'fair'). The name was confined to Ireland until the early 20th century when it was first taken up by English speakers on a wider basis. It reached a peak in popularity in the 1960s but has since fallen out of fashion and has even become the subject of ridicule (a 'Kevin' being anyone lacking intelligence or sophistication in 1980s slang). Well-known bearers of the name have included a 7th-century Irish saint remembered as the patron saint of Dublin, US film actor Kevin Kline (b.1947), British footballer Kevin Keegan (b.1951) and US film actor Kevin Costner (b.1955). Commonly shortened to **Kev**. Also found as **Kevan**.

Kez *See* KEZIA.

Kezia (f) Biblical name derived from the Hebrew Qetsiah, meaning 'cassia' (the name of a tree that produces cinnamon). It appears in the Bible as the name of the second of Job's three beautiful daughters and was consequently among the many biblical names taken up by the Puritans in the 17th century. Sometimes shortened to **Kez**, **Kiz**, **Kizzie**, **Kizzy**, **Kissie** or **Kissy**. Also spelled **Keziah** – as borne by Keziah Wesley (d.1741), sister of the 18th-century English Methodist leader John Wesley – and as **Keshia**, **Cassia** or **Kasia**.

Keziah *See* KEZIA.

Khadija (f) Arabic name derived from *khadija* ('premature child'). Records of the name go back to pre-Islamic times but it is most famous today as the name of Muhammad's respected first wife – an identification that has resulted in the name remaining consistently popular throughout the Islamic world over succeeding centuries, right up to the present day. Variant forms include **Khadiga**.

Khalid (m) Arabic name derived from *khalid* ('eternal'). The name was borne in the 7th century by the military commander Khalid ibn al-Walid, who won the praise of Muhammad himself for his conquests on behalf of Islam. As a result of this association the name has long been one of the most popular of all Arabic names. More recent bearers of the name have included King Khalid of Saudi Arabia (1913–81), ruler of the country from 1975 to 1981. **Khalida** is a rare feminine form of the name.

Khalifa (m) Arabic name derived from *khalifa* ('caliph' or 'successor'). The name was often used to refer to the successors of Muhammad and thus acquired strong religious significance. In the 16th century the title caliph was taken up by the Ottoman sultans, whose so-called 'caliphate' was not finally abolished until 1924.

Khalil (m) Arabic name derived from *khalil* ('bosom friend'). An Indian variant is **Khaleel**.

Khayrat (m) Arabic name derived from *khayra* ('good deed').

Khayri (m) Arabic name derived from *khayri* ('benevolent'). A feminine form of the name is **Khayriyya**.

Khurshid (m) Indian name derived from the Persian *khurshid* ('sun'). A Muslim name, it is intended to suggest that the bearer has a bright, sunny disposition.

Khwaja (m) Indian name derived from the Persian *khwaja* ('lord' or 'master'). The name was borne by a Muslim prophet who is sometimes identified with the biblical Elijah.

Kiaran *See* KIERAN.

Kid (m) English nickname that has gradually won acceptance as a legitimate first name, especially in the USA. Originally a nickname for any man notable for his youthful good looks, it evokes memories of the Wild West and the various legendary outlaws who bore the name, such as Billy the Kid. It remains confined largely to Canada and the USA. Well-known bearers of the name since the early 20th century have included the US bandleader Kid Ory (Edward Ory; 1886–1973).

Kiera *See* KIERAN.

Kieran (m) English version of the Gaelic Ciaran, itself derived from the Irish *ciar* ('black') and usually interpreted to mean 'little dark-haired one'. The name was largely confined to Ireland until the middle of the 20th century when it began to be taken up more widely among English speakers. Notable bearers of the name have included twenty-six Irish saints. Also spelled **Kieron**, **Cieran**, **Keiran**, **Kiaran** or **Kyran**. **Kiera**, **Ciera**, **Ciara** and **Kiara** are rare feminine versions of the name.

Kilie *See* KYLIE.

Killian (m) Irish first name that represents an Anglicization of the Irish Gaelic **Cillian**, meaning 'church'. It was borne by several early Irish saints. Also encountered as **Kilian**.

Kim (m/f) English first name that evolved as a diminutive form of KIMBERLEY. In Scandinavia it may also be encountered as an abbreviated form of Joakim (*see* JOACHIM). It emerged among English speakers as a name in its own right towards the end of the 19th century, when it was usually given as a masculine name – as given by the central character, a young Indian boy, in Rudyard Kipling's novel *Kim* (1901). In Kipling's book it was explained that the full version of the boy's name was **Kimball** – originally a surname probably derived from the Old English *cynebeald* ('kin bold'). From the 1920s the name became well known as a name for girls, particularly in the USA, again as an abbreviation of Kimberley. It enjoyed a peak in popularity on both sides of the Atlantic in the 1960s.

Notable bearers of the name have included (among males) British spy Kim Philby (Harold Adrian Russell Philby; 1912–88) and British cricketer Kim Barnett (b.1960) and (among females) US actresses Kim Novak (Marilyn Novak; b.1933) and Kim Basinger (Kimila Basinger; b.1954) and British pop singer Kim Wilde (b.1960). Sometimes spelled **Kym**. Diminutive forms of the name include **Kimmy** and **Kimmie**.

Kimball See KIM.

Kimberley (m/f) English first name derived from the name of the South African town of Kimberley. The town was itself named after British statesman John Wodehouse, 1st Earl of Kimberley, whose family came from a place in England called Kimberley (meaning 'Cyneburga's wood' in Old English). It was taken up as a first name in celebration of the British army's relief of the town from siege in 1900 during the course of the Boer War. Like its diminutive form KIM, it was used initially as a boys' name but later came to be adopted as a name for girls, chiefly from the 1940s. It enjoyed a peak in popularity in the 1980s and 1990s. Also encountered in the forms **Kimberleigh** and **Kimberly** (the usual spelling of the name in Canada and the USA).

Kimmie/Kimmy See KIM.

Kinborough (f) English name derived from the Old English for 'royal fortress'. As **Cyneburga** it was borne by a 7th-century English abbess from Northamptonshire who was later venerated as a saint. It remained in use in England until the 18th century but now appears to be defunct.

King (m) English first name derived from the royal title that has gradually won acceptance since the 19th century, chiefly in the USA. It evolved in parallel with such equivalent names as DUKE and EARL, presumably in the belief that the bearer would thereby be distinguished by aristocratic qualities. Early in its history it was probably borne chiefly by servants in royal households. Its popularity among US Blacks since the 1960s owes much to the reputation of the US Black civil rights leader Martin Luther King (1929–68). Other well-known bearers of the name have included US jazz musician King Oliver (Joseph Oliver; 1885–1938) and US film director King Vidor (1894–1982).

Kingsley (m) English place name (from Cheshire, Hampshire and Staffordshire) that was subsequently taken up as a surname and first name. The original place name meant 'king's wood' in Old English. It was taken up by English speakers around the middle of the 19th century, perhaps promoted by the popularity of British novelist Charles Kingsley (1819–75). Notable bearers of the name have included British novelist Kingsley Amis (1922–95).

Kiran (m) Indian name derived from the Sanskrit *kirana* ('dust' or 'thread') and usually interpreted to mean 'ray of light'. It appears to have been a medieval invention.

Kirby (m/f) English place name derived from the Old Norse *kirkja* ('church') that was subsequently taken up as a surname and, from the 19th century, as an occasional first name borne by both sexes.

Kirill See CYRIL.

Kirk (m) Scottish and English place name that was subsequently adopted as a surname and then as a first name among English speakers around the middle of the 19th century. The original place name came from the Old Norse *kirkja* ('church') and the surname was usually reserved for people living near a church. As a first name it enjoyed a peak in popularity in the 1980s. Well-known bearers of the name have included US film actor Kirk Douglas (Issur Danielovitch Demsky; b.1916).

Kirsten (f) Scandinavian version of CHRISTINE that was taken up as a first name among English speakers during the 19th century. It became increasingly frequent in the English-speaking world from the 1950s. Famous bearers of the name have included

Norwegian soprano Kirsten Flagstad (1895–1962). Commonly shortened to KIRSTY. Also encountered as **Kirstin** and **Kirsteen**.

Kirstie See KIRSTY.

Kirstin See KIRSTEN.

Kirsty (f) English first name that is thought to have developed as a Scottish diminutive of CHRISTINE. Early instances of its appearance in the English-speaking world included its use in the form **Kirstie** as a familiar version of CHRISTINA in the Robert Louis Stevenson novel *The Weir of Hermiston* (1896). It won wide acceptance as a first name in its own right in the 1960s. Well-known bearers of the name in its two variant forms in modern times have included Scottish television presenter Kirsty Wark (b.1955), US television actress Kirstie Alley (b.1955) and Scottish singer-songwriter Kirsty MacColl (1959–2000). *See also* KIRSTEN.

Kishen See KRISHNA.

Kishore (m) Indian name derived from the Sanskrit *kisora* ('colt'). **Kishori** is a feminine version of the name and is usually interpreted as meaning 'filly'.

Kissie/Kissy See KEZIA.

Kistna See KRISHNA.

Kit See CHRISTOPHER.

Kitty (f) English first name that developed as a diminutive of CATHERINE and its variant derivatives, such as KATHLEEN. It emerged as a familiar form of these names among English speakers in the 18th century and has remained popular ever since (chiefly in the USA). Well-known bearers of the name have included English actress Kitty Clive (1711–85), the fictional Kitty Bennet in Jane Austen's novel *Pride and Prejudice* (1813), British tennis player Kitty Godfree (1896–1992) and US country singer Kitty Wells (Muriel Ellen Deason; b.1919).

Kiz/Kizzie/Kizzy See KEZIA.

Kjeld/Kjell See KETTIL.

Klaas/Klaes See CLAUS.

Klara See CLARA.

Klaudia See CLAUDIA.

Klaus See CLAUS.

Klemens/Kliment See CLEMENT.

Knud See KNUT.

Knut (m) Scandinavian first name (pronounced 'kunoot') derived from the Old Norse Knutr, itself possibly from *knutr* ('knot') or else from the Old German *knt* ('kind' or 'race'). The name was originally reserved for men of short, stocky build but is now frequently borne by males in Denmark and Norway regardless of their stature. Notable bearers of the name have included two kings named Knut (or **Canute**). Usually spelled in Danish as **Knud**.

Kodey/Kody See CODY.

Kolya See NICHOLAS.

Konrad See CONRAD.

Konstantin/Konstantyn See CONSTANTINE.

Kora See CORA.

Korbinian (m) German first name derived ultimately from the Latin *corvus* ('raven'). It is best known as the name of a 7th-century Frankish saint who lived at Freising near Munich. **Körble** is a familiar form of the name.

Korey/Korrie/Kory See COREY.

Kornel See CORNELIUS.

Kort See KURT.

Kostya See CONSTANTINE.

Kreszenz (f) German first name (pronounced 'krechence') derived from the Latin Crescentia, itself from the Latin *crescere* ('to grow'). According to German tradition it is a lucky name that guarantees the child concerned will always enjoy robust health. **Zenzi** is a familiar version of the name.

Kriemhild (f) German first name derived from *grim* ('mask') and *hild* ('battle'). It appears in the *Nibelungenlied* legends as the name of Siegfried's wife. Also found as **Kriemhilde** and **Krimhilde**.

Kris *See* CHRISTOPHER.

Krishna (m) Indian name derived from the Sanskrit *krsna* ('black' or 'dark'). As the name of the most popular and widely venerated of all Hindu gods, it has unique religious significance for Indians. **Kistna** is a variant found in central India. **Kishen** is a modern version of the name now common in northern India. **Kannan** is another variant form.

Kristeen *See* CHRISTINE.

Kristen/Kristian *See* CHRISTIAN.

Kristie *See* CHRISTIE.

Kristin/Kristine *See* CHRISTINE.

Kristina *See* CHRISTINA.

Kristoffer *See* CHRISTOPHER.

Krystal/Krystle *See* CRYSTAL.

Krystof *See* CHRISTOPHER.

Krystyna *See* CHRISTINA.

Krzysztof *See* CHRISTOPHER.

Kumar (m) Indian name derived from the Sanskrit *kumara* ('boy' or 'son'). Borne in Indian mythology by one of the sons of Shiva, it is sometimes interpreted to mean 'prince'. **Kumari** is a feminine form of the name, taken to mean 'maiden' or 'warrior'.

Kumari *See* KUMAR.

Kunigunde (f) German first name derived from the Old Germanic *kuoni* ('brave') and *guard* ('strife'). It was borne by an 11th-century saint, the wife of Holy Roman Emperor Henry II and, as **Cunégonde**, by the heroine of Voltaire's satirical novel, *Candide* (1759). Sometimes shortened to **Kinge** or **Kinga**. Variants in other languages include

the Dutch **Kunigonde** or **Cunegonde**.

Kurt (m) German first name that evolved as a diminutive of Konrad (*see* CONRAD). It was taken up on a limited scale among English speakers in the 1950s. Famous bearers of the name have included German-born US composer Kurt Weill (1900–1955), US novelist Kurt Vonnegut (b.1922) and US rock singer Kurt Cobain (1965–94). Also encountered as **Curt**. Variants in other languages include the Dutch **Kort**.

Kyle (m/f) English first name derived from a Scottish surname, itself based on a place name from Ayrshire derived from the Gaelic *caol* ('narrow'), as applied to narrow straits or channels. When it was first taken up by English speakers in the 1940s it was usually bestowed upon boys, but from the 1960s it has appeared with increasing regularity as a name for girls, often being treated as a diminutive of KYLIE. Well-known bearers of the name have included US actor Kyle MacLachlan (b.1959).

Kylie (f) Australian first name that has become more widely accepted throughout the English-speaking world since the late 1970s. The name is popularly associated with the Aborigine word for 'boomerang' but it probably in fact evolved from KYLE or possibly KELLY. Its popularity in the UK in the 1980s owed much to the huge success enjoyed by the imported Australian television soap opera *Neighbours*, in which one of the main characters was played by Australian actress Kylie Minogue (b.1968), who was subsequently launched as an international pop star. Occasionally spelled **Kyly**, **Kilie** or **Kyleigh**.

Kym *See* KIM.

Kynaston (m) English place name derived from the Old English meaning 'settlement of Cynefrith' that was subsequently taken up as a surname and first name in medieval times.

Kyra *See* CYRUS.

Kyran *See* KIERAN.

L

Laban (m) Hebrew name meaning 'white'. It features in the Bible, in the form Labhan, as that of the father of Jacob's wives Leah and Rebecca. As a result of its biblical connections it was taken up by English Puritans in the 17th century but is rare today. There is a character called Laban Tall in Thomas Hardy's novel *Far From the Madding Crowd* (1874).

Labhrainn/Labhras *See* LAURENCE.

Lacey (m/f) English surname that has made occasional appearances as a first name among English speakers since medieval times. The original source of the surname was a Norman place name, Lassy in Calvados. When used as a feminine name it is often assumed that there is a link with the ordinary vocabulary word 'lace'. Also found as **Lacy,** usually when adopted as a masculine name.

Lachlan (m) English version of the Scottish Lachlann or Lochlann which means 'land of lochs' or 'land of fjords' and was originally reserved for settlers from Norway. Another derivation suggests the name originally came from the Gaelic *laochail* ('warlike'). The name has retained its Scottish associations into modern times but is now encountered much more widely, particularly in Australia and Canada and other countries that received many Scottish emigrants. Notable bearers have included the British colonial administrator Lachlan Macquarie (1761–1824), who served as governor of New South Wales. Sometimes shortened to **Lachie** or, in Canada, to **Lockie**. A rare feminine equivalent of the name in Scotland is **Lachina**.

Lachtna (m) Irish first name derived from the Gaelic for 'milk-coloured'. It features in

Irish legend as the name of an ancestor of King Brian Boru.

Lacy *See* LACEY.

Ladislao/Ladislas *See* LASZLO.

Laelia (f) Roman name meaning 'cheerful' or 'chatty'. Also found as a variant of AURELIA. It was borne by a 5th-century Irish saint, and was taken up by English speakers in the 19th century. Also found as **Lelia** – as in George Sand's novel *Lélia* (1833). Other variant spellings include **Lela**.

Laetitia *See* LETITIA.

Laila *See* LEILA.

Laird (m) Scottish name meaning 'landowner'. It has made rare appearances as a first name, mostly in the USA.

Lajos *See* LOUIS.

Lakshman (m) Indian name derived from the Sanskrit *laksmana* ('having auspicious marks'). It appears in the *Mahabharata* and in the *Ramayana*, in which the name became identified with the qualities of brotherly love. Occasionally found in the variant form **Laxman**.

Lakshmi (f) Indian name derived from the Sanskrit *laksmi* ('mark' or 'sign'). In Indian legend the goddess Lakshmi, Vishnu's wife, represents beauty, good luck and wealth. Occasionally encountered in the form **Laxmi**.

Lal (m) Indian name derived from the Sanskrit *lal* ('to play' or 'to caress') or else from the Prakrit *lala* ('king'). It is commonly used by modern Hindus as a term of endearment meaning 'darling'. *See also* LALAGE.

Lala (f) Slav name meaning 'tulip flower'.

Also encountered as a familiar version of HELEN.

Lalage (f) Greek name derived from *lalagein* ('to chatter' or 'to babble'). Usually pronounced 'lalagee', it featured in the *Odes* of the 1st-century BC Roman poet Horace and appeared sporadically among English speakers from the 19th century. There is a character with the name in John Fowles' novel *The French Lieutenant's Woman* (1969). Diminutive forms of the name include **Lal**, LALA, **Lallie** and **Lally**.

Lalita (f) Indian name derived from the Sanskrit *lalita* ('amorous' or 'charming'). Borne by one of Krishna's lovers, it is also one of the names borne by Shiva's wife Durga. Also found in the variant form **Lalit**.

Lalla/Lallie/Lally *See* EULALIA; LALAGE.

Lambert (m) English, French, German and Dutch name derived from the Old German *lant* ('land') and *berht* ('famous' or 'bright') and thus meaning 'famous landowner'. The name was borne by a 7th-century saint living in Flanders and came to England with the Normans. It became increasingly frequent during medieval times under the influence of Dutch immigrants, sometimes appearing as **Lambard**, and was still in occasional use as late as the beginning of the 20th century. Notable bearers of the name have included English imposter Lambert Simnel (1475–1535), who made a fraudulent claim to the throne of England as Edward VI, and the central character Lambert Strether in *The Ambassadors* (1903) by Henry James. Sometimes shortened to BERT. Variants in other languages include the Dutch **Lammert** and the German **Lamprecht**.

Lana (f) English name derived either via Alana from ALAN, meaning 'shining', 'harmony' or 'rock', or else as an independent name without any particular meaning. Russians sometimes use it as an abbreviation of SVETLANA. It seems to have made its first appearance, in the USA, in the 1920s and became well known in the 1940s as the name of US actress Lana Turner (Julia Turner; 1920–95).

Lance (m) English name that exists either as a diminutive of LANCELOT or as a name in its own right, derived from the Old German *lant* ('land') or possibly from the French *lance* ('lance'). It was recorded in use in England by the 13th century, when it also appeared as **Launce**, but was subsequently eclipsed by Lancelot or Launcelot. It was revived by English speakers towards the end of the 19th century. Well-known bearers of the name have included British actor Lance Percival (b.1933). Diminutive forms include **Lancelin** and the German **Lanzo**.

Lancelot (m) English first name possibly derived from the old French *l'ancelle* ('servant') or else from an unknown Celtic name. Also spelled **Launcelot**, it became famous as the name of Sir Lancelot, the most prominent of King Arthur's Knights of the Round Table (thought to have been created by Chrétien de Troyes as the character does not feature in earlier Arthurian mythology). Other bearers of the name in literature have included William Shakespeare's Launcelot Gobbo in *The Merchant of Venice* (1596–8) and the central character in Tobias Smollett's *The Life and Adventures of Sir Launcelot Greaves* (1762). It is rare today. Commonly shortened to LANCE or, formerly, to **Launce** – as borne by a character in Shakespeare's *Two Gentlemen of Verona* (1592–3).

Lanty *See* LAURENCE.

Laoise *See* LUCY.

Lara (f) English version of the Russian Larissa, which itself is thought to have come from the name of an ancient Greek city (meaning 'citadel') or else from the Latin for 'cheerful'. Also found as a variant of LAURA. The name was borne in Roman myth by a nymph who was punished by Jupiter after she declined to assist him in his amorous pursuits and exiled to the Underworld, becoming mother of the

Roman household gods called the Lares. The name was popularized throughout the English-speaking world in the late 1960s and 1970s by a character called Lara in the film *Doctor Zhivago* (1965), based on the novel (1957) by Boris Pasternak. Notable bearers of the name since then have included US actress Lara Flynn Boyle (b.1970).

Laraine *See* LORRAINE.

Larissa *See* LARA.

Lark (f) English first name derived from the name of the songbird. It has made rare appearances among English speakers since the early 20th century.

Larrie/Larry *See* LAURENCE.

Lars (m) Scandinavian variant of LAURENCE. It emerged as one of the most popular of all masculine names in Scandinavia in the 1960s and 1970s.

Lasse *See* LAURENCE.

Laszlo (m) Hungarian version of the Polish WLADYSLAW. The name was borne by an 11th-century king of Hungary who was long admired for his chivalric behaviour. Variants include the Italian **Ladislao** and the Latinate **Ladislas** or **Ladislaus**.

Lata (f) Indian name derived from the Sanskrit *lata*, the name of a creeping plant. Through this botanical association, it is often interpreted to mean 'curvy' or 'sinuous' and has thus become identified with notions of feminine beauty.

Latasha (f) English first name apparently resulting from a combination of LATISHA and NATASHA. It first established itself as a favourite within the Black population of the USA in the early 1980s and is just one of several similar names that were created by adding the prefix 'La-' to existing names (others including **Lakisha** and **Latoya**).

Latimer (m) English first name derived from the Old French for 'interpreter'

Latisha (f) English first name of relatively recent invention, probably influenced by LETITIA. Sometimes shortened to **Tisha**. *See also* LATASHA.

Latoya *See* LATASHA.

Launce/Launcelot
See LANCE; LANCELOT.

Laura (f) English, Spanish and Italian first name derived from the Latin *laurus* ('laurel' or 'bay'). In ancient Rome victorious emperors wore crowns of laurel leaves and the name thus became associated with the notions of 'victory' or 'triumph'. The love poetry that the 14th-century Italian poet Petrarch addressed to 'Laura' – in reality probably Laure de Sade (Laure de Noves; 1308–48) – did much to make the name popular in medieval Europe, especially in literary contexts. Other medieval forms of the name included Lora. It made its debut as a first name among English speakers around the 16th century and subsequently enjoyed peaks in popularity in the 19th century and again from the 1960s.

Notable bearers of the name have included a 9th-century Spanish martyr, British artist Dame Laura Knight (1877–1970), British fashion designer Laura Ashley (1925–85) and US film actress Laura Dern (b.1967). **Laurie**, **Lowri**, **Lori** and **Lolly** are all familiar forms of the name. **Loreen**, **Laurene**, **Lorena**, **Laurice**, **Laurissa**, **Laurina**, **Laurinda**, **Lorelle**, **Lorinda** and **Lorita** are among diminutive versions. Variants in other languages include the French **Laurie**, the Catalan **Llora** and the German **Lore**. *See also* LAUREN; LAURETTA.

Lauraine *See* LORRAINE.

Laureen *See* LAURA.

Laurel (f) English first name, derived from the name of the tree, that has become increasingly frequent since the middle of the 20th century. The early development of the name is thought to have been influenced by LAURA and it is sometimes considered to be a straightforward variant of that name. Also found as **Laurelle**. **Laurie** can appear as a shortened form.

Lauren (f) English first name that developed as a variant of LAURA. It appeared with increasing frequency among English speakers from the 1960s, familiar from the name of US film actress Lauren Bacall (Betty Joan Perske; b.1924), and reached a peak in popularity in the 1990s. Occasionally encountered as **Loren** (the usual spelling when the name is, rarely, given to boys).

Laurence (m) English first name derived ultimately from the Latin Laurentius, which means 'man from Laurentum' (Laurentum being a town in Latium that probably took its name from 'laurel'). It was borne by a 3rd-century Roman saint who according to tradition was burnt to death on a gridiron. An English saint also bore the name in the 7th century, and its connection with the 12th-century Archbishop of Dublin St Laurence O'Toole made it lastingly popular in Ireland – although the archbishop's name was originally Lorcan (meaning 'fierce'). The name became more frequent in England in medieval times but subsequently fell from favour. Also appearing (since the 16th century) as **Lawrence,** it was revived in the 19th century and became increasingly popular in the 20th century on both sides of the Atlantic, promoted by among others the celebrated British soldier and writer T. E. Lawrence ('Lawrence of Arabia'; 1888–1935). The 'w' spelling is now the usual rendering of the name in the USA and Canada.

Notable bearers of the name in its two forms have included British artist Sir Lawrence Alma-Tadema (1836–1912), British actor Sir Laurence Olivier (1907–89) and British novelist Lawrence Durrell (1912–90). The usual shortened version of the name is **Larry** (or **Larrie**) – as borne by US harmonica player Larry Adler (Lawrence Adler; 1914–2001), British television presenter Larry Grayson (William White; 1923–95) and US actor Larry Hagman (b.1930). Other abbreviated versions include **Lauri, Laurie, Lawrie** (or **Lori**) – as borne by British novelist Laurie Lee (1914–97) – as well as **Loren, Lorin,**

Lorrin, Lol, Laz and the Irish **Lanty**. Variants in other languages include the Irish Gaelic **Labhras,** the Scottish Gaelic **Labhrainn,** the French **Laurent,** the Italian **Lorenzo,** the Spanish **Lorencio,** the German **Lorenz** (shortened to **Lenz**), the Dutch **Lorens** and **Laurens,** the Russian **Lavrenti,** the Finnish **Lasse** (or **Lassi**) and the Scandinavian LARS. **Laurencia** and **Laurentia** are infrequent feminine versions of the name.

Laurencia See LAURENCE.

Laurene See LAURA.

Laurens/Laurent/Laurentia
See LAURENCE.

Lauretta (f) Diminutive version of LAURA. It made its first appearances in medieval times but did not appear with any frequency among English speakers until the middle of the 19th century. Sometimes shortened to **Laurie** or **Lorrie**. Variants include **Lorette** and **Laurette. Loretta** – as borne by US actress Loretta Young (Gretchen Young; 1913–2000) – is the most popular form of the name in Canada and the USA.

Laurette See LAURETTA.

Lauri/Laurie See LAURA; LAUREL; LAURENCE; LAURETTA.

Laurina/Laurinda/Laurissa/Laurita
See LAURA.

Lavena See LAVINIA.

Lavender (f) English first name derived from that of the scented plant. Like a number of other flower names it was taken up by English speakers towards the end of the 19th century. It is very rare today.

Laverne (f) English first name that resulted from the addition of the prefix 'La-' to the established VERNE. This was one of a series of names that appeared by a similar process in the middle of the 20th century, chiefly in the USA. The fact that there was an ancient Italian goddess of thieves called Laverna is almost certainly coincidental.

Lavina *See* LAVINIA.

Lavinia (f) Roman name derived from the name of the ancient Roman town of Lavinium (itself of unknown origin). According to legend, Lavinia was the name of the wife of Aeneas, and thus that of the mother of the Roman people. Long considered an aristocratic name, it was popular during the late Renaissance, then went out of fashion for a time before being taken up by English speakers once more in the 18th century. Notable bearers of the name in literature have included characters in William Shakespeare's *Titus Andronicus* (1590–94), Charles Dickens' *David Copperfield* (1849–50) and Henry James' *Washington Square* (1880). Sometimes shortened to **Vinnie** or **Vinny**. **Lavina** and **Lavena** are variant forms.

Lavrenti/Lawrence/Lawrie
See LAURENCE.

Lawson (m) English surname that was taken up on an occasional basis as a first name around the middle of the 19th century. The surname itself evolved from Law, a nickname derived from Lawrence.

Laxman *See* LAKSHMAN.

Laxmi *See* LAKSHMI.

Layla (f) Arabic name meaning 'wine' or 'intoxication'. The name became widely familiar throughout the Arabic world through the poetry of Qays ibn-al-Mulawwah (d.688), whose works were often addressed to his cousin Layla. Many centuries later the name enjoyed a new lease of life among English speakers through the classic Eric Clapton hit single 'Layla' (1970), which was addressed to George Harrison's wife Pattie Boyd, who subsequently married Clapton. *See also* LEILA.

Layton *See* LEIGHTON.

Laz *See* LAURENCE.

Lazarus (m) Biblical name derived via the Greek Lazaros and the Aramaic Lazar from the Hebrew Eleazar or Eliezer (meaning

'God has helped' or 'God is my help'). In the Bible the name is borne by a diseased beggar and by the brother of Mary and Martha whom Jesus raises from the dead. Because of its link with the biblical beggar, described as 'full of sores', the name came to be associated with lepers in medieval times and was thus an unpopular choice of name. It has made sporadic appearances among English-speakers since the 17th century but is rarely if ever encountered today outside the Jewish community. Variants in other languages include the French **Lazare** and the Italian **Lazzaro**.

Lea *See* LEAH; LEE.

Leah (f) Hebrew name meaning 'antelope', 'gazelle' or even 'cow' – although another derivation suggests it means 'languid' or 'weary'. It appears in the Bible as the name of Jacob's first wife, the daughter of Laban and sister of Rachel. It was taken up by English Puritans in the 17th century and has continued in irregular use ever since, predominantly within the Jewish community. Variants include **Lea**, a form that has become more common since the middle of the 20th century, LEE and the Italian LIA.

Léan *See* HELEN.

Leander (m) Latin version of the Greek Leandros, itself derived from *leon* ('lion') and *andros* ('man') and thus meaning 'strong brave man'. The name is famous from the Greek myth of Hero and Leander, in which the youthful Leander drowns in a storm while swimming the Hellespont in order to pay his customary nightly visit to his lover the priestess Hero. Subsequent bearers of the name included a 6th-century Spanish saint and several characters in the comedies of the 17th-century French playwright Molière. The name has enjoyed a limited revival in the 20th century among Black Americans. Variants in other languages include the French **Léandre** and the Italian, Spanish and Portuguese **Leandro**.

Leanna/Leanne *See* LIANNE.

Leanora/Leanore *See* LEONORA.

Leberecht (m) German name meaning 'live rightly'. It was taken up by German speakers in the 17th century. The most notable bearer of the name to date has been the Prussian field marshal Gebhard Leberecht von Blücher (1742–1819), who led the Prussian forces at the Battle of Waterloo (1815).

Lech (m) Polish name (pronounced 'lek') of uncertain origin. It was borne by the legendary founder of the Polish people. The most famous bearer of the name in modern times has been Polish trade unionist and President Lech Walesa (b.1943). **Leszek** is a familiar form of the name.

Leda (f) Greek name possibly derived from the Lycian for 'woman'. The name is best known from the Greek myth of Leda and the Swan, in which Leda is ravished by Zeus in the guise of a swan and becomes the mother of two sets of twins – Helen of Troy and Hermione and Castor and Pollux. The name has made relatively few appearances among English speakers over the centuries.

Lee (m/f) English surname derived from the Old English *leah* ('wood', 'meadow' or 'clearing') that has been in use among English speakers as a first name for boys since the 19th century and for girls since the early 20th century. In the USA the name was promoted by association with the famous Confederate general Robert E. Lee (1807–70). Other notable bearers of the name have included US actors Lee J. Cobb (Leo Jacoby; 1911–76) and Lee Marvin (1924–87), US actress Lee Remick (1935–91), US golfer Lee Trevino (b.1939) and British footballer Lee Sharpe (b.1971). Also found as **Lea** or **Leigh** (usually treated as a feminine version of the name, although Australians tend to treat it as a masculine form). *See also* LEAH.

Lee-Ann *See* LIANNE.

Leela (f) Indian name derived from the Sanskrit *lila* ('play'). Also found as **Lila**, it is usually interpreted to be a reference to love-play.

Leesa *See* LISA.

Leif (m) Scandinavian name (pronounced 'leef') derived from the Old Norse Leifr (meaning 'descendant' or 'heir'). Notable bearers of the name have included the Norse seaman Leif Ericsson, who discovered the New World around the year 1000.

Leigh *See* LEE.

Leighton (m) English place name and surname derived from the Old English *leac* ('leek') and *tun* ('settlement') and thus meaning 'herb garden'. It has been in use as a first name among English speakers since the late 19th century. Also found as **Layton** or **Leyton**.

Leila (f) Arabic name meaning 'night' and thus meaning 'dark-haired', 'swarthy' or 'dark-eyed'. As **Leilah** it features in the Persian legend of Leilah and Mejnoun, which is in many respects a parallel for the myth of Cupid and Psyche. Lord Byron depicted a beautiful slave called Leila in his poem *The Giaour* (1813) and Edward Bulwer-Lytton wrote a novel about another oriental beauty entitled *Leila* (1838), promoting the occasional adoption of the name among English speakers throughout the 19th century. The name has continued in sporadic use into modern times. Also found as **Laila**, **Lela** or **Lila**. British model Kate Moss gave the name Lila to her baby in 2002. *See also* LAYLA.

Lela *See* LAELIA; LEILA.

Leland (m) English surname derived from the Old English *laege* ('fallow') and *land* ('land') that has also been in use as a first name, particularly in the USA, since the 19th century.

Lelia *See* LAELIA.

Lemmy *See* LEMUEL.

Lemuel (m) Hebrew name meaning 'devoted to God'. It features in the Bible as the name of a king mentioned in the Book of

Proverbs. It was taken up by English speakers in the middle of the 19th century but seems to have disappeared from use since the 1930s. The most famous bearer of the name is Lemuel Gulliver in Jonathan Swift's *Gulliver's Travels* (1725). Commonly shortened to **Lemmy**.

Len *See* LENNOX; LEONARD; LIONEL.

Lena (f) English, Scottish, German, Dutch and Scandinavian name that exists as a diminutive of various longer names ending '-lena' or '-lina', such as HELENA. It was taken up by English speakers in the middle of the 19th century. Well-known bearers of the name have included US singer Lena Horne (b.1917) and Scottish singer and dancer Lena Zavaroni (1963–99). Also found as LINA and **Leni** – as borne by German film director Leni Riefenstahl (Helene Riefenstahl; 1902–2003). Variants in other languages include the German and Danish LENE.

Lenda *See* LINDA.

Lene (f) German and Danish first name (pronounced 'leeni'), sometimes regarded as an abbreviated form of names ending '-lene', such as Magdalene. It ranked among the top five feminine names used in Denmark in the 1960s. Variants include **Leni**.

Leni *See* LENA; LENE.

Lennard/Lennart/Lennie
See LEONARD.

Lennox (m) Scottish and English surname that has also been taken up as an occasional first name. Also found as **Lenox**, it is particularly associated with Scotland, where there is an earldom of the same name, referring to a district near Loch Lomond. Notable bearers of the name have included British composer Sir Lennox Berkeley (1903–89) and British boxer Lennox Lewis (b.1965). Sometimes shortened to **Len** or **Lenny**.

Lenny *See* LENNOX; LEONARD; LIONEL.

Lenora *See* LEONORA.

Lenore *See* ELEANOR.

Lenox *See* LENNOX.

Lenz *See* LAURENCE.

Leo (m) English first name derived from the Latin *leo* ('lion'). It made its first appearances among English speakers in the medieval period and enjoyed a peak in popularity in the late 19th and early 20th centuries. Notable bearers of the name have included several early saints, six emperors of Constantinople, thirteen popes, including Pope Leo the Great (*c*.390–461), and in more recent times US actor Leo G. Carroll (1892–1972) and the Australian-born actor Leo McKern (Reginald McKern; 1920–2002). It enjoyed a boost in popularity in 2001 after British Prime Minister Tony Blair and his wife Cherie chose it for their fourth child. Variants in other languages include the Russian **Lev** or **Lyov** and the Czech **Leos** – as borne by the Czech composer Leos Janacek (1854–1928). Feminine versions of the name include **Lea** and **Leola**. *See also* LEON; LEOPOLD.

Leocadia (f) Spanish name derived from the Greek *leukos* ('light' or 'clear'). It was borne by a 4th-century virgin martyr from Toledo. Variants include the Portuguese **Laocadia**. **Leocadio** is a masculine version of the name.

Leofric (m) Old English name (pronounced 'lee-ofrik') derived from *leof* ('dear') and *ric* ('ruler'). The name survived the Norman Conquest and continued in use during the medieval period and even beyond. The most famous bearer of the name was the 11th-century husband of Lady Godiva, remembered for riding naked through the streets of Coventry in order to persuade her husband to reduce the heavy taxes he had recently imposed upon the townspeople.

Leolin/Leoline *See* LLEWELLYN.

Leon (m) English, German and Irish Gaelic name derived from LEO and thus meaning 'lion'. It became fairly common among English speakers in the 19th century but is today rare outside the Jewish community, who use the name in remembrance of the dying words of Jacob, in which he likened the kingdom of Judah to a lion. Well-known bearers of the name have included British children's writer Leon Garfield (1921–96), US novelist Leon Uris (1924–2003) and British politician Sir Leon Brittan (b.1939). Variants include the French **Léon**, the Italian **Leone** and the Spanish **León**. **Leonie** and **Leona** are feminine forms of the name. *See also* LEONTINE; LIONEL.

Leona *See* LEON.

Leonard (m) English first name derived via Old French from the Old German *leon* ('lion') and *hard* ('strong' or 'brave') and thus meaning 'brave as a lion'. It was borne by a 5th-century French saint, the patron saint of prisoners, and came to England with the Normans. It appeared infrequently during the medieval period but enjoyed a considerable revival in the 19th century and continued in popular use until the middle of the 20th century before going into decline.

Notable bearers of the name have included US composer Leonard Bernstein (Louis Bernstein; 1918–90), US actor Leonard Nimoy (b.1931) and Canadian singer-songwriter and author Leonard Cohen (b.1934). Common abbreviations of the name are **Len**, **Lennie** and **Lenny** – as borne by British cricketer Len Hutton (1916–90), US comedian Lenny Bruce (1926–66), British thriller writer Len Deighton (b.1929) and British comedian Lenny Henry (b.1958). Also encountered as **Lennard**. Variants in other languages include the French **Léonard**, the German **Leonhard**, the Scandinavian **Lennart** and the Italian, Spanish, and Portuguese **Leonardo** – as borne by the Renaissance artist and engineer Leonardo da Vinci (1452–1519).

Leonardo *See* LEONARD.

Leone *See* LEON.

Leonid (m) Russian first name derived from the Greek Leonidas, which was in turn derived ultimately from *leon* ('lion'). The name was made famous in ancient history by Leonides, the king of Sparta who died fighting the Persians at the Battle of Thermopylae (480 BC). Other bearers of the name in its various forms have included two early saints and Soviet President Leonid Brezhnev (1906–82).

Leonie *See* LEON.

Leonora (f) English first name that developed via Eleanora as a variant of ELEANOR. It made its first appearances among English speakers in the 19th century, promoted by characters of the same name in three celebrated operas – Beethoven's *Fidelio* (1806, 1814), Donizetti's *La Favorita* (1840) and Verdi's *Il Trovatore* (1853). Another Leonora appeared in the novel *Joseph Andrews* (1742) by Henry Fielding. Sometimes shortened to NORA, **Norah** or **Nornie**. Variants include **Leanora**, **Leanore**, **Lenore**, **Lenora** and the German **Leonore**.

Leontina *See* LEONTINE.

Leontine (f) English version of the French Léontine, itself derived from the Italian Leontina, which in turn evolved from the Latin Leontius – a derivation of the Latin *leo* ('lion'). Alternatively, the name is considered to have resulted from the combination of LEONORA and CLEMENTINE. Also found as **Leontyne**, it was taken up by English speakers in the 19th century. Notable bearers of the name have included US opera singer Leontyne Price (Mary Leontine Price; b.1927).

Leontyne *See* LEONTINE.

Leopold (m) German and English first name derived from the Old German Liutpold, from *liut* ('people') and *bald* ('bold') and thus meaning 'of a bold people'. Popular among several European royal families, it was taken up on an irregular basis by English speakers around the middle of the 19th century but has become rare since the early years of the 20th century and is now usually considered to be a non-English name. Notable bearers of the name have included King Leopold of the Belgians (1790–1865), Queen Victoria's third son Prince Leopold (1853–84), British-born US conductor Leopold Stokowski (1882–1977) and the fictional Leopold Bloom in James Joyce's novel *Ulysses* (1922). Commonly shortened to LEO or, more rarely, to **Poldie**. Variants in other languages include the modern German **Luitpold**, the French **Léopold** and the Italian, Spanish and Portuguese **Leopoldo**.

Leos *See* LEO.

Leroy (m) English first name derived from the Old French *le roy* ('the king'). Used initially as a nickname, it is thought to have been given initially to royal servants. It was taken up as a first name in the USA in the 19th century and subsequently in the UK in the 1960s, winning particular approval in recent years among the Black population. Variant forms include **LeRoy** and **LeRoi**. *See also* DELROY; ELROY.

Les *See* LESLIE; LESTER.

Lesbia (f) Greek name meaning 'woman of Lesbos' (Lesbos being one of the Greek islands). The island of Lesbos was the home of the 7th-century BC poetess Sappho, whose love poems to other women resulted in the creation of the word 'lesbian' to describe such feelings. The name was also used by the 1st-century Roman poet Catullus for his otherwise unidentified lover and has since made occasional appearances in English literature. Because of its connection with lesbianism the name is extremely rare today.

Lesley *See* LESLIE.

Leslie (m/f) Scottish place name (from Lesslyn in Aberdeenshire) that was subsequently taken up as a surname and first name in both England and Scotland. The original place name may have been derived from the Gaelic *leas cuilinn* ('garden of hollies'). As a surname it was borne by a

famous Scottish family, whose members included the celebrated Civil War general David Leslie (d.1682). Also encountered as **Lesley**, it was first recorded in use as a first name in the 18th century, promoted by the Robert Burns poem 'Bonnie Lesley'. It became increasingly popular in the late 19th century, reaching a peak in the 1950s and 1960s, since when it has held its own as a name for girls but has gone into a sharp decline as a boys' name. Although the spelling Lesley is now chiefly reserved for girls, Leslie is still used for both sexes.

Notable bearers of the name in its various forms have included British actors Leslie Howard (1890–1952) and Leslie Henson (1891–1957), British crime writer Leslie Charteris (1907–93), British comedian Leslie Phillips (b.1924), French actress Leslie Caron (b.1931) and British actresses Lesley-Anne Down (b.1954) and Leslie Ash (b.1960). Commonly shortened to **Les**.

Lester (m) English place name (now given as Leicester) that was subsequently taken up as a surname and occasional first name. The original place name was derived from the Old English *Ligora* (a tribal name of unknown meaning) and *caester* ('Roman fort'). It appears to have made its debut as a first name around the middle of the 19th century. Notable bearers of the name have included US jazz musician Lester Cole (1904–85) and British jockey Lester Piggott (b.1935). Commonly shortened to **Les**.

Leszek *See* LECH.

Leta (f) English first name derived from the Latin *letus* ('glad').

Letitia (f) English first name derived from the Latin *laetitia* ('gladness' or 'joy'). Also spelled **Leticia**, **Laetitia** or **Lecia**, it was taken up by English speakers during the medieval period and has continued in use into modern times, although it has become increasingly rare since the early 20th century. Well-known bearers of the name over the centuries have included the fictional Laetitia Prism in Oscar Wilde's comedy *The Importance of Being Earnest* (1895) and

British television actress Letitia Dean (b.1967). Commonly shortened to **Lettie**, **Letty**, **Titty**, **Tish** or **Tisha**. *See also* LETTICE.

Letizia *See* LETTICE.

Lettice (f) English first name derived from LETITIA. This diminutive form of the name has medieval roots and was the more popular form of the name between the 12th and 17th centuries. It remained in occasional use into the 20th century but is now very rare, perhaps because of its similarity with 'lettuce', which is pronounced identically. There is a character called Lettice Beardsall in D. H. Lawrence's novel *The White Peacock* (1911) and the name also featured in the Peter Shaffer play *Lettice and Lovage* (1987). Sometimes shortened to **Lettie** or **Letty**. An Italian variant is **Letizia**. *See also* LETITIA.

Lettie/Letty *See* ALETHEA; LETITIA; LETTICE.

Lev *See* LEO.

Levi (m) Jewish name derived from the Hebrew *lewi* ('associated', 'attached' or 'pledged'). It features in the Bible as the name of the third son of Jacob and Leah and founder of the Levite tribe and as a name by which the apostle Matthew was sometimes known. It was in use among English Jews as early as the 17th century and has since made occasional appearances among non-Jewish English speakers. There is a character called Levi Everdene in Thomas Hardy's novel *Far From the Madding Crowd* (1874). Also spelled **Levy**.

Levy *See* LEVI.

Lew *See* LEWIS.

Lewella *See* LLEWELLYN.

Lewin (m) English first name derived from the Old English meaning 'beloved friend'.

Lewis (m) English version of the French LOUIS, also encountered in Wales as an Anglicization of LLEWELLYN. First recorded in use among English speakers during the medieval period, it enjoyed a peak in popularity in the 1990s. Notable bearers of the name have included British children's writer Lewis Carroll (Charles Lutwidge Dodgson; 1832–98 – Lutwidge itself being an unusual variant of Louis). Commonly shortened to **Lew** – as borne by Russian-born British television producer Lew Grade (Louis Winogradsky; 1906–98).

Lex (m) English first name that is thought to have evolved as a diminutive of ALEXANDER, influenced perhaps by REX. The name made its first appearances among English speakers in the 19th century. Well-known bearers of the name have included Superman's sworn enemy Lex Luther in the *Superman* stories. **Lexie** and **Lexy** are familiar versions of the name. A rare feminine variant is the English and Scottish **Lexine**.

Lexie/Lexine/Lexy *See* ALEXIS; LEX.

Leyton *See* LEIGHTON.

Lia (f) Italian variant of LEAH, also found as a diminutive of Rosalia. Since the 1950s the name has also been encountered among English speakers as a diminutive of various longer names, such as AMELIA and DELIA.

Liam (m) Irish variant (pronounced 'lee-am') of WILLIAM, via the Gaelic Uilliam. Long popular among the Irish, it has appeared with increasing frequency elsewhere in the English-speaking world since the 1930s. Notable bearers of the name have included the Irish novelist Liam O'Flaherty (1897–1984), Northern Ireland actor Liam Neeson (b.1952) and British rock musician Liam Gallagher (b.1972).

Liana (f) French first name derived from JULIANA or from various other names ending in '-liana'. It is rare among English speakers, who generally prefer the related name LIANNE.

Lianne (f) English first name that evolved either out of the French Julianne (*see* JULIANA) or through the combination of LEE and ANNE. It was taken up by English speakers in the 1940s and has since become fairly popular in Australia. **Leanne** is a commonly encountered variant form of the name in increasing use since the 1960s. **Leanna**, **Lee-Ann** and **Leigh-Ann** are less common versions.

Lib/Libby *See* ELIZABETH.

Liddy *See* LYDIA.

Liese/Liesel/Leisl *See* ELIZABETH.

Lil *See* LILIAN; LILY.

Lila *See* LEELA; LEILA; LILY.

Lilac (f) English first name derived from that of the scented shrub. The name of the plant came ultimately via French and Spanish from the Arabic *lilak*, itself derived from the Persian *nilak* ('bluish').

Lili *See* ELIZABETH.

Lilian (f) English first name that is thought to have developed from ELIZABETH or else through the combination of LILY and ANNE (although the name Lily was not adopted until the 19th century). Already known in Italy in the form **Liliana**, it was first recorded in use among English speakers towards the end of the 16th century. It enjoyed a peak in popularity among English speakers towards the end of the 19th century. It has been largely out of favour since the 1920s. Also found (especially in the USA) as **Lillian**. Commonly shortened to **Lil** or **Lily**. Notable bearers of the name have included British actress Dame Lilian Braithwaite (1873–1948), British theatre manager Lilian Bayliss (1874–1934), US film actress Lillian Gish (1893–1993) and US playwright Lillian Hellman (1905–84). Variants include the Scottish **Lilias** or **Lillias**.

Lilias *See* LILIAN.

Lilith (f) Biblical name derived from the Hebrew for 'serpent' or 'belonging to the night' but otherwise variously interpreted to mean 'night monster', 'storm goddess' or 'screech owl'. In medieval times it was commonly believed that Adam had had a wife called Lilith before Eve but that she had been turned into a hideous demon in punishment for refusing to obey her husband. As a result of its biblical history, the name was not taken up as a first name until the 20th century, by which time the legend of Lilith had been forgotten by most people and the name was being treated more often as a variant of LILY. Well-known bearers of the name have included the fictional Lilith in the 1980s hit US television comedy series *Cheers* and the 1990s spin-off *Frasier*.

Lilla/Lillah *See* LILY.

Lilli *See* ELIZABETH.

Lillian/Lillias *See* LILIAN.

Lily (f) English first name derived from the flower, itself a symbol of purity. Also encountered occasionally as a diminutive form of ELIZABETH. It was taken up by English speakers around the middle of the 19th century when there was a considerable fashion for such flower names. The music hall song 'Lily of Laguna' (1898) helped to promote the name towards the end of the century but it went into a lasting decline after the early years of the 20th century. Familiar forms of the name include **Lil**, **Lilly** and **Lillie** – as borne by the Jersey-born actress and royal mistress Lillie Langtry (Emilie Charlotte Le Breton; 1853–1929), who was widely known as 'the Jersey Lily'. An unusual elaboration of the name is **Tiger Lily**, in which form it was bestowed upon Tiger Lily Hutchence (b.1996), the daughter of British television presenter Paula Yates and Australian rock star Michael Hutchence. Other variants include **Lilla**, **Lillah** and **Lila**. *See also* LILIAN.

Lin *See* LINDA; LINDSAY; LYNN.

Lina (f) English first name that developed as a diminutive of ADELINA, CAROLINA and other names ending '-lina' around the middle of the 19th century. It is sometimes also encountered as a variant of LENA.

Lincoln (m) English place name (from the city of Lincoln) that was subsequently taken up as a surname and, from the 19th century, as an occasional first name. The city of Lincoln was originally known as *Lindum colonia* ('lake settlement'). It is more common in the USA than elsewhere, being bestowed in many cases in honour of President Abraham Lincoln (1809–65).

Linda (f) English first name that appears to have developed in the late 19th century as a diminutive form of BELINDA and other names with similar '-linda' endings. It is sometimes suggested that the emergence of the name may also have been influenced by the Spanish *linda* ('pretty'), the Italian *linda* ('neat') or even the Old German *lindi* ('snake') – the snake being considered a personification of wisdom in various ancient cultures. It enjoyed a peak in popularity during the 1950s and 1960s, when it ranked among the top five favourite names across the English-speaking world. Well-known bearers of the name have included US pop singer Linda Ronstadt (b.1946), US photographer Linda McCartney (Linda Louise Eastman; 1942–98; wife of singer-songwriter Paul McCartney), and Canadian-born US model Linda Evangelista (b.1965). Occasionally spelled since the early 20th century **Lynda** or **Lenda**. Sometimes shortened to **Lin**, **LYNN** or **Lynne**. **Lindie**, **Lyndi** and **Lindy** are diminutive forms of the name.

Linden (f) English first name that appears to have developed as a 20th-century variant of LINDA. It is also the common name for the lime tree (from the Old English *linde*) and so could also be a 'flower' name. Also found as **Lindon**. *See also* LYNDON.

Lindon *See* LINDEN; LYNDON.

Lindsay (m/f) Old English place name (from Lindsey in Lincolnshire) meaning 'island of Lincoln' or 'wetland belonging to Lincoln' that was later taken up as a surname in Scotland and as a first name by English speakers around the world. Lindsey in Lincolnshire was the original home of Sir Walter de Lindesay, one of the followers of David I of Scotland, who subsequently accompanied his master to Scotland when he became king. Also spelled **Lindsey,** it was taken up as a first name by English speakers in the 19th century, usually reserved initially for males. Since the 1930s it has been used with increasing frequency as a name for girls and has been employed less and less as a masculine name. Notable bearers of the name have included British film director Lindsay Anderson (1923–94) and Scottish actress Lindsay Duncan (b.1950). Sometimes shortened to **Lin** or **Lyn**. Also spelled **Linsay**, **Linsey**, **Linzi**, **Lyndsay**, **Lynsay**, **Lindsie** or **Lynsey** – as borne by British pop singer Lynsey de Paul (b.1951).

Lindsey *See* LINDSAY.

Lindy *See* LINDA.

Linette *See* LYNETTE.

Linford (m) English place name (from Berkshire) derived from the Old English *lin* ('flax') or *lind* ('lime tree') and *ford* ('ford') that was subsequently taken up as a surname and first name. Well-known bearers of the name in modern times have included the British athlete Linford Christie (b.1960).

Linnea (f) Swedish first name derived from that of the noted Swedish botanist Linnaeus (Carl von Linné; 1707–70), who devised the Linnaean system of classification. When the name first appeared in the middle of the 19th century it was usually spelled **Linnaea**. Sometimes shortened to **Nea**.

Linnet (f) English first name derived from that of the songbird, or else encountered as a variant form of LYNETTE or of the Welsh ELUNED. The bird name came ultimately from the Old French *linotte*, itself from *lin* ('flax'), the seeds of which are the bird's usual food. Its use was promoted among English speakers by an appearance in Alfred, Lord Tennyson's *Idylls of the King* (1859).

Linnette See LYNETTE.

Linton (m) English place name probably

derived from the Old English *lin* ('flax' or 'cotton') or *lind* ('lime tree') and *tun* ('enclosure') that was subsequently taken up as a surname and occasional first name. It is commonest within the Black community in the UK. Famous bearers of the name include Jamaican poet Linton Kwesi Johnson (b.1952). *See also* LYNTON.

Linus (m) English first name derived from the Greek Linos, itself possibly derived from *lineos* ('blond' or 'flaxen-haired'). The name features in the Bible as that of a Roman Christian greeted by St Paul and in Greek myth as that of Hercules' music teacher. The fact that today the name is more familiar in the USA than elsewhere in the English-speaking world reflects the popularity of the Charles Schulz comic strip *Peanuts*, in which there is a character called Linus. Notable bearers of the name in real life have included the second pope (d.*c.*76) and US chemist Linus Pauling (1901–94).

Linzi *See* LINDSAY.

Lionel (m) English first name derived via French from LEON and meaning 'little lion'. It was first recorded in use among English speakers in the medieval period but remained relatively unknown until the early years of the 20th century, when it enjoyed considerable favour before falling out of fashion again after the 1930s. Well-known bearers of the name have included one of the Knights of the Round Table (otherwise known as Sir Lyon), British composer Lionel Monckton (1861–1924), US actor Lionel Barrymore (1878–1954), British composer Lionel Bart (1930–99) and US soul singer Lionel Richie (b.1949). Sometimes shortened to **Len** or **Lenny**.

Lis *See* FELICITY.

Lisa (f) English first name (pronounced 'leesa' or 'lihza') that developed as a diminutive of ELIZABETH. It emerged as a popular first name in its own right in the 1960s but fell out of fashion somewhat after the 1980s. Also found as **Liza** and, rarely, **Leesa**. Notable bearers of the name in its various forms have included US actress and singer Liza Minnelli (b.1946), British actress Liza Goddard (b.1950) and British soul singer Lisa Stansfield (b.1965). Diminutive forms include **Liz, Lizzie, Lisette** and **Lysette** – as borne by British actress Lysette Anthony (b.1963).

Lisbet/Lisbeth/Lise *See* ELIZABETH.

Lisette *See* ELIZABETH; LISA.

Lisha (f) English first name that developed as a diminutive form of such names as DELICIA and Felicia.

Liss *See* FELICITY.

Lissa *See* MELISSA.

Lissie *See* FELICITY.

Lita *See* LOLITA.

Liv (f) Scandinavian first name probably derived from the Old Norse *hlif* ('defence' or 'protection') although the link is often made today with *liv* ('life'). The name featured in Norse legend and was revived towards the end of the 19th century. Well-known bearers of the name have included the Norwegian actress Liv Ullmann (b.1939).

Livia (f) English first name derived from the Roman Livius, itself possibly from the Latin *lividus* ('leaden-coloured' or 'bluish'). It is also encountered as a diminutive form of OLIVIA. It featured as the name of a character in William Shakespeare's *Romeo and Juliet* (1595) and subsequently made a number of further appearances in English literature from the 16th century onwards. **Livy** and **Livvy** are familiar forms of the name.

Livvy/Livy *See* LIVIA.

Liz/Liza *See* ELIZABETH; LISA.

Lizbeth *See* ELIZABETH.

Lizzie/Lizzy *See* ELIZABETH; LIZA.

Lleu (m) Welsh name (pronounced 'hlu') meaning 'bright' or 'shining'. It was borne by the Celtic Irish god Lugh and also appears in the *Mabinogi*. It was revived among Welsh speakers in the 20th century.

Llew *See* LLEWELLYN.

Llewella *See* LLEWELLYN.

Llewellyn (m) Welsh name (pronounced 'hluwelin') often thought to mean 'leader' or else to be derived from the Welsh *llyw* ('lion') and *eilun* ('likeness') but probably, in fact, descended from the much older Old Celtic name Lugobelinos (of uncertain meaning). Originally spelled **Llywelyn**, it has retained its strong association with Wales and is rarely if ever encountered outside families with Welsh connections. The name is most famous as that of two 13th-century princes of Gwynedd. Sometimes shortened to **Lew**, **Lyn** or **Llew**. **Lewella** and **Llewella** are feminine versions of the name. Variant forms include **Leolin**, **Leoline** and **Fluellen** (an attempt to reproduce the pronunciation of the Welsh 'll').

Lloyd (m) English first name derived from a Welsh surname that in turn evolved as a nickname meaning 'grey' or 'grey-haired'. It was taken up by English speakers in the early years of the 20th century, when it became widely known from the name of Prime Minister David Lloyd George (1863–1945), who inherited it as his mother's maiden name. It has remained in use ever since, becoming particularly popular in the USA. Notable bearers of the name in recent times have included US actor Lloyd Bridges (1913–98). Occasionally spelled **Loyd**. *See also* FLOYD.

Llywelyn *See* LLEWELLYN.

Lo *See* LOIS; LOLA; LOLITA.

Lochlann/Lockie *See* LACHLAN.

Lodewijk/Lodovico *See* LOUIS.

Logan (m) Scottish place name (from Ayrshire) that was subsequently taken up as a surname and first name. The original place name may have come from the Gaelic for 'hollow'. It remains confined largely to Scotland. Well-known bearers of the name have included US-born British writer Logan Pearsall Smith (1865–1949).

Lois (f) Biblical name (pronounced 'lowis') possibly derived from the Greek *loion* ('better' or 'good') but also encountered as a diminutive form of LOUISA or LOUISE (despite the fact that they are of entirely different Germanic origin). The name features in the Bible as that of Timothy's grandmother and consequently was taken up by English speakers in the 17th century. Since the early 20th century the name has been found more frequently in Canada and the USA than elsewhere in the English-speaking world, enjoying a peak in popularity in the 1920s. Well-known bearers of the name have included the fictional Lois Lane in the *Superman* stories. Sometimes shortened to **Lo**.

Lol *See* LAURENCE.

Lola (f) Spanish and English first name that developed alongside LOLITA as a diminutive of DOLORES. Occasionally also found as a familiar form of Carlotta (*see* CHARLOTTE). Long established across the Spanish-speaking world, particularly in the Hispanic countries of South America, it has made occasional appearances among English speakers since the 19th century. Famous bearers of the name have included the Irish-born American dancer Lola Montez (Marie Dolores Eliza Rosanna Gilbert; 1818–61), who wielded considerable power as the mistress of King Ludwig I of Bavaria. The British pop group The Kinks released a hugely successful hit single entitled 'Lola' in 1970. Sometimes shortened to **Lo**. Variants include the rare **Lolicia**.

Lolicia *See* LOLA.

Lolita (f) Spanish first name that developed alongside LOLA as a diminutive of DOLORES. It first entered English-speaking use in the USA in the 19th century. Today it is closely associated with the notoriety that surrounded Vladimir Nabokov's novel

Lolita (1955), about an ageing academic's love for a young girl. Commonly shortened to **Lo** or **Lita**.

Lolly *See* LAURA.

Loman (m) Irish first name derived from *lomm* ('bare'). It was borne by several early Irish saints.

Lonan (m) Irish first name derived from *lon* ('blackbird'). It was borne by a number of little-known Irish saints.

Lone (f) Danish first name that developed as a diminutive of Magdelone and other names with similar endings.

Lonnie (m) English first name that developed as an Anglicized diminutive of Alonzo (*see* ALPHONSE) or as a variant of Lennie (*see* LEONARD). Also found as **Lonny**, it appears to have been a 20th-century invention. Famous bearers of the name have included US blues musician Lonnie Johnson (Alonzo Johnson; 1899–1970) and Scottish pop musician Lonnie Donegan (1931–2002). Sometimes shortened to **Lon** – as borne by US actor Lon Chaney (Alonzo Chaney; 1883–1930).

Lope (m) Spanish first name (pronounced 'loh-pay') derived from the Roman Lupus, from the Latin *lupus* ('wolf'). Spanish speakers took up the name during the medieval period and in its Latin version it was borne by several early French and Spanish saints.

Lora *See* LAURA.

Loraine *See* LORRAINE.

Lorcan *See* LAURENCE.

Lore *See* LAURA.

Loredana (f) Italian first name that is thought to have made its first appearance as the name of the heroine in the novel *L'amore de Loredana* (1908) by Luciano Zuccoli. Zuccoli may have based the name on the Venetian surname Loredan, itself ultimately derived from the Latin *laureum* ('laurel grove').

Loreen/Lorelle *See* LAURA.

Loren *See* LAUREN; LAURENCE.

Lorena *See* LAURA.

Lorenz/Lorenzo *See* LAURENCE.

Loreto (f) English and Irish first name derived ultimately from an Italian place name. It was to Loreto in central Italy that in the 13th century angels were supposed to have carried the Holy House of the Virgin from Nazareth – hence the popularity of the name among Roman Catholics.

Loretta/Lorette *See* LAURETTA.

Lori *See* LAURA; LORRAINE.

Lorin *See* LAURENCE.

Lorinda *See* LAURA.

Loris (f) English first name of obscure origins, but possibly a diminutive form of LAURA. It seems to have made its first appearance in the latter half of the 20th century, winning particular approval in Australia.

Lorn *See* LORNE.

Lorna (f) English first name that is thought to have been invented by the British novelist R. D. Blackmore for the heroine of his romantic novel *Lorna Doone* (1869). According to Blackmore, the name was based on the Scottish place name Lorn (in Argyll) and may have been intended to bring to mind the Marquis of Lorne as well as the Old English *lorn* ('lost' or 'forsaken'). The huge success of the novel guaranteed the popularity of the name on both sides of the Atlantic, particularly Scotland, from the late 19th century. *See also* LORNE.

Lorne (m) English first name that may have developed out of LORNA or may simply share the same origin in the Scottish place name Lorn (in Argyll). It is particularly popular in Canada and other countries with strong Scottish connections. Famous bearers of the name have included Canadian actor Lorne Greene (1915–87), star of the US television cowboy series *Bonanza*. Also found as **Lorn**.

Lorraine (f) English first name derived from a Scottish surname that may in turn have been borrowed from the name of the eastern French province of Lorraine, itself derived from the Latin Lotharingia (meaning 'territory of the people of Lothar'). It is often assumed to be a variant of LAURA. The name may have become familiar to English speakers in the 16th century through Mary, Queen of Scots' mother Mary of Lorraine, but it was not taken up as a first name until the 19th century. It enjoyed a peak in popularity in the 1950s and 1960s but has since gone into decline. Well-known bearers of the name have included US playwright Lorraine Hansberry (1930–65) and British actress Lorraine Chase (b.1951). Familiar forms of the name are **Lori** and **Lorri**. Also spelled **Lauraine**, **Laraine**, **Lorain**, **Loraine** or **Lorayne**.

Lorri *See* LORRAINE.

Lorrie *See* LAURETTA.

Lorrin *See* LAURENCE.

Lothair *See* LOTHAR.

Lothar (m) German first name derived from the Old German *hlud* ('fame') and *hari* ('army' or 'warrior'). It was borne by an 8th-century French saint and two Holy Roman Emperors – one of whom bequeathed the name to the province Lotharingia (meaning 'territory of the people of Lothar'), which later became LORRAINE. Sometimes appears in the Anglicized form **Lothair**. Another variant is the Italianate **Lothario**, which is best known to English speakers as a nickname for any male with a licentious disposition. This association goes back to two fictional characters – both of them debauched libertines – who bore the name respectively in William Davenant's play *The Cruel Brother* (1630) and Nicholas Rowe's tragedy *The Fair Penitent* (1703). *See also* LUTHER.

Lothario *See* LOTHAR.

Lotta/Lottie/Lotty *See* CHARLOTTE.

Lotus (f) English first name that refers to the lotus fruit of Greek mythology, which was reputed to induce a state of indolent forgetfulness in those who ate it.

Lou *See* LOUIS; LOUISA; LOUISE.

Louella (f) English first name derived from the combination of Lou (from LOUISA or LOUISE) and the feminine suffix '-ella' (*see* ELLA). It was taken up by English speakers in the 19th century and remains in circulation chiefly in the USA. Notable bearers of the name have included US Hollywood gossip columnist Louella Parsons (1880–1972). Also spelled **Luella**.

Louie *See* LOUIS; LOUISA; LOUISE.

Louis (m) French first name derived from the Old German Hlutwig (*see* LUDWIG), itself from the Old German *hlut* ('fame') and *wig* ('warrior') and thus meaning 'famous warrior'. It was Latinized as Ludovicus (*see* LUDOVIC). As CLOVIS, the name was borne by the founder of the French monarchy and in the form Louis it was borne by a total of eighteen subsequent French kings. The name was Anglicized as LEWIS after it came to England in the medieval period under the influence of the Normans. The French form of the name, however, made a comeback among English speakers from the 18th century and enjoyed peaks in popularity in the late 19th and early 20th centuries, and again in the 1990s. When spelt Louis, the name is still usually pronounced in the French manner ('loo-ee'), without the final 's' being sounded.

Notable bearers of the name have included the Scottish writer Robert Louis Stevenson (1850–94), Russian-born US film producer Louis B. Mayer (Eliezer Mayer; 1885–1957) and US jazz musician Louis Armstrong (1901–71). Commonly shortened to **Louie** or **Lou** – as borne by US film comedian Lou Costello (Louis Cristillo; 1906–59). Variants in other languages include the Hungarian **Lajos**, the Italian

Luigi and the Spanish and Portuguese **Luis**. *See also* ALOYSIUS; LOUISA; LOUISE.

Louisa (f) Feminine form of LOUIS, adopted by English speakers in the 18th century. A popular name in the late 19th century, at its peak in the 1870s, it has been eclipsed since the early years of the 20th century by LOUISE. Notable bearers of the name have included the US children's author Louisa M. Alcott (1832–88). Also found as **Louiza** and **Luisa**. Commonly shortened to **Lou** or **Louie**. Variants in other languages include the German **Luise**, the Swedish **Lovisa** and the Danish and Norwegian **Lovise**. A familiar form of the name in German is LULU. *See also* LOIS; OUIDA.

Louise (f) French feminine variant of LOUIS that has largely replaced LOUISA among English speakers since the early 20th century. Borne by the French saint Louise de Marillac (1591–1660), this French version of the name seems to have made its first appearance among English speakers in the 17th century when the mistresses of Charles II included Louise de Kéroualle, Duchess of Portsmouth. It subsequently gave way to Louisa in the 18th century and did not re-emerge until the end of the 19th century. At a peak in the USA in the 1920s, it increased steadily in frequency in the UK from the 1950s, reaching a high point in popularity in the 1980s. Well-known bearers of the name have included US film actress Louise Brooks (1906–85). Commonly shortened to **Lou** or **Louie** and occasionally to LULU. **Luise** is a German variant occasionally found in use among English speakers.

Lourdes (f) Spanish first name derived from the name of the celebrated shrine in southern France, where numerous miracles are claimed to have taken place since a young French peasant girl had visions of the Virgin Mary there in the 1850s. It is confined chiefly to the Catholic community and is only rarely encountered among English speakers. Also found in Spanish as **Lurdes**.

Loveday (f) English first name referring to the medieval 'lovedays' on which disputes were traditionally settled. First recorded in use during the early 13th century, the name was usually reserved for children born on one of these days. Although very rare, it is still encountered from time to time today, mainly in Cornwall (where it may also be found as **Lowdy**).

Lovell (m) English first name derived from a surname based on the Old French nickname Louvel ('wolf-cub' or 'little wolf'). Its use among English speakers dates back to at least the 11th century, although it has appeared only infrequently since the 15th century. Shortened to **Love**, it enjoyed some popularity among English Puritans during the 17th century. It has strong Scottish connections. Sometimes appears as **Lowell**, **Lovel** or **Lovet**.

Lovisa *See* LOUISA.

Lowell *See* LOVELL.

Lowri (f) Welsh first name representing a regional variant of LAURA. Also encountered as **Lowry**. Notable bearers of the name in recent years have included English television presenter Lowri Turner (b.1965).

Loyd *See* LLOYD.

Lu *See* LULU.

Luana *See* LUANNE.

Luanne (f) English and Italian first name apparently without any specific meaning. Also found as **Luana** (or **Luanna**), it was taken up as a first name by English and Italian speakers after it was used (as the name of a Polynesian maiden) in the King Vidor film *The Bird of Paradise* (1932), for which it appears to have been invented.

Lubna (f) Arabic name derived from *lubna* ('storax tree'). The storax was formerly prized among Arab peoples as a source of ingredients for incense and perfume. The name is best known from the 7th-century legend of Lubna and Qays, a loving husband and wife forced to divorce because of their childlessness.

Luc/Luca *See* LUKE.

Lucan (m) Irish first name meaning 'place of elms'. As a first name, it would appear to have been borrowed from a place name.

Lucas (m) English first name derived either from the surname or else from the Roman Lucas, also the source of LUKE. During the medieval period it appeared in the Authorized Version of the New Testament and other documents as a formal version of Luke. It came into vogue among English speakers briefly in the 1930s but has otherwise remained relatively rare.

Lucasta (f) English first name invented by English poet Richard Lovelace (1618–57). It is thought that the original Lucasta of Lovelace's poem 'Lucasta' (1649) was probably called LUCY or else bore the surname LUCAS. A rare name by the 20th century.

Luce *See* LUCIA; LUCY.

Lucetta (f) English first name that developed as a diminutive form of LUCIA or LUCY. It would appear to be of mainly historical interest, with records of its use among English speakers going back to the 16th century but relatively few appearances in succeeding centuries with the exception of a brief period in vogue in the 19th century. Notable bearers of the name have included a minor character in William Shakespeare's *The Two Gentlemen of Verona* (1594). A variant form is the French **Lucette**.

Lucette *See* LUCETTA.

Lucia (f) Roman name that developed as a feminine version of LUCIUS, derived from the Latin *lux* ('light'). Because of its meaning it is thought that the name was originally reserved for children born at dawn. The Romans also used the name in the variant form **Lucina**, the name of a goddess who was also the patroness of childbirth. Borne

by the 4th-century martyr St Lucia of Syracuse, who is traditionally supposed to have had her eyes put out and thus became the patroness of eye-disease sufferers, it continued in use in Italy and was taken up by English speakers towards the end of the 19th century, often as an alternative to LUCY. Variously pronounced 'loocheea' or 'loosia', the name was popularized as that of the heroine of Donizetti's opera *Lucia di Lammermoor* (1835) and subsequently in the *Mapp and Lucia* novels of E. F. Benson (1867–1940). Sometimes shortened to **Luce**. *See also* LUCETTA.

Lucian (m) English version of the French Lucien and the Italian Luciano, which are both descendants of the Roman Lucianus, derived from LUCIUS. As Lucianus, the name appeared among English speakers as early as the 12th century, although it was not until the 19th century that the modern form of the name started to make infrequent appearances. Famous bearers of the name have included the celebrated 2nd-century Greek satirist Lucian of Samosata, a martyred 3rd-century saint and the German-born British painter Lucian Freud (b.1922). **Luciana** is a rare feminine form of the name that appears in the works of William Shakespeare. **Lucienne** is a feminine variant from France.

Luciana/Luciano *See* LUCIAN.

Lucie *See* LUCY.

Lucien/Lucienne *See* LUCIAN.

Lucilla *See* LUCILLE.

Lucille (f) French variant of the Roman Lucilla, itself a feminine derivative of LUCIA. As Lucilla, the name was borne by several minor early saints and was recorded in use among English speakers as early as the 16th century – as shown by its appearance in, for instance, John Lyly's prose romance *Euphues, The Anatomy of Wit* (1578). The modern form of the name, Lucille, took over in the 19th century. Notable bearers of the name have included US television comedienne Lucille Ball (1911–89), star of the popular *I Love Lucy* shows of the 1950s and 1960s. Occasionally also spelled **Lucile**. The usual abbreviated form of the name is LUCY.

Lucina *See* LUCIA.

Lucinda (f) English first name that developed as a variant of LUCIA or LUCY. The earliest records of the name go back to Cervantes' classic work *Don Quixote* (1605). It made its first appearances in English, French and German literature in the 17th century but was not taken up as a popular choice of first name among English speakers until the 18th century. It has always been considered an aristocratic name. Well-known bearers of the name have included Lucinda Roanoke in Anthony Trollope's *The Eustace Diamonds* (1873) and British television presenter and social historian Lucinda Lambton (b.1943). Sometimes shortened to Lucy or to CINDY, **Cindi** or **Sindy**. Variants in other languages include the French **Lucinde**.

Lucio *See* LUCIUS.

Lucius (m) Roman name derived from the Latin *lux* ('light'). It appears in the Bible as the name of a Roman consul, of a prophet of Antioch and of a companion of St Paul and was also borne by three popes. It made its first appearances in English in the 16th century and was borne by several characters in the Roman plays of William Shakespeare. Subsequently Richard Brinsley Sheridan gave the name to the comical Irishman Sir Lucius O'Trigger in his play *The Rivals* (1775). LUCKY is a familiar diminutive variant. In Ireland the name is sometimes used as an Anglicized form of the Irish LACHTNA. Variants in other languages include the Italian, Spanish and Portuguese **Lucio**. *See also* LUCIA.

Lucky (m/f) English first name that developed either as a nickname or else as a familiar derivative of such names as FELICITY, LUCIUS, LUCY or LUKE. It has made irregular appearances as a first name since the early 20th century, chiefly

in the USA. One well-known bearer of the name was the notorious US gangster Charles 'Lucky' Luciano (1897–1962), who was considered remarkably fortunate not to have spent more of his career behind bars.

Lucrece *See* LUCRETIA.

Lucretia (f) Roman name that developed as a feminine form of the masculine Lucretius, itself possibly derived from LUCIUS but otherwise of unknown origin. According to legend, it was the name borne by the 5th-century BC wife of Tarquinius Collatinus, who committed suicide after she was raped by a son of Tarquinius Superbus, King of Rome, causing a scandal that resulted in the end of the Roman monarchy. The tale was later related by William Shakespeare in his poem *The Rape of Lucrece* (1594) – **Lucrece** being a French form of the name. It was also borne by the notorious Lucretia Borgia (1480–1519), who was popularly believed to have been involved in incestuous relationships with her father Pope Alexander VI and her brother Cesare and suspected of being guilty of using poison to dispose of her political enemies. The name appeared irregularly among English speakers between the 16th and 18th centuries but perhaps because of its historical associations it has never been very common and is today encountered only rarely, chiefly in the USA. **Lucrezia** is an Italian variant.

Lucy (f) English version of the Roman LUCIA. It also exists as a diminutive of LUCILLE or LUCINDA. It was taken up by English speakers during the medieval period and became increasingly popular from the 18th century, reaching peaks in frequency on both sides of the Atlantic in the late 19th and late 20th centuries. Well-known bearers of the name have included the fictional Lucy Lockit in John Gay's comic opera *The Beggar's Opera* (1728), the maid Lucy in Richard Brinsley Sheridan's *The Rivals* (1775) and Lucy Ashton in Sir Walter Scott's *The Bride of Lammermoor* (1819).

Familiar forms of the name include **Luce** (in which form it appears in Shakespeare's *The Comedy of Errors*), LUCKY and LULU. Variants include LUCETTA, **Lucette**, the French **Lucie** (taken up as an alternative to Lucy among English speakers from the 1980s) and the Irish Gaelic **Laoise**.

Ludger *See* LUITGER.

Ludmila (f) Russian name derived from the Old Slavonic *lud* ('people') and *mil* ('grace' or 'favour'). It was borne by a 10th-century Bohemian saint and has since made occasional appearances among English speakers. Also encountered as **Ludmilla**.

Ludo *See* LUDOVIC.

Ludovic (m) English version of the Latin Ludovicus (*see* LOUIS), also found in Scotland as an Anglicization of the Gaelic Maol Domhnaich, meaning 'devotee of the Lord'. It was taken up by English speakers in the 19th century, becoming commonest in Scotland where it is particularly associated with the Grant clan. Well-known bearers of the name have included Scottish broadcaster and writer Sir Ludovic Kennedy (b.1919). Commonly abbreviated to **Ludo**. Also found as **Ludovick**. **Ludovica** is a rare feminine form of the name. *See also* LUDWIG.

Ludvig *See* LUDWIG.

Ludwig (m) German name derived from the Old German Hlutwig, itself from *hlut* ('fame') and *wig* ('warrior'). A German equivalent of the French LOUIS, it became well known through its adoption by the royal house of Bavaria. Perhaps the most famous bearer of the name to date has been the German composer Ludwig van Beethoven (1770–1827). **Lutz** is a familiar German form of the name. Variants in other languages include the Scandinavian **Ludvig**, the Dutch **Lodewijk**, the Polish **Ludwik**, the Czech **Ludvik** and the Italian **Lodovico**. *See also* CLOVIS; LUDOVIC.

Ludwik *See* LUDWIG.

Luella *See* LOUELLA.

Luigi/Luis *See* LOUIS.

Luise *See* LOUISA; LOUISE.

Luitgard (m) German first name derived from the Old German *liut* ('people') and *gard* ('protection'). A common medieval name still in use today, although now relatively rare.

Luitger (m) German first name derived from the Old German *liut* ('people') and *gari* ('spear'). Variants include the Dutch **Ludger**.

Luitpold *See* LEOPOLD.

Luka/Lukas *See* LUKE.

Luke (m) English first name derived via the Roman LUCAS ultimately from the Greek Loukas, meaning 'man from Lucania' (Lucania being an area in southern Italy). It features in the Bible as the name of one of the four evangelists, author of the third gospel and the patron saint of doctors and painters – the reason why the name was formerly often given to the sons of craftsmen. The name came to England with the Normans, emerging in its modern form around the 12th century. It has remained in circulation ever since, with a recent peak in popularity since the early 1990s. Well-known bearers of the name have included Luke Moggs in George Eliot's *The Mill on the Floss* (1860), Luke Skywalker in the *Star Wars* film trilogy of the 1970s and 1980s and US actor Luke Perry (b.1967). LUCKY is a familiar form of the name. Variants in other languages include the French **Luc,** the Italian **Luca,** the German **Lukas** and the Russian **Luka**.

Lulu (f) German first name that developed as a diminutive form of Luise, the German version of LOUISA. Also found in use among English speakers as a familiar form of LUCY, it is a relatively recent introduction to the English-speaking world, of 20th-century origin. It is best known in the UK as the stagename of the pop singer Lulu

(Marie Lawrie; b.1948). **Lu** is a diminutive form.

Luned *See* ELUNED; LYNETTE.

Lupita *See* GUADALUPE.

Lurdes *See* LOURDES.

Luther (m) German surname derived from the Old German *liut* ('people') and *heri* ('warrior') and thus meaning 'people's warrior' that was taken up as a first name among English speakers from the 19th century. As the surname of the German religious reformer and theologian Martin Luther (1483–1546) it has always had a special significance for Protestants throughout Europe and the USA and was taken up by Puritans on both sides of the Atlantic. Following the assassination of the Black US civil rights leader Martin Luther King (1929–68), who was himself (like his father) named in honour of Martin Luther, the name was taken up by many Black Americans in tribute to his efforts on their behalf. Other well-known bearers of the name have included US soul singer Luther Vandross (b.1951). *See also* LOTHAR.

Lutz *See* LUDWIG.

Luz (f) Spanish first name derived from the Spanish *luz* ('light'). Its popularity is largely based on the fact that it is also a title borne by the Virgin Mary ('Our Lady of Light').

Lyall (m) Scottish surname derived from the Old Norse name Liulfr (possibly meaning 'wolf') that has also made occasional appearances as a first name, chiefly among Scots. *See also* LYLE.

Lydia (f) English first name derived ultimately from a Greek name meaning 'woman of Lydia' (Lydia being a region in Asia Minor). The name features in the Bible as that of a widow who became one of St Paul's converts and was consequently taken up by Puritans on both sides of the Atlantic in the 17th century. It remained popular through the 18th and 19th centuries but subsequently suffered a lengthy decline before being revived in the 1990s. Notable bearers of the name in English literature have included Lydia Languish in Richard Brinsley Sheridan's comedy *The Rivals* (1775), Lydia Bennet in Jane Austen's novel *Pride and Prejudice* (1813) and the heroine of H. E. Bates' novel *Love for Lydia* (1952). **Liddy** is a familiar form of the name. Variants in other languages include the French **Lydie** and the Polish **Lidia**.

Lyle (m) English surname derived from the French *de l'isle* ('of the island') that was taken up as a first name among English speakers in the 19th century. As a surname it was originally used to refer to someone who came from any raised area of land, not just islands. Its popularity in Scotland may have been influenced by confusion with the otherwise unconnected Scottish name LYALL.

Lyn *See* LINDSAY; LLEWELLYN; LYNN.

Lynda *See* LINDA.

Lyndon (m) English place name (from Rutland) that was subsequently taken up as a surname and first name. The original place name was derived from the Old English *linde* ('linden' or 'lime tree') and *dun* ('hill'). Its popularity in the USA in the 20th century was influenced to some extent by the fact that it was borne by US President Lyndon Baines Johnson (1908–73). Also found as **Lindon**. *See also* LINDEN.

Lynette (f) English first name that developed as a diminutive of LYNN. The addition of the '-ette' ending suggests a French influence. It was taken up by English speakers during the 19th century and was promoted by Alfred, Lord Tennyson's 1872 poem 'Gareth and Lynette', part of the Arthurian epic *The Idylls of the King* (1859–85). Tennyson, however, was alluding to a much older Celtic name derived from an old Welsh word meaning 'image' and variously given as **Linet**, **Lunet**, **Luned** or **Lunete**. The name is also popularly linked with the

French *lune* ('moon') and the songbird called the linnet – hence such variants as LINNET, **Linette** and **Linnette**. Sometimes spelled **Lynnette**.

Lynn (m/f) English first name that developed variously as a diminutive of the masculine names LLEWELLYN or LINDSAY or else from the feminine names LINDA, LINDEN or **Lynda** (*see* LINDA). As a masculine name it is rarely used outside Wales, where it seems to have made early appearances in the 19th century. It is rather more widespread as a name for females, having made its first appearance around the same time but going on to enjoy a peak in popularity in the 1950s and 1960s. Well-known bearers of the name have included British actress Lynn Fontanne (Lillie Louise Fontanne; 1887–1983), Canadian ballet dancer Lynn Seymour (b.1939) and British actress Lynn Redgrave (b.1943). Also found as **Lin**, **Lyn** or **Lynne**.

Lynne *See* LYNN.

Lynnette *See* LYNETTE.

Lynsey *See* LINDSAY.

Lynton (m) English place name derived from the Old English for 'place on the torrent' that was subsequently taken up as a surname and first name. Notable bearers of the name include British Prime Minister Anthony Charles Lynton Blair (b.1953). Also spelled LINTON.

Lyov *See* LEO.

Lysette *See* LISA.

Lyssa *See* ALICIA.

Lytton (m) English first name meaning 'loud torrent'. Also found as **Litton**, it is best known through the English biographer Lytton Strachey (1880–1932).

Lyubov (f) Russian name meaning 'love'. **Lyuba** is a familiar form of the name.

M

Maarten *See* MARTIN.

Maas *See* THOMAS.

Mab *See* MABEL; MAEVE.

Mabel (f) English first name derived from the Old French *amabel* or *amable* ('lovely'). Early medieval versions of the name included the Latin Mabella, Amabilia, Mabilia, Mabilla and Mably (the first letter of the name being dropped as early as the 12th century). Pronounced originally with a short 'a' (as in 'gabble'), as Mabel it was found fairly frequently between the 12th and 15th centuries, after which it fell into disuse before being revived in the 19th century, when the pronunciation of the name was changed to rhyme with 'table'. After a peak between 1870 and 1920, the name went into a lasting decline.

Well-known bearers of the name have included children's writer Mabel Lucy Atwell (1879–1964) and US actress Mabel Normand (1894–1930). Also found as **Mable** or **Mabelle** (although this version of the name is sometimes alternatively derived from the French *ma belle*, meaning 'my lovely'). Other variants of relatively recent invention are **Maybelle** and **Maybelline**. The name is also known in Spain as a combined version of MARIA ISABEL. Common diminutive forms of the name include **Mab**, **Mabs** and MAY. *See also* AMABEL.

Mabella/Mabelle/Mable *See* MABEL.

Mabon (m) Welsh first name derived from the Old Celtic *mab* ('son'). It probably began as the name of a Celtic god. Like other ancient Celtic names it was revived in the 20th century.

Macario *See* MAKARI.

Mackenzie (m/f) Scottish first name meaning 'son of Kenneth'. It is particularly associated with Canada, where it is chiefly applied to girls and is understood to be a reference to the Mackenzie River.

Macsen *See* MAXIM.

Mädchen (f) German first name meaning 'girl'. It was taken up by English speakers on an occasional basis in the 1960s.

Maddie *See* MADELEINE; MADONNA.

Maddison *See* MADISON.

Maddy *See* MADELEINE; MADONNA.

Madeleine (f) French and English first name derived from the Hebrew Magdalene, meaning 'of Magdala' (Magdala being a town on the Sea of Galilee). The biblical Mary Magdalene was the New Testament figure who according to long-standing tradition washed Christ's feet with her tears. As Magdalen, Madeline or Madlin, it was first imported to England from France in the 13th century, when veneration of St Mary Magdalene was at a height following the discovery of her supposed relics. Other early versions of the name included Maudlin, reflecting the pronunciation of the name in post-Reformation England, but this variant disappeared after the ordinary vocabulary word came to mean 'sentimental' in reference to the story of St Mary Magdalene's tears.

The name became significantly popular among English speakers around the middle of the 19th century and has remained in currency ever since, with Madeleine the more usual spelling since the beginning of the 20th century. Also found occasionally as **Madolina**, **Madoline**, **Madelaine** and

Madlyn. Variants in other languages include **Magda**, **Magdala**, **Magdalena**, the Italian **Maddalena** and the French **Madelon**. Often shortened to **Mad**, **Madge**, **Maddie**, **Maddy** and LENA. Famous bearers of the name in its various forms have included the fictional Madoline who is the subject of John Keats's poem 'The Eve of St Agnes' (1819), British actress Madeleine Carroll (1906–87), US actress Madeline Kahn (1942–99) and the French schoolgirl created by Ludwig Bemelmans in his children's book *Madeline* (1952).

Madelina/Madeline *See* MADELEINE.

Madge *See* MADELEINE; MARGARET.

Madhav (m) Indian name derived from the Sanskrit *madhava* ('vernal'). In mythology it was borne by one of Krishna's ancestors and subsequently by Krishna, Vishnu, Shiva and Indra as well as by a celebrated 14th-century Hindu teacher and philosopher. **Madhavi** is a feminine form of the name.

Madhur (f) Indian name derived from the Sanskrit *madhura* ('sweet'). A relatively recent introduction as a first name, it is well known to English speakers as the name of the Indian-born cookery writer Madhur Jaffrey (b.1937). Related names include **Madhu**, a masculine name that dates from the medieval period, and **Madhukar**, another masculine name meaning 'bee' or 'honey-maker'.

Madison (m/f) English surname derived either from Magdalen (*see* MADELEINE) or meaning 'son of Maud' that was subsequently taken up as a first name. Also found as **Maddison**, it is largely confined to the USA, where it was promoted as a first name in the early 19th century through James Madison (1751–1836), who served as the country's fourth President (New York's Madison Avenue and Madison Square were named after him).

Madoc (m) Welsh first name meaning 'fortunate', or else derived from the Celtic *aodh* ('fire'). Recorded as early as the 11th century, it remains rare outside Wales. Also found as **Madog**.

Madonna (f) English first name derived from the Italian title for the Virgin Mary, meaning 'my lady'. As a first name it appears to have been a 20th-century introduction, being taken up initially by Italian Americans. The name enjoyed renewed worldwide exposure in the 1980s and 1990s as that of the US pop singer and film actress Madonna (Madonna Louise Veronica Ciccone; b.1958). Diminutive forms of the name include DONNA and **Maddy**.

Mae *See* MARY; MAY.

Mael (m) Welsh first name (pronounced 'mile') derived from the Gaelic vocabulary word *mael* ('prince').

Maeve (f) English version of the Irish Meadhbh, possibly derived from the Irish *meadhbhan* ('intoxication') and thus meaning 'she who intoxicates'. It is the name of a legendary queen of Connacht and is still largely confined to Ireland. Famous bearers of the name have included Irish novelist Maeve Binchy (b.1940). Pronounced 'mave', it is also found as **Maev**, **Mave**, **Meave**, **Meaveen**, **Medbh** and **Mab**. According to English legend, Mab was the name of the queen of the fairies (Shakespeare identifies her as such in *Romeo and Juliet*).

Magda/Magdalen/Magdalena/ Magdalene *See* MADELEINE.

Maggie *See* MARGARET.

Magnolia (f) English flower name that like many other flower names made its first appearance among English speakers in the late 19th century. It has never been common and is very rare today.

Magnus (m) Roman name meaning 'great' that was revived as a first name among English speakers early in the 20th century. The name is usually traced back to the 9th-century Holy Roman Emperor Charlemagne, who was also known as *Carolus Magnus* ('Charles the Great'). Subsequently the name was taken up in medieval Scandinavia and was borne in honour of Charlemagne by seven kings of Norway and several saints. The name subsequently reached Scotland and Ireland via the Shetlands, where it remains very common. It became more widespread among English speakers from the 1960s. Variant forms include the Irish **Manus**, the Danish **Mogens** and the Finnish **Mauno**. Well-known bearers of the name in relatively recent times have included British scientist and television presenter Magnus Pyke (1908–92) and Icelandic-born British television presenter Magnus Magnusson (b.1929).

Maha (f) Arabic name derived from *maha* ('wild cow'). The name evokes the large expressive eyes of cattle, often considered a metaphor for feminine beauty in the Arab world.

Mahalia (f) English first name derived from the Hebrew Mahalah and Mahali, which is thought to mean 'tenderness' (although other suggestions are that it was based on a musical term or on an ordinary vocabulary word meaning 'barren'). The name features in the Bible as that of the wife of Esau and also of a wife of King Rehoboam. It seems to have made its first appearances among English speakers in the 17th century and is now commonest in the USA. A famous bearer of the name was the US gospel singer Mahalia Jackson (1911–72). Variants of the name include **Mahala**, **Mehala**, **Mehalah** and **Mehalia**.

Mahavir (m) Indian name derived from the Sanskrit *maha* ('great') and *viru* ('hero') and thus meaning 'great hero'. Notable bearers of the name have included the 6th-century BC founder of Jainism (accounting for the name's popularity among Jains).

Mahendra (m) Indian name derived from the Sanskrit *maha* ('great') and INDRA and thus meaning 'the great god Indra'. Also found as **Mahinder** and **Mohinder**.

Mahinder *See* MAHENDRA.

Mahmud (m) Arabic name derived from *hamida* ('to praise') and thus meaning 'praiseworthy'. The name was popularized at an early date by Mahmud of Ghazna (971–1030), a Muslim commander of Turkish origin who conquered India but who also left a lasting legacy of hatred between Muslims and Hindus throughout the Indian sub-continent. Also found as **Mahmood**, **Mehmud** and **Mehmood**. *See also* MUHAMMAD.

Mahon (m) English version of the Irish Mathuin, itself descended from Mathghambain, meaning 'bear'. In its earliest form it was borne by a brother of Brian Boru, a king of Ireland in the 11th century.

Mai *See* MAY.

Maia *See* MAYA.

Maidie (f) Scottish and Irish first name apparently derived from the ordinary vocabulary word 'maid', possibly influenced by MAISIE. It may also be encountered as a rare diminutive form of MARY (probably because the Virgin Mary is sometimes referred to as a 'maid of God' or 'Maid Mary' etc.). It enjoyed a minor vogue among English speakers in the late 19th and early 20th centuries. Occasionally found as **Maidy**.

Maire *See* MARY.

Mairead *See* MARGARET.

Mairi *See* MARY.

Mairin *See* MAUREEN.

Mairwen (f) Welsh first name derived from MARY and *wen* ('white' or 'blessed').

Maisie (f) Diminutive form of the Scottish Mairead, a variant of MARGARET. It came into fashion among English speakers in the late 19th century, reached a peak in the 1920s, but fell from favour again after the 1930s. Henry James wrote a novel under the title *What Maisie Knew* (1897). Also found as **Mysie**.

Maitland (m) English surname of uncertain meaning that has also been adopted infrequently as a first name. The original surname is of Norman-French origin.

Maja *See* MAYA.

Makari (m) Russian first name derived from the Greek Makarios, itself from *makaros* ('blessed'). It was borne by several early saints and has variants in many languages, including the Italian, Spanish and Portuguese **Macario,** the French **Macaire** and the Polish **Makary**. Also found as **Makar**.

Makepeace (m) English first name meaning 'peacemaker'. A relatively rare first name, it is best known as the middle name of English novelist William Makepeace Thackeray (1811–63).

Makram (m) Arabic name derived from *makram* ('generous' or 'noble').

Mal *See* MALCOLM; MALDWYN.

Malachi (m) Hebrew name (pronounced 'malak-eye') meaning 'my messenger'. It features in the Bible as the name of the last of the twelve minor Old Testament prophets. It was taken up among other biblical names by the Puritans in the 17th century. Malachi Malagrowther was a pseudonym used by Sir Walter Scott in the 19th century. The name is only rarely encountered today. Also found as **Malachy**, although this version of the name (as borne by an early Irish king) can also be interpreted to mean 'devotee of St Seachnall'.

Malandra (f) English first name apparently devised through the combination of ALEXANDRA and MELANIE. It received a boost in the UK in the 1990s through British television actress Malandra Burrows (b.1965), although in her case the name resulted from the combination of her parents' names Malcolm and Sandra.

Malati (f) Indian name derived from the Sanskrit *malati* ('jasmine'), also interpreted as 'the night' or 'moonlight'.

Malcolm (m) English version of the Gaelic Mael Colum ('disciple of St Columba'). It is also found in Scotland as an Anglicized

version of COLUM. The name Columba itself means 'dove' in Latin. St Columba's conversion of the Scots to Christianity in the 6th century ensured the name's lasting popularity in Scotland, where notable early bearers included four kings (one of whom succeeded Macbeth). The name was taken up elsewhere in the English-speaking world on a significant scale in the 1920s and 1930s and reached a peak in popularity in the 1950s before going into decline.

Famous bearers of the name have included British land speed record holder Sir Malcolm Campbell (1885–1948), British conductor Sir Malcolm Sargent (1895–1967), US Black activist Malcolm X (Malcolm Little; 1925–65) and British novelist Malcolm Bradbury (1932–2000). Diminutive forms of the name include **Mal** and **Malc**. **Malcolmina** and **Malina** are rare feminine versions.

Maldwyn (m) Welsh variant of the English BALDWIN. The name is relatively unknown outside Wales, where it is also a county name (named after the Norman knight Baldwyn de Boller, and known in English as Montgomeryshire). **Mal** is a common diminutive form of the name.

Malina *See* MALCOLM.

Malinda *See* MELINDA.

Malise (f) Gaelic name meaning 'servant of Jesus'. In Scotland it is traditionally associated with the Gordon family.

Mallory (m) English surname derived from a Norman French nickname meaning 'unfortunate', from the French *malheure* ('unhappy' or 'unlucky'). It is usually encountered as a masculine name, but is occasionally also given to girls, most often in the alternative spelling **Malory**.

Malone (m) Irish first name, originally a surname, meaning 'follower of St John'.

Malvina (f) First name devised by the Scottish poet James Macpherson (1736–96) for a character in the celebrated poetry he claimed was the work of the legendary

Gaelic bard Ossian. Macpherson may have based the name on the Gaelic *mala mhin* ('smooth brow'). Like several other 'Ossianic' names it became popular throughout Scandinavia in the early 19th century as an indirect result of the French Emperor Napoleon's enthusiasm for Macpherson's work (Norway and Sweden were then under French domination). Modern bearers of the name have included the US singer-songwriter Malvina Reynolds (1900–1978). Variants in other languages include the German **Malwine**. **Malvin** is a masculine version of the name.

Malvolia (f) English first name that developed as a feminine equivalent of **Malvolio**, an invention of William Shakespeare's, meaning 'ill-will'. The name made rare appearances among English speakers in the 19th century.

Mamie (f) English first name that developed as a diminutive of several different names, including MARGARET, MARY and MAY, although it is often assumed to be based on 'mammy' or 'mummy'. It made its first appearances in the USA during the 19th century but is rarely heard today. Notable bearers of the name have included the fictional Mamie Pocock in the novel *The Ambassadors* (1903) by Henry James, US blues singer Mamie Smith (1883–1946) and Mamie Eisenhower (1896–1979), wife of US President Dwight D. Eisenhower. Also found as **Mame**, as in the musical *Mame* (1966).

Man *See* EMANUEL.

Manasseh (m) Hebrew name meaning 'causing to forget'. It appears in the Bible as the name of several people, including Joseph's elder son. It was recorded in use in England in the 11th and 12th centuries and was later taken up by Puritans on both sides of the Atlantic. Instances of the name in subsequent centuries have included a character in William Makepeace Thackeray's *Vanity Fair* (1847–8). Also found as **Manasses**.

Mandy *See* AMANDA; MIRANDA.

Manette *See* MARY.

Manfred (m) English, German and Dutch first name derived from the Old German *mana* ('man') or *magin* ('strength') and *fridu* ('peace') and thus meaning 'man of peace' or 'strong peace'. The name was brought to Britain by the Normans but subsequently fell into disuse until its import from Germany in the 19th century. It was popularized in the English-speaking world by Horace Walpole's use of the name for the central character in his novel *The Castle of Otranto* (1765) and a few years later Lord Byron made Count Manfred the central character of his poetic drama *Manfred* (1817). Other well-known bearers of the name have included the German First World War airman Manfred von Richthofen (1882–1918) and South African-born British pop musician Manfred Mann (Michael Lubowitz; b.1940). Variants in other languages include the German **Manfried** and **Manfrid** and the Italian **Manfredo**.

Mani (m) Indian name derived from the Sanskrit *mani* ('jewel'). It appears in the *Mahabharata* as the name of a serpent and also as that of one of Shiva's sons. It is very common in southern India.

Manley (m) English surname possibly derived from 'manly' or else from an English place name based on the Old English *maene* ('common') and *leah* ('wood' or 'clearing'). It made an early appearance in William Wycherley's comedy *The Plain-Dealer* (1676) and continued in use into the 20th century, although it is now rare. Well-known bearers of the name have included British poet Gerard Manley Hopkins (1844–89).

Manlio (m) Italian first name derived from the Latin Manlius, which was itself derived either from *mane* ('morning') or *man* ('good'). In ancient times Manlius was the name of a prominent Roman family. Bearers of the name in later centuries have included a son of the 19th-century Italian revolutionary Giuseppe Garibaldi.

Manny *See* EMANUEL.

Manon *See* MARIE.

Mansel (m) English surname that is occasionally encountered as a first name. It may have come originally from the French place name Le Mans. Also found as **Mansell**.

Mansoor *See* MANSUR.

Mansur (m) Arabic name derived from *mansur* ('victorious' or 'triumphant'). Notable bearers of the name have included the caliph Al-Mansur Abu Jafar (*c*.712–75), builder of Baghdad. Also found as **Mansoor**.

Manuel/Manuela *See* EMANUEL.

Manus *See* MAGNUS.

Mara (f) Hebrew name supposedly meaning 'bitter', although it is often assumed to be a variant of MARY. The name appears in the Bible as the name that Ruth's mother-in-law Naomi (meaning 'sweetness') gives herself when she complains that God has treated her badly: 'call me not Naomi, call me Mara: for the Almighty hath dealt very bitterly with me'. It has made occasional appearances in the English-speaking world since the 17th century. Also found as **Marah**.

Maralyn *See* MARILYN.

Marc *See* MARCUS; MARK.

Marcel (m) French first name derived from the Latin Marcellus, itself a diminutive of MARCUS. It was popularized in France through a 3rd-century missionary from Gaul who bore the name and was martyred for his faith at Bourges and it was among the names officially approved after the 1789 Revolution. It was adopted on an occasional basis by English speakers in the late 19th century and is today relatively common in Canada. Notable bearers of the name have included French writers Marcel Proust

(1871–1922) and Marcel Pagnol (1895–1974) and French mime artist Marcel Marceau (b.1923). Variants in other languages include the Italian **Marcello** and the Spanish and Portuguese **Marcelo**. **Marcella** (or, in France, **Marcelle**) is a feminine version of the name also found in English-speaking countries, especially Ireland – as borne by US rock singer Marcella Detroit (b.1956).

Marcella/Marcelle *See* MARCEL.

Marcia (f) English feminine variant of the Latin Marcius (or MARIUS). The name became current in the English-speaking world in the late 19th century, notably in the USA (where the usual spelling since the 1920s has been **Marsha**). There were three early Christian saints with the name. Well-known bearers of the name in more recent times have included the heroine of Thomas Hardy's novel *The Well-Beloved* (1897) and British Prime Minister Harold Wilson's secretary Marcia Falkender (b.1932). **Marcine** is a variant. Familiar forms of the name include **Marcie** and **Marcy**.

Marcie *See* MARCIA.

Marco/Marcos *See* MARK.

Marcus (m) Roman name which, like MARIUS, was possibly from that of Mars, the Roman god of war. Common in ancient Rome, it was subsequently taken up by English speakers around the middle of the 19th century and reached a peak in popularity in the 1970s. Notable bearers of the name over the centuries have included Roman Emperor Marcus Aurelius (121–180), Marcus Andronicus in Shakespeare's *Titus Andronicus* (1590–94), US Black activist Marcus Garvey (1887–1940) and British politician Sir Marcus Fox (1927–2002). Sometimes shortened to **Marc**. *See also* MARK.

Marcy *See* MARCIA.

Mared *See* MARGARET.

Maredudd *See* MEREDITH.

Marek *See* MARK.

Margaret (f) English and Scottish version of the Roman Margarita, which was itself descended from the Greek *margaron* ('pearl'). Some authorities have traced the word back further to a Hebrew source or else to a Persian word meaning 'child of light'. St Margaret of Antioch was a Hungarian-born 3rd-century martyr who was a popular subject of worship in medieval times (she also became the patron saint of childbirth). The name was taken up first in Scotland in the 11th century, when bearers included St Margaret and the wife of Malcolm III of Scotland. It was subsequently adopted by numerous English speakers in medieval times, becoming one of the most lastingly popular of all girls' names – although, being a saint's name, it suffered a temporary decline after the Reformation. It enjoyed peaks in popularity in the 17th century and again in the early part of the 20th century, since when it has faltered somewhat.

Famous bearers of the name have included members of many of Europe's royal families, including the English queens Margaret of Anjou (1430–82) and Margaret Tudor (1489–1541). Among notable Margarets in more recent times have been British Prime Minister Margaret Thatcher (b.1925), Queen Elizabeth II's sister Princess Margaret (1930–2002) and British novelist Margaret Drabble (b.1939). Diminutive forms of the name include **Madge**, **Maggie** (or **Maggi**), **Marge**, **Margi**, **Margie**, **Meg**, **Meggie**, **Megs**, **Meta**, **Moggy**, MAY, PEGGY and RITA. As well as Margarita, variants include **Margareta**, **Margaretta**, **Marghanita**, MARJORIE, the Welsh MEGAN and **Mared**, the Scottish MAISIE, the Gaelic **Mairead**, the French **Marguerite** and MARGOT (Anglicized as **Margo**), the Italian **Margherita**, the Scandinavian **Marit**, the Swedish GRETA and the German **Margret**. *See also* DAISY; PEARL; PEGEEN.

Margareta/Margaretta/Margarita *See* MARGARET.

Margaux *See* MARGOT.

Marge *See* MARGARET; MARJORIE.

Margery *See* MARJORIE.

Marghanita/Margi/Margie *See* MARGARET.

Margot (f) French diminutive of Marguerite (*see* MARGARET). It was first adopted from the French by English speakers in medieval times but remained rare until the 19th century, when it increased in frequency. It is still pronounced in the French manner (as 'Margo'). Notable bearers of the name have included British political hostess Margot Asquith (1864–1945) and British ballerina Dame Margot Fonteyn (Margaret Hookham; 1919–91). Also found as **Margo**. The unusual spelling **Margaux** was invented by US actress Margaux Hemingway (Margot Hemingway; 1955–96), who wished to honour the bottle of Margaux red wine that her mother and father (novelist Ernest Hemingway) drank on the night she was conceived.

Margret *See* MARGARET.

Marguerita/Marguerite *See* MARGARET.

Mari *See* MARIE.

Maria (f) Latin name from which the English MARY emerged. The Latin name in turn was descended from the Greek Mariam, which was itself derived from the Hebrew Miryam. The original meaning of the name may possibly have been 'to swell' (as in pregnancy). Also the modern Spanish, Portuguese, Italian, German, Dutch, Scandinavian, Polish and Czech form of the name, Maria owes its international popularity across the Christian world to the Virgin Mary. This form of the name was taken up by English speakers by the 16th century and remained fashionable through the 18th and 19th centuries, although it has always been less popular than the usual English version Mary. It enjoyed a minor resurgence in popularity in the 1960s. The usual pronunciation of the name has changed since the 19th century from

'Mar-eye-a' to 'Mar-ee-a', probably under the influence of the Italian, Spanish and Portuguese pronunciation.

Notable bearers of the name over the centuries have included characters in Shakespeare's plays *Much Ado About Nothing* (1598–9) and *Twelfth Night* (1601), Greek-born US opera singer Maria Callas (1923–77), British actress Maria Aitken (b.1945) and the heroine of Leonard Bernstein's musical *West Side Story* (1957). Variants include **Mariel** and **Mariah** – as borne by US actress Mariel Hemingway (b.1961) and US soul singer Mariah Carey (b.1970). Sometimes shortened to MIA, **Mitzi** or **Ria**, abbreviated forms that may be treated as names in their own right. Among the name's diminutive forms are the Irish **Moya**, the Italian **Mariella** (or **Marielle**) and **Marietta** (also found as **Mariette**) and the Spanish **Marita**. The name is often encountered in combination with other names, for instance the Italian **Giammaria** (a boys' name) and the Spanish **Maribel** (from Maria and ISABEL). *See also* MARIE; MARIUS.

Mariabella (f) First name combining MARIA and BELLA, usually assumed to mean 'beautiful Mary'. It was taken up by English speakers in the 17th century and has made occasional appearances since then.

Mariah *See* MARIA.

Mariam/Mariamne *See* MIRIAM.

Marian (f) English version of the French MARION, which was itself derived from MARIE. It is sometimes also considered to be a combined form of MARY and ANN. The name was recorded in use in England in medieval times and was subsequently popularized through Maid Marian, a central character in the Robin Hood legend (although she did not feature in the earliest versions of the tales). Notable bearers of the name since the medieval period have included a character in Thomas Hardy's novel *Tess of the D'Urbervilles* (1891) and US opera singer Marian Anderson (1897–1993). Occasionally encountered as Marion

(although this is today more often considered to be a masculine form of the name). *See also* MARIANNE.

Mariana/Marianna *See* MARIANNE.

Marianne (f) Variant form of MARIAN, often treated as a combination of MARY and ANNE. It was first taken up by English speakers in the 18th century, when it existed alongside **Mary-Ann**. In France the name has been adopted for the symbolic woman representing the Republic itself. Also found as **Mariane**, **Maryanne**, Mariana (recorded among English speakers as early as the 16th century) and **Marianna**. Notable bearers of the name in its various forms have included characters in William Shakespeare's *Measure for Measure* (1604) and *All's Well That Ends Well* (1603–4), one of the heroines in Jane Austen's *Sense and Sensibility* (1811), the subject of Tennyson's 'Mariana' (1830) and 'Mariana in the South' (1832), US poet Marianne Moore (1887–1972) and British pop singer Marianne Faithfull (b.1947).

Maribel *See* MARIA.

Marie (f) French equivalent of MARY, derived from the Latin MARIA. It was taken up by English speakers in the 19th century, initially in the USA. It reached a peak in popularity in the 1960s and 1970s. Notable bearers of the name have included French physicist Marie Curie (1867–1934) and British music-hall performer Marie Lloyd (Matilda Alice Victoria Wood; 1870–1922). Also found as **Maree** and **Mari**. **Mimi** is a diminutive form, famous from Giacomo Puccini's opera *La Bohème* (1896), in which the Parisian seamstress Mimi is a central character. Variants include the French **Manon** – as in the Massenet opera *Manon* (1884). It also appears in combination with many other names, as in **Jean-Marie** and **Marie-France**.

Mariel *See* MARIA; MURIEL.

Mariella/Marielle/Marietta/Mariette *See* MARIA.

Marigold (f) English flower name that was among many similar names taken up by English speakers towards the end of the 19th century. The flower itself was originally named *golde* (after the precious metal, because of its colour) but was renamed in the medieval period in honour of the Virgin Mary, with whom the flower was associated. Rarely encountered today. Also found as **Marygold**. GOLDIE is an accepted diminutive form of the name.

Marika (f) Slavonic variant of MARIA, now recognized as an independent name.

Marilyn (f) English first name based on a combination of MARY and LYNN (or ELLEN), or simply an elaboration of Mary with the suffix '-lyn'. Occasionally found as **Maralyn** and **Marolyn**, it is a relatively recent introduction dating from the early 20th century. Its early history was mostly confined to the USA, but it was taken up on an increasing scale elsewhere in the English-speaking world from the 1950s in response to the international popularity of US film actress Marilyn Monroe (Norma Jean Baker; 1926–62). A rare instance of the name being adopted by a man is US rock singer Marilyn Manson (Brian Warner; b.1969). Other variants include **Marilene**, **Marylin**, **Marylyn**, **Merilyn** and **Merrilyn**.

Marina (f) Italian, Spanish, German and English name representing a feminine equivalent of the Latin family name Marinus, itself derived from MARIUS. Because of its similarity to the Latin *marinus* ('of the sea') it has always had maritime associations – as shown by Shakespeare's use of it for Pericles' daughter in *Pericles* (1607–8), with the explanation that she was born at sea. The earliest records of the name among English speakers date from the 14th century, when its introduction was perhaps inspired by the Greek martyr St Marina of Alexandria. Notable bearers of the name in more recent times have included Princess Marina of Greece, Duchess of Kent (1906–68), who was a daughter-in-law of George V, British writer Marina

Warner (b.1946) and Marina Mowatt (b.1966), daughter of Princess Alexandra. Sometimes shortened to **Rena**. *See also* MARNIE.

Mario (m) Modern Italian, Spanish and Portuguese version of the Latin MARIUS. The name owes its considerable international popularity to the notion that it is a masculine form of MARIA. Well-known bearers of the name have included US singer Mario Lanza (Alfredo Cocozza; 1921–59) and US motor-racing driver Mario Andretti (b.1940).

Marion (m/f) English surname derived via Marianus from the Latin MARIUS that has also made rare appearances as a first name since the 19th century. It also exists as an alternative spelling of MARIAN. The most famous bearer of the name to date has been US film actor John Wayne (Marion Michael Morrison; 1907–79).

Maris (f) English name of uncertain origin. It is thought that it may have had its roots in the Latin *stella maris* ('star of the sea'). The name became familiar to many in the late 1990s through an unseen character called Maris in the hit US television comedy series *Frasier*.

Marisa (f) Italian, Spanish and English first name that evolved through the combination of MARIA or MARINA and LISA. Also found as **Marissa**, it is a relatively recent introduction to the English-speaking world, dating from the 1950s, and is uncommon outside the USA. Variants in other languages include the Dutch **Marijse**.

Marit *See* MARGARET.

Marita *See* MARIA.

Marius (m) Roman name that may have come from that of Mars, the Roman god of war, or else possibly from the Latin *maris* ('male' or 'manly'). A suggestion that it comes from the Latin *mare* ('sea') is usually discounted. Also found in several other European languages since the Renaissance, it has made occasional appearances as a first name among English speakers since the 19th century. Well-known bearers of the name have included British actor Marius Goring (1912–98). *See also* MARCIA; MARCUS; MARK; MARIO.

Marje/Marji *See* MARJORIE.

Marjolaine (f) French first name derived from the name of the herb marjoram. The name is today often assumed to be a variant form of MARJORIE.

Marjorie (f) English version of the French Marguerite (*see* MARGARET), regarded as a separate name since at least the 13th century. A derivation from the 17th century suggests it comes from the name of the herb marjoram (*see* MARJOLAINE). The earliest record of the name in England dates back to 1194, when it was given as Margerie or Margery. The spelling Marjorie was adopted initially in Scotland at the end of the 13th century, promoted by the fact that it was borne by a daughter of Robert the Bruce (destined to found the royal house of Stuart). The traditional medieval spelling Margery virtually disappeared in the 18th and 19th centuries, except among isolated rural communities, but was revived in the early 20th century when various forms of the name enjoyed a peak in popularity. Also found as **Marjory** and, in Scottish Gaelic, as **Marsali**. Notable bearers of the name in its different forms have included British crime novelist Margery Allingham (1904–66). Abbreviated versions of the name include **Marje**, **Marji**, **Marge**, **Margy** and **Margie**.

Mark (m) English version of the Latin MARCUS, possibly derived from the name of the Roman god of war Mars and thus meaning 'warlike'. The name appears in the Bible as that of one of the four evangelists, author of the second Gospel, and it later enjoyed some currency among English Puritans from the 17th century, although it was not until the 1960s that it suddenly emerged as one of the most popular choices of boys' names. An early bearer of the name

was King Mark of Cornwall, who figures in Arthurian legend in the story of Tristram and Isolde – it may have been this association with King Mark that prevented the name being taken up on any scale by English speakers until well after the medieval period. In more recent times the name has been borne by luminaries as diverse as US writer Mark Twain (Samuel Langhorne Clemens; 1835–1910) and British rock musician Mark Knopfler (b.1949). Twain explained that in taking the name Mark he was imitating a Mississippi boatman's cry for 'two fathoms deep'.

In France the name usually appears as **Marc**, as borne by Russian artist Marc Chagall (1889–1985) and by British pop singers Marc Bolan (Mark Feld; 1947–77) and Marc Almond (b.1957). Versions of the name in other languages include the Italian and Spanish **Marco**, as borne by Venetian explorer Marco Polo (1254–1324), the Portuguese **Marcos**, the Romanian **Marku**, the German **Markus**, the Ukrainian **Marko**, the Finnish **Markku** and the Polish and Czech **Marek**. Among familiar versions of the name commonly heard are **Markie** and **Marky**. *See also* MARIUS.

Marla *See* MARLENE.

Marlene (f) German diminutive form (pronounced 'marleen' or 'marlayna') of Maria Magdalene that was taken up by English speakers in the 1930s. Long before the name was adopted in the English-speaking world it was familiar to Germans. Its acceptance throughout the English-speaking world was a reflection of the international fame enjoyed by German-born US actress Marlene Dietrich (Maria Magdalene von Losch; 1904–92), whose greatest hit song was 'Lili Marlene'. Also found as **Marlena**, **Marleen** and **Marline**. Sometimes shortened to **Marla** or **Marley**. *See also* MADELEINE.

Marley (m) English place name derived from the Old English for 'pleasant wood' that has also been taken up as a surname and occasional first name. It has appeared more frequently in recent decades in tribute to Jamaican reggae musician Bob Marley (1945–81).

Marlin *See* MARLON; MERLIN.

Marlon (m) English first name of uncertain origin, possibly derived either from Marc (*see* MARK) or else from MARION or MERLIN. It made its first appearance among English speakers in the 1950s, when it received a huge boost through the massive popularity of US film actor Marlon Brando (b.1924), who inherited the name from his father. Also found as **Marlo** and **Marlin**.

Marmaduke (m) English and Irish first name of uncertain origin. Attempts have been made to trace the name back to the Celtic name Mael Maedoc meaning 'disciple of Maedoc' (Maedoc, or MADOC, being the name of several early Irish saints). Records of its use among English speakers date back to the 12th century, but it has never been a very frequent choice and is rare today (except as a name for family pets). Always considered an aristocratic name, it is associated traditionally with Yorkshire. Bearers of the name over the centuries have included fictional characters in Anthony Trollope's *Phineas Finn* (1869) and in Virginia Woolf's *Orlando* (1928). Sometimes abbreviated to DUKE.

Marna *See* MARNIE.

Marnie (f) English first name of uncertain origin. Also found as **Marni**, it may have developed, via **Marna**, as a variant of MARINA. Alfred Hitchcock's film *Marnie* (1964) helped to promote the name, particularly in the USA. Famous bearers of the name have included US singer Marni Nixon, who provided the singing voice for Audrey Hepburn in the film *My Fair Lady* (1964).

Marsali *See* MARJORIE.

Marsha *See* MARCIA.

Marshal *See* MARSHALL.

Marshall (m/f) English surname derived from the Old French *marechal* ('marshal') that has been been in occasional use as a masculine name since the 19th century and as a name for girls since the 1940s. The surname was ultimately Germanic in origin, coming from *marah* ('horse') and *scalc* ('servant'), and was thus originally reserved for people whose jobs were connected with looking after horses – although later it was used for anyone who filled any official ceremonial position. Also found as **Marshal**, it is more common in Canada and the USA than it is in the UK. Notable bearers of the name have included Canadian writer Marshall McLuhan (Herbert Marshall McLuhan; 1911–80).

Marta *See* MARTHA.

Martha (f) English first name derived from the Aramaic for 'lady'. It appears in the Bible as the name of Lazarus' sister, who complains to Jesus that everyone has left her to do all the housework while they listen to his words – and thus became forever identified with domestic drudgery. The popularity of the name in medieval France reflected the legend that St Martha had come to Provence after Christ's crucifixion. It was among the biblical names taken up by Puritans on both sides of the Atlantic in the 17th century and later enjoyed a marked resurgence in popularity in the USA in the 19th century in tribute to Martha Washington (1732–1802), wife of President George Washington. It has declined in use since the middle of the 20th century. Other notable bearers of the name have included the US dancer Martha Graham (1894–1991). Sometimes shortened to **Marti**, **Martie**, **Marty**, **Mattie** or **Matty** as well as to **Patty** or **Pattie**. Variants in other languages include the French and German **Marthe**, the Spanish, Italian and Scandinavian **Marta** and its diminutive **Martita**.

Marti/Martie *See* MARTHA; MARTINA.

Martin (m) English, French and German first name derived from the Roman Martinus which probably developed from the name of the Roman god of war Mars and thus may be interpreted to mean 'warlike'. Borne by the 4th-century St Martin of Tours, who was famed for dividing his cloak in two in order to share it with a beggar, it was later adopted as the name of five popes and became a popular choice of name throughout Europe in medieval times (when a cult of St Martin prospered in Britain). It has remained in currency among English speakers ever since the 12th century, with a recent peak in popularity in the 1960s and 1970s.

Notable bearers of the name have included German Protestant theologian Martin Luther (1483–1546), US President Martin van Buren (1782–1862), the central characters in the novels *Martin Chuzzlewit* (1843–4) by Charles Dickens and *Martin Eden* (1909) by Jack London, US Black activist Martin Luther King (1929–68) and British novelist Martin Amis (b.1949). Variant spellings include **Martyn**, originally a Welsh version of the name but now regularly encountered throughout the English-speaking world. Commonly abbreviated to **Marty** – as borne by British comedian Marty Feldman (1933–83) and British pop singer Marty Wilde (Reginald Smith; b.1939). Variants in other languages include the Dutch **Maarten**, the Italian **Martino,** the Portuguese **Martinho,** the German **Merten** and the Scandinavian **Morten**. *See also* MARTINA.

Martina (f) Feminine equivalent of MARTIN, first used by the Romans and subsequently taken up by English speakers around the middle of the 19th century. Notable bearers of the name have ranged from an obscure 3rd-century saint to Czech-born US tennis player Martina Navratilova (b.1956). Customarily abbreviated to **Marti**. Variants include **Martine**, **Martinella** and the Polish **Martyna**.

Martine *See* MARTINA.

Martita *See* MARTHA.

Marty *See* MARTHA; MARTIN.

Martyn *See* MARTIN.

Marvin (m) English surname of uncertain origin that has been in use as a first name since the 19th century. It may have emerged as a variant of MERVYN, although another theory traces it back to the Old English name Maerwine, which meant 'famous friend'. The name is most frequently found in Canada and the USA, where it made its first appearances. Also found as **Marvyn**, it reached a peak in popularity in the 1920s, since when it has gone into decline. Notable bearers of the name have included US soul singer Marvin Gaye (1939–84), US popular composer Marvin Hamlisch (b.1944), US boxer Marvin Hagler (b.1952) and the fictional Marvin the Paranoid Android in Douglas Adams' novel *The Hitchhiker's Guide to the Galaxy* (1979). Sometimes shortened to **Marv**.

Marwa (f) Arabic name derived from *marw* or *marwa*, the name of a fragrant plant, or else meaning 'shiny pebble' or 'flint'. The mountain of Al-Marwa in Mecca has strong ritual significance for Muslims.

Mary (f) English version of the French MARIE, derived from the Latin MARIA. The ultimate source of the name is thought to have been the Hebrew name Miryam, which may originally have had the meaning 'good/full' or 'to swell', thus evoking the idea of pregnancy and motherhood. This derivation of the name is supported by the similarity it bears with the word for 'mother' in various languages, such as the French *mère* and the Spanish *madre*. Another derivation traces the name back via MIRIAM to the Latin *stella maris* ('star of the sea'). According to St Jerome the name came from the Latin *stilla maris* ('drop of the sea'). Other derivations suggest that the name means 'wished-for child' or 'rebellion' and that it may have ancient Egyptian roots, meaning 'beloved of Amun' (Amun being an Egyptian god).

The name is borne by six biblical characters, of whom the Virgin Mary is by far the most significant. As a name of great religious importance it was borne by several early saints but was considered unsuitable for secular use for several centuries. Attitudes eventually changed, however, and the name became well established throughout much of Europe around the 12th century. It faltered in popularity among English speakers after the Reformation, partly because of its association with Mary Tudor, otherwise known as 'Bloody Mary' for the religious persecution that took place during her reign. The Puritans also had doubts about the name because of its strong Catholic connotations. It subsequently regained its status as one of the most frequent choices of name for girls across the English-speaking world in the 17th century and by the middle of the 18th century around one-fifth of all female children being born in England were being given the name. It kept its status as the most popular girls' name among English speakers until around the 1920s, since when it has suffered a marked decline and has been eclipsed to a large extent by the alternative Marie. It has made many appearances among royalty over the centuries, being borne by England's Mary I (1516–58) and Mary II (1662–94), Mary, Queen of Scots (1542–87) and British monarch George V's wife Mary of Teck (1867–1953). Other notable bearers of the name in more recent times have included Canadian film actress Mary Pickford (Gladys Mary Smith; 1893–1976) and British fashion designer Mary Quant (b.1934).

The name has many variant and diminutive forms, including the English **Mae**, MAY, MAIDIE, MAISIE, MAMIE, MOLLY, **Mimi**, **Minnie**, **Poll** and POLLY, the French **Manette**, the Italian **Marietta** and **Mariella**, the German **Mitzi**, the Dutch **Marieke** and **Mieke**, the Danish MIA, the Swedish **Maj**, the Russian **Masha** and the Polish MARIKA. It also appears in combination with a variety of other names, as in **Mary Ann**, **Mary Jane** and **Marylou**. Variants in other languages include the Irish Gaelic **Maire** and **Maura**, the Scottish **Mairi** and MOIRA, the Welsh **Mair** and **Mari** and the Russian **Marya**.

Maryam (f) Arabic name of uncertain meaning, but usually considered to be an Arabic version of MIRIAM. It has been suggested instead that the original source may have been a Syriac word meaning 'elevated'.

Maryann/Maryanne *See* MARIANNE.

Marylou *See* MARY.

Marylyn *See* MARILYN.

Masha *See* MARY.

Mason (m) English surname, originally an occupational name for anyone working with stone, that has made occasional appearances as a first name on both sides of the Atlantic. It is more often encountered in the USA than elsewhere.

Masood *See* MASUD.

Massimo *See* MAXIM.

Masterman (m) Scottish and English surname meaning 'master's man' or 'servant' that has made occasional appearances as a first name. Traditionally considered an aristocratic name sometimes given by barons to their first sons, it has never been very common. Captain Frederick Marryat gave the name to the hero of his novel *Masterman Ready* (1841).

Masud (m) Arabic name meaning 'fortunate' or 'lucky'. Also found as **Masood**.

Mat *See* MATILDA; MATTHEW.

Mateusz/Mathew *See* MATTHEW.

Mathias *See* MATTHIAS.

Mathilda *See* MATILDA.

Mathuin *See* MAHON.

Matilda (f) English first name derived via Norman French from the Old German Mahthildis, itself from *macht* ('might') and *hiltja* ('battle') and thus meaning 'mighty in battle'. It came to England with the Normans, being borne by William the Conqueror's wife Matilda (d.1083), and was later borne by a daughter of Henry I. It fell from favour after the medieval period and it was not until the 18th century that it was revived with any enthusiasm by English speakers. It declined in use once more after the early 20th century. Recent instances of the name have included the heroine of Roald Dahl's popular children's story *Matilda* (1988). The 'Matilda' of the Australian song 'Waltzing Matilda' does not, incidentally, refer to a person but to a slang term for a bushman's pack. Sometimes shortened to **Mat**, **Mattie** (or **Matty**), **Pattie** (or **Patty**), **Tilda** or **Tilly**. Variants include the English **Mathilda**, the French, Spanish and Portuguese **Mathilde**, the Italian **Mafalda**, the German **Mechtilde** and the Polish **Matylda**. *See also* MAUD.

Matrona (f) Russian name derived from the Latin for 'lady', itself descended from *mater* ('mother'). It was borne by several early Christian martyrs. Variants include **Matryona** and the Jewish **Madrona**.

Matt *See* MATTHEW.

Matthew (m) English first name derived from the Hebrew Mattathiah, meaning 'gift of God'. The name features in the Bible as that of one of the four evangelists, author of the first Gospel. It came to England with the Normans, usually in such forms as Matheu or Mathiu, and was relatively common in medieval times. It received a boost after the Reformation, although it was rather less popular than some of the other biblical names adopted at that time. It was not until the 1960s and 1970s, in fact, that the name claimed a position among the most frequent names in use – a position it has since retained.

Early instances of the name included appearances in Ben Jonson's comedy *Every Man in his Humour* (1598) and in Tobias Smollett's novel *Humphry Clinker* (1771). Notable bearers of the name since then have included British writer Matthew Arnold (1822–88) and US general Matthew B. Ridgway (1895–1993). A common diminutive form is **Mat** or **Matt** – as borne by British footballer Sir Matt Busby (1909–94) and British singer Matt Monro (Terry Par-

sons; 1930–85). Variants in other languages include the French **Mathieu,** the Italian **Matteo**, the Spanish **Mateo**, the Portuguese **Mateus**, the German **Mattäus**, the Dutch **Matthijs**, the Scandinavian **Mats**, the Danish **Mads**, the Polish **Mateusz** and the Russian **Motya**. *See also* MATTHIAS.

Matthias (m) Greek version of the Hebrew Mattathiah (also the source of MATTHEW). The usual Latin form of the name was Matthaeus. It appears in the Bible as the name of the apostle who took the place of Judas Iscariot and was subsequently among the biblical names taken up by the Puritans in the 17th century. It has never been very common among English speakers. Also found as **Mathias**.

Mattie/Matty *See* MARTHA; MATILDA.

Maud (f) English, French, German and Dutch diminutive form of MATILDA. It came to England as the name of William the Conqueror's granddaughter and was subsequently well known as that of Henry I's daughter Maud or Matilda (1102–67), who challenged her cousin Stephen for the English throne. Throughout the medieval period Maud was the usual vernacular version of the more formal Matilda. Alfred, Lord Tennyson helped to revive use of the name in the 19th century through his much-read poem *Maud* (1855), from which came the popular song 'Come into the garden, Maud'. Other notable bearers of the name have included Maud (1869–1938), the daughter of Edward VII and Queen Alexandra who married Haakon VII of Norway, and Irish nationalist Maud Gonne (1865–1953), to whom Irish poet W. B. Yeats dedicated several celebrated poems. Also found as **Maude**. A familiar version of the name is **Maudie**.

Maudie *See* MAUD.

Mauno *See* MAGNUS.

Maura *See* MARY; MOIRA.

Maureen (f) English version of the Irish Mairin, itself derived from MARY and meaning 'little Mary'. It was taken up by English speakers towards the end of the 19th century and enjoyed a peak in popularity in the 1930s, since when it has been largely out of favour – although it is still fairly common in Scotland and Ireland. Notable bearers of the name have included US actresses Maureen O'Sullivan (1911– 98) and Maureen O'Hara (b.1920) and British actress Maureen Lipman (b.1946). Also found as **Maurene**, **Maurine** and **Moreen**. Sometimes shortened to **Mo** or **Reenie**.

Maurice (m) English and French version of the Roman Mauricius, itself derived from the Latin *maurus* ('moor', 'dark-skinned' or 'swarthy'). It may also be encountered in Ireland as an Anglicized version of Muirgheas, from *muir* ('sea') and *gus* ('choice'). The 3rd-century St Maurice was the commander of a Roman legion of Christian soldiers who were martyred in Switzerland after they refused to participate in pagan sacrifices (the resort of St Moritz was named after him). The name came to England with the Normans, in the form Meurisse, and was relatively popular in medieval times, when it was usually given as Morris, but subsequently appeared only irregularly until the middle of the 19th century, when it enjoyed a minor vogue. By then it had evolved into the modern spelling, though usually still pronounced 'morris' in Britain; in the United States the French-style 'mow-reece' is more common. The name became relatively rare once more after the 1930s. Notable bearers of the name have included several 16th-century dukes of Saxony, French composer Maurice Ravel (1875–1937), French singer and actor Maurice Chevalier (1888–1972), the central character of E. M. Forster's novel *Maurice* (1913) and British actor Maurice Denham (1909–2002). Sometimes shortened to **Mo**, **Moss**, **Maurie** or **Morrie**. Variants in other languages include the Welsh **Meuric** or **Mourig**, the Irish **Muiris**, the German **Moritz**, the Italian **Maurizio**, the Spanish and Portuguese **Mauricio**, the Scandi-

navian **Maurits** and the Russian **Mavriki**.

Maurine *See* MAUREEN.

Mave *See* MAEVE; MAVIS.

Mavis (f) English and Scottish first name derived from a traditional name for the song thrush, itself originally from the Old French *mauvis*. It made its first appearance among English speakers towards the end of the 19th century after it was used by novelist Marie Corelli for her character Mavis Clare in *The Sorrows of Satan* (1895). It reached a peak in popularity in the 1930s, since when it has been in decline. **Mave** is a shortened form of the name.

Mavourneen (f) Irish first name derived from the Irish Gaelic for 'darling little one'. Also found in the form **Mavourna**.

Max *See* MAXIMILIAN; MAXINE; MAXWELL.

Maxene *See* MAXINE.

Maxie *See* MAXIMILIAN; MAXINE; MAXWELL.

Maxim (m) Russian first name derived from the Latin *maximus* ('greatest'). Numerous early Christian saints bore the name. Notable bearers of the name in succeeding centuries have included the Russian writer Maxim Gorki (Alexei Maximovich Peshkov; 1868–1936) and the romantic central character of Daphne du Maurier's novel *Rebecca* (1938). Variants in other languages include the Welsh **Macsen**, the Italian **Massimo** and the French **Maxime**.

Maximilian (m) English and German version of the Roman Maximilianus, derived from the Latin *maximus* ('greatest'). There were two St Maximilians in the 3rd century but it has also been suggested that the name was invented in the 15th century by the Holy Roman Emperor Frederick III for his son the future Maximilian I (1459–1519), through the combination of the names of the celebrated Roman generals Quintus Fabius Maximus and Scipio Aemillianus. The name subsequently became well known as a favourite choice of the Habsburgs and also, from the 16th century, of the royal house of Bavaria. It was recorded in use among English speakers in the early 17th century, although it has always been very rare. The diminutive form **Max** first appeared as an independent version towards the end of the 19th century. It is also shortened to **Maxie**.

Bearers of the name in its various forms have included the ill-fated Austrian-born Maximilian, Emperor of Mexico (1832–67), who was deposed and shot by his enemies, British critic and wit Sir Max Beerbohm (Henry Maximilian Beerbohm; 1872–1956), Austrian theatrical producer Max Reinhardt (1873–1943), British comedian Max Miller (Harold Sargent; 1895–1963) and Austrian actor Maximilian Schell (b.1930). A rare feminine variant of the name is **Maximiliane**.

Maxine (f) Feminine version of **Max** (*see* MAXIMILIAN). It emerged as a popular girls' name among English speakers in the 1930s and remained a fairly frequent choice until the 1960s, after which it went into decline. Also found as **Maxene,** as borne by US singer Maxene Andrews (1916–95), one of the Andrews Sisters. Sometimes shortened to **Maxie** (or **Maxy**) or **Micki** (or **Mickie**).

Maxwell (m) Scottish place name meaning 'Magnus' well' or 'large spring' that was subsequently taken up as a surname and, from the 19th century, as a first name throughout the English-speaking world. Often shortened to **Max** or **Maxie**. Notable bearers of the name have included Canadian-born newspaper proprietor Max Aitken, 1st Baron Beaverbrook (William Maxwell Aitken; 1879–1964), US playwright Maxwell Anderson (1888–1959) and British comedian Max Wall (Maxwell George Lormier; 1908–90).

May (f) Diminutive form of MARGARET and MARY that is now often treated as a name in its own right, invoking either the hawthorn or may tree and its blossom or else the name of the month. It was taken up by English speakers towards the end of the 19th century and reached a peak in popularity in the early years of the 20th century, when George V's wife Queen Mary (Princess Mary of Teck; 1867–1953) was usually addressed as May by her friends and family. It has since suffered a decline. It is also found as **Mae** – a variant popularized by US film actress Mae West (1892–1980), whose statuesque figure resulted in the name 'Mae West' being taken up for the inflatable life-jackets worn by RAF flight crew. Variants in other languages include **Mai** – as borne by the Swedish film actress and director Mai Zetterling (1925–94).

Maya (f) English first name of ancient Greek and Roman origin, possibly meaning 'nurse' or else derived from the Latin *mai* ('great'). It is also possible to derive it from the Sanskrit for 'illusion'. Also found as **Maia** and **Maja**, it was borne in Greek mythology by the daughter of Atlas and Pleione who became the mother of Hermes by Zeus. The month of May is thought to have been named after Maia, the Roman goddess of spring who was also identified as the mother of Jupiter. Pronounced 'my-a', the name made its first appearances among English speakers in the early 20th century and remains rare outside the USA. Notable bearers have included the US writer Maya Angelou (Marguerite Annie Johnson; b.1928), who acquired it originally as a nickname bestowed upon her by her younger brother, who referred to her as 'mya sister'.

Maybelle/Maybelline *See* MABEL.

Mayer (m) German and French first name derived from the German for 'farmer' or the French for 'physician'. Also encountered as **Meyer** or **Myer**.

Maynard (m) English surname derived via Norman French from the Old German Maganhard, itself based on *magin* ('strength') and *hard* ('brave' or 'hardy'), that has been in occasional use as a first name since the Norman Conquest. The German version of the name replaced the earlier Old English equivalent Maegenheard. Notable bearers of the name have included British economist John Maynard Keynes (1883–1946). Variants in other languages include the modern German **Meinard** or **Meinhard**.

Meadhbh/Meave/Meaveen *See* MAEVE.

Mechtilde *See* MATILDA.

Medbh *See* MAEVE.

Meena (f) Indian name derived from the Sanskrit *mina* ('fish'). It is borne in Indian mythology by the daughter of Usha, the goddess of the dawn, by Kubera, the god of wealth, and by Durga, wife of Shiva.

Mefodi (m) Russian first name derived from the Greek Methodios, from *meta* ('with') and *hodos* ('road') and thus meaning 'fellow traveller'. St Methodius was a 9th-century evangelist working in Moravia and author of a Slavonic translation of the Bible. Variants in other languages include the Polish **Metody** and the Russian **Mefodya** or **Modya**.

Meg *See* MARGARET.

Megan (f) Welsh variant via Meg of MARGARET. It was largely confined to Wales until the late 20th century, when it began to appear much more widely throughout the English-speaking world. The name became well known in the UK through British Prime Minister David Lloyd George's daughter Lady Megan Lloyd George (1902–66). Commonly shortened to **Meg** or **Meggie** (or **Meggy**). Variants include **Meghan**, **Meaghan** and **Meagan** – forms that have been taken up in Australia and Canada as a result of a mistaken belief that the name has Irish roots.

Meggie *See* MARGARET; MEGAN.

Meghan *See* MEGAN.

Megs *See* MARGARET; MEGAN.

Mehalia *See* MAHALIA.

Mehitabel (f) Hebrew name meaning 'God makes happy' or 'God benefits'. As Mehetabel, the name gets a brief mention

in the Bible. It was subsequently taken up by English speakers after the Reformation, early records of its use going back at least to 1578. It disappeared from regular use in Britain in the 19th century, but has subsequently resurfaced sporadically in the USA. The best known bearer of the name is the cat who is Archy the cockroach's friend in the poem *Archy and Mehitabel* (1927) by Don Marquis.

Mehmud *See* MAHMUD.

Meical *See* MICHAEL.

Meinard/Meinhard *See* MAYNARD.

Meinrad (m) German first name derived from the Old German *magin* ('strength') and *rad* ('counsel'). The name is best known as that of a 9th-century saint who was a member of the famous Hohenzollern royal family.

Meinwen (f) Welsh first name (pronounced 'mine-wen') meaning 'white' or 'fair'.

Meir (m) Jewish name derived from the Hebrew for 'giving light'. Variants include **Meier**, **Meyer**, **Myer**, **Maier** and **Mayr**.

Meirion (m) Welsh first name (pronounced 'myrion') that may have its roots ultimately in the Roman Marianus, itself derived from MARIUS. The former Welsh county of Merionethshire or Merioneth ('seat of Meirion') was named after a Meirion who was the son or grandson of the 5th-century chieftain Cunedda. Also found as **Merrion**. Relatively recent feminine versions of the name are **Meiriona** and **Meirionwen**.

Mel *See* MELANIE; MELINDA; MELISSA; MELVILLE; MELVIN.

Melanie (f) French, English and Dutch first name adapted via Old French from the Roman Melania, which itself was derived from the Greek *melas* ('black' or 'dark'). The name was originally reserved for children with dark hair, dark eyes or a swarthy complexion. It was borne by two 5th-century

Roman saints and made its first appearance among English speakers in medieval times, perhaps introduced by French Huguenot immigrants, but failed to catch on. It made a comeback, however, in the middle of the 17th century – although it remained relatively rare outside the southwestern counties of England until the 1960s since when it has become a frequent choice of name throughout the English-speaking world. It ranked among the top 50 girls' names among English speakers in the 1970s. Its emergence in relatively recent times may owe something to the fact that it was among the unusual names that were chosen for characters in Margaret Mitchell's highly successful novel *Gone with the Wind* (1936), subsequently filmed. Often shortened to **Mel**.

Notable bearers of the name have included US pop singer Melanie (Melanie Safka; b.1947), US film actress Melanie Griffith (b.1957) and two members of the 1990s British pop group The Spice Girls. Variants include **Melany**, **Mellony** and the French **Mélanie**.

Melba (f) English first name of Australian origin. The name appears to have been taken up initially in tribute to the celebrated Australian opera singer Dame Nellie Melba (Helen Mitchell; 1861–1931), who adopted the name from her home city, Melbourne.

Melchior (m) Hebrew name derived from that of one of the Three Magi in the Bible. It is thought to have resulted from the combination of the Persian *melk* ('king') and *quart* ('city'). An Italian variant is **Melchiorre**.

Melek (m) Jewish first name derived from the Hebrew for 'king'.

Melesina/Melicent *See* MILLICENT.

Melina (f) Diminutive version of several different names, such as EMMELINE, MELINDA and MELISSA. It has made rare appearances among English speakers since the 19th century. Notable bearers of the name have included Greek-born actress Melina Mercouri (1925–94).

Melinda (f) English first name that is thought to have developed as a variant form of BELINDA and other similar names. A link with the Latin *mel* ('honey') has been suggested. Also found as **Malinda**, it was first taken up by English speakers in the 18th century – there is a character of the name in Tobias Smollett's novel *Roderick Random* (1748). Today it is heard most frequently in Australia and the USA. Bearers of the name in more recent times have included British model Melinda Messenger (b.1971). Sometimes shortened to **Mel**.

Meliora (f) English first name derived from the Latin *melior* ('better'). It has made rare appearances in Britain since medieval times, confined chiefly to Cornwall.

Mélisande *See* MILLICENT.

Melissa (f) Greek name derived via *melissa* ('bee') from *meli* ('honey') that has been in use among English speakers since the 16th century. It became widely popular in the latter half of the 20th century, especially in the USA and Australia. Instances of the name in literature have included characters in Ariosto's *Orlando Furioso* (1532), Edmund Spenser's *The Faerie Queene* (1590–96), Charles Dickens' *The Old Curiosity Shop* (1840–41) and Lawrence Durrell's *The Alexandria Quartet* (1957–60). In real life the name has strong aristocratic associations, having been adopted by several of Britain's most prominent noble families. Occasionally shortened to **Mel**, **Missie** or **Lissa**.

Mellony *See* MELANIE.

Melody (f) English first name derived from the ordinary vocabulary word 'melody', itself descended from the Greek *melodia* ('singing of songs'). It made its first appearances among English speakers in the late 18th century and became increasingly popular in the 1920s, perhaps inspired by the Irving Berlin song 'A pretty girl is like a melody' (1919), and again from the 1950s. Also found as **Melodie**.

Melor (m) Russian first name that was devised in the 20th century in a self-conscious attempt to replace traditional names with modern names celebrating the creation of the Soviet state in Russia. The letters of the name stand for Marx, Engels, Lenin, October and Revolution. The name became defunct with the dismantling of the Communist state in Russia in the late 1980s.

Melva (f) English first name of uncertain origin, sometimes encountered as a diminutive form of **Melvina** (*see* MELVIN). It has been suggested that the name may have developed from a Celtic word for 'chief'.

Melville (m) English and Scottish surname and first name derived ultimately from the Norman French place name Malville, meaning 'bad settlement'. It appeared as a surname in Scotland as early as the 12th century and was taken up as a first name from the 19th century. Often shortened to **Mel**.

Melvin (m) Scottish surname that was taken up as a first name among English speakers towards the end of the 19th century. Its roots are obscure, but it may be descended in part from the Old English *wine* ('friend'). Another theory links the name with the Gaelic Malvin ('smooth brow'). It became increasingly popular from the 1950s. Also found as **Melvyn** – as borne by US actor Melvyn Douglas (1901–81) and British writer and broadcaster Melvyn Bragg (b.1939). Both forms of the name are commonly shortened to **Mel** – as borne by US film director Mel Brooks (Melvin Kaminsky; b.1926), British comedian Mel Smith (Melvyn Smith; b.1952) and Australian actor Mel Gibson (b.1956). **Melvina** is a rarely encountered feminine version of the name.

Melvyn *See* MELVIN.

Menahem (m) Jewish name derived from the Hebrew for 'comforter'. It features in the Bible as the name of a king of Israel who ordered the murder of all the pregnant women in his kingdom, but this has not

militated against it becoming a popular name within the Jewish community. Because of its original Hebrew meaning it was traditionally reserved for children born after the death of an older sibling. Also found as **Menachem** – as borne by Israeli Prime Minister Menachem Begin (1913–92).

Mendel (m) Jewish variant of the Hebrew MENAHEM, meaning 'comforter'.

Menuha (f) Jewish name derived from the Hebrew for 'peace' or 'tranquillity'. Variants include **Menuhah**.

Meraud (f) English first name of uncertain origin. It is often assumed that the name was originally derived from 'emerald', but others suggest that it is more likely to have evolved from an earlier Celtic name, perhaps based on *mur* ('the sea'). Confined largely to Cornwall, where records of it go back to the 13th century.

Mercedes (f) Spanish and French first name derived from the Spanish *merced* ('mercy'), itself descended from the Latin *mercedes* ('wages' or 'ransom'). Christ's crucifixion was sometimes interpreted as a form of ransom for the sins of mankind, and it was this notion that linked 'ransom' with 'mercy'. In Spain the Virgin Mary is often addressed as *Maria de las Mercedes* ('Mary of the Mercies') and this no doubt played a key role in the name becoming popular among Catholics, particularly in Spain and the USA from the 19th century. Today the name is automatically associated by many people with the Mercedes Benz motor car, which was named after the daughter of the company's top executive. Familiar forms of the name include MERCY and SADIE.

Mercia *See* MERCY.

Mercy (f) English virtue name also encountered as a diminutive form of MERCEDES. It was one of the many virtue names adopted by English Puritans in the 17th century, and like several of the others it has long since fallen from favour. The name features in John Bunyan's *A Pilgrim's Progress* (1684). MERRY is a diminutive form of the name. A rare Latinate variant of the name is **Mercia**, coincidentally also the name of a powerful early Anglo-Saxon kingdom, derived from the Old English *Merce* ('people of the borderland').

Meredith (m/f) English version of the Welsh Maredudd or Meredydd, which may have been based on a combination of *mawredd* ('greatness') and *iudd* ('lord' or 'chief'), thus meaning 'great chief'. The Welsh form of the name is little known outside Wales itself, although the English form can be found across the English-speaking world. Today the name is perhaps commoner among females than it is among men, especially in the USA, promoted by a female character called Meredith in Enid Bagnold's popular novel *National Velvet* (1935). Sometimes shortened to MERRY.

Merfyn *See* MERVYN.

Meriel *See* MURIEL.

Merilyn *See* MARILYN.

Merle (m/f) English first name that probably developed initially as a variant of MERYL or MURIEL. It is often related to the French *merle* ('blackbird'). As a first name for girls it was taken up towards the end of the 19th century. It made its first appearances as a boys' name early in the 20th century, largely confined to the USA. Notable bearers of the name have included US actress Merle Oberon (Estelle Merle O'Brien Thompson; 1911–79) and US country singer Merle Haggard (b.1937).

Merlin (m) English version of the Welsh Myrddin, which is thought to have been based upon the Old Celtic words for 'sea' and 'fort' or 'hill', thus meaning 'seahill fort'. It is most famous as the name of the magician who plays a major role in Arthurian legend. Also found as **Marlin** and **Merlyn** – as borne by Welsh politician Merlyn Rees (b.1920). Merlyn is occasionally found as a girls' name.

Merrilyn *See* MARILYN.

Merrion *See* MEIRION.

Merry (m/f) English first name that exists as a diminutive form of various other names, including MARY, MERCY and MEREDITH. It first won acceptance among English speakers in the 19th century, when it also appeared in Charles Dickens' novel *Martin Chuzzlewit* (1844) as an informal version of Mercy. It is usually found in the USA as a variant of Mary, from which it is indistinguishable in normal US pronunciation.

Merten *See* MARTIN.

Merton (m) English place name derived from the Old English for 'settlement by a lake' that was subsequently taken up as a surname and occasional first name.

Merv *See* MERVYN.

Mervyn (m) English version of the Welsh Merfyn, probably from the Old Celtic words for 'sea' and 'great' and usually interpreted as meaning 'sea ruler'. It was largely confined to Wales until the 1930s, when it began to be heard more widely among English speakers. Notable bearers of the name have included Welsh actor Mervyn Johns (1899–1992) and British novelist Mervyn Peake (1911–68). Also found as **Mervin**. Often shortened to **Merv**. *See also* MARVIN.

Meryl (f) Diminutive form of MURIEL that has emerged as an independent name among English speakers since the early 20th century. The most well-known bearer of the name to date has been the US film actress Meryl Streep (Mary Louise Streep; b.1949).

Meshulam (m) Jewish name derived from the Hebrew for 'friend' or 'paid for'. It features in the Bible, also appearing as **Meshullam**.

Meta *See* MARGARET.

Methuselah (m) Hebrew name meaning 'man of the dart'. Famed as the name of the oldest man in the Bible, who is said to have died at the age of 969, it appeared sporadically as a first name among English speakers in the 17th and 18th centuries.

Metody *See* MEFODI.

Meuric/Meurig *See* MAURICE.

Meyer *See* MAYER.

Mia (f) Italian and Spanish name adopted by English speakers in the early 20th century. It may come from the Italian and Spanish *mia* ('mine') but is also often treated as a diminutive form of MARIA (Scandinavian in origin). The most famous bearer of the name to date has been the US film actress Mia Farrow (b.1945). It enjoyed a significant boost in popularity in 2001 after it was chosen by English actress Kate Winslet for her daughter and ranked among the thirty most popular girls' names for that year.

Micah (m) Hebrew equivalent of MICHAEL, meaning 'who is like Yah?' (Yah being an alternative name for Jehovah). It appears in the Bible as the name of one of the prophets and subsequently made occasional appearances among English Puritans from the 17th century. Sir Arthur Conan Doyle brought the name new exposure with the publication of his novel *Micah Clarke* (1889).

Michael (m) English and German first name derived from the Hebrew for 'who is like God?'. The biblical St Michael was the archangel who led the angels against the army of Satan and who in consequence of this became the patron saint of soldiers. The name was borne by eight Byzantine emperors and by the founder of the Romanov dynasty in Russia among others. It was taken up by English speakers in the 12th century and remained consistently popular until the 19th century, when it went out of fashion. It came back into favour in the 1930s and has since maintained its status as one of the most frequently encountered of all English names, often present in lists of the top five boys' names in English-speaking countries. It has always been particularly popular in the

USA (where it was the most popular of all boys' names in the 1970s) and in Ireland, to the extent that the abbreviated form **Mick** has long been a nickname for any Irishman. There are also numerous surnames based on the name.

Notable bearers of the name have included British scientist Sir Michael Faraday (1791–1867), British actors Sir Michael Redgrave (1908–85) and Michael Caine (Maurice Micklewhite; b.1933), Prince Michael of Kent (b.1942), British television presenter Michael Barrymore (b.1952) and US pop singer Michael Jackson (b.1958). As well as Mick, the name is commonly shortened to **Mickey** (or **Micky**), **Mike**, **Mikey** or MIDGE, any of which may be treated as independent names in their own right – as in the case of British rock singers Mick Jagger (b.1943) and Mick Hucknall (b.1960) or US crime writer Mickey Spillane (Frank Morrison Spillane; b.1918) and US actors Mickey Rooney (Joe Yule; b.1920) and Mickey Rourke (b.1950) or US boxer Mike Tyson (b.1966). **Misha** is a familiar Russian version of the name (spelled **Mischa** in Germany).

Variants include the English **Mitchell** (or **Mitch**), the Welsh **Meical**, the French **Michel**, the Italian **Michele**, the Spanish and Portuguese **Miguel**, the Russian **Mikhail**, the Finnish **Mikko** and the Hungarian **Mihaly**. A feminine version of the name is **Michaela** or **Mikaela** (pronounced, with the emphasis on the second syllable, as 'mikayla'), which appears to have made its debut in the 1930s. Very rarely Michael itself has also been employed as a name for girls. *See also* MICAH; MICHELLE.

Michaela *See* MICHAEL.

Michèle *See* MICHELLE.

Michelle (f) Feminine variant of the French **Michèle**, itself a feminine equivalent of Michel (*see* MICHAEL). The original French Michèle was taken up by English speakers in the 1940s, but was soon eclipsed by its Anglicized form Michelle (although it is still occasionally found in the French spelling, with or without the accent). As Michelle the name enjoyed a peak in popularity between 1950 and 1980, in part as a result of the Beatles song 'Michelle' (1965). Notable bearers of the name in its variant forms have included British actress Michele Dotrice (b.1947) and US film actress Michelle Pfeiffer (b.1957). Often shortened to **Chelle**, **Shell** or SHELLEY. **Micheline** is a rare variant of the name.

Mick/Mickey *See* MICHAEL.

Micki/Mickie *See* MAXINE.

Micky *See* MICHAEL.

Midge (m/f) English first name that developed as a diminutive form of several other names, including MADGE, MICHELLE and Mick (*see* MICHAEL). It was taken up among English speakers in the 20th century. Well-known bearers of the name have included 1980s British pop musician Midge Ure (James Ure; b.1953).

Mieczyslaw (m) Polish first name (pronounced 'michislav') derived from the Old Polish *miecz* ('man') or *mieszka* ('bear') and *slav* ('glory'). Notable bearers of the name have included two early kings of Poland. Variants include **Maslaw**. **Mietek** and **Mieszko** are familiar forms of the name also used in Poland.

Mignon (f) English first name (pronounced 'meen-yon') derived from the French *mignon* ('darling' or 'cute'). Because of its closeness to Mignonette, it is often treated as a flower name and as a result was taken up on a small scale by English speakers in the 19th century. Awareness of the name was promoted through the opera *Mignon* (1866) by Charles Thomas, based on Goethe's novel *Wilhelm Meisters Lehrjahre* (*Wilhelm Meister's Apprenticeship*; 1796).

Miguel/Mihaly/Mikaela/Mike/ Mikey/Mikhail/Mikko *See* MICHAEL.

Miklos *See* NICHOLAS.

Milagros (f) Spanish first name derived

from a title of the Virgin Mary, *Nuestra Señora de los Milagros* ('Our Lady of Miracles').

Milborough (f) English first name derived from the Old English *milde* ('mild') and *burg* ('borough' or 'fortress'). Also found as Mildburgh, Mildburga and Milbury, it was well known as the name of a 7th-century English saint. As Milborough, the name made occasional reappearances among English speakers from medieval times until the 18th century, when it was last recorded in use in Shropshire.

Milburn (m) English place name derived from the Old English for 'mill stream' that was subsequently adopted as a surname and occasionally as a first name.

Mildred (f) English first name derived from the Old English Mildthryth, itself based on *milde* ('mild') and *thryth* ('strength') and thus meaning 'gentle strength'. It was borne by a daughter of the 7th-century King Merowald of the Old English kingdom of Mercia who became an abbess and was later honoured as a saint. The name was revived by English speakers in the 17th century and again in the 19th century. It enjoyed a peak in popularity in the USA in the 19th century but fell into disuse in the UK around the middle of the 20th century and is now very rare. Notable bearers of the name have included US jazz and blues singer Mildred Bailey (1907–51) and the heroine of James M. Cain's novel *Mildred Pierce* (1941). Commonly shortened to **Millie** or **Milly**.

Milena (f) Czech name derived from *mil* ('grace' or 'favour'). In Italy, where it has been taken up since 1900, it is treated as a combined form of the names MARIA and Elena (*see* HELEN). Variants include **Milana**, **Milada** and **Mladena**.

Miles (m) English first name of uncertain origin. Attempts have been made to trace it back to the Roman Milo, itself possibly from the Latin *miles* ('soldier'), although a link has also been suggested with the Slavonic *mil* ('dear' or 'beloved'). Other derivations from Old German suggest it means 'merciful' or 'generous'. The name came to England with the Normans and often appeared as Milo in medieval times. It has remained in use ever since, enjoying a minor vogue in the 18th century. It has long been a popular name in Ireland, perhaps through association with the legendary King Milesius of Spain, an early invader of Ireland. The Irish have also used it as a translation for such names as Maoileas ('servant of Jesus'), Maolmuire ('servant of Mary') or Maelmore ('majestic chief'). In recent years it enjoyed a resurgence in popularity among English speakers in the 1960s and again in the 1990s.

Notable bearers of the name have included a character in the 15th-century Coventry mystery plays, English Bible translator Miles Coverdale (1488–1568), one of the children in *The Turn of the Screw* (1898) by Henry James, British actor and playwright Miles Malleson (1888–1969) and US jazz musician Miles Davis (1926–91). Also found as **Myles** – as borne by English colonist Myles Standish (1584–1656), a leader of the Pilgrim Fathers. Milo came back into fashion in the 19th century, but is rarely encountered today. An uncommon female version of the name is **Mileese**.

Milford (m) English first name meaning 'mill ford'. Relatively rare as a first name, it is also in use as a surname and place name.

Miller (m) English first name derived from the ordinary vocabulary word. It is generally more familiar as a surname.

Millicent (f) English version of the French Mélisande, itself derived from the Old German Amalswint, from *amal* ('industry') and *swind* ('strong') and thus meaning 'hard worker'. It came to England from France in the late 12th century (as Melisende or Melisenda) and remained in use until the 17th century, when it fell from fashion. It was revived in the 19th century but is rare today. Notable bearers of the name have

included one of Charlemagne's daughters, British suffragette Dame Millicent Fawcett (1847–1929) and British singer Millicent Martin (b.1934). Commonly shortened to **Millie** or **Milly**. Variants include **Melicent**, **Melisent** and **Melesina**.

Millie/Milly *See* AMELIA; CAMILLA; EMILY; MILDRED; MILLICENT.

Milo *See* MILES.

Milos *See* MILOSZ.

Miloslaw (m) Polish first name (pronounced 'meeloslav') derived from the Slavonic *mil* ('grace' or 'favour') and *slav* ('glory'). Also found as **Miloslav**. **Miloslava** is a feminine form of the name.

Milosz (m) Polish diminutive form (pronounced 'meelosh') of various longer names based on the Slavonic *mil* ('grace' or 'favour'). Variants in other languages include the Czech **Milos**.

Milton (m) English place name derived from the Old English *mylentun* ('settlement with a mill') that was subsequently adopted as a surname and, since the early 19th century, as a first name on both sides of the Atlantic. The name's popularity was greatly influenced by respect for the English poet John Milton (1608–74). Today it is more common in the USA than elsewhere. Notable bearers of the name have included US comedian Milton Berle (Mendel Berlinger; 1908–2002), US economist Milton Friedman (b.1912) and Ugandan Prime Minister Milton Obote (b.1934). Sometimes shortened to **Milt**.

Mima *See* JEMIMA.

Mimi *See* MARIE.

Mina *See* WILHELMINA.

Mindy (f) English first name that appears to have developed under the influence of Mandy (*see* AMANDA) and CINDY. The name enjoyed international exposure in the late 1970s through the US television comedy series *Mork and Mindy*.

Minerva (f) Roman name, borne by the goddess of wisdom and possibly derived from the Latin *mens* ('mind') or else from an unknown Etruscan source. Records of its use as a first name date from the Renaissance. It has made rare appearances as a first name among English speakers since the 19th century. There is a character called Minerva Potts in the novel *Pickwick Papers* (1837) by Charles Dickens. Sometimes shortened to **Minnie**.

Minna (f) English first name derived either from the Old German *minna* ('memory' or 'love') or else from the Old German *min* ('small'). Also adopted as a diminutive of WILHELMINA. Its use among English speakers was for many years confined largely to Scotland – as shown by Sir Walter Scott's Minna Troil in *The Pirate* (1822).

Minne *See* WILHELMINA.

Minnie *See* MINERVA; WILHELMINA.

Minta/Minty *See* ARAMINTA.

Mira *See* MYRA.

Mirabel (f) English first name derived from the Latin *mirabilis* ('wonderful'). It was taken up by English speakers in the 12th century and was often employed as a masculine name until the 18th century – as borne by the hero Mirabell in William Congreve's comedy *The Way of the World* (1700). Also found as **Mirabelle**. An early feminine variant was the Italianate **Mirabella**, in which form the name appears in Edmund Spenser's poem *The Faerie Queene* (1590, 1596). The modern spelling was adopted in the 19th century.

Mirabella/Mirabelle *See* MIRABEL.

Miranda (f) English name derived from the Latin *mirari* ('to wonder at') and thus meaning 'adorable' or 'fit to be loved'. The name was invented by William Shakespeare for Prospero's daughter in his play *The Tempest* (1611) and was subsequently among several Shakespearean names to be taken up throughout the English-speaking world. It has appeared with increasing frequency since the middle of the 19th century. Notable bearers of the name have included British actress Miranda Richardson (b.1958). Sometimes shortened to **Mira**, **Mandy** or **Randy**.

Mireille (f) French first name probably derived from the Provençal *mirar* ('to admire'). It appeared initially as Mireio in the poems of Frédéric Mistral (1830–1914), who declared it to be a variant of MIRIAM and thus an acceptable name in the eyes of the Christian church. An Italian variant is **Mirella**.

Miriam (f) Hebrew name, originally MARYAM, of uncertain meaning. Closely related to MARY, which came from the same source, it is usually interpreted as meaning 'good', 'full' or 'to swell' (as in pregnancy) and may have been descended ultimately from an unknown Egyptian root. The name features in the Bible as that of a prophetess who was the sister of Aaron and Moses and it has always been a favourite within the Jewish community. It was taken up by English speakers during the 17th century. Notable bearers of the name have included a character in D. H. Lawrence's novel *Sons and Lovers* (1913), British actress Miriam Karlin (b.1925), British television presenter Miriam Stoppard (b.1937) and British actress Miriam Margolyes (b.1941). Also encountered as **Myriam**, **Mariam** or **Mariamne**. A familiar form of the name is **Mitzi**.

Miroslav (m) Czech, Polish and Russian name derived from the Slavonic *meri* ('great' or 'famous') and *slav* ('glory'). **Miroslava** is a feminine form of the name.

Mirza (m) Indian name derived from a Persian honorific title meaning 'prince'.

Mischa/Misha *See* MICHAEL.

Missie *See* MELISSA.

Misty (f) English first name derived from the ordinary English vocabulary word. The word made its debut as a first name among English speakers in the 1970s, inspired by the Clint Eastwood film *Play Misty For Me* (1971) – 'Misty' being the name of a hit single (1954) that features centrally in the plot.

Mitch/Mitchell *See* MICHAEL.

Mitzi *See* MARIA; MARY; MIRIAM.

Mo *See* MAUREEN; MAURICE; MOSES.

Moreen *See* MAUREEN.

Modest *See* MODESTY.

Modesty (f) English virtue name that appears to have made its debut among English speakers only in the 20th century. It appears to be a modern equivalent of the Late Latin name Modestus, which had much the same meaning. Notable bearers of the name have included the 1960s British cartoon character Modesty Blaise. Related names include the Russian **Modest**, a name borne by a handful of early Christian saints, the French **Modestine** and the Italian, Spanish and Portuguese **Modesto**. A diminutive form of the Russian variant is **Desya**.

Modya *See* MEFODI.

Mogens *See* MAGNUS.

Moggy *See* MARGARET.

Mohammed *See* MUHAMMAD.

Mohan (m) Indian name derived from the Sanskrit *mohana* ('bewitching'). In Indian mythology it is borne by Shiva, Kama and Krishna. **Mohana** is the usual feminine form of the name.

Mohinder *See* MAHENDRA.

Mohini (f) Indian name derived from the Sanskrit *muh* ('to bewitch'). The name is borne in Indian mythology by Vishnu and is also the name of a style of classical Indian dancing.

Moina (f) Irish and Scottish first name possibly derived from the Gaelic for 'girl of the peat-moss'.

Moira (f) English version of the Irish Maire, itself a variant of MARY. It probably evolved through the usual pronunciation of Mary in Irish. As **Maura**, the name was borne by a 5th-century martyr. English speakers took up Moira in the 19th century, since when it has established itself as a particular favourite in Scotland. Notable bearers of the name have included South African-born British actress Moira Lister (b.1923), Scottish-born ballerina Moira Shearer (b.1926) and Scottish singer Moira Anderson (b.1940). Also found in the USA as **Moyra**.

Mollie *See* MOLLY.

Molly (f) English first name that had emerged as a diminutive of MARY by the 18th century. The change of 'r' to 'll' is a standard evolution shared with several other names, such as Sarah, which produced Sally in much the same way. Early instances of the name included the celebrated London beauty Molly Mog (1699–1766), about whom John Gay wrote the ballad 'Fair Maid of the Inn', and a gamekeeper's daughter in the novel *Tom Jones* (1749) by Henry Fielding, the first of a series of housemaids and other domestic servants to share the name in English literature. Other notable bearers of the name have included Irish novelist Molly Keane (1905–96) and US actress Molly Ringwald (b.1968). Also found as **Moll**, best known from Daniel Defoe's novel *Moll Flanders* (1722), and **Mollie** – as borne by the fictional Mollie Malone (the central character in the Irish song 'Cockles and Mussels') and British comedy actress Mollie Sugden (b.1924).

Mona (f) English version of the Irish Muadhnait, itself derived from *muadh* ('noble' or 'good'). Occasionally also encountered as a diminutive form of MONICA. It took root initially in Ireland and was subsequently taken up by English speakers elsewhere towards the end of the 19th century, when Irish names were in vogue. Notable bearers of the name have included British actress Mona Washbourne (1903–88). Also found as **Moyna**.

Monday (f) English first name that was

formerly reserved for girls born on a Monday. Little used since medieval times.

Monica (f) English first name of uncertain origin. Attempts have been made to trace it back to the Greek *monos* ('alone') or the Latin *monere* ('to warn' or 'to advise'). The 4th-century St Monica, who came from Carthage, was the mother of St Augustine of Hippo and was later venerated for her matronly virtues. Having been taken up by English speakers in the 19th century, it increased in frequency in the 1930s, since when it has remained moderately popular. Notable bearers of the name have included British novelist Monica Dickens (1915–92), one of the girls in Muriel Spark's novel *The Prime of Miss Jean Brodie* (1961), Yugoslavian-born tennis player Monica Seles (b.1973) and a character in the popular 1990s US television series *Friends*. Sometimes shortened to MONA. Variant forms include the French **Monique**, the German and Scandinavian **Monika** and the familiar form **Monny**.

Monique/Monny *See* MONICA.

Monroe (m) English and Scottish first name that is thought to have had its roots in a Scottish place name and surname originally meaning 'mouth of the Roe' (a reference to the River Roe in Ireland's County Derry, from which the Scottish Munro clan are supposed to have come). The name is especially popular in the USA, promoted by US President James Monroe (1758–1831), author of the Monroe Doctrine opposing European interference in the Americas, and subsequently by film actress Marilyn Monroe (1926–62). Also found as **Monro**, **Munroe** and **Munro**.

Montague (m) English surname that was taken up as a first name among English speakers in the early 19th century. It began as a Norman place name, Mont Agigu near Caen, itself derived from the Old French *mont* ('hill') and *aigu* ('pointed'), and was borne by the lords of Montaigu in La Manche, one of whom – Drogo de Montacute – came to England with William the

Conqueror in the 11th century. The name still has strong aristocratic associations, being the surname of a celebrated noble family of England. Also found as **Montagu**. Often shortened, like MONTGOMERY, to **Monty** or **Monte**.

Montgomery (m) English surname and former Welsh county name that has appeared occasionally as a first name among English speakers since the 1920s. It began life as a Norman place name, Mont Goumeril, derived from the Old French *mont* ('hill') and the Germanic *gomeric* ('man power') and thus meaning something like 'mountain of the powerful one'. A character called Montgomery Ward Snopes appears in several novels written by William Faulkner in the 1940s and 1950s, but later appearances of the name probably owed more to the popularity of British wartime army commander Field Marshal Bernard Montgomery (1887–1976), who was widely known by the usual diminutive form of the name, **Monty**. Other notable bearers of the name have included the US film actor Montgomery Clift (1920–66). *See also* MALDWYN.

Montmorency (m) French surname that made occasional appearances as a first name among English speakers in the 19th century. The surname came originally from a Norman place name derived from the Old French *mont* ('hill') and the Gallo-Roman name **Maurentius**. Sometimes shortened to **Monty**. The name appears in Jerome K. Jerome's *Three Men in a Boat* (1889) as that of a pet dog.

Montserrat (f) Catalan name derived ultimately from the Latin *mons serratus* ('jagged hill'). It refers specifically to a mountain near Barcelona on which stands a celebrated Benedictine monastery dedicated to the Virgin Mary, built in 976. Notable bearers of the name have included Spanish soprano Montserrat Caballé (b.1933). Sometimes shortened to **Montse** or **Monse**.

Monty *See* MONTAGUE; MONTGOMERY; MONTMORENCY.

Mor (f) Scottish and Irish name derived from the Gaelic for 'large' or 'great'. In late medieval times this was the most popular of all Irish girls' names and it has remained in regular use in Scotland and Ireland into modern times. Variants include MORAG and **Moreen** (*see* MAUREEN).

Morag (f) Scottish first name derived from *mor* ('great'). Another derivation suggests it comes from the Gaelic for 'sun'. Some authorities have also described it as a Scottish equivalent of MARY or SARAH. It has appeared with increasing frequency both in Scotland and elsewhere in the English-speaking world in the 20th century, although it is still thought of as a predominantly Scottish name.

Moray *See* MURRAY.

Morcant *See* MORGAN.

Mordecai (m) Hebrew name probably derived from Persian and meaning 'devotee of Marduk' (Marduk being the most important of the gods of ancient Babylon). It features in the Bible as the name of Esther's foster father. It was taken up by English Puritans in the 17th century and remained in currency among Nonconformists until the end of the 19th century. Today it is rare outside the Jewish community. Notable bearers of the name have included a character in George Eliot's novel *Daniel Deronda* (1876) and Canadian novelist Mordecai Richler (b.1931). Sometimes shortened to **Mordy** or **Morty**. Among Jews it is sometimes abbreviated to **Motke** or **Motl**.

Mordy *See* MORDECAI.

Moreen *See* MAUREEN.

Morgan (m/f) English first name derived from the Welsh Morcant, which may have come from the words *mor* ('sea') and *cant* ('circle' or 'edge') but is otherwise of unknown origin. It is sometimes suggested that the name means 'seabright'. The name has a long history among the Welsh and was famous as the name of a 7th-century Welsh prince commemorated today in the name of Glamorgan in south Wales. Though still commonly encountered in Wales, the name is now found throughout the English-speaking world. Its use as a girls' name was promoted by the appearance of the name in Arthurian legend, borne by Arthur's stepsister, the sorceress Morgan le Fay. A feminine variant is **Morgana**. Notable bearers of the name have included British novelist E. M. Forster (Edward Morgan Forster; 1879–1970), US actor Morgan Freeman (b.1937) and US actress Morgan Fairchild (Patsy McClenny; b.1950).

Moriarty (m) English first name derived from the Irish Muirchertach, which means 'seafarer'. Today it is usually associated with Professor Moriarty, the arch-enemy of Sir Arthur Conan Doyle's celebrated detective Sherlock Holmes.

Moritz *See* MAURICE.

Morley (m) English place name derived from the Old English *mor* ('moor' or 'marsh') and *leah* ('wood' or 'clearing') that was subsequently taken up as a surname and on occasion as a first name.

Morna *See* MYRNA.

Morrie/Morris *See* MAURICE.

Mort *See* MORTIMER; MORTON.

Morten *See* MARTIN.

Mortimer (m) English surname that was taken up as a first name among English speakers in the 19th century. It probably had its roots in a Norman place name derived from the Old French for 'dead sea' (referring to a stagnant lake or marsh) that came to be borne by the lords of Mortemer in Normandy. Another suggestion is that it is of Celtic origin, meaning 'sea warrior'. Notable bearers of the name have included characters in Anthony Trollope's novel *Doctor Thorne* (1858), Charles Dickens' novel *Our Mutual Friend* (1865), Scottish-born archaeologist and broadcaster Sir

Mortimer Wheeler (1890–1976) and the male lead in Joseph Kesselring's play *Arsenic and Old Lace* (1941). Sometimes shortened to **Mort**.

Morton (m) English place name derived from the Old English *mortun* ('settlement on a moor') that was subsequently taken up as a surname and, from the middle of the 19th century, as a first name. It is most frequently found today within the Jewish community, as an Anglicized version of MOSES. **Mort** and **Morty** are familiar forms of the name.

Morty *See* MORDECAI; MORTON.

Morven (f) English name of uncertain Scottish derivation. It may have been taken from the name of the Morvern district in north Argyll, Scotland, itself based on the Gaelic for 'great gap', or else from the Gaelic *mor bheinn* ('great peak'). Its use as a first name was promoted by its identification as Fingal's kingdom in the notorious but much admired Ossianic poems of James Macpherson published in the 18th century.

Morwenna (f) Cornish and Welsh name derived either from the Welsh *morwyn* ('maiden') or else from the Welsh *mor* ('sea') and *gwaneg* ('wave'). Several Cornish churches are named after the Celtic St Morwenna, who lived in the 5th century. The name was revived around the middle of the 20th century. Also appears as **Morwen**.

Moses (m) Hebrew name of uncertain origin. It may have evolved, via the Hebrew Moshel, from the Egyptian *mes* ('child' or 'born of'). The story of the biblical Moses, who led the Israelites out of Egypt and passed on the Ten Commandments, established the name as a traditional favourite among Jews. Early records of the name in English, dating from the 11th century, give it as Moyses. Also found as **Moyse** or **Moss**, it was adopted by English Puritans in the 17th century, but is rare today. Notable bearers of the name have included fictional characters in Oliver Goldsmith's novel *The Vicar of Wakefield* (1766) and Richard

Brinsley Sheridan's comedy *The School for Scandal* (1777). Abbreviated forms of the name include **Mo**, **Mose** and **Moy**. **Moshe** (or **Moishe**) is a Yiddish variant – as borne by the Israeli military commander Moshe Dayan (1915–81). *See also* MORTON.

Moshe *See* MOSES.

Moss *See* MAURICE; MOSES; MOSTYN.

Mostafa *See* MUSTAFA.

Mostyn (m) Welsh first name derived from a place name in Clwyd, itself derived from the Old English *mos* ('moss') and *tun* ('settlement'). Sometimes abbreviated to **Moss**.

Motke/Motl *See* MORDECAI.

Motya *See* MATTHEW.

Moy *See* MOSES.

Moya *See* MARIA.

Moyna *See* MONA.

Moyra *See* MOIRA.

Mstislav (m) Czech and Russian first name (pronounced 'musheeslav') derived from an old Slavonic name based on *mshcha* ('vengeance') and *slav* ('glory'). Variants include the Polish **Mscislaw**.

Muhammad (m) Arabic name derived from *hamida* ('to praise') and thus meaning 'praiseworthy'. As the name of the founder of Islam, it has long been one of the most popular masculine names among Muslims around the world. Notable bearers of the name in the English-speaking world have included US boxer Muhammad Ali (Cassius Marcellus Clay; b.1942). Also found as **Mahomet**, **Mohammad** or **Mohammed**. *See also* AHMED; HAMID; MAHMUD.

Muhsin (m) Arabic name derived from *muhsin* ('beneficent' or 'charitable'). Also found in the feminine version **Muhsina**, this is a traditional favourite across the Arab-speaking world.

Muir (m) Scottish place name meaning 'moor' that was subsequently taken up as a surname and is occasionally encountered in use as a first name. Notable bearers of the name have included the Scottish film music director Muir Mathieson (1911–72).

Muireann (f) Irish first name (pronounced 'mwirran') derived from the Irish Gaelic *muir* ('sea') and *fionn* ('white' or 'fair'). Also found as **Muirinn** or **Morann** and frequently equated with MAUREEN.

Muiris *See* MAURICE.

Muirne *See* MYRNA.

Mukesh (m) Indian name of uncertain origin. It may be derived from the Sanskrit *isa* ('ruler') or else mean 'conqueror of the demon Muka', in reference to a legendary battle between the god Shiva and a wild boar.

Mukhtar (m) Arabic name derived from *khara* ('to choose') and thus meaning 'chosen'.

Muna (f) Arabic name meaning 'hope' or 'object of desire'.

Mungo (m) Scottish name possibly derived from the Welsh *mwyn* ('dear', 'gentle' or 'kind'). It was borne as a nickname meaning 'most dear' by a 6th-century Scottish saint, otherwise known as St KENTIGERN, and to this day is rare outside Scotland itself. Notable bearers of the name have included Scottish explorer Mungo Park (1771–1806), a character called Sir Mungo Malagrowther in Sir Walter Scott's novel *The Fortunes of Nigel* (1822) and 1970s British pop group Mungo Jerry.

Munir (m) Arabic name derived from *nawara* ('to illuminate') and thus meaning 'bright' or 'shining'. **Munira** is a feminine form of the name.

Munro/Munroe *See* MONROE.

Murali (m) Indian name derived from the Sanskrit *murali* ('flute'). In Indian mythology, the name is sometimes borne by the flute-playing Krishna.

Murdo *See* MURDOCH.

Murdoch (m) English surname and first name derived from the Scottish Gaelic Murdo or Muireadhach itself based on the

Gaelic *muir* ('sea') and usually interpreted to mean 'seaman' or 'mariner'. Sometimes shortened to **Murdy** or **Murdie**. Rare feminine forms include **Murdag** and **Murdina**. **Murtagh** is an Irish equivalent.

Murgatroyd (m) English place name (from Yorkshire) that was subsequently adopted as a surname and from the 19th century as an occasional first name. The original place name – unlocated – was derived from the first name Margaret and the Yorkshire dialect *royd* ('clearing') and the name thus means 'Margaret's clearing'.

Muriel (f) English version of the Irish Gaelic Muirgheal and the Scottish Gaelic Muircall derived from *muir* ('sea') and *geal* ('bright') and thus meaning 'sea-bright'. The earliest records of the name come from Brittany, Scotland and Ireland, although it also appears to have been in use in England by medieval times (William the Conqueror is supposed to have had a half-sister with the name). It began to appear with increasing frequency among English speakers in the 19th century and won particular favour in Scotland. It reached a peak in popularity during the 1920s and 1930s but has since suffered a sharp decline. Notable bearers of the name have included a character in Mrs Craik's very popular novel *John Halifax, Gentleman* (1856) and Scottish-born novelist Muriel Spark (b.1918). Also found as **Mariel, Meriel, Merrill** and MERYL.

Murphy (m/f) Irish first name derived from the Irish Gaelic for 'sea hound'.

Murray (m) Scottish surname that was taken up on an occasional basis as a first name among English speakers in the 19th century. The surname (borne by the Dukes of Atholl among others) came originally from the Scottish place name Moray, derived from *mor* ('sea'), although as a first name Murray may also be found as an Anglicized version of the Gaelic **Muireach**. Well-known bearers of the name have included British television sports commentator Murray Walker (b.1923) and US pianist Murray Perahia (b.1947). Also found as **Moray** or **Murry**.

Murtagh *See* MURDOCH.

Musad (m) Arabic name derived from *saida* ('to be lucky'). Also found as **Misid**.

Mustafa (m) Arabic name meaning 'chosen'. As a title of MUHAMMAD, it has long been one of the most popular names among Muslims. Notable bearers of the name have included Mustafa Kemal (1881–1938), the founder of the modern Turkish state. Also found as **Mostafa**.

Mutasim (m) Arabic name meaning 'faithful to God'.

Myer *See* MAYER.

Myf *See* MYFANWY.

Myfanwy (f) Welsh name (pronounced 'murvanwee') derived from the Welsh *my* ('my dear') and *manwy* ('fine' or 'precious') and thus meaning 'my fine one' or 'my dear precious one'. Alternatively, the name may have developed from *menyw* ('woman'). It is largely confined to Wales and was little known before the 20th century. It is best known to English speakers as the name of Myfanwy Price, a character in Dylan Thomas' celebrated poetic play *Under Milk Wood* (1954). Sometimes shortened to **Myf** (pronounced 'muv'), **Myfi** or FANNY.

Myles *See* MILES.

Myra (f) English first name possibly derived from the Greek *muron* ('myrrh') or the Latin *mirari* ('to wonder at'), or else as an anagram of MARY or a variant of MOIRA. In Scotland it is sometimes used as an Anglicization of Mairead. The name appears to have been invented by the English poet Fulke Greville (1554–1628) for the subject of his love poems and for many years it remained a predominantly literary name used only by poets and novelists. It was taken up as a first name by English speakers in the 19th century, when it became particularly popular in Scotland. Notable bearers of the name have included the British pianist Dame Myra Hess (1890–

1965) and the central character in Gore Vidal's novel (later filmed) *Myra Breckinridge* (1968). The fact that the name was also borne by notorious 1960s British child killer Myra Hyndley (1942–2002) may have dampened enthusiasm for the name in recent decades. Also found as **Mira**.

Myrddin *See* MERLIN.

Myriam *See* MIRIAM.

Myrna (f) English version of the Irish Muirne, a name derived from the Gaelic *muirne* ('affection' or 'tenderness'). The name of the mother of the legendary Irish hero Finn MacCool, it was taken up by English speakers in the 19th century. Well-known bearers of the name have included US film actress Myrna Loy (1905–93). Also found as **Morna** and **Muirre**.

Myron (m) Greek name meaning 'myrrh' that was taken up as a first name by English speakers in the 20th century. Sometimes today interpreted to mean 'fragrant'. Borne by a celebrated 5th-century Greek sculptor, it was popular among early Christians because of its link with myrrh, one of the gifts presented to the baby Jesus. Notable bearers of the name have included several early saints and, in modern times, US film producer Myron Zelznick (1898–1944).

Myrrha (f) Arabic name meaning 'myrtle'. It has made occasional appearances among English speakers since the early 20th century.

Myrtill/Myrtilla *See* MYRTLE.

Myrtle (f) English plant name derived from the name of the garden shrub, which was a symbol of victory in ancient Greece. Like many other flower names, it was adopted as a first name among English speakers in the middle of the 19th century. It has fallen out of favour since the middle of the 20th century. Notable bearers of the name have included characters in Thomas Hardy's novel *The Hand of Ethelberta* (1876) and P. G. Wodehouse's *Meet Mr Mulliner* (1927). Variants of the name include **Myrtill** and **Myrtilla**.

Mysie *See* MAISIE.

N

Nada/Nadezhda *See* NADIA.

Nadia (f) Russian first name that developed as a diminutive of Nadezhda, meaning 'hope', or alternatively from the Arabic for 'moist with dew'. The name was virtually unknown in the English- and French-speaking worlds before the early 20th century, when the hugely successful tours of Sergei Diaghilev's Ballets Russes did much to promote Russian names in Europe. Famous bearers of the name have included the wife of Russian Bolshevik leader Lenin, French conductor and musician Nadia Boulanger (1887–1979) and Romanian gymnast Nadia Comaneci (b.1961). Variant forms of the name include **Nada**, **Nadya**, **Nadja** and the French **Nadine** – as borne by South African novelist Nadine Gordimer (b.1923).

Nadim (m) Arabic name derived from *nadama* ('to drink') and thus interpreted as meaning 'drinking companion' or 'confidant'. It is in common use in Indian communities, also appearing in such variants as **Nadeem**.

Nadine/Nadya *See* NADIA.

Nagendra (m) Indian name derived from the Sanskrit *naga* ('serpent' or 'elephant') and *indra* ('greatest' or 'mightiest'). It does not appear to have been adopted as a first name until the late medieval period.

Nahum (m) Hebrew name meaning 'comforter'. It appears in the Bible as the name of an Old Testament prophet who lived in the 7th century BC and has always been popular among Jews. It was among the biblical names that were taken up by the Puritans in the 17th century. Notable bearers of the name have included English playwright

Nahum Tate (1652–1715), remembered today chiefly for the happy ending he attached to his adaptation of Shakespeare's tragedy *King Lear*. Variants of the name include the Russian **Naum**.

Na'il (m) Arabic name meaning 'winner'. The feminine version of the name, **Na'ila**, was borne by the wife of the Caliph Uthman ibn-Affan: in the year 656 she tried in vain to prevent her husband being murdered by his enemies and then, although herself injured by the assassins' swords, shouted out news of his death from the rooftops.

Nairn (m) Celtic first name meaning 'dweller by the alder tree'.

Nairne (f) Gaelic first name meaning 'from the river'.

Najib (m) Arabic name meaning 'of noble descent' or 'high-minded'. A modern Arabic derivation of the name suggests it means 'bright' or 'clever'. Also found as **Nagib**.

Nan *See* ANN; ANNE; NANCY; NANETTE.

Nana *See* ANN; ANNE.

Nance *See* NANCY.

Nancy (f) English first name that probably evolved as a familiar form of ANN. It emerged as an independent name in its own right during the 18th century. Particularly popular in the USA and Canada in the middle years of the 20th century, the name has suffered something of a decline in popularity since it became established as a slang term for a homosexual. Notable bearers of the name have included a character in the Charles Dickens novel *Oliver Twist* (1837–8), US-born politician Nancy Astor (1879–1964), who became Britain's first woman member of parliament, British novelist

Nancy Mitford (1907–73), the fictional teenage detective Nancy Drew and US First Lady Nancy Reagan (Anne Frances Reagan; b.1921), wife of US President Ronald Reagan. Also found as **Nancie**, **Nanci** and **Nanny**. A Gaelic version of the name is **Nandag**. Diminutive forms include **Nan** and **Nance**. *See also* HANNAH.

Nanda (m) Indian name derived from the Sanskrit *nanda* ('joy'), although it is sometimes understood to mean simply 'son'. It is borne in legend by Krishna's foster-father and by Vishnu as well as a number of other lesser characters. It was also a royal name, borne by an early king of Magadha.

Nandy *See* FERDINAND.

Nanette (f) English and French first name that probably evolved via Nan from ANN. It seems to have made its first appearance in the early years of the 20th century. Its popularity was much promoted by the success of Vincent Youman's operetta *No, No, Nanette* (1925). Well-known bearers of the name have included British actress Nanette Newman (b.1939). Variants include **Nannette**.

Nanny *See* NANCY.

Naoise (m) Irish Gaelic name of uncertain meaning, pronounced 'neesha'. It is best known as the name of the lover of Deirdre in ancient Irish legend: on Naoise's death at the hands of Conchobar, king of Ulster, Deirdre died of grief.

Naomi (f) Hebrew name meaning 'sweetness', 'pleasantness', 'pleasure' or 'my delight'. It appears in the Old Testament Book of Ruth as the name of Ruth's mother-in-law. A common Jewish name, it was among the many biblical names adopted by the Puritans in the 17th century and has enjoyed renewed popularity in non-Jewish communities (especially in Australia) since the 1970s. Well-known bearers of the name have included British yachtswoman Dame Naomi James (b.1949) and British model Naomi Campbell (b.1970). A rare variant is

Naomia. Others include the French **Noémie** and the Italian **Noemi**.

Napier (m) English and French first name derived from the Greek for 'of the new city'.

Napoleon (m) French name derived via the Italian Napoleone from the Greek *nea polis* ('new city') and *leone* ('lion'). In Italy, where the name is relatively rare, the name is often linked with that of the city of Naples. As the first name of the Corsican-born French Emperor Napoleon Bonaparte (1769–1821), it became one of the best known, and feared, names in Europe. It has occasionally been adopted as a first name in English-speaking countries since the early 19th century, chiefly within the Black community in the USA. Notable bearers of the name in fiction have included Napoleon, leader of the pigs in George Orwell's *Animal Farm* (1945) and General Napoleon Aufsteig in George Bernard Shaw's *Back to Methuselah* (1920).

Narayan (m) Indian name derived from the Sanskrit *nara* ('man') and *ayana* ('path') and thus interpreted as meaning 'son of man'. In ancient myth, Narayana is the lord of creation, later synonymous with Brahma. The name has also been associated with Vishnu and (mostly formerly) with Krishna.

Narcissus (m) English version of the Greek Narkissos, which may have developed from the Greek *narke* ('numbness'). The name is thought to be of pre-Greek origin but is now indelibly associated with the Greek legend of Narcissus, the beautiful youth who fell in love with his own reflection and was eventually transformed into the flower bearing his name. The name is mentioned in the Bible and was popular among slaves and freedmen in Roman times. Two men are venerated as St Narcissus – the first a 2nd-century bishop of Jerusalem and the second a 4th-century Spanish bishop and martyr. It is encountered only very rarely as a first name today. Variants include the Italian, Portuguese and Spanish **Narciso** and the French **Narcis**. A rare feminine form is **Narcissa** – perhaps best known as the name Alexander Pope gave to the actress Anne Oldfield in his *Moral Essays* and also that of a character in Tobias Smollett's *The Adventures of Roderick Random* (1748).

Narelle (f) Australian first name of obscure meaning. A relatively recent introduction, it ranked among the most popular girls' names in Australia in the 1970s.

Narendra (m) Indian name derived from the Sanskrit *nara* ('man') and *indra* ('mighty'). Later derivations suggest it means 'physician'. As a first name, its history dates back to the medieval period. Variants include **Narender**, **Narendhra** and **Narinder**.

Nash (m) English first name meaning 'ash tree'. A relatively rare choice as a first name, it is more familiar as a surname.

Nasir (m) Arabic name meaning 'helper' or 'supporter'. The name derives from the verb *nasara* ('to render victorious'). An Indian variant is **Nasr**.

Nastassia *See* NATASHA.

Nat *See* NATHAN; NATHANIEL.

Natalia *See* NATALIE.

Natalie (f) English, French and Russian first name derived from the Latin *natale domini* ('birthday of the Lord'). A traditional favourite in Russia, where it is often encountered as **Natalya**, the name is often given to girls born on or near Christmas Day and is now equally common in French- and English-speaking countries. It was borne by a 4th-century saint whose feast day is celebrated on 1 December. The earliest records of the name's introduction to Britain date from the late 19th century and it enjoyed a peak in popularity in the English-speaking world in the 1970s. Well-known bearers of the name have included Russian-born US ballerina Natalia Makarova (b.1940), US actress Natalie Wood (Natasha Gurdin; 1938–82) and US pop singer Natalie Cole (b.1950). Alternative forms include **Natalia**, **Nathalie**,

Natalee and **Natelie**. Among the name's diminutives are **Talia**, **Talya** and **Tally**. *See also* NATASHA.

Natalya *See* NATALIE.

Nataraj (m) Indian name derived from the Sanskrit for 'king of dancers'. It appears to have medieval roots and is one of the names borne by Shiva, who is often depicted dancing. It is the name of one of the central characters in R. K. Narayan's *The Man-Eater of Malgudi* (1961).

Natasha (f) Russian first name that evolved initially as a familiar variant of Natalya (*see* NATALIE) but went on to win acceptance as a distinct name in its own right not only in Russia but also in French-, German- and English-speaking cultures. Notable instances of the name in literature have included Natasha Rostova in Leo Tolstoy's epic novel *War and Peace* (1863–9). The popularity of the name in the UK in the 1960s and 1970s reflected in part the success enjoyed by television adaptations of Tolstoy's novel. Diminutive forms include **Tasha**. Among variant forms of the name are **Natacha**, **Natashia**, **Natasja** and **Nastassia** – as borne by German film actress Nastassia Kinski (b.1959).

Nathalie *See* NATALIE.

Nathan (m) Hebrew name meaning 'gift' or 'he has given'. An Old Testament name, it was borne by the prophet Nathan – who criticized King David for engineering the death in battle of Uriah so that he could marry his widow Bathsheba – and also by one of David's sons. It was among the biblical names that were adopted by Puritans in England and America in the 17th century and subsequently enjoyed a resurgence in popularity on both sides of the Atlantic and in other parts of the English-speaking world around 1900. It became widely popular once more in the 1970s and 1980s. It is sometimes treated as a diminutive form of NATHANIEL or JONATHAN. Notable bearers of the name have included US general

Nathan B. Forrest (1821–77). **Nat** is a common diminutive form.

Nathanael *See* NATHANIEL.

Nathaniel (m) Hebrew name meaning 'gift of God' or 'God has given'. It appears in the New Testament as the personal name of the apostle Bartholomew. The name was first adopted in English-speaking countries after the Reformation and its use was substantially promoted by William Shakespeare's employment of it for a character in his play *Love's Labour's Lost* (1594). It is, however, commoner today in the USA than it is on the British side of the Atlantic. Famous bearers of the name have included US writers Nathaniel Hawthorne (1804–64), Nathanael West (Nathan Wallenstein Weinstein; 1903–40) and Nathaniel Benchley (1915–81). Sometimes found as **Nathanael** and, in Italy, as **Natanaele**. **Nat** and **Natty** are the most common diminutive forms – as borne by US jazz singer and pianist Nat King Cole (1917–65) and the fictional Natty Bumppo in James Fenimore Cooper's *Leather-Stocking Tales* (1823–46). *See also* NATHAN.

Natty *See* NATHANIEL.

Naum *See* NAHUM.

Nazario (m) Italian, Portuguese and Spanish name derived via the Roman Nazarius from the place name Nazareth (based on the Hebrew for 'branch'), the home village of Mary and Joseph. It was popular among the early Christians and borne by several saints. Variants in other languages include the French **Nazaire** and the Spanish **Nazaret**.

Neacal *See* NICHOLAS.

Neal *See* NEIL.

Neassa (f) Irish Gaelic name of uncertain but undoubtedly ancient origin. It was borne by the mother of King Conchobar of Ulster.

Ned *See* EDMUND; EDWARD.

Nehemiah (m) Hebrew name meaning 'comfort of the Lord' or 'consoled by Yah'. The name of a 5th-century governor of Jerusalem whose efforts to rebuild Jerusalem were recorded in the Old Testament book of Nehemiah, it was taken up by the Puritans in the 17th century but has surfaced only rarely since then.

Neil (m) English first name derived from the Irish Niall, itself from the Gaelic *niadh* (variously thought to mean 'champion', 'cloud' or 'passionate'). Also found as **Neal**, **Neale**, **Neill** and the Scottish **Neilie** or **Neillie**, it predated the Norman Conquest and can be found in the 'Domesday Book' in various forms, giving rise to such surnames as Neild and Nielson. It appeared with more frequency from the 19th century and has remained consistently popular throughout the English-speaking world since then, reaching a peak in the 1960s. Famous bearers of the name have included US playwright Neil Simon (b.1927), US astronaut Neil Armstrong (b.1930), British politician Neil Kinnock (b.1942) and US singer-songwriter Neil Young (b.1945). Variants include the Scandinavian and Icelandic **Njal**, the French **Nel** or **Nele** and the rare feminine form **Neilina**. *See also* NIGEL.

Neirin *See* ANEURIN.

Nell (f) English first name that developed as a diminutive form of various longer girls' names, including ELEANOR, ELLEN and HELEN. The initial 'N' is thought to have attached itself through the repeated use of such everyday phrases as 'mine Ell'. Now considered a name in its own right, it is rarely found today in such older forms as **Nelly** or **Nellie**. It was fairly common in Victorian England, but has suffered a decline in popularity since the 1930s. Famous bearers of the name have included Nell Gwyn (Elinor Gwyn; 1650–87), the much-loved actress who became the mistress of Charles II, Little Nell (christened Elinor Trent) in the Charles Dickens novel *The Old Curiosity Shop* (1840–41), Australian opera singer Dame Nellie Melba (Helen Mitchell;

1861–1931), the heroine of the popular song 'Nellie Dean' (1906) and 'Nellie the Elephant' in a popular children's song of the same title.

Nelly *See* ELEANOR; ELLEN; NELL.

Nelson (m) English surname, meaning 'son of Neil' or 'son of Nell', that was adopted as a first name in tribute to the great naval hero Admiral Horatio Nelson (1758–1805) after his death at the Battle of Trafalgar. It has remained in occasional use ever since, becoming more common in the USA than elsewhere. Notable bearers of the name since Admiral Nelson have included US politician Nelson Rockefeller (1908–79), US singer Nelson Eddy (1901–67) and South African President Nelson Mandela (b.1918).

Nena *See* NINA.

Nerina (f) Italian first name that may represent a development of the now redundant Nerino, which was itself derived from Nero or Nerio (of obscure meaning), or else had its origins in Nereus, the name of a Greek sea god. It can also be considered a variant of NERISSA, meaning 'sea nymph'. Also found as **Nerine**, it has never been very widespread.

Nerissa (f) English first name that was probably originally derived from the Greek *nereis* ('sea nymph'). It is thought to have been coined by English playwright William Shakespeare when he needed a name for Portia's sharp-witted maidservant in *The Merchant of Venice* (1596–8). *See also* NERINA; NERYS.

Nero (m) Italian first name meaning 'dark' or 'black'. Its limited application as a first name over the centuries reflects the notoriety of the Roman Emperor Nero (AD 37–68).

Nerys (f) Welsh first name of uncertain origin but possibly derived from the Welsh *ner* ('lord') and thus usually interpreted as meaning 'lady'. Alternatively, it may be regarded as a development of NERISSA. A

relatively modern invention, it is little encountered outside Wales. Well-known bearers of the name include the British actress Nerys Hughes (b.1941).

Nessa *See* VANESSA.

Nessie/Nesta *See* AGNES.

Nestor (m) Greek first name derived from the Greek *nostos* ('homecoming') and thus interpreted as meaning 'he who remembers'. It appears in Homer's *Iliad* as the name of one of the Greek commanders at the siege of Troy and was borne by several early Christian martyrs. **Nestore** is a modern Italian variant of the name.

Netta/Nettie *See* ANNETTE; HENRIETTA; JANET; JEANETTE.

Nev *See* NEVILLE.

Neville (m) English first name derived from the French place name Neuville, meaning 'new town', that was adopted as a surname by English speakers after the Norman Conquest and as a first name from the 17th century. The name has strong aristocratic associations and recalls one of William the Conqueror's knights, Gilbert de Nevil, as well as Richard Neville (1428–71), who as Earl of Warwick acquired the nickname 'Warwick the Kingmaker' during the Wars of the Roses. Having made its debut as a first name in English-speaking countries in the 17th century it was at its most frequent between the middle of the 19th century and the 1960s, since when it has suffered a marked decline. Famous bearers of the name have included British Prime Minister (Arthur) Neville Chamberlain (1869–1940) and British novelist Neville Shute (1899–1960). **Nev** is a common diminutive of the name. Variant forms include **Nevil**, **Nevile** and **Nevill**.

Nevin (m) Irish first name derived from the Irish Gaelic for 'little saint'. Also found as **Niven**.

Newell (m) English first name, originally a surname, meaning 'new field'.

Newt *See* NEWTON.

Newton (m) English place name, meaning 'new town', that was subsequently adopted as a surname and (from the 19th century) as an occasional first name. Sometimes bestowed in honour of the English scientist Sir Isaac Newton (1642–1727), it is today rare outside the USA. The usual abbreviated form is **Newt** – as borne by US politician Newt Gingrich (b.1943).

Ngaio (f) New Zealand name (pronounced 'nayo' or 'nigh-o') derived from a Maori tree name (or alternatively interpreted as meaning 'clever'). The most famous bearer of the name to date has been the New Zealand crime novelist Dame Ngaio Marsh (1899–1982).

Ngaire *See* NYREE.

Nia *See* NIAMH.

Niall *See* NEIL.

Niamh (f) Irish first name meaning 'radiance' or 'brightness'. Pronounced 'Neev' or 'Nee-av', it is very popular within Ireland but relatively rare elsewhere in the English-speaking world. The name was borne by a pagan goddess and appeared in Ossianic legend as the name of a fairy who fell in love with Ossian and carried him off to the mythical land of Tir nan Og. More recent bearers of the name have included Irish actress Niamh Cusack (b.1953). Sometimes abbreviated to **Nia** in Wales.

Nichol *See* NICHOLAS.

Nichola *See* NICOLA.

Nicholas (m) English first name derived from the Greek Nikolaos, itself from the Greek *nike* ('victory') and *laos* ('people') and thus interpreted as meaning 'victory of the people'. The name was borne by a 4th-century bishop of Myra, who later achieved sainthood and immortality as the original 'Father Christmas' or 'Santa Claus'. He is now the patron saint of children, merchants, pawnbrokers, sailors, and of Greece and Russia. The name became popular in

England from the 12th century and as 'Old Nick' it was one of the familiar nicknames bestowed upon the Devil (although this use of the name probably comes from German *nickel*, meaning 'goblin'). It suffered a decline after the Reformation but revived once more around the middle of the 20th century. It reached a peak in popularity in the 1960s and 1970s, then fell from favour for a few years before regaining lost ground in the 1990s.

Among the many well-known bearers of the name have been five popes and two emperors of Russia, and in fiction a young student in Geoffrey Chaucer's *The Canterbury Tales* (*c*.1387) and the title character in Charles Dickens' *Nicholas Nickleby* (1838–9). Variants include **Nicolas**, **Nickolas**, **Nichol** and **Nicol** (the most common version of the name in medieval England and a popular form of the name in Scotland). The Latin version of the name **Nicholaus** also gave rise to the German **Niklaus** and **Klaus** or CLAUS. Scandinavian variants include the Swedish and Norwegian **Nils**, the Finnish **Launo** or **Niilo** and the Danish **Niels**, while the Russians usually render the name as **Nikolai** (the familiar form of which is **Kolya**). Italians have the version **Nicolò**, while Hungarians know the name as **Miklos**. A Scottish Gaelic version is **Neacal**. The most common diminutive form of the name in the English-speaking world is **Nick** (or **Nicky**) – as borne by US film actor Nick Nolte (b.1940) and British golfer Nick Faldo (b.1957), among many others. Less common diminutives include **Nik** and **Nico**. *See also* COLIN; NICODEMUS.

Nick/Nicky *See* NICHOLAS; NICOLA.

Nico *See* NICHOLAS; NICODÈME.

Nicodemus (m) English first name derived from the Greek Nicodemus, which has its origins in the Greek *nike* ('victory') and *demos* ('people') and thus has the same meaning as NICHOLAS. The Greek version of the name features in the New Testament as the name of the man who helped Joseph of Arimathea bury Jesus Christ and it was consequently among the many biblical names adopted by Puritans on both sides of the Atlantic in the 17th century. It has been little used since then in the English-speaking world. **Nicodemo** is an Italian, Spanish and Portuguese version of the name; **Nicodème** a French one. **Nico** is a diminutive form.

Nicol *See* NICHOLAS.

Nicola (f) English and Italian first name representing a feminine equivalent of NICHOLAS. It is fairly common in English-speaking countries, where it has been used since the 12th century, and, as **Nicole**, in France. It enjoyed a peak in popularity in the UK in the 1970s. Famous bearers of the name in its various forms have included British actress Nicola Pagett (b.1945) and Australian actress Nicole Kidman (b.1967). The French version of the name received a boost in the 1990s when it was borne by a pretty French girl featured in a long-running series of television advertisements for a French car company. Other variants include **Nichola**, **Nikola**, **Nicholette** and **Nicolette** (a French version of the name sometimes shortened to COLETTE that occurs as far back as the medieval romance *Aucassin and Nicolette*). Among common diminutive forms of the name are **Nick**, **Nickie**, **Nicky** and **Nikki**.

Nicolas *See* NICHOLAS.

Nicole/Nicolette *See* NICOLA.

Niels *See* NICHOLAS.

Nigel (m) English first name that is thought to have been taken up as a Latinized version of NEIL soon after the Norman Conquest. In early writings it is found as Nigellus, sometimes incorrectly derived from the Latin *niger* ('black'). Other early versions of the name include Nygell and Nigelle. The name can be found in the 'Domesday Book' and was in frequent use during the medieval period but subsequently tailed off somewhat until a revival in the 19th century, when Nigel was widely accepted as the usual form of the name. It enjoyed a more recent

peak in popularity in the late 1950s and early 1960s but has been less in favour since then. Famous bearers of the name have included the hero of Sir Walter Scott's novel *The Fortunes of Nigel* (1822), British actor Nigel Hawthorne (1929–2001), British racing driver Nigel Mansell (b.1953), British Conservative politician Nigel Lawson (b.1932) and British violinist Nigel Kennedy (b.1956). Commonly abbreviated to **Nige**. **Nigella**, as borne by British cook and journalist Nigella Lawson (b.1960), and **Nigelia** are relatively uncommon feminine versions of the name.

Nigelia/Nigella *See* NIGEL.

Nikita (f) Russian first name derived from the Greek name Aniketos, meaning 'unconquerable'. The name was borne by a 2nd-century pope and many centuries later by Russian premier Nikita Khrushchev (1894–1971). Instances of the name in literature have included a character in Joseph Conrad's *Under Western Eyes* (1911).

Nikki *See* NICOLA.

Niklaus/Nikolai *See* NICHOLAS.

Nils *See* NICHOLAS.

Nina (f) Russian first name that may have evolved from ANN or simply as a diminutive form of various longer Russian names ending in '-nina', such as Antonina. An alternative derivation suggests the name developed from the Spanish *niña* ('little girl'). It was first adopted in English-speaking countries in the 19th century. Notable bearers of the name have ranged from a Babylonian sea goddess and the heroine of Anton Chekhov's play *The Seagull* (1896) to British novelist Nina Bawden (b.1925) and US jazz singer Nina Simone (Eunice Kathleen Wayman; 1933–2003). Variant forms include **Nena**, **Ninetta**, **Ninita** and **Ninette** – as borne by the Irish-born ballet dancer Dame Ninette de Valois (Edris Stannus; 1898–2001).

Ninette *See* NINA.

Ninian (m) Scottish and Irish first name

of uncertain origin. It may possibly be related to VIVIAN, itself derived from the Latin *vivus* ('alive'). It was borne by a 5th-century saint who was responsible for bringing Christianity to the Picts of southern Scotland and was in general use in Scotland until the 16th century. It is now very rare even within Scotland and Ireland.

Nissa (f) Hebrew first name meaning 'sign'. This is a relatively modern invention.

Nita *See* ANITA; JUAN.

Niven *See* NEVIN.

Nizar (m) Arabic name of obscure derivation. Famous bearers of the name have included the poet Nizar Al-Qabbani (b.1923).

Noah (m) Hebrew name meaning 'long-lived' or, alternatively, 'rest' or 'comfort'. Best known as the name of the Old Testament builder of the Ark at the time of the Great Flood, the name was taken up by English Puritans on both sides of the Atlantic during the 17th century. Notable bearers of the name, which is still in occasional use, have included the American lexicographer Noah Webster (1758–1843) and the fictional Noah Claypole in the Charles Dickens novel *Oliver Twist* (1837–8). **Noë** is a French variant.

Noam (m) Hebrew name meaning 'pleasantness', 'delight' or 'joy' that has enjoyed some popularity, chiefly among Jewish families in the USA. Famous bearers have included the US linguist Noam Chomsky (b.1928).

Noble (m) English surname of medieval origin that has also, rarely (and chiefly in the USA), been applied as a first name. The intention behind the name was presumably the same as that behind such equivalents as DUKE and EARL, meant to convey a notion of social status and nobility of character.

Noel (m) French and English first name derived from the French *Noël* ('Christmas'). Variously given with or without the diaer-

esis, the name has been reserved traditionally for children born on Christmas Day or during the Christmas period, although this is by no means a strict rule. In medieval times it was given to both boys and girls, but since the 17th century it has been reserved increasingly for boys, although the feminine versions **Noele**, **Noelle** and **Noelene** (or **Noeleen**) are still encountered with a fair degree of frequency. Famous bearers of the name have included British playwright, actor and singer Noël Coward (1899–1973) and British television presenter Noel Edmonds (b.1948) – both of whom were born in the month of December. Female bearers of the name have included British children's writer Noel Streatfeild (1895–1986) and British television actress Noele Gordon (1923–85). Variants of the masculine name include **Nowell**.

Noele/Noeleen/Noelene/Noelle
See NOEL.

Nola *See* FENELLA.

Nolan (m) Australian, English and Irish surname meaning 'descendant of a noble' or 'famous' that has also been in occasional use as a first name. A feminine version of the name popular in Australia is **Nolene** (or **Noleen**).

Noleen/Nolene *See* NOLAN.

Noll *See* OLIVER.

Nona (f) English first name derived from the Latin *nonus* ('ninth'). Usually reserved for ninth-born children in the 19th century, it is rarely encountered today. A familiar variant of the name is **Nonie**.

Nonie *See* NONA; NORA.

Nora (f) Irish first name derived from HONOR, which has since been adopted in Scotland, Scandinavia and many English-speaking countries. Also found as **Norah**, it is sometimes treated as an abbreviation of ELEANOR and LEONORA or as a feminine version of NORMAN. It made its debut among English speakers in the 19th century and enjoyed a peak in popularity in the first half of the 20th century but has since fallen out of favour. Notable bearers of the name have included Nora Helmer in the Henrik Ibsen play *A Doll's House* (1879), Nora Clitheroe in Sean O'Casey's *The Plough and the Stars* (1926), US screenwriter Nora Ephron (b.1941), the fictional Nora Batty in the long-running British television comedy series *The Last of the Summer Wine* and US pop singer Norah Jones (b.1979). Familiar variants of the name in Ireland include **Nonie** and **Noreen**.

Norbert (m) English first name derived from the Old German *nord* ('north') and *berht* ('bright' or 'famous') and thus interpreted as meaning 'famous northman'. The name was borne by a German saint (1080–1134) who founded the Premonstratensian Canons. It came to England with the Normans in the 11th century and was subsequently revived on both sides of the Atlantic towards the end of the 19th century, when many medieval names came back into vogue. It has since disappeared, at least on the British side of the Atlantic. Familiar forms of the name include BERT, BERTIE and **Norrie**.

Noreen *See* NORA.

Norm *See* NORMAN.

Norma (f) English and Italian first name possibly derived from the Latin *norma* ('rule', 'pattern' or 'standard'). It is also sometimes considered (especially in Scotland) to be a feminine version of NORMAN. The name became popular in the wake of the great success enjoyed by Vincenzo Bellini's opera *Norma* (1831), in which Norma is a Druid priestess, and reached a peak in the English-speaking world in the 1920s, since when it has become relatively rare. Well-known bearers of the name have included Canadian-born US actress Norma Shearer (1900–1983), US actress Norma Jean Baker (better known as Marilyn Monroe; 1926–62) and Norma Major, wife of British Prime Minister John Major.

Norman (m) English first name derived

from the Old English *nord* ('north') and *man* ('man') and thus meaning 'Northman' or 'Viking'. It also exists as an Anglicization of the Norse name Tormod (from the name of the god Thor and the Old Norse for 'wrath'). The name was fairly frequently used in Anglo-Saxon England and remained common until the 14th century. Although it virtually disappeared in England over the ensuing 400 years, it remained popular in Scotland (particularly among members of the McLeod clan) and was among the many medieval names that were later revived by the Victorians. It was in widespread use in the first half of the 20th century, but has tailed off somewhat since the 1950s. Notable bearers of the name have included British fashion designer Norman Hartnell (1901–79), British film comedian Norman Wisdom (b.1918), US novelist Norman Mailer (b.1923) and British politicians Norman Tebbitt (b.1931) and Norman Lamont (b.1942). **Norm** and **Norrie** are common diminutive forms. Feminine versions of the name include **Normanna** and **Normina**. *See also* NORA; NORMA; NORRIS.

Nornie *See* LEONORA.

Norrie *See* NORBERT; NORMAN.

Norris (m) English surname that evolved as a variant of NORMAN and was later adopted as an occasional first name. It was fairly popular during the 19th century but has since fallen out of fashion. Notable bearers of the name have included British author and publisher Norris McWhirter (b.1925), founding editor (with his brother) of the *Guinness Book of Records*.

Northcliffe (m) English first name, originally a surname, meaning 'north cliff'.

Norton (m) English place name combining the Old English *nord* ('north') and *tun* ('settlement') that was subsequently adopted both as a surname and occasional first name. It has made sporadic appearances as a first name since the 19th century but has never been in widespread use.

Nowell *See* NOEL.

Nuala *See* FENELLA.

Nur (m/f) Arabic name meaning 'light'. The name is used for both boys and girls, although **Nura** is a version reserved for girls alone.

Nuria (f) Spanish first name derived from a Catalan title for the Virgin Mary – 'Our Lady of Nuria' – relating Mary to Nuria in Gerona, site of the celebrated 'black madonna' (a statue of Mary blackened by candle smoke).

Nye *See* ANEURIN.

Nyree (f) Anglicized version of the Maori name Ngaire (of unknown origin). The popularity of New Zealand-born actress Nyree Dawn Porter (1940–2001) in the British television series *The Forsyte Saga* did much to promote the increasing use of the name throughout the English-speaking world in the 1970s, although curiously it has remained relatively uncommon in New Zealand.

O

Obadiah (m) English first name derived from the Hebrew for 'servant of the Lord'. There is a Book of Obadiah in the Old Testament and the name is borne by around a dozen biblical characters, including a palace official who shielded a hundred prophets from the threats of Queen Jezebel by hiding them in a cave. It was subsequently among the many biblical names adopted by the Puritans in the 17th century, although it has rarely surfaced since then. As a result of its popularity among Puritans, 'Obadiah' became a common slang term for anyone with Puritan leanings. Notable literary bearers of the name have included Tristram Shandy's clumsy but faithful servant in Laurence Sterne's picaresque novel *Tristram Shandy* (1759–67) and the hypocritical Revd Obadiah Slope in Anthony Trollope's *Barchester Towers* (1857). A modern Hebrew variant is **Ovadia**.

Oberon *See* AUBERON.

Ocean (m/f) English first name derived from the ordinary vocabulary word 'ocean'. This very uncommon and relatively recent invention may have been inspired by Oceanus, the name of a Greek sea-god depicted as an old man with a long beard and bull's horns.

Ocky *See* OSCAR.

Octavia (f) Roman name derived from the Latin for *octavus* ('eighth') and thus often reserved for eighth-born children. The most famous Octavias in Roman history included the sister of the Emperor Augustus, who was noted for her great beauty, the second wife of Mark Antony and the young wife of the Emperor Nero, who was among the many people murdered on his orders. The use of the name in English-speaking countries dates mainly from the 19th century, and notable bearers have included British social reformer Octavia Hill (1838–1912). The notion that the name relates especially to eighth-born children might have threatened it with redundancy in the modern world, but parents continue to choose it regardless of how many children they have. An Italian variant is **Ottavia**. Masculine versions of the name include the Roman **Octavian** and **Octavius** – names that enjoyed a brief vogue in the English-speaking world during the 19th century but now rarely encountered. Octavius is the name of a character in the George Bernard Shaw play *Man and Superman* (1903). The Italian **Octavio** has never won wide acceptance among English speakers.

Octavius *See* OCTAVIA.

Odell (m) English surname derived from the Old English for 'hill of woad' that was subsequently adopted as a surname and occasional first name. It also exists as a masculine version of ODETTE. Rare feminine versions are **Odella**, ODILE and **Odelyn**.

Odette (f) French first name derived via the Old French masculine name Oda from the Old German *od* ('riches'). The name appears to have been imported to the English-speaking world towards the end of the 19th century. The most famous Odette of recent times has been the Second World War French Resistance heroine Odette Churchill (1912–95), whose wartime adventures were related in the film *Odette* (1950). Variants include **Odetta**.

Odile (f) French first name (pronounced 'oh-deel') that may have been derived from the German OTTO, meaning 'riches' or 'wealth', or may alternatively be descended

269

from the Old German *othal* ('fatherland'). It is sometimes considered to be a feminine version of ODELL. The name is rare outside French-speaking countries. Also found as **Odilia**. *See also* OTTILIE.

Odo *See* OTTO.

Ofra *See* OPRAH.

Ogden (m) English place name derived from the Old English for 'valley of oak' that was subsequently adopted as a surname and, from the 19th century, as an occasional first name. The most famous bearer of the name to date has been US humorous poet Ogden Nash (1902–71).

Ogilvie (m) Celtic first name, also a surname, meaning 'high peak'. Also encountered as **Ogilvy**.

Oighrig *See* ERICA; EUPHEMIA; HENRIETTA.

Oisin *See* OSSIAN.

Olaf (m) Scandinavian name derived from the Old Norse *anleifr* ('family descendant'). Borne by several Scandinavian kings, it came to Britain with the Vikings and was subsequently introduced to the USA by Scandinavian immigrants in the 19th century. It has maintained its status as one of the most popular of all Scandinavian names but is now found only occasionally elsewhere in the world. Variant forms include **Olav**, **Olave**, the Swedish **Olov** and the Scottish **Aulay** (from the Gaelic **Amhlaigh**).

Oleg (m) Russian variant of the Scandinavian Helge (*see* HELGA). The name came to Russia with Scandinavian settlers but never won the approval of the Russian Orthodox Church, unlike its feminine equivalent OLGA. This reflected the fact that it was borne by the 10th-century Prince Oleg of Kiev, who promoted the prosperity of Kiev but refused to convert to Christianity.

Olga (f) Russian variant of the Scandinavian HELGA, and a feminine equivalent of OLEG. Notable bearers of the name have included the 10th-century St Olga, wife of the Prince of Kiev, who was instrumental in bringing Christianity to Russia. The name was imported to England in the late 19th century. Notable bearers of the name in recent times have included Russian gymnast Olga Korbut (b.1955) and the British politician Lady Olga Maitland (b.1944). Also found as **Olya**.

Olive (f) English first name derived from the Latin *oliva* ('olive tree'). The earliest records of the name date back to the 13th century, when it was usually given as Oliva – although other versions included Oliff and Olivet. It became popular during the 19th century, probably because the plant has long been a symbol of peace, and reached a peak in the 1920s before being eclipsed by the related OLIVIA. Well-known bearers of the name have included the fictional Olive Oyl, girlfriend of the cartoon character Popeye. Other variants include **Olivette**.

Oliver (m) English first name that is thought to have developed either from the Scandinavian OLAF or alternatively from the Old German *alfihar* ('elf host'). It was in common use among English speakers in medieval times, when it was well known as the name of the legendary knight companion of Roland (hero of the medieval *Song of Roland*). Because of its subsequent association with Oliver Cromwell (1599–1658), who ruled England during the period of the Commonwealth following the Civil War, the name was little used between the 17th and 19th centuries but it has since enjoyed a substantial revival. By the late 1980s it was firmly established as one of the most popular modern boys' names. Notable bearers of the name since Cromwell's time have included British writer Oliver Goldsmith (1728–74), US film comedian Oliver Hardy (1892–1957), British actor Oliver Reed (1938–99), US film director Oliver Stone (b.1946) and the central character in the Charles Dickens novel *Oliver Twist* (1837). Variants include the French **Olivier** and the Welsh HAVELOCK. Among the name's diminutives are **Noll, Nollie** and the more common **Ol** or **Ollie**.

Olivette *See* OLIVE.

Olivia (f) English and Italian first name derived ultimately from the Latin *oliva* ('olive tree'). It appeared in medieval times in the variant form Oliva – as borne by St Oliva, the patron saint of olive groves – and was promoted in the English-speaking world through William Shakespeare's character Olivia in *Twelfth Night* (1601) and subsequently by Oliver Goldsmith's Olivia in *The Vicar of Wakefield* (1766). The name was, however, in relatively modest use in the English-speaking world until the 1970s, since when it has enjoyed a strong resurgence in popularity. Well-known bearers of the name in recent times have included the British-born US film actress Olivia de Havilland (b.1916) and the British-born Australian pop singer and actress Olivia Newton-John (b.1948). Diminutive forms include **Libby** and **Livvy** (or **Livy**). *See also* OLIVE.

Olivier/Ollie *See* OLIVER.

Olof *See* OLAF.

Olwen (f) Welsh first name derived from the Welsh *ol* ('footprint') and *wen* ('white' or 'blessed'). The name refers to the Welsh legend of the beautiful Olwen, whose footprints sprouted white clover wherever she went. The name is confined chiefly to Wales, although it was popular for a time in England following the 1849 English translation of the *Mabinogion*, which includes an account of the legend. Also found as **Olwin** and **Olwyn**.

Olya *See* OLGA.

Olympia (f) Greek name derived from Olympus (the home of the gods in Greek mythology). The original form of the name was Olympias, in which guise it was borne by a 4th-century saint and by Alexander the Great's mother. As Olympia the name spread through the French- and English-speaking worlds, although it has never been very common. Many people are familiar with it from Edouard Manet's painting *Olympia*, a frankly realistic portrait of a reclining nude woman that caused a scandal in the art world when it was exhibited in 1865. More recent bearers of the name have included US actress Olympia Dukakis (b.1931). A French variant is **Olympe**.

Om (m) Indian name based on the Sanskrit syllable *om* that has long had special mystical and religious associations. Hindus believe that it includes all the sounds that the human voice can make and that it invokes the names of the supreme gods Vishnu, Shiva and Brahma.

Omar (m) Hebrew name meaning 'eloquent', or alternatively an Anglicization of the Arabic UMAR (meaning 'flourishing' or 'prosperous'). A biblical name, it has surfaced occasionally in English-speaking countries since the 19th century, although it is the Arabic form of the name that is now more common. Over the centuries the name has been borne by such luminaries as the Persian poet and scientist Omar Al-Khayyám (*c*.1048–*c*.1122), author of the *Rubaiyat*, and the Egyptian-born film actor Omar Sharif (Michael Shalhoub; b.1932).

Omega (f) Greek name derived from the last letter of the Greek alphabet. It has been employed from time to time for last-born children, just as ALPHA has been reserved on occasion for the first-born.

Ona *See* UNA.

Onora *See* HONORA.

Oona/Oonagh *See* UNA.

Opal (f) Indian name derived from the Sanskrit for 'precious stone'. The name Opal was borrowed from that of the gemstone around the end of the 19th century, when there was a considerable vogue for jewel names among English speakers, and it is considered particularly appropriate for girls born in October (opal being the birthstone for that month). Folklore insists that it is unlucky for people born in any other month to wear opal (although one superstition suggests this is safe enough if it is worn alongside a diamond). The name is now rarely encountered outside the USA. Variants include the rare **Opaline**.

Opaline *See* OPAL.

Ophelia (f) English and Italian first name derived from the Greek Ophelos, meaning 'help' or 'profit' (or alternatively – though less plausibly – from *ophis*, meaning 'a serpent'). It has been speculated that the name was a 16th-century invention, appearing for the first time in the works of Jacopo Sannazzaro (1458–1530). In English-speaking countries at least it is indelibly associated with the doomed heroine in William Shakespeare's tragedy *Hamlet* (1599) – although Shakespeare may have got the name from Sannazzaro. The name was extremely rare before the 19th century, when it was increasingly adopted by Black Americans in particular. It has enjoyed a resurgence in popularity since the 1980s.

Oprah (f) Hebrew first name of obscure meaning. One suggestion speculates that it means 'she who turns her back' while another claims it means 'fawn'. Originally given as Orpah, it features in the Old Testament (where, curiously, it is a man's name) and includes among its other variants **Orpa**, **Orpha**, **Ophrah**, **Ofra**, **Orphy** and **Orfa**. The best-known bearer of the name in recent times has been US television chat show host Oprah Winfrey (b.1954), who acquired the name through a misspelling of Orpah on her birth certificate.

Ora (f) English first name of obscure origin, possibly derived from the Latin *orare* ('to pray'). Alternatively, the name may have evolved as a diminutive of CORA or DORA.

Oralie (f) English first name of obscure origin. It is sometimes treated as a variant of AURELIA. Also found as **Oralee**.

Oran (m) Irish first name, originally Odhran, derived from the Gaelic *odhar* ('green' or 'sallow'). The name was borne by one of St Columba's most loyal followers.

Orfa *See* OPRAH.

Orfeo (m) Italian first name derived from the Greek Orpheus (of obscure meaning). The name recalls the Greek legend in which the musician Orpheus visits the underworld in the hope of reclaiming the dead Eurydice but loses her forever on disobeying a command not to look back as she follows him back to the mortal world.

Oria *See* ORLA.

Oriana (f) English first name derived from the Latin *oriri* ('to rise') and thus interpreted as meaning 'dawn' or 'sunrise'. Another suggestion is that the name was based originally on the French *or* or Spanish *oro* ('gold'). The name enjoyed a considerable vogue during the 16th century and was one of the poetic names bestowed upon Elizabeth I by her admirers (for instance, in the case of a 1601 collection of madrigals entitled *Triumphs of Oriana*). It has remained relatively uncommon in succeeding centuries, although Alfred, Lord Tennyson attracted new attention to the name with his ballad 'Oriana' (1830). Variants include **Ariane**.

Oriel (f) English first name derived either from the Latin for 'porch' or alternatively from the Old German for 'battle heat'. The name came to Britain with the Normans in the 11th century and made a limited comeback in the 20th century, but has otherwise been a relatively rare choice of name over the centuries. Variants include **Auriel** and **Oriole**.

Orinthia (f) Greek name derived from *orinein* ('to excite'). George Bernard Shaw gave the name to the female lead in his play *The Apple Cart* (1929). The variant **Orinda** was well known in the 17th century as the pseudonym of the English poet and letter-writer Katherine Philips (1631–64), who won the admiration of Cowley, Dryden and others and was popularly dubbed 'The Matchless Orinda'.

Oriole *See* ORIEL.

Orla (f) Irish first name derived from the Gaelic for 'golden princess'. Also found as **Orlaidh**, **Oria** and **Orlagh**, it remains confined to Ireland.

Orlagh/Orlaidh *See* ORLA.

Orlando (m) Italian version of ROLAND, meaning 'famous land'. It has been in occasional use among English speakers since medieval times. Notable bearers of the name in the English-speaking world have included the English organist and composer Orlando Gibbons (1583–1625). It has also figured prominently in literature – notably in Boiardo's *Orlando Innamorato* (1487), in Ariosto's epic poem *Orlando Furioso* (1516–33), as the name of one of the main characters in William Shakespeare's *As You Like It* (1600) and as the name of the eponymous fictional hero/heroine of the Virginia Woolf novel *Orlando* (1928). *See also* URSULA.

Ormerod (m) English place name derived from the Old English for 'Orm's place' that has been in occasional use both as a surname and first name over the centuries.

Ormonde (m) Irish surname variously derived from the Gaelic for 'red' or else from a Gaelic place name (meaning 'East Munster').

Orpah *See* OPRAH.

Orrell (m) English place name derived from the Old English for 'ore hill' that was subsequently adopted as a surname and occasional first name.

Orsina *See* ORSON.

Orson (m) English and French first name derived via the Old French *ourson* ('bearcub') from the Latin *ursus* ('bear'). In the medieval legend of the twin brothers Valentine and Orson, Orson was a small child who was carried off and raised in the wild by a family of bears. Among the most notable carriers of the name in recent times have been US film actor and director Orson Welles (George Orson Welles; 1915–85). Variants include the Italianate **Orsino** and

Orso and the feminine versions **Orsina** and URSULA.

Ortho (m) English first name derived from the Greek *ortho* ('straight'). The name is little known outside Cornwall.

Orval *See* ORVILLE.

Orville (m) English first name that was invented by the novelist Fanny Burney for the central character in her book *Evelina* (1778) – although it is just possible that she may have taken it from a French place name. In Burney's eyes the name evoked aristocratic associations and was thus ideal for her hero, Lord Orville. The name is today more common in the USA than it is in the UK. The most famous bearer of the name to date has been US flight pioneer Orville Wright (1871–1948). Also found as **Orval**.

Osbert (m) English first name derived from the Old English *os* ('god') and *beorht* ('famous') and thus interpreted as meaning 'famous as a god'. Originally spelled Osbeorht, it was recorded in use in Northumberland before the Norman Conquest and remained in currency until around the 15th century. It was revived along with other Saxon names during the 19th century. Well-known bearers of the name in relatively recent times have included the British writer Osbert Sitwell (1892–1969) and British cartoonist Osbert Lancaster (1908–86). Diminutive forms include **Oz** and **Ozzie**.

Osborne (m) English surname derived from the Old English *os* ('god') and *beorn* ('bear' or 'warrior'), and thus interpreted as meaning 'god-like warrior', that has also made infrequent appearances as a first name (chiefly in the USA). It emerged as a first name during the 19th century but has never enjoyed wide popularity and is still usually thought of as a surname. Occasionally found as **Osborn** or **Osbourne**.

Oscar (m) English and Irish first name derived from the Gaelic *os* ('deer') and *cara* ('friend') and thus interpreted as meaning 'gentle friend'. Alternatively, it may be

English in origin, having its roots in the Old English *ansfar* ('god-spear'). The name became popular after the poet James Mac-Pherson (1736–96) bestowed it upon the warrior son of the mythical ancient bard OSSIAN in the poems he fraudulently published in the 1760s as the original work of Ossian himself. Napoleon, an admirer of the Ossian legend, gave the name to one of his godsons and as Oscar I the latter was crowned King of Sweden and Norway, thus guaranteeing the adoption of the name throughout Scandinavia (where it sometimes appears as **Oskar**). Later still the Irish playwright and wit Oscar Wilde (1854–1900) was given the name in honour of his godfather Oscar II of Sweden (who received treatment from Wilde's father, an eye surgeon) and brought the name notoriety as well as lasting literary fame. After Wilde's trial for homosexuality the name fell into disfavour in the UK, although it remained in currency in the USA and later in the century it regained much lost ground among the British. Other bearers of the name have included US lyricist Oscar Hammerstein II (1895–1960) and US jazz musician Oscar Peterson (b.1925).

The Oscar statuettes awarded in Hollywood each year to prominent personalities in the cinema are alleged to owe their name to the similarity they bore to the 'Uncle Oscar' of the executive secretary of the Academy of Motion Picture Arts and Sciences. Another story, however, suggests the statuettes were named after Oscar Wilde, who when asked if he had ever won the Newdigate Prize for Poetry quipped that 'while many people have won the Newdigate, it is seldom that the Newdigate gets an Oscar'.

Occasionally shortened to **Os** or **Ossie**. Diminutives include **Ocky**.

Osheen *See* OSSIAN.

Osip *See* JOSEPH.

Osmond (m) English first name derived from the Old English *os* ('god') and *mund* ('protection'). The name was recorded in use in England before the Norman Conquest, when it acquired its modern form. Early bearers of the name included St Osmond, who served as Chancellor under William the Conqueror. The name was revived in the 19th century but is today infrequently encountered except as a surname. **Osmund** is a rare variant form, and **Ossie** a diminutive.

Ossian (m) Irish first name derived from the Gaelic for 'little deer'. The name was borne by a figure from Irish legend but first attracted significant public attention throughout the English-speaking world when the poet James MacPherson (1736–96) identified an ancient Gaelic bard called Ossian as the original author of recently discovered poems that he had published. The poems, which caused a sensation when they first appeared, became the subject of a considerable literary scandal when it was proved to most people's satisfaction that they had been written by MacPherson himself. Variant spellings include the Irish **Oisin** and **Osheen**. **Ossia** is a feminine version. *See also* OSCAR.

Ossie *See* OSCAR; OSMOND.

Oswald (m) English first name derived from the Old English *os* ('god') and *weald* ('rule') and thus interpreted as meaning 'divine power' or 'rule of God'. The frequency of the name in pre-Norman England owed much to St Oswald of Northumbria (605–41), the first Anglo-Saxon king to achieve sainthood. Another St Oswald served as Archbishop of York in the 10th century. The name fell into disuse after the Middle Ages and remained redundant for some centuries before it was eventually revived in the 19th century. In William Shakespeare's tragedy *King Lear* (c.1607), Oswald is the malicious steward described by Edgar as 'a serviceable villain'. In the 20th century the name's popularity suffered from identification with the British fascist leader Oswald Mosley (1896–1980). Diminutive forms are **Oz** and **Ozzie**.

Oswin (m) Old English first name derived

from *os* ('god') and *wine* ('friend'). The name of a 7th-century King of Northumbria who achieved sainthood as a Christian martyr when he was murdered by his own brother, it has been little used since the 19th century.

Otho *See* OTTO.

Otilie *See* OTTILIE.

Otis (m) English first name derived via the German OTTO from the Old German *ot* ('riches') – or alternatively from the Greek for 'keen-eared'. As a first name it is rare outside the USA, where its use was promoted by James Otis (1725–83), a hero of the American War of Independence. It has been bestowed occasionally upon girls as well as boys. Notable bearers of the name have included US actor Otis Skinner (1858–1942) and US soul singer Otis Redding (1941–67).

Ottavia *See* OCTAVIA.

Ottilie (f) French and German first name derived from ODILE. Sometimes interpreted as meaning 'of the fatherland'. The name of the 7th-century patron saint of Alsace, it is common to both the Germanic and French cultures but rare in English-speaking countries. Also found as **Otilie** (a central European variant) and **Ottilia**. *See also* OTTOLINE.

Otto (m) German first name derived from the Old German *ot* ('riches' or 'possessions'). The name recalls Otto the Great (912–73), the German king who established control over the nomadic Magyar tribes and thus founded the Holy Roman Empire. The name came to Britain with the Normans in the 11th century and remained fairly common through the medieval period. It enjoyed a partial revival in the English-speaking world in the 19th century. Like other Germanic names, it vanished almost completely from the English-speaking world following the outbreak of the First World War and is now little heard outside Germany itself. Famous bearers of

the name have included several members of the German and Austrian royal families, the German statesman Prince Otto von Bismarck (1815–98) and Austrian-born US film director Otto Preminger (1906–86). Literary Ottos have included a central character in *A High Wind in Jamaica* (1929) by Richard Hughes. The name is occasionally used insultingly of Germans in general. Variants include **Odo**, **Oddo** and **Otho**.

Ottokar (m) German first name derived from the Old German *ot* ('riches' or 'prosperity') and *wacar* ('watchful'). A king of this name ruled the Goths in the 5th century and it was also the name of two kings of Bohemia in the 13th century. Also found as **Otokar**.

Ottoline (f) French and English variant of OTTILIE. Notable bearers of the name have included the British literary figure Lady Ottoline Morrell (1873–1938).

Ouida (f) French variant (pronounced 'ooeeda') of LOUISA, derived from a childish mispronunciation of the name. It was the pseudonym of the hugely popular French novelist Ouida (Marie Louise de la Ramée; 1839–1908).

Owain *See* OWEN.

Owen (m) Welsh first name that may have been evolved from EUGENE, meaning 'well-born', or else from the Welsh *oen* ('lamb'). Another theory suggests that the name came from the Old Celtic for 'born of Esos' (Esos being a minor Celtic deity from Gaul). Originally spelt **Owain**, in which form it is still sometimes encountered, it was borne by the great Welsh rebel Owen Glendower (1359–1416) and has long been one of the most popular Welsh names, although it is also found with some frequency in other parts of the English-speaking world. The British novelist Edward Bulwer Lytton (1831–91) published several books under the pseudonym 'Owen Meredith'. **Owena** is a rare feminine version.

Oz/Ozzie *See* OSBERT; OSWALD.

P

Paavo/Pablo *See* PAUL.

Pacifica *See* PEACE.

Paco *See* FRANCIS.

Paddy *See* PATRICIA; PATRICK.

Padma (m/f) Indian flower name derived from the Sanskrit *padma* ('lotus'). The name features in ancient Sanskrit literature and legend. It is most frequently encountered in Kashmir, Nepal and northern India and is today almost exclusively reserved for females. Related names include the feminine **Padmavati**, which combines *padma* ('lotus') with *vati* ('resembling') to mean 'lotus-like', and **Padmini**, which combines *padma* ('lotus') with *ini* ('having') to mean 'full of lotuses'.

Padmavati/Padmini *See* PADMA.

Padraic/Padraig *See* PATRICK.

Page/Paget *See* PAIGE.

Paige (f) English surname meaning 'page' or 'servant' that has been taken up as a first name in relatively recent times. Medieval pages were young men serving in the households of the noble families of England and were always male, although curiously in modern times the name has been reserved exclusively for girls. Also encountered as **Page** and **Paget**, the name is especially popular in the USA.

Palmer (m) English surname meaning 'pilgrim' that is occasionally found as a first name. The surname can be traced back ultimately to the Latin *palma* ('palm') and thus referred to palm-bearing pilgrims to the Holy Land.

Paloma (f) Spanish first name derived from the Latin *palumba* ('dove'). Well-

known bearers of the name have included Paloma Picasso (b.1949), daughter of the celebrated Spanish painter Pablo Picasso.

Pam *See* PAMELA.

Pamela (f) English first name that was invented by the English poet and soldier Sir Philip Sidney in his pastoral romance *Arcadia* (1590). Sidney (who put the stress on the second syllable) apparently derived the name from the Greek words *pan* ('all') and *meli* ('honey'), thus creating a name meaning 'all sweetness'. The use of the name (with its modern pronunciation) by British novelist Samuel Richardson in his hugely successful *Pamela* (1740), which depicted the amorous adventures of the virtuous Pamela Andrews, did much to promote the popularity of the name from the mid-18th century onwards, reaching a peak around 1950. More recent bearers of the name have included US diplomat Pamela Harriman (1921–97), New Zealand-born comedienne Pamela Stephenson (b.1951) and Canadian television actress Pamela Anderson (b.1967). Variant forms include **Pamala**, **Pamelia**, **Pamella**, **Pamilia**, **Pamila** and **Pammala**. **Pam** is a common diminutive form of the name – as borne by British versifier Pam Ayres (b.1947) and US tennis player Pam Shriver (b.1962). It may also be found shortened to **Pammy**, chiefly in Australia.

Pamelia *See* PAMELA.

Pancho *See* FRANCIS.

Pancras (m) English version of the Greek Pankratios, itself derived from the Greek *pan* ('all') and *kratein* ('to rule') and thus interpreted as meaning 'ruler over all'. The Greek version of the name was used by Byzantine Greeks as a title for Christ himself and the name was consequently popular among early Christians. It was also borne by a 1st-century Christian saint martyred at Taormina and by a less well-known 3rd-century Christian saint, whose remains were sent to England on the orders of the Pope in the 7th century. This latter saint is now remembered chiefly through the name of London's St Pancras railway station. The modern Italian equivalent of the name is **Pancrazio**. Other variants include the Russian **Pankrati** and the German **Pankraz**.

Pancrazio *See* PANCRAS.

Pandora (f) Greek first name derived from the Greek words *pan* ('all') and *doron* ('gift') and thus interpreted as meaning 'all-gifted' or 'many-gifted'. According to Greek legend, Pandora was the name of the very first mortal woman, created out of earth by the fire god Hephaistos expressly to punish man after Prometheus stole the gift of fire from him. Pandora was offered to Prometheus' brother Epimetheus as a wife, together with a mysterious box that Pandora was forbidden to open. Unable to control her curiosity as to what was inside, Pandora opened the box and out flew all the troubles and woes that mankind has been subject to ever since. All that remained in the box was hope. Because of its rather negative classical associations, the name does not appear to have been taken up by English speakers before the 20th century. Notable bearers of the name in modern times have included the girlfriend of Adrian Mole in Sue Townsend's *Diary of Adrian Mole* (1980).

Pansy (f) English flower name that was adopted as a first name alongside many other flower names in the 19th century. It is sometimes derived from the French *pensée* ('thought'). Although it is still occasionally encountered, it has never been as popular as some of the other Victorian flower names, such as POPPY, and its use as a slang term for an effeminate male has done nothing to improve its chances of being revived.

Notable bearers of the name have included the fictional Pansy Osmond in *The Portrait of a Lady* (1881) by Henry James.

Paolo *See* PAUL.

Paris (m) Greek name borne by the son of King Priam of Troy, a central character in the story of the Trojan War. It was Paris' abduction of the beautiful Helen that provoked the start of the epic conflict between the Greeks and the Trojans, destined to end in the sacking of the city of Troy after ten years of fighting. The name was also borne by a 4th-century Greek-born Neapolitan bishop who subsequently achieved sainthood. Also found as **Parris**, the name has been popular chiefly in the USA.

Parker (m) English surname meaning 'park keeper' that has been in occasional use (chiefly in the USA) as a first name since the 19th century. There is a Dr Parker Peps in the novel *Dombey and Son* (1848) by Charles Dickens.

Parnel *See* PETRONELLA.

Parry (m) Welsh surname derived from *ap Harry* (meaning 'son of HARRY'), which was subsequently adopted as a first name. It is rarely encountered outside the principality of Wales itself.

Parsifal *See* PERCIVAL.

Parthenia (f) Greek name derived from the Greek *parthenos* ('virgin'). Popularly associated with the Parthenon in Athens, which was dedicated to the goddess Athena Parthenos (Athena the Maid), the name was borne by a character in Sir Philip Sidney's *Arcadia* (1590) and has made sporadic reappearances among English speakers since the late 19th century.

Parthenope (f) Greek name (pronounced 'parthenopee') derived from the Greek *parthenos* ('virgin') and *ops* ('face') and thus interpreted as meaning 'maiden-faced'. In Greek legend, Parthenope was a siren who drowned herself in despair after she failed to lure Odysseus with her singing because he had had himself tied to the mast of his ship; her body was eventually washed ashore at Naples. The name was taken up by English speakers in the 19th century.

Parvais (m) Indian Muslim name derived from the Persian *parvaiz* ('fortunate' or 'happy'). Notable bearers of the name have included a son of the Mogul emperor Jahangir, who died in 1626 and is remembered for the fine (though now ruined) buildings he erected at Sultanpur near Agra.

Parvati (f) Indian name derived from the Sanskrit *parvati* ('of the mountain'). One of the chief names borne by Shiva's wife, it is particularly popular in the states of southern India.

Pascal (m) French first name derived from the Latin *Paschalis* ('of Easter'). It was taken up as a first name by the early Christians, usually reserved for boys born in the Easter season. Subsequently it was borne by two medieval popes and became especially popular in medieval Cornwall. Little encountered today, it retains its association with Roman Catholicism. Occasionally found as **Paschal**. Another variant form (for boys) is **Pascoe**. The usual Italian version is **Pasquale**, while in France the name is found as **Pascale**, in which form it has sometimes been given to girls in English-speaking countries since the 1960s.

Pascoe *See* PASCAL.

Pat *See* PATIENCE; PATRICIA; PATRICK.

Patience (f) English 'virtue' name derived ultimately from the Latin *pati* ('to suffer'). It was popular with the early Christians and was subsequently taken up by the Puritans on both sides of the Atlantic in the 16th and 17th centuries. At first it was given to boys as well as girls but it has long since been reserved exclusively for females, surviving rather better than many of the other virtue names adopted by the Puritans. The name appears in Shakespeare's *Henry VIII* (1613) and in the 19th century Gilbert and Sullivan used the name for the title and central character of their comic opera *Patience; or, Bunthorne's Bride* (1881), thus promoting its

use at the end of the century. It has suffered a marked decline in popularity in the 20th century. Notable bearers of the name have included British poet Patience Strong (Winifred May; 1905–90). Sometimes shortened to **Pat** or **Patty**.

Patrice *See* PATRICIA.

Patricia (f) Feminine version of PATRICK, derived from the Latin *patricius* ('nobleman'). The name was introduced initially in written records by the Romans to distinguish female members of noble families from males. It was borne by a 7th-century saint but was only accepted as a first name among English speakers from the 18th century, especially in Scotland. It became more widespread after it was bestowed upon Queen Victoria's granddaughter Princess Victoria Patricia Helena Elizabeth of Connaught (1886–1974), reaching a peak in popularity in the 1950s before suffering a marked decline. More recent bearers of the name have included British actresses Patricia Neal (b.1926), Patricia Routledge (b.1929) and Patricia Hodge (b.1946).

Familiar diminutive forms include **Pat**, **Patsy**, **Patty**, **Patti**, **Pattie**, **Paddy**, **Tricia** and **Trisha**. The diminutive Patsy may or may not be related to the US slang term for a person who has been fooled or hoodwinked but has certainly suffered in the USA at least through association with the term. In much the same way Patsy is avoided in Australia, where it is a slang term for a homosexual. Variants of the name in other languages include **Patrika**, **Patrice** (a French form sometimes also encountered in Canada and the USA), **Patrishka** and the Italian **Patrizia**.

Patrick (m) English and Irish first name derived from the Latin *patricius* ('nobleman'). The name is particularly popular in Ireland in tribute to St Patrick (*c*.385–461), the patron saint of Ireland who first came to the country from England as a captive but later, after a dream, returned voluntarily to bring Christianity to the Irish. It seems likely, however, that

St Patrick derived his name from Celtic rather than Latin origins. Such was the reverence the Irish had for St Patrick that initially his name was thought too holy for general use and it was left to the Scots and subsequently people living in northern England to be the first to take the name up on a significant scale. However, after the 17th century it established itself as one of the most common of all first names in use throughout Ireland and it is now thought of as a primarily Irish name. The earliest records of the name's use in England date from the 12th century and it has remained popular throughout the rest of the English-speaking world into modern times. The Irish variant **Padraic** – as borne by Irish poet and playwright Padraic Colum (1881–1972) – has returned to favour in Ireland in recent decades in preference to the Anglicized Patrick, as have the alternatives **Padraig**, **Patric** and **Patraic**.

Notable bearers of the name in relatively recent times have included British actor Patrick Macnee (b.1922), British astronomer Patrick Moore (b.1923) and US actor Patrick Swayze (b.1954). Often shortened to **Pat** – as borne by Australian tennis player Pat Cash (b.1965) – or **Paddy** – as borne by British politician Paddy Ashdown (Jeremy Ashdown; b.1941); **Packy** is another, rarer, diminutive form. The use of Paddy as a nickname for any Irish person dates from the 19th century.

Patsy *See* HYPATIA; PATRICIA.

Patti/Pattie/Patty *See* MARTHA; PATIENCE; PATRICIA.

Paul (m) Roman name derived from the Latin *paulus* ('little' or 'small'). The name started life as a nickname but was subsequently borne by several saints and by the apostle St Paul (who changed his name from Saul on his conversion to Christianity), thus guaranteeing its lasting popularity with Christians in succeeding centuries. It was recorded in Britain before the Norman Conquest and made infrequent appearances during medieval

times but only became significantly popular from the 17th century (although it has never been as common in Britain as it has been in some other countries). It has remained in circulation throughout the English-speaking world ever since, reaching a peak in frequency since the middle of the 20th century when it began to appear for the first time in the top twenty most popular boys' names.

Well-known bearers of the name in recent times have included US singer Paul Robeson (1898–1976), British actor Paul Scofield (b.1922), US actor Paul Newman (b.1925), British singer-songwriter Paul McCartney (b.1942) and British footballer Paul Gascoigne (b.1967). Versions in other languages include the Irish **Pól**, the French **Paule**, the Finnish **Paavo**, the Russian **Pavel** (and its diminutive forms **Pava** and **Pasha**), the Italian **Paolo** and the Spanish **Pablo**, as borne by the Spanish painter Pablo Picasso (1881–1973) and Spanish cellist Pablo Casals (1876–1973). *See also* PAULA; PAULETTE; PAULINE.

Paula (f) Germanic first name, a feminine version of PAUL. St Paula (347–404) was venerated for the assistance she gave to St Jerome and for her good works, which included the building of a hospice for pilgrims in Bethlehem. The name was also borne by several early Christian martyrs. It was first taken up by English speakers in medieval times but only emerged as a significantly popular choice from the 1950s. It has been in decline since the 1970s. Notable bearers of the name have included the fictional Paula Tanqueray in Arthur Wing Pinero's play *The Second Mrs Tanqueray* (1893) and, in more recent times, British actress Paula Wilcox (b.1949) and television presenter Paula Yates (1959–2000), who was formerly married to rock star Bob Geldof. POLLY is sometimes heard as a familiar variant of the name.

Pauleen/Paulene *See* PAULINE.

Paulette (f) French first name, a feminine version of PAUL. Although French in origin this version of the name may now be encountered in many English-speaking countries. It became fairly popular in the 1920s and enjoyed another peak in popularity in the 1960s, tending to eclipse the longer-established PAULINE. Famous bearers of the name have included the US actress Paulette Goddard (Pauline Marion Goddard Levy; 1911–90). Also found as **Pauletta**.

Paulina *See* PAULINE.

Pauline (f) French first name, a feminine version of PAUL. Although Paulina, the original Roman version of the name, became the traditional English version (popular from the 19th century onwards) the French spelling is now much more common among English speakers. The name became popular in the USA before it was taken up on a significant scale elsewhere in the English-speaking world. Notable bearers of the name in its two forms have included the 4th-century Christian martyr St Paulina, a character in Shakespeare's *The Winter's Tale* (1611), Pauline Bonaparte (1780–1825; sister of the French Emperor Napoleon Bonaparte), the heroine in the highly successful silent film series *The Perils of Pauline* (1914) and the fictional Pauline Fowler in the long-running British television soap series *Eastenders*. Also found as **Paulene**, **Pauleen** and **Paulanne**. *See also* PAULETTE.

Pavel *See* PAUL.

Peace (f) English first name that was among the names celebrating a variety of abstract qualities favoured by the Puritans on both sides of the Atlantic in the 17th century. It is now found only very infrequently. A very rare variant is **Pacifica**.

Peadar *See* PETER.

Pearce *See* PIERS.

Pearl (f) English jewel name, which was first adopted as a first name among English speakers in the late 19th century. The jewel itself represents tears and unhappiness, but this has not affected the popularity of the name. It is also encountered occasionally as a diminutive of MARGARET, which was itself derived from the Greek for 'pearl'. Having reached a peak in popularity in the 1920s, it has since fallen out of favour and is now rarely encountered. The name has sometimes been applied to males, especially in the USA. Notable bearers of the name have included US novelist Pearl Buck (1892–1973) and US singer Pearl Bailey (1918–90). Also found as **Pearle**. Familiar forms include **Pearlie**, **Pearly** and **Perlie**. Versions of the name in other languages include the Italian and Spanish **Perla**.

Pedro *See* PETER.

Peers *See* PIERS.

Peg *See* PEGGY.

Pegeen (f) Irish first name that evolved as a diminutive form of MARGARET. There is a character of the name in J. M. Synge's *The Playboy of the Western World* (1907).

Peggy (f) Diminutive form of MARGARET. Also found as **Peg** and **Peggie,** this has long been treated as an independent name in its own right as well as an abbreviation of Margaret. It probably arose originally as a rhyming version of Meggy, although the precise mechanism by which the M was replaced by a P is not known. Records of its use date back at least to the 16th century but it remained relatively uncommon until the 1920s when it reached a peak in popularity. It has since fallen out of use. Famous bearers of the name have included the British actresses Dame Peggy Ashcroft (1907–91) and Peggy Mount (1916–2001).

Pelham (m) English place name meaning 'Peola's place or settlement' that was subsequently taken up as a surname and first name. Notable bearers of the name have included British novelist P. G. Wodehouse (Pelham George Wodehouse; 1881–1975), the creator of Jeeves and Bertie Wooster who was known to his close friends by the nickname 'Plum'.

Pen *See* PENELOPE.

Penelope (f) English name of uncertain

origin, probably derived from the Greek *pene* (meaning 'thread' or 'bobbin'), or else just possibly from the Greek *penelops* (the name of a species of duck). According to Greek legend, Penelope was the loving wife of the great hero Odysseus, who waited patiently at home while her husband spent ten years fighting at Troy and then another ten years making his way slowly home, hampered and delayed by the gods he had offended. Penelope's wait was made more difficult by the persistent attentions of the Hundred Suitors, who occupied her home and tried to persuade her to choose one of them as her husband in the belief that after so many years Odysseus must be dead. To fend off their demands Penelope insisted that before she could choose a husband she must first complete the weaving of a shroud for her beloved father-in-law – each night she unpicked the work she had done during the day to ensure the weaving went on without ever reaching an end. When Odysseus eventually reached home he praised Penelope for her loyalty to him and murdered every one of the Hundred Suitors. The name was taken up by English speakers in the 16th century and has remained consistently popular ever since, with a peak in the 1950s and 1960s. In Ireland it is sometimes considered to be an Anglicization of the Gaelic Fionnuala or Fionnghuala (*see* FENELLA).

Notable bearers of the name in recent times have included British writers Penelope Fitzgerald (1916–2000) and Penelope Lively (b.1933), British actress Penelope Keith (b.1939) and Spanish actress Penelope Cruz (b.1974). The name is often shortened to **Pen** or **Penny**.

Penny *See* PENELOPE.

Peony (f) English flower name that made its debut as a first name in the 19th century. Unlike some of the other flower names, this one has never enjoyed significant popularity. The flower may have got its original (Greek) name from Paion, physician to the gods.

Pepe *See* JOSÉ.

Pepita (f) Diminutive form of the Spanish first name Josefina (*see* JOSEPHINE), now treated as a name in its own right. The literal meaning of the name in Spanish is 'she who adds'.

Peppi *See* PERPETUA.

Per *See* PETER.

Perce *See* PERCIVAL; PERCY.

Percival (m) English first name, apparently invented originally by the 12th-century French poet Chrétien de Troyes for the central character of his poem *Percevale, a knight of King Arthur* (*c.*1175). Chrétien himself indicated that the name came from the Old French *perce-val* ('one who pierces the valley'), although some people seem to have borne it as a surname derived from the place name Percheval in Normandy and another theory plausibly links the name to the Celtic name Peredur (meaning 'hard steel'). According to Arthurian legend, Sir Percival was the most pure of all the knights of the Round Table and was destined to be the hero who finds the Holy Grail (later versions of the legend, however, grant this privilege to Sir Galahad). **Perceval** remains the usual French spelling of the name, while the Germans render it as **Parsifal**. As Percival, the name was first heard in England in the 14th century and was subsequently popularized among English speakers during the 19th century by Alfred, Lord Tennyson's Arthurian poems published as *Idylls of the King*. It has since fallen from favour in the UK but is still fairly popular in the USA. Often shortened to PERCY, **Perce** or **Val**.

Percy (m) French place name that was later adopted both as a surname and first name among French and English speakers. It also exists as a diminutive form of PERCIVAL, although the two names have different origins. The source place name, Perci in Normandy, appears to have had its roots in the Roman personal name Persius. The name has strong aristocratic connections:

William de Perci was one of William the Conqueror's closest companions and in time the Percy family became one of the most powerful baronial houses of England. As a first name Percy was first adopted by members of the aristocratic Seymour family, who married into the Percy line in the early 18th century. It was subsequently taken up on a much wider basis. The name has declined in popularity since it reached a peak in the early 20th century and is now relatively rare.

Famous bearers of the name over the years have ranged from the British Romantic poet Percy Bysshe Shelley (1792–1822), who claimed a distant connection with the noble Percy family, and Australian composer Percy Grainger (George Percy Grainger; 1882–1961) to British television gardener Percy Thrower (1913–88) and the fat green engine in the *Thomas the Tank Engine* railway stories of the Revd W. Awdry. Like Percival, the name is sometimes shortened to **Perce**.

Perdita (f) English first name derived from the Latin *perditus* ('lost'). William Shakespeare is thought to have invented the name for the castaway heroine in his play *The Winter's Tale* (1611). It has never been common but has continued to appear sporadically into modern times. One of the dogs in Dodie Smith's *One Hundred and One Dalmatians* (1956), later filmed by Walt Disney, is called Perdita. **Purdie** is an accepted diminutive form.

Peregrine (m) English first name ultimately derived via Italian from the Latin *peregrinus* ('stranger' or 'foreigner'). The name was recorded in use among early Christians, apparently selected to emphasize the transitory nature of man's existence on earth. It was also borne by three saints, including a 7th-century hermit living near Modena in Italy, and by a 2nd-century Greek philosopher. Its use in England dates from the 13th century. Notable bearers of the name have included the central character in Tobias Smollett's *Peregrine Pickle* (1751) – the success of this book did

much to make the name popular in the later 18th and 19th centuries, although it has never been common (possibly because of its traditional association with Roman Catholicism). Famous bearers of the name have included British journalist Peregrine Worsthorne (b.1923). Sometimes shortened to PERRY. The usual Italian variant is **Pellegrino**.

Perlie *See* PEARL.

Pernel/Peronel/Peronelle
See PETRONELLA.

Perpetua (f) Roman name derived from the Latin *perpetuus* ('perpetual'). The name was borne by a 3rd-century Christian martyr and since then has been largely confined to members of the Roman Catholic community. Sometimes shortened to **Peppi**.

Perrine *See* PETER.

Perry (m) English surname derived from the Old English *pirige* ('man who lives by a pear tree'), which has also been adopted fairly infrequently as a first name. It is also encountered as a diminutive of PEREGRINE or PETER. The name is especially popular in Canada and the USA, partly in tribute to two 19th-century American admirals of the name who respectively beat the British in battle on the high seas and opened up trade with Japan. The name has enjoyed peaks in popularity in the 1930s and again since the 1980s. Notable bearers of the name in relatively recent times have included the US singer Perry Como (Pierino Como; 1912–2001) and the fictional television detective Perry Mason, created by US crime writer Earle Stanley Gardner in the 1930s.

Persephone (f) Greek first name (pronounced 'pur-sef-o-nee') derived from the Greek *pherein* ('to bring') and *phone* ('death') and thus meaning 'bringing death'. According to Greek legend, Persephone was the beautiful daughter of Zeus and Demeter who was carried off to the Underworld by Hades and had to be rescued from there by her mother. Unfortunately Persephone had eaten six pomegranate seeds while in the Underworld and was therefore doomed to spend six months of each year with Hades as goddess of the dead (which is how winter came about). The literal meaning of the name explains why it has never been very popular as a first name.

Persis (f) English first name derived from the Greek *Persis* ('Persian woman'). As it is mentioned briefly in the Bible by St Paul, the name was taken up by the Puritans in the 17th century but never enjoyed wide popularity and has long since fallen out of favour.

Pet *See* PETRA; PETRONELLA; PETULA.

Peta/Petena *See* PETER.

Pete *See* PETER.

Peter (m) English, German and Scandinavian first name derived via the Latin name Petrus from the Greek *petros* ('rock' or 'stone'). The lasting popularity of the name owes much to the apostle St Peter, the author of two New Testament Epistles, who was credited with founding the Christian Church and to whom hundreds of churches were subsequently dedicated. Originally named Simon, he was given the name by Christ himself, who chose it to reflect the fact that he would be the 'rock' on which the Christian Church would be built. The original Aramaic rendering of the name was Cephas.

The name was very common throughout the Christian world during medieval times and was closely linked with the Papacy. It appeared in the 'Domesday Book' in the Latin form Petrus and was subsequently usually rendered in England as PIERS or in other variant forms until the 14th century, when the modern version of the name became generally accepted. It suffered a prolonged decline after the Reformation because of its association with Roman Catholic saints, but continued to surface from time to time both in real life and in fiction, as illustrated by the characters Sir Peter Teazle in Richard Brinsley Sheridan's comedy *The School for Scandal* (1777) and Peter Featherstone in George Eliot's novel *Middlemarch* (1872). It finally returned to favour among English speakers in the early 20th century through the huge popularity of two fictional characters: Peter Rabbit in the children's stories of Beatrix Potter and Peter Pan in J. M. Barrie's novel and play *Peter Pan: or the Boy Who Would Not Grow Up* (1904). It has been in decline since the 1960s.

Notable bearers of the name since 1904 have included the British actors Sir Peter Ustinov (b.1921) and Peter Sellers (1925–80), Irish actor Peter O'Toole (b.1932) and US film director Peter Bogdanovich (b.1939). Commonly shortened to **Pete**. Rare feminine versions of the name are **Peta** (apparently a modern Australian invention), **Petena**, **Peterina**, **Peternella** and **Perrine**. Variants in other languages include the Spanish **Pedro**, the French **Pierre**, the Italian **Piero** and **Pietro**, the Dutch **Piet**, the Swedish **Per**, the Russian **Pyotr** and the Scottish and Irish Gaelic **Peadar**. *See also* PERRY; PETERKIN; PETRA; PETRONELLA; PETULA; PIERS; PIRAN.

Peterina *See* PETER.

Peterkin (m) English first name that evolved as a variant form of PETER. Of chiefly historical interest today, it was borne by a character in R. M. Ballantyne's adventure novel *The Coral Island* (1857).

Peternella *See* PETER.

Petra (f) Feminine equivalent of the boys' name PETER, derived from the Latin *petros* ('rock'). The appeal of the name was bolstered in 1812 by the discovery of the romantic ruins of the ancient Jordanian city of Petra, where substantial buildings were set into cliff faces. As a first name it seems to have been first adopted by English speakers in the 1940s. Famous bearers of the name have included German environmental campaigner Petra Kelly (1947–92). Variants include **Petrina** and **Petrona**. **Pet** is a diminutive.

Petrina *See* PETRA.

Petronella (f) Roman family name (originally *Petronius*) of uncertain meaning that has been used as a first name in the English-speaking world since the 12th century. It was supposedly borne by an early Christian martyr, said by some to be the daughter of the apostle Peter, and as such enjoyed some popularity in medieval times. Also found as **Petranella**, **Petronilla**, **Petronel** or **Peronelle**, it is treated sometimes as a feminine version of PETER. Sometimes shortened to **Pet**. The abbreviated forms **Parnel** and **Pernel** were historically associated with prostitutes and vanished from use after the 18th century.

Petula (f) English first name of uncertain origin, though possibly from the Latin *petere* ('to seek' or 'to attack'), root of the word 'petulant', or else inspired by the flower name *petunia*. Apparently a 20th-century invention, it is more frequently treated as a feminine equivalent for the boys' name PETER. Notable bearers of the name have included British pop singer Petula Clark (Sally Owen; b.1932). Sometimes shortened to **Pet**.

Peyton (m) English place name meaning 'farm of Paega' that was subsequently taken up as a surname and first name. The name is more frequently found in the USA than elsewhere in the English-speaking world, promoted perhaps by the popularity of the US television drama series *Peyton Place* in the 1960s.

Phebe *See* PHOEBE.

Phelan (m) Irish first name derived from the Irish Gaelic for 'wolf'.

Phelim *See* FELIX.

Phemie *See* EUPHEMIA.

Pheobe *See* PHOEBE.

Phil *See* FELICITY; PHILIP; PHILIPPA; PHILOMENA; PHYLLIDA; PHYLLIS.

Philadelphia (f) Greek name meaning 'brotherly love'. The name was borne by an ancient city in Asia Minor and was subsequently taken up as a first name by the Puritans. It is popular chiefly in the USA, perhaps because it was chosen by William Penn as the name of the city of Philadelphia, Pennsylvania.

Philander (m) Greek first name meaning 'lover of men'. The name is borne by one of the central characters in Ariosto's *Orlando Furioso* (1532).

Philemon (m) Hebrew first name derived from the Greek *philema* ('kiss'). In Greek legend the elderly Philemon was the husband of Baucis, and the couple unwittingly offered hospitality to the disguised gods Zeus and Hermes and were duly rewarded for their kindness. One of the Epistles of St Paul was addressed to a man named Philemon, 'a dearly beloved fellow-labourer'. The name was subsequently taken up by the Puritans and enjoyed some popularity in the USA in the 19th century but is now rarely encountered.

Philip (m) English first name derived from the Greek *Philippos*, itself derived from the Greek words *philein* ('to love') and *hippos* ('horse'), and thus meaning 'lover of horses'. Alexander the Great's father was Philip II of Macedonia (382–336 BC) and the name was also borne by one of the twelve apostles and several saints. It is also a familiar name among European royalty, being borne by kings of France and Spain and, today, by Elizabeth II's Greek-born husband Philip, Duke of Edinburgh (b.1921). In medieval times the name was shared by both sexes, although distinct feminine versions of the name – such as PHILIPPA – were introduced for use in written records. It suffered a decline in popularity among English speakers in the 16th century through its association with England's enemy Philip II of Spain, but regained lost ground when it was revived in the 19th century. It reached a peak in popularity in the 1950s and 1960s and has since declined once more.

Other notable bearers of the name over

the centuries have included the English Renaissance poet and soldier Sir Philip Sidney (1554–86), US television comedian Phil Silvers (1912–85), British poet Philip Larkin (1922–85) and British rock musician Phil Collins (b.1951). Common diminutives include **Phil**, **Pip** and **Flip**. Variants include **Phillip** (the usual spelling in Australia and when it is found as a surname), the German **Philipp**, the French **Philippe**, the Spanish **Felipe** and the Italian **Filippo**.

Philippa (f) Feminine version of PHILIP, meaning 'lover of horses'. It was introduced originally for use in medieval written records to distinguish male and female bearers of the name Philip, which was formerly common to members of both sexes. Notable medieval bearers of the name included Edward III's queen Philippa of Hainault (1314–67) and the wife of English poet Geoffrey Chaucer, among others, but it was only in the 19th century that the name was adopted on a significant scale throughout the English-speaking world. Well-known bearers of the name in recent times have included British television presenter Philippa Forrester (b.1968). Also found as **Phillipa** and **Philipa**. **Phil** is a diminutive. *See also* PHILIPPINA; PIPPA.

Philippina (f) English and German first name that emerged as a diminutive of PHILIPPA. Also found in France as **Philippine**, in medieval times it was sometimes suggested that the name came from the Greek words *philein* ('to love') and *poine* ('pain') and referred to the Christian practices of self-flagellation and the wearing of hairshirts, etc. as methods of purging sin.

Philis *See* PHYLLIS.

Phillida *See* PHYLLIDA.

Phillie *See* PHILOMENA; PHYLLIDA; PHYLLIS.

Phillip *See* PHILIP.

Phillipa *See* PHILIPPA.

Phillis *See* PHYLLIS.

Philly *See* PHILOMENA; PHYLLIDA; PHYLLIS.

Philo (m) English and German rendering (pronounced 'fihlo') of the ancient Greek name *Philon*, derived from the Greek prefix *phil-* ('love') and meaning 'loved'. The name was borne by a 2nd-century saint and was subsequently adopted by English speakers in the 18th century, enjoying widest acceptance in the USA. Well-known bearers of the name have included US typewriter and sewing-machine manufacturer Philo Remington (1816–89).

Philomela (f) Greek name derived from the Greek words *philos* ('dear' or 'sweet') and *melos* ('song'), and thus meaning 'sweet singer'. Another derivation suggests the word means 'nightingale', a theory that is supported by the ancient Greek myth of King Pandion's daughter Philomela, who was transformed into a nightingale. The name was taken up by English speakers in the 16th century, as reflected by Robert Greene's romance *Philomela* (1592). Also found as **Philomel**.

Philomena (f) English and German first name derived from the Greek words *philein* ('to love') and *menos* ('strength') and thus meaning 'strongly beloved' or 'strength-loving'. The name was formerly popular in Italy and in Ireland, where it was associated with two early saints. The first saint lived in Italy in the 3rd century; what were presumed to be her bones were discovered beneath the altar in the church at San Severino in 1527. What purported to be the remains of the second St Philomena were unearthed in Rome in 1802, inspiring the foundation of a cult. Eventually, however, it was realized that the Latin inscription on the tomb, *Filumena pax tecum* ('Peace be with you, beloved'), was not in fact a reference to the saint's name and the cult was disbanded. As a result the name fell into disuse, although it has continued to make rare reappearances throughout the English-speaking world into recent times. Variants include **Philomene**, **Philomina** and **Filomena**.

Philomena

285

Sometimes shortened to **Phil** and **Phillie** (or **Philly**).

Phineas (m) Biblical name possibly derived from the Hebrew *Phinehas* ('serpent's mouth' or 'oracle'), but more likely descended from the Egyptian *Panhsj* ('the black'), a name used for Nubians. It appears in the Old Testament as the name of one of Eli's sons and of a grandson of Aaron. The name was adopted as a first name among English speakers in the 16th century but has never been common and had virtually disappeared from use by the late 19th century, except among members of the world's Jewish communities. Notable bearers of the name have included the central character in Anthony Trollope's novels *Phineas Finn* (1869) and *Phineas Redux* (1874) and US showman Phineas T. Barnum (1810–91). Occasionally also found as **Phinehas**, the original biblical spelling, or as the Yiddish **Pinchas**.

Phoebe (f) Latin version (pronounced 'feebee') of a Greek first name derived from the Greek *phoibe* ('bright' or 'shining'). According to Greek legend, Phoebe was a daughter of Uranus and Gaia. Artemis and the Roman moon goddess Diana were also sometimes known by the name. It features in the New Testament as the name of the carrier of one of St Paul's letters, which was the reason why the name was adopted with some enthusiasm in post-Reformation England. The name also features in Shakespeare, as the name of a shepherdess. It reached a peak in popularity in the late 19th century but has been less frequently encountered since then, although it enjoyed a resurgence in popularity in the 1990s. Notable bearers of the name in modern times have included the US actress Phoebe Cates (b.1963). Sometimes encountered in the forms **Phebe** and **Pheobe** and occasionally as a diminutive form of EUPHEMIA.

Phoenix (m/f) English first name that alludes to the legendary bird of Arabian mythology, which was believed to burst periodically into flames and arise renewed from its own ashes. Among those to choose the name for their offspring in recent years has been English Spice Girl pop singer Melanie Brown who in 1999 named her new daughter Phoenix Chi.

Phyllida (f) Variant form of PHYLLIS, which emerged as a distinct name in its own right in the 15th century. Also encountered in the variant form **Phillida**, it was particularly popular among English speakers in the 17th century. Well-known bearers of the name in recent times have included Scottish actress Phyllida Law (b.1932). Sometimes shortened to **Phil** and **Phillie** (or **Philly**).

Phyllis (f) English and German first name derived from the Greek *phullis* ('foliage' or 'green branch'). In Greek legend, Phyllis was a beautiful country girl who hanged herself when she was disappointed in love. The gods took pity on her and transformed her into an almond tree, fated to bear no leaves until her lover returned. The name was borne by several beautiful rustic heroines in classical poetry and was later revived by John Milton in his poem *L'Allegro* (1645). In the 16th century it appears to have become confused with Felicia to produce such variants as **Felis** and **Phillice**. The name dipped in popularity in the 18th century because of its unsophisticated rustic associations, but it revived in the late 19th century, reached a peak in the 1920s and has continued to appear sporadically up to the present day. Notable bearers of the name have included the British actresses Phyllis Calvert (1915–2002) and Phyllis Logan (b.1954). Also found as **Phillis, Philis** and **Phyliss**. Sometimes shortened to **Phil** and **Phillie** (or **Philly**). *See also* PHYLLIDA.

Pia (f) Italian first name derived from the Latin *pia* ('pious', 'dutiful' or 'godly'), a feminine equivalent of the now effectively defunct masculine Pius. It has made occasional appearances among English speakers in the 20th century, especially since the 1970s, although it remains less common than it is in other countries, notably Italy and Scandinavia. Notable bearers of the name in recent times have included US singer and actress Pia Zadora (b.1956).

Piaras/Pierce *See* PIERS.

Piero/Pierre *See* PETER.

Piers (m) Norman French equivalent of PETER that has long since been adopted among English speakers as an alternative to the English form of the name. The name became familiar in England after the Norman Conquest and quickly established its place, as shown by William Langland's poem *Piers Plowman* (*c*.1362). It became increasingly popular from the 1930s. Variant forms in use among the English and Irish include **Pearce, Pierce** and **Peers**. Notable bearers of the name in its various forms have included Irish-born film actor Pierce Brosnan (b.1953). The Irish also have the less common Gaelic variant **Piaras**.

Pietro *See* PETER.

Piety (f) English 'virtue' name that was adopted by the Puritans in the 17th century. Piety was one of the characters representing different virtues depicted in John Bunyan's *The Pilgrim's Progress* (1678, 1684). Unlike some of the other virtue names, Piety has long since fallen into disuse.

Pilar (f) Spanish first name derived from *Nuestra Señora del Pilar* ('Our Lady of the Pillar'), one of the titles used in Spain for the Virgin Mary. The title relates to the legend that Mary appeared on a pillar to St James the Greater at Saragossa. Sometimes shortened to **Pili**.

Pinchas *See* PHINEAS.

Pip *See* PHILIP; PIPPA.

Pippa (f) Diminutive form of PHILIPPA, now also used as a name in its own right. It became popular with English speakers after the publication of Robert Browning's poetic drama *Pippa Passes* (1841), in which Pippa is a naïve young Italian silk worker. Ironically, although Browning clearly believed the name had Italian roots, the name is not actually used in Italy. Sometimes shortened to **Pip**.

Piran (m) Cornish place name (pronounced 'pirrun') of unknown meaning that has also on occasion been taken up as a first name. It is suggested that the original place name was itself derived from the name PETER. Also found as **Perran**, the name was born by the Celtic abbot St Piran, the patron saint of Cornish miners.

Pitambar (m) Indian name derived from the Sanskrit words *pita* ('yellow') and *ambara* ('garment') and thus meaning 'wearing yellow garments'. Hindus wear yellow robes at various holy celebrations and the name is particularly popular with followers of Vishnu or Krishna, who include the name among their many epithets.

Pius (m) Italian first name meaning 'holy'. It has been borne by several popes over the centuries.

Placido (m) Italian, Spanish and Portuguese name derived from the Latin *placidus* ('calm' or 'untroubled'). Popular among early Christians, it is best known today from the name of the celebrated Spanish tenor Placido Domingo (b.1941). **Placida** is an equivalent name for girls.

Plaxy (m) Cornish name supposedly descended from the Greek name Praxedes, which was itself derived from the Greek *praxis* ('action' or 'doing') and is usually taken to mean 'active'. It has been encountered occasionally outside Cornwall in the 20th century. The science-fiction writer Olaf Stapledon selected the name for Plaxy Trelone in his novel *Sirius* (1944).

Pleasance (f) English first name derived from the Old French *plaisance* ('pleasure'). The name was introduced to England by the Normans. **Pleasant** is a rare variant – as borne by Pleasant Riderhood, a character in Charles Dickens' novel *Our Mutual Friend* (1865).

Pol *See* POLLY.

Pól *See* PAUL.

Poldie *See* LEOPOLD.

Poll *See* POLLY.

Polly (f) Variant form of MARY, influenced by MOLLY. This familiar form of Mary has been known for several centuries, as illustrated by its use in 'Polly put the kettle on' and other traditional nursery rhymes, and there have been suggestions that it is not in fact dependent upon Mary for its existence but came from a distinct, forgotten source. Notable bearers of the name have included the fictional Polly Peachum in John Gay's hugely successful *The Beggar's Opera* (1728). It has also long been a traditional name for parrots, for obscure reasons. Also found as **Pollie**. Sometimes shortened to **Pol** or **Poll**.

Pollyanna (f) English first name combining POLLY and ANNA that is popular chiefly in the USA. It appears to have been invented by Eleanor H. Porter in her novel *Pollyanna* (1913), in which the central character Pollyanna Whittier is an irrepressibly optimistic girl.

Poppy (f) English flower name derived from the Old English *popaeg* that was first introduced towards the end of the 19th century. The name was very popular in Edwardian England and reached a peak in the 1920s, despite the association between the flower and the thousands who died in the poppy fields of north-eastern France during the First World War – commemorated ever since on 'Poppy Day'.

Portia (f) Anglicization (pronounced 'porsher') of the Latin name Porcia, a feminine form of the Roman family name Porcius, which was itself probably derived from the Latin *porcus* ('hog' or 'pig'). Borne by a famous Roman family whose most notable member was the courageous wife of Marcus Junius Brutus, it was selected by William Shakespeare for the heroine of *The Merchant of Venice* (1598), one of his most successful female characters. Like many other Shakespearean names it has made occasional re-appearances as a first name ever since, despite its unfortunate literal meaning (although another theory suggests it originally meant 'safe harbour').

Posie *See* POSY.

Posy (f) English flower name that seems to have made its first appearance among English speakers in the 1920s. Sometimes treated as a diminutive of JOSEPHINE. Notable bearers of the name have included the fictional Posy Fossil in Noel Streatfield's much-loved children's story *Ballet Shoes* (1936) and British newspaper cartoonist Posy Simmonds (b.1945). Also found as **Posie**.

Prabhakar (m) Indian name derived from the Sanskrit *prabha* ('light') and *kara* ('maker') and thus meaning 'maker of light' or 'illuminator'. Often given to the sun in early texts, it appears in the *Mahabharata* as the name of a serpent-god and is also one of the names borne by Shiva.

Prabhu (m) Indian name derived from the Sanskrit *prabhu* ('mighty'). It was later interpreted to mean 'king' and borne by various gods in classical texts.

Prabodh (m) Indian name (pronounced 'prabod') derived from the Sanskrit *prabodha* (awakening). A medieval introduction, it evokes the blooming of flowers and the awakening of the conscience.

Pradeep (m) Indian name derived from the Sanskrit *pradipa* ('light' or 'lantern'). Although this name appears in ancient classical texts, its use as a first name is a relatively recent innovation.

Prakash (m) Indian name derived from the Sanskrit *prakasa* ('light' or 'famous'). It appears in several ancient texts, including the *Mahabharata*.

Pramod (m) Indian name derived from the Sanskrit *pramoda* ('joy' or 'pleasure'). The name appears in various classical texts as that of a variety of characters, including a demon-serpent.

Pran (m) Indian name derived from the Sanskrit *prana* ('breath' or 'life'). It was borne by various minor deities in classical literature and subsequently became a well-known term of endearment.

Prasad (m) Indian name derived from the Sanskrit *prasada* ('brightness'). Long associated with the quality of tranquillity, its use as a first name is a relatively recent innovation. It is often encountered as part of longer compound names, such as **Ramprasad**.

Pratap (m) Indian name derived from the Sanskrit *pratapa* ('heat' or 'majesty').

Pratibha (f) Indian name derived from the Sanskrit *pratibha* ('light' or 'wit'). This appears to have been a medieval introduction.

Prem (m) Indian name derived from the Sanskrit *prema* ('love'). Notable bearers of the name have included several early kings of Kashmir. Often encountered as part of longer compound names, such as **Premshankar**. Variants include the feminine **Prema**.

Presley (m) English first name, also a surname, meaning 'priest's meadow'.

Preston (m) English place name derived from the Old English *preost* ('priest') and *tun* ('enclosure'), thus meaning 'priest's farm' or 'priest's place', that was subsequently adopted as a surname and first name. It made its debut as a first name in the 19th century. Notable bearers of the name have included US film director and screenwriter Preston Sturges (Edmund Preston Biden; 1898–1959).

Price (m) Welsh surname meaning 'son of RHYS' that has also won wide acceptance as a first name. Often found as **Pryce**.

Primo (m) Italian, Spanish and Portuguese first name derived from the Latin *primus* ('first'). It was borne by several early Christian martyrs. Well-known bearers of the name in modern times have included the Italian writer Primo Levi (1919–87).

Primrose (f) English flower name derived from the Latin *prima rose* ('first rose') that made its debut as a first name towards the end of the 19th century and reached a peak in popularity during the 1920s. In Scotland the name appeared as a surname before being adopted as a first name. It is the family name of the earls of Rosebery.

Primula (f) English flower name derived from the Latin *primus* ('first') that made its debut as a first name towards the end of the 19th century.

Prince (m) English surname that was subsequently adopted as a first name. Taken from the royal title (derived from the Latin *princeps*, 'one who takes first place'), it was used originally as a surname by families with royal connections and by those who were in the service of a prince. It was also taken up (somewhat ironically) among the black slaves of 19th-century America. Notable bearers of the name have included the fictional Prince Turveydrop in *Bleak House* (1853) by Charles Dickens and US pop star Prince (Prince Rogers Nelson; b.1958), who in the 1990s dropped the name in favour of an unpronounceable symbol – prompting the media to dub him 'the artist formerly known as Prince' for the sake of convenience.

Princess (f) Feminine equivalent of the boys' name PRINCE. Similarly derived from the royal title, it has never enjoyed significant acceptance as a first name.

Prisca *See* PRISCILLA.

Priscilla (f) Roman first name derived via a Roman family name from the Latin *priscus* ('ancient' or 'old'). The intention behind the name seems to have been to suggest that the bearer will enjoy a very long life. The name features variously as Priscilla or **Prisca** in the New Testament as that of one of St Paul's companions. As Prisca, it was also borne by a Christian martyr put to death during the reign of Claudius II. The name appears in Edmund Spenser's *The Faerie Queene* (1590, 1596) and in the 17th century was taken up by the Puritans. It came back into fashion in the 19th century, although it has dipped in popularity somewhat since the 1960s. Well-known bearers of the name in recent times have included US actress Priscilla Presley (b.1945), wife of singer Elvis Presley. Diminutive forms include CILLA and the less common **Pris**, **Prissy** and **Scilla**.

Priya (f) Indian name derived from the Sanskrit *priya* ('beloved'). In ancient texts the name is often used to denote a wife or mistress.

Proserpine (f) Roman version (pronounced 'proserpeen') of the Greek PERSEPHONE. It has been suggested that the name may be linked to the Latin *proserpere* ('to creep forth'), evoking the idea of spring flowers emerging after winter. The name was taken up on an occasional basis by English speakers in the 19th century. There is a character of the name in George Bernard Shaw's play *Candida* (1894). Sometimes shortened to **Pross** or **Prossy**.

Prosper (m) French and English first name derived from the Latin *prosper* ('fortunate' or 'prosperous'), which itself came from *pro spe* ('according to one's wishes'). It was commonly found among the saints of the early Christian church and was later adopted by the Puritans. Famous bearers of the name have included the French writer Prosper Mérimée (1803–70). Variants of the name in other languages include the Italian, Spanish and Portuguese version **Prospero**, in which form Shakespeare used it in his last play *The Tempest* (1612).

Prospero *See* PROSPER.

Pross/Prossy *See* PROSERPINE.

Pru *See* PRUDENCE; PRUNELLA.

Prudence (f) English first name derived from the Roman name Prudentia, itself derived from the Latin *prudens* ('provident'). It made occasional appearances in medieval England, including one in the works of Geoffrey Chaucer, before establishing itself

as one of the most popular 'virtue' names espoused by the Puritans in the 17th century. Unlike some of the other virtue names, such as CHASTITY and TEMPERANCE, Prudence has retained its appeal into modern times, although appearing with less frequency than it did formerly. Notable bearers of the name have included a 15th-century Italian abbess now remembered as the Blessed Prudentia, an allegorical character in John Bunyan's *The Pilgrim's Progress* (1674, 1684), the fictional subject of the Beatles' single 'Dear Prudence' (1968) and South African-born British cookery writer Prue Leith (Prudence Leith; b.1940). Sometimes shortened to **Pru**, **Prue** and **Purdy**. **Prudencio** is a Spanish and Portuguese version of the name that was borne by two male Spanish saints and which is still sometimes given to boys.

Prue *See* PRUDENCE; PRUNELLA.

Prunella (f) English first name probably derived from the Latin *pruna* ('little plum'). The name was first adopted by English speakers in the 19th century, although the word had been familiar for at least a century before that as the name of a type of smooth woollen fabric used for clerical and academic gowns, of the wild flower selfheal (*Prunella vulgaris*), and also as an alternative name for the hedge sparrow or dunnock. The most widely known bearer of the name in modern times has been British actress Prunella Scales (b.1932), who co-starred with John Cleese in the classic television comedy series *Fawlty Towers*. Sometimes shortened to **Pru** or **Prue**.

Pryce *See* PRICE.

Pryderi (m) Welsh first name (pronounced 'pridairee') meaning 'caring for' or 'anxiety'. There is a character of the name in the *Mabinogion*.

Psyche (f) Greek name derived from the Greek *psukhe* ('soul'). In Greek mythology, Psyche represented the human soul, falling in love with Eros (or Cupid). English speakers adopted the name in the 19th century. There are characters named Psyche in Alfred, Lord Tennyson's poem 'The Princess' (1847) and in Gilbert and Sullivan's comic opera *Princess Ida* (1884), which was based on Tennyson's work.

Pugh (m) Welsh first name, also a surname, meaning 'son of Hugh'.

Purdie *See* PERDITA.

Purdy *See* PRUDENCE.

Puroshottam (m) Indian name derived from the Sanskrit words *purusa* ('man') and *uttama* ('highest') and thus meaning 'the best of men'. The name is sometimes bestowed upon Vishnu or Krishna and is especially popular among the Jains.

Pyotr *See* PETER.

Q

Queenie (f) English first name that began life as a nickname derived from REGINA (which means 'queen' in Latin), although it may ultimately have descended from the Old English *cwene* ('woman'). The name became popular in medieval times and was revived in the 19th century in reference to Queen Victoria (as a result of which it became an accepted nickname for anyone called VICTORIA). Also found as **Queeny** and rarely, chiefly in the USA, as **Queena**.

Quentin (m) English and French name derived from the Latin *quintus* ('fifth') and thus often given to fifth sons. Roman versions of the name were Quintus and Quintinus, while fifth daughters might be called Quintilla or Quintina. St Quentin was a 3rd-century martyr, after whom the town of St Quentin in northern France was named. The name came to England with the Normans but disappeared during medieval times, only to be revived in the 19th century (particularly in Scotland). Well-known bearers of the name (which is also found as **Quintin**) have included British politician and lawyer Quentin Hogg, Viscount Hailsham (1907–2001) and British writer Quentin Crisp (Denis Pratt; 1910–99). Notable instances of the name in fiction have included the central character in Sir Walter Scott's novel *Quentin Durward* (1823). The name is also found in the variant form **Quinton** and in the feminine variants **Quintella** and **Quinetta**. Diminutive forms include **Quin** and QUINN.

Quincy (m) French place name derived from the Roman Quintus, itself from the Latin *quintus* ('fifth'), that was later adopted in the English-speaking world both as a surname and first name. The name is particularly popular in the USA, reflecting admiration for President John Quincy Adams (1767–1848), who in turn acquired the name from his maternal great-grandfather John Quincy (who died in the year the future President was born). More recent bearers of the name have included US jazz musician Quincy Jones (b.1933). Variants include **Quincey** and **Quintus**.

Quinn (m) Irish first name derived from a Gaelic surname meaning 'counsel'. *See also* QUENTIN.

Quinton *See* QUENTIN.

Qusay (m) Arab name meaning 'distant'. This name is of pre-Islamic origin, but is supposed to have been borne by an ancestor of Muhammad who introduced a new lunar calendar.

R

Rab *See* ROBERT.

Rabab (f) Arabic and Indian name derived from the name of a traditional stringed musical instrument called the *rababah*. It was borne by Muhammad's grandson Rabab (d 861)

Rabbie *See* ROBERT.

Rachael *See* RACHEL.

Rachel (f) Hebrew name meaning 'ewe' (symbolizing innocence and gentleness). As Rahel it appears in the Old Testament as the name of Jacob's beautiful second wife, the mother of Joseph and Benjamin. It was subsequently taken up as a first name by Christians, Jews and Moslems alike. Also found as **Rachael** or **Racheal** (and occasionally **Rachelle**), it was largely confined to the Jewish community before being more widely adopted in post-medieval times. The name was adopted in England by the Puritans after the Reformation and enjoyed peaks in popularity among English speakers in the 17th, 19th and 20th centuries, with a considerable boom since 1970. In Scotland it is sometimes treated as an Anglicization of the Gaelic **Raoghnald**, which had its roots in the Norse **Ragnhildr**. The usual Spanish variant of the name is **Raquel**.

Notable bearers of the name in its various forms have included the French actress Rachel (Elizabeth Félix; 1820–58), the British actress Rachel Kempson (1910–2003), the US film actress Raquel Welch (Raquel Tejada; b.1940) and the British cricketer Rachael Heyhoe Flint (b.1939). Sometimes shortened to **Rach**, **Rachie**, **Rae**, **Ray** and SHELLEY. *See also* ROCHELLE.

Rachelle *See* RACHEL.

Raclaw/Rada *See* RADOSLAW.

Radcliff (m) English place name derived from the Old English for 'red cliff' that was subsequently adopted as a surname and first name. Also found as **Radcliffe** or **Radclyffe** – as borne by the British novelist [Marguerite] Radclyffe Hall (1886–1943), author of the notorious novel *The Well of Loneliness* (1928).

Radha (m/f) Indian first name derived from Sanskrit *radha* ('success'). The name appears in the *Mahabharata* and was borne by one of Krishna's favourite female companions. Also found as part of the compound name **Radhakrishna**.

Radoslaw (m) Polish first name (pronounced 'radoslav') of Slavonic origin, derived from *rad* ('glad') and *slav* ('glory'). Commonly shortened to **Raclaw**. Variants include the Czech and Russian **Radoslav** and the feminine versions **Radoslawa** (Polish) and **Radoslava** (Czech), which are sometimes abbreviated to **Rada**.

Radu (m) Romanian diminutive form of various Slavonic names beginning Rad-, including RADOSLAW and RADZIMIERZ.

Radzimierz (m) Polish first name (pronounced 'rad-jim-yersh') derived from the Slavonic *rad* ('glad') and *meri* ('great' or 'famous'). Sometimes shortened to RADU. Variants in other languages include the Czech **Radomir** or **Radim** and the Russian **Radimir**.

Rae *See* RACHEL; RAELENE.

Raelene (f) Australian compound name combining **Rae** (a diminutive of RACHEL) with the standard feminine suffix -lene. A relatively recent introduction dating from the middle of the 20th century, it was probably inspired by such parallel names as DAR-LENE. It is rarely found outside Australia.

Rafa/Rafael *See* RAPHAEL.

Rafe *See* RALPH.

Rafiq (m) Arabic and Indian name derived from *rafiq* (variously meaning 'companion', 'friend' or 'kind', 'gentle'). Also found as **Rafi** or **Rafee**.

Raghnaid/Raghnailt *See* RAGNHILD.

Raghnall *See* RONALD.

Raghu (m) Indian first name derived from the Sanskrit *raghu* ('swift'). It appears in classical texts and was also borne by Buddha's son.

Ragna (f) Scandinavian diminutive for various first names beginning with the Old Norse *regin* (meaning 'advice', 'decision' or 'the gods'). Examples include RAGNBORG and RAGNHILD. It was in common use in Viking times and was subsequently revived in the 19th century.

Ragnar *See* RAYNER.

Ragnborg (f) Scandinavian first name derived from the Old Norse *regin* ('advice', 'decision' or 'the gods') and *borg* ('fortification'). It was used by the Vikings and was subsequently revived in the 19th century. Also found (in Sweden) as **Ramborg**.

Ragnhild (f) Scandinavian first name derived from the Old Norse *regin* ('advice', 'decision' or 'the gods') and *hildr* ('battle'). Also encountered as **Ragnild** or as **Raghnailt** (Irish Gaelic) or **Raghnaid** (Scottish Gaelic).

Ragnvald (m) Scandinavian first name derived from the Old Norse Rognvaldr, which combined *regin* ('advice', 'decision' or 'the gods') with *valdr* ('ruler'). Often considered to be a Scandinavian equivalent of REYNOLD.

Raibert *See* ROBERT.

Raimondo/Raimundo *See* RAYMOND.

Raina/Raine *See* REGINA.

Rainer/Rainier *See* RAYNER.

Raisa (f) Russian first name (pronounced 'rye-eesa') possibly derived from the Greek *rhadios* ('adaptable' or 'easy-going'). Also found as **Raya**, it was borne by an early Christian martyr put to death in 308. Recent bearers of the name have included Raisa Gorbachev (1932–99), wife of the former Soviet leader.

Raj (m) Indian first name derived from the Sanskrit *raja* ('king'). It was borne by various gods and was later used to denote anyone bearing military rank. It appears as a component of many longer names. In southern India it also appears in the forms **Raja, Rajan** and **Rajam**.

Rajani (f) Indian first name derived from the Sanskrit *rajani* ('the night'). It appears in classical texts and in the *Mahabharata* is borne by Durga or Kali, the wife of Shiva.

Rajendra (m) Indian first name derived from the Sanskrit *raja* ('king') and *indra* ('mighty'). Taken to mean 'emperor' in ancient texts, it is also found as **Rajender** and **Rajinder**.

Rajesh (m) Indian first name derived from the Sanskrit *raja* ('king') and *isa* ('ruler'). It does not appear to have been used before medieval times.

Rajiv (m) Indian first name derived from the Sanskrit *rajiva* ('striped'). It appears in classical texts and made its debut as a first name in medieval times. The most notable bearer of the name in recent times has been the Indian Prime Minister Rajiv Gandhi (1944–91).

Rajnish (m) Indian first name derived from the Sanskrit *rajani* ('night') and *isa* ('ruler') and thus meaning 'ruler of the night'. It appears in classical texts as a name for the moon and made its debut as a first name only in relatively recent times. Also found as **Rajneesh**.

Rakesh (m) Indian first name derived from

the Sanskrit *raka* ('full-moon day') and *isa* ('ruler') and thus meaning 'ruler of the full-moon day'. In classical texts the name was borne by a moon goddess and it also appears as one of Shiva's names.

Raleigh (m) English place name (pronounced 'ralee') derived from the Old English for 'clearing with roe deer' that was later adopted as a surname and occasional first name. The name evokes the memory of the celebrated English seafarer, writer and explorer Sir Walter Raleigh (*c.*1552–1618), who was a favourite of Elizabeth I.

Ralph (m) English first name derived via Norman French from the Old Norse Rathulfr, from *raed* ('counsel') and *wulf* ('wolf') and thus meaning 'wise and strong'. In such early forms as Radulf and Raedwulf the name predated the Norman Conquest. As **Ralf** or **Rauf** (pronounced 'rayf') it remained popular through medieval and post-medieval times, as shown by Nicholas Udall's comedy *Ralph Roister-Doister* (1566) and by the appearance of the name for a minor character in William Shakespeare's *Henry VI* (1597). **Rafe** was the usual form of the name in the 17th century, reflecting its contemporary pronunciation, but it eventually gave way to Ralph in the 18th century, when several names ending -f were changed to -ph in deference to the contemporary enthusiasm for (Greek) classical-looking names. Having reached a peak in popularity in the 1920s, the name has since gone into decline. The current pronunciation of the name with a short 'a' and with the 'l' sounded is relatively recent, dating only from the early 20th century (although the older pronunciation is still heard occasionally). A familiar version of the name is **Ralphie**. **Ralphina** is a rare feminine variant.

Notable bearers of the name have included the US philosopher Ralph Waldo Emerson (1803–82), the British composer Ralph Vaughan Williams (1872–1958), the British actor Sir Ralph Richardson (1902–83), the British cartoonist Ralph Steadman

(b.1936) and British actor Ralph Fiennes (b.1962). *See also* RAOUL.

Ralston (m) English place name that was subsequently adopted as a surname and, since the 19th century, as a first name.

Rama (m) Indian first name derived from the Sanskrit *rama* ('pleasing'). It was borne in classical texts by Vishnu, by an elder brother of Krishna and by RAMACHANDRA. It is also found as part of several compound names beginning Ram-. **Ram** is a variant form.

Ramachandra (m) Indian first name derived from the Sanskrit *ramacandra* ('Rama-moon'). It was borne by Vishnu and by the central character in the *Ramayana* – a popular figure of worship since the medieval period; and subsequently by numerous kings, writers and religious authorities in medieval times. Also found as **Ramachander** in southern India.

Ramakrishna (m) Indian first name combining the names RAMA and KRISHNA. It appears to have made its debut in the medieval period. Notable bearers of the name have included the Bengali mystic Sri Ramakrishna Paramahamsa (1836–86), whose teaching is continued today by an order of monks and by a religious organization called the Ramakrishna Mission.

Ramborg *See* RAGNBORG.

Ramesh (m) Indian first name derived from RAMA combined with the Sanskrit *isa* ('ruler'). It is one of the names borne by Vishnu and became a popular choice of first name in the medieval period.

Rameshwar (m) Indian first name derived from RAMA and the Sanskrit *isvara* ('lord') and thus meaning 'lord Rama'.

Ramiro (m) Spanish first name derived from the Old German *ragin* ('advice' or 'decision') and *mari* ('famous'). The name was borne by an early Christian martyr killed by the Visigoths in the 5th or 6th century.

Ramón/Ramona *See* RAYMOND.

Ramsay (m) English place name derived from the Old English *hramsa* ('wild garlic' or 'ram') and *eg* ('island') that was later taken up, chiefly in Scotland, as a surname and first name. The name's Scottish connections date back to the 12th century, when the young David I, King of Scots lived at the English court and owned estates in eastern England: when he inherited the throne of Scotland he took with him several courtiers with English names, including Ramsay. Also encountered as **Ramsey**. Notable bearers of the name have included British Labour Prime Minister James Ramsay MacDonald (1866–1937).

Ramsden (m) English first name meaning 'ram's valley'.

Ran *See* RANDOLPH; RANULPH.

Ranald *See* RONALD.

Randal/Randall *See* RANDOLPH.

Randolph (m) English first name derived from the Old English *rand* ('shield edge') and *wulf* ('wolf') and thus meaning, roughly, 'strong defender'. The original Old English form of the name, itself an English equivalent of the earlier Scandinavian Rannulfr, was Randwulf. In the 'Doomsday Book' the name was Latinized as Randulfus. In medieval times English versions of the name included **Randal**, **Randall**, **Randel** and **Randle**. After several centuries of disuse the name enjoyed a revival in the 19th century, by which time the -f ending had largely given way to -ph in response to the 18th-century enthusiasm for (Greek) classical-looking names. It has since been more popular in Canada and the USA than elsewhere in the English-speaking world. Sometimes shortened to **Ran** or to **Randy** (or **Randi**), especially in the USA, regardless of the latter's slang meaning of 'lustful' or 'lecherous'.

Notable bearers of the name in its various forms have included the fictional Randal Olifaunt in Sir Walter Scott's *The Fortunes of Nigel* (1822), both the father (1849–95) and the son (1911–68) of British Prime Minister Winston Churchill, US film actor Randolph Scott (1898–1987) and US singer-songwriter Randy Newman (b.1944).

Randy *See* MIRANDA; RANDOLPH.

Rani (f) Indian first name derived from the Hindi for 'queen'. Also encountered as **Ranee**.

Ranjit (m) Indian first name derived from the Sanskrit *ranjita* ('coloured' or 'painted'). Another derivation suggests it means 'charmed' or 'delighted'. It made its debut as a first name in the medieval period. Notable bearers of the name have included Ranjit Singh (1780–1839), founder of the Sikh kingdom of Punjab.

Ranulf *See* RANULPH.

Ranulph (m) English version of the Old Norse Reginulfr, which was itself derived from *regin* ('advice' or 'decision') and *ulfr* ('wolf') thus meaning 'well-counselled and strong'. The original English form of the name was Ranulf, which subsequently developed into Ranulph in the 18th century in response to the contemporary enthusiasm for (Greek) classical-looking names. Notable bearers of the name in recent times have included British explorer Sir Ranulph Fiennes (b.1944). Sometimes shortened to **Ran**.

Raoghnald *See* RACHEL.

Raoul (m) French version of RALPH, now found occasionally in the English-speaking world as a name in its own right. Also found as **Raul**.

Raphael (m) Hebrew name meaning 'God has healed'. As the name of a biblical archangel it became very popular among early Christians but was subsequently confined largely to the Jewish community until the 16th century, when it reappeared in many Christian countries, particularly in Italy, Spain and Portugal where it is spelled **Rafael** or **Raffaele**. It was taken up by English speakers in the 16th and 17th centuries but was frowned upon by the Puritans and has remained rare among English speakers up to the present day, despite a brief vogue in the late 19th century. It is found much more frequently today in southern European countries. Notable bearers of the name have included the celebrated Italian Renaissance painter Raphael (Raffaello Santi; 1483–1520). Sometimes abbreviated (in Spain) to **Rafa**. A rare feminine variant is **Raffaella** (or **Raphaela**).

Raphaela See RAPHAEL.

Raquel See RACHEL.

Rashid (m) Arabic and Indian first name meaning 'rightly guided' or 'mature'. Also found as **Rasheed**. A feminine equivalent of the name is **Rashida**.

Rastus See ERASTUS.

Ratan (m) Indian first name derived from the Sanskrit *ratna* ('jewel'). It was taken up as a first name in the medieval period and is most common today in northern India. Variants include **Ratnam,** the usual form in the southern part of the subcontinent.

Rati (f) Indian first name derived from the Sanskrit *rati* ('rest' or 'repose'), although the name is commonly interpreted today to signify 'pleasure', notably of a sexual nature. The name is sometimes borne by Kama, the god of love.

Rauf See RALPH.

Raul See RAOUL.

Ravi (m) Indian first name derived from the Sanskrit *ravi* ('sun'). It was borne by a sun god, among other Indian deities.

Ravindra (m) Indian first name derived from the Sanskrit *ravi* ('sun') and *indra* ('mighty'). Variants include the Bengali **Rabindra** and **Rabindranath** – as borne by the Indian poet and philosopher Rabrindranath Tagore (1861–1941).

Ray See RACHEL; RAYMOND.

Raya See RAISA.

Raymond (m) English first name derived via the French Raimont from an Old German name combining *ragin* ('advice' or 'decision') and *mund* ('protection') and thus meaning 'well-advised protector'. As Raimund or Reimund, the name came to England with the Normans and was also borne by two 13th-century Spanish saints, one of whom became the patron saint of midwives. In its modern form it re-emerged among English speakers in the middle of the 19th century and subsequently enjoyed a peak in popularity between the 1920s and the 1950s.

Well-known bearers of the name have included US crime writer Raymond Chandler (1888–1959), who created the sleazy private detective Philip Marlowe, Canadian actor Raymond Massey (1896–1983) and British broadcaster Raymond Baxter (b.1922). Often shortened to **Ray** – as borne by Welsh-born US film actor Ray Milland (Reginald Truscott-Jones; 1905–86), US science-fiction writer Ray Bradbury (b.1920) and US soul singer Ray Charles (b.1930).

Redmond and **Redmund** are two Irish versions of the name. Other foreign language variants include the Spanish **Ramón** or **Raimundo** and the Italian **Raimondo**. Feminine versions of the name include **Raymonde** and the Spanish **Ramona**, which became popular in Canada and the USA after the publication of Helen Hunt Jackson's novel *Ramona* in 1884.

Raymund See RAYMOND.

Rayner (m) English first name derived from the Old German *ragin* ('advice' or 'protection') and *hari* ('army' or 'warrior'). The name was introduced to England by the Normans in the 11th century and it remained in fairly frequent use until the 14th century, since when it has been relatively rare among English speakers and more common in Germany and elsewhere. Also found as **Raynor** and **Rainier** (a French version), as borne by Prince Rainier III of Monaco (b.1923). A German variant is **Rainer**, as borne by German poet Rainer Maria Rilke (1875–1926). The usual Scandinavian version of the name is **Ragnar**. **Raina** and **Raine** are feminine variants.

Raza (m) Indian first name derived from the Arabic *riza* ('contentment' or 'satisfaction'). It was borne by the Shiite leader Ali Musi Raza (764–818) and is today a popular name among Muslims. Also found as **Riza**.

Read *See* REID.

Reanna (f) English first name of obscure origins. A recent introduction, it may have evolved from RHEA and was probably influenced by DEANNA and the Welsh RHIANNON. Also found as **Reanna** and **Rheanna**.

Rearden *See* RIORDAN.

Reba *See* REBECCA.

Rebecca (f) Hebrew name possibly meaning 'heifer' or, according to another theory, 'binding', 'knotted cord' or 'noose' (perhaps in reference to the marriage bond). In fact, the name probably has an older lost Aramaic source. It appears (as Rebekah) in the Old Testament as the name of the wife of Isaac and mother of Jacob and Esau and has always been a popular Jewish name. Because of its religious associations it was among the many biblical names favoured by the Puritans in England and America in the 16th and 17th centuries. The name enjoyed a new lease of life in the wake of the publication of Daphne du Maurier's novel *Rebecca* (1938), also a popular film (1940), and enjoyed another significant revival in the 1970s, by which time its religious connotations were largely forgotten.

Famous bearers of the name have included central characters in William Makepeace Thackeray's *Vanity Fair* (1848), Henrik Ibsen's *Rosmersholm* (1886) and Kate Douglas Wiggin's *Rebecca of Sunnybrook Farm* (1903), as well as British writer Dame Rebecca West (Cicily Isabel Fairfield; 1892–1983) and US actress Rebecca DeMornay (b.1962).

Occasionally found as **Rebeccah**, **Rebeckah** or **Rebekka**. Commonly shortened to **Becky**, **Becca** or, less frequently, to

Reba. Variants in other languages include the Hebrew **Rivka**.

Red (m) English first name that began life as a nickname for any person with red hair or alternatively as a derivative of names with 'r' and 'd' in them, especially EDWARD and RICHARD. Also found as **Redd**, it is more common in the USA than elsewhere. Well-known bearers of the name have included US actors Red Skelton (Richard Skelton; 1910–97) and Red Buttons (Aaron Chwatt; b.1918).

Redmond/Redmund *See* RAYMOND.

Redvers (m) English surname with strong aristocratic associations that has also appeared occasionally as a first name. It appears to have made its debut as a first name in the 19th century, when notable bearers of it included the British general Sir Redvers Buller (1839–1908).

Reece *See* RHYS.

Reed *See* REID.

Reenie *See* DOREEN; MAUREEN; RENÉ.

Rees *See* RHYS.

Reg *See* REGINALD.

Regan (f) English first name of unknown origin, though conceivably derived from REGINA. Possibly linked with the Irish surname Regan or Reagan, it was most famously employed by William Shakespeare for one of the king's three daughters in his tragedy *King Lear* (1605).

Reggie *See* REGINA; REGINALD.

Regina (f) English first name derived from the Latin *regina* ('queen'). One of the titles bestowed upon the Virgin Mary was *Regina Coeli* ('Queen of Heaven') and St Regina was a 3rd-century Christian virgin martyr. As a result of these religious associations Regina was a fairly popular choice of girls' name in medieval times, when it was also encountered occasionally as **Reina**, an Anglicization of the French **Reine**. It fell from favour after the Reformation because of its

Catholic links, only to be revived in the 18th century and then to become relatively widespread in the 19th century, largely in tribute to Queen Victoria. Today it is mostly confined to the USA. Notable bearers of the name have included the fictional Regina Giddens in Lillian Hellman's play *The Little Foxes* (1939). Sometimes shortened to **Reggie**. A relatively recent variant form, possibly derived from a surname, is **Raine** – as borne by Countess Spencer, stepmother of Diana, Princess of Wales. The usual modern French version of the name is **Régine**. A Russian variant is **Raina** (introduced to English speakers by George Bernard Shaw as the name of a character in his 1894 play *Arms and the Man*). *See also* GINA; QUEENIE; REGAN; REX.

Reginald (m) English first name derived from the Old English Regenweald, itself derived from *regen* ('counsel') and *weald* ('power') and thus meaning 'well-counselled ruler'. The name was in occasional use among the Anglo-Saxons but became much more popular after the Norman Conquest through its French equivalents **Reinald** and **Reynaud**, Anglicized as REYNOLD, the usual form of the name until it was eclipsed by Reginald (and the Latin form **Reginaldus**) in the 15th century. After three centuries of neglect the name Reginald came back into fashion during the 19th century as a result of its appearance in Sir Walter Scott's *Ivanhoe* (1820). It remained a common choice of name through the first half of the 20th century but has suffered a marked decline in recent decades. Notable bearers of the name have included the central character in several short stories by 'Saki' (H. H. Munro), British politician Reginald Maudling (1917–79), British television newsreader Reginald Bosanquet (1932–84) and the fictional Reginald Perrin in the popular 1970s British television comedy series *The Fall and Rise of Reginald Perrin*. Commonly shortened to **Reg**, **Reggie** or **REX**. *See also* ROALD; RONALD.

Régine *See* REGINA.

Régis (m) French first name derived from the Old Provençal for 'ruler'. Its popularity in France was greatly promoted by St Jean-François Régis of Narbonne (d.1640), who was famous for his work reforming prostitutes.

Reid (m) English surname derived from the Old English *read* ('red') or alternatively from an Old English place name that evolved from *hreod* ('reeds') or *reod* ('cleared land'). It was subsequently adopted as a first name, often reserved for children with red hair or a ruddy complexion. Today it is more common in the USA than elsewhere. Occasionally encountered as **Read** or **Reed**.

Reina/Reine *See* REGINA.

Reinhard *See* REYNARD.

Reinhold *See* REYNOLD.

Remedios (f) Spanish first name derived from a title bestowed upon the Virgin Mary, *Nuestra Señora de los Remedios* (*remedio* in Spanish meaning 'remedy' or 'help').

Remo *See* REMUS.

Remus (m) English name possibly derived from the Latin *remus* ('oar') or else from Romulus' brother Remus, legendary founder of Rome. It made sporadic appearances as a first name among English speakers in the 19th century. The most famous bearer of the name is the fictional former black slave Remus in Joel Chandler Harris' *Uncle Remus* tales (1880–1910). An Italian variant is **Remo**.

Rémy (m) French name derived from the Latin Remigius, from *remex* ('oarsman'). It was borne by a celebrated 6th-century French bishop of Rheims and by an 8th-century bishop of Rouen. Related names in other languages include the Italian, Spanish and Portuguese **Remigio**.

Rena/Renata *See* RENÉ.

René (m) French first name derived from the Latin *renatus* ('reborn'). As **Renatus** it was popular among the early Christians and was later taken up by the Puritans in the 17th century. Its frequency in Canada and the USA reflects the influence of the French missionary St René Goupil (d.1642), who was killed by North American Iroquois Indians after he made the sign of the cross. Other celebrated bearers of the name have included the French philosopher René Descartes (1596–1650). Both René and the feminine version **Renée** (or **Reenie**) have been adopted among English speakers in the 20th century, becoming especially popular in Australia. The name may or may not appear with an accent. Other variants include **Renato** (an Italian, Spanish and Portuguese version) and the feminine **Rena** (or **Rina**), **Renata** (found in Italy, Poland, Germany and the Czech Republic as well as in English-speaking countries) and **Renate** (found chiefly in Germany).

Renée See RENÉ.

Renie See IRENE.

Reuben (m) Hebrew name meaning 'behold, a son'. The name appears in the Bible as that of Jacob's eldest son and of the founder of one of the twelve tribes of Israel and it has always been popular among the world's Jewish communities. Also found as **Ruben**, it was among the many biblical names adopted by English-speaking Puritans in the 17th century. It remained common well into the 19th century, by which time it had acquired strong rural connotations, but has since become rare. Well-known bearers of the name have included characters in Sir Walter Scott's *The Heart of Midlothian* (1818), Thomas Hardy's *Under the Greenwood Tree* (1872) and Anna Sewell's children's novel *Black Beauty* (1877). **Rube** and **Ruby** are common abbreviations of the name. Variants in other languages include the Jewish **Reuven**, the Scandinavian **Ruben** and the Finnish **Ruupeni** and **Ruuppo**.

Rex (m) English first name derived from the Latin *rex* ('king'). It is largely a 20th-century introduction, although it is also sometimes considered to be a shortened

form of REGINALD. Famous bearers of the name have included British artist Rex Whistler (Reginald John Whistler; 1905–44) and British actor Rex Harrison (Reginald Carey Harrison; 1908–90). *See also* REGINA.

Rexanne (f) English first name derived from REX, probably influenced by ROXANNE.

Reynard (m) French name derived from the Old German *ragin* ('counsel') and *hard* ('hard') and thus meaning 'mighty and brave'. Also found as **Rainard**, it was popular among the Norman French, who introduced it to England, but was eventually eclipsed by REYNOLD. It is virtually extinct today although it is still remembered through Reynard the Fox in Aesop's *Fables* and it remains a traditional name for foxes. **Reinhard** is a German variant.

Reynaud See REYNOLD.

Reynold (m) English first name derived via Norman French from the Old German *ragin* ('advice' or 'decision') and *wald* ('ruler') and thus meaning 'well-counselled ruler'. Also encountered as a variant form of REGINALD, it was originally spelled as the French **Reynaud** before the modern version of the name became the standard English form. It has been in irregular use among English speakers since the 19th century. Variants in other languages include the Welsh **Rheinallt**, the Italian **Rinaldo** and the German **Reinhold**. *See also* RAGNVALD; REYNARD.

Rhea (f) Greek name meaning 'flow' and originally borne by an earth goddess identified as the mother of Zeus. Another legend names Rhea Silva as the mother of Romulus and Remus, founders of Rome. It is relatively rare today. Well-known bearers of the name have included US actress Rhea Perlman (b.1948), one of the stars of the long-running 1980s US television comedy series *Cheers*. *See also* REANNA; SILVIA.

Rheanna See REANNA.

Rhett (m) English first name of uncertain

origin, possibly derived from the older BRETT or else from the Dutch surname de Raedt, itself derived from the Middle Dutch *raet* ('advice'). A more fanciful suggestion traces the name back rather tentatively to the Greek *rhetor* ('speaker' or 'orator'). Whatever its ultimate origins, the name seems to have made its first appearance as that of one of the leading characters in Margaret Mitchell's novel *Gone with the Wind* (1936), which was later turned into a classic film starring Clark Gable as Rhett Butler. As a result of the film's huge success the name was taken up on both sides of the Atlantic in the 1940s and has continued to make sporadic appearances ever since. A relatively recent feminine version of the name is **Rhetta**. *See also* SCARLETT.

Rhian (f) Welsh first name meaning 'maiden'. This appears to be a modern innovation. A variant is **Rhianu**.

Rhiannon (f) Welsh first name meaning 'nymph' or 'goddess', probably derived from *rigantona*, a Celtic royal title meaning 'great queen'. The name is thought to have been borne by a Celtic goddess associated with horses and was later carried by the legendary Celtic Princess Rhiannon, who was falsely accused of murdering her own infant son (the boy had in fact been kidnapped and she was cleared of the charge when he was returned after seven years). In modern times it has been taken up by many English speakers without Welsh connections. Older forms of the name include **Riannon**. A recently introduced variant is **Rhianna**.

Rhianu *See* RHIAN.

Rhoda (f) Hebrew name derived from the Greek *rhodon* ('rose'), or alternatively possibly meaning 'a woman from Rhodes' (the name of the island of Rhodes having itself been taken from the Greek *rhodon*). It appears in the New Testament as the name of a servant girl in the house of Mary, mother of John, who barred the door to St Peter after his miraculous escape from prison. The name was adopted by Puritans in England

in the 17th century and has enjoyed a modest revival in the 20th century. In Scotland the name is often treated as a feminine equivalent of RODERICK. Notable bearers of the name have included characters in George Meredith's *Rhoda Fleming* (1845), William Makepeace Thackeray's *Vanity Fair* (1848) and George Bernard Shaw's *Man and Superman* (1903). In the 1970s the name was further popularized by the US television series *Rhoda*, starring Valerie Harper.

Rhodri (m) Welsh first name derived from the Old Welsh *rhod* ('wheel') and *rhi* ('ruler'), or alternatively treated as a Welsh variant of RODERICK. Notable bearers of the name have included a 9th-century Welsh king and Welsh politician Rhodri Morgan (b.1939).

Rhona (f) Scottish first name that developed either from a place name (from Rona, an island in the Hebrides) or as a feminine variant of RONALD or Raghnaid. It seems to have made its debut as a first name around 1870. Although also found as **Rona**, the usual variant spelling of the name may have resulted from the influence of RHODA. Its use is still largely confined to Scotland. *See also* ROWENA.

Rhonda (f) Welsh first name derived from the Welsh *rhon* ('pike' or 'lance') and *da* ('good') that has made occasional appearances as a first name since the early 20th century. It was probably influenced by RHODA and RHONA and acquired extra significance through the link with the Rhondda valley (named after a local river) in south Wales. The decline of heavy industry in the Rhondda since the 1960s, with the accompanying problems of unemployment and lack of investment in the area, has tended to make the name a less attractive choice in the UK in recent decades and it is now more often encountered in other parts of the English-speaking world such as Australia, Canada and the USA, where it seems to have made its debut in the 1940s. Famous bearers of the name have included the US film star Rhonda Fleming (Marilyn Louis Fleming; b.1922).

Rhonwen *See* ROWENA.

Rhydderch *See* RODERICK.

Rhys (m) Welsh first name (pronounced 'reece') meaning 'ardour' or 'rashness'. Also found as **Reece** and in the Anglicized form **Rees**, the name was borne by an 11th-century King of Wales, Rhys ap Tewdwr (d.1093), and by his grandson Rhys ap Gruffud (1132–97) but remains little used today outside the Welsh community around the world. It has also given rise to several surnames, such as Rees, Rice and PRICE.

Ria *See* MARIA.

Rian *See* RYAN.

Riannon *See* RHIANNON.

Riaz (m) Indian first name derived from the Arabic *riyad* ('meadow' or 'garden'). A predominantly Muslim name, it is best known from its use for the capital of Saudi Arabia, Al-Riyadh.

Rica *See* ERICA; FREDERICA.

Ricard/Ricardo/Riccardo
See RICHARD.

Rich *See* RICHARD.

Richard (m) English first name derived via France from the Old German Ricohard, a combination of the German words *ric* ('power') and *hard* ('strong') and thus meaning 'powerful ruler'. As Ricehard (root of the modern **Ricard**), the name was familiar to the Anglo-Saxons, but it was the Normans who introduced the modern form and established it as one of the most lastingly popular of all English names. Its status as a standard English first name is reflected in the traditional 'Tom, Dick and Harry' list of common English names, DICK or **Dickie** being a common diminutive form. In medieval times it was also occasionally found as **Richer**. After a dip in the 19th century it recovered lost ground in the 20th century,

with peaks in the years 1900–1910 and 1950–80. The name has also given rise to numerous surnames, including Rich, Richards, Richardson, Dixon and Hitchcock (this last via Rich and its rhyming variant Hitch).

Among the most famous bearers of the name have been three English kings, the English essayist Richard Steele (1672–1729), US President Richard Nixon (1913–94), Welsh actor Richard Burton (1925–84), British film director and actor Sir Richard Attenborough (b.1923), British entrepreneur Richard Branson (b.1950) and US film actor Richard Gere (b.1949).

Other common diminutive forms include **Rich**, **Richie** (or **Ritchie**), **Rick** (or **Rik**) and **Ricky** (or **Rikki**). Among well-known bearers of the name in these reduced versions have been US country singer Rick Nelson (Eric Nelson; 1940–85), British pop musician Rick Wakeman (b.1949) and British television comedian Rik Mayall (b.1958). Historical diminutives of the name no longer in use today include **Dickon**, **Hick**, **Hickon** and **Ricket**. Variants in other languages include the Spanish **Ricardo**, the Italian **Riccardo**, the Scandinavian **Rikard** and the Polish **Ryszard**. Rare feminine versions of the name include **Ricarda**, **Richelle** and **Richenda**, an 18th-century coinage possibly modelled on such names as BRENDA and GLENDA. *See also* RICHMAL.

Richenda/Richie *See* RICHARD.

Richmal (f) English combination of MICHAEL and RICHARD. A relatively recent introduction, known chiefly from British children's author Richmal Crompton (1890–1969), writer of the *Just William* stories.

Richmond (m) English first name, also a place name, derived from the Old French for 'strong hill'. Commonly abbreviated to **Rich** or **Richie**.

Rick *See* ERIC; RICHARD.

Rickie *See* FREDERICA.

Ricky *See* ERIC; FREDERICA; RICHARD.

Rider (m) English first name, also a sur-name, derived from the ordinary vocabu-lary word. The most famous bearer of the name to date has been English novelist Sir Henry Rider Haggard (1856–1925).

Ridley (m) English place name (shared by towns and villages in several English counties) that was itself derived from Old English *hreod* ('reeds') and *leah* ('wood' or 'clearing') and was subsequently taken up as a surname and first name. The name enjoyed some popularity among Prot-estants in 16th-century England after the burning of the Protestant Bishop Nicholas Ridley (*c*.1500–1555) during the reign of Mary Tudor.

Rik *See* RICHARD.

Rika *See* ERICA; FREDERICA.

Rikard *See* RICHARD.

Rike (f) German diminutive (pronounced 'reeka') of various first names ending -rike, such as **Friederike** and **Ulrike**.

Rikki *See* RICHARD.

Riley (m) English place name, derived from the Old English *ryge* ('rye') and *leah* ('clearing' or 'meadow'), that was sub-sequently taken up as a surname and first name. In Ireland it may also represent a development of the surname Reilly or be descended from the Irish first name Raghal-lach (of obscure meaning).

Rilla (f) German first name meaning 'brook'.

Rina *See* RENÉ.

Rinaldo *See* REYNOLD.

Riona *See* CATRIONA.

Riordan (m) English version of the Irish Gaelic name Rordan, derived from *riogh* ('king') and *bard* ('poet'). Also encountered as **Rearden**.

Rita (f) English and Scandinavian first name that developed originally as an Italian and Spanish variant of Margarita (*see* MAR-GARET) and is now considered to exist as a name in its own right. It has been adopted by English speakers since the beginning of the 20th century and is much more common among English speakers than the full version of the name. Early bearers of the name included St Rita of Cascia (1381–1457), a nun who was credited with numerous miraculous acts and, because of her own early marriage to a violent hus-band, became the patron saint of unhappy marriages. More recent bearers of the name have included US film star Rita Hayworth (Margarita Carmen Cansino, 1918–87), whose popularity did much to promote the name in the 1940s, British actress Rita Tush-ingham (b.1942), the central character in British playwright Willy Russell's *Educating Rita* (1980) and US pop singer Rita Coolidge (b.1945).

Ritchie *See* RICHARD.

Rivka *See* REBECCA.

Roald (m) Norwegian name derived from the Old German *hrod* ('fame') and *valdr* ('ruler') and thus meaning 'famous ruler'. First adopted by English speakers in the 20th century, it is sometimes linked with the names RONALD and REGINALD. Famous bearers of the name have included the Nor-wegian polar explorer Roald Amundsen (1872–1928) and the Norwegian-born British children's author Roald Dahl (1916–90).

Rob/Robb/Robbie/Robby *See* ROBERT.

Robert (m) English, Scottish and French first name derived via Norman French from the Old German Hrodebert, from *hrod* ('fame') and *berht* ('bright' or 'famous') and thus meaning 'bright famous one' or simply 'famously famous'. Although the Anglo-Saxons had an equivalent form of the name, Hreodbeorht, in its modern form it arrived in England via France – William the Con-queror's father was called Robert. It made numerous appearances in the 'Domesday Book' and subsequently retained its status as a favourite choice into medieval times. The Scottish king Robert the Bruce (1274–1329) made the name especially popular in Scotland, where it is also occasionally found in the form **Raibert**. The name has ranked consistently among the most popular first names in the English-speaking world right up to the present day.

Notable bearers of the name since Bruce have included the Scottish outlaw Robert 'Rob Roy' MacGregor (1671–1734), British Prime Minister Robert Peel (1788–1850), Scottish poet Robert Burns (1759–96), US general Robert E. Lee (1807–70), Scottish writer Robert Louis Stevenson (1850–94), US politician Robert Kennedy (1925–68) and US film actor Robert Redford (b.1936). Common diminutive forms of the name include **Rob** (or **Robb**), **Robbie** (or **Robby**), BOB (or BOBBY) and BERT (or BERTIE). Other diminutive forms now of historical interest only are Dob, Hob and Nob. Long-established Scottish diminutives are **Rab** and **Rabbie**. *See also* ROBERTA; ROBIN; RUPERT.

Roberta (f) Feminine equivalent of ROBERT. It was introduced in the 1870s and became especially popular in Scotland and the USA, where it was further popularized by the Jerome Kern musical *Roberta* (1933). Notable bearers of the name in recent times have included US singer Roberta Flack (b.1939). Often shortened to BOBBIE or **Berta**. **Robertina** is a rare variant form.

Robin (m/f) English first name that developed as a diminutive form of ROBERT but has long had its own independent existence. The name came to England from France in medieval times and subsequently emerged as a separate boys' name in its own right. It has been bestowed upon members of both sexes only since the 1950s and possibly as a result of this has become less common among boys since then. Its popularity for girls may have been partly inspired by the name of the garden bird. Notable bearers of the name have included the legendary English outlaw Robin Hood, Robin Goodfellow (or Puck) in Shake-

speare's *A Midsummer Night's Dream* (1595–6), Christopher Robin in the *Winnie-the-Pooh* stories of A. A. Milne, Batman's young lieutenant in the *Batman* stories first published in 1939, British television presenter Sir Robin Day (1919–2000), US film actor Robin Williams (b.1952) and US actress Robin Givens (b.1964). The exclusively feminine versions of the name **Robyn**, **Robynne** and **Robina** (also found as **Robena** and **Robinia**) go back to the 15th century or earlier. English Parliamentarian leader Oliver Cromwell had a sister named Robina.

Robina/Robyn *See* ROBIN.

Rocco (m) Italian first name derived from the Old German *hrok* ('repose'). St Rocco lived in France in the 14th century and spent much of his life tending to plague victims in northern Italy before finally returning home and dying in prison after his family failed to recognize him. He is now the patron saint of the sick. Variant forms of the name include the US **Rocky**, which evokes the idea of physical toughness or strength of character. It is particularly popular among boxers and others engaged in rigorous physical endeavour – partly in tribute to the US boxer Rocky Marciano (Rocco Marciano; 1923–69). Versions of the name in other languages include the French **Roch**, the Spanish and Portuguese **Roque** and the Catalan **Roc**.

Rochelle (f) French first name that is alternatively a feminine diminutive form of the French Roch (*see* ROCCO), a variant of RACHEL, or else derived from a place name (from the French port of La Rochelle) meaning 'little rock'. It is little heard today in France but is heard occasionally among the black population of the USA.

Rocky *See* ROCCO.

Rod/Roddie/Roddy *See* RODERICK; RODNEY.

Roderick (m) English first name derived from the Old German Hrodic, from the words *hrod* ('fame') and *ric* ('power') and thus meaning 'famously powerful'. It was first brought to England by the Normans but virtually disappeared from use in the post-medieval period. It was subsequently revived in the early 19th century following the publication of Sir Walter Scott's poem 'The Vision of Don Roderick' (1811). The name was originally considered to be Scottish rather than English, but has become widespread throughout the English-speaking world since the 19th century.

A famous bearer of the name in its Spanish incarnation **Roderigo** or **Rodrigo** (imported to Spain by the Goths as early as the 8th century and sometimes shortened to **Ruy**) was a king of Spain who died fighting the Saracens in 711 and whose adventures were recounted not only by Sir Walter Scott but also by Robert Southey in his poem 'Roderick, the Last of the Goths' (1814). Other literary Rodericks have included the central characters in Tobias Smollett's *Roderick Random* (1748) and Henry James' *Roderick Hudson* (1876). Also found as **Rodrick** and **Roderic** and commonly shortened to **Rod** or **Roddy** – as borne by British actor Roddy McDowall (Roderick McDowall; 1928–98) and British pop singer Rod Stewart (Roderick Stewart; b.1945). Versions in other languages include the Russian RURIK and the Welsh RHODRI and **Rhydderch** (meaning 'reddish-brown'). In Scotland the name is sometimes treated as an equivalent of the Gaelic **Ruairi** (*see* RORY). The Scottish **Rodina** and RHODA are feminine versions of the name.

Roderigo *See* RODERICK.

Rodge/Rodger *See* ROGER.

Rodion (m) Russian first name derived from the Greek name Herodion, which itself evolved from Hera, the name of the goddess who was the wife of Zeus in Greek mythology. As Herodion the name features in the New Testament as that of a martyred bishop of Patras. Sometimes shortened to **Rodya**.

Rodney (m) English place name (from Somerset) meaning 'reed island' that was subsequently adopted as a surname and first name. Its popularity in England dates from the 19th century when it was associated with the naval exploits of Admiral Lord George Rodney (1719–92), who secured major victories against the French and Spanish fleets. It has suffered a marked decline in popularity since the 1950s. Well-known bearers of the name have included British composer Richard Rodney Bennett (b.1936), British actor Rodney Bewes (b.1937) and the fictional Rodney Trotter in the popular 1980s British television comedy series *Only Fools and Horses*. Commonly shortened to **Rod**, **Roddie** or **Roddy** – as borne by US actor Rod Steiger (Rodney Steiger; 1925–2002) and Australian tennis player Rod Laver (Rodney Laver; b.1938).

Rodolf/Rodolfo/Rodolph/Rodolphe *See* RUDOLPH.

Rodrigo *See* RODERICK.

Rodya *See* RODION.

Rogelio (m) Spanish first name derived from the Latin Rogelius or Rogellus (of unknown meaning). It has been suggested that the name may be linked to the Latin Rogatus (meaning 'requested' or 'prayed for'). A Spanish St Rogellus was put to death by the Moors in 852.

Roger (m) English and French first name derived via Norman French from the Old German *hrod* ('fame') and *gar* ('spear') and thus meaning 'famous warrior'. As Hrothgar (modelled on the Old German Hrodgar), the name was familiar to the Anglo-Saxons and was also the name of a legendary king. The modern form of the name was introduced to England by the Normans and it appeared in the 'Domesday Book' in the Latinized form Rogerus. Roger became a popular choice in medieval times but went into a gradual decline from the 16th century, being considered a peasant name, before being revived from the 1840s. It reached a peak in the 1950s but has gone into a gradual decline since the 1970s.

Notable bearers of the name have included the 12th-century Roger of Salisbury, who was chancellor of England under Henry I, English philosopher Roger Bacon (1214–94), the fictional Sir Roger de Coverley, a character created in the early 18th century by the essayist Sir Richard Steele, French film director Roger Vadim (1927–2000) and British television and film actor Roger Moore (b.1927). The black and white skull-and-crossbones traditionally associated with pirates has long been nicknamed the 'Jolly Roger'.

The name is occasionally encountered as **Rodger**, which is sometimes shortened to **Rodge**, the modern form of the old diminutive **Hodge** (a generic term for a farm labourer). Variants in other languages include the Italian **Ruggiero**, the Spanish **Rogerio**, the Dutch **Rutger** and the Scandinavian **Roar**. *See also* RORY.

Rohan (m) French place name and surname that was subsequently adopted as a first name. Another derivation links it with the Irish Gaelic for 'red'. Also found as ROWAN.

The name is also common in India, where it evolved from the Sanskrit *rohana* ('ascending'). There is a holy mountain bearing the name in Sri Lanka.

Roisin *See* ROSE.

Roland (m) English first name derived via Norman French from the Old German Hrodland, from *hrod* ('fame') and *land* ('land' or 'territory') and thus meaning 'famous landowner'. It was introduced to England by the Normans in the 11th century and appeared in the 'Domesday Book' as Rolland. In medieval legend, Roland was the most gallant of all the knights in the court of the Emperor Charlemagne and the hero of many adventures, as celebrated in the 12th-century *Chanson de Roland*, in Ariosto's *Orlando Furioso* (1516) and later in poems by Lord Byron. Since a brief resurgence in the 1920s, the name has been largely out of favour. Also found as **Row-**land, in which form it was borne by Sir Rowland Hill (1795–1879), founder of the penny post in 1840. Diminutive forms include **Roly**, **Rowley** and **Rollo**. The usual French version is **Rolande**. An Italian variant is ORLANDO.

Rolf (m) English, German and Scandinavian variant of RUDOLPH, derived from *hrod* ('fame') and *wulf* ('wolf'). In the Latinized form **Rollo** the name dates at least as far back as the Vikings, being borne by Rollo, son of Rognvald of Norway (d.932), who invaded northern France and established Viking rule over Normandy. As Rolf, it subsequently reached England at the time of the Norman Conquest. It continued to appear in the Latinized form Rollo during medieval times and became confused with RALPH before re-establishing its independent existence in the late 19th century. Well-known bearers of the name in recent times have included Australian artist and television presenter Rolf Harris (b.1930). Rarely found in the variant form **Rolph**.

Rollo *See* ROLAND; ROLF.

Rolph *See* ROLF.

Roly *See* ROLAND.

Roma (f) Roman name derived from that of the city of Rome. The Emperor Hadrian built a temple in Rome to the goddess Roma and she was worshipped throughout Roman territories. It has appeared sporadically as a first name since the 19th century.

Romaine (f) French first name meaning 'Roman woman'. The French equivalent of the masculine ROMAN, it was first adopted by English speakers in the 19th century and is also encountered as **Romayne**. The Latinate **Romana** is a variant form.

Roman (m) Russian, Polish and Czech first name derived from the Latin Romanus ('man from Rome'). It remains rare among English speakers, but is occasionally imported from other languages. Notable bearers of the name familiar in the English-speaking world have included several saints and the Polish-born US film director Roman Polanski (b.1933). Variants in other languages include the French ROMAIN and the Italian **Romano**.

Romayne *See* ROMAINE.

Romeo (m) Italian first name meaning 'pilgrim to Rome'. It became widely known among English speakers through William Shakespeare's character of the name in his tragedy *Romeo and Juliet* (1595) but it has never been in more than occasional use. Shakespeare himself is thought to have got the name from Arthur Brooke's earlier *The Tragicall Historye of Romeus and Juliet*, which in turn made use of a story by the Italian Matteo Bandello (1485–1561). A relatively rare choice of first name over the centuries despite its romantic overtones, it achieved new prominence in 2002 when English footballer David Beckham and his popstar wife Victoria Beckham chose it for their second son, not, however, because of its literary connections, but simply because they liked the name.

Romey *See* ROSEMARY.

Romilda (f) Italian first name derived from the Old German *hrom* ('fame') and *hild* ('battle').

Romola (f) Italian first name, meaning 'woman of Rome', derived ultimately from the Roman Romulus. It became known in the English-speaking world through George Eliot's novel *Romola* (1863), set in Renaissance Florence, and it has made sporadic appearances as a first name ever since. A masculine form of the name is **Romolo**.

Romy *See* ROSEMARY.

Ron *See* RONALD.

Rona *See* RHONA.

Ronald (m) English and Scottish equivalent of REGINALD that developed from the Old Norse Rognvaldr. Also found in Scotland as **Ranald** and **Raghnall**, the name has become widespread among English speakers since the late 19th century and is

no longer thought of as uniquely Scottish. It reached a peak in popularity in the UK in the 1920s and in the USA in the 1940s. Famous bearers of the name have included British film actor Ronald Colman (1891–1958), US film actor and President Ronald Reagan (b.1911) and British cartoonist Ronald Searle (b.1920). Often shortened to **Ron** or **Ronnie** (or **Ronni**), as borne by the British television comedians Ronnie Barker (b.1929) and Ronnie Corbett (b.1930), who were known as 'The Two Ronnies'. Rare feminine variants include **Ronalda**, **Ronna** and **Ronnette**. *See also* RHONA; ROALD.

Ronalda *See* RONALD.

Ronan (m) Irish name derived from the Irish Gaelic *ron* ('little seal'). The most famous of several Irish saints to bear the name was a 5th-century Irish missionary working in Cornwall and Brittany. Modern bearers of the name have included Irish pop singer Ronan Keating (b.1977).

Ronna/Ronnette *See* RONALD.

Ronnie *See* RONALD; VERONICA.

Roo *See* RUE; RUTH.

Roque *See* ROCCO.

Rory (m) Irish and Scottish name derived from the Gaelic name Ruairi or Ruaidhri, from the Gaelic *ruadh* ('red' or 'red-haired') and *ri* ('king') and thus meaning 'red king'. It is sometimes considered to be an equivalent of ROGER and it is also used as a diminutive form of RODERICK. The reign of the celebrated 12th-century Irish king Rory O'Connor did much to popularize the name in medieval Ireland but it is now in general use throughout the English-speaking world, becoming increasingly common in the 1990s. Notable bearers of the name have included Irish rock musician Rory Gallagher (1948–95) and British television impersonator Rory Bremner (b.1961). Sometimes found as **Rorie** or in the Gaelic forms **Ruari** or **Ruaridh**.

Ros *See* ROSALIND; ROSAMUND.

Rosa/Rosabel/Rosabella/Rosalba *See*
ROSE.

Rosaleen *See* ROSALIND.

Rosalie (f) French first name that developed from the older Latin Rosalia, the
name of a Roman festival in which people
decorated the tombs of the dead with garlands of roses. The Latin form of the name
is encountered only rarely in English-
speaking communities, having been replaced fairly comprehensively by the
French form in the middle of the 19th century. Notable bearers of the name have included the 12th-century hermit St Rosalia
of Palermo. There are also characters with
the name in Anne Brontë's *Agnes Gray*
(1847) and Oscar Wilde's *Lady Windermere's
Fan* (1892). The success of the Hollywood
musical *Rosalie* in the 1930s, starring Nelson
Eddy, did much to popularize the name in
the mid 20th century.

Rosalind (f) English first name that had
its origins in the Old German Roslindis,
derived from *hros* ('horse') and either *lind*
('tender' or 'soft') or *linta* ('lime'), in which
case it means 'horse shield made of lime
wood'. The Goths introduced the name to
Spain, where it acquired a much more
attractive new derivation from *rosa* and
linda, meaning 'pretty rose'. The name
came to England with the Normans in the
11th century, but it was not until the late
16th century that it began to appear with
any frequency. Its use was much promoted
by its appearance in various literary works
of the period, notably Edmund Spenser's
The Shephearde's Calendar (1579), Thomas
Lodge's romance *Rosalynde* (1590) and William Shakespeare's *As You Like It* (1599),
which was based on Lodge's work. There
are also characters called **Rosaline** in
Shakespeare's *Love's Labour's Lost* (c.1595)
and *Romeo and Juliet* (1595). The name subsequently went out of fashion, but was revived in the 20th century when notable
bearers included US actress Rosalind Russell
(1908–76) and British opera singer Rosalind
Plowright (b.1949). Other variants include

Rosalyn, **Rosalynne**, **Rosalin**, **Rosalinda**, **Roslyn**, **Rosslyn** and **Rosaleen**.
Often shortened to **Ros** or **Roz**.

Rosalinda/Rosaline/Rosalyn
See ROSALIND.

Rosamund (f) English first name combining the Old German *hros* ('horse') and
mund ('protection'), although a more
popular derivation of medieval origin suggests that it comes from the Latin *rosa mundi*
('rose of the world') or *rosa munda* ('pure
rose'). It was introduced to England by the
Normans in the 11th century and has remained in circulation ever since, though it
has been in decline since the early 20th
century. Also found as **Rosamond**, the
name was famously borne by the 'Fair Rosamund' Clifford (d.1176), who was the mistress of Henry II and who is rumoured to
have been poisoned by Henry's jealous
queen Eleanor of Aquitaine. Centuries later
she was the subject of Joseph Addison's
opera *Rosamond* (1707) and of Algernon
Swinburne's play *Rosamond* (1860). Other
famous bearers of the name have included
British novelist Rosamond Lehmann
(1901–90). Sometimes shortened to **Ros** or
Roz.

Rosanna (f) English first name combining
ROSE and ANNA. It was first adopted in the
18th century and has remained popular
ever since, often appearing as **Rosanne**,
Rozanne or **Roseanne**. Other variants
include **Roseanna** and **Rosannah**
(suggesting a combination of Rose with
HANNAH). Famous bearers of the name in
its various forms have included US comedienne Roseanne Barr (b.1953) and US actress Rosanna Arquette (b.1959).

Rosario (m/f) Spanish first name derived
from a title bestowed upon the Virgin Mary,
Nuestra Señora del Rosario ('Our Lady of the
Rosary'). The name is reserved for females
in Spain, but in southern Italy and Sicily is
sometimes given to male children. **Charo**
is a familiar form of the name.

Roscoe (m) English place name derived

from the Old Norse *ra* ('roe-deer') and *skogr* ('wood' or 'copse') that was subsequently adopted as a surname and occasional first name.

Rose (f) English first name derived from the Old German *hros* ('horse') or *hrod* ('fame'). Now associated universally with the flower, from the Latin *rosa*, the name came to England (as Roese and Rohese) with the Normans in the 11th century and has remained consistently popular, in part because the flower is a symbol of the Virgin Mary. It reached a peak in popularity in the late 19th and early 20th centuries and again in the 1990s. Notable bearers of the name have included St Rose of Lima (1586–1617), who was the first American saint, and British novelists Dame Rose Macaulay (1881–1958) and Rose Tremain (b.1943). It is also a royal name, being borne by Princess Margaret Rose (1930–2002) and Lady Rose Windsor (b.1980). Sometimes used in the forms **Rosie** or **Rosy**. Other variants include **Rosa**, **Rosabel** and **Rosabella** ('beautiful rose'), **Rosalba** ('white rose'), **Rosetta** ('little rose'), **Roselle**, **Rosette**, the Italian **Rosina** and the Spanish **Rosita**. An Irish variant of the name, meaning 'little rose', is **Roisin** (alternatively spelled **Rosheen**, reflecting its pronunciation). Sometimes encountered as an abbreviation of ROSEMARY and other names beginning with Rose-.

Roseanna/Roseanne *See* ROSANNA.

Roseline *See* ROSALIND.

Roselle *See* ROSE.

Roselyn *See* ROSALIND.

Rosemarie *See* ROSEMARY.

Rosemary (f) English flower name derived from the Latin *ros marinus* ('sea dew'), a reference to the plant's blue-green foliage. It is sometimes also considered to be a simple combined form of ROSE and MARY. Like other flower names, it became an increasingly popular choice of first name from the late 19th century. The success of the musical *Rose Marie* (1924) did much to promote the name in the 1920s and it remained frequent until the 1960s, since when it has been in decline. Notable bearers of the name have included British children's author Rosemary Sutcliff (1920–92) and US singer Rosemary Clooney (1928–2002). Sometimes encountered as **Rosemarie**. Diminutive forms of the name include ROSE, **Rosie** and the rare **Romey** and **Romy** – as borne by the Austrian film actress Romy Schneider (Rosemarie Schneider; 1938–82).

Rosetta *See* ROSE.

Roshanara (f) Indian first name derived from the Persian *roshanara* ('light of the assembly') and thus suggesting great personal beauty in the bearer. Popular among Muslims, it is often identified with Roshan Ara Begum, daughter of the 17th-century Mogul emperor Shah Jahan.

Rosheen *See* ROSE.

Rosie *See* ROSE; ROSEMARY.

Rosina/Rosita *See* ROSE.

Roslyn *See* ROSALIND.

Ross (m) Scottish place name derived from the Scottish Gaelic *ros* ('peninsula' or 'promontory') that was subsequently adopted as a surname and, from the 19th century, as a first name. Other derivations suggest that it came from the Old German *hrod* ('fame'), the French *roux* ('red') or the Anglo-Saxon *hros* ('horse'). It has become increasingly popular since the 1970s. Notable bearers of the name have included a character in the popular 1990s US television series *Friends*. As a surname it is a well-known Scottish clan name with numerous members not only in Scotland but also in Ireland, Canada and Australia.

Rosslyn *See* ROSALIND.

Roswitha (f) German first name derived from *hrod* ('fame') and *swinth* ('strength'). It became widely known as the name of a

10th-century German nun who is remembered for her verse and plays written in Latin.

Rosy *See* ROSE.

Rowan (m/f) English version of the Irish Gaelic Ruadhan, meaning 'little red-haired one'. The name comes ultimately from the Gaelic *ruadh* ('red'). It is sometimes derived instead from the alternative name of the mountain ash, which bears red berries. The popularity of the name in Ireland was boosted by the fact that it was borne by two early Irish saints. It seems to have made its first appearances among English speakers in the middle of the 20th century. It used to be an exclusively boys' name but is now used for both sexes, although it is sometimes altered to **Rowanne** when applied to girls. Well-known bearers of the name have included British television comedian Rowan Atkinson (b.1955). *See also* ROHAN.

Rowena (f) English first name derived from the Old English *hrod* ('fame') and *wynn* ('joy') or, alternatively, a Celtic first name derived from the Welsh Rhonwen, based on *rhon* ('pike' or 'lance') and *gwen* ('white' or 'fair') and thus meaning 'slender and fair'. In the legend of Vortigern and Rowena, the beautiful Rowena was the cause of the great 5th-century British king's downfall. Having fallen into disuse, Sir Walter Scott's use of the name for his character Lady Rowena of Hargottstanstede in his novel *Ivanhoe* (1819) did much to make the name popular in the 19th century. Sometimes encountered as **Rowina**. Diminutive forms of the name include **Ron**, **Ronnie**, **Rona** and RHONA.

Rowland/Rowley *See* ROLAND.

Roxana (f) Latinized version of the Persian first name Roschana, meaning 'dawn' or 'light'. The most famous Persian bearer of the name was Roxana, Persian wife of Alexander the Great, who lived in the 4th century BC. The popularity of the name was boosted among English speakers by the publication of Daniel Defoe's novel *Roxana*

(1724). As **Roxane** or **Roxanne**, now the most common English and French versions of the name, it subsequently appeared as the name of the heroine of Edmond Rostand's play *Cyrano de Bergerac* (1897). Commonly shortened to **Roxie** or **Roxy**.

Roxane/Roxanne/Roxie/Roxy
See ROXANA.

Roy (m) English first name of uncertain derivation. According to one theory the name comes from the French *roi* ('king'); according to another it developed as an Anglicization of the Gaelic RORY, coming ultimately from the Gaelic *ruadh* ('red') and thus being reserved primarily for children with red hair or a ruddy complexion. The celebrated Scottish outlaw Robert MacGregor (1671–1734) was known as 'Rob Roy' because of his red hair and Sir Walter Scott's novel *Rob Roy* (1817) did much to familiarize the name in the 19th century, particularly in Scotland. It reached a peak in popularity in the 1920s. More recent bearers of the name have included the US 'singing cowboy' Roy Rogers (Leonard Slye; 1912–98), US pop artist Roy Lichtenstein (1923–97), US country musician Roy Orbison (1936–88) and British Labour politician Roy Hattersley (b.1932). *See also* LEROY.

Royal (m) English first name derived either from the adjective 'royal' or from a surname meaning 'rye hill'. It is relatively rare as a first name and is little known outside the USA. *See also* ROYLE.

Royce (m) English surname, derived from an obsolete Germanic variant of ROSE, that has also appeared occasionally as a first name since the late 19th century. *See also* ROYSTON.

Royle (m) English place name (from Lancashire) derived from Old English *ryge* ('rye') and *hyll* ('hill') that was subsequently taken up as a surname and occasional first name. It probably developed under the influence of such similar-sounding names as Doyle (*see* DOUGAL) and because of the link with the ordinary vocabulary word 'royal'. *See also* ROYAL.

Royston (m) English place name (from Hertfordshire) meaning 'settlement of Royce' that was subsequently taken up as a surname and first name. It appears to have made its debut as a first name in the 18th century and continues to appear sporadically today, chiefly in England and Australia.

Roz *See* ROSALIND; ROSAMUND.

Rozanne *See* ROSANNA.

Ruadhan *See* ROWAN.

Ruairi/Ruari/Ruaridh *See* RORY.

Rube *See* REUBEN; RUBY.

Rubina *See* RUBY.

Ruby (f) English jewel name derived from the Latin *rubeus* ('red') that was taken up as a first name in the late 19th century. It largely fell out of fashion after the 1920s. Notable bearers of the name have included Canadian-born US singer and dancer Ruby Keeler (Ethel Keeler; 1909–93) and US television comedienne Ruby Wax (b.1953). Variant forms include **Rubie** and **Rubina**. *See also* REUBEN.

Rudi/Rudolf *See* RUDOLPH.

Rudolph (m) English first name derived from the Old German Hrodulf, from *hrod* ('fame') and *wulf* ('wolf') and thus meaning 'famous warrior'. The name has made occasional appearances among English speakers since the 19th century, occasionally appearing as Rodolph, or in the modern Germanic form **Rudolf**. The name is also known in many other countries, including the Netherlands, Scandinavia, Poland and the Czech Republic.

A family name of the Habsburg line of Holy Roman Emperors, its popularity in the English-speaking world was greatly enhanced by its appearance in Anthony Hope's adventure novels *The Prisoner of Zenda* (1894) and *Rupert of Hentzau* (1898). It subsequently received further boosts through public adulation for US film star Rudolph Valentino (Rodolfo di Valentina d'Antonguolla; 1895–1926) and Russian-born ballet dancer Rudolf Nureyev (1939–93). The appearance of the name in the children's Christmas song 'Rudolph the Red-nosed Reindeer' may have made the name more familiar but is less likely to have encouraged parents to choose it as a name for their offspring.

Commonly shortened to **Ruud**, **Rudy** or **Rudi** (the German version), as borne by US singer Rudy Vallee (Hubert Vallee; 1901–86). Variants in other languages include the French **Rodolphe**, the German and Dutch **Rodolf** and the Italian and Spanish **Rodolfo**. *See also* ROLF.

Rudy *See* RUDOLPH.

Rudyard (m) English place name (from Rudyard Lake in Staffordshire) that was subsequently adopted as an occasional first name. The name was made lastingly famous by the British writer Rudyard Kipling (1865–1936).

Rue (f) English plant name that is sometimes also considered to be a diminutive form of RUTH. Also encountered as **Roo**, it only emerged as a first name among English speakers in the 20th century.

Rufina (f) Russian first name derived ultimately from the Latin name **Rufinus**, meaning 'rosy' or 'reddish'. It is fairly popular in Russia, but has made only a handful of appearances among English speaking people. The masculine version of the name, **Rufino**, is common to the Italian, Spanish and Portuguese cultures.

Rufus (m) English first name derived from the Latin for 'red-haired'. A biblical name, it was later borne by William Rufus (1056–1100), who as William II succeeded his father William the Conqueror as king of England and died in mysterious circumstances when hunting in the New Forest. It is unclear whether William acquired the name through the colour of his hair or through the colour of his complexion. The name reappeared among English speakers in the 19th century but remains rare.

Ruggiero *See* ROGER.

Rukmini (f) Indian first name derived from the Sanskrit *rukmini* ('adorned with gold'). The name features in the *Mahabharata* as that of one of Krishna's lovers.

Rune (m) Scandinavian first name derived from the Old Norse *run* ('secret lore'). It was revived in the late 19th century and has since become very popular. The feminine equivalent of the name is **Runa**.

Rupert (m) English version of the Dutch Rupprecht, which like ROBERT comes ultimately from the Old German for 'bright fame'. The name came to England with Prince Rupert of the Rhine (1619–92), the nephew of Charles I who fought on behalf of his uncle in the English Civil War. Other notable bearers of the name have included the central character in Anthony Hope's adventure novel *Rupert of Hentzau* (1898), the British war poet Rupert Brooke (1887–1915), the children's cartoon character Rupert the Bear and the Australian media tycoon Rupert Murdoch (b.1931). **Ruperta** is a rare feminine version of the name.

Ruperta *See* RUPERT.

Rupinder (f) Indian first name derived from the Sanskrit *rupa* ('beauty') and *indra* ('mighty') and thus meaning 'great beauty'. It is found most frequently among Sikhs.

Ruqayya (f) Arabic name derived from *ruqiy* ('ascent' or 'progress') or else from *ruqyah* ('spell' or 'charm'). It was borne by one of Muhammad's daughters (d.624).

Rurik (m) Russian first name that evolved from a Scandinavian equivalent of RODERICK. It became famous as the name of a 9th-century warlord who founded the Russian monarchy and whose house held the throne of Russia until the 16th century. The name is also known in Finland and Sweden.

Russ *See* RUSSELL.

Russell (m) English surname and first name derived from the French nickname *rousel* ('little red one'). It was originally reserved for children with red hair or a ruddy complexion. Also found as **Russel**, it has strong aristocratic connections and is the family name of the dukes of Bedford. As a first name its history dates from the 19th century, with a peak in popularity (notably in the USA) in the late 20th century. Wellknown bearers of the name in its various forms have included the British television presenter Russell Harty (1934–88) and British pianist Russ Conway (Trevor Stanford; 1927–2000). Sometimes shortened to **Russ** or **Rusty**.

Rusty *See* RUSSELL.

Rut *See* RUTH.

Rutger *See* ROGER.

Ruth (f) Hebrew name of uncertain origin, variously interpreted as meaning 'companion', 'friend' or 'vision of beauty'. The name appears in the Old Testament as that of King David's great-grandmother and the subject of the Book of Ruth. It was subsequently among the biblical names taken up by Puritans in England after the Reformation, perhaps because in its otherwise unrelated ordinary vocabulary sense it also evoked the concepts of pity and compassion. Notable bearers of the name have included the central character in Elizabeth Gaskell's novel *Ruth* (1853), the Anglo-Indian novelist Ruth Prawer Jhabvala (b.1927) and the British crime novelist Ruth Rendell (b.1930). Also encountered in the familiar forms **Roo**, **Ruthie** and, in Italy, Spain, Germany, the Netherlands, Scandinavia and Poland, as **Rut**. *See also* RUE.

Ruthie *See* RUTH.

Rutland (m) English place name and surname that has made occasional appearances as a first name since the 19th century.

Ruud *See* RUDOLPH.

Ruy *See* RODERICK.

Ryan (m) Irish surname of uncertain origin that was subsequently adopted as a first name throughout the English-speaking world. The original Gaelic surname meant 'descendant of Rian', Rian probably coming from *ri*, meaning 'king'. An alternative derivation links the name with that of an ancient sea or river god (also the inspiration behind the name of the River Rhine). The name reached a peak in popularity in the 1990s, when it appeared in the top ten boys' names. Famous bearers of the name in the 20th century have included US film actor Ryan O'Neal (b.1941) and British footballer Ryan Giggs (b.1973). Occasionally found in the form **Rian**.

Ryszard *See* RICHARD.

S

Sabah (f) Arabic name derived from *sabah* ('morning'). Also found as **Saba**, the name has enjoyed a peak in popularity in recent times through the fame of the Lebanese singer and actress Sabah (b.1933).

Sabella (f) English first name that is thought to have developed from ISABELLA. This is a relatively recent introduction, of 20th-century invention.

Sabia (f) Irish first name that developed as a Latinized version of the Gaelic SADHBH. The earliest records of the name go back to the medieval period.

Sabina (f) Roman name meaning 'Sabine woman' that was first adopted by English speakers in the 17th century. The Sabines were an Italic race who were absorbed by their neighbours the Romans early in the history of that nation. The forcible abduction of Sabine women by Romans seeking wives is remembered in legend and art as 'The Rape of the Sabine Women'. The name has never been very common among English speakers although it enjoyed a minor vogue in the 19th century. Notable bearers have included Nero's mistress Poppaea Sabina and St Sabina, a 2nd-century Christian martyr from Rome. It is also used as an Anglicized form of the Irish SADHBH. Diminutive forms of the name include **Sabbie**, **Sabby** and **Bina**. A French version of the name is **Sabine**.

Sabine *See* SABINA.

Sabra (f) Hebrew first name meaning 'restful'.

Sabrina (f) Welsh first name that has been in occasional use among English speakers since the 19th century. The name features in Welsh legend as that of an illegitimate daughter of King Locrine who as an infant was drowned in the River Severn (subsequently named after her) on the orders of Locrine's widow Gwendolen. In fact, if the legendary Sabrina lived at all, she probably got her name from that of the river rather than vice-versa. The legendary Sabrina was later the subject of several celebrated literary works, including John Milton's masque *Comus* (1637), in which she appears in the guise of the nymph of the Severn. A film entitled *Sabrina*, based on Samuel Taylor's play *Sabrina Fair* (a quotation from Milton's work), was released in 1954 and there was a character of the same name in the 1970s US television series *Charlie's Angels*. The name enjoyed a resurgence in popularity in the 1980s, especially in the USA.

Sacha *See* SASHA.

Sachairi *See* ZACHARY.

Sacheverell (m) English surname that was subsequently taken up as a first name. The original surname is thought to have come from a place name in Normandy, Saute-Chevreuil (meaning 'roebuck leap'). The name was popularized in the 18th century by the celebrated English political preacher Henry Sacheverell (c.1674–1724). Other famous bearers of the name have included the British writer Sacheverell Sitwell (1897–1985). Sometimes shortened to **Sachie**.

Sachie *See* SACHEVERELL.

Sad (m) Arabic name derived from *saida* ('lucky' or 'happy'). Notable bearers of the name have included a warrior-cousin of Muhammad and Sad Zaghlul (1857–1927), a prominent Egyptian nationalist who was instrumental in expelling the British from

Egypt and served briefly as the country's Prime Minister.

Sadhbh (f) Irish first name (pronounced 'save') derived from the Gaelic for 'sweet'. It was commonly given to girls in medieval Ireland. Today it is more likely to be found in such Anglicized forms as SABIA and SABINA.

Sadie (f) English first name that developed as a diminutive form of SARAH. It emerged from the shadow of Sarah in the late 19th century and enjoyed a peak in popularity in the 1970s, notably in the USA. Notable bearers of the name have included the fictional Sadie Thompson in Somerset Maugham's short story 'Rain' (1921), which was the source of several films. *See also* MERCEDES.

Saffie/Saffrey *See* SAFFRON.

Saffron (f) English first name that has been in occasional use among English speakers since the 1960s. The origin of the name lies in the golden-yellow crocus pollen long used as a spice. Diminutive forms include **Saffie** and **Saffrey**.

Sagar (m) Old English name derived from words meaning 'victory' and 'people'.

Said (m) Arabic name derived from *said* ('happy' or 'lucky').

Saints *See* SANCHO.

Sakhr (m) Arabic name derived from *sakhr* ('solid rock'). It featured prominently in the poems that the 7th-century poet Al-Khansa wrote about her brother Sakhr after he died in battle and today it remains one of the most popular names used in Saudi Arabia.

Sal *See* SALLY; SALVADOR; SARAH.

Salah (m) Arabic name derived from *salah* ('goodness' or 'righteousness'). Also found as **Saleh**, it is most familiar to English speakers in the older form Salah al-Din, or Saladin – the name of the famous 12th-century Arab leader who led the Muslim forces in the Third Crusade. In its modern form it is one of the most popular of all Arab

names today. **Salih** or **Salha** is a feminine equivalent.

Salamon *See* SOLOMON.

Salena *See* SELINA.

Salih *See* SALAH.

Salim (m) Arabic name derived from *salim* ('safe' or 'secure'). Also found as **Saleem** and **Selim**. **Salma** is a feminine equivalent.

Salina *See* SELINA.

Sally (f) English first name that began life as a diminutive form of SARAH. The process by which the 'r' in the name became 'll' is fairly standard among English first names (*see also* MOLLY). The name was well established by the 18th century, when it was further boosted by the ballad 'Sally in Our Alley' by the English poet and composer Henry Carey (1687–1743). It enjoyed a peak in popularity in the 1920s and received another boost in the 1930s with the release of the Gracie Fields film *Sally in Our Alley* (1931), with its memorable theme song 'Sally'. Since its last resurgence in the 1960s it has been eclipsed once more by Sarah, from which it originally came. Notable bearers of the name have included the fictional Sally Bowles in Christopher Isherwood's *Sally Bowles* (1937), the basis of the stage musical (1961) and film (1972) *Cabaret*, British politician Sally Oppenheim (b.1930) and British athlete Sally Gunnell (b.1966). Also found as **Sallie** and **Salley**. Commonly shortened to **Sal**. The name is also often encountered in combination with other names, as for instance in **Sallyann** (or **Sally-Anne**) and **Sally-Jane**.

Sallyann/Sally-Anne/Sally-Jane *See* SALLY.

Salman *See* SOLOMON.

Salome (f) Greek version of an Aramaic name of unknown meaning, possibly linked to the Hebrew *shalom* ('peace'). The name was common in biblical times, but its association with Herod's granddaughter, whose demand for the head of John the Baptist brought about his execution, has militated against it ever becoming a popular choice. It was occasionally included among the biblical names taken up by the Puritans in the 16th and 17th centuries, probably because it was also borne in the New Testament by the mother of the apostles James and John, who was one of the women present at Jesus' tomb on Easter Sunday. Oscar Wilde's play *Salome* (1894) and Richard Strauss' opera *Salome* (1905) did something to rehabilitate the name. Today the stress is almost always placed on the second syllable, although historically it was often placed on the first syllable, with the final '-e' left silent. Variant forms of the name in other languages include the French **Salomé** and the Polish **Salomea**.

Salud (f) Spanish first name derived from a title bestowed upon the Virgin Mary, *Nuestra Señora de la Salud* ('Our Lady of Salvation').

Salvador (m) Spanish first name derived from the Latin *salvator* ('saviour'). A popular name in Roman Catholic countries, it is also found in Italian as **Salvatore**. Famous bearers of the name have included the Spanish surrealist painter Salvador Dali (1904–89). Sometimes shortened to **Sal**.

Salvatore *See* SALVADOR.

Sam *See* SAMANTHA; SAMPSON; SAMSON; SAMUEL.

Samantha (f) English variant of SAMUEL. It appears to have first entered use in the southern states of the USA, perhaps under the influence of ANTHEA, during the 18th century, but it was not until the 1960s that the name became widespread throughout the English-speaking world. Its popularity was boosted in 1956 by the Cole Porter song 'I love you, Samantha' from the film *High Society*. Well-known bearers of the name have included the fictional Samantha Stephens, the beautiful witch played by Elizabeth Montgomery in the 1960s US

television series *Bewitched*, and the British model and singer Samantha Fox (b.1966). Sometimes shortened to **Sam** or **Sammy** (or **Sammie**).

Sammy *See* SAMANTHA; SAMPSON; SAMSON; SAMUEL.

Samoyla *See* SAMUEL.

Sampson (m) English surname that was subsequently adopted as a first name. It may also be found as a variant of SAMSON. It made sporadic appearances among English speakers in the 19th century. Sometimes shortened to **Sam** or **Sammy**.

Samson (m) English version of the Hebrew Shimshon, which was itself derived from *shemesh* ('sun'), thus meaning 'sun child'. It features in the Bible as the name of the immensely powerful leader of the Israelites who was deceived by Delilah but got his revenge by pulling down the temple of the Philistines on their heads – as described in John Milton's *Samson Agonistes* (1671). A 6th-century Welsh saint also bore the name, although in this instance the name may have come from an unknown Celtic source. It made sporadic appearances among English speakers throughout medieval times and was revived by the Puritans in the 17th century. It is still occasionally encountered today, often as the stagename of circus performers. Sometimes found as SAMPSON. An Italian variant is **Sansone**. **Sam** and **Sammy** are common familiar forms of the name.

Samuel (m) English version of the Hebrew Shemuel or Shmuel, variously meaning 'name of God' or 'He has hearkened'. Another derivation suggests the name comes from the Hebrew *shaul meel* ('asked of God'). It features in the Bible as the name of the 11th-century BC prophet after whom two books of the Old Testament were named and as a result was taken up by Puritans on both sides of the Atlantic in the 17th century. It has retained its status as a popular choice ever since, particularly among Jews and Nonconformists. In Scotland and Ireland it is sometimes considered to be an Anglicized version of the Gaelic Somhairle, derived from the Old Norse for 'summer wanderer' or 'Viking' (*see* SOMERLED). Celebrated bearers of the name have included English diarist Samuel Pepys (1633–1703), English novelist Samuel Richardson (1689–1761), English lexicographer Dr Samuel Johnson (1709–84), English poet Samuel Taylor Coleridge (1772–1834) and Irish playwright and novelist Samuel Beckett (1906–89). Variants in other languages include the Russian **Samoyla** and **Samuil** and the Welsh **Sawyl**.

The diminutive form **Sam** is in common use and is sometimes treated as an independent name in its own right. Notable bearers of the name in its reduced form have included the fictional Sam Weller in Charles Dickens' *Pickwick Papers* (1837), US film director Sam Peckinpah (1926–85) and US actor Sam Shepard (b.1943). It is also widely known from 'Uncle Sam', the familiar personification of the United States whose name probably came about because it produced the initials US. Another familiar variant is **Sammy** – as borne by US singer and entertainer Sammy Davis Jr (1925–90). *See also* SAMANTHA.

Sancha/Sanchia *See* SANCHO.

Sancho (m) Spanish first name of uncertain derivation. It has been speculated that the name may be descended ultimately from the Latin Sanctius, from *sanctus* ('holy'). The Spanish and Latin forms of the name were used as alternatives for one another in medieval times, but the two variants may not in fact come from the same source. The name was borne by a Spanish saint martyred by the Moors in 851 and in fiction by Sancho Panza, the comical squire in the novel *Don Quixote* (1605–15) by Miguel Cervantes. **Sancha** and **Sanchia** are feminine versions of the name. Sanchia was introduced to English speakers in the 13th century when the Earl of Cornwall married Sanchia, the daughter of the Count of Provence. It appears to have caused some confusion, however, in the English-

speaking world and over the centuries it has appeared in such divergent forms as **Science**, **Sence**, **Saints** and **Sens**.

Sandalio (m) Spanish first name derived from the Latin Sandalus, which may itself have come from the Germanic *sand* ('true') and *ulf* ('wolf'). A Spanish saint bearing the name was put to death by the Moors at Cordoba in the 9th century.

Sandford *See* SANFORD.

Sandhya (f) Indian name derived from the Sanskrit *sandhya* ('junction' or 'twilight'). The hour of twilight has special ritual significance for Brahmins and other religious castes and the name is also borne by a daughter of the god Brahma.

Sandie *See* SANDRA.

Sandor *See* ALEXANDER.

Sandra (f) English first name derived from the Italian Alessandra (*see* ALEXANDRA). It made early appearances in the English-speaking world in the 19th century, notably in George Meredith's novel *Sandra Belloni* (1886). It became widespread in the 1930s and enjoyed a peak in popularity in the 1950s before going into a slow decline. Also found in the form **Zandra** – as borne by British fashion designer Zandra Rhodes (b.1940). Variants include the Scottish **Saundra** and the chiefly US **Sondra**. Familiar versions of the name are **Sandy** and **Sandie** – as borne by British folk-rock singer Sandy Denny (1941–78) and British pop singer Sandie Shaw (Sandra Goodrich; b.1947). *See also* CASSANDRA.

Sandro *See* ALEXANDER.

Sandy *See* ALEXANDER; SANDRA; SAWNEY.

Sanford (m) English place name, originally Sandford, from Old English *sand* ('sand') and *ford* ('ford') that was subsequently taken up as a surname and first name. It is more common in the USA than elsewhere, sometimes appearing in tribute to an early governor of Rhode Island called Peleg Sanford.

Sanjay (m) Indian name derived from the Sanskrit *samjaya* ('triumphant'). It is borne by several characters in Indian mythology and figures in the *Mahabharata*. Bearers of the name in more recent times have included Indira Gandhi's son Sanjay Gandhi (1948–80).

Sankar *See* SHANKAR.

Sanna *See* SUSANNAH.

Sansone *See* SAMSON.

Santiago (m) Spanish first name meaning 'Saint James' (IAGO being an archaic Spanish version of JAMES). The intention behind giving the name to newborn male children was to win for them the protection of St James, the patron saint of Spain, who is supposed to have visited the country. DIEGO is a variant.

Santos (m) Spanish and Portuguese name meaning 'saints'. The name is usually chosen in the belief that this will ensure a newborn child is granted divine protection. It is sometimes given to children born on All Saints' Day.

Santuzza (f) Italian diminutive version of Santa, which was itself derived from the Latin *sanctus* ('holy'). It appears to have been heard first in Sicily.

Saoirse (f) Irish first name meaning 'freedom'. Pronounced 'sairsha', it appears to be a relatively recent introduction as a first name, inspired by the establishment of Ireland as an independent nation.

Sapphira *See* SAPPHIRE.

Sapphire (f) English jewel name derived from the Hebrew *sappir* ('sapphire' or 'lapis lazuli'). It was first taken up by English speakers along with other jewel names in the 19th century, but has never been common. A variant of the name, in which form it may be found in the New Testament, is **Sapphira**.

Sappho (f) Greek first name, borne originally by a celebrated Greek lyric poet who lived in the 7th century BC and is believed to have been a lesbian, which may have inhibited take-up of the name.

Sara *See* SARAH.

Sarah (f) Hebrew name meaning 'princess', and pronounced 'sah-rah' or 'sare-ruh'. It appears in the Bible as the name of the 90-year-old wife of Abraham and mother of Isaac, although with an earlier derivation – from *sarai* ('contentious' or 'quarrelsome'). God gave the woman her new name before the birth of her son. As a result of its religious associations the name was taken up by English-speaking Puritans in the 16th century, when it often appeared as **Sarey**, **Sarra** or **Sara** (a variant of Greek origin). It reached a peak in popularity in Britain in the late 19th century, becoming – with ELIZABETH and MARY – one of the top three most popular girls' names of the 1870s. Almost as popular in the USA, it maintained its position into the early 20th century, then declined before enjoying another resurgence in the 1960s, when Sara again became a popular variant. It remained among the most popular girls' names in the English-speaking world through the 1970s and 1980s.

Notable bearers of the name have included the English actress Sarah Siddons (1755–1831), the fictional Sarah Gamp in Charles Dickens' novel *Martin Chuzzlewit* (1843–44), the French actress Sarah Bernhardt (1844–1923), the US jazz singer Sarah Vaughan (1924–90) and Princess Margaret's daughter Lady Sarah Armstrong-Jones (b.1964). Familiar forms of the name include SALLY, **Sal** and **Sassie**. Among rarer variants are **Sarina** and **Sarita**. In Ireland the name is sometimes accepted as an equivalent for **Saraid** (meaning 'excellent') and SORCHA. *See also* SADIE; ZARA.

Saraid *See* SARAH.

Saranna (f) English first name, a combined form of SARAH and ANNA. It seems to have made its first appearance among English speakers in the 18th century, but remains rare.

Saraswati (f) Indian name derived from the Sanskrit *saras* ('fluid' or 'lake') and -*vati* ('watery'). The name was borne by a goddess identified with the River Indus and also with education and the arts and sciences.

Sarey/Sarina/Sarita/Sarra *See* SARAH.

Sasha (m/f) Diminutive form of ALEX- ANDER or ALEXANDRA. Originally a Russian variant, it was introduced to the English- speaking world in the early 20th century through the international tours of Sergei Diaghilev's Ballets Russes. One of the main characters in Virginia Woolf's novel *Orlando* (1928) is a Russian princess called Sasha. **Sacha** – as borne by the French film director and actor Sacha Guitry (1885– 1957) and the French singer Sacha Distel (b.1933) – is a common French version. A German variant is **Sascha**. Occasionally shortened to **Sy**.

Sashi *See* SHASHI.

Saskia (f) Dutch first name of obscure origin that was taken up by English speakers in the 1950s. Recorded in use among the Dutch in medieval times, the name may have evolved from the Old German *sachs* ('Saxon'). Notable bearers of the name have included the Dutch artist Rembrandt's wife, the subject of several of his paintings, and British actress Saskia Wickham (b.1967).

Sassa/Sassie *See* SARAH.

Saturnino (m) Italian, Spanish and Portu- guese first name derived from the Latin Sat- urnus, the name of the Roman god of agriculture. As Saturninus, the name was borne by numerous early Christian saints.

Saul (m) Hebrew name meaning 'asked for' or 'desired'. It features in the Bible as the name of one of the first kings of Israel and as the Jewish name of St Paul (Paul being his Roman name). John Dryden has a character of the name in his poem *Absalom and Achitophel* (1681) and Handel wrote an oratorio entitled *Saul* (1739). Revived by the Puritans in the 17th century, it has been encountered only sporadically among Eng-

lish speakers since the 19th century, almost exclusively within the Jewish community. Notable bearers of the name in recent times have included US novelist Saul Bellow (b.1915).

Saundra *See* SANDRA.

Sava (m) Russian first name derived via Greek from the Hebrew *saba* ('old man'). Notable bearers of the name have included two early Christian saints.

Savanna (f) English first name derived from the Spanish *zavana* ('grassland' or 'plain'). Popular chiefly in the USA, where it is also the name of a port in east Georgia. Also found as **Savannah** and **Zavanna**.

Saveli (m) Russian first name derived from the Latin Sabellius, which came from the ancient Italic tribe known as the Sabelli. The name was borne by a 4th-century Christian martyr.

Savitri (f) Indian name derived from the Sanskrit *savitri* ('of the sun-god Savitr'). The name was borne by the wife or daughter of Brahma and has come to be associated with the virtues of married love and fidelity.

Sawney (m) Scottish variant of **Sandy** (*see* ALEXANDER). The name has lost ground since the 19th century, perhaps because it came to mean 'fool'. Notable bearers of the name have included the notorious Scottish cannibal Sawney Beane, who was executed around 1600.

Sawyl *See* SAMUEL.

Saxon (m) English first name derived from the name of the 5th-century Germanic in- vaders of Britain, the Saxons. The Old German *sachs* originally meant 'dagger' or 'short sword'. It was taken up as a first name during the 19th century, when there was a considerable enthusiasm for archaic names from the medieval period or earlier.

Sayyid (m) Arabic name derived from *sayyid* ('master' or 'lord'). Notable bearers of the name have included the Egyptian composer and singer Sayyid Darwish (1893–1923).

Scarlett (f) English surname that was taken up as a first name in the middle of the 20th century. It was originally reserved for dealers in scarlet cloth or for people habitually wearing scarlet-coloured clothing – as borne, for instance, by Robin Hood's fellow outlaw Will Scarlett. As a first name it was popularized by the US novelist Margaret Mitchell, who selected it for the central character Scarlett O'Hara in the celebrated novel (1936) and film (1940) *Gone with the Wind*. Scarlett's full name, it is explained, is Katie Scarlett O'Hara – Scarlett being her grandmother's maiden name. The huge popularity of Mitchell's character, played on film by Vivien Leigh, has inspired many people on both sides of the Atlantic to select the name for their own children since 1940. The name has also appeared as **Scarlet**, reflecting the ordinary vocabulary word 'scarlet', although its popularity may have been held back in some quarters by association with the 'scarlet woman' (meaning 'prostitute') criticized in the biblical Book of Revelation. *See also* ASHLEY; RHETT.

Scevola (m) Italian first name supposedly derived from the Latin *scaevus* ('left-handed'). The name was borne by the 6th-century BC hero Gaius Mucius Scaevola, the subject of various semi-legendary stories. Myth had it that he thrust his right hand into a fire in order to prove to Lars Porsenna the strength of his mental powers. The name was passed on by his descendants and was later taken up by others impressed by his courage.

Science *See* SANCHO.

Scilla *See* PRISCILLA.

Scott (m) Scottish and English surname meaning 'Scotsman' or 'Scottish' that was formerly commonly applied to anyone from Scotland. It appears that Scott was appearing as a first name in this context before the Norman Conquest. In Scotland itself it was sometimes applied to Gaelic-speaking people from Ireland. Also found as **Scot,** the name increased in popularity as a choice of first name around the middle of the 20th century, perhaps in tribute to US novelist F. Scott Fitzgerald (1896–1940), who reportedly inherited the name from the US songwriter Francis Scott Key (1780–1843), whose compositions included 'The Star-Spangled Banner'. Other notable bearers of the name have included British explorer Robert Falcon Scott (1868–1912), US ragtime pianist and composer Scott Joplin (1868–1917), US pop singer Scott Walker (b.1944) and the fictional Scott Tracy, the eldest of the Tracy brothers in the children's 1960s television adventure series *Thunderbirds*. Familiar variants include **Scottie** and **Scotty** – as borne by Montgomery 'Scottie' Scott in the long-running US film and television series *Star Trek*.

Seaghdh (m) Scottish first name derived from the Gaelic for 'fine' or 'hawk-like'. **Seaghdha** is an Irish Gaelic variant. Anglicized versions of the name include SETH and SHAW.

Seamus (m) English version of the Irish Seamas, itself an equivalent of the English JAMES. Commonly encountered in Ireland, it remains rare elsewhere in the English-speaking world, although it has made occasional appearances among people with no Irish links since the middle of the 20th century. Well-known bearers of the name have included Irish poet Seamus Heaney (b.1939). Also found as **Seumas** and as **Shamus,** a variant reflecting the usual pronunciation of the name. *See also* HAMISH.

Sean (m) Irish first name that is an equivalent of the English JOHN. Pronounced 'shawn', it retains its position as a typically Irish name but since the 1920s has also been found fairly frequently outside the Irish community, increasingly since the 1960s. Notable bearers of the name have included Irish playwright Sean O'Casey (1880–1964), Scottish film actor Sean Connery (Thomas Connery; b.1929), British actor

Sean Bean (b.1958) and US film actor Sean Penn (b.1960). Also encountered in the variant forms **Shane** (from the Northern Irish pronunciation of the name), **Shaun** and **Shawn**. The release of the classic western *Shane* (1953) did much to popularize Shane as an accepted version of the name. Rare feminine versions of the name are **Shauna** and **Shani,** although the variant Shane has been given to girls with increasing frequency since the 1950s, chiefly in Australia.

Seaton (m) English first name, originally a place name and surname, meaning 'farmstead at the sea'. Also found as **Seton**.

Seb *See* SEBASTIAN.

Sebastian (m) English form of the Latin Sebastianus, meaning 'of Sebasta' (a town in Asia Minor). Another derivation suggests the name comes from the Greek *sebastos* ('respected' or 'august'). As the name of the 3rd-century Christian martyr St Sebastian, who was shot with arrows and then beaten to death, it was widely known to English speakers in medieval times and later. Shakespeare has two characters named Sebastian in his plays – in *Twelfth Night* (1601) and *The Tempest* (1611). In more recent times it has acquired an aristocratic gloss, as shown by Evelyn Waugh's adoption of it for his character Lord Sebastian Flyte in *Brideshead Revisited* (1945). The adulation accorded to a British television adaptation of Waugh's book in 1981 may have contributed to a resurgence in the name's popularity in the 1980s and 1990s. Other notable bearers of the name have included British novelist Sebastian Faulks (b.1953) and British athlete Sebastian Coe (b.1956). Variants in other languages include the French **Sébastien**, the Spanish **Sebastián**, the Italian **Sebastiano** and the Russian **Sevastian**. **Seb**, **Sebbie**, **Bastian**, **Baz**, **Bazza** and the French **Bastien** are diminutive forms of the name.

Seeta/Seetha *See* SITA.

Sefton (m) English place name meaning 'settlement in the rushes' that was subsequently taken up as a surname and from the 19th century as a first name.

Seirian (f) Welsh first name meaning 'bright one'. It is pronounced 'syereean'. A masculine equivalent is **Seiriol**.

Sekar (m) Indian first name derived from the Sanskrit *sekhara* ('peak' or 'crest'). Often found as part of longer compound names, such as Chandrasekhar. **Shekhar** is a common variant.

Selby (m) English place name meaning 'willow farm' that was subsequently taken up as a surname and from the 19th century as a first name.

Selena *See* SELINA.

Selig (m) Jewish first name derived from the Yiddish *selig* ('happy' or 'fortunate'). Also found as **Zelig**.

Selima (f) English first name derived from the Arabic *selim* ('peace'), although it is also commonly assumed to be a variant of SELINA. The earliest records of its use among English speakers date from the 18th century. It became widely known after the publication of Thomas Gray's poem 'Ode on the Death of a Favourite Cat' (1748), about the demise of Horace Walpole's cat Selima. In Gray's poem the stress is placed on the first syllable. A modern variant of the name is SELMA, a contracted version that emerged in the 18th century under the influence of THELMA. This form of the name received a boost following the publication of the Ossianic poems of James MacPherson, in which Selma was the name of a romantic castle – when the poems were translated into Swedish many readers were misled into assuming Selma was a personal name and consequently it was adopted by them for their own use.

Selina (f) English version of the Greek Selene, from the Greek *selene* ('moon') – or alternatively from the Latin Caelina (*see* CELINE), from *caelum* ('heaven'). The name of the Greek goddess of the moon, it was adopted as a first name among English speakers in the 17th century and increased in frequency in the 19th century. It reached peaks in popularity in the 1830s and more recently in the 1980s. Notable bearers of the name have included the British Calvinist leader Selina Hastings, Countess of Huntingdon (1707–91) and British television presenter Selina Scott (b.1951). **Salena**, **Selena** and **Salina** are variant forms.

Selma English first name of uncertain origin. It is sometimes presumed to be a contracted form of SELIMA. Also found as **Zelma**.

Selwyn (m) English surname of uncertain origin that has been in occasional use as a first name since medieval times. The name may originally have come from the Old English *sele* ('prosperity') or *sele* ('hall') and *wine* ('friend') or else, via Old French, from the Latin Silvanus, derived from *silva* ('wood'). A third derivation links the name to Welsh words meaning 'ardour' and 'fair'. Famous bearers of the name have included British politicians Selwyn Lloyd (1904–78) and John Selwyn Gummer (b.1939). Also found as **Selwin**.

Semyon *See* SIMON.

Senan (m) English version of the Irish Seanan, from the Gaelic *sean* ('old' or 'wise'). Pronounced 'shannon', the name was borne by several early Irish saints.

Sence/Sens *See* SANCHO.

Senga (f) Scottish first name that probably evolved from the Gaelic *seang* ('slender'). Another theory links the name with AGNES, which it spells when read backwards.

Sepp *See* JOSEPH.

Septimus (m) Latin name meaning 'seventh'. It was taken up by English speakers in the 19th century, when it was often reserved for seventh-born male children. Notable bearers of the name have included the fictional Rev. Septimus Harding in Anthony Trollope's novel *The Warden* (1855) and Rev. Septimus Crisparkle in

Charles Dickens' *Edwin Drood* (1870). **Septima** is a relatively infrequent feminine version of the name.

Seraphina (f) Latin first name derived from the Hebrew *seraphim* ('fiery' or 'burning ones'). In the Bible the name is borne by an order of angels. In the 5th century it was also associated with a saint venerated in southern Europe, about whom little is now known. Sometimes found as **Serafina** and shortened to **Fina**. Variants in other languages include the Russian **Serafima** and the Italian **Serafino**.

Serena (f) English first name derived from the Latin *serenus* ('calm' or 'serene'). It was borne by an early saint and later featured as the name of a character in Edmund Spenser's *The Faerie Queene* (1590, 1596). It is sometimes considered to be an aristocratic name and in recent times has even been selected for use within the royal family as the name of Serena Stanhope, Viscountess Linley (b.1970). Rare variant forms include **Serina**, **Serenah** and **Serenna**.

Serge *See* SERGEI.

Sergei (m) Russian first name derived from the Latin Sergius, which is of uncertain origin. The Latin form of the name was borne by four popes and an early Christian martyr and came to Russia with St Sergius in the 14th century. Variants in other languages include the Italian **Sergio** and the French **Serge**, as borne by Russian ballet dancer Serge Lifar (1905–86).

Sergio *See* SERGEI.

Seth (m) English first name derived from the Hebrew *sheth* ('appointed' or 'set'). It appears in the Bible as the name of the third son of Adam and Eve and is sometimes interpreted to mean 'compensation' – the birth of Seth compensating to some extent for the loss of their murdered second son, Abel. It was taken up by English speakers on both sides of the Atlantic in the 17th century but has largely fallen out of use since the 1870s, by which time it was widely understood to be a traditional country name. Notable bearers of the name have included Seth Bede in George Eliot's novel *Adam Bede* (1859) and Seth Starkadder in the satirical novel *Cold Comfort Farm* (1932) by Stella Gibbons. The name is also used by Indian peoples, who trace it back to the Sanskrit *setu* ('bridge') or *sveta* ('white').

Seton *See* SEATON.

Seumas *See* SEAMUS.

Seve *See* SEVERIANO.

Severiano (m) Italian, Spanish and Portuguese first name derived from the Latin name Severinus. Borne by several early saints, it is relatively uncommon today. A well-known diminutive form of the name is **Seve,** as borne by Spanish golfer Seve Ballesteros (b.1957). Variant forms of the name include **Severino,** which also exists in the feminine forms **Severina** (Latin) and **Séverine** (French).

Severo (m) Italian, Spanish and Portuguese name derived from the Latin name Severus, meaning 'stern' or 'severe'. It was borne by many early saints, guaranteeing its popularity in Catholic countries in later centuries.

Seward (m) English surname derived from the Old English for 'sea' or 'victory' and 'guard' that was adopted as a first name in the 19th century.

Sexton (m) English first name derived from the Old French for 'sacristan'. It is most familiar from Harry Blyth's fictional detective Sexton Blake, whose adventures were hugely popular on the radio in the postwar years.

Sextus (f) Latin name meaning 'sixth'. It was revived by English speakers in the 19th century, when it was reserved chiefly for sixth-born male children. As **Sixtus,** it was borne by three early popes (although this version of the name is sometimes alternatively traced back to the Greek *xystos*, meaning 'polished').

Seymour (m) English surname that has been in occasional use as a first name since the 19th century. The surname came originally from a Norman French place name, Saint-Maur in Normandy, which itself took its name from the little-known 6th-century North African St Maurus (Maurus meaning 'Moor'). Notable bearers of the name have included British actor-manager Sir Seymour Hicks (1871–1949). Occasionally found as **Seamor**, **Seamore** or **Seamour**.

Shadi (m) Arabic first name derived from *shada* ('to sing'). **Shadya** is a feminine version of the name.

Shafiq (m) Arabic and Indian first name derived from *shafiq* ('compassionate' or 'sympathetic'). **Shafiqa** is a feminine version of the name.

Shahira (f) Arabic first name derived from *shahira* ('renowned' or 'famous').

Shahjahan (m) Indian name derived from the Persian *shah* ('king' or 'emperor') and *jahan* ('world') and thus meaning 'king of the world'. The most famous historical bearer of the name was the Mogul emperor Shah Jahan (1592–1666), builder of the Taj Mahal, where he now lies buried. Also found as **Shahjehan**.

Shahnaz (f) Indian name derived from the Persian *shah* ('king' or 'emperor') and *naz* ('glory' or 'grace') and thus meaning 'glory of a king'. The name implies that the bearer is beautiful enough to grace a king.

Shahrazad (f) Arabic first name derived from the Persian *shahr* ('city') and *zad* ('person'). As **Sheherazade,** the name is well known around the world from the *Thousand and One Nights*, in which Sheherazade delays her execution by telling the vizier compelling stories until eventually he falls in love with her. Also found as **Shahrizad**.

Shakti (f) Indian name derived from the Sanskrit *sakti* ('power'). The name of Shiva's wife, it is understood to represent various kinds of power, from the power wielded by monarchs to the creative power of poets.

Shakuntala (f) Indian name derived from the Sanskrit *sakunta* ('bird'). In Kalidasa's classical drama the heroine Shakuntala is brought up by the birds of the forest after she is abandoned there. Later she marries King Dushyanta, only to be parted from him by a curse, but eventually re-united to live happily ever after as his queen.

Shamus *See* SEAMUS.

Shane *See* SEAN; SHANNON.

Shanel/Shanelle *See* CHANEL.

Shankar (m) Indian name derived from the Sanskrit *sam* ('auspicious') and *kara* ('making') and meaning 'one who brings happiness'. It is one of SHIVA's names and features in various classical texts; it was also borne by a celebrated 8th- or 9th-century religious teacher. Also found as **Sankar**. *See also* JAYASHANKAR.

Shanna *See* SUSANNAH.

Shannon (f) English first name that probably developed as a combination of Shane (*see* SEAN) and SHARON, although it is often assumed that it comes from the name – meaning 'the old one' – of the Irish river (despite the fact that the name is little used in Ireland). It seems to have made its debut as a first name in the 1950s and is today commoner in Canada and the USA than elsewhere.

Shanta (f) Indian name derived from the Sanskrit *santa* ('calm' or 'pacified'). It appears in the *Mahabharata* and is understood to denote a person in full control of their emotions.

Shantel/Shantelle *See* CHANTEL.

Shanti (f) Indian name derived from the Sanskrit *santi* ('tranquillity'). It describes the state of peace achieved through meditation and yoga and appears in various ancient religious texts.

Shari *See* SHARON.

Sharif (m) Arabic name derived from *sharif* ('eminent' or 'virtuous'). Borne as a title by descendants of Muhammad, it is best known today as the surname of the Egyptian film actor Omar Sharif (Michael Shalhouz; b.1932). Also found as **Shareef**. **Sharifa** is a feminine version of the name.

Sharlene *See* CHARLENE.

Sharlott *See* CHARLOTTE.

Sharma (m) Indian name derived from the Sanskrit *sarman* ('protection' or 'refuge'). Adopted as a first name only in relatively recent times, it is now often interpreted to mean 'comfort' or 'joy'.

Sharmain/Sharmaine *See* CHARMAINE.

Sharmila (f) Indian name derived from the Sanskrit *sarman* ('protection' or 'refuge'). A relatively recent introduction as a first name, it is sometimes interpreted to mean 'bashful' or 'modest'.

Sharon (f) English first name derived ultimately from the Hebrew Saron, from *sar* ('to sing' or 'singer'). The name features in the Bible as the name of a valley in Palestine, famed for its natural beauty, and is often interpreted to mean 'the plain'. It was taken up by English speakers in the 1930s and reached a peak in popularity in the 1960s and 1970s before falling rapidly out of favour. Notable bearers of the name have included US film actresses Sharon Tate (1943–69) and Sharon Stone (b.1957). Variant forms of the name include **Sharron**, as borne by British swimmer Sharron Davies (b.1962), **Sharona**, **Sharonda** and **Sharyn**. Sometimes shortened to **Shari**.

Sharron *See* SHARON.

Shashi (m) Indian name derived from the Sanskrit *sasin* ('having a hare'). It is a traditional Indian name for the moon, the features of which are sometimes thought to resemble a hare. Sometimes found as

Sashi, it also appears as part of longer compound names such as **Shashikant**.

Shaun/Shauna *See* SEAN.

Shaw (m) English surname derived from the Old English *sceaga* ('wood' or 'copse') and used as a first name since the 19th century. It can also be found in Scotland as an Anglicized equivalent of SEAGHDH.

Shawn *See* SEAN.

Shayna (f) Jewish first name derived from the Yiddish for 'beautiful'. Also found as **Sheine**.

Sheba *See* BATHSHEBA.

Sheela (f) Indian name derived from the Sanskrit *sila* ('character' or 'conduct'). In Buddhist teaching the word represents the ideal of 'piety'. As a first name it seems to have been first used in medieval times. Today it sometimes appears as SHEILA through confusion with the Western name.

Sheelagh *See* SHEILA.

Sheena (f) English version of the Scottish and Irish Gaelic Sine, itself an equivalent of the English JANE or JEAN. It was taken up by English speakers in the 1930s, chiefly in Scotland. The US comic book character Sheena, introduced in 1938 and subsequently the subject of a television series and film (1984), did much to popularize the name on a wider basis. Also found in the forms **Shena**, **Sheenagh**, **Sheona** and **Shona**. Notable bearers of the name have included Scottish television presenter Sheena McDonald (b.1954) and Scottish pop singer Sheena Easton (b.1959).

Sheila (f) English version of the Irish Gaelic Sile, an equivalent of the English CELIA. It made its debut among English speakers in the late 19th century and reached a peak in the UK in the 1930s, by which time it was no longer thought of as distinctly Irish. It has since gone into decline, in part thanks to the fact that in Australia the name has become a slang term for any woman. Well-known bearers of the

name have included British actress Sheila Hancock (b.1933) and South African actress Sheila Steafel (b.1935). Also found as SHEELA, **Sheelah** and **Shelagh**, as borne by the Irish playwright Shelagh Delaney (b.1939).

Shekhar *See* SEKAR.

Shelagh *See* SHEILA.

Sheldon (m) British place name (from Derbyshire, Devon and the West Midlands) meaning 'steep-sided valley' or 'flat-topped hill' that was subsequently adopted as a surname and has been in occasional use as a first name on both sides of the Atlantic since the early 20th century. As a first name it appears to have been adopted initially in the USA.

Shell *See* MICHELLE.

Shelley (f) English place name (from Essex, Suffolk and Yorkshire) meaning 'wood on a slope' that was subsequently adopted as a surname and first name. It may also be encountered as a familiar form of MICHELLE and RACHEL. As a first name it emerged in the mid-19th century under the influence of the British Romantic poet Percy Bysshe Shelley (1792–1822). It enjoyed a peak in the 1970s and 1980s before going into decline. The fact that it is now reserved almost exclusively for girls reflects the influence of SHIRLEY. Well-known bearers of the name have included the US actresses Shelley Winters (Shirley Schrift; b.1922) and Shelley Long (b.1949). Also found as **Shelly**.

Shem (m) Hebrew name meaning 'renown' or 'name'. The name features in the Bible as that of Noah's eldest son but has never enjoyed widespread acceptance in the English-speaking world and remains rare.

Shena/Sheona *See* SHEENA.

Sher (m) Indian name derived from the Persian *sher* ('lion'). Notable bearers of the name have included the Mogul Emperor Sher Shah (1486–1545). *See also* CHER.

Sherborne (m) English first name, also a surname, meaning 'clear stream'. Also encountered as **Sherbourne**.

Sheree/Sheri *See* CHERIE.

Sheridan (m) Irish surname of uncertain meaning that was subsequently adopted as a first name throughout the English-speaking world. One suggestion is that the name came originally from the Gaelic *sirim* ('to seek'). It made its debut as a first name in the middle of the 19th century, boosted by the popularity of the works of Irish playwright Richard Brinsley Sheridan (1751–1816) and later of Irish novelist Sheridan Le Fanu (Joseph Sheridan Le Fanu; 1814–73), who shared family links. More recent bearers of the name have included British critic and biographer Sheridan Morley (b.1941). Sometimes shortened to **Sherry**.

Sherie *See* CHERIE.

Sherill *See* CHERYL.

Sherilyn *See* CHERYL.

Sherley *See* SHIRLEY.

Sherlock (m) English first name derived from Middle English for 'shear lock' (possibly reserved for people with closely cropped hair). The name is strongly associated with Sherlock Holmes, the fictional detective created by Sir Arthur Conan Doyle in the late 19th century. As a result of this identification use of the name in real life has been infrequent, although it is not unknown.

Sherman (m) English surname derived from the Old English *sceara* ('shears') and *mann* ('man') that was subsequently adopted as a first name. It began as a medieval trade name reserved for those whose job it was to trim the nap of woollen cloth after weaving. Its popularity in the USA was boosted by the exploits of US general William Tecumseh Sherman (1820–91) in the US Civil War.

Sherri/Sherry *See* CHERIE; SHIRLEY.

Sherwin (m) English first name, also a surname, meaning 'loyal friend' or 'fast-footed'.

Sheryl *See* CHERYL.

Shevaun *See* SIOBHAN.

Shifra (f) Jewish name derived from the Hebrew *shifra* ('beauty' or 'grace'). It features in the Bible as **Shiphrah**.

Shimon *See* SIMON.

Shiphrah *See* SHIFRA.

Shirin (f) Indian name derived from the Persian *shirin* ('sweet' or 'charming'). The most famous bearer of the name was the daughter of the Byzantine emperor Maurice (*c.*539–602) whose amorous adventures were the subject of several later romances.

Shirl *See* SHIRLEY.

Shirley (f) English place name (from Derbyshire, Hampshire, Surrey and the West Midlands) that was subsequently adopted as a surname and, from the 1860s, as a first name. The name came originally from the Old English *scir* ('county' or 'bright') and *leah* ('wood' or 'clearing'). The name was formerly reserved for boys, but it was transferred to girls soon after the publication of Charlotte Brontë's novel *Shirley* (1849), in which the heroine's parents chose the name for their unborn son and decided to keep to their choice even when the baby turned out to be a girl. The name enjoyed a peak in popularity in the 1930s, largely through the screen success of US child star Shirley Temple (b.1928). It remained popular until the 1950s, since when it has suffered a marked decline. Well-known bearers of the name in recent times have included British politician Shirley Williams (b.1930), US actress Shirley Maclaine (b.1934) and British singer Shirley Bassey (b.1937). Variant forms include **Sherley** and **Shirlee**. SHELLEY, **Sherry**, **Sherri** and **Shirl** are popular diminutive forms of the name.

Shiva (m) Indian name derived from the Sanskrit *siva* ('benign' or 'auspicious').

Borne by one of the principal Indian gods, representing both regeneration and destruction, the name is found in a number of variant forms, including **Shiv**, **Sib** and **Sheo**.

Shlomo *See* SOLOMON.

Shmuel *See* SAMUEL.

Shobha (f) Indian first name derived from the Sanskrit *sobha* ('brilliance' or 'beauty'). It was adopted as a first name in medieval times. The usual feminine version of the name is **Shobhana**.

Sholto (m) English version of the Scottish Gaelic Sioltach (meaning 'sower' or 'fruitful'). Largely confined to Scotland, where it first emerged in the 19th century and is traditionally associated with the Douglas family. A character of the name appears in Walter Scott's *The Bride of Lammermoor* (1819).

Shona *See* SHEENA.

Shripati (m) Indian first name derived from the Sanskrit Sri, the name of a goddess of fortune and beauty, and *pati* ('husband' or 'lord') and thus meaning 'husband of the goddess Sri'. In various classical texts it is borne by Vishnu or Krishna.

Shug/Shuggie *See* HUGH.

Shukri (m) Arabic first name derived from *shakara* ('to thank'). A feminine version of the name is **Shukriyya**.

Shula *See* SHULAMIT.

Shulamit (f) Jewish name derived from the Hebrew for 'peacefulness', coming ultimately from *shalom* ('peace'). The name features in the biblical Song of Solomon and is today a common Hebrew name. Also found as **Shulamith** and **Shulamite**. A diminutive form is **Shula,** a name long familiar to British listeners to the BBC radio series *The Archers* as that of Shula Archer, one of the leading characters – although in this case the name was devised by her parents picking five letters at random from the alphabet and rearranging them until they formed an acceptable name.

Shushana/Shushanna *See* SUSANNAH.

Shyam (m) Indian first name derived from the Sanskrit *syama* ('black' or 'dark') but later understood to mean 'beauty'. Also found as **Sham** and **Sam**. A feminine form of the name is **Shyama**.

Siân (f) Welsh version of JANE, also in existence as a feminine variant of SEAN. Pronounced 'sharn', it was taken up in Wales in the 1940s and has since made occasional appearances elsewhere in the English-speaking world. It may appear with or without the accent. Well-known bearers of the name have included Welsh actress Siân Phillips (b.1934). **Siana** is a recognized diminutive form.

Sib/Sibb/Sibella/Sibilla/Sibyl/ Sibylla *See* SYBIL.

Sid *See* SIDNEY.

Siddharta (m) Indian first name derived from the Sanskrit *siddha* ('accomplished') and *artha* ('aim' or 'goal') and thus meaning 'he who has accomplished his goal'. It appears several times in Indian legend and is an alternative name for Buddha. It was also borne by a celebrated Indian poet.

Sidney (m/f) English surname that became increasingly popular as a first name from the middle of the 19th century. It may originally have begun as a Norman French place name, Saint-Denis, or, more likely, came from the Old English *sidan* ('wide') and *eg* ('river island'), so meaning 'wide island'. As a surname it was borne by a famous English family, whose most notable members included the English poet Sir Philip Sidney (1554–86). Another celebrated bearer of Sidney as a surname was the 17th-century English politician Algernon Sidney (c.1622–83), who achieved the status of a political martyr after his execution for his participation in the Rye House Plot to kill Charles II. Also found from the 19th century as **Sydney**, it reached a peak in popularity as a first name in the late 19th and early 20th centuries, boosted perhaps by the character Sydney Carton in Charles Dickens' *A Tale of Two Cities* (1859). It has since become infrequent. Today the spelling Sydney is usually reserved for females.

Notable bearers of the name have included Australian painter Sir Sidney Nolan (1917–92) and US actor Sidney Poitier (b.1924). Commonly shortened to **Syd** or **Sid** – as borne by British comedian Sid James (Sydney James; 1913–73), US comedian Sid Caesar (b.1922) and British punk rock musician Sid Vicious (John Simon Ritchie; 1957–79). As a name for girls, it may have been influenced by SIDONIE and similarly made its first appearance in the 19th century. A variant form of the feminine version of the name is **Sydne**.

Sidonie (f) French version of the Latin Sidonia (meaning 'of Sidon', Sidon being the capital of Phoenicia). Another derivation suggests it comes from the Greek *sindon* ('linen'), probably in reference to the linen shroud of Jesus Christ. There were two saints called Sidonius in the 4th and 7th centuries. The French version of the name was taken up by English speakers in the 19th century. Famous bearers of the name have included the French novelist Colette (Sidonie Gabrielle Colette; 1873–1954). Also found as **Sidony**.

Siegbert (m) German first name derived from the Old Germanic *sige* ('victory') and *berht* ('bright' or 'famous'). It was borne by a 7th-century French king admired for his saintly works and in an Old English variant by an early Christian king of East Anglia. The name is now particularly popular among Jews. Sometimes shortened to **Sigi**.

Siegfried (m) German first name derived from the Old Germanic *sige* ('victory') and *frid* ('peace'). It was commonly encountered during medieval times and was subsequently revived in the 19th century, when the story of the legendary Siegfried was celebrated in Richard Wagner's *Ring*

cycle. The name has made rare appearances among English speakers, being borne by, among others, the British war poet Siegfried Sassoon (1886–1967). There was also a leading character called Siegfried in the vet novels of James Herriot, televised in the 1980s. Sometimes shortened to **Sigi**.

Siegmund *See* SIGMUND.

Siena (f) Italian first name derived from that of the city. As a first name it appears to have made its debut in the 19th century.

Sierra (f) Spanish first name meaning 'mountain range'. It appears to be a relatively late introduction among English speakers.

Sigi *See* SIEGBERT; SIEGFRIED; SIGMUND.

Sigismund *See* SIGMUND.

Sigmund (m) German and English first name derived from the Old German *sige* ('victory') and *mund* ('defender') and thus meaning 'victorious defender'. Famous as the name of a legendary German hero later celebrated in the operas of Richard Wagner and as the name of Austrian psychiatrist Sigmund Freud (1856–1939), it has made occasional appearances among English speakers since before the Norman Conquest. In medieval times it became confused with SIMON and virtually disappeared from use. The usual modern German form of the name is **Siegmund**, with **Sigismund** being a variant. The Polish version is **Zygmunt**. Sometimes shortened to **Sigi**.

Sigourney (f) English surname that was taken up as a first name in the 1920s. The name appears to have been introduced by US novelist F. Scott Fitzgerald via his character Sigourney Howard in *The Great Gatsby* (1925). Fitzgerald is thought to have taken the name from the writer Lydia Howard Sigourney (1791–1865). In due course the name was adopted by US film actress Sigourney Weaver (Susan Alexandra Weaver; b.1949) and it was due to her that the name emerged as an increasingly popular choice in the 1990s.

Sigrid (f) Scandinavian first name derived from the Old Norse *sigr* ('victory') and *frithr* ('fair' or 'beautiful'). The name reached Britain many centuries ago but subsequently fell into disuse until its revival in relatively recent times, when it has been imported from Scandinavia where it is still common. Sometimes shortened to **Siri**.

Sigurd (m) Scandinavian first name derived from the Old Norse *sigr* ('victory') and *vörthr* ('guardian'). A Norwegian variant is **Sjurd**. Sometimes shortened to **Sigge**.

Silas (m) English first name derived via Hebrew from the Latin Silvanus, from *silva* ('wood'). Silvanus was the Roman god of trees. The name was originally applied to people who lived in wooded areas or who worked with wood in some way. It features in the New Testament as the name of a prophet who was a companion of St Paul, and as a consequence was among the biblical names taken up by the Puritans in the 17th century. The name appeared in several notable literary works of the 19th century, including George Eliot's novel *Silas Marner* (1861), in which Silas is a miserly linen weaver, and Sheridan Le Fanu's novel *Uncle Silas* (1864), in which Silas Ruthyn is the main villain. It has since fallen into disuse.

Sile *See* SHEILA.

Silke *See* CELIA.

Silvain *See* SILVANO.

Silvana *See* SILVANO.

Silvano (m) Italian first name derived from the Latin Silvanus, from *silva* ('wood'). It was borne by several early saints. A French variant is **Sylvain**. **Silvana** is a feminine version of the name.

Silver (m) English first name derived from the Old English *siolfor* ('silver'). It was reserved originally for children with silvery hair.

Silvester *See* SYLVESTER.

Silvia (f) Italian and English first name derived from the Latin Silvius, itself from *silva* ('wood'). According to Roman legend, Rhea Silvia was the mother of Romulus and Remus, the founders of Rome, and as a result the name has been consistently popular in Italy ever since the Renaissance. It was also borne by a 6th-century saint who became the mother of Gregory the Great. There is a character called Silvia in Shakespeare's *Two Gentlemen of Verona* (1592–3) and another in William Congreve's *The Old Bachelor* (1693), but it was not until the 19th century that the name was taken up as a first name by English speakers on a significant scale. It has since gone into decline and is rarely encountered among the younger generation today. The variant form **Sylvia** is now the more common spelling of the name – as borne by the British suffragette leader Sylvia Pankhurst (1882–1960) and US poet Sylvia Plath (1932–63). **Sylvie** is the French version of the name, as borne by the actress Sylvie (Louise Sylvain; 1883–1970). Sometimes shortened to **Syl**.

Silvio (m) Italian and English first name derived from the Latin **Silvius**, itself from *silva* ('wood'). Notable early bearers of the name included an early Christian saint put to death in Egypt.

Sim/Simeon *See* SIMON.

Simon (m) English version of the Hebrew Simeon or Shimon, meaning 'hearkening' or 'he who hears' (although another derivation traces it back to the Greek *simos*, meaning 'snub-nosed'). The name is borne by several biblical figures, including the ancestor of one of the twelve tribes of Israel and two apostles. Both Simon and Simeon were in use among English speakers in medieval times and remained consistently popular until the Reformation when both forms of the name went into decline. Simon returned to favour early in the 20th century and it has since kept its place among the most popular choices, with a peak throughout the English-speaking world in the 1960s and 1970s. Notable bearers of the name over the centuries have included the English parliamentarian Simon de

Montfort, Earl of Leicester (c.1208–65), who led a rebellion against the crown in 1265, the fictional adventurer Simon Templar created in the 1930s by British novelist Leslie Charteris in *The Saint* series, and British conductor Sir Simon Rattle (b.1955). Often shortened to **Si** or **Sim**. Variants in other languages include the Russian **Semyon** and the Dutch **Siemen**. *See also* SIMONE.

Simone (f) French variant of SIMON that has also won acceptance among English speakers. It was first taken up in the English-speaking world in the 1940s. Celebrated bearers of the name have included the French writer Simone de Beauvoir (1908–86) and the French actress Simone Signoret (1921–85). Also encountered in the form **Simona**.

Sinclair (m) Scottish surname that has also made sporadic appearances throughout the English-speaking world as a first name. The surname itself came from a Norman French place name, Saint-Clair, which in turn may have been named after the French St Clair. It appears to have made its debut as a first name towards the end of the 19th century. Well-known bearers of the name have included the US novelist Sinclair Lewis (Harry Sinclair Lewis; 1885–1951).

Sindy *See* CINDY.

Sine *See* SHEENA.

Sinead (f) Irish version (pronounced 'shinnayd') of the English JANET. It retains its identification as an essentially Irish name and is only rarely found elsewhere in the English-speaking world. Famous bearers of the name have included the Irish actress Sinead Cusack (b.1948) and Irish singer-songwriter Sinead O'Connor (b.1966).

Siobhan (f) Irish version of the English JOAN. Pronounced 'shivaun', it is more common in Ireland than elsewhere, although it has been taken up on an occasional basis elsewhere in the English-

speaking world. Notable bearers of the name have included the Irish actress Siobhan McKenna (1923–86). Also found as **Shevaun** and the modern form **Chevonne**. *See also* JUDITH.

Siri *See* SIGRID.

Sis/Sissy *See* CECILIA; CISSIE.

Sita (f) Indian first name derived from the Sanskrit *sita* ('furrow'). In ancient mythology Sita is variously identified as a goddess of agriculture and as another name of the goddess Lakshmi. She appears in the *Mahabharata* and is a central character in the *Ramayana*. Today she remains one of the central figures of worship among Hindus. Also found as **Seeta** and **Seetha**, and as part of longer compound names such as **Sitaram**.

Sitaram *See* SITA.

Skeeter (m/f) English first name that began as a nickname for any small or energetic person. It may have come from 'mosquito' or else from 'skeets' or 'scoots'. It is a 20th-century introduction of US origin and remains relatively rare. A well-known bearer of the name is US country singer Skeeter Davis (Mary Frances Penick; b.1931).

Skip (m) English first name adopted as a diminutive of **Skipper**. It may have come ultimately from a Dutch word meaning 'ship's captain'.

Sly *See* SYLVESTER.

Sofia/Sofie *See* SOPHIA.

Sol *See* SOLOMON.

Solange (f) French version of the Latin Solemnia, derived from *solemnis* ('solemn' or 'religious'). The name was born by the 9th-century St Solange, who was sanctified after she was murdered by her own master while resisting his advances.

Solly *See* SOLOMON.

Solomon (m) Hebrew name derived from *shalom* ('peace') and meaning 'man of peace'. It appears in the Bible as the name of the son of David and Beersheba, whose wise rule over Israel brought about a lengthy peace. Almost exclusively a Jewish name, it was first adopted by English speakers in the 16th century. Well-known bearers of the name have included the Solomon Grundy of nursery rhyme fame and the British classical pianist Solomon (Solomon Cutner; 1902–88). Commonly abbreviated to **Solly** or **Sol**. Variants include the medieval **Salamon**, the Hebrew **Shlomo** and the Arabic **Sulayman**. Another variant familiar today is **Salman** – as borne by Indian-born British novelist Salman Rushdie (b.1947).

Solveig (f) Norwegian name derived from the Old Norse *salr* ('house' or 'hall') and *veig* ('strength'). Variant forms include the Swedish **Solvig** and the Danish **Solvej**. Notable bearers of the name have included the fictional heroine of Henrik Ibsen's *Peer Gynt* (1867).

Somerled (m) Scottish name derived from an Old Norse name meaning 'summer traveller'. The name is traditionally associated with the Macdonald clan. Variant forms include **Summerlad** and the Gaelic **Somhairle** (sometimes Anglicized as **Sorley**). *See also* SAMUEL.

Somerset (m) English first name, also a place name, meaning 'summer farmstead'. The most notable bearer of the name to date has been English novelist William Somerset Maugham (1874–1965).

Somhairle *See* SAMUEL; SOMERLED.

Sondra *See* SANDRA.

Sonia (f) Russian diminutive of Sofiya, an equivalent of the English SOPHIA. It was taken up by English speakers in the early 20th century and it now exists as an independent name. It enjoyed a peak in popularity in the 1960s and 1970s. Also found as **Sonya** and **Sonja** (or **Sonje**). One of the central characters in Dostoyevsky's novel *Crime and Punishment* (1866) is called Sonya Marmeladova.

Sonny (m) English diminutive of SAUL, SOLOMON and several other names. It is also in frequent use as a familiar nickname for any young person. Largely a 20th-century introduction, it was promoted by the song 'Sonny Boy' in the Al Jolson film *The Singing Fool* (1928). Also found as **Sonnie**. Notable bearers of the name in its various forms have included British actor Sonnie Hale (John Robert Hale-Monro; 1902–59), US boxer Sonny Liston (Charles Liston; 1932–70) and US pop singer Sonny Bono (Salvatore Bono; 1935–98).

Sonya *See* SONIA.

Sophia (f) Greek first name meaning 'wisdom' now common to numerous cultural traditions. St Sophia is a saint in the Eastern Orthodox Church – she was probably not a real person but came about rather as a result of a misinterpretation of the phrase *Hagia Sophia* ('holy wisdom'). The name spread from Greece through Hungary to Germany and was taken up by English speakers in the 17th century, promoted by James I's granddaughter Sophia, Electress of Hanover (1630–1714), who gave birth to George I. It reached a peak in popularity in the 18th century but suffered a decline from the late 19th century. Variant forms include **Sofia**, **Sofie** and **Sophie** (or **Sophy**), a French version of the name that since the 1960s has become more widely accepted than the original Sophia. Well-known bearers of the name in its various forms have included such luminaries as US variety star Sophie Tucker (Sophia Abuza; 1885–1966), US actress Sophia Loren (Sofia Scicolone; b.1934), British food writer Sophie Grigson (b.1959) and British model and writer Sophie Dahl (b.1979). Diminutive forms of the name include SONIA.

Sophie *See* SOPHIA; SOPHRONIA.

Sophronia (f) Greek name derived from *sophron* ('prudent' or 'sensible'). First recorded in the 14th century, the name was taken up by English speakers in the 19th century but is now rare. Sometimes shortened to **Sophie** or **Sophy**.

Sophy *See* SOPHIA; SOPHRONIA.

Sorcha (f) Irish and Scottish Gaelic name meaning 'brightness'. In Ireland it is often treated as a Gaelic variant of SARAH. In Scotland it is sometimes assumed to be a variant of CLARA.

Sorley *See* SOMERLED.

Sorrel (f) English plant name adopted as a first name in the 1940s. The plant name is thought to have come originally from the German *sur* ('sour'), a reference to the sour taste of its leaves. Also found as **Sorrell**, **Sorell** and **Sorel**.

Spencer (m) English surname meaning 'dispenser' that was subsequently adopted as a first name. It was originally reserved for the stewards who dispensed supplies in English manor houses. The name is closely identified with the Churchill family and also with Diana, Princess of Wales, whose maiden name was Spencer. It was taken up as a first name in the 19th century. Notable bearers of the name have included British Prime Minister Spencer Perceval (1762–1812), British Prime Minister Winston Spencer Churchill (1874–1965) and US film actor Spencer Tracy (1900–1967).

Spike (m) English first name that began life as a nickname for anyone with tufty or spiky hair. It has also been used traditionally as a nickname for anyone whose real name is not known. Of early 20th-century origin, it is rarely given at birth but adopted later. Famous bearers of the name have included British comedian Spike Milligan (Terence Alan Milligan; 1918–2002) and US film director Spike Lee (Shelton Jackson; b.1956).

Spring (f) English first name derived either from the name of the spring season or from natural springs or wells. A 19th-century introduction, it remains relatively rare.

Squire (m) English first name, also a surname, meaning 'shield bearer'. Famous bearers of the name have included English

actor-manager Squire Bancroft (1841–1926).

Sri (f) Indian name (pronounced 'Sree') derived from the Sanskrit *sri* ('beauty', 'light' or 'prosperity'). It was borne in legend by the goddess Lakshmi and later came to be used as an honorific before the names of various gods (for example, Sri Krishna). Also found as **Shree** and **Shri**, and forming part of various longer compound names, such as **Sridhar**, **Srikant**, **Srinivas** and **Sriram**.

Stacey (f) English first name that evolved as a feminine equivalent of STACY. It may also be found as a diminutive form of ANASTASIA. It enjoyed a minor vogue among English speakers from the 1960s, reaching a peak in the 1970s and 1980s. Also found as **Stacy**, **Stacie** and **Staci**. Commonly shortened to **Stace**.

Stacy (m) English surname derived from EUSTACE that was taken up as a first name in the 19th century. Well-known bearers of the name have included US actor Stacy Keach (Walter Stacy Keach; b.1941). Also found as STACEY.

Stafford (m) English place name derived from the Old English *staeth* ('landing place') and *ford* ('ford') that was later taken up as a surname and, from the middle of the 19th century, as a first name. In the 15th and 16th centuries it was famous primarily as the surname of the dukes of Buckingham. Notable bearers of the name have included British politician Sir Stafford Cripps (Richard Stafford Cripps; 1889–1952).

Stan *See* STANLEY.

Stanford (m) English place name derived from the Old English for 'stony ford' that was subsequently taken up as a surname and first name. Occasionally found as **Stamford**.

Stanhope (m) English first name, also a surname, meaning 'stony hollow'.

Stanislas (m) Latinized version of a Slavonic name derived from *stan* ('government' or 'camp') and *slav* ('glory'). Notable bearers of the name have included the 11th-century martyr St Stanislas of Cracow and two kings of Poland. Variants include **Stanislaus**, **Stanislaw** (Polish) and **Stanislav** (Russian). Feminine forms include the Polish **Stanislawa** and the Czech **Stanislava**.

Stanley (m) English place name derived from the Old English *stan* ('stone') and *leah* ('wood' or 'clearing') and thus meaning 'stony field' that was subsequently taken up as a surname and, from the 18th century, as a first name. As a surname it was strongly associated with the earls of Derby. As a first name it enjoyed a peak in popularity between 1880 and 1930, since when it has become less frequent. Interest in the name in the Victorian period was much boosted by the exploits of the British journalist and explorer Sir Henry Morton Stanley (John Rowlands; 1841–1904), discoverer of the 'lost' Dr Livingstone in 1869. Other notable bearers of the name have included British Prime Minister Stanley Baldwin (1867–1947), British comedian Stanley Holloway (1890–1982) and British footballer Sir Stanley Matthews (1915–2000). Commonly shortened to **Stan** – as borne by British-born US comedian Stan Laurel (Arthur Stanley Jefferson; 1890–1965) and US jazz musician Stan Getz (1927–91).

Star *See* STELLA.

Steenie *See* STEPHEN.

Stef *See* STEPHANIE.

Stefan *See* STEPHEN.

Stefanie/Steffie *See* STEPHANIE.

Stella (f) English first name derived from the Latin *stella* ('star'). The name was first used as a title for the Virgin Mary, *Stella Maris* ('star of the sea'). It made its debut as a first name among English speakers in medieval times but it was not until the 18th century that it started to be used on a significant scale. It remained in vogue until the 1920s, since when it has become less

frequent. The name has a proud literary history, being used by Sir Philip Sidney as a pseudonym for Penelope Devereux in his sonnet sequence *Astrophel and Stella* (1582), in which he was Astrophel (meaning 'star-lover'), and by Jonathan Swift in his *Journal to Stella* (1710–13), which was addressed to Esther Johnson (Esther, like Stella, meaning 'star'). Other notable bearers of the name have included British novelist Stella Gibbons (1902–89). Modern diminutive forms of the name include **Star**. *See also* ESTELLE.

Sten (m) Swedish name derived from the Old Norse *steinn* ('stone'). It also appears as part of many longer compound names, such as **Stenbjörn** and **Stenulf**. A Norwegian variant is **Stein**.

Steph *See* STEPHANIE.

Stephan/Stéphane *See* STEPHEN.

Stephanie (f) English version of the French Stéphanie, itself derived from the Latin Stephania or Stephana, an equivalent of the English STEPHEN. It was taken up by English speakers in the late 19th century and, after a temporary fall from favour from the 1950s, enjoyed a peak in popularity in the 1990s. Well-known bearers of the name have included British actress Stephanie Beacham (b.1949). Also found as **Stefanie** – as borne by US actress Stefanie Powers (Stefania Federkiewicz; b.1942) – and **Steffany**. Diminutive forms of the name include **Steph**, **Stef**, **Steffie**, **Stevi** and **Stevie** – as borne by British poet Stevie Smith (Florence Margaret Smith; 1902–71) and US rock singer Stevie Nicks (b.1948).

Stephen (m) English version of the Greek name Stephanos, meaning 'garland', 'wreath' or 'crown', and the Latin Stefanus. The name features in the Bible as that of the first Christian martyr, who was stoned to death on false charges, and it was later borne by several other saints and ten popes. It appeared in the 11th-century 'Domesday Book' and was borne by England's King Stephen (c.1097–1154). The name has been consistently popular among English speakers since medieval times, with its most recent peak around 1960.

Notable bearers of the name have included British poet Sir Stephen Spender (1909–95), the fictional Stephen Dedalus in James Joyce's novel *Ulysses* (1922), the US composer and lyricist Stephen Sondheim (b.1930), US horror writer Stephen King (b.1947) and British comedian and writer Stephen Fry (b.1957). Also found as **Steven** – as borne for instance by US film director Steven Spielberg (b.1946). It is commonly abbreviated to **Steve** or **Stevie** – as in the cases of US film actor Steve McQueen (1930–80), US pop singer Stevie Wonder (Steveland Morris, b.1950) and British snooker player Steve Davis (b.1957). Variants of the name in other languages include **Stephan**, the Welsh **Steffan**, the Irish **Steafan**, the Scottish **Steenie**, the French **Stéphane**, the Italian **Stefano**, the German **Steffen**, the Polish **Stefan**, the Hungarian ISTVÁN and the Spanish **Estéban**. *See also* ÉTIENNE.

Sterling *See* STIRLING.

Steve/Steven *See* STEPHEN.

Stevie *See* STEPHANIE; STEPHEN.

Stew *See* STEWART; STUART.

Stewart (m) English first name that developed either from a Scottish surname, derived from the Old English *stigweard* ('steward'), or as a variant of STUART. Although long-established as a surname, it only emerged as a first name in the early 19th century. It enjoyed a minor vogue in the 1950s but has become less common since the 1970s. Well-known bearers of the name have included British film actor Stewart Granger (James Lablanche Stewart; 1913–93). **Stew**, **Stu** and **Stewie** are common diminutive forms.

Stig (m) Scandinavian name derived from the Old Norse Stigr, which was itself a diminutive form of Stigandr meaning 'wanderer'. English speakers know the name from the children's novel *Stig of the Dump* (1963) by Clive King.

Stirling (m) English and Scottish surname and first name that can be variously derived from the place name Stirling (of uncertain meaning) or from the ordinary vocabulary word 'sterling', which itself developed from the Middle English *sterrling* ('little star'). The term 'sterling' became linked with money in Norman times when coins sometimes bore a small star pattern and the word thus came to mean 'valuable' or 'excellent'. As a first name Stirling (or **Sterling**) is a relatively recent introduction, which does not seem to have been taken up before the early 20th century. Notable bearers of the name have included British motor-racing driver Stirling Moss (b.1929).

St John (m) English first name derived from the French place name Saint-Jean, and ultimately from the name of John the Baptist. Usually pronounced 'sinjun' and confined to the Roman Catholic English-speaking world, it has been in occasional use since the late 19th century. Notable bearers of the name have included British politician Norman St John-Stevas (b.1929).

Storm (f) English first name derived from the ordinary vocabulary word, suggesting perhaps a passionate, lively nature. The name does not seem to have been used before the early 20th century.

Strachan (m) Scottish first name, also a surname, meaning 'little valley'. Also rendered in the form **Strahan**.

Stratford (m) English first name, also a place name, meaning 'ford on a Roman road'. Notable bearers of the name have included English actor Stratford Johns (1925–2002).

Struan (m) Scottish first name derived from the Scottish Gaelic *sruthan*, meaning 'streams'.

Stu *See* STEWART; STUART.

Stuart (m) Scottish surname that developed as a French version of STEWART and has been in use as a first name throughout the English-speaking world since the early

19th century. It came to Scotland in the 16th century with Mary Stuart, Queen of Scots, who had spent her childhood in France, and among the Scots is still closely identified with the royal house of Stuart. Elsewhere it has lost its uniquely Scottish character. It reached a peak in popularity in the 1950s and 1960s and is still fairly popular. Well-known bearers of the name in recent times have included British footballer Stuart Pearce (b.1962). **Stew**, **Stu** and **Stewie** are common diminutive forms.

Su *See* SUSAN; SUSANNAH.

Subhash (m) Indian name derived from the Sanskrit *su* ('good') and *bhasa* ('speech') and thus meaning 'eloquent'. Notable bearers of the name have included the Indian nationalist leader Subhash Chandra Bose (1897–1945).

Sue *See* SUSAN; SUSANNAH.

Suha (f) Arabic name derived from *suha* ('star').

Suhayl (m) Arabic name derived from *suhayl*, the Arabic name for the star Canopus. Also found as **Suhail**.

Sukie/Suky *See* SUSAN.

Sulayman *See* SOLOMON.

Sullivan (m) Irish first name, also a surname, derived from the Irish Gaelic for 'black-eyed'.

Suman (m) Indian name derived from the Sanskrit *su* ('good') and *manas* ('mind') and thus meaning 'cheerful' or 'well-disposed'.

Sumantra (m) Indian name derived from the Sanskrit *su* ('good') and *mantra* ('advice') and thus meaning 'one who gives good advice'. It is particularly popular in Bengal.

Sumati (f) Indian name derived from *su* ('good') and *mati* ('mind') and thus meaning 'intelligent'. In ancient times it was used mainly as a boys' name, but today it is almost exclusively female.

Summer (f) English first name derived from the name of the season, itself originally a Sanskrit word.

Sunday (f) English first name derived from the day of the week. Never common, this appears to be a 20th-century invention, confined to children born on a Sunday.

Sunder (m) Indian name derived from the Sanskrit *sundara* ('beautiful'). A popular choice of name today, it is also found in such variant forms as **Sundar**, **Sundara**, Sundaram and **Sundaran**.

Sunil (m) Indian name derived from the Sanskrit *su* ('good' or 'very') and *nila* ('dark blue'). It is a relatively recent introduction but is now established as a popular choice of name in northern India.

Sunita (f) Indian name derived from the Sanskrit *su* ('good') and *nita* ('led' or 'conducted') and thus meaning 'of good conduct'. It was used originally as a masculine name but is today reserved for females. Related names include **Suniti**.

Sunny (m) English first name derived from the ordinary vocabulary word 'sunny', suggesting that the bearer has a cheerful, optimistic personality. Clearly influenced by SONNY, this does not appear to date from earlier than the beginning of the 20th century. It may have evolved from the nickname 'Sunny Jim', a familiar form of address for anyone called JAMES.

Suresh (m) Indian name derived from the Sanskrit *sura* ('god') and *isa* ('ruler' or 'lord') and thus meaning 'ruler of the gods'. It is one of the names borne in mythology by INDRA, SHIVA and Vishnu.

Surinder (m) Indian name derived from the Sanskrit *sura* ('god') and *indra* ('mighty') and thus meaning 'mightiest of the gods'. Also found as **Surendra**.

Surya (m) Indian name (pronounced 'sureea') derived from *surya* ('sun'). In mythology it is the name of the sun-god and father of the first man and woman. It may also be found as part of such longer compound names as **Suryakent** and **Suryanarayana**.

Susan (f) English first name derived originally from SUSANNAH but now accepted as an independent name in its own right. It made its first appearances in the 17th century but did not enjoy great popularity until the middle of the 20th century, when it suddenly became a very frequent choice of name. It remained consistently popular for three decades or more before falling from favour in the 1980s. Notable bearers of the name have included the fictional Susan Mountford in Thomas Heywood's tragedy *A Woman Killed with Kindness* (1603), US writer Susan Sontag (b.1933) and British actresses Susan Hampshire (b.1938) and Susan George (b.1950). Occasionally found as **Suzan**. Common diminutives include **Sue** or **Su** – as borne by British writer Sue Townsend (b.1946) and by British actress Su Pollard (b.1949) – as well as **Susie** (or **Suzie**), **Suzy**, **Sukie** and **Suky**.

Susanna *See* SUSANNAH.

Susannah (f) English version of the Hebrew Shushannah, derived from *shoshan* ('lily'). In the Bible Susannah is the wife of Joachim, wrongly suspected of adultery. It was taken up by English speakers as early as the 13th century and remained in currency until the 18th century when it was largely replaced by SUSAN. Well-known bearers of the name in recent times have included British actress Susannah York (b.1941). The name also appears as **Susanna** – as in the Stephen Foster song 'O, Susanna' (1848) – and **Suzanna**. Other variants include **Suzanne** and **Suzette** (both originally French), the German **Susanne**, the Polish **Zuzanna**, and the Hebrew **Shushana** and **Shushanna**. Among diminutives of the name are **Sue** (or **Su**), **Susie**, **Suzie** (or **Suzy**) and the more unusual **Sanna** and **Shanna**.

Sushil (m) Indian name derived from the Sanskrit *su* ('good') and *sila* ('conduct') and thus meaning 'good-tempered'. **Sushila**

(or **Susheela**) is a feminine version of the name.

Susie *See* SUSAN; SUSANNAH.

Suzanne/Suzette *See* SUSANNAH.

Suzie/Suzy *See* SUSAN; SUSANNAH.

Sven (m) Swedish first name derived from the Old Norse *sveinn* ('boy' or 'lad'). It has since spread throughout the German-speaking world and has also reached the USA. Notable bearers of the name in recent times have included Swedish football manager Sven-Goran Eriksson (b.1948). Also found as the Danish **Svend** and the Norwegian **Svein**.

Svetlana (f) Russian first name ultimately derived via the Slavonic *svet* ('light') from the Greek Photine, itself from *photos* ('light'). The Greek form of the name was borne by a 1st-century saint who was put to death in Rome. Sometimes shortened to LANA.

Swaran (m) Indian name derived from the Sanskrit *su* ('good') and *varna* ('colour') and thus meaning 'beautiful in colour'.

Swithin (m) English first name derived from the Old English *swith* ('strong' or 'mighty'). Originally given as Suitha, it dates back to before the Norman Conquest but is very rare today. The most famous bearer of the name was St Swithin (or **Swithun**), the 9th-century bishop of Winchester whose feast day falls on 15 July: according to tradition, if it rains on St Swithin's Day then it will continue to rain for another forty days. This belief has its roots in the legend that when attempts were made to move the saint's remains from their humble resting place outside Winchester cathedral to a more prestigious location inside the building the workers were prevented from completing the task by persistent rain (although curiously a second attempt many years later met with no such difficulties).

Sy *See* CYRUS; SASHA.

Sybella *See* SYBIL.

Sybil (f) English version of the Latin Sibilla, Sibylla, Sybella or Sybilla, derived ultimately from the Greek for 'prophetess'. The name was borne by the prophetesses who were guardians of the oracles at various locations in the ancient world. This essentially pagan name was made acceptable to Christians by St Augustine, who included a sibyl in his work *The City of God*. A sibyl is also said to have predicted the coming of Christ. The name was later taken up by the Normans, and William the Conqueror himself had a daughter-in-law called Sibylla. As Sibylla or **Sibyl**, it remained in common circulation in a variety of forms until the Reformation but then fell into disuse. The publication of Benjamin Disraeli's novel *Sybil* (1845) did much to revive the name (in its modern spelling) in the 19th century. Notable bearers of the name have included the British actress Dame Sybil Thorndike (1882–1976) and the fictional Sybil Fawlty played by Prunella Scales in the 1970s British television comedy series *Fawlty Towers*. Variant spellings include **Sybille** and **Cybill** – a form popularized by US actress Cybill Shepherd (b.1949). Diminutive forms of the name include **Sib** and **Sibb**.

Syd/Sydne/Sydney *See* SIDNEY.

Sylvain *See* SILVANO.

Sylvana *See* SILVANO.

Sylvester (m) English and German first name derived from the Latin for 'wood-dweller' or 'of the woods'. It was the name of several early saints and of three popes. It was first taken up by English speakers in medieval times and has remained in sporadic use ever since. Notable bearers of the name have included US film actor Sylvester Stallone (b.1946). Also found as **Silvester**. Variants in other languages include the Italian **Silvestro** and the Spanish **Silvestre**. **Silvestra** is a rare feminine form. It is occasionally shortened to **Syl** or **Sly**.

Sylvia/Sylvie *See* SILVIA.

T

Tabitha (f) Aramaic name meaning 'doe' or 'gazelle'. It was revived in 17th-century England by the Puritans, inspired by the story of the biblical Tabitha, a worthy and charitable Christian woman of Joppa who was brought back to life by the prayers of St Peter. It has suffered a sharp decline in popularity, however, in the 20th century, perhaps because of the identification of the name with the fictional Tabitha Twitchit, Tom Kitten's mother in the children's stories of Beatrix Potter. Another fictional bearer of the name in relatively recent times was Tabitha Stephens, Elizabeth Montgomery's daughter in the 1960s US television comedy series *Bewitched* – about a beautiful witch attempting to adapt to life in modern US suburbia – and the central character in the sequel *Tabitha*. Also found as **Tabatha**. A Greek equivalent of the name is DORCAS. **Tabbie** and **Tabby** are common diminutive forms.

Tacey (f) English first name derived from the Latin *tacere* ('to be silent'). The Puritans adopted the name in the form **Tace** (meaning 'hush') and it continued in occasional use until the 18th century since when it has become extremely rare. Variant forms include **Tacy** and **Tacita**.

Tad *See* THADDEUS.

Tadhg (m) Irish name (pronounced 'tige', as in 'tiger') meaning 'poet' or 'philosopher'. Common in medieval times, it also appears as **Taig**, **Teige** or **Teague** and may be used by Northern Irish Protestants when referring to Catholics.

Taffy (m) Welsh version of DAVID that has made occasional appearances as a name in its own right. Also widely known as a nickname for anyone with Welsh ancestry, the name evolved from David and its Welsh equivalent **Dafydd** in the 19th century and is variously used as a nickname with either friendly or antagonistic intent. Centuries ago, when English farmers living on the Welsh borders were suffering the depredations of Welsh cattle raids a popular English rhyme ran: 'Taffy was a Welshman, Taffy was a thief, Taffy came to my house and stole a leg of beef'. Also found as **Taff**. Rather curiously, in George du Maurier's novel *Trilby* (1894) the name appears as a familiar form of TALBOT.

Talbot (m) English surname possibly derived from the Old French *taille-botte* ('cleave faggot' or 'cut bundle') or else from obscure Germanic roots, which has also been adopted occasionally as a first name since the 19th century. The name has strong aristocratic connections, being the family name of the earls of Shrewsbury and in medieval times was often given to dogs (the symbol of the aristocratic earls of Shrewsbury is in fact a white dog). A medieval variant of the name was **Talebot**. *See also* TAFFY.

Talfryn (m) Welsh place name derived from the Welsh *tal* ('high') and *bryn* ('hill') that has been adopted as a first name in relatively recent times.

Talia *See* NATALIE; THALIA.

Taliesin (m) Welsh first name (pronounced 'tally-ai-sin') derived from the Welsh *tal* ('high') and *iesin* ('shining') and thus interpreted as meaning 'shining brow'. The most famous bearer of the name was a legendary 6th-century Welsh poet, sometimes credited as the author of the celebrated *Book of Taliesin*. It is very rare today.

Talitha (f) Aramaic name meaning 'little girl' or 'maiden'. It appears in the New Testament as the name of a young girl raised from the dead by Jesus and has made infrequent appearances in the English-speaking world since the mid-19th century.

Tallulah (f) English first name derived from an American Indian place name (Tallulah Falls in Georgia) meaning 'running water'. The most famous bearer of the name to date has been Tallulah Bankhead (1903–68), the beautiful and outrageous US actress and wit who inherited the name from her grandmother. It is sometimes treated as a variant of the Irish Gaelic **Tallula**, from words meaning 'abundance' and 'lady' or 'princess', as borne by two Irish saints.

Tally/Talya *See* NATALIE.

Tam *See* THOMAS.

Tamara (f) Russian version of the Hebrew Tamar, meaning 'palm tree' or 'date palm'. It was introduced to the English-speaking world by the Puritans in the 17th century, and was revived in the 20th century. It is borne in the Old Testament by four women, including a daughter of King David and a sister of Absalom, who is raped by her half-brother Amnon. Perhaps the most influential biblical bearer of the name was Absalom's daughter Tamar, who was praised for her 'fair countenance'. It was also borne by a 12th-century Queen of Georgia and by a demon queen described in verse by Mikhail Lermontov. Lermontov's poem *Tamara* subsequently provided the basis for a ballet with music by the Russian composer Mily Balakirev (1837–1910) – a tragedy depicting the murderous habits of a beautiful Caucasian princess. Other notable bearers of the name have included the Queen of the Goths in William Shakespeare's *Titus Andronicus* (c.1589) and the Russian ballerina Tamara Karsavina (1885–1978). *See also* TAMMY.

Tammy (f) Diminutive form of TAMARA and TAMSIN that is now often considered a name in its own right. Its popularity was much boosted in 1957 when the pop song 'Tammy' (sung by Debbie Reynolds in the film *Tammy and the Bachelor*) topped the US charts for three weeks. Well-known bearers of the name have included US country singer Tammy Wynette (Virginia Wynette Pugh; 1942–98). Also found as **Tammie**. *See also* THOMAS.

Tamsin (f) Cornish version of the medieval Thomasin, Thomasina or Thomasine (a feminine form of THOMAS) that has enjoyed a considerable vogue in popularity since the 1950s. **Tasmin** is a modern variant of the name, probably influenced by JASMINE. Older versions of the name include **Tamsine**, **Tamasine**, **Tamzin** and **Tamzen**. TAMMY is a common diminutive form. Bearers of the name in its various forms have included the fictional Thomasin Yeobright in Thomas Hardy's *The Return of the Native* (1878).

Tancred (m) German first name derived from the Old German Thancharat, itself from the Old German *thank* ('thought') and *rad* ('counsel'). The name came to England with the Normans but has since made only infrequent appearances among English speakers. Notable bearers of the name have included a German hero of the First Crusade, whose adventures were later celebrated in Torquato Tasso's *Gerusalemme Liberata* (1581) and Rossini's opera *Tancredi* (1813) among other works. The usual Italian version of the name is **Tancredo**.

Tania *See* TANYA.

Tanisha (f) English first name derived ultimately from the Hausa for 'born on Monday'.

Tanith (f) First name derived ultimately from that of the Phoenician goddess of love. Also found as **Tanit**, it has made infrequent appearances as a first name in the English-speaking world.

Tansy (f) English first name derived from that of the strongly perfumed colourful yellow garden flower. The original source of the plant name is the Greek *athanasia* ('immortality'). In the 16th century it was customary to scatter tansy flowers and leaves on the floor to perfume the room. Also found as a diminutive form of ANAS-TASIA, its use as a first name dates only from the late 19th century. Instances of the name in fiction have included T. Edwardes' novel *Tansy* (1921).

Tanya (f) Anglicization of the Russian TAT-IANA, which has won acceptance as a name in its own right since the 1940s. The name has increased steadily in popularity into the 1990s. Also found as **Tania**, **Tonya** (also an abbreviated form of ANTONIA) and, in Germany, as **Tanja**.

Tara (f) Irish place name meaning 'hill', which was adopted as a first name by English speakers in the late 19th century. An alternative derivation suggests a link with the Irish earth goddess Temair, whose name means 'dark one'. The castle on the hill of Tara in County Meath was until the 6th century the time-honoured meeting-place of the Irish royal court and the site of coronations; it features prominently in Irish legend. Thomas Moore made the name widely known in the early 19th century through his poem 'The harp that once through Tara's halls' (1807). As a first name, Tara enjoyed a considerable vogue in Canada and the USA after the release of the film *Gone with the Wind* (1939), in which it was the name of the estate inherited by the central character, Scarlett O'Hara. British television audiences of the 1960s were equally likely to know the name from the fictional Tara King in the popular adventure series *The Avengers*. Real-life bearers of the name in recent times have included British actress Tara Fitzgerald (b.1967). It has also made rare appearances as a boy's name.

Tara is also a popular first name for males and females in India, where it is usually traced back to the Sanskrit for 'carrying' or 'saviour' or else from another word meaning 'shining' or 'star' (this last is the usual derivation of the girls' name). The name makes various appearances in re-ligious writings as a name for Vishnu and for a general in Rama's army and also as an alternative name for Shiva's wife DURGA or for Buddha's wife.

Tariq (m) Arabic first name meaning 'one who knocks at the door at night'. The name is borne by the morning star and also by a celebrated 8th-century Berber leader, Tariq ibn Ziyad (d.*c*.720). The place where he landed in Spain in 711 was named Jabal-Tariq in his honour (now called Gibraltar). Sometimes found as **Tari**. Notable bearers of the name in recent times have included Indian-born British political activist Tariq Ali (b.1943).

Tarquin (m) Roman family name of obscure Etruscan origin which remains in occasional use as a first name. Two early Roman kings bore the name. The second of them, Lucius Tarquinius Superbus, went into exile in 510 BC when the Roman Republic was founded. In Arthurian legend, Tarquin makes an appearance as the name of a 'recreant knight'.

Tasgall (m) Scottish Gaelic name derived from the Old Norse *fas* ('god') and *ketill* ('sacrificial cauldron'). The name is particularly associated with the Scottish MacAskill clan and is sometimes spelled **Taskill** by English speakers.

Tasha *See* NATASHA.

Taskill *See* TASGALL.

Tate (m) English first name, also a surname, derived ultimately from the Old Norse for 'cheerful'. Also encountered as **Tait** or **Teyte**.

Tatiana (f) Russian name of uncertain origin that has enjoyed considerable popularity in various forms in the English-speaking world since the early 20th century. It may have Asian roots, although one derivation suggests it comes ultimately from the Roman family name Tatius or else from the Greek *tatto* ('I arrange'). Titus Tatius was, according to legend, joint ruler with Romulus of the Sabine and Latin peoples.

The name was borne by a 3rd-century female Christian martyr and in its masculine form Tatianus by several male saints. The name of William Shakespeare's Titania in *A Midsummer Night's Dream* (*c*.1594) is thought to have been a corrupted form of the Russian original. It was also borne by the fictional Tatiana Larina in Pushkin's novel *Eugene Onegin* (1823–31) and in real life by the Grand Duchess Tatiana (1897–1918), the second daughter of Czar Nicholas II who was executed by the Bolsheviks with the rest of the Russian royal family in Ekaterinburg after the Russian Revolution. Familiar shortened versions of the name include TANYA.

Tawny (f) English first name derived from Old French *tané* ('tanned'). Like GINGER it was traditionally reserved for people with a certain hair colour – in this case brown. Also found as **Tawney**.

Taylor (m/f) English surname that is also in existence as a first name for both sexes. Reserved originally for members of the tailoring profession, it was formerly given only to boys. Notable bearers of the name over the centuries have included British poet Samuel Taylor Coleridge (1772–1834). Also found as **Tayler**.

Teague *See* TADHG.

Teal (f) English first name derived from that of the teal duck. Virtually unknown today, it was recorded in use in Britain as early as the 14th century. Also found as **Teale**.

Teasag *See* JESSIE.

Ted/Teddy *See* EDMUND; EDWARD; THEODORE.

Teena *See* TINA.

Tegan *See* TEGWEN.

Tegwen (f) Welsh first name derived from the Welsh *teg* ('fair' or 'beautiful') and *wen* ('white' or 'blessed'). It appears to have been a relatively modern invention. Variants include **Tegan**.

Teigue *See* TADHG.

Tekla *See* THEKLA.

Tel *See* TERENCE; TERRY.

Temperance (f) English first name that was among the many 'virtue' names that were adopted by the Puritans in the 17th century. It remained in use on both sides of the Atlantic until the late 19th century but is now rarely encountered.

Tempest (f) English first name derived from the ordinary vocabulary word meaning 'severe storm'.

Terence (m) English first name derived ultimately from the Roman Terentius, itself of obscure origin. Terentius was the family name adopted by the Carthaginian-born Roman playwright Terence (Publius Terentius Afer; 185–159 BC), who as a slave borrowed the name from his erstwhile master, senator Terentius Lucanus, out of gratitude when the latter granted him his freedom. It was only widely adopted as a first name among English speakers in the late 19th century and reached a peak in popularity in the 1950s. In Ireland it has been regarded for many years as an Anglicized form of the Gaelic Turlough (meaning 'instigator' or 'one who initiates an idea'). Notable bearers of the name have included British playwright Terence Rattigan (1911–77), British designer Sir Terence Conran (b.1931) and British actor Terence Stamp (b.1938). Also found as **Terance**, **Terrance**, **Terrence** and **Terrell**. Common diminutive forms are **Tel** and TERRY.

Teresa (f) English, Italian and Spanish first name possibly derived ultimately from one of two Greek words variously meaning 'reaper'/'harvest' and 'guarding'/'watching' – or else conceivably derived from the name of the Greek island of Thera. Alternatively spelt **Theresa** or **Theresia,** it was borne by the wife of the 5th-century St Paulinus – the first recorded instance of the name. It was also borne by two well-known Christian saints – St Teresa of Avila (1515–82), a mystic who reformed the Carmelite order, and St Theresa of Lisieux (1873–97), who was credited with various miracles and acts of prophecy before her premature death from tuberculosis. The name was confined chiefly to Italy and Spain until the 16th century, but later spread throughout the Roman Catholic world in response to the popularity of the two saints bearing the name. English speakers adopted the name in the 18th century and it largely lost its Catholic associations in English-speaking countries, reaching a peak in popularity in Britain and elsewhere in the 1960s and 1970s. It has since experienced a marked decline in frequency.

Notable bearers of the name in relatively recent times have included the world-famous Albanian-born Indian missionary Mother Teresa of Calcutta (Agnes Gonxha Bojaxhiu; 1910–97). The usual French form of the name is **Thérèse** – as borne by the French Queen Marie-Thérèse (1638–83) and by the central character in Emile Zola's *Thérèse Raquin* (1867), while the Irish sometimes render it as **Treasa**. Teresa and Theresa are the usual spellings of the name in the UK; Theresa is the usual version in Ireland and the USA. Common diminutives of the name include **Teri**, **Terry**, **Tess**, **Tessie** and TESSA, all of which are sometimes considered to be distinct names in their own right. *See also* TRACY.

Teri *See* TERESA.

Terrell/Terrence *See* TERENCE.

Terry (m) English first name of Germanic origin, derived from words meaning 'tribe' and 'power'. It is also a diminutive form of several other names, including TERENCE, THEODORE and the feminine TERESA. Notable bearers of the name have included Irish radio and television presenter Terry Wogan (b.1938), British theatre director Terry Hands (b.1941) and British football player and manager Terry Venables (b.1943). A French version is **Thierry**. Variant spellings include **Terri** and **Teri**. The name is sometimes shortened to **Tel**.

Tertius (m) Roman first name (pro-

nounced 'tershus') meaning 'third', and thus usually reserved for third-born children. Rare occurrences of the name since classical times have included the doctor in the George Eliot novel *Middlemarch* (1871).

Tess *See* TERESA; TESSA.

Tessa (f) English first name that exists both as a diminutive form of TERESA and as an independent name derived from obscure European (possibly Italian) origins. It made its first appearance among English speakers towards the end of the 19th century. Notable bearers of the name and its variant forms **Tess** and **Tessie** have included the fictional heroine of Thomas Hardy's novel *Tess of the D'Urbervilles* (1891), a character in George Eliot's *Romola* (1863), British comedienne Tessie O'Shea (1914–95) and Jamaican-born British athlete Tessa Sanderson (b.1956).

Tetty *See* ELIZABETH.

Tex (m) English first name derived as an abbreviation of the state name Texas and today in fairly frequent use as a nickname for inhabitants of that state. It is still confined largely to the USA, where notable bearers of the name have included US film actor Tex Ritter (Woodward Ritter; 1905–74) and US cartoon director Tex Avery (Frederick Bean; 1908–80).

Teyve (m) Jewish first name (pronounced 'toyvee') representing a Yiddish version of the Hebrew Tuvia, which is itself a version of Tobias (*see* TOBY). The most famous bearer of the name to date has been the fictional milkman who is the central character in the highly successful musical *Fiddler on the Roof* (1967), as played on stage and film by Topol. Also found as **Teive**.

Thaddeus (m) Hebrew first name possibly meaning 'valiant' or 'wise' or else derived from THEODORE. The name occurs in the New Testament as the name of one of the apostles and has consequently been adopted from time to time in various parts of the English-speaking world since the 19th century. Variants in other languages include the Spanish **Tadeo**, the Portuguese **Tadeu**, the Italian **Taddeo**, the Russian **Faddei** and the Polish **Tadeusz**. The Irish sometimes use the name as an Anglicized form of TADHG. **Tad**, **Thad** and **Thadis** are common diminutive forms.

Thady *See* THADDEUS.

Thalia (f) Greek name derived from the Greek *thallein* ('to flourish'). It was borne by Thalia, the Muse of comedy, and has made occasional appearances among English speakers in the latter half of the 20th century. Also found as **Talia**.

Thane (m) Old English name meaning 'servant'. Thane was originally an Anglo-Saxon title for a noble holding land with the king's permission. In Scotland it was a title borne by clan chiefs. It made its debut as a first name in the 19th century, when there was a considerable fashion for names with apparently ancient English origins.

Thea *See* DOROTHY; THEODORA.

Theda *See* THEODORA.

Thekla (f) English version of the Greek Theokleia, derived from the Greek *theos* ('god') and *kleia* ('glory'). The name was borne by a 1st-century Christian saint who is supposed to have been converted by St Paul and who became the Church's first female martyr. Also found as **Thecla**. A Scandinavian variant is **Tekla**.

Thel *See* ETHEL; THELMA.

Thelma (f) English first name invented by the British popular novelist Marie Corelli (1855–1924) for the Norwegian central character in her novel *Thelma* (1887). It is speculated that Corelli may have based the name on the Greek *thelema* ('will' or 'wish'). The name enjoyed a vogue in the 1920s and 1930s but has since lost ground. Applications of the name in recent years have included the name of one of the leading characters in the US film *Thelma and Louise* (1991). Sometimes shortened to **Thel**.

Thelonius (m) English first name that was taken up initially as a Latinized version of the German Till or Tillo, themselves diminutives of DIETRICH. It is also found as **Thelonious**, in which form it was borne by the celebrated US jazz musician Thelonious Monk (1920–82).

Theo *See* THEOBALD; THEODORE.

Theobald (m) German first name descended from the Old German Theudobald, which was itself derived from Old German *theud* ('people' or 'race') and *bald* ('bold' or 'brave'). An Old English variant was Theodbald. The name featured in the 'Domesday Book' and was borne by a 12th-century Archbishop of Canterbury. It continued to be found fairly regularly among English speakers through medieval times, often in such variants as Tebald, Tibald, Tedbald, Tibert and Tybalt – in which form it was chosen by William Shakespeare for a character in his play *Romeo and Juliet* (1591–6). The use of the name for the cat in the medieval French fable *Reynard the Fox* led to the diminutive forms **Tibby** and **Tibs**, now common cat names. The usual diminutive form for human bearers of the name is **Theo**.

Theodora (f) Feminine version of THEODORE, itself meaning 'God's gift'. It shares the same roots as Dorothea (*see* DOROTHY), with the two parts of the name put in reverse order. The name was borne by the beautiful but notorious wife of the Byzantine Emperor Justinian I (500–548) and also by the wife of the 9th-century Roman Emperor Theophilus. It was first adopted by English speakers in the 17th century but has never been very common. A related variant is **Theodosia,** which has similarly made occasional appearances in the English-speaking world since the 17th century. A character named Theodosia appears in William Makepeace Thackeray's novel *The Virginians* (1857–9). The two forms of the name are sometimes abbreviated to **Thea**, DORA or **Theda** – as borne by the US film actress Theda Bara (Theodosia Goodman;

1890–1955). The usual form of the name in Russia is **Fedora** (or **Feodora**).

Theodore (m) English first name derived from the Greek *theos* ('god') and *doron* ('gift') and thus interpreted as meaning 'God's gift'. The name was popular with early Christians and was borne by no less than twenty-eight saints, including St Theodore of Canterbury (602–90). Because it was so closely associated with saints, the name was not favoured by the Puritans in the 17th century, but it enjoyed a resurgence in popularity on both sides of the Atlantic in the 19th century and has since continued to make regular appearances, often in the abbreviated form **Theo**. In the USA the name is commonly shortened to **Ted** or **Teddy**. In Russia it usually appears as **Fyodor** (sometimes shortened to **Fedya**) – as borne by the celebrated Russian novelist Fyodor Dostoevsky (1821–81). The most famous bearers of the name have included a leading character in Horace Walpole's *The Castle of Otranto* (1764) and US President Theodore Roosevelt (1858–1919), after whom the 'teddy bear' was named – apparently after he declined to shoot a small bear tied up for him to make an easy kill when out hunting. *See also* TERRY; THADDEUS; THEODORA; TUDOR.

Theodoric (m) Old German name meaning 'ruler of the people'. An Old English version was Theodric, from which came the medieval French name **Thierry**. The name was adopted sporadically in Britain in the 18th century but subsequently fell out of use among English speakers. The most notable bearer of the name was Theodoric the Great, the 6th-century King of the Ostrogoths. *See also* DEREK.

Theodosia *See* THEODORA.

Theophania *See* TIFFANY.

Theophila *See* THEOPHILUS.

Theophilus (m) Greek first name derived from the Greek *theos* ('god') and *philos* ('loving' or 'friend') and thus variously interpreted as meaning 'loved by God' or 'one

who loves God'. It features in the New Testament as the name of the recipient of St Luke's Gospel and the Acts of the Apostles and was also borne by two saints – a 2nd-century Bishop of Antioch and the 9th-century Greek St Theophilus of Nicomedia. The name was taken up by the Puritans in the 16th century but has never been a very popular choice in the English-speaking world. It was borne by the fictional Revd Theophilus Grantly in Anthony Trollope's *Barchester* novels and in the 1980s British television comedian Lenny Henry (b.1958) turned the name to comedic purposes in the guise of the 'hip' sex symbol Theophilus P. Wildebeest. An equally rare feminine version of the name is **Theophila**. Often shortened to **Theo**. *See also* FILAT.

Theresa/Thérèse *See* TERESA.

Thierry *See* THEODORIC.

Thirsa *See* THIRZA.

Thirza (f) English first name descended from the Hebrew Tirzah, which may have had its origins in a place name or else in Hebrew words meaning 'acceptance' or 'pleasantness'. The name was taken up by the Puritans in the 17th century, since when it has appeared only sporadically. Also found as **Thirsa**.

Thom *See* THOMAS.

Thomas (m) English first name derived via the Greek Didymos from the Aramaic for 'twin'. The name appears several times in the Bible, notably as the name of one of the apostles – 'Doubting Thomas', who was originally called Judas but acquired his new name to differentiate him from Judas Iscariot and Jude. According to the New Testament account, Thomas was one of twins. Prior to the Norman Conquest the name was largely reserved in England for clergymen. It was further revered for its religious connections in medieval times as the name of the English martyr St Thomas à Becket (1118–70), who was famously put to death by knights acting on behalf of Henry II, as that of the English theologian

St Thomas Aquinas (1225–74), and later as that of Sir Thomas More (1478–1535), who was executed for opposing Henry VIII's Reformation, and became a Catholic saint.

Commonly shortened since medieval times to **Tom** or **Tommy** (or more unusually **Thom**), the name has long been a favourite choice of forename among English speakers (as its inclusion in the proverbial 'Tom, Dick and Harry' list of archetypal boys' names shows). After something of a decline between the 1960s and the 1980s, it reclaimed its long-established place high in lists of the top ten names for boys in the 1990s.

Notable bearers of the name over the centuries have included British poet Thomas Gray (1716–71), British artist Thomas Gainsborough (1727–88), US Presidents Thomas Jefferson (1743–1826) and Thomas Woodrow Wilson (1856–1924), British novelist Thomas Hardy (1840–1928), Anglo-American poet Thomas Stearns Eliot (1888–1965), Welsh singer Tom Jones (b.1940), British pop singer and actor Tommy Steele (b.1936) and US film actor Tom Cruise (b.1962). Fictional bearers of the name have included the central character in Henry Fielding's novel *Tom Jones* (1749), Thomas the Tank Engine in the children's stories of the Revd W. Awdry and Tom the Cat in the *Tom and Jerry* cartoons. In the 19th century 'Thomas Atkins' was written on army enlistment forms as a specimen signature and consequently 'Tommy Atkins' and simply 'Tommy' became well-known nicknames for British soldiers.

Scottish variants of the name include **Tammy** or **Tam** – as borne by the central character in Robert Burns' celebrated poem 'Tam o'Shanter' – and **Tomas**. Versions in other languages include the Italian **Tommaso**, the Russian **Foma** and the Dutch **Maas**.

Thomasina *See* TAMSIN.

Thora (f) Scandinavian name derived from Thor, as borne by the Norse god of thunder. It appeared only infrequently among English speakers before the 20th century and is today indelibly associated with the veteran British film and television actress Dame Thora Hird (1913–2003). Historical variants of the name included **Thyra** and **Tyra**.

Thorley (m) English place name meaning 'thorn wood' that was subsequently adopted as a surname and occasional first name. It has made rare appearances as a first name among English speakers since the 19th century.

Thornton (m) English place name meaning 'settlement among the thorns' that was subsequently adopted both as a surname and occasional first name. Notable bearers of the name have included the US writer Thornton Wilder (1897–1975).

Thurstan (m) English place name derived from the Old Norse for 'Thor's stone' that was subsequently taken up as a surname and occasional first name. Also spelled **Thurston**, the name came to England with the Vikings and made rare appearances as a first name from the 19th century. *See also* DUSTIN.

Thyra *See* THORA.

Tia (f) English first name that evolved as a diminutive of various longer names, such as LETITIA.

Tiarnan (m) Irish first name derived from the Gaelic for 'lord'. Also found in the forms **Tiernan** and **Tierney**.

Tibby *See* ISABEL; THEOBALD.

Tibor (m) Hungarian first name descended from the Latin Tiberius, derived from the name of the River Tiber (itself of obscure meaning). As Tiberius the name was borne by an early Roman emperor and also by a Christian martyr executed under the Emperor Diocletian in 303.

Tiernan *See* TIARNAN.

Tiffany (f) English first name derived via the French variant Titaine from the Greek Theophania, itself from the Greek *theos* ('god') and *phainein* ('to appear') and thus interpreted as meaning 'manifestation of God'. It was traditionally reserved for girls born on the feast of Epiphany (6 January), which celebrates the young Christ's visit to the Temple, but is bestowed fairly indiscriminately today. Relatively common in medieval times, it subsequently fell into disuse before enjoying a lasting resurgence in popularity in the wake of the success of the film *Breakfast at Tiffany's* (1961), starring Audrey Hepburn – Tiffany's being the name of a select jewellery shop in New York. Sometimes shortened to **Tiff**, **Tiffy** or **Tiffie**.

Tiger Lily *See* LILY.

Tilda/Tilly *See* MATILDA.

Tim *See* TIMOTHY.

Timon (m) Greek name derived from *time* ('honour') that has made occasional appearances among English speakers as a fanciful variant of TIMOTHY in relatively recent times. It is widely known as the name of the central character in William Shakespeare's *Timon of Athens* (c.1607).

Timothy (m) English first name derived ultimately from the Greek Timotheos, itself from the Greek *time* ('honour') and *theos* ('god') and thus interpreted as meaning 'honouring God' or 'honoured by God'. The name was borne by a biblical saint, a close companion of St Paul who was later stoned to death in AD 97 when he spoke out against the worship of the goddess Diana. The name was apparently unknown in England prior to the Reformation and enjoyed a peak in popularity between 1950 and 1980, although it has gone into something of a decline in recent years. **Timothea** is a rare feminine version of the name. Common diminutives include **Tim**, as borne by Tiny Tim in Charles Dickens' *A Christmas Carol* (1843), and **Timmy**, in which form it was borne by the fictional Timmy Tiptoes, the foolish squirrel in Beatrix Potter's *The Tale of Timmy Tiptoes* (1911). Other famous bearers of the name have included British actor

Timothy West (b.1934), British lyricist Sir Tim Rice (b.1944) and British tennis player Tim Henman (b.1974). *See also* TIMON.

Tina (f) English first name that evolved as a diminutive of CHRISTINA and other names ending '-tina' and has long enjoyed acceptance as a name in its own right. First adopted by English speakers in the 19th century, it reached a peak in popularity among English speakers in the 1960s and 1970s and is also a popular choice in Scandinavia. Famous bearers of the name have included US rock singer Tina Turner (Annie Mae Bullock; b.1939). Occasionally found as **Teena**.

Tirzah *See* THIRZA.

Tish/Tisha *See* LATISHA; LETITIA.

Titty *See* LETITIA.

Titus (m) Roman first name of uncertain origin, possibly derived from the Latin *titulus* ('title of honour') and thus interpreted as meaning 'honoured'. St Titus was a disciple of St Paul, and another notable bearer of the name in ancient times was the Roman Emperor Titus Flavius Vespasianus (40–81). The name was adopted by English speakers after the Reformation and was borne by, among others, the 17th-century English conspirator Titus Oates (1649–1705), whose involvement in the Popish Plot against Charles II may have been responsible for the name failing to become a great favourite among the British. It was also borne in fiction by the central character in William Shakespeare's tragedy *Titus Andronicus* (1590–94) and, in the 20th century, by Titus Groan, the central character in the *Gormenghast* trilogy (1946–59) by British novelist Mervyn Peake. Variants in other languages include **Tito**, the usual version of the name in Italy, Portugal, Spain and several other continental European countries.

Tobias/Tobin *See* TOBY.

Toby (m) English version of the Hebrew Tobias (meaning 'the Lord is good'). The biblical tale of 'Tobias and the Angel' – in which Tobias earns the help of an angel and returns home very rich – did much to ensure the name's popularity in medieval times (the traditional English puppet character Punch's dog is called Toby in reference to this story). The name also features in William Langland's poem *Piers Plowman* (late 14th century) but does not appear to have become widely popular until after the Reformation. It enjoyed a marked revival in popularity in the 1980s and 1990s. Famous bearers of the name have included the fictional Sir Toby Belch in William Shakespeare's *Twelfth Night* (1601), Uncle Toby in Laurence Sterne's *Tristram Shandy* (1759–67) and the British novelist Tobias Smollett (1721–71), author of *Roderick Random* among other books. The decorative mugs called Toby jugs are supposed to have got their name from the fictional Toby Philpot, who appeared in a poem (1761) adapted by Francis Fawkes from a Latin original. Variants include **Tobin**.

Todd (m) English surname derived from a dialect word meaning 'fox' that has made occasional appearances as a first name into modern times. It enjoyed a considerable vogue during the 1970s, especially in Canada and the USA where it ranked among the fifty most popular boys' names. Also encountered as **Tod**. Well-known bearers of the name have included US actor Tod Andrews (1920–72) and British television actor Todd Carty (b.1963).

Toinette *See* ANTOINETTE.

Tolly *See* BARTHOLOMEW.

Tom/Tomas/Tommy *See* THOMAS.

Toni *See* ANTOINETTE; ANTONIA.

Tonia *See* ANTONIA; TANYA.

Tony *See* ANTHONY.

Tonya *See* ANTONIA; TANYA.

Topaz (f) English jewel name that has made occasional appearances as a first name since the late 19th century. During medi-

eval times the name was sometimes encountered as a variant of the boys' name **Tobias**. Also found as **Topaze**.

Topsy (f) English first name of obscure origin. One derivation suggests it evolved from the word 'topsail' and thus became associated with the Black slaves formerly transported in sailing ships from Africa to the Americas. Harriet Beecher Stowe's selection of the name for the Black orphan slave girl in her novel *Uncle Tom's Cabin* (1852) supports this theory, but her sentimental and patronizing attitude towards race relations tended to limit the name's appeal for subsequent generations. It has, however, made a reappearance in relatively recent times in the *Topsy and Tim* books for young children.

Torcall *See* TORQUIL.

Toria *See* VICTORIA.

Torkel *See* TORQUIL.

Tormod *See* NORMAN.

Torquil (m) Scottish version (pronounced 'torkwil') of the Old Norse Thorketill (meaning 'Thor's cauldron'). The name came to Britain with the Danes and also entered Gaelic culture as **Torcall**, **Torcul** or **Torcail**, being adopted in the Outer Hebrides and especially by members of the Scottish Macleod clan, who claim descent from a man named Torquil. A character named Torquil of the Oak appears in Sir Walter Scott's *The Fair Maid of Perth* (1828). **Torkel** is another variant.

Tory *See* VICTORIA.

Totty *See* CHARLOTTE.

Tracey *See* TRACY.

Tracy (m/f) French place name (meaning 'place of Thracius') that was subsequently adopted as a surname and, from the early 19th century, as a first name in the English-speaking world. Another derivation suggests it also evolved as a diminutive of TERESA. The name was borne originally by boys as well as girls, but is now virtually unknown as a masculine name. The fact that it is a relatively recent introduction may have been in part the result of a long-standing prejudice against the name since it was borne by William de Tracy, the leader of the four knights who murdered St Thomas à Becket in Canterbury Cathedral in 1170. Because of this misdeed, anyone who bears the name Tracy is, according to time-honoured superstition, fated to have the wind always blowing in their faces.

The name enjoyed a considerable boost in popularity in the 1940s and 1950s following the release of the highly successful films *The Philadelphia Story* (1940) and *High Society* (1956), respectively starring Katharine Hepburn and Grace Kelly in the role of heiress Tracy Samantha Lord. It may also have benefited from the popularity of US film star Spencer Tracy (1900–1967) and of the fictional US detective Dick Tracy during the same era. Having maintained its popular status through the 1960s and 1970s, when the more usual spelling was **Tracey**, it suffered a sharp decline and is now rare among the young. **Tracie** is another variant form. Well-known bearers of the name have included US tennis player Tracy Austin (b.1962), British comedienne Tracey Ullman (b.1959) and US rock singer-songwriter Tracy Chapman (b.1964). **Trace** is a common diminutive form.

Trafford (m) English first name of Germanic origin meaning 'dweller beyond the ford'. It enjoyed some exposure in the early 1980s through the Claire Luckham play *Trafford Tanzi* (1980), in which the central character is a female wrestler.

Trahearn (m) Welsh first name derived from the Welsh *haearn* ('iron'). Also found as **Traherne**.

Travers *See* TRAVIS.

Travis (m) English surname meaning 'toll-keeper' or 'crossing', that emerged as a popular first name in the late 20th century. Also spelled **Travers**, the name came originally from the French *traverser* ('to cross').

By the 1970s the name ranked among the fifty most popular boys' names in Australia and was also well established in the USA.

Treasa *See* TERESA.

Trefor *See* TREVOR.

Tremaine (m) Cornish first name, also a surname, meaning 'homestead on the rock'. Also encountered as **Tremayne**.

Trent (m) English place name (from the River Trent in northwest England) that was subsequently adopted as a surname and occasional first name. The name of the river came originally from a Celtic source meaning 'trespasser' (a reference to the river's tendency to flood). As a first name, Trent is more commonly encountered in Canada and the USA than it is on the British side of the Atlantic.

Trev *See* TREVOR.

Trevelyan (m) English place name derived from the local Cornish name Elian and the Cornish dialect word *tref* ('settlement'), and thus interpreted as meaning 'place of Elian', that has made occasional appearances over the centuries both as a surname and first name. Its use is still largely confined to Cornwall.

Trevor (m) Welsh place name – originally Trefor – derived from the Welsh words *tref* ('homestead') and *mawr* ('great'), which was subsequently adopted both as a surname and, from the 1860s, as a first name among both Welsh and English speakers. It enjoyed a peak in popularity around the middle of the 20th century. Notable bearers of the name have included British actor Trevor Howard (1916–88), whose success in the popular romantic film *Brief Encounter* (1945) did much to popularize the name in the years following the Second World War, British television newsreader Trevor McDonald (b.1939) and British footballer and sports commentator Trevor Francis (b.1954). The usual diminutive form of the name is **Trev**.

Tricia *See* PATRICIA.

Trilby (f) English first name apparently derived from the Italian for 'to sing with trills'. It was invented by the British novelist George du Maurier for the central character – a singer – in his novel *Trilby* (1894) and it has made infrequent appearances as a first name since then. It was du Maurier's character, incidentally, who inspired the name of the trilby hat.

Trina *See* CATRIONA.

Tris *See* BEATRICE; TRISTRAM.

Trish/Trisha *See* PATRICIA.

Triss *See* BEATRICE.

Tristan *See* TRISTRAM.

Tristram (m) English version of the Celtic Drystan, itself derived from the Celtic *drest* or *drust* (meaning 'din' or 'tumult') or alternatively (possibly via Old French) from the Latin *tristis* ('sad'). As Tristram the name made its first appearance in England in the 12th century. It was borne by Sir Tristram of Lyoness, one of the most noble of King Arthur's legendary knights of the Round Table. The tragic story of Sir Tristram and his fatal passion for Princess Isolda, who was betrothed to King Mark of Cornwall but fell in love with Tristram after they both accidentally drank a love potion intended for the betrothed couple, was later celebrated by Alfred, Lord Tennyson in his *The Idylls of the King* (1859), which further promoted the popularity of the name. Wagner also based his opera *Tristan und Isolde* (1865) on the legend, which may originally have come from the French (thus supporting a French origin for the name). Instances of the name elsewhere in fiction have included the central character in Laurence Sterne's picaresque novel *Tristram Shandy* (1759–67) and one of the central characters in the comical vet stories of James Herriott (d.1995). In recent years **Tristan** has tended to replace Tristram as the usual version of the name. Also found as **Tristran** and **Trystan**. **Tris** is a common diminutive form.

Trix/Trixie *See* BEATRIX.

Troy (m) Norman French surname derived from the name of the French city of Troyes that is occasionally encountered among English speakers as a first name. Another derivation suggests the name comes from the Irish for 'foot soldier' or else from a phrase meaning 'from the place of the people with curly hair'. The romantic association of the name with that of the ancient city besieged by the Greeks for ten years, as celebrated by Homer, has undoubtedly done much to keep the name in use. The name is especially popular today in Australia and the USA but remains rare in the UK. Well-known bearers of the name in fiction have ranged from Sergeant Troy in Thomas Hardy's *Far From the Madding Crowd* (1874) to Troy Tempest, the hero of Gerry Anderson's 1960s puppet adventure television series *Stingray*.

Trudy (f) Diminutive form of GERTRUDE, meaning 'ruler of the spear', or alternatively of ERMINTRUDE ('wholly beloved'), that is now widely accepted among English speakers as a first name in its own right. Also found as **Trudi** and **Trudie**.

Truman (m) English surname derived from the Old English *treowe* ('true' or 'trusty') and *mann* ('man'), and thus meaning 'trusty man', that has also made occasional appearances as a first name. It is little used outside the USA, where notable bearers of the name have included the writer Truman Capote (1924–84). Also found as **Trueman**.

Tryphena (f) English first name derived from the Greek for 'daintiness' or 'delicacy'. It features in the New Testament and has made occasional appearances among English speakers since the Reformation. Well-known bearers of the name have included Tryphena Sparks, the girl with whom British novelist Thomas Hardy fell in love as a young man.

Trystan *See* TRISTRAM.

Tudor (m) Welsh first name that is often

erroneously treated as a version of THEO-
DORE, a name of Greek origin meaning
'God's gift', but which is more correctly
assumed to be a development of the Celtic
Teutorix (meaning 'people's ruler'). Also
found in Wales in the form **Tudur**, it has
strong royal connections as the name of the
royal house of Tudor, beginning with Henry
VII (1457–1509) and ending with the death
of Elizabeth I in 1603.

Tuesday (f) English first name based on
the day of the week and usually reserved
for children born on that day. Well-known
bearers of the name have included US film
actress Tuesday Weld (b.1943).

Turlough See TERENCE.

Ty See TYRONE.

Tybalt See THEOBALD.

Tycho (m) Scandinavian first name (pronounced 'tye-ko') derived from the Greek

tychon ('hitting the mark'). Notable bearers
of the name have included the Danish astronomer Tycho Brahe (1546–1601).
Variant forms include **Tyko**, **Tyge** and the
Russian **Tikhon**.

Tyler (m/f) English surname originally denoting a worker employed to tile roofs that
has also made occasional appearances as a
first name. Famous bearers of the name in
relatively recent times have included US
film actress Mary Tyler Moore (b.1936). Also
encountered as **Tylar**.

Tyra See THORA.

Tyrone (m) Irish county name, meaning
'Eoghan's (or Owen's) land', which was subsequently adopted as a surname and occasional first name, chiefly in Ireland and
the USA. Celebrated bearers of the name
have included US film star Tyrone Power
(1913–58) and British theatre director and
critic Tyrone Guthrie (1900–1971). Sometimes shortened to **Ty** or **Tye**.

U

Udo (m) German first name meaning 'prosperous'.

Uilleam *See* WILLIAM.

Ulf *See* WOLF.

Ulick *See* ULYSSES; WILLIAM.

Ulrica (f) Scandinavian first name that developed as a feminine version of the masculine Ulric, itself derived from the Norse Wulfric (meaning 'wolf ruler'). The name Ulric was borne by three saints, but it is the feminine form that is more often encountered today. Variant forms include the Scandinavian **Ulrika**, popularized in the 1990s through Swedish-born British television personality Ulrika Jonsson (b.1967). The name is sometimes abbreviated to **Ulla**.

Ulrich (m) German first name meaning 'fortune and power'.

Ulysses (m) Roman version of the Greek Odysseus, famous as the name of the legendary Greek hero of Homer's *Odyssey*. The name (possibly meaning 'hater' in the original Greek) is rarely encountered outside Ireland, where diminutive forms include **Ulick**, although it is occasionally encountered in the USA in tribute to US President Ulysses S. Grant (1822–85). In modern literature the name has been immortalized by James Joyce in his novel *Ulysses* (1922). Variants include the Italian **Ulisse** and the Spanish **Ulises**.

Uma (f) English first name that appears to have made its first appearance towards the end of the 19th century in a story entitled 'The Beach of Falesa' by Robert Louis Stevenson. Famous bearers of the name have included US film actress Uma Thurman (b.1970).

Umar (m) Arabic name meaning 'populous' or 'flourishing'. Also encountered as OMAR, this is one of the most common names in the Arab world. The name recalls Umar ibn-al-Khattab (*c*.581–644), who was one of Muhammad's most loyal followers.

Umberto *See* HUMBERT.

Una (f) Irish and Scottish first name possibly derived from the Irish *uan* ('lamb') or else from the Latin *unus* ('one'). Also encountered as JUNO, **Ona**, **Oonagh** and **Oona**, the name features prominently in Edmund Spenser's epic poem *The Faerie Queene* (1596), in which the character Una represents the unity of religion. Well-known bearers of the name in recent times have included British television personality Una Stubbs (b.1937).

Undine (f) Roman first name (pronounced 'undeen') derived from the Latin for 'of the waves'. The legendary Undine was a watersprite who sought to win a soul by bearing a child by a human husband and thus became acquainted with all the perils of a mortal existence.

Unice *See* EUNICE.

Unity (f) English first name derived ultimately from the Latin *unus* ('one'). It was enthusiastically adopted along with other 'virtue' names by English Puritans in the 16th and 17th centuries, although it is relatively uncommon today. Famous bearers of the name have included Unity Mitford (1914–48), the English socialite who attracted notoriety for her links with top German Nazis before the Second World War.

Upton (m) English place name derived from the Old English for 'upper settlement' or 'town on the heights' that was subsequently adopted as a surname and first name. It has been used as a first name since the 19th century. Among the best-known bearers of the name has been US novelist Upton Sinclair (1878–1968).

Urban (m) Roman first name derived from the Latin *urbanus* ('citizen'). In the New Testament St Paul addresses Urban in his letter to the Romans and the name was subsequently borne by several saints and eight popes. The name has been adopted in many countries, including Scandinavia and England. A feminine equivalent is **Urbana**.

Uri (m) Hebrew first name meaning 'light'. The most famous bearer of the name in recent years has been Israeli illusionist Uri Geller (b.1943).

Uriah (m) Hebrew name meaning 'God is light'. The name appears in the Bible as that of a Hittite warrior betrayed by King David and was revived by English Puritans in the 17th century and once again in the early 19th century. Today it is indelibly associated with Uriah Heep, the obsequious clerk in the Charles Dickens novel *David Copperfield* (1849–50), and has consequently been long out of favour (although a rock band of the 1970s chose Uriah Heep as their name). *See also* URIEL.

Uriel (m) Hebrew name meaning 'God is light'. The name appears in the Bible, but is today confined mostly to the Jewish community, although it is not unknown in English and American literature, featuring in both John Milton's *Paradise Lost* (1667) and Henry Wadsworth Longfellow's *The Golden Legend* (1851). *See also* URIAH.

Ursula (f) English, German and Scandi-navian first name derived from the Latin *ursa*, and meaning 'little she-bear'. Also used as a feminine equivalent of ORLANDO, the name enjoyed some popularity among English speakers in medieval times under the influence of the legend of the 4th-century St Ursula, Cornish leader of a doomed crusade who was martyred by the Huns alongside her 11,000 female companions (or just eleven, as the figure of 11,000 may have been the result of an early mistranslation) when she reached Cologne. Well-known Ursulas of more recent times have included the US science-fiction writer Ursula Le Guin (b.1929) and Swiss-born film actress Ursula Andress (b.1936). Notable Ursulas in literature have included characters in William Shakespeare's plays *Two Gentlemen of Verona* (1592–3) and *Much Ado About Nothing* (1598–9), the heroine in Mrs Craik's *John Halifax, Gentleman* (1856) and Ursula Brangwen in D. H. Lawrence's *The Rainbow* (1915). Occasionally encountered as **Ursella**. Diminutive forms include **Urse** and **Ursie**.

Usha (f) Indian name derived from the Sanskrit for 'dawn'. In the Rig-Veda dawn is described as the beautiful daughter of heaven. The name also features in the legend of the demon princess Usha, who falls in love with Vishnu's grandson Aniruddha. The popularity of the name in Britain was bolstered in the 1990s when it was borne by a character in the long-running radio soap opera *The Archers*.

Uthman (m) Arabic name meaning 'baby bustard'. Frequently encountered throughout the Islamic world, the name recalls the caliph Uthman ibn-Affan (*c*.574–656), Muhammad's son-in-law. Centuries later the name was adopted by the Ottomans.

V

Vadim (m) Russian first name of uncertain origin, though possibly a variant of VLA-DIMIR. The name has been in use since medieval times.

Val *See* PERCIVAL; VALENTINE; VALERIE.

Valary *See* VALERIE.

Valda (f) German first name derived from the Old German *vald* ('power' or 'rule'). It has never been very common and may be a 20th-century invention. VELDA is a variant. The equivalent name for men is WALDO.

Valdemar *See* WALDEMAR.

Valentina *See* VALENTINE.

Valentine (m/f) English and French first name derived ultimately from the Latin *valens* ('strong' or 'healthy'). St Valentine was a 3rd-century martyr who was executed under the Roman Emperor Claudius II around AD 269, reportedly for opposing a prohibition against young men of soldiering age being allowed to marry. His feast day is celebrated on 14 February. The name is inextricably linked with romance and St Valentine's Day has long been a day for lovers to exchange unsigned cards and gifts (this tradition actually predates Valentine and has its origins in celebrations connected with the goddess Juno).

The earliest records of Valentine being in use as a first name in England date back to the 13th century and it has always been applied to members of both sexes (though less commonly now for girls). Famous bearers of the name have included British actor Valentine Dyall (1908–85), otherwise known as radio's 'Man in Black'. Literary instances of the name have included the medieval French romance *Valentine and Orson*, which tells the adventures of twin

brothers: Valentine is raised at the court of King Pepin and eventually marries the sister of a giant. There are also characters named Valentine in William Shakespeare's plays *Two Gentlemen of Verona* (1592–3) and *Twelfth Night* (1601) and in J. M. Barrie's play *Quality Street* (1902). **Valentia** and **Valentina** – as borne by Soviet cosmonaut Valentina Tereshkova (b.1937) – are feminine variants of the name. A diminutive form is **Val**, as borne in recent times by Irish singer Val Doonican (b.1932) and US film actor Val Kilmer (b.1959).

Valeria *See* VALERIE.

Valerie (f) English and French first name descended ultimately from the Latin name Valeria (from the Latin for 'strong' or 'healthy'). The name was borne by a powerful Roman family and by an early Christian saint (the French St Valeria) long before it was introduced to the English-speaking world in the 17th century, when it appeared initially as Valeria. By the end of the 19th century Valeria had largely given way to the French variant Valerie. The name reached a peak in popularity between the two world wars. Notable bearers of the name have included British film actress Valerie Hobson (1917–98) and British television presenter Valerie Singleton (b.1937). Variants include **Valarie**, **Valery** and **Valary**. The most common diminutive is **Val**; less common abbreviated forms include **Vallie**.

Van (m) First name of unknown origin, possibly descended from VANCE or IVAN. When treated as a prefix to a surname it means 'of' or 'from' in Dutch. Famous bearers of the name have included US actor Van Heflin (Emmett Evan Heflin; 1910–71) and Northern Ireland singer-songwriter Van Morrison (George Ivan Morrison; b.1945).

Vance (m) English surname derived from the Old English for 'fen-dweller', which was subsequently taken up as a surname and occasional first name. Sometimes shortened to VAN.

Vanda *See* WANDA.

Vanessa (f) English first name that began life as an invention of the poet and satirist Jonathan Swift (1667–1745). Dean Swift devised the name when writing to his close friend Esther Vanhomrigh, taking 'Van' from Vanhomrigh and 'Essa' from Esther. The name became popular after the publication of his poems *Cadenus and Vanessa* (1713), 'Cadenus' being an anagram of *Decanus*, the Latin for 'dean' and thus his own poetical name for himself. Hugh Walpole also gave the name to a central character in his historical novels *Judith Paris* (1931), *The Fortress* (1932) and *Vanessa* (1933) and in recent years the name has been encountered with increasing frequency in Australia, Canada and other parts of the English-speaking world. Famous bearers of the name since Swift's day have included British painter Vanessa Bell (1879–1961) and British actress Vanessa Redgrave (b.1937). Variants of the name include **Vanetta** and **Venessa**. Common diminutives are **Nessa**, **Nessie** and **Vanny**.

Vanya *See* IVAN.

Varda (f) Hebrew first name meaning 'rose'. Also found in the variant form **Vardah**.

Vasant (m) Indian name derived from the Sanskrit *vasanta* ('spring'). In Indian mythology Spring is the close companion of Kama, the god of love. The name was popular in medieval times and is sometimes a component of longer names, such as **Vasantakumar**. Variants include the Bengali **Basant** and the feminine version **Vasanta**.

Vasco (m) Spanish, Portuguese and Italian first name derived from the medieval Velasco or Belasco. The medieval forms of the name are thought to have evolved from the Basque for 'crow'.

Vashti (f) Persian name meaning 'beautiful' or 'best'. A biblical name, it was adopted by English Puritans after the Reformation but has never ranked among the most popular European names.

Vasili *See* BASIL.

Vasu (m) Indian first name derived from the Sanskrit *vasu* ('bright' or 'excellent'). The name of several Indian deities, including a son of Krishna, it was also borne by one of the authors of the Rig-Veda. It is sometimes treated as an abbreviation of **Vasudeva**, one of the alternative names for Vishnu. Variants include the Bengali **Basu**.

Vaughan (m/f) Welsh surname (pronounced 'vorn') derived from the Welsh *fychan* ('small' or 'little one') that has been in use as a first name since the 19th century. The name is rarely used for girls except in the USA. Famous bearers of the name have included the British composer Ralph Vaughan Williams (1872–1958). Also found as **Vaughn**.

Velda (f) German first name meaning 'inspired' or 'wise', or possibly a variant of VALDA. It has never been in frequent use.

Velma *See* WILHELMINA.

Velvet (f) English first name inspired by the luxurious soft cloth of the same name.

Venetia (f) English first name derived from the Latin name for the city of Venice. A less likely explanation suggests that it developed rather tortuously from the Welsh name GWYNETH. As a first name, Venetia first appeared in the 16th century, when noted bearers of the name included the celebrated beauty Venetia Stanley, the wife of courtier Sir Kenelm Digby who is said to have drunk 'viper wine' to preserve her admired appearance. After her premature death at the age of thirty-three she acquired literary immortality as the subject of poems by Ben Jonson and others. Four centuries later Benjamin Disraeli wrote a novel entitled *Venetia* (1837) and the name enjoyed renewed popularity.

Venkat (m) Indian first name derived from the Sanskrit Venkata, the name of a sacred hill near Madras and the site of one of the most important holy shrines in India. The name was also borne by a celebrated king of Vijayanagara in medieval times and is today sometimes found as a component of longer names, such as **Venkatesh** and **Venkataraman**.

Venus (f) Roman name for the goddess of love. It has only rarely been adopted among English speakers as a first name, appearing infrequently in this role ever since the 16th century. Well-known bearers of the name in modern times have included the 1990s US tennis star Venus Williams (b.1980).

Vera (f) English first name derived either from the Russian *viera* ('faith') or else from the Latin *verus* ('true'). The name – sometimes treated as a diminutive of VERONICA – was taken up in the English-speaking world in the 19th century, promoted by characters of the same name in the novels *Moths* (1880), by the British novelist Ouida, *A Cigarette-Maker's Romance* (1890), by Marion Crawford, and *Vera* (1921), by Elizabeth von Arnim. It has undergone something of a decline since reaching a peak in the 1920s, however. Famous bearers of the name have included British novelist Vera Brittain (1893–1970) and British wartime singer Dame Vera Lynn (b.1917).

Vere (m) French place name derived from the Old French *ver* ('alder') that was subsequently adopted as a baronial surname and has been in use as a first name in the English-speaking world since the 17th century. The name came to Britain with one of William the Conqueror's companions and has appeared infrequently as a first name since the 18th century.

Verena (f) Swiss first name of unknown meaning, though possibly sharing the same roots as VERA. The name is still fairly common in Switzerland, the homeland of the 3rd-century St Verena, who is supposed to have been Egyptian in origin. Its use among English speakers was promoted by its appearance in the Henry James novel *The Bostonians* (1886). A familiar variant of the name is **Vreni**.

Vergil *See* VIRGIL.

Verity (f) English first name derived from the Latin *verus* ('truth'). It was one of various 'virtue' names that were adopted with some enthusiasm by English Puritans in the 17th century and has survived subsequent changes of fashion to be encountered on an occasional basis today. Well-known bearers of the name in recent times have included British television producer Verity Lambert (b.1935). A rare variant is **Verily**.

Verna (f) English first name of uncertain origin. It is thought that it may have emerged as a feminine version of VERNON, or alternatively that it evolved from the Latin *vernus* ('spring'). It was first adopted in English-speaking countries in the 1880s but seems to have vanished from use since the 1960s. Holders of the name include US actress Verna Bloom (b.1939). *See also* WERNER.

Verner *See* WERNER.

Vernon (m) French place name, meaning 'place of alders' or 'alder grove', that was subsequently taken up as a surname and has also been in fairly widespread use as a first name in English-speaking countries. Richard de Vernon was one of William the Conqueror's closest companions and the name has retained its strong aristocratic associations into modern times. It appears to have been adopted as a first name in the 19th century. Famous bearers of the name have included British-born US dancer Vernon Castle (1887–1918) and British poet Vernon Scannell (b.1922). **Verne** and **Vern** are common diminutive forms.

Verona (f) English first name derived from the name of the Italian city (itself of uncertain origin). Alternatively, it is sometimes considered to be a variant of VERONICA. Bearers of the name since it was first adopted by English speakers in the late 19th century have included the fictional Verona Babbitt in the novel *Babbitt* (1922) by Sinclair Lewis.

Veronica (f) English first name probably derived from the Latin *vera icon* ('true image'), but possibly a variant of the Greek Pherenike ('victory bringer') – *see* BERNICE. St Veronica was the name later given to the unidentified woman who wiped Christ's face with a cloth when he was on his way to be crucified (tradition claims that an image of Christ's face was thus left on the material). The name arrived in Scotland from France (where it is found as **Véronique**) in the 17th century but was not taken up in England until the late 19th century. It reached a peak in popularity in the years between 1920 and 1960 but has since gone out of fashion. Among those to favour the name early in its history was Dr Johnson's biographer James Boswell (1740–95), who named his daughter Veronica. More recent bearers of the name have included US actress Veronica Lake (Constance Ockleman; 1919–73). Variants include VERONA and **Veron**. **Ron** and **Ronnie** are common diminutive forms. *See also* VERA.

Vesta (f) English first name derived from that of the Roman goddess of the hearth and fire, itself ultimately from the Greek *hestia* ('hearth'). It was adopted by English speakers in the 19th century. Famous bearers of the name have included British music hall singer Vesta Tilley (Matilda Alice Powles; 1864–1952).

Veva *See* GENEVIÈVE.

Vi *See* VIOLET.

Vic *See* VICTOR; VICTORIA.

Vicky *See* VICTORIA.

Victor (m) English first name derived from the Roman Victorius, itself from the Latin for 'conqueror'. Commemorating Christ's victory over death and sin, the name was fairly common among early Christians and was borne by several martyrs as well as a pope. It fell into disuse during medieval times but re-emerged in the English-speaking world in the 19th century in tribute to Queen Victoria. The name has suffered a decline in subsequent years, although it remained fairly popular in the USA until the 1950s. Well-known bearers of the name have included the French novelist Victor Hugo (1802–85), British dance-band leader Victor Sylvester (1900–1978), US film actor Victor Mature (1915–99) and Danish-born pianist and comedian Victor Borge (1909–2000). European variants include the German and Scandinavian **Viktor** and the Italian **Vittore**. The usual diminutive form is **Vic** – as borne by British comedian and musician Vic Oliver (1898–1964), US actor Vic Morrow (1932–82) and British television comedian Vic Reeves (Jim Moir; b.1959).

Victoria (f) English and Spanish first name derived from the Latin *victoria* ('victory'). The name was borne by an early Christian martyr but was more or less unknown in England prior to the 19th century. It became fairly popular in the English-speaking world following the accession to the British throne of Queen Victoria (1819–1901), who inherited the name from her German mother Princess Maria Louisa Victoria of Saxe-Coburg-Gotha. The name enjoyed a peak in popularity in the 1970s, since when it has maintained its status as a favourite choice of new parents. Other well-known bearers of the name have included British writer Victoria Glendinning (b.1937), US actress Victoria Principal (b.1945) and British comedienne Victoria Wood (b.1953). **Victorine** and the French **Victoire** are variant forms. Diminutives include **Vic**, **Vikki**, **Vicky**, **Vickie**, **Viti**, **Toria** and **Tory**. *See also* QUEENIE; VITA.

Vidal (m) Spanish first name (pronounced

'veedarl') derived ultimately from the Hebrew *hayyim* ('life'). Well-known bearers of the name have included hairdresser Vidal Sassoon (b.1928). Variants include **Vitale**.

Vijay (m) Indian first name (pronounced 'veejay') derived from the Sanskrit *vijaya* ('victory' or 'booty'). The name of a province of eastern India that in time became the heart of the Vijayanagara empire, it was also the name of one of Krishna's grandchildren. It has been popular as a first name for many centuries and may also be found as a component of longer names, such as **Vijayakumar**, **Vijakalakshmi** and **Vijayashankar**. Variants include the Bengali **Bijay** and **Bijoy**. A feminine version of the name is **Vijaya**, an alternative name for the goddess Durga, the wife of Shiva.

Vikki *See* VICTORIA.

Vikram (m) Indian first name derived from the Sanskrit *vikrama* ('stride' or 'pace'). Later interpreted to mean 'heroism' or 'strength', it was borne by Vishnu in the *Mahabharata*. This use of the name comes from the word *trivikrama*, meaning 'thrice stepping' – a reference to the legend that Vishnu could travel the entire length of the universe in just three steps. The name was also borne by a celebrated king of Ujjain, who expelled the Scythians from India and who in 58 BC ushered in the Vikrama era. Notable bearers of the name in recent times have included Indian novelist Vikram Seth (b.1952).

Vilma *See* WILHELMINA.

Vin *See* VINCENT.

Vina *See* DAVINA.

Vinay (m) Indian first name derived from the Sanskrit *vinaya* ('leading asunder' or 'guidance'). To Buddhists the name denotes the code of behaviour to which monks must adhere. Variants include **Vinayak** (related to **Vinayaka**, an alternative name for the elephant-headed god Ganesh).

Vince *See* VINCENT.

Vincent (m) English, French, Dutch and Scandinavian first name derived from the Latin *vincens* ('conquering'). The name was borne by several saints, the most notable of whom were the 4th-century Spanish martyr St Vincent of Saragossa and St Vincent de Paul (c.1580–1660), the French founder of the Vincentian Order of the Sisters of Charity, who were dedicated to helping the poor. The name was fairly well known in the late medieval period and enjoyed a resurgence in popularity among English speakers in the 19th century. Famous bearers of the name have included the Dutch painter Vincent Van Gogh (1853–90), whose celebrated life and tragic death were recalled in the pop song 'Vincent' by Don Maclean in 1971, and the US film actor Vincent Price (1911–93). Variants include **Vinny** and **Vinnie** – as borne by British footballer Vinnie Jones (b.1965). **Vin** and **Vince** are diminutive forms. Feminine versions include **Vincetta** and **Vincentia**.

Vinnie *See* LAVINIA; VINCENT; VIRGINIA.

Viola (f) English first name derived from the Latin *viola* ('violet'). The popularity of the name in the English-speaking world was largely the result of the influence of the character Viola in William Shakespeare's *Twelfth Night* (1601). It was also the title of an unfinished opera by the Czech composer Bedrich Smetana (1824–84). The name reached a peak in popularity in the early 20th century (inspired by the popularity of the pansy-like flower) but has since tailed off considerably.

Violet (f) English first name derived from the Latin plant name (a traditional symbol of modesty). It was first adopted in England in medieval times, when it was sometimes rendered as Violante. Notable bearers of the name in more recent times have included British politician Lady Violet Bonham Carter (1887–1969), Vita Sackville-West's lover novelist Violet Trefusis (1894–1971) and the British-born Violette Szabo (1921–45), who was executed by the Germans as a spy during the Second World War and whose story was told in the film *Carve Her Name with Pride* (1958). The name has undergone a marked decline since the 1920s. A French variant is **Violette** and the name is also found, chiefly in Italy, as **Violetta**. A common diminutive is **Vi**.

Violetta *See* VIOLET.

Virgil (m) Roman family name of obscure meaning that has been in occasional use as a first name among English speakers since medieval times. Initially spelled Vergil or Vergilius, it appears to have been taken up at an early date more often in tribute to a revered French bishop or a celebrated Irish monk of the same name than it was to the great 1st-century BC Roman poet Publius Vergilius Maro (or Virgil) with whom the name is usually associated today. English settlers subsequently took the name with them to the USA and other parts of the English-speaking world and it has remained in currency into modern times. Notable bearers of the name have included US composer Virgil Thomson (1896–1989), the fictional Virgil Tibbs in John Ball's detective novel *In the Heat of the Night* (1964) and one of the Tracy brothers in the popular 1960s British animated television series *Thunderbirds*. A Spanish variant is **Virgilio**.

Virginia (f) English first name derived from the Latin name Verginius, itself from the Latin for 'maiden' or 'virgin'. In Roman legend Verginius or Virginius was a beautiful young woman who was murdered by her father to save her from seduction by the unsuitable Appius Claudius. The name was subsequently given by Sir Walter Raleigh to the first English possessions in America in the 16th century in tribute to England's 'Virgin Queen', Elizabeth I. In 1587 the first child born in Virginia was given the name Virginia Dare (although she was fated to perish along with the rest of the colony in mysterious circumstances soon after). The popularity of the name was further promoted in England – and as **Virginie** in France – by the novel *Paul et Virginie* (1787) by the French writer Bernardin

de Saint-Pierre. Notable bearers of the name in more recent times have included British novelist Virginia Woolf (1882–1941), British actress Virginia McKenna (b.1931), British tennis player Virginia Wade (b.1945) and British politician Virginia Bottomley (b.1948). Diminutive forms include GINGER, **Ginny** or **Jinny** and **Vinnie** or **Vinny**.

Vita (f) English and Scandinavian first name derived from the Latin *vitus* ('life'), or alternatively from the Sanskrit for 'desire' or 'wish'. The name is also sometimes regarded as a diminutive of VICTORIA. Notable bearers of the name have included British writer Vita Sackville-West (1892–1962), who acquired the name as a familiar form of VIRGINIA. **Vitus** is a masculine form.

Vittore *See* VICTOR.

Vitus *See* VITA.

Viv *See* VIVIAN; VIVIEN.

Vivian (m/f) English first name derived ultimately from the Latin *vivus* ('alive' or 'lively'). The name was borne by a little-known 5th-century Christian martyr called St Vivianus but was otherwise little used until after medieval times. Also found as **Vivyan** and **Vyvyan**, the name was originally given solely to men, but later to members of both sexes. The earliest records of its use in England date to the 12th century. Celebrated bearers of the name have included the central character in the novel *Vivian Grey* (1826) by Benjamin Disraeli and British explorer Sir Vivian Fuchs (1908–99). The most common diminutive form is **Viv** – as borne by West Indian cricketer Viv Richards (b.1952). *See also* VIVIEN.

Viviana *See* VIVIEN.

Vivien (f) English first name that developed as a feminine variant of VIVIAN. Also found as **Vivienne**, **Viviette**, **Viviana** or **Vivianne**, the name was popularized by Alfred, Lord Tennyson's poem 'Vivien and Merlin' (1859), in which he identifies Vivien, Lady of the Lake as the object of Merlin's passion. Tennyson's Vivien rewards Merlin's interest in her by using her magic to imprison him in a castle of air. Famous bearers of the name in recent times have included British actress Vivien Leigh (Vivian Leigh; 1913–67) and British fashion designer Vivienne Westwood (b.1941). The usual diminutive is **Viv**.

Viviette *See* VIVIEN.

Vladimir (m) Russian first name derived from the Slavonic *volod* ('rule') and *meri*

('great'). Its popularity was greatly enhanced by St Vladimir (956–1015), the Russian prince who was largely responsible for the Christianization of his country. Variants include the Dutch WALDEMAR and the diminutive forms VADIM and **Volya**. A feminine version is **Vladimira**.

Vladislav (m) Slavonic first name meaning 'great ruler'.

Volya *See* VLADIMIR.

Vonda *See* WANDA.

Vyvyan *See* VIVIAN.

W

Wade (m) Old English surname, meaning 'dweller by the ford' or simply 'ford', that has appeared as a first name in relatively recent times (chiefly in the USA). It was the name of a legendary medieval hero and first emerged as a first name in the 19th century. It was further popularized by the US novelist Margaret Mitchell after she used it for one of the characters in *Gone with the Wind* (1936).

Wal *See* WALLACE; WALTER.

Walburga (f) Old Germanic name derived from *wald* ('rule') or *wal* ('foreign' or 'strange') and *burg* ('fortress'). St Walburga (also given in Old English as Wealdburgh and Wealburh) was an 8th-century abbess whose feast day is celebrated on 1 May – Walpurgis Night, the eve of her feast day, is traditionally linked with witchcraft rites in Germany. The name has long since fallen from favour.

Waldemar (m) Old German name meaning 'power', derived from the words *wald* ('rule') and *mari* ('famous'). The name is encountered throughout Germany, Scandinavia and the Netherlands and is an equivalent of the Russian VLADIMIR. **Valdemar** is a Scandinavian variant. Diminutive forms include WALDO.

Waldo (m) Diminutive form of the German WALDEMAR, meaning 'power' or 'rule'. An early English form for the name was Waltheof. It is little used outside the USA, where famous bearers have included the writer and philosopher Ralph Waldo Emerson (1803–82). Emerson's father was a Lutheran clergyman and probably named his son after the 12th-century reformist Peter Waldo, founder of the Waldensian religious sect. A female variant is VALDA.

Walid (m) Arab name meaning 'newborn baby'. The popularity of the name was much promoted by military victories in the Middle East and Spain that Arab armies enjoyed during the reign of Walid I (d.715).

Walker (m) English first name, also a surname, meaning 'fuller'.

Wallace (m) Scottish surname, meaning 'Welsh' or 'Welshman' or (from Old French *waleis*) simply 'foreign' or 'stranger', which was subsequently adopted throughout the English-speaking world as a first name. The emergence of the name in Scotland owed much to the popularity of Scottish patriot Sir William Wallace (1274–1305), who was executed by the English after leading a rebellion against English rule. It has been in use as a first name since the 19th century. Notable bearers of the name in more recent times have included US actor Wallace Beery (1885–1949) and the fictional Wallace in Nick Park's Oscar-winning *Wallace and Gromit* animated films of the 1990s. Diminutive forms include **Wal** and **Wally** and the association between this and the ordinary slang term 'wally', denoting a stupid or foolish person, would seem to have been partly responsible for the name's sharp decline since the 1970s. *See also* WALLIS.

Wallis (m/f) Infrequently encountered variant of WALLACE. The name is more common in the USA than it is in the UK and is particularly associated with Wallis Simpson (1896–1986), the US divorcee for whom Edward VIII gave up the British throne in 1936.

Wally *See* WALLACE; WALTER.

Walt *See* WALTER.

Walter (m) English, German and Scandinavian name derived from the Old German *waldhar* ('army ruler' or 'folk ruler'). Rendered in Old English as Wealdhere, it was introduced to England in its modern form by the Normans in the 11th century. The name was originally pronounced with a silent 'l' (as 'water') and thus gave rise to such variants as **Watkin** and its diminutives **Wat** – as borne by Wat Tyler (d.1381), leader of the Peasants' Revolt of 1381 – and **Wattie** (a Scottish variant). It reached a peak in popularity in the late 19th century, but has become increasingly rare since the 1930s.

Notable bearers of the name have included English sailor Sir Walter Raleigh (1554–1618), Scottish poet and novelist Sir Walter Scott (1771–1832), British artist Walter Sickert (1860–1942) and British poet Walter de la Mare (1873–1956). Diminutive forms include **Wal**, the English **Wally** and the US **Walt** – as borne by US poet Walt Whitman (1819–92) and US cartoon and film maker Walt Disney (1901–66). Variants in other languages include the German **Walther**, the French **Gautier**, the Dutch **Wouter** and the Scandinavian **Valter**.

Wanda (f) English first name of obscure origin, possibly derived from the Slavonic tribal name Wend or otherwise of Polish origins (a legendary 8th-century queen of Poland bore the name). Alternatively the name may have come from the Old German for 'young shoot' or 'family'. It first appeared among English-speaking communities in the 19th century, when it became well known as the title of a popular novel (1883) by the British novelist Ouida, but it is uncommon today – although it is occasionally encountered as a diminutive of WENDY. In more recent times it has resurfaced in the title of the film *A Fish Called Wanda* (1988). Notable bearers of the name have included Polish keyboard player Wanda Landowska (1887–1959). Variants include **Vanda**, **Venda**, **Vonda** and **Wenda**.

Ward (m) English surname derived from the Old English *weard* ('guard' or

'watchman'), which was adopted as a first name in the mid 19th century. It remains in occasional use on both sides of the Atlantic.

Warner (m) English surname, derived from the German tribal name Warin (meaning 'to protect') and the German *harja* (meaning 'people'), that was taken up as a first name in the 19th century. The surname was introduced to England by the Normans in the variant forms Warin and Guarin, from which the English surnames Warren, Warner, Waring and Garnett all developed. It represents an English equivalent of the German WERNER.

Warren (m) English surname of disputed Norman origin that may have evolved from the Norman French La Varenne ('game park') or else from the Old German Warin (a tribal name that originally meant 'to protect'). As a first name it faded from view after the Norman era but was revived in the 19th century and enjoyed particular popularity in the USA, where it ranked among the fifty most popular names in the 1870s and again in the 1920s. Famous bearers of the name have included British statesman Warren Hastings (1732–1818), US film actor Warren Beatty (b.1937) and British television actor Warren Mitchell (b.1926).

Warwick (m) English surname (pronounced 'worrik') derived from the county town of Warwickshire, which itself means 'farm by the weir'. It was adopted as a first name in the 19th century and subsequently enjoyed particular popularity in Australia. Diminutive forms include **Warric**.

Washington (m) Old English place name meaning 'settlement of Wassa's people' that was later adopted as a surname and ultimately as a first name. Its popularity as a first name in the USA reflects the fame of the country's first president, George Washington (1732–99), whose family came from Northamptonshire in England. Other notable bearers of the name have included the US writer Washington Irving (1783–1859). Diminutive forms include **Wash**.

Wasim (m) Arab and Indian name meaning 'handsome' or 'good-looking'. An Indian variant is **Waseem**.

Wat/Watkin/Wattie *See* WALTER.

Wayne (m) English surname meaning 'carter' or 'cart-maker' which became a popular choice of first name in the 1940s. Use of the name was promoted by the popularity of US film actor John Wayne (Marion Michael Morrison; 1907–79), who took his stage name from Anthony Wayne (1745–96), a general in the American War of Independence. It enjoyed a peak in popularity in the 1970s, when it ranked among the twenty most popular names in the English-speaking world, but has since suffered a sharp decline in popularity. Famous bearers of the name have included British pop singer Wayne Fontana (b.1945) and British ballet dancer Wayne Sleep (b.1948).

Webster (m) English surname meaning 'weaver' that emerged as a first name on both sides of the Atlantic during the 19th century. Its use in the USA was promoted by such famous bearers of the name as US lexicographer Noah Webster (1758–1843) and US statesman Daniel Webster (1782–1852).

Wenda *See* WANDA; WENDY.

Wendel *See* WENDELL.

Wendell (m) Old German surname, thought to have been derived originally from Wend (the name of a Slavonic tribe), and usually interpreted as meaning 'wanderer', that has been in occasional use as a first name among English speakers since the 19th century. Famous bearers of the name have included US writer Oliver Wendell Holmes (1809–94) and his identically-named son (1841–1935), who achieved fame as a lawyer. Also found in Germany as **Wendel**.

Wendy (f) English first name that was invented by the Scottish playwright J. M. Barrie in his classic children's story *Peter Pan* (1904). The name was inspired originally by Margaret Henley, the young daughter of one of Barrie's friends, who was in the habit of calling the writer her 'fwendy-wendy'. Margaret died young and Barrie intended the fictional Wendy Darling to be a memorial to her (one of his god-daughters was also subsequently named Wendy after the character). Some authorities have, however, speculated that the name may have been heard before 1904 as a diminutive form of GWENDA or GWENDOLEN. To poet laureate John Betjeman the name conjured up cherished images of middle-class England in the 1920s, as celebrated in 'Indoor Games near Newbury': 'Oh but Wendy, when the carpet yielded to my indoor pumps/There you stood, your gold hair streaming...' Since Barrie invented the name Wendy has maintained its status as one of the most popular girls' names on both sides of the Atlantic, especially in Scotland (although it has fallen out of favour since reaching a peak in popularity in the 1960s and 1970s).

Well-known bearers of the name have included Australian tennis player Wendy Turnbull (b.1952), British poet Wendy Cope (b.1945) and British actresses Wendy Hiller (1912–2003), Wendy Craig (b.1934), and Wendy Richard (b.1946). It has also been bestowed upon children's playhouses – 'Wendy houses' – in imitation of the house constructed by the Lost Boys for Barrie's Wendy in the original story. The name has been appropriated in slang to infer that a person is weak, inept and unpopular. Diminutive forms of the name include **Wend**, while variants include **Wenda** and **Wendi**.

Wenonah *See* WINONA.

Werner (m) German, Dutch and Scandinavian first name (pronounced 'verna') derived ultimately from the Old German tribal name Warin. Famous bearers of the name in recent times have included German film director Werner Herzog (b.1942). Also found as **Verner** and **Wernher**, as borne by German rocket scientist Wernher von

Braun (1912–77). *See also* WARNER; WARREN.

Werther (m) German first name (pronounced 'verta') derived from the Old German *wert* ('worthy') and *heri* ('warrior'). The name was fairly common in medieval times and reappeared in the 18th century after Goethe chose it for the name of the central character in *Die Leiden des jungen Werther* ('The Sorrows of Young Werther', 1774).

Wesley (m) Old English place name meaning 'west meadow', which was later adopted as a surname and first name. Many Methodists chose the name for their children in tribute to the founder of the Methodist movement John Wesley (1703–91). It has since been adopted by a wider variety of communities and is especially popular in the USA and among West Indian families. Famous bearers of the name have included US actor Wesley Snipes (b.1962). **Wes** is a diminutive form.

Whitney (m/f) English place name meaning 'at the white island', which was later adopted as both a surname and first name. The name has been used for both sexes, particularly by Black Americans, since at least the 1920s. Famous bearers of the name in recent times have included US pop singer and film actress Whitney Houston (b.1964).

Wilberforce (m) English place name (from North Yorkshire) meaning 'Wilbur's ditch', which was subsequently adopted as a surname and first name. Its adoption was promoted by the popularity of William Wilberforce (1759–1833), the English politician who led the campaign to end the slave trade.

Wilbert (m) English first name derived from the Old English *will* ('will') and *beorht* ('bright'). It has never enjoyed widespread popularity but is occasionally encountered in the USA.

Wilbur (m) English surname of obscure origins, possibly from the Old English *will*

('will') and *burh* ('defence'), that was subsequently taken up as a first name. The name is rarely encountered today outside the USA, where it may have been imported by Dutch settlers. Famous bearers of the name have included US flying pioneer Wilbur Wright (1867–1912) and Zambian-born US novelist Wilbur Smith (b.1933).

Wilf *See* WILFRED.

Wilfred (m) English first name derived from the Old German *wil* ('will' or 'desire') and *frid* ('peace') and thus interpreted as meaning 'desiring peace'. Old English forms included Walfrid and Wilfrith. The name largely disappeared after the Norman Conquest, but reappeared in Victorian times and remained popular (especially in northern Britain) until the mid 20th century, in part because it was also a saint's name – that of the 8th-century St Wilfred, Archbishop of York. Among notable bearers of the name since him have been First World War British poet Wilfred Owen (1893–1918) and British radio personality Wilfred Pickles (1904–78). Bearers of the name in literature have included Walter Scott's Wilfred of Ivanhoe in *Ivanhoe* (1819). Variants include **Wilfrid**, as borne by the British actors Wilfrid Hyde White (1903–91) and Wilfrid Brambell (1912–85), and the (rare) feminine forms **Wilfreda** and **Wilfrida**. The usual German version is **Wilfried** and it can also be found in Scandinavia as **Vilfred**. Among diminutive forms are **Wil**, **Wilf** and **Wilfie**. *See also* WILKIE.

Wilfreda/Wilfrid *See* WILFRED.

Wilhelm *See* WILLIAM.

Wilhelmina (f) German first name that is infrequently encountered among English-speaking people except in the variant form **Wilma**. It is the feminine equivalent of the German Wilhelm (*see* WILLIAM) and is generally confined in the English-speaking world to Scotland, Canada and the USA. Famous bearers of the name have included Queen Wilhelmina of the Netherlands (1880–1962). Variants include the Anglicized **Williamina** and the diminutive forms **Willa**, **Velma**, **Vilma**, **Ilma**, **Mina**, MINNA, **Minne**, **Minnie** and ELMA, which are all commoner in the USA than they are in the UK.

Wilkie (m) English surname derived from WILFRED or WILLIAM, which made its debut as a first name in the 19th century. Notable bearers of the name have included British novelist Wilkie Collins (1824–89).

Will *See* WILLIAM.

Willa *See* WILHELMINA.

Willard (m) English surname derived from the Old German *wil* ('will') and *helm* ('helmet' or 'protection') that is occasionally encountered as a first name in the USA but is virtually unknown except as a surname elsewhere. Notable bearers of the name include Jamaican-born opera singer Willard White (b.1946).

Willem *See* WILLIAM.

William (m) English first name derived from the Old German *wil* ('will') and *helm* ('helmet' or 'protection') that is usually interpreted as meaning 'defender'. The name came to England (as Willelm) in 1066 with the Normans, who were led by William the Conqueror (1027–87), and was for some two centuries the most common of all first names before being overtaken by JOHN. It went into a temporary decline in the UK (though not in the USA) in the late 19th century but revived later in the following century. Its lasting popularity among English speakers owes something to the fact that it has appeared many times in the British royal family and may be expected to enjoy a new lease of life when the present Prince William (b.1982) eventually takes the throne as William V. Other famous bearers of the name have included English playwright and poet William Shakespeare (1564–1616), British poets William Blake (1757–1827) and William Wordsworth (1770–1850), British novelist William

Makepeace Thackeray (1811–63), British prime minister William Gladstone (1809–98) and US novelist William Burroughs (1914–97).

Variant forms include the feminine version WILLA, the Scottish Gaelic **Uilleam,** the Irish Gaelic **Uilliam**, **Ulick** and LIAM, the Welsh **Gwilim**, **Gwill**, **Gwilym** and **Gwyllim**, the French **Guillaume**, Italian **Guglielmo**, the Spanish **Guillermo** and **Guillem** and the Germanic **Wilhelm** or **Willem** (and the feminine WILHELMINA). Among the most frequently encountered diminutive forms are **Bill** (and **Billy** or **Billie**) and **Will** (and **Willy** or **Willie**). Famous Bills and Billys have included Austrian-born US film director Billy Wilder (Samuel Wilder; 1906–2002), Scottish football manager Bill Shankly (1913–81), US rock and roll star Bill Haley (1926–81), US television comedian Bill Cosby (b.1937) and US President Bill Clinton (b.1946). Among notable bearers of the names Will, Willie and Willy have been US humorist Will Rogers (1879–1935), British film actor Will Hay (1888–1949), British humorist Willie Rushton (1937–96), Scottish jockey Willie Carson (b.1942) and British playwright Willy Russell (b.1947). *See also* WILKIE; WILLARD; WILLIS.

Williamina *See* WILHELMINA.

Willie *See* WILLIAM.

Willis (m) English surname meaning 'son of Will', which made its debut as a first name in the 19th century. It has never ranked among the most popular first names. Notable bearers of the name have included British playwright Willis Hall (b.1929).

Willoughby (m) English place name derived from the Old English *welig* ('willow') and the Old Norse *byr* ('settlement'), and thus interpreted as meaning 'farm among the willows', that was later adopted as a surname and first name. It only emerged as a first name in the 19th century, although it was little used even then outside the upper classes. It effectively disappeared from use after the early years of the 20th century.

Instances of the name in fiction have included Willoughby in Jane Austen's *Sense and Sensibility* (1811).

Willow (f) English first name of relatively recent coinage. Taken from the name of the tree (*welig* in Old English), it remains rare.

Willy *See* WILLIAM.

Wilma *See* WILHELMINA.

Wilmer (m) English first name of obscure origin, possibly a masculine version of Wilma (*see* WILHELMINA). Alternatively, the name may have evolved from the Old German *wil* ('will' or 'desire') and *meri* ('famous').

Wilmot (m) Medieval English name probably derived from WILLIAM or else from the Old German *wil* ('will' or 'desire') and *muot* ('mind' or 'courage') that was first adopted as a surname. The name reappeared as a first name in the 19th century but it remains relatively uncommon.

Wilson (m) English first name, also a surname, meaning 'son of Will'. Also found as **Willson**.

Win *See* WINIFRED; WINSTON; WINTHROP.

Windsor (m) Old English place name meaning 'river bank with a windlass (for hauling boats)' that was subsequently adopted both as a surname and first name. The surname of the British royal family since 1917, it has enjoyed only desultory popularity as a first name (in which form it first appeared in the 19th century). Notable bearers have included the Welsh actor Windsor Davies (b.1930).

Winifred (f) English and Welsh first name derived from the Old English *wynn* ('joy') and *frith* ('peace') and sometimes interpreted as meaning 'blessed reconciliation'. In Old English the name became united with the masculine Winfrith, meaning 'friend of peace'. The 7th-century Welsh martyr St Winifred (or **Gwenfrewi** in Welsh) was beheaded by the Welsh Prince Caradoc after she refused his advances but

was restored to life; a holy spring broke from the ground at the place where her head fell – Holywell, in North Wales). The name – occasionally also found as **Winifrid** or **Winnifred** – became increasingly common from the 16th century, although it has fallen out of favour somewhat since reaching a peak in popularity in the years 1880–1930. Notable bearers of the name have included Trinidad-born British pianist Winifred Atwell (1914–83). Diminutive forms include FREDA, **Win**, **Winn** and **Winnie** – as borne by Winnie Mandela (b.1934), former wife of South African President Nelson Mandela.

Winnie *See* WINIFRED; WINSTON.

Winnifred *See* WINIFRED.

Winona (f) Sioux Indian name meaning 'eldest daughter'. The name of a legendary American Indian princess, it later became the name of a city in Minnesota and reappeared in Henry Wadsworth Longfellow's epic poem *Hiawatha* (1855), where it is given as **Wenonah**. Another variant is **Wynona**. The spelling Winona dates back to H. L. Gordon's poem 'Winona' (1881). Well-known bearers of the name have included US film actress Winona Ryder (b.1971).

Winston (m) English first name derived ultimately from that of a village in Gloucestershire. Several local families took the name of the village of Winestone (meaning '(boundary) stone of a man called Wynna' or simply 'friend's settlement') as their surname in medieval times and it was a daughter of one of these, Sarah Winston, who eventually married into the Churchill family in the early 17th century. In 1620, when she gave birth to a son, the boy was christened Winston in her honour. This first Sir Winston Churchill in time became father of the 1st Duke of Marlborough, whose illustrious descendants included another Sir Winston – Britain's wartime leader Sir Winston Leonard Spencer Churchill (1874–1965).

The name has never been overly popular

in the UK, perhaps because its association with Winston Churchill is so overwhelming. It is, however, sometimes encountered in other parts of the world that have long-established links with Britain, particularly the Caribbean. Notable bearers of the name apart from Churchill have included British singer-songwriter John Winston Lennon (1940–80) and the fictional Winston Smith, the central character in George Orwell's nightmarish novel about the future *1984* (1949).

Diminutive forms of the name include **Win** and **Winnie** – although as a girls' name Winnie has different roots. Bearers of the informal versions of Winston include Winnie-the-Pooh, the teddy-bear hero of the children's stories written by A. A. Milne in the 1920s.

Winthrop (m) English place name meaning 'village of Wynna', which was later adopted as a surname and has occasionally appeared as a first name (chiefly in the USA). The Winthrop family were one of the most prominent colonial families in 17th-century Massachusetts. The most common diminutive form is **Win**.

Winton (m) English place name (common to Cumbria and North Yorkshire), variously interpreted as meaning 'pasture enclosure' or 'willow enclosure', that was later adopted both as a surname and first name.

Witold (m) German and Polish name (pronounced 'vitold'), derived from the Old German *wida* ('wide') or *witu* ('wood') and *wald* ('ruler'). Variants in other languages include the Lithuanian **Vytautas**.

Wladyslaw (m) Polish name (pronounced 'vladishlav') derived from the Old Slavonic *volod* ('rule') and *slav* ('glory'). In Poland the name has long been associated with the upper classes and was borne by four Polish kings. Variants include the Czech **Vladislav** and **Ladislav**. *See also* LASZLO.

Wolf (m) German and Jewish first name (pronounced 'volf'), possibly an abbreviated version of WOLFGANG. Alternatively,

it may always have had an independent existence, based on the ordinary vocabulary word 'wolf'. Notable bearers of the name in the English-speaking world have included British screenwriter Wolf Mankowitz (1924–98). The British television comedy *Citizen Smith* in the late 1970s had a central character nicknamed 'Wolfie' (although his real first names were Walter Henry). Variants include **Wolfe**, as borne by the Irish nationalist Wolfe Tone (1763–98), and the Scandinavian **Ulf** and **Ulv**.

Wolfgang (m) German first name (pronounced 'volfgang') derived from the Old German *wolf* ('wolf') and *gang* ('going'). The most famous bearer of the name to date has been German composer Wolfgang Amadeus Mozart (1756–91).

Woodrow (m) English place name derived from the Old English for 'row of houses by a wood', which later appeared both as a surname and first name. The name received a considerable boost through US President Thomas Woodrow Wilson (1856–1924), who acquired the name from his maternal grandfather Thomas Woodrow. Other notable bearers of the name have included British politician Woodrow Wyatt (1918–97). Diminutive forms include WOODY.

Woody (m) Diminutive form of WOODROW (or otherwise a familiar version of the surname Woods). Notable bearers of the name in the 20th century have included US folk singers Woody Guthrie (1912–67) and Woody Herman (1913–87), US comedian and director Woody Allen (Allen Stewart Konigsberg; b.1935) and US film and television actor Woody Harrelson (b.1962).

Wouter *See* WALTER.

Wyatt (m) English surname derived from the Old German *wido* ('wood' or 'wide'), which subsequently emerged as a first name (chiefly in the USA) in the 19th century. It comes from the same roots as GUY and in medieval times was also encountered in the forms **Guyat** and **Wyat**. Famous bearers of the name have included US lawman Wyatt Earp (1848–1929).

Wybert (m) Old English name derived from *wig* ('battle') and *beorht* ('bright' or 'famous'). It is extremely rare today.

Wyn *See* WYNN.

Wyndham (m) English place name (from Norfolk) that was subsequently adopted as a surname and first appeared as a first name in the middle of the 19th century. As the place name Wymondham it means 'Wyman's homestead' – the Anglo-Saxon name Wyman having been derived from the Old English *wig* ('battle') and *mund* ('protection'). Famous bearers of the name have included British novelist Percy Wyndham Lewis (1882–1957).

Wynfor *See* GWYNFOR.

Wynford (m) Welsh place name meaning 'white stream' or 'holy stream', which sub-

sequently appeared both as a surname and first name. Its use as a first name appears to date from the early 20th century.

Wynn (m) English first name variously derived from a Welsh surname, from the Welsh *wyn* ('white' or 'blessed'), or else from an Old English surname meaning 'friend'. It also exists as a variant of GWYN and is sometimes encountered as **Wyn**. The feminine version **Wynne** is little known outside Wales.

Wynne *See* WYNN.

Wynona *See* WINONA

Wystan (m) Old English name derived from the Old English *wig* ('battle') and *stan* ('stone'). It was the name of a murdered 9th-century boy saint who was a Prince of Mercia, but is only encountered rarely today. The most notable bearer of the name in modern times has been British poet Wystan Hugh Auden (1907–73).

X

Xanthe (f) Greek name (pronounced 'Zanthee') derived from *xanthos* ('golden' or 'yellow'). The name is borne by several minor characters in tales from Greek mythology.

Xara *See* ZARA.

Xavier (m) Spanish name (pronounced 'zayveeuh' or 'zavveeuh' in English) probably derived from the Basque place name Etcheberria (meaning 'new house') or else possibly from the Arabic for 'bright'. The popularity of the name in Catholic France and Spain came about through the fame of the Basque Jesuit missionary St Francis Xavier (1506–52), who acquired his name from the family home in Navarre. Notable bearers of the name have included US bandleader Xavier Cugat (Francisco de Asis Javier Cugat de Bru y Deulofeo; 1900–1990). Occasionally found as **Javier** or **Zavier**, it also has several feminine versions, including **Xavia**, **Xaviera**, **Xaverine** and **Zavia**.

Xenia (f) English first name (pronounced 'zeeneea') derived from the Greek *xenia* ('hospitable'), infrequently encountered. Variant forms include ZENA, **Zenia** and **Zina**.

Y

Yael (f) Jewish first name, which has ranked among the most popular of all Jewish names since biblical times. It is derived from the Hebrew name for a female wild goat. **Jael** is a variant form.

Yatta *See* JAFFE.

Yakim *See* JOACHIM.

Yakov *See* JACOB.

Yale (m) Welsh place name meaning 'fertile upland' that was subsequently adopted as a surname and first name. The name is occasionally encountered in the USA, where it is associated with Yale University, founded by Elihu Yale (who had Welsh ancestry) in 1701.

Yasmin *See* JASMINE.

Yehiel (m) Jewish first name derived from the Hebrew for 'God lives'. The name appears as that of a minor character in the Bible and has remained popular among Jews ever since. Also found as **Jehiel**.

Yehudi *See* JUDAH.

Yermolai (m) Russian first name derived from the Greek name Hermolaos (meaning 'people of Hermes'). St Hermolaos was a 3rd-century martyr.

Yevgenie *See* EUGENE.

Yitzhak (m) Jewish first name representing a modern Hebrew version of ISAAC. Well-known bearers of the name in modern times have included the Polish-born Israeli Prime Minister Yitzhak Shamir (b.1915).

Volanda (f) Medieval French name of Germanic origins, derived ultimately from the Greek for 'violet flower'. Or it may well have developed originally from VIOLA, via Violante. Variant forms include the French **Yolande**, **Yalonda**, **Jolanda**, **Jolantha**, **Jolan**, **Jolana**, **Yalinda**, **Yolette**, **Iolanda** and IOLANTHE. The name, which has been encountered chiefly in Canada and the USA since 1900, is sometimes abbreviated to **Yola** or **Jola**.

Yorath *See* IORWERTH.

Yorick (m) Danish equivalent of the English GEORGE. The name is widely familiar from the deceased court jester in William Shakespeare's *Hamlet* (1599) but is infrequently encountered today.

York (m) English place name derived from the Old English for 'yew' that was subsequently adopted as a surname and occasional first name. The name's links with British royalty are thought to have been influential in the name's infrequent appearances as a first name.

Ysabel *See* ISABEL.

Ysanne (f) English first name that is thought to have evolved through the combination of ISABEL and ANNE.

Yseult/Ysolde *See* ISOLDE.

Yuri (m) Russian equivalent of the English GEORGE. Well-known bearers of the name have included Russian President Yuri Andropov (1914–84). Also encountered as **Yury**. A Polish variant is **Juri**.

Yusuf *See* JOSEPH.

Yves (m) French first name (pronounced 'eve') derived ultimately from the Old Norse *yr* ('yew'). The name came to Britain with the Normans in the 11th century. Notable bearers of the name in modern times have included French fashion designer Yves Saint Laurent (b.1936) and French film actor Yves Montand (Ivo Livi; 1921–91). Variants include the Cornish **Ives** and the German **Ivo**.

Yvette *See* YVONNE.

Yvonne (f) English and French first name that developed as a feminine equivalent of YVES. Unlike Yves, the name has enjoyed relatively widespread acceptance in English-speaking countries since 1900, reaching a peak in frequency in the 1950s and 1960s, and is now rarely thought of as a foreign import. Famous bearers of the name have included the French actresses Yvonne Arnaud (1892–1958) and Yvonne Printemps (1895–1977) and the US pop singer Yvonne Elliman (b.1951). Variant forms include **Evette**, **Evon**, **Evonne** and **Yvette** (a popular form among French speakers). A diminutive form is **Vonnie**.

Z

Zacchaeus (m) Aramaic name meaning 'innocent' or 'pure', or else a variant of Zachariah (*see* ZACHARY). The name was adopted by English Puritans in 17th-century England and America. Diminutives include **Zack** and **Zak**.

Zachariah *See* ZACHARY.

Zachary (m) Anglicized version of the Hebrew Zachariah, Zechariah or Zacharias, meaning 'Jehovah has remembered'. Often shortened to **Zac**, **Zack** and **Zak**, it features in the Bible as the name of John the Baptist's father and of around thirty other people. It appeared regularly in England and America after the Puritans adopted it in the 17th century. Notable bearers of the name have ranged from St Zachary, who became pope in 741, to US President Zachary Taylor (1784–1850). Rare variants include ZACCHAEUS and **Zakki**. The name is sometimes rendered in Gaelic as **Sachairi**.

Zack/Zak *See* ISAAC; ZACCHAEUS; ZACHARY.

Zakki *See* ZACHARY.

Zandra *See* ALEXANDRA; SANDRA.

Zane (m) Either a variant form of JOHN, which may be Danish in origin, or from a place name or surname of obscure origin. Famous bearers of the name have included US western writer Zane Grey (1875–1939), who hailed from Zanesville – itself named after ancestors of his.

Zara (f) Arabic name meaning 'splendour' or 'flower', but also in use as a variant of SARAH. The name has been adopted occasionally by English speakers since the 1960s and attracted renewed attention in the UK in 1981 when Princess Anne be-

stowed the name upon her daughter, Zara Phillips. Also found as **Xara**.

Zavanna *See* SAVANNA.

Zavia *See* XAVIER.

Zayd (m) Arabic name derived from *zada* ('to increase'). The name is of pre-Islamic origins and is still commonly encountered today. Zayd ibn-Haritha was an early convert to Islam who died in battle against the Byzantines in 629.

Zaynab (f) Arabic name derived from *zaynab* (the name of a sweet-scented plant). It was the name of several friends and relations of Muhammad, notably his granddaughter by Fatima, and has maintained its status as one of the most popular of Arab names.

Zeb (m) Hebrew name that developed as a shortened form of Zebuwn (meaning 'exaltation') or alternatively as a diminutive of ZEBEDEE.

Zebedee (m) Hebrew name meaning 'my gift'. A biblical name, it was taken up by English Puritans in the 17th century and enjoyed a minor vogue in the 1960s when it appeared as the name of a character in the popular British children's television series *The Magic Roundabout*. The usual diminutive form is ZEB.

Zechariah *See* ZACHARY.

Zedekiah (m) Hebrew name meaning 'the Lord is righteous' or 'the Lord is just'. Found in the Old Testament as the name of a king of Judah and three others, it was subsequently adopted by Puritans in the 17th century but is rare today. Sometimes shortened to **Zed**.

Zeke *See* EZEKIEL.

Zelda (f) Jewish name of obscure origins that is in use on both sides of the Atlantic. The name may have come originally from the Yiddish for 'happiness' (as does **Zelde**) or may be a familiar form of the German GRISELDA. The most notable bearer of the name to date has been Zelda Fitzgerald (1900–1947), the schizophrenic wife of US novelist F. Scott Fitzgerald.

Zelde *See* ZELDA.

Zelig *See* SELIG.

Zelma *See* SELMA.

Zena (f) Persian name meaning 'woman'. It may have developed as a familiar form of Zinaida but is sometimes adopted as a variant of XENIA or of ROSINA. Also encountered as **Zina** – as borne by US tennis player Zina Garrison (b.1963).

Zenia *See* XENIA.

Zenobia (f) Greek name meaning 'power of Zeus' or 'life from Zeus'. It was in use among the ancient Syrians, being the name of a beautiful but ruthless 3rd-century Queen of Palmyra whose opposition to Rome provoked a Roman invasion of the country. The reasons why the name re-emerged in Cornwall in the 16th century remain obscure but it continued to appear sporadically among English speakers, particularly in the south-western part of Britain, until the end of the 19th century. Variants include the Russian **Zinovia**.

Zephania (f) Hebrew name, also found as Zephaniah, meaning 'Jehovah protects' or 'Jehovah conceals'. There is a Book of Zephania in the Old Testament and the name was later revived by the Puritans after the Reformation, although it is rare today. A diminutive form is **Zeph**.

Zeta *See* ZITA.

Zia (m) Muslim name derived from the Arabic for 'light' or 'splendour'. Notable bearers of the name have included the historian Zia ud-Din Barni (1282–1356) and,

more recently, President Zia-ul-Haq (1924–88) of Pakistan. Also found as **Ziya**.

Zillah (f) Hebrew name meaning 'shade' or 'shadow'. A biblical name also found as **Zilla**, it enjoyed a brief period of popularity in the English-speaking world following the Reformation but fell from fashion after the 19th century (although it is still occasionally encountered among Romany families).

Zina *See* XENIA; ZENA.

Zinnia (f) English flower name that has been adopted infrequently as a first name in the 20th century.

Zinovia *See* ZENOBIA.

Zipporah (f) Hebrew name meaning 'bird'. It appears in the Bible as the name of the wife of Moses.

Zita (f) English and Italian first name derived from the medieval Tuscan *zita* ('little girl'). Borne by a 13th-century patron saint of domestic servants, Zita was also the name of the last Empress of Austria. Also encountered as **Zeta**, as borne by Welsh film actress Catherine Zeta Jones (b.1969).

Zoë (f) Greek name meaning 'life' that has been in regular use as a first name among English speakers since the 19th century. When the Bible was translated from Hebrew into Greek by Alexandrian Jews they selected Zoë as the nearest equivalent they could find for EVE and the name was consequently in use among Christians in ancient Rome. A saint's name that may or may not appear with a diaeresis, it has a relatively short history among English speakers, only achieving significant popularity since the Second World War. It reached a peak in popularity in the 1970s, when it briefly ranked among the most commonly selected girls' names. Famous bearers of the name have included US writer Zoë Akins (1886–1958) and British actress Zoe Wanamaker (b.1949). Occasionally found as **Zoey** or even **Zowie** (as borne by a child of British rock star David Bowie).

Zola (f) English name of obscure origins,

though possibly beginning life as an Italian surname or else as a variant of ZOË. Popularized as the surname of French novelist Emile Zola (1840–1902), it became well known as a first name in the 1980s when it was borne by South African runner Zola Budd (b.1966).

Zoltan (m) Hungarian first name of obscure origin. It is speculated that the name may have developed from the Turkish *sultan*. Famous bearers of the name have included the Hungarian-born film director Zoltan Korda (1895–1961).

Zona (f) English first name of obscure origins, though possibly a variant of ZENA. It has only rarely been found outside the USA.

Zora (f) Arabic name meaning 'dawn', or alternatively a biblical place name, that has been employed occasionally as a first name among English speakers.

Zowie *See* ZOË.

Zuleika (f) Persian name (pronounced 'zoo-like–a') meaning 'brilliant beauty' that has been in occasional use among English speakers since at least the early 19th century. The name of Potiphar's wife in the Bible, it was popularized centuries later in the English-speaking world by Lord Byron's use of the name in *The Bride of Abydos* (1813) and later still by Max Beerbohm's novel *Zuleika Dobson* (1911), which is about a young woman whose beauty drives her lovers to suicide. Beerbohm made it clear that he preferred the name to be pronounced 'Zuleeka'. An Arabic variant of the name is **Zulekha**.

Zygmunt *See* SIGMUND.

SAINTS' DAYS

January

1   Basil, Fulgentius, Justin, Telemachus
2   Abel, Basil, Caspar, Gregory, Macarius, Seraphim
3   Daniel, Frances, Geneviève
4   Angela, Benedicta, Roger
5   Paula, Simeon
6   Balthasar, Gaspar, Raphaela
7   Cedda, Crispin, Lucian, Raymond, Reynold, Valentine
8   Atticus, Gudule, Lucian, Severinus
9   Adrian, Alix, Hadrian, Peter
10 Agatho, Marcian, William
11 Brandan
12 Ailred, Benedict, Tatiana
13 Godfrey, Hilary
14 Felix, Hilary, Kentigern, Malachi
15 Isidore, Ita, Macarius, Maurus, Micah, Paul
16 Henry, Honoratus, Marcellus, Otto, Priscilla
17 Antony, Roseline
18 Dermot, Faustina, Priscilla, Susanna
19 Gerontius, Henry, Marius, Martha, Pia, Wulfstan
20 Euthymius, Fabian, Sebastian
21 Agnes, Fructuosus, Josepha, Maximus, Meinrad
22 Dominic, Timothy, Vincent
23 Aquila, Bernard, Ildefonsus, Raymond
24 Babylas, Francis, Timothy
25 Artemas, Gregory, Joel
26 Aubrey, Conan, Paula, Timothy, Titus, Xenophon
27 Angela, Candida, John, Julian, Marius, Theodoric
28 Ephraem, Paulinus, Peter, Thomas
29 Francis, Gildas
30 Hyacintha, Martina, Matthias
31 Adamnan, Aidan, Cyrus, John, Julius, Marcella, Tryphena

February

1   Bridget, Ignatius, Pionius
2   Joan, Theodoric
3   Anskar, Blaise, Ives, Laurence, Margaret, Oliver, Simeon, Werburga

4   Andrew, Gilbert, Isidore, Joan, Joseph, Nicholas, Phileas, Theophilus
5   Adelaide, Agatha, Avitus, Caius, Joachim, Matthias
6   Dorothy, Gerald, Luke, Mel, Paul, Silvanus, Titus, Vedast
7   Juliana, Luke, Moses, Richard, Theodore
8   Isaiah, Jerome, Sebastian, Stephen, Theodore
9   Apollonia, Cyril, Teilo
10   Hyacinth, Scholastica, Silvanus
11   Benedict, Blaise, Caedmon, Gregory, Jonas, Lazarus, Lucius, Theodore, Victoria
12   Alexis, Eulalia, Julian, Marina, Meletius
13   Agabus, Beatrice, Catherine, Priscilla
14   Abraham, Adolf, Cyril, Methodius, Valentine
15   Claud, Georgia, Jordan, Sigfrid
16   Elias, Flavian, Gilbert, Jeremy, Juliana, Pamphilus, Philippa, Samuel, Valentine
17   Reginald
18   Bernadette, Colman, Flavian, Leo, Simeon
19   Boniface, Conrad
20   Amata, Wulfric
21   George, Peter
22   Margaret
23   Lazarus, Martha, Mildburga, Milo, Polycarp
24   Adela, Lucius, Matthias
25   Ethelbert, Tarasius, Walburga
26   Alexander, Isabel, Porphyrius, Victor
27   Gabriel, Leander
28   Antonia, Hedwig, Hilary, Louisa, Oswald

March

1   Albinus, David, Felix, Roger
2   Agnes, Chad, Simplicius
3   Ailred, Anselm, Camilla, Marcia, Owen
4   Adrian, Casimir, Humbert, Lucius, Peter
5   Kieran, Piran, Virgil
6   Chrodegang, Colette, Cyril, Felicity, Jordan, Perpetua
7   Felicity, Paul, Perpetua, Thomas
8   Beata, Felix, Humphrey, John, Julian, Philemon, Pontius, Stephen
9   Catherine, Dominic, Frances, Gregory, Pacian
10   Anastasia, Caius, John, Macarius, Simplicius
11   Alberta, Aurea, Constantine, Oengus, Sophronius, Teresa
12   Bernard, Gregory, Maximilian, Paul, Seraphina
13   Gerald, Nicephorus, Patricia, Roderick, Solomon
14   Benedict, Eustace, Matilda
15   Clement, Louise, Lucretia, Zachary
16   Abraham, Julian, René
17   Gertrude, Joseph, Patrick, Paul
18   Alexander, Anselm, Christian, Cyril, Edward, Egbert, Narcissus, Salvator
19   Joseph

20 Alexandra, Claudia, Cuthbert, Euphemia, Herbert, Hippolytus, John, Martin, Sebastian, Theodosia
21 Benedict, Clementia, Serapion
22 Basil, Catherine, Nicholas, Octavian
23 Aquila, Theodosia, Turibius
24 Catherine, Gabriel, Simon
25 Harold, Humbert, Lucy, Richard
26 Basil, Emmanuel
27 Augusta, John, Lydia, Matthew
28 Gwendoline, John
29 Berthold, Gladys, Jonas, Mark, Rupert
30 John
31 Aldo, Amos, Benjamin, Cornelia, Guy

April

1 Gilbert, Hugh, Ludovic, Mary, Melito
2 Constantine, Drogo, Francis, Leopold, Mary, Theodosia, Urban
3 Alexandrina, Irene, Richard
4 Benedict, Isidore
5 Gerald, Juliana, Vincent
6 Celestine, William
7 George, Hegesippus, Herman, John, Llewellyn
8 Agabus, Dionysius, Walter
9 Hugh, Mary, Reginald
10 Ezekiel, Fulbert, Hedda, Michael, Terence
11 Gemma, Guthlac, Hildebrand, Isaac, Leo, Stanislaus
12 Damian, Julius, Zeno
13 Ida, Martin
14 Bernard, Caradoc, Eustace, Justin, Lambert
15 Anastasia, Aristarchus, Pudus, Silvester, Trophimus
16 Benedict, Bernadette, Drogo, Hervé, Lambert, Magnus
17 Agapetus, Elias, Robert, Stephen
18 Andrew, James
19 Alphege, Leo
20 Agnes
21 Anastasius, Anselm, Beuno, Conrad, Januarius, Simeon
22 Alexander, Caius, Theodore
23 Fortunatus, George, Gerard, Giles, Helen
24 Egbert, Fidelis, Ives, Mellitus
25 Mark, Phaebadius
26 Alda, Franca, Stephen
27 Zita
28 Louis, Patrick, Paul, Peter, Theodora, Valeria, Vitalis
29 Antonia, Ava, Catherine, Hugh, Peter, Robert, Wilfrid
30 Catherine, Hildegard, James, Miles, Pius, Sophia

May

1 Asaph, Bertha, Isidora, Joseph, Peregrine, Sigismund, Walburga
2 Athanasius, Zoë
3 Antonina, James, Maura, Philip, Timothy
4 Ethelrad, Florian, Gotthard, Monica, Silvanus
5 Angelo, Hilary
6 Benedicta, Prudence
7 Augustus, Flavia, Gisela, John, Stanislas
8 Benedict, Boniface, John, Michael, Peter, Victor
9 Gerontius
10 Antoninus, Aurelian, Beatrice, Comgall, Job, John, Simon
11 Aloysius, Cyril, Ignatius, James, Mamertus, Methodius, Philip, Walter
12 Achilleus, Dominic, Epiphanius, Gemma, Nereus, Pancras
13 Robert
14 Carthage, Giles, Mary, Matthias, Michael, Petronilla
15 Bertha, Dionysia, Dympna, Hilary, Isidore, Magdalen, Rupert, Silvanus
16 Brendan, John, Peregrine, Simon
17 Basilla, Paschal, Robert
18 Alexandra, Camilla, Claudia, Eric, John, Julitta
19 Celestine, Dunstan, Pudens, Pudentia, Yves
20 Aquila, Basilissa, Bernardino, Ethelbert, Orlando
21 Helena, Theobald, Theophilus
22 Julia, Rita
23 Ivo, William
24 David, Joanna, Patrick, Susanna, Vincent
25 Aldhelm, Bede, Dionysius, Gregory, Madeleine, Urban
26 Augustine, Lambert, Philip, Quadratus, Zachary
27 Augustine, Frederick, John, Julius
28 Augustine, Bernard
29 Theodosia, William
30 Felix, Ferdinand, Hubert, Isaac, Joan
31 Camilla, Petronilla

June

1 Angela, Justin, Pamphilus, Simeon, Theobald
2 Erasmus, Eugene, Marcellinus, Nicephorus, Nicholas, Peter, Pothinus
3 Charles, Clotilda, Isaac, Kevin, Matthias, Paula
4 Cornelius, Francis, Optatus, Petrock, Vincentia, Walter
5 Boniface, Ferdinand, Franco, Marcia, Valeria
6 Claud, Felicia, Martha, Norbert, Philip
7 Paul, Robert, Willibald
8 Melania, William
9 Amata, Cecilia, Columba, Cyril, Diana, Ephraem, Richard
10 Margaret, Olive, Zachary

11 Barnabas, Bartholomew, Fortunatus
12 Antonia, Christian, Humphrey, Leo
13 Anthony, Lucian
14 Basil
15 Alice, Germaine, Guy, Orsisius, Vitus, Yolanda
16 Aurelian, Julitta
17 Alban, Botolph, Emily, Harvey, Manuel, Sanchia, Teresa
18 Elizabeth, Fortunatus, Guy, Marina, Mark
19 Bruno, Gervase, Jude, Juliana, Odo, Protasius, Romuald
20 Alban, John
21 Alban, Aloysius, Lazarus, Ralph, Terence
22 Alban, Ederhard, John, Niceta, Pantaenus, Paulinus, Thomas
23 Audrey
24 Bartholomew, Ivan, John
25 Prosper, Solomon, William
26 John
27 Cyril, Ferdinand, Ladislaus, Madeleine, Samson
28 Irenaeus, Marcella, Paul
29 Emma, Judith, Paul, Peter, Salome
30 Bertrand, Lucina, Theobald

July

1 Aaron, Cosmas, Damian, Oliver, Simeon, Theodoric
2 Marcia, Otto, Reginald
3 Aaron, Anatolius, Julius, Leo, Thomas
4 Andrew, Aurelian, Bertha, Elizabeth, Odo, Ulrich
5 Anthony, Blanche, Grace, Gwen, Philomena, Zoë
6 Isaiah, Mary
7 Cyril, Hedda, Palladius, Pantaenus
8 Adrian, Aquila, Arnold, Edgar, Elizabeth, Kilian, Morwenna, Priscilla, Raymund
9 Alberic, Barnabas, Cornelius, Everild, Godfrey, Jerome, Nicholas, Thomas, Veronica
10 Amelia, Emmanuel, Maurice
11 Benedict, Olga, Oliver, Pius
12 Fortunatus, Jason, John, Monica, Veronica
13 Eugene, Henry, Joel, Mildred, Silas
14 Camillus, Deusdedit, Humbert, Nicholas, Ulric
15 Baldwin, Bonaventure, David, Donald, Edith, Henry, Jacob, Swithin, Vladimir
16 Eustace, Milo, Valentine
17 Alexis, Antoinette, Ennodius, Kenelm, Leo, Marcellina, Margaret, Nahum
18 Arnulf, Bruno, Camillus, Edith, Frederick, Marina, Philastrius
19 Ambrose, Aurea, Jerome, Symmachus, Vincent
20 Aurelius, Elias, Elijah, Jerome, Margaret, Marina
21 Angelina, Constantine, Daniel, Julia, Laurence, Praxedes, Victor
22 Joseph, Mary, Theophilus
23 Anne, Apollinaris, Balthasar, Bridget, Gaspar, Susanna
24 Boris, Christiana, Christina, Declan, Felicia
25 Anne, Christopher, James, Joachim, Thea, Valentina

26 Anne, Joachim
27 Berthold, Celestine, Natalia, Pantaleon, Rudolph, Theobald
28 Innocent, Samson, Victor
29 Beatrice, Felix, Flora, Lucilla, Lupus, Martha, Olaf, Urban
30 Everard, Julitta, Peter, Silas
31 Giovanni, Helen, Ignatius, Joseph

August

1 Alphonsus, Charity, Eiluned, Ethelwold, Faith, Hope, Justin, Kenneth
2 Alphonsus, Eusebius, Stephen
3 Gamaliel, Lydia, Nicodemus
4 Dominic, Jean-Baptiste, Perpetua
5 Afra, Oswald
6 Hormisdas, Octavian
7 Albert, Cajetan, Claudia, Sixtus
8 Dominic, Myron
9 Matthias, Oswald, Samuel
10 Geraint, Laurence, Oswald, Philomena
11 Alexander, Blane, Clare, Lelia, Susanna
12 Clare, Murtagh
13 Hippolytus, Maximus, Pontian, Radegunde
14 Marcellus, Maximilian
15 Arnulf, Mary, Napoleon, Stanislaus, Tarsicius
16 Joachim, Roch, Serena, Simplicianus, Stephen, Titus
17 Benedicta, Cecilia, Clare, Hyacinth, Myron, Septimus
18 Evan, Helena, Milo
19 John, Louis, Magnus, Sebaldus, Thecla, Timothy
20 Bernard, Herbert, Oswin, Philibert, Ronald, Samuel
21 Abraham, Jane, Pius
22 Andrew, Hippolytus, Sigfrid, Timothy
23 Claudius, Eleazar, Eugene, Philip, Rose, Sidonius, Zacchaeus
24 Alice, Bartholomew, Emily, Jane, Joan, Nathanael, Ouen
25 Joseph, Louis, Lucilla, Menas, Patricia
26 Dominic, Elias, Elizabeth, Zephyrinus
27 Caesarius, Gabriel, Hugh, Margaret, Monica, Rufus
28 Adelina, Alexander, Augustine, Julian, Moses, Vivian
29 Basilla, John, Merry, Sabina
30 Felix, Pammachius, Rose
31 Aidan, Paulinus, Raymund

September

1 Anna, Augustus, Gideon, Giles, Joshua, Simeon, Verena
2 John, René, Stephen, William
3 Dorothy, Euphemia, Gabriel, Gregory, Phoebe, Simeon

4 Babylas, Boniface, Candida, Hermione, Ida, Marcellus, Moses, Rosalia, Rose
5 Laurence, Urban, Vitus, Zacharias
6 Beata, Magnus, Zechariah
7 Eustace, Regina
8 Adrian, Natalia, Sergius
9 Isaac, Kieran, Louise, Peter, Seraphina, Sergius, Wilfrida
10 Aubert, Candida, Finnian, Isabel, Nicholas, Pulcheria
11 Daniel, Ethelburga, Hyacinth, Paphnutius, Theodora
12 Guy
13 Amatus, John
14 Cormac
15 Albinus, Catherine, Roland
16 Cornelius, Cyprian, Edith, Eugenia, Euphemia, Lucy, Ninian, Victor
17 Ariadne, Columba, Hildegard, Justin, Lambert, Narcissus, Robert, Satyrus, Theodora
18 Irene, Sophia
19 Constantia, Emily, Januarius, Susanna, Theodore
20 Candida, Eustace, Philippa, Vincent
21 Jonah, Matthew, Maura
22 Felix, Jonas, Maurice, Thomas
23 Adamnan, Helen, Linus, Thecla
24 Gerard
25 Albert, Aurelia, Herman, Sergius
26 Cosmas, Cyprian, John, Justina, René
27 Adolphus, Caius, Cosmas, Damian, Frumentius, Terence, Vincent
28 Exuperius, Solomon, Wenceslas
29 Gabriel, Michael, Raphael
30 Jerome, Otto, Simon, Sophia

October

1 Francis, Nicholas, Remigius, Romanos, Teresa
2 Leodegar, Theophilus
3 Gerard, Thérèse, Thomas
4 Ammon, Aurea, Berenice, Francis, Petronius
5 Flavia, Flora
6 Aurea, Bruno, Faith, Magnus, Mary, Thomas
7 Augustus, Julia, Justina, Mark
8 Bridget, Laurentia, Sergius, Simeon
9 Abraham, Demetrius, Denis, Dionysius, Gunther, James, John, Louis
10 Daniel, Francis, Paulinus, Samuel
11 Atticus, Bruno, Juliana, Kenneth, Nectarius
12 Cyprian, Edwin, Maximilian, Wilfrid
13 Edward, Gerald, Magdalen, Maurice, Theophilus
14 Callistus, Cosmas, Dominic
15 Aurelia, Leonard, Lucian, Teresa, Thecla, Willa
16 Baldwin, Bertrand, Gall, Gerard, Hedwig, Lullus, Margaret
17 Ignatius, Margaret, Rudolph, Victor
18 Blanche, Candida, Gwen, Gwendoline, Luke

19 Cleopatra, Isaac, John, Laura, Lucius, Paul, Peter
20 Adelina, Andrew, Irene, Martha
21 Hilarion, Ursula
22 Abercius, Philip
23 Bartholomew, Ignatius, James, John, Josephine
24 Anthony, Martin, Raphael, Septimus
25 Balthasar, Crispin, Crispinian, Dorcas, Gaudentius, George, Tabitha, Thaddeus, Theodoric
26 Albinus, Cuthbert, Damian, Demetrius, Lucian
27 Antonia, Sabina
28 Anastasias, Firmilian, Godwin, Jude, Simon, Thaddaeus
29 Narcissus, Terence
30 Alphonsus, Artemas, Dorothy, Marcellus, Serapion, Zenobia
31 Quentin, Wolfgang

November

1 Cledwyn, Cosmas, Damian, Mary
2 Eustace, Maura, Tobias, Victorinus
3 Hubert, Malachy, Martin, Pirminius, Sylvia, Valentine, Winifred
4 Agricola, Charles, Frances, Vitalis
5 Cosmo, Elizabeth, Martin, Zacharias
6 Illtyd, Leonard, Paul
7 Carina, Florentius, Gertrude, Rufus, Willibrord
8 Elizabeth, Godfrey, Willehad
9 Simeon, Theodore
10 Florence, Justus, Leo, Tryphena
11 Bartholomew, Martin, Menas, Theodore
12 Josaphat, Martin, Matthew, Nilus, René
13 Abbo, Brice, Eugene, John, Nicholas, Stanislaus
14 Dubricius, Gregory, Laurence
15 Albert, Leopold, Machutus
16 Agnes, Edmund, Eucherius, Gertrude, Margaret, Matthew
17 Dionysius, Elizabeth, Gregory, Hilda, Hugh, Victoria, Zacchaeus
18 Constant, Odo, Romanus
19 Crispin, Elizabeth, Mechtild, Nerses
20 Edmund, Octavius, Silvester
21 Albert, Gelasius, Rufus
22 Cecilia, Philemon
23 Amphilochius, Clement, Columban, Felicity, Gregory, Lucretia
24 Flora, John, Thaddeus
25 Catherine, Clement, Mercurius, Mesrob, Moses
26 Conrad, Leonard, Peter, Silvester, Siricius
27 Barlam, Fergus, James, Josaphat, Virgil
28 James, Simeon, Stephen
29 Blaise, Brendan, Cuthbert, Frederick
30 Andrew, Frumentius, Maura

December

1 Eligius, Nahum, Natalia, Ralph
2 Aurelia, Chromatius, Viviana
3 Claudius, Francis Xavier, Jason, Lucius
4 Ada, Barbara, Bernard, John, Osmond
5 Bartholomew, Clement, Sabas
6 Abraham, Dionysia, Gertrude, Nicholas, Tertius
7 Ambrose, Josepha
8 Mary
9 Peter
10 Brian, Eulalia, Gregory, Julia, Miltiades, Sidney
11 Damasus, Daniel, Franco
12 Agatha, Cormac, Dionysia, Jane Frances, Spyridon, Vicelin
13 Aubert, Judoc, Lucy, Ottilia
14 Conrad, John, Spyridon
15 Christiana, Mary
16 Adelaide, Albina, Azariah, Eusebius
17 Florian, Lazarus, Olympias
18 Frumentius, Rufus
19 Thea, Urban
20 Dominic, Ignatius
21 Peter, Thomas
22 Adam, Anastasia, Chrysogonus
23 John, Victoria
24 Adam, Adela, Eve
25 Anastasia, Eugenia
26 Christina, Dionysius, Stephen, Vincentia
27 Fabiola, John, Stephen, Theodore
28 Theophila
29 David, Marcellus, Thomas, Trophimus
30 Sabinus
31 Columba, Cornelius, Fabian, Melania, Sextus, Silvester

POPULAR FIRST NAMES

England and Wales

Boys

1700		1800		1900	
1	John	1	William	1	William
2	William	2	John	2	John
3	Thomas	3	Thomas	3	George
4	Richard	4	James	4	Thomas
5	James	5	George	5	Charles
6	Robert	6	Joseph	6	Frederick
7	Joseph	7	Richard	7	Arthur
8	Edward	8	Henry	8	James
9	Henry	9	Robert	9	Albert
10	George	10	Charles	10	Ernest

1920s		1950s		1960s	
1	John	1	David	1	Paul
2	William	2	John	2	David
3	George	3	Peter	3	Andrew
4	James	4	Michael	4	Stephen
5	Ronald	5	Alan	5	Mark
6	Robert	6	Robert	6	Michael
7	Kenneth	7	Stephen	7	Ian
8	Frederick	8	Paul	8	Gary
9	Thomas	9	Brian	9	Robert
10	Albert	10	Graham	10	Richard

1970s		1980s		1990s	
1	Stephen	1	Christopher	1	Daniel
2	Mark	2	Matthew	2	Matthew
3	Paul	3	David	3	James
4	Andrew	4	James	4	Christopher
5	David	5	Daniel	5	Adam
6	Richard	6	Andrew	6	Thomas
7	Matthew	7	Steven	7	David
8	Daniel	8	Michael	8	Luke
9	Christopher	9	Mark	9	Jamie
10	Darren	10	Paul	10	Robert

2001		2002		2003	
1	Jack	1	Jack	1	Jack
2	Thomas	2	Joshua	2	Joshua
3	Joshua	3	Thomas	3	Thomas
4	James	4	James	4	James
5	Daniel	5	Daniel	5	Daniel
6	Harry	6	Benjamin	6	Oliver
7	Samuel	7	William	7	Benjamin
8	Joseph	8	Samuel	8	Samuel
9	Matthew	9	Joseph	9	William
10	Lewis	10	Oliver	10	Joseph

Girls

1700		1800		1900	
1	Mary	1	Mary	1	Florence
2	Elizabeth	2	Ann	2	Mary
3	Ann	3	Elizabeth	3	Alice
4	Sarah	4	Sarah	4	Annie
5	Jane	5	Jane	5	Elsie
6	Margaret	6	Hannah	6	Edith
7	Susan	7	Susan	7	Elizabeth
8	Martha	8	Martha	8	Doris
9	Hannah	9	Margaret	9	Dorothy
10	Catherine	10	Charlotte	10	Ethel

1920s		1950s		1960s	
1	Joan	1	Susan	1	Tracey
2	Mary	2	Linda	2	Deborah
3	Joyce	3	Christine	3	Julie
4	Margaret	4	Margaret	4	Karen
5	Dorothy	5	Carol	5	Susan
6	Doris	6	Jennifer	6	Alison
7	Kathleen	7	Janet	7	Jacqueline
8	Irene	8	Patricia	8	Helen
9	Betty	9	Barbara	9	Amanda
10	Eileen	10	Ann	10	Sharon

1970s		1980s		1990s	
1	Claire	1	Sarah	1	Emma
2	Sarah	2	Claire	2	Sarah
3	Nicola	3	Emma	3	Laura
4	Emma	4	Laura	4	Charlotte
5	Joanne	5	Rebecca	5	Amy
6	Helen	6	Gemma	6	Rebecca
7	Rachel	7	Rachel	7	Gemma
8	Lisa	8	Kelly	8	Katharine
9	Rebecca	9	Victoria	9	Lauren
10	Karen / Michelle	10	Katharine	10	Hayley

2001		2002		2003	
1	Chloe	1	Chloe	1	Emily
2	Emily	2	Emily	2	Ellie
3	Megan	3	Jessica	3	Chloe
4	Jessica	4	Ellie	4	Jessica
5	Sophie	5	Sophie	5	Sophie
6	Lauren	6	Megan	6	Megan
7	Charlotte	7	Charlotte	7	Lucy
8	Hannah	8	Lucy	8	Olivia
9	Olivia	9	Hannah	9	Charlotte
10	Lucy	10	Olivia	10	Hannah

Scotland

Boys		*Girls*	
2003		2003	
1	Lewis	1	Emma
2	Jack	2	Ellie
3	Cameron	3	Amy
4	James	4	Sophie
5	Kyle	5	Chloe
6	Ryan	6	Erin
7	Ben	7	Rachel
8	Callum	8	Lucy
9	Matthew	9	Lauren
10	Jamie/Adam	10	Katie

USA

Boys

1900

1	John
2	William
3	Charles
4	Robert
5	Joseph
6	James
7	George
8	Samuel
9	Thomas
10	Arthur

1920s

1	Robert
2	John
3	William
4	James
5	Charles
6	Richard
7	George
8	Donald
9	Joseph
10	Edward

1940s

1	Robert
2	James
3	John
4	William
5	Richard
6	Thomas
7	David
8	Ronald
9	Donald
10	Michael

1950s

1	Robert
2	Michael
3	James
4	John
5	David
6	William
7	Thomas
8	Richard
9	Gary
10	Charles

1960s

1	Michael
2	David
3	Robert
4	James
5	John
6	Mark
7	Steven
8	Thomas
9	William
10	Joseph

1970s

1	Michael
2	Robert
3	David
4	James
5	John
6	Jeffrey
7	Steven
8	Christopher
9	Brian
10	Mark

1990s

1	Michael
2	Christopher
3	Matthew
4	Joshua
5	Jacob
6	Andrew
7	Daniel
8	Nicholas
9	Tyler
10	Joseph

2001

1	Jacob
2	Michael
3	Matthew
4	Joshua
5	Christopher
6	Nicholas
7	Andrew
8	Joseph
9	Daniel
10	William

2002

1	Matthew
2	Tyler
3	Joshua
4	Michael
5	Nicholas
6	Alex
7	Jacob
8	Andrew
9	Brandon
10	Taylor

2003

1 Jacob
2 Michael
3 Joshua
4 Matthew
5 Ethan
6 Joseph
7 Andrew
8 Christopher
9 Daniel
10 Nicholas

Girls

1900		1920s		1940s	
1	Mary	1	Mary	1	Mary
2	Ruth	2	Barbara	2	Patricia
3	Helen	3	Dorothy	3	Barbara
4	Margaret	4	Betty	4	Judith
5	Elizabeth	5	Ruth	5	Carol
6	Dorothy	6	Margaret	6	Sharon
7	Catherine	7	Helen	7	Nancy
8	Mildred	8	Elizabeth	8	Joan
9	Frances	9	Jean	9	Sandra
10	Alice / Marion	10	Ann	10	Margaret

1950s		1960s		1970s	
1	Linda	1	Mary	1	Michelle
2	Mary	2	Deborah	2	Jennifer
3	Patricia	3	Karen	3	Kimberly
4	Susan	4	Susan	4	Lisa
5	Deborah	5	Linda	5	Tracy
6	Kathleen	6	Patricia	6	Kelly
7	Barbara	7	Kimberly	7	Nicole
8	Nancy	8	Catherine	8	Angela
9	Sharon	9	Cynthia	9	Pamela
10	Karen	10	Lori	10	Christine

1990s		2001		2002	
1	Ashley	1	Emily	1	Emily
2	Jessica	2	Madison	2	Jessica
3	Emily	3	Hannah	3	Hannah
4	Sarah	4	Ashley	4	Alyssa
5	Samantha	5	Alexis	5	Amanda
6	Brittany	6	Samantha	6	Samantha
7	Amanda	7	Sarah	7	Madison
8	Elizabeth	8	Abigail	8	Megan
9	Taylor	9	Elizabeth	9	Katie
10	Megan	10	Jessica	10	Alexis

2003	
1	Emily
2	Madison
3	Hannah
4	Emma
5	Alexis
6	Ashley
7	Abigail
8	Sarah
9	Samantha
10	Olivia

Australia

Boys

1950s		1970s		1990s	
1	John	1	Matthew	1	Matthew
2	Peter	2	Andrew	2	Daniel
3	Michael	3	David	3	Michael
4	David	4	Michael	4	Thomas
5	Robert	5	Paul	5	Benjamin
6	Stephen	6	Adam	6	James
7	Paul	7	Christopher	7	Samuel
8	Phillip	8	Daniel	8	Nicholas
9	Christopher	9	Mark	9	Joshua
10	Ian	10	Scott	10	Christopher

2001		2002		2003	
1	Jack	1	Jack	1	Joshua
2	Lachlan	2	Joshua	2	Jack
3	Joshua	3	Lachlan	3	Thomas
4	James	4	Thomas	4	Ethan
5	Benjamin	5	William	5	Liam
6	Matthew	6	Liam	6	Jacob
7	Thomas	7	Ethan	7	Matthew
8	Nicholas	8	James	8	Mitchell
9	William	9	Benjamin	9	Lachlan
10	Samuel	10	Matthew	10	Daniel

Girls

1950s		1970s		1990s	
1	Susan	1	Michelle	1	Jessica
2	Margaret	2	Catherine	2	Sarah
3	Anne	3	Kylie	3	Emma
4	Elizabeth	4	Nicole	4	Lauren
5	Christine	5	Rebecca	5	Rebecca
6	Jennifer	6	Melissa	6	Ashleigh
7	Judith	7	Lisa	7	Amy
8	Patricia	8	Belinda	8	Emily
9	Catherine	9	Rachel	9	Kate
10	Helen	10	Sarah	10	Katherine

2001		2002		2003	
1	Emily	1	Emily	1	Chloe
2	Georgia	2	Chloe	2	Jessica
3	Jessica	3	Georgia	3	Emma
4	Chloe	4	Jessica	4	Grace
5	Olivia	5	Olivia	5	Sarah
6	Sophie	6	Ella	6	Shakira
7	Hannah	7	Sophie	7	Emily
8	Grace	8	Charlotte	8	Amy
9	Sarah	9	Isabella	9	Hannah
10	Ella	10	Hannah	10	Hayley